VISUAL PERCEPTION
Physiology, Psychology and Ecology
2nd Edition

VISUAL PERCEPTION
Physiology, Psychology and Ecology
2ND EDITION

Vicki Bruce and Patrick Green
Department of Psychology
University of Nottingham
Nottingham NG7 2RD, England

[EA] **LAWRENCE ERLBAUM ASSOCIATES, PUBLISHERS** [EA]
Hove and London (UK)   Hillsdale (USA)

Reprinted 1991, 1992 (twice), 1993

Lawrence Erlbaum Associates Ltd., Publishers
27 Palmeira Mansions
Church Road
Hove
East Sussex, BN3 2FA
UK

British Library Cataloguing in Publication Data

Bruce, Vicki
Visual perception: physiology, psychology and ecology
2nd ed.
1. Visual perception
I. Title II. Green, Patrick, R.
152.14

ISBN 0-86377-145-9 (Hbk)
ISBN 0-86377-146-7 (Pbk)

Typeset by Litholink Ltd., Welshpool, Powys
Printed and bound by BPCC Wheatons Ltd., Exeter

To Michael
and
To the memory of Rodney Green

CONTENTS

Preface to the first edition   xi

Preface to the second edition   xiii

Part I: The Physiological Basis of Visual Perception

1 Light and Eyes   1
Light and the Information it Carries   2
The Evolution of Light-Sensitive Structures   7
The Adaptive Radiation of the Vertebrate Eye   16
Conclusions   28

2 The Neurophysiology of the Retina   31
The Retina of the Horseshoe Crab   31
The Vertebrate Retina   36
The Output of the Retina   38
Retinal Mechanisms   45
Conclusions   48

3 Visual Pathways in the Brain   49
The Visual Cortex   52
The Functions of the Visual Pathway   60
Beyond the Striate Cortex   65
Conclusions   72

Part II: Processing Retinal Images

4 Introduction: Approaches to the Psychology of Visual Perception   73
Overview of Marr's Theory of Vision   78

5 The Raw Primal Sketch   81
The Marr-Hildreth Algorithm   87
Other Routes to the Raw Primal Sketch   94
Conclusions   103

6 Perceptual Organisation   105
Ambiguous Pictures   106
Gestalt Laws of Organisation   110
Recent Approaches to Perceptual Organisation   115
Concealment and Advertisement   121
Perceptual Organisation in Other Species   125
Why do the Gestalt Laws Work?   127
Artificial Intelligence Approaches to Grouping   128
Conclusions   139

7 Perceiving Depth and Movement   141
Perceiving the Third Dimension   141
Observer Movement and Object Motion   159
Marr's Theory of the 2½D Sketch   168
Integrating Information from Successive Fixations   170

8 Object Recognition   175
Simple Mechanisms of Recognition   177
More Complex Recognition Processes   179
Marr and Nishihara's Theory of Object Recognition   190
Beyond Generalised Cones   196
Conclusion   202

**9 Connectionist Models of Visual
Perception   203**
Satisfying Constraints—Marr and Poggio's (1976)
Algorithm   204
Mapping Between Coordinate Systems   206
Learning to Recognise Patterns   211
Concluding Remarks   219

Part III: Detecting Information in the Transforming Optic Array

10 Introduction to the Ecological Approach to Visual Perception   223
J. J. Gibson's Theory of Perception   224

11 Visual Guidance of Animal Locomotion   241
How Animals Move About   241
How Insects Steer a Straight Course   243
Detecting Surfaces   251
Detecting Distance   255
Conclusions   265

12 Visual Guidance of Human Action   267
Postural Adjustments   268
Walking, Running and Jumping   272
Driving Cars   278
Ball Games: Catching and Hitting   282

13 The Computation of Image Motion   287
Early Motion Computation   289
The Integration of Motion Measurements   298
More Complex Properties of Optic Flow   305
Conclusions   309

14 Theories of the Control of Action   311
The Optomotor Response   312
The Control of Human Action   314
Conclusions   320

15 Event Perception   321
The Perception of Relative Motion   321
Biological Motion   327
The Perception of Causality   333
Perception and Attribution   338

16 Perception of the Social World   343
Perceiving Other Animals' Behaviour   344
Recognition of Individuals   357
Human Face Perception   360
Concluding Remarks   374

Part IV: Conclusions

**17 Contrasting Theories of Visual
Perception   375**
The Nature of the Input   376
Direct and Indirect Theories of Perception   377
Concluding Comments   389

References   393

Glossary   413

Author Index   419

Subject Index   425

PREFACE TO THE FIRST EDITION

Our primary aim in writing this book has been to present a wide range of recent evidence and theoretical developments in the field of visual perception to an advanced undergraduate readership. The material covered is drawn from three areas; the neurophysiological analysis of vision, the "computational" accounts of vision which have grown out of traditional experimental approaches and artificial intelligence, and work on vision which shares at least some of J.J. Gibson's "ecological" framework.

In the first part of the book we discuss the evolution of different types of eye, the neurophysiological organisation of visual pathways, particularly in mammals, and contrasting theoretical interpretations of single unit responses in visual systems.

We turn in the second part to psychological and computational models of the interpretation of information in retinal images, discussing perceptual organisation, the perception of depth and of movement, and pattern and object recognition. The contribution of David Marr's work to these problems is emphasised.

In the third part we discuss how extended patterns of light can provide information for the control of action and to specify events; topics covered are the visual guidance of animal and human locomotion, theories of the control of action, and the role of vision in animal social behaviour and human event perception.

We have assumed that our readers will have had some prior knowledge of basic neurophysiology (for Part I of the book) and experimental psychology (for Parts II and III), such as might have been gained from an introductory psychology course.

Our choice of topics differs in some respects from that of most textbooks of visual perception. Some topics are excluded. In particular, we do not discuss sensory physiology and psychophysics in as much detail as other texts. We do include material on animal perception which would usually be found in an ethology text, and consider in detail research on human and animal reactions to patterns of optic flow. Our choice of topics is governed by a consistent theoretical outlook. We have been committed to the value of an ecological approach in its *wider* sense; that espoused by David Marr as much as by James Gibson, who both argued for the need to consider the structure of the world in which an animal or person lives and perceives. It is this commitment which has guided the overall plan of the book.

We have attempted to go beyond exposition of theoretical and empirical developments in each of our three areas, and to discuss promising issues for further research and to present an analysis and critique of the theories we discuss. We have been most speculative about future possibilities for the ecological approach in Chapters 11 and 12, and address global theoretical issues most fully in Chapter 13. Our final conclusion is that an ecological perspective offers valuable insights, but that a "direct" theory of perception is not adequate.

These are exciting times in the study of visual perception, and we believe that there is much to be gained by cross-fertilisation between research areas. There are real and important issues dividing different theoretical camps, which must continue to be debated vigorously, but it is also worthwhile to mark out some potential common ground.

Although the readers we have in mind are advanced psychology students, we have designed the book to also be useful to zoology students specialising in neurophysiology and in animal behaviour, and particularly to students in the increasingly popular courses which combine zoology and psychology. We hope that research workers may also find the book useful; although it will surely be superficial in their areas of primary interest, it may be helpful in approaching the literature in adjoining areas.

Our manuscript has been improved considerably as a result of critical comments from a number of people. Our colleague Alan Dodds read the entire manuscript, and Robin Stevens read parts. A number of anonymous reviewers furnished further comments. We would like to thank all these people most sincerely. They spotted blunders, and suggested ways of making points more clearly, which would not have occurred to us alone; any remaining errors are, of course, our own responsibility. Mike Burton helped us with our own, and other people's, mathematical reasoning. He was also one of several people who introduced us to the mysteries of word-processing; Chris Blunsdon, Roger Henry and Anne Lomax are the others.

Roger Somerville (WIDES Advertising and Design) drew all those figures not otherwise acknowledged, and thus contributed enormously to the text. Sam Grainger took many photographs, and E. Hildreth, D. H. Hubel, Fergus Campbell, John Frisby and Paul Ekman all provided photographs for us to use. Penny Radcliffe typed endless letters and helped in many other ways when we ourselves were flagging. Mike Forster and Rohays Perry encouraged us to see this project through, and gave us editorial help.

PREFACE TO THE SECOND EDITION

As the first edition went to press in 1984, research on visual perception was progressing rapidly in a number of areas. The second wave of research inspired by Marr's work was just developing; research into the computation of optical flow was already accelerating; and the connectionist revival was gathering momentum. We have tried to mention all these developments in our new edition by including three (largely) new chapters. In Chapter 5, we bring our earlier discussion of Marr and Hildreth's theory of edge detection together with the more recent work of Watt and Morgan to review approaches to raw primal sketch computation. Chapter 9 is entirely new, and in it we show how "connectionist" modelling can be applied to the problems raised in the second part of the book. Chapter 13 considers accounts of how the optic flow field, so central to the third part of the book, could actually be computed by the visual systems of different species.

In addition to these new chapters, we have reorganised the second half of Part III somewhat, and have considerably expanded our discussion of imprinting and face perception in the resulting Chapter 16. We have updated other material throughout the text, and particularly in Chapter 3 where we have brought our treatment of the physiology of vision up to date. We have also emphasised the recent convergence between theoretical developments and physiological evidence at a number of points in Parts II and III.

Our thanks are due again to all those who helped us with the first edition, and additionally to those who reviewed or otherwise commented on the text after its publication; they have done much to encourage us to embark upon this revision. We thank Mark Georgeson and Roger Watt for their expert scrutiny of our draft second edition; their suggestions have helped us to improve the accuracy and thoroughness of our new material. We also thank Mark Georgeson for providing a valuable illustration. Our thanks are due again to Mike Burton, who gave us considerable help in interpreting the connectionist literature. Any errors remaining after help from these colleagues are, of course, entirely our own responsibility. Finally, we thank Mike Forster, Rohays Perry and Melanie Tarrant for their support and editorial work.

Part I

THE PHYSIOLOGICAL BASIS OF VISUAL PERCEPTION

Chapter One

LIGHT AND EYES

All organisms, whether bacteria, oak trees or whales, must be adapted to their environments if they are to survive and reproduce. The structure and physiology of organisms are not fixed at the start of life; to some extent, adjustments to changes in the environment can occur so as to "fine-tune" the organism's adaptation. One way of achieving this is through the regulation of growth processes, as when plants grow so that their leaves face the strongest available light. Another way, which is much more rapid and is only available to animals, is movement of the body by contraction of muscles.

If the movement of an animal's body is to adapt it to its environment, it must be regulated, or guided, by the environment. Thus the swimming movements of a fish's body, tail and fins are regulated so as to bring it into contact with food and to avoid obstacles; or the movement of a person's throat, tongue and lips in speaking are regulated by the speech of other people, linguistic rules and so on.

In order for its movement to be regulated by the environment, an animal must be able to detect structures and events in its surroundings. We call this ability *perception*, and it in turn requires that an animal be sensitive to at least one form of energy which can provide information about the environment. One source of information is provided by chemical substances diffusing through air or water. Another is mechanical energy, whether pressure on the body surface, forces on the limbs and muscles or waves of sound pressure in air or water. Further information sources, to which some animals are sensitive but people probably are not, are electric and magnetic fields.

An animal sensitive to diffusing chemicals can detect the presence of nearby food or predators, but often cannot pinpoint their exact location, and cannot detect the layout of its inanimate surroundings. Pressure on the skin and mechanical forces on the limbs can provide information about the environment in immediate contact with an animal, while sound can provide information about more distant animals but not usually about distant inanimate structures.

Sensitivity to diffusing chemicals and to mechanical energy gives an animal considerable perceptual abilities, but leaves it unable to obtain information rapidly about either its inanimate world or about silent animals at a distance from itself (there are a few exceptions, however; see Chapter 11, p. 243). The form of energy that can provide these kinds of information is *light*, and consequently most animals have some ability to perceive their surroundings through vision. We will begin our discussion of visual perception in animals and people by considering first the physical nature of light and then how the environment structures the light that reaches an observer.

LIGHT AND THE INFORMATION IT CARRIES

Light is one form of *electromagnetic radiation*; a mode of propagation of energy through space which includes radio waves, radiant heat, gamma rays and X-rays. One way in which we can picture the nature of electromagnetic radiation is as a pattern of waves propagated through an imaginary medium. It therefore has a velocity, 3×10^{-8} m/sec in a vacuum, and a wavelength, which ranges from hundreds of metres in the case of radio waves to 10^{-12} or 10^{-13} m in the case of cosmic rays. Only a very small part of this range is visible; for human beings, radiation with wavelengths between 400 and 700 nanometres (1 nm = 10^{-9} m) can be seen (Fig. 1.1).

For some purposes, however, the model of electromagnetic radiation as a wave is not appropriate and we must instead treat it as a stream of tiny particles called *photons* travelling in a straight

The spectrum of electromagnetic radiation. Wavelengths are given in nanometres (1 nm = 10^{-9} m). The visible part of the spectrum is shown on the right, with the colours of different wavelengths of light.

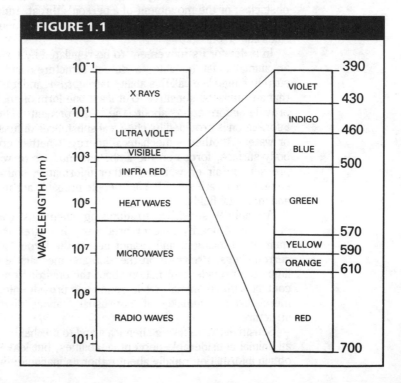

FIGURE 1.1

line at the speed of light. Each photon consists of a quantum of energy (the shorter the wavelength of the light the larger the energy quantum), which is given up as it strikes another particle. We need these two conceptions of the nature of electromagnetic radiation because nothing in our experience is analogous to the actual nature of it and we must make do with two imperfect analogies at the same time.

These problems are of no concern in understanding how light is propagated around the environment. For these purposes we can think of light as made up of rays, which vary in both their intensity and their wavelength. Rays are emitted from light sources and would, in a vacuum, travel in a straight line without attenuation. A vacuum is not a congenial environment for animals, however, and the fate of light rays travelling through natural habitats is more complex.

First, as light passes through a medium, even a transparent one such as air or water, it undergoes *absorption*, as photons collide with particles of matter, give up their energy and disappear. Absorption is much stronger in water than in air and even in the clearest oceans there is no detectable sunlight below about 1000 metres. Longer wavelengths are absorbed more strongly, so that available light becomes progressively bluer in deeper water.

Secondly, light is *diffracted* as it passes through a transparent or translucent medium. Its energy is not absorbed, but rather rays are scattered on striking small particles of matter. Diffraction of sunlight by the atmosphere is the reason why the sky is blue; light of shorter wavelengths is scattered more and so a greater proportion of light reaching the ground is blue. Without an atmosphere, the sky would be completely dark, as it is on the moon.

Thirdly, the velocity of light falls when it passes through a transparent medium; the greater the optical density of the medium, the greater the decrease. As a result, when rays of light pass from a medium of one optical density to a medium of a different density, they are bent, or *refracted*, unless they strike the boundary between the two media perpendicularly. Refraction occurs, for example, at the boundary between air and water or between air and glass, and we will consider it in more detail when we describe the structure of eyes.

Finally, when light strikes an opaque surface, some of its energy is absorbed and some of it is *reflected*. A matt black surface absorbs most of the light falling on it and reflects little, while a silvery surface does the opposite. The way surfaces reflect light varies in two important ways. First, a surface may reflect some wavelengths more strongly than others, so that the spectral composition of the reflected light (the relative proportions of wavelengths it contains) differs from that of the incident light. A leaf, for example, absorbs more (and hence reflects less) red light than light of other wavelengths. Note that surfaces do not reflect single wavelengths and absorb all others, but alter the spectral composition of the light reflected from them, increasing the proportions of some wavelengths relative to others.

Secondly, the *texture* of a surface determines how coherently it reflects light. A perfectly smooth surface such as a mirror reflects light uniformly, but most natural surfaces have a rougher texture, made up of a mosaic of tiny reflecting surfaces set at different angles. Light striking such a surface is therefore reflected in an incoherent way (see Fig. 1.2).

Now that we have described the nature of light and the processes governing its travel through space, we turn to ask how it carries information for animals about their environments. A useful concept in understanding this is the *ambient optic array*, a term coined by Gibson (1966). Imagine an environment illuminated by sunlight and therefore filled with rays of light travelling between surfaces. At any point, light will converge from all directions, and we can imagine the point surrounded by a sphere divided into tiny solid angles. The intensity of light and the mixture of wavelengths will vary from one solid angle to another, and this spatial pattern of light is the optic array. Light carries information because the structure of the optic array is determined by the nature and position of the surfaces from which it has been reflected.

Figure 1.3 illustrates the relationship between environment and optic array. At a point just above the ground, there is a simple pattern in the array, with light in the upper part coming directly from the sun or scattered by the atmosphere, and light in the lower part having been reflected from the surface of the ground. The array is therefore divided into two segments differing in the intensity and spectral composition of light arriving through them. The boundary between these two areas specifies the horizon.

Each of these two segments can be further subdivided, and finer levels of spatial pattern in the optic array carry further information.

FIGURE 1.2

Regular reflection of rays of light from a polished surface such as a mirror (a) and irregular reflection from a textured surface (b).

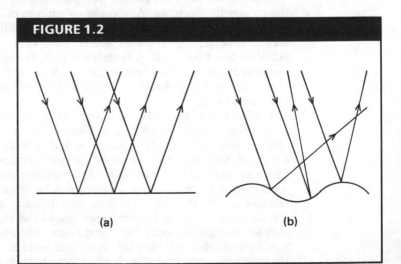

(a)   (b)

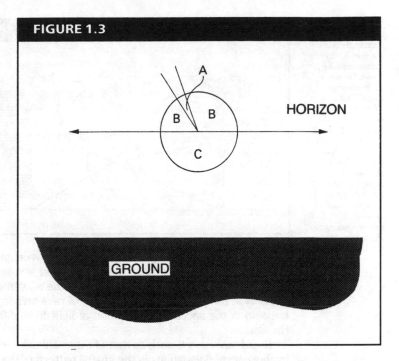

FIGURE 1.3

HORIZON

GROUND

Section through the optic array at a point above the ground in an open environment. In angle A incident light arrives directly from the sun, in angles B it has been scattered by the atmosphere and in angle C it has been reflected from the ground. The arrows point to the distant horizon.

The upper segment contains a region in which light of very high intensity arrives from the sun, and its position relative to the horizon specifies time of day. The pattern of light intensities and wavelengths in the lower segment will not be uniform unless the surface is smooth and mirror-like; the rays of light in the array reflected from a natural, textured surface will differ in intensity and wavelength from point to point in the array. In other words, there will be a fine structure in the optic array, characteristic of the surface from which the light has been reflected. A sandy surface and a stony surface, for example, would give different patterns of fine structure in the optic array.

If we add objects to this simple environment (Fig. 1.4) we get an optic array with a more complex spatial pattern. It is divided into many segments, containing light reflected from different surfaces, and differing in the average intensities and spectral compositions of light passing through them. The boundaries between these segments of the optic array provide information about the three-dimensional structure of objects in the world. Again, at a finer level of detail, each segment of the array will be patterned in a way determined by the texture of the surface that its light is reflected from. At this level, the optic array can carry information about further properties of objects and terrain.

So far, we have considered how a static optic array provides information about the world. Most natural environments contain movement, however, and most animals need to detect it. Any movement in the environment will be specified by a change in the

FIGURE 1.4

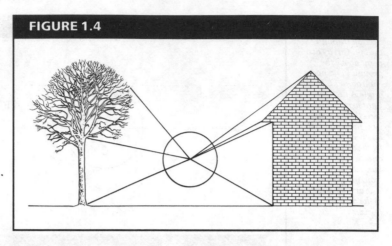

spatial pattern of the optic array. Some movement in nature is slow, such as the daily movement of the sun across the sky. The optic array in Figure 1.3 will change with the movement of the sun, not only in the position of the segment of rays arriving from the sun but also in the spectral composition of light from different parts of the sky.

Rapid movement, such as that of other animals, will be specified in short-term fluctuations in the spatial pattern of the optic array. If one of the objects in Figure 1.4 moves, the boundaries of some segments in the optic array will move relative to the others. This spatiotemporal pattern in the optic array can carry further information about the direction, speed and form of movement involved.

We have been looking at simple optic arrays in daylight in open terrestrial environments, but the same principles apply in any illuminated environment. At night, the moon and stars illuminate the world in the same way as does the sun, though with light that is many orders of magnitude less intense. In water, however, there are some differences. First, refraction of light at the water surface means that the segment of the optic array specifying "sky" is of a narrower angle than on land. Second, light is absorbed and scattered much more by water than by air, so that information about distant objects is not specified in the pattern of intensities and wavelengths in the optic array. Third, in deep water, light from below is not reflected from the substrate but scattered upwards (Fig. 1.5).

These examples all illustrate one important point; the spatial and temporal *pattern* of light converging on a point in a land or water environment provides information about the structure of the environment and events occurring in it. The speed of light ensures that, effectively, events in the environment are represented in the optic array instantaneously. Only in deep oceans and completely dark caves is no information at all available in light, although the phenomenon of *bioluminescence*—the emission of light by

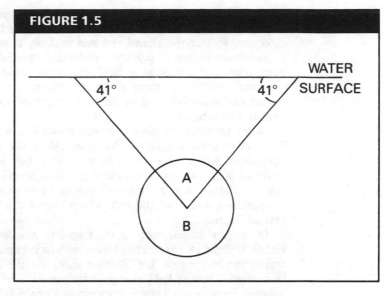

FIGURE 1.5

Section through the optic array at a point below the water surface. Because light rays from the sky and sun are refracted at the air–water boundary, they are "compressed" into an angle (A) of 98°. Incident light in angle B has been scattered by water or reflected from underwater objects.

organisms—means that even in these habitats light may carry information about the biological surroundings.

Up to this point we have considered a point just above the ground, or in open water, and asked what sort of information is available in the optic array converging on that point. Now, we must put an animal at the centre of this optic array and ask how it can detect the information available in it. If it is to detect any information at all, it must first have some kind of structure sensitive to light energy, and our next topic is the evolution of such structures among animals. How do different kinds of light-sensitive structures allow light energy to influence the activity of animals' nervous systems, and what scope do these structures have for detecting the fundamental information-carrying features of optic arrays; spatial pattern and changes in spatial patterns?

THE EVOLUTION OF LIGHT-SENSITIVE STRUCTURES

Many biological molecules absorb electromagnetic radiation in the visible part of the spectrum, changing in chemical structure as they do so. Various biochemical mechanisms have evolved which couple such changes to other processes. One such mechanism is photosynthesis, in which absorption of light by chlorophyll molecules powers the biochemical synthesis of sugars by plants. Animals, on the other hand, have concentrated on harnessing the absorption of light by light-sensitive molecules to the mechanisms which make them move.

In single-celled animals, absorption of light can modulate processes of locomotion directly through biochemical pathways. *Amoeba* moves by a streaming motion of the cytoplasm to form extensions of the cell called pseudopods. If a pseudopod extends into bright light, streaming stops and is diverted in a different direction, so that the animal remains in dimly lit areas. *Amoeba* possesses no known pigment molecules specialized for light sensitivity, and presumably light has some direct effect on the enzymes involved in making the cytoplasm stream. Thus, the animal can avoid bright light despite having no specialized light-sensitive structures.

Other protozoa do have pigment molecules with the specific function of detecting light. One example is the ciliate *Stentor coeruleus*, which responds to an increase in light intensity with a reversal of the waves of ciliary beat which propel it through the water. Capture of light by a blue pigment causes a change in the membrane potential of the cell, which in turn affects ciliary beat (Wood, 1976).

Other protozoans, such as the flagellate *Euglena*, have more elaborate light-sensitive structures, in which pigment is concentrated into an eyespot, but *Stentor* illustrates the basic principles of *transduction* of light energy which operate in more complex animals. First, when a pigment molecule absorbs light, its chemical structure changes. This, in turn, is coupled to an alteration in the structure of the cell membrane, so that the membrane's permeability to ions is modified, which in turn leads to a change in the electrical potential across the membrane.

In a single cell, this change in membrane potential need travel only a short distance to influence processes that move the animal about. In a many-celled animal, however, some cells are specialized for generating movement and some for detection of light and other external energy. These are separated by distances too great for electrotonic spread of a change in membrane potential, and information is instead transmitted by neurons with long processes, or axons, along which action potentials are propagated.

In many invertebrates, particularly those with translucent bodies, the motor-and interneurons, which generate patterns of muscle contraction, contain pigment and are directly sensitive to light. This sensitivity is the basis of the diffuse "dermal" light sense of various molluscs, echinoids and crustacea which do not possess photoreceptor cells but nevertheless are sensitive to light, and particularly to a sudden dimming of light caused by an animal passing overhead (Millott, 1968).

Most animals sensitive to light possess *photoreceptor* cells, specialised for the transduction of light into a receptor potential. Photoreceptor cells may be scattered over the skin, as in earthworms, or may be concentrated into patches called *eyespots*, such as those along the mantle edge of some bivalve molluscs.

Recall that it is the spatial pattern of light in the optic array which provides information about the environment. To what extent can an animal with single receptor cells or patches of cells in eyespots detect spatial pattern? The answer is that it cannot, since a single receptor cell samples the *total* light reaching it from all directions.

It can, however, detect changes over time in total intensity and invertebrates with a dermal light sense or simple eyespots probably do no more than this. For an aquatic animal, a sudden reduction in light intensity is likely to mean a potential predator is passing overhead, and clams and jellyfish respond to such dimming with defensive responses.

If any spatial pattern in the optic array is to be detected, an animal must have a *number* of photoreceptors and each must be sensitive to light in a narrow segment of the array. In practice, any photoreceptor cell has some such directional sensitivity. The way pigment is arranged in the cell makes it more sensitive to light from some directions than from others, and further directional sensitivity is achieved in simple eyespots by screening the receptor cells with a layer of dark pigment.

An animal with eyespots distributed over its body, each screened by pigment, therefore has some ability to detect spatial pattern in the light reaching it (see Fig. 1.6). It would, for example, be able to use the pattern of activity in its eyespots to maintain its swimming orientation by keeping the source of greatest light intensity above it, or to orient defensive responses according to the rough direction of approach of a predator.

The evolution of greater complexity in eyes can be thought of as the invention of various ways of improving directional sensitivity. One simple way of doing this is to sink a patch of receptor cells into the skin to make an "eye-cup" or *ocellus* (Fig. 1.7). Many invertebrates possess eye-cups, particularly coelenterates, flatworms, molluscs and annelid worms. Eye-cups vary in the detail of their structure; some are open to the water, others are filled with gelatinous material, while many contain a crystalline lens.

A hypothetical transparent disc-shaped animal with patches of photoreceptor cells around its edge. The lengths of the bars in the lower diagram represent the intensities of light falling on each patch. In (a) each patch is sensitive to light through 360° and so each receives the same amount of light. In (b) and (c), screening of the patches by pigment reduces the angle through which they are sensitive to light. The amounts of light striking each receptor now differ, and the differences specify the direction of the water surface (b) or an overhead object (c).

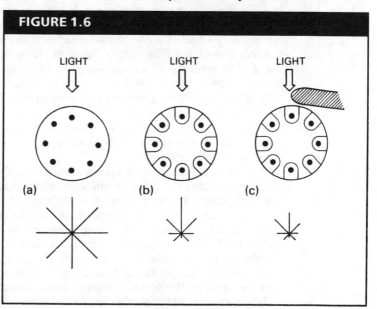

FIGURE 1.6

Examples of eye—
cups, from the
limpet Patella (a)
and the snail
Murex (b). Fig.
10.37 from
Invertebrate
Zoology, Third
Edition by Robert
D. Barnes,
copyright © 1974
by Saunders
College
Publishing, a
division of Holt,
Rinehart and
Winston, Inc.,
reprinted by
permission of the
publisher.

FIGURE 1.7

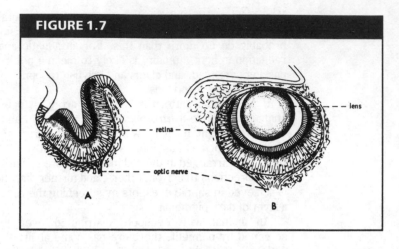

The receptor cells in an eye-cup are clearly sensitive to light from a narrower angle than if they were on the surface of the skin, and the presence of a refractile lens further helps to reject light rays at a large angle from the axis. An animal with eye-cups distributed over its body can, because of this greater directional sensitivity, detect finer spatial pattern in the optic array than can the animal in Figure 1.6 with its eye-spots. Some molluscs have rows of regularly spaced eye-cups along the body—examples are the marine gastropod *Corolla* and some bivalves with eye-cups along the mantle edge—and these animals are potentially able to detect nearby moving objects through successive dimming of light in adjacent eye-cups.

Because the angles through which eye-cups are sensitive to light are wide, and overlap a good deal, the degree of directional sensitivity achieved by an animal with many eye-cups is not great. Further directional sensitivity requires the possession of a true *eye*. The eye-cups of molluscs appear to be miniature eyes, but their function differs from that of eyes in a crucial way. A true eye forms an *image* on a layer of photoreceptor cells. When an image is formed, all light rays reaching the eye from one point in space are brought together at one point in the image, so that each receptor cell in the eye is struck by light coming from a different narrow segment of the optic array.

In most mollusc eye-cups possessing a lens, the image lies some distance behind the layer of photoreceptors (Land, 1968) and so spatial pattern in the optic array is not mapped on to the array of receptors in a single eye-cup. Instead, following the principle illustrated in Figure 1.6, it is mapped onto the array of eye-cups over the body. In a sense, it is the whole animal that is an eye. To build a true eye requires *both* concentrations of photoreceptor cells into one part of the body *and* some apparatus for forming an image on them. We describe the two basic structural plans of eyes, the compound and the single-chambered eye.

The Compound Eye

A compound eye can be constructed by continuing the process of making eye-cups more directionally sensitive, while at the same time making them smaller and grouping them all together into a single structure. Eyes of this kind have evolved in some bivalve molluscs (e.g. *Arca*) and in the marine annelid *Branchioma*, but the most elaborate eyes based on this principle are those of crustaceans and insects. A compound eye is made up of a number of *ommatidia*; each one is a small, elongated eye-cup with a crystalline cone at the tip and the light-sensitive *rhabdom* below it. Transparent cuticle—the cornea—covers the whole array of ommatidia (Fig. 1.8a).

Compound eyes vary in several ways around this basic plan. The number of ommatidia varies greatly, and the structure of the cone differs in the eyes of different insect groups, some eyes not having a cone at all. A particularly important kind of variability in the compound eye is the degree of optical isolation between adjacent ommatidia. This is greatest in the *apposition* type of eye, characteristic of some crustaceans and of diurnal insects, in which the rhabdoms and cones touch and there is absorptive screening pigment between the ommatidia. These two features reduce the amount of light that can reach a rhabdom from cones other than that above it and so keeps the angle of acceptance of light of each ommatidium low.

At the other extreme is the *superposition* eye, which has less pigment between ommatidia and a clear space between the layer of

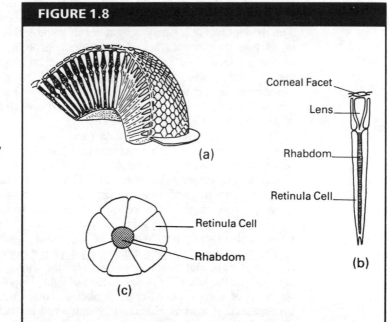

FIGURE 1.8

(a) Schematic diagram of the compound eye of an insect. (b) The structure of a single ommatidium. (c) Cross section through an ommatidium, showing the rhabdom made up from overlapping folds of retinula cell membrane. Adapted from Wigglesworth (1964).

cones and the layer of rhabdoms, so that there is more opportunity for light to reach a rhabdom from neighbouring cones. The difference in structure between apposition and superposition eyes reflects an important difference in the means by which they form an image on the layer of rhabdoms. In the apposition eye, light striking the cone of an ommatidium from outside its narrow angle of acceptance does not reach the rhabdom, but is either reflected or absorbed. This mechanism yields an image in bright light, but has the disadvantage that, in dim light, each ommatidium cannot gather sufficient light to stimulate the receptors.

In a superposition eye, on the other hand, light rays from one point in space striking *many* adjacent cones are brought to a focus on the same rhabdom. Three different types of superposition eye have been identified, which use different optical arrangements to focus light rays in this way, and their details are described by Nilsson (1988). The result in all three cases is that each rhabdom gathers light over a wide area of the eye without losing directional sensitivity. Superposition eyes can therefore provide vision in dimmer light than can apposition eyes, and accordingly are commonly found in nocturnal insects and in marine crustacea.

So far, we have seen how the structure of a compound eye ensures that each rhabdom samples a small segment of the optic array. How do the rhabdoms transduce the light striking them into electrical changes in nerve cells which can ultimately modulate behaviour? Figures 1.8b and 1.8c show the structure of a typical rhabdom, made up of between six and eight *retinula* cells arranged like the slices of an orange. The inner membrane of each retinula cell is folded into a tubular structure called the *rhabdomere*.

The rhabdomeres contain molecules of *rhodopsin* pigment. The rhodopsins are a family of light-sensitive molecules, each made up of two components linked together; a protein, opsin, and a smaller molecule, retinal. The shape of retinal changes when it absorbs light, and this change is coupled to an increase in membrane conductance and consequently a wave of depolarisation. The size of this *receptor potential* is proportional to the logarithm of the intensity of light striking the cell.

Most diurnal insects and crustaceans possess more than one type of retinula cell, each type having a pigment with a different relationship between wavelength of light and the probability of absorption, or *absorption spectrum*. Commonly, there are three types of pigment, with peak absorption at different points in the range of wavelengths from yellow through blue to ultraviolet. As we will see later, possession of two or more pigments with different absorption spectra makes colour vision possible.

The response of single retinula cells does not depend only upon the wavelength and intensity of light striking them; they are also sensitive to the *plane of polarisation* of light. Unpolarised light is made up of waves vibrating in all planes around the direction of propagation. If light is absorbed or diffracted in such a way that some planes of vibration are represented more than others, the light is said to be polarised. One piece of information that the plane of polarisation of light from the sky can provide is the position of the sun, even when completely blocked by cloud, and bees make use of this information in navigating.

Single-Chambered Eyes

The second basic structural plan for eyes is that of the single-chambered eye, which can be derived by enlargement and modification of a *single* eye-cup rather than by massing eye-cups together. Figure 1.9 shows three devices — a pinhole camera, a concave mirror and a convex lens — which can form an image, and all three designs can be achieved by modifying an eye-cup in different ways.

A pinhole camera can be made from an eye-cup by nearly closing off its opening, and the cephalopod *Nautilus* possesses an eye of this kind. The design has not been a popular one in the animal kingdom because the aperture of a pinhole camera must be small to form an image and so can admit only small amounts of light.

A concave mirror can be made by coating the back of an eye-cup with reflecting material and moving the photoreceptors forward to

FIGURE 1.9

The optics of image formation. An image is formed when rays of light arriving at one point I in the image plane (IP) all come from the same point O in space. In the pinhole camera (a) this occurs because the aperture is so small that each point in the image plane is illuminated by light arriving through a narrow cone. A concave mirror (b) reflects light in such a way that all rays striking it from one point are brought to a focus at the same point in the image plane. A convex lens (c) achieves the same result by refraction of light.

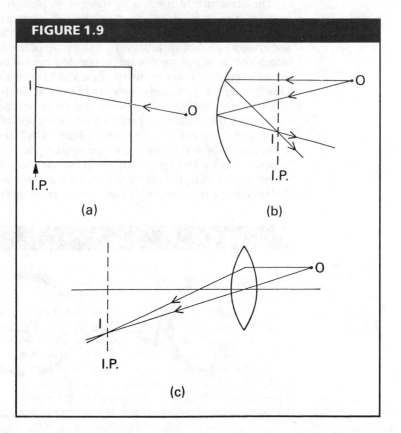

the image plane. The eyes of the scallop *Pecten* are arranged in this way, with a silvery layer of guanine crystals at the back of the eye forming an image at the level of the retina (Land, 1968). This is also a rare tactic, and only one other animal, the deep-sea ostracod crustacean *Gigantocypris*, is known to adopt it.

By far the most evolutionarily successful type of single-chambered eye uses a convex lens, as a camera does, and is found in the vertebrates and the cephalopod molluscs (octopus and squid). This type of eye has evolved by the enlargement of the eye-cup so that the image formed by the lens falls on the receptor cells and not behind them. Intermediates on the evolutionary route from eye-cup to single-chambered eye can be seen in gastropod molluscs such as *Pterotrachea* and in the alciopid annelids.

For the moment, we will only outline the basic structure of the vertebrate eye, before looking at it in detail in the next section. Figure 1.10 shows the important components of this kind of eye—the cornea, iris, lens and retina—and also the remarkable degree of convergent evolution of the eye in two unrelated groups of animals, the cephalopods and the vertebrates (a convergence so close that dilation of the pupil of the eye signals sexual arousal in cuttlefish just as in people).

The structure of the retina, the mat of photoreceptors at the back of the eye, does differ in the two groups. Cephalopod photoreceptors are built on the same rhabdomeric plan as those of the arthropods, but vertebrate receptors are of the *ciliary* type, in which the layers of membrane containing light-sensitive pigment are stacked in an outer segment of the cell. There are two types of ciliary receptor, rods and cones, and they have differently shaped outer segments (Fig. 1.11). Rods and cones are packed into the retina with their long axes parallel to the direction of incident light, and a layer of absorptive pigment behind, which reduces internal reflection. Whereas receptors in the cephalopod eye are arranged sensibly, facing the light from the lens, the vertebrate retina is "inverted"; that is, the rods and cones are in the layer of the retina furthest from the lens, with their outer segments pointing away

Section through (a) an octopus eye and (b) a human eye. (a) Adapted from Barnes (1968). (b) Adapted from Walls (1942).

FIGURE 1.10

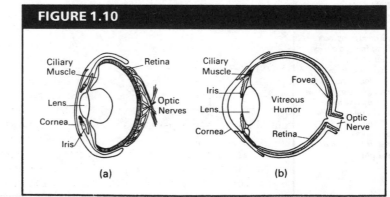

(a)   (b)

FIGURE 1.11

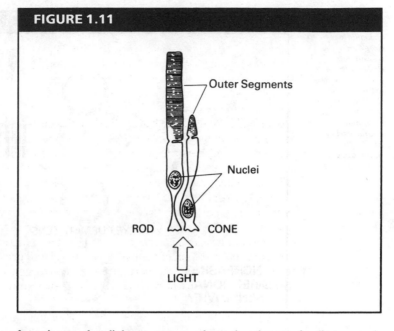

Structure of rod and cone in the vertebrate retina. The outer segments contain folded layers of membrane packed with light—sensitive pigment. Adapted from Uttal (1981).

from it, so that light must pass through a layer of cells to reach them.

The pigments in rods and cones belong to the rhodopsin family, and transduction begins in the same way as in the retinula cells of insects; photons absorbed by the retinal part of the rhodopsin molecule cause it to change in shape and to detach from the opsin part. This change triggers a cascade of enzymatic processes in the outer segment which result in the breakdown of cyclic guanosine monophosphate (cGMP). This in turn causes the conductance of a channel in the cell membrane, gated by cGMP, to fall, and the membrane is hyperpolarised. In darkness, cGMP is resynthesised and the membrane potential returns to its resting level. The details of these biochemical processes are described by Pugh and Cobbs (1986); note that the overall effect of light striking a rod or cone is to cause a hyperpolarising receptor potential (in contrast to the depolarisation of a rhabdomeric receptor).

Conclusions

The pattern of evolution of light-sensitive structures in animals, as we have outlined it, is summarised in Figure 1.12, and the interested reader will find further details in Land (1981). The central theme in this pattern is increasing directional sensitivity of photoreceptors and therefore increasing ability to detect spatial pattern and movement in the optic array. At one extreme, a jellyfish can detect dimming of the total light reaching it in order to escape from an overhead predator, while at the other a hawk can spot a mouse running through grass hundreds of feet below.

Schematic diagram of the evolution of different types of eye. (a) "Pinhole" eye of Nautilus; (b) Reflecting eye of Pecten; (c) Single-chambered eye; (d) Single ommatidium; (e) Compound eye.

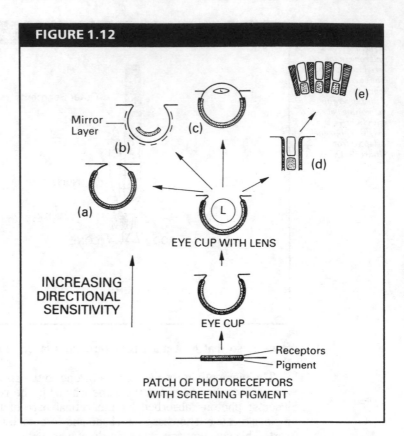

FIGURE 1.12

As we have seen, increased directional sensitivity has been achieved in a variety of ways, through the evolution of two quite differently constructed eyes, and the modification of each type to form an image in more than one way. It would be mistaken to attempt to rank these different types of eye in order of merit, and in particular to see the vertebrate eye as an evolutionary pinnacle. As Kirschfeld (1976) has shown, the eyes of vertebrates and insects achieve comparable directional sensitivity, but the two designs are most appropriate for large and small animals respectively. We see here an example of diverse biological solutions to the common problem of image formation.

THE ADAPTIVE RADIATION OF THE VERTEBRATE EYE

In the remainder of this chapter we examine in more detail the workings of the vertebrate eye and particularly the differences between the eyes of different species. In the course of evolution, many variations on the basic single-chambered plan have evolved and, to some extent, these variations are related to the demands of each species' environment and way of life. This kind of evolutionary modification of a basic structure is called *adaptive radiation*.

Focusing the Image

The fundamental job of a single-chambered eye is to map the spatial pattern in the optic array onto the retina by forming an image; all light rays striking the eye from one point in space are brought to a focus at one point on the retina. What influences how efficiently vertebrate eyes do this?

The ability of a person or animal to detect fine spatial pattern is expressed as their *visual acuity*. This can be measured by the use of a *grating*; a pattern of parallel vertical dark bars equal in width and separated by bright bars of the same width. As the dark and bright bars are made narrower, there comes a point when an observer is no longer able to *resolve* the grating; that is, to distinguish it from a uniform field of the same average brightness. Since the width of the bars at which this happens will depend on how far the observer is from the grating, we do not measure width as a distance but as a *visual angle*; the angle which a bar subtends at the eye. Figure 1.13 shows how size, distance and visual angle are related. Under optimal lighting conditions, the minimum separation between the centres of adjacent dark and bright bars which a person can resolve is about 0.5 min of arc.

Visual acuity is limited by several processes. The first is the efficiency with which the optical apparatus of the eye maps the spatial pattern of the optic array on to the retina. The second is the efficiency with which receptor cells convert that pattern into a pattern of electrical activity; and the third is the extent to which information available in the pattern of receptor cell activity is detected by the neural apparatus of retina and brain. For the moment, our concern is with the first of these processes, and the important consideration is how sharply the eye focuses an image on the retina. As an image becomes more blurred, spatial pattern in the optic array is smoothed out in the pattern of light at the retina and the detection of fine differences is compromised.

Before considering how the eyes of different species achieve optimal focusing, we need to explain in more detail the optical principles governing the formation of an image by a single-chambered eye. An image is formed because light is bent, or

The formula relating visual angle θ subtended by an object to its height h, and its distance from a lens d, and also to the height i of its image on a projection plane at a distance r from the lens. For small visual angles, the retinal surface approximates to a projection plane, and r is the diameter of the eye and i the height of the retinal image. For larger visual angles, the curvature of the retina is significant, and the relationship tan θ = i/r does not hold.

FIGURE 1.13

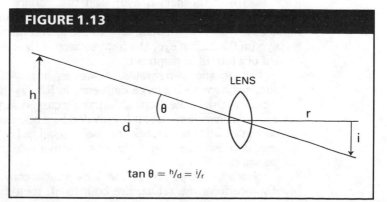

$$\tan \theta = {}^h\!/_d = {}^i\!/_r$$

refracted, at the boundary between two transparent media of different optical densities, such as air and glass. The degree of bending of light is determined by the difference in refractive index of the two media. In a convex lens, the two air–glass boundaries are curved in such a way that parallel rays of light are bent through a greater angle the greater their distance from the axis (Fig. 1.9c). Rays of light from one point on an object at optical infinity, arriving at the lens in parallel, therefore converge to the focal plane of the lens. The distance of the focal plane from the centre of the lens is its focal length, f.

The greater the degree to which a lens bends parallel light rays to converge at the focus, the shorter its focal length. A convenient measure of a lens' performance is its *power*, defined as the reciprocal of its focal length (power is measured in dioptres if focal length is measured in metres).

An image of an object at infinity is therefore formed at a distance f from the lens, and we say that the *image plane* lies at this distance. If the object is brought closer to the lens, the relationship between its distance u from the lens and the distance v of the image plane is given by:

$$\frac{1}{f} = \frac{1}{u} + \frac{1}{v}$$

As the object comes nearer to the lens, the image plane will therefore move further back from it, so that the image formed on a surface located in the focal plane will be blurred. In a camera, the image is kept focused on the film as object distance varies by changing the distance between the lens and the film. As we shall see, the vertebrate eye solves the problem in a different way.

In a vertebrate eye, there are four refracting surfaces as light passes from medium to cornea to aqueous humour to lens to vitreous humour. The refracting power of each surface is determined both by its curvature (a fatter lens is more powerful) and by the difference in refractive indices (RIs) of the media on either side of it. For an animal living in air, there is a large difference in RI between the medium (RI = 1) and the cornea (RI = 1.376 in the human eye), and this surface has considerable refracting power. Accordingly, the eyes of land vertebrates have a flattened lens contributing little to the total refracting power of the eye (in the human eye, the front surface of the cornea provides 49 out of a total of 59 dioptres).

For aquatic vertebrates, however, none of the refracting surfaces have such a large difference in RIs, as the RI of water is similar to that of the cornea. A strongly curved surface is therefore needed somewhere, and it is provided by a near-spherical lens, not only in aquatic vertebrates but also in squid and octopus. Also, the lens of a fish eye is of a higher refractive index than that of the human eye.

Now, if the power of the lens-cornea combination, and its distance from the retina, are both fixed, then a sharply focused image will only be formed of objects lying at a certain range of distances from the eye. This range is called the *depth of field*, and is the distance over which the object can move to and from the eye without the image plane falling outside the layer of retinal receptors. For a human eye focused at infinity, this range is from about 6 metres to infinity. The reason why we can focus on objects less than 6 metres from the eye is that its optics can be adjusted by a process called *accommodation*.

Three different mechanisms of accommodation are known in vertebrate eyes. One is to alter the radius of curvature of the cornea, a mechanism used by some bird species (Schaeffel & Howland, 1987). The second, used by fish, amphibians and snakes, is to move the lens backwards and forwards to keep the image plane on the retina, and the third, used by other reptiles, birds and mammals, is to alter the power of the lens by changing its shape. In the human eye, contraction of the *ciliary muscles* attached to the lens causes it to thicken, increasing its curvature and therefore its power, so that nearby objects are brought into focus. When the ciliary muscles are fully relaxed, the lens takes on a flattened shape and the eye is focused at infinity.

In this way, the power of the human lens can be adjusted over a range of up to 15 dioptres, a figure which falls with age. The ability to accommodate over a wide range is clearly useful to primates, animals which characteristically examine the detail of objects at close range. The ability of other vertebrates to accommodate does not always need to be as great, and this is true particularly of fish and other aquatic animals. Because light is scattered and absorbed by water, there is no need for the eye to focus on distant objects, and it can be somewhat myopic (unable to bring an object at infinity into focus) without missing out on any information available in the optic array.

In contrast, the need for accommodation is especially great for animals which live both on land and in water, and need to achieve acuity in two media of different refractive index. Diving birds, seals, and amphibious fish and turtles show a fascinating variety of adaptations in eye structure and function to solve this problem.

The problem can be overcome by brute force, as in otters, cormorants and turtles, which possess a highly flexible lens and powerful ciliary muscles, allowing accommodation of up to 50 dioptres. Another tactic, used in the eyes of penguins and the flying fish *Cypselurus*, is to flatten the cornea so that it has little or no refractive power in air or water, and rely largely on the lens for refraction.

Still another solution is to divide the eye into separate image-forming systems with different optical properties. Such eyes are found in the "four-eyed" fish *Anableps*, which swims at the surface with the upper part of the eye, adapted for vision in air, above the surface, and the lower part, adapted for vision in water, below it. Finally, a fourth solution is found in the eyes of seals, which have a spherical lens suitable for underwater vision, but a narrow slit pupil which closes in air to form small apertures which act as pinhole cameras, so that the lens no longer forms the image. More details of these and other adaptations of the eye in amphibious animals are given by Sivak (1978).

Even when an eye is optimally focused, there is a certain degree of blur in the image caused by optical imperfections in the eye. For several reasons, lenses do not bring light rays to a focus in the ideal way we have described so far. First, parallel rays may be brought to a slightly different focus depending on how far from the axis they strike the lens (spherical and comatic aberration) or depending on their orientation relative to the lens (astigmatic aberration). The refractive index of a medium varies with the wavelength of light, so that different wavelengths are brought to a focus in slightly different planes (chromatic aberration). Finally, scattering of light in the fluids of the eye and in the retinal layers overlying the receptors further blurs the image.

A boundary between two segments of the optic array differing in intensity is therefore spread out on the retina to some extent, even with optimal focus. Given the figure for the acuity of the human eye mentioned earlier, however, the impact of these aberrations is not great, at least in optimal conditions. One way in which some sources of aberration, particularly spherical aberration, can be reduced is by constricting the pupil so that light only enters the lens through a narrow aperture. This means of reducing aberration, however, is not available in dim light.

Vision in Bright and Dim Light

If an eye is optimally focused, the spatial pattern in the optic array is transformed into a pattern of light intensity on the retina with a minimum degree of blur. The second constraint on an animal's or a person's visual acuity now comes into play; the efficiency with which this pattern of light on the retina is transformed into a pattern of electrical activity in receptor cells.

One factor which will influence this efficiency will clearly be the density of packing of receptor cells in the retina. The more densely receptors are packed, the finer the details of a pattern of light intensities that can be transformed into differences in electrical activity. If acuity were limited by receptor spacing and not by optical factors, the minimum distance between adjacent dark and bright bars for a grating to be resolved would be equal to the average distance between adjacent receptors (assuming receptors are packed in a rectangular array). The difference in acuity between people and falcons is the result of a difference in receptor packing. The photoreceptors in the falcon's eye are packed three times more densely than in the human eye, and the falcon can resolve a grating with a spacing of 0.2 min of arc, as compared with the figure for a human observer of 0.5 min (Fox, Lehmkuhle & Westendorff, 1976).

A second factor, which we need to dwell on at more length, is the intensity of light striking the retina. It makes a difference to the detectability of a spatial difference in light intensity on the retina whether two neighbouring cells are being struck by 5 and 10 photons per second or by 5000 and 10,000. The reason is that, even under constant illumination, the rate at which photons strike a receptor fluctuates around an average value, and this variability increases as the square root of the average value. If light intensity is high, so that the average rates of photon flux striking two adjacent receptors are also high, then the difference between the two rates will therefore be large relative to the fluctuation in each.

As the light reaching the eye becomes dimmer, the difference in photon flux at adjacent receptors eventually becomes comparable to the extent of fluctuation, and so is detectable only if the two rates of flux are averaged over a period of time. Now, if this difference is caused by a moving boundary in the optic array, the difference in photon flux may not be present in any part of the retina long enough to be detected. As light becomes dimmer, the maximum speed of movement in the optic array which can be detected will fall.

One solution to this problem would be to increase the cross-sectional area of receptor cells so that each sampled a larger segment of the optic array and so received a larger flux of photons. Alternatively, the outputs of neighbouring receptors could be "pooled" by connection to one interneuron, so that they effectively acted as a single receptor. Either solution would increase the *sensitivity* of the eye, but, as we discussed above, they would both decrease its *acuity*. The design of an eye is therefore subject to a trade-off between sensitivity and acuity; what are the implications of this constraint for the evolution of vertebrate eyes?

Many vertebrate species use only part of the daily cycle for their activities, being either nocturnal or diurnal. Nocturnal animals need eyes with high sensitivity in dim moon-and starlight, and this is true also of deep-sea fish. Diurnal animals, on the other hand, can have eyes with high acuity. Even so, it is unusual for a species' vision to operate in a very narrow band of light intensities. The intensities encountered by either a diurnal or a nocturnal animal vary over several orders of magnitude (see Fig. 1.14), and so in either case vision must be adapted to operate in a *range* of light intensities. Strict specialisation is likely to be found only in animals such as deep-sea fish and bats living in dark caves by day.

The most striking way in which the vertebrate eye is adapted for vision in a range of light intensities is in the structure of the retina. We noted earlier the two kinds of vertebrate photoreceptor—rods and cones—and saw that a rod has a deeper stack of pigment-filled layers of folded membrane in its outer segment than has a cone. A photon passing through a rod therefore stands a lower chance of coming out the other end than one passing through a cone, and so the membrane potential of a rod will be influenced by levels of light too low to affect a cone.

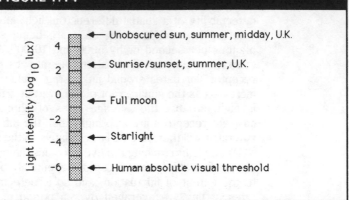

FIGURE 1.14

Typical values for light intensity at different times of day and under different conditions. Note that intensity varies over several log units in both daytime and night−time conditions. Adapted from Martin (1985).

It is therefore not surprising that there is a correlation between the ratio of rods to cones in an animal's retina and its ecology. Diurnal animals have a higher proportion of cones than do nocturnal animals, though pure-cone retinas are rare, found mostly in lizards and snakes. Pure-rod retinas are also rare, found only in animals—deep-sea fish and bats—which never leave dark habitats.

A further adaptation of the retina in animals active in dim light is the presence of a silvery *tapetum* behind the retina, which reflects light back through it and so gives the rods a second bite at the stream of photons, though at the cost of increasing blur through imperfect reflection. The glow of a cat's eyes in the dark is caused by reflection of light by a tapetum behind its retina.

A possibility exploited by a few nocturnal animals is to use infrared (IR) radiation, which can provide information about the environment in the absence of visible light, subject to some limitations. First, IR is rapidly absorbed by water, and therefore only potentially useful on land. Secondly, the IR radiation emitted by a warm-blooded animal would screen any radiation it detected, and so we would only expect sensitivity to IR in cold-blooded animals. Thirdly, it could only be used to detect objects differing in temperature from the rest of the environment.

The one group of vertebrates which do detect information carried by IR radiation are a group of snakes, the pit vipers, which hunt for small birds and mammals at night. The cornea and lens of the vertebrate eye are opaque to IR, and so a different kind of sensory organ is required. These snakes have specialized organs alongside the eyes, acting as pinhole cameras to form an IR image of their surroundings, which enable them to detect the location of nearby warm-blooded animals.

So, a retina containing only rods or only cones adapts an animal for vision in a narrow range of light intensities. How is retinal structure adapted for vision over a wider range? Imagine that we start with an animal which is basically diurnal but needs to be equipped with some night vision. We add rods to the pure-cone retina, scattering them about evenly among the cones. We discover, though, that to capture much light at night, we need a great many rods. In the human eye, for example, there are 120 million rods as opposed to only 7 million cones.

Now, if we have added the rods evenly over the retina, we would find the distances between the cones are now much larger than when we started and that acuity in daytime vision is reduced. The way out of this problem in many vertebrate eyes is to divide the retina into two regions. One small area is rich in cones, with little or no pooling of the outputs of adjacent receptors, while the other, larger, area is rich in rods, with considerable pooling of outputs. The cone-rich region provides high acuity vision in bright light, whilst the rod-rich area provides high sensitivity vision in dim light.

This pattern is found especially in birds and in primates, where the cone-rich area is usually circular, and sometimes contains a pit-like depression in the retina, called a *fovea*. The cone-rich area of the human eye is called the *macula lutea*, and it contains a fovea. There are only cones in the centre of the fovea, and their proportion and density of packing decrease further out into the retina. At more than about 10° from the centre, outside the macula, there are few cones, and the peripheral part of the retina contains almost all rods.

There are other ways in which vertebrate eyes are adapted to operate over a range of light intensities. One is movement of cells containing pigment, and sometimes also the receptor cells, in the retina. These *retinomotor* responses are found in fish, and in some reptiles and birds, and act to screen the rods with pigment in bright light and to expose them in dim light.

A second mechanism, rare in fish but more common in birds and especially mammals, is dilation and constriction of the pupil by the muscular tissue of the iris. In diurnal mammals, the pupil is usually round, and its function is to reduce the aperture of the lens in bright light and so reduce blur of the retinal image due to spherical and other optical aberrations. In dim light, when sensitivity and not acuity is at a premium, the pupil opens to admit more light. Mammals active in both day and night often have a slit pupil, which, for mechanical reasons, can close more completely than a round one. A cat's eye has a retina adapted for nocturnal vision and a slit pupil which allows it to operate in the daytime.

A third process, known as *adaptation*, occurs in the retinas of many animals to adjust the sensitivity of photoreceptors and interneurons to varying intensities of light. In the human eye, the iris does not play a major role in regulating the intensity of light reaching the retina, and so adaptation is the main means by which sensitivity is adjusted. We can see over a range of approximately 7 log units of light intensity (a 10^7 -fold range), but at any one time, our vision is effective over a range of only one or two log units, and this range can shift upwards (light adaptation) or downwards (dark adaptation). We return to adaptation in Chapter 2.

To conclude, vertebrate eyes are subject to the basic physical constraint that greater sensitivity in dim light can only be won at the cost of reduced acuity. Different species strike different bargains between these two factors, depending upon their ecology, but many manage to operate over a range of light intensities. Humans are an example of a basically diurnal species with acute *photopic* (bright light) vision and some degree of low acuity *scotopic* (dim light) vision. We are fairly adaptable, though not as much as cats!

Sampling the Optic Array

An animal with simple eye-cups distributed over its body can detect light reaching it from any direction, and therefore, at any instant, it samples the entire optic array. As soon as an animal's photo-receptors are concentrated into a pair of compound or single chambered eyes at the front of the body, constraints arise on how the optic array can be sampled.

Some insects, such as the dragonfly, have large compound eyes wrapped almost completely around the head and so can gather light from almost the entire optic array without moving. The angle through which light striking a single vertebrate eye is focused onto the retina can be as great as 200°, and so the same opportunity exists for nearly panoramic vision. This is achieved by placing the eyes *laterally*, on either side of the head with their axes perpendicular to the body.

All vertebrate groups include species having laterally placed eyes. By and large, the arrangement is characteristic of animals especially vulnerable to predation, such as fish living in open water, ground living birds such as quail and chickens, and grazing mammals such as rabbits and horses. The dominant consideration in the arrangement of these animals' eyes is the need to detect predators approaching from any direction.

In other species, however, there are other demands on eye structure and position which reduce the angle through which light reaching the eye is focused on the retina. First, animals with a small, cone-rich area in the retina can sample only a small segment of the optic array at any instant, under photopic conditions. Second, some species need to make the image at the retina larger in order to increase acuity. This is particularly true of predatory birds needing to spot prey from a considerable height; such birds have a deeper eye than that of ground-living birds. Just as in a telephoto lens, however, increased magnification is achieved at the cost of a reduced field of view.

Third, animals with laterally placed eyes have only a small degree of *binocular overlap*—that segment of the optic array which is sampled by both eyes. For reasons which we discuss in Chapter 7, binocular overlap can contribute to the perception of depth, and the eyes of some species are swung forward from the lateral position in order to take advantage of this possibility. The greatest extent of binocular overlap is found in primates, which have their eyes at the front of the head with parallel axes. The human eye, for example, accepts light through an angle of about 150°, but binocular overlap means that the angle for two eyes is not much greater.

Many birds have an arrangement of eyes which compromises between binocular and lateral placement, with some degree of overlap of the angles of admission of light of the eyes. Examples are hummingbirds and various birds of prey, which often have two cone-rich areas in each retina, one corresponding to an area of acute monocular vision, and one corresponding to the area of overlap between the two eyes.

If, for one or more of these reasons, an animal has less than panoramic vision, it can only sample the entire optic array over time, by moving its eyes. In some vertebrates, such as frogs, the eyes cannot move relative to the body to any appreciable extent. For such animals, sampling the optic array through eye movement would mean moving the whole body, which would clash with other concurrent demands on body movement. Consequently, animals with immobile eyes usually have them laterally placed to allow panoramic vision.

One means of moving the eyes is available when the head can move relative to the body, and most birds use head movement to scan through the optic array. Birds of prey, in particular, can rotate their heads through large angles. A second means comes with the ability to move the eyes relative to the head. Most vertebrates can do this to some extent, although few can move their eyes through large angles. The chameleon is an animal with strikingly mobile eyes; its angle of vision is small, and, as it searches for prey, its two laterally placed eyes swivel about quite independently, giving a distinctly creepy impression!

The chameleon apart, the eyes of primates make the largest, most rapid and most precisely controlled eye movements. The human eye is held in position by a dynamic balance between three pairs of antagonistic muscles, and instability in this balance causes a continuous small-amplitude *tremor*. As a result, the image on the retina is in constant motion, any point on it moving by about the distance between two adjacent foveal cones in 0.1 sec.

Sampling of the optic array is achieved by three kinds of eye movement. First, rapid and intermittent jumps of eye position called *saccades* are made in order to fixate an object with foveal vision. As a person reads or looks at a picture, their eyes make several saccades each second to scan the page or screen.

Once an object is fixated, *pursuit* movements keep it in foveal vision as it moves, or as the observer moves. If the distance of an object from the observer changes, *convergence* movements keep it fixated by the foveas of both eyes. As an object comes closer, convergence movements turn the directions of gaze of both eyes towards the nose. If an object comes within a few inches of the face, further convergence is impossible and "double vision" occurs (we say more about convergence and stereoscopic vision in Chapter 7). Whereas saccades are sudden, intermittent changes of eye position, both pursuit and convergence are smooth, continuous eye movements.

In conclusion, the human eye at any instant samples a relatively large segment of the optic array (the *peripheral* field) with low acuity, and a much smaller segment (the *central*, or foveal field) with high acuity. Smooth and saccadic eye movements shift this high-acuity segment about rapidly, so that acute vision over a wide angle is achieved. Further details of human eye movements, their anatomical and neural mechanisms, and models of their control may be found in Carpenter (1977).

This highly specialised way in which we sample the optic array makes it difficult for us to appreciate the different ways in which other animals do so. We are used to detecting what another person is looking at from the direction in which their eyes are pointing, but this direction may mean something quite different in other species. A horse, sheep or rabbit does not need to look straight at something in order to see it, while the angle of a bird's head may be related to what it is looking at in quite a different way depending on whether it is fixating monocularly or binocularly. It is only when watching animals such as cats and apes looking that we are on familiar ground!

Detecting Colour

A vertebrate eye maps not only the pattern of light intensities in the optic array onto the retina but also the pattern of different spectral compositions of light. We have already seen that the spectral composition of light in a segment of the optic array can carry information about the kind of surface the light was reflected from. The intensities of light reflected from a leaf and from an insect resting on it might be equal, but if they reflected different mixtures of wavelengths it would pay a bird searching for food to be able to detect this difference; in other words, to detect the difference in *colour* between the two surfaces.

It is important to note that our perception of the colour of a surface is not determined only by the spectral composition of light reflected from it, but also by the intensity and composition of light from surrounding surfaces (see Chapter 3, p. 68). Even so, for colour vision to be possible at all, an animal or person must possess a retina which is sensitive to differences in wavelength of light independently of differences in intensity, and this requires the presence of at least two sets of receptor cells, each containing a pigment with a different absorption spectrum.

Why are two or more types of receptor required for colour vision? The absorption spectrum of a receptor's pigment determines how the receptor potential varies with the wavelength of light striking it. A difference in the spectral composition of light falling on two neighbouring receptors containing the same pigment will therefore cause a difference in their electrical response, but an appropriate difference in light intensity alone will cause exactly the same difference in response. In a retina containing only one type of receptor cell, the pattern of receptor potentials therefore does not carry information about the patterns of intensity and of spectral composition in the optic array independently, and an animal with such a retina is incapable of colour vision.

We have already seen that insects usually possess three types of retinula cell, each with a different pigment. In any one vertebrate species, all rods in the retina contain the same pigment type, and so animals with pure-rod retinas cannot detect wavelength and intensity differences independently. This need not be a handicap; for deep-sea fish, the spectrum of available light is narrow, and such fish usually have a pure-rod retina in which the peak of the absorption spectrum of the pigment matches the blue light available.

Species capable of colour vision may have cones with a pigment different from that in the rods, or they may have two or three types of cone, each with different pigments. The cones of birds and some reptiles additionally contain coloured oil droplets through which light must pass to reach the outer segment, and these coloured filters will further differentiate the wavelength sensitivities of cones.

Coloured oil droplets in bird and reptile cones may have two further functions. The droplets are always red, orange or yellow, and Walls (1942) argues that they act to screen out short wavelength light and thereby improve acuity in two ways; by reducing chromatic aberration and by filtering out light scattered from the sky in the same way as a skylight filter on a camera does. He suggests that the yellow pigmentation of the lens in the human eye and of the macula lutea may have similar functions. Alternatively, Kirschfeld (1982) proposes that the function of such pigments is to screen short wavelength light which damages receptor cells through photooxidation.

The presence of different pigments in different cone types is the most common basis for vertebrate colour vision. Some fish and turtle species have cones large enough for direct recording with a microelectrode, and this method reveals three types of cone with different wavelength sensitivities. The cones in the primate retina are too small for direct recording, but they fall into three classes having pigments with different absorption characteristics. In the case of the human retina, these pigments have peak absorption at 419, 531 and 558 nm (Fig. 1.15), and presumably cones containing these pigments have corresponding peaks in their sensitivity spectra. In photopic conditions, we are able to distinguish colours because of this differential sensitivity of cones, while in scotopic conditions, when only rods are stimulated, we have no colour vision.

We have explained how the possession of photoreceptors with two or more pigments differing in their absorption spectra is a

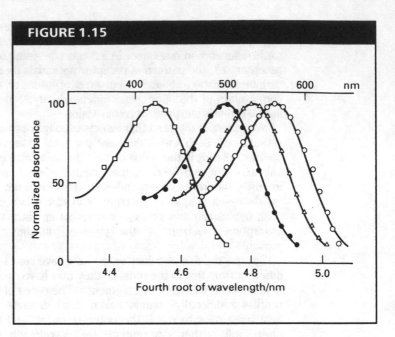

Absorption spectra of the four types of human photoreceptor. From left to right, curves are for: blue–sensitive cones, rods, green–sensitive cones and red–sensitive cones. Reproduced from Dartnall, Bowmaker and Mollon (1983) with permission of author and publishers.

FIGURE 1.15

necessary precondition for colour vision, and we deal further with this topic in Chapter 3 (p. 68). A full introduction to psychophysical studies of colour vision, and to the relationships between their findings and the properties of cone pigments, is given by Mollon (1982).

CONCLUSIONS

We have followed the workings of the vertebrate eye from the entry of light through the cornea to the formation of a pattern of receptor potentials in the receptor cells of the retina. We have seen how the eye is adapted in different ways in different species to maximise the amount of information in the optic array captured in this pattern of excitation, and that the extent to which this can be achieved is constrained by various factors, especially the amount of available light. A more detailed account of the adaptive radiation of the vertebrate eye is given in Walls' (1942) classic work, and a fuller treatment of the anatomy, physiology and optics of the human eye can be found in Barlow and Mollon (1982).

The reason why the spatial pattern of the optic array is captured in the pattern of retinal activity is that each receptor is influenced by light from a narrow segment of the array. This in turn happens because the optics of the eye form an image on the retina. The same thing happens in a camera, where the light striking each light-sensitive grain in the film comes from a narrow segment of the optic array, and so the camera is a useful analogy for understanding the optics of the eye.

It is important to realise, however, that the analogy between camera and eye has serious limitations. First, there are differences in quality between retinal images and images formed by cameras. Judged by the same standards as a camera, even the most sophisticated eye forms an image of extremely poor quality, and would be put to shame by an Instamatic camera. As well as the optical aberrations causing blur which we have already mentioned, there are aberrations of lens and cornea causing distortion of the image. Together with the curvature of the retina, these mean that images of straight lines are curved and metrical relations in the image do not correspond to those in the world.

In addition, the movements of the eye consist not just of a series of fixations, during which the image is static, but of smooth movements and tremor, causing the image to move continually; a camera which moved in this way would produce blurred pictures. The image also has a yellowish cast, particularly in the macular region, and it contains shadows of the blood vessels overlying the layer of receptor cells in the retina.

In principle, as these factors cause predictable distortions of the retinal image, it would be possible to correct for them and to recover the right metrical relations, colours and other properties of the image (although any pattern lost through blurring could not be recovered). To think in terms of "cleaning up" the retinal image to the point where it resembles a photograph implies, however, that the role of the eye is to take a snapshot of the world at each fixation and to send a stream of pictures to the brain to be examined there.

This conception of the eye's role betrays a second, more serious, limitation to the analogy between camera and eye. The purpose of a camera is to produce a picture to be viewed by people, but the purpose of the eye and brain is to extract the information from the changing optic array needed to guide an animal's or a person's actions, or to specify objects or events of importance. Although this could be achieved by first converting the retinal image into a neural "image" of photograph-like quality and then extracting information from this second image, such a process seems implausible on grounds of economy; it would be wasteful.

Blurring apart, the imperfections of the retinal image do not result in the loss of any information about spatial pattern and changes in spatial pattern in the optic array, and a more plausible design for a visual system would involve the extraction of important variables of pattern directly from the pattern of electrical activity in rods and cones, without first correcting distortions. As we show in Chapter 2, the extraction of information about pattern begins in the retina itself, and the optic nerve does not transmit a stream of pictures to the brain, as a television camera does to a television set, but instead transmits *information* about the pattern of light reaching the eyes.

Chapter Two

THE NEUROPHYSIOLOGY OF THE RETINA

*I*nformation is available to animals, in the spatial and temporal pattern of the optic array, to specify the structure of their surroundings and events occurring in them. Compound and single-chambered eyes map this spatiotemporal pattern onto an array of light-sensitive receptor cells, so transforming it into a pattern of electrical activity in these cells. This pattern of receptor cell activity must in its turn be transformed so that information needed to guide the animal's actions is made available.

These further transformations take place in the central nervous system, and one way of studying them is to record the electrical activity of single nerve cells in retina, optic nerve and brain in response to stimulation by light. The ultimate aim of this approach is to understand how information important to an animal is detected by networks of nerve cells and represented in patterns of neural activity. For all but the simplest animals, this is a distant goal indeed, and our knowledge does not yet extend beyond the early stages of neural transformation of patterns of light. In this chapter we describe the first of these stages, the transformation which the pattern of receptor cell activity undergoes in the retina. We consider first a relatively simple example, and then go on to the more complex retina of vertebrates.

THE RETINA OF THE HORSESHOE CRAB

The horseshoe crab *Limulus* has two compound eyes placed laterally on its shell, each made up of several hundred ommatidia. Each of these contains 10 or more retinula cells arranged radially around the dendrite of an eccentric cell (Fig. 2.1). The axons of the eccentric and retinula cells form a bundle, the optic nerve, which runs to the brain. What information passes down the axons making up the optic nerve when light falls on the eye?

FIGURE 2.1

Section through the base of an ommatidium in the Limulus *eye. Retinula cells are packed like the slices of an orange around the dendrite of the eccentric cell, and their inner edges make up the light–sensitive rhabdom. Adapted from Ratliff, Hartline and Lange (1966).*

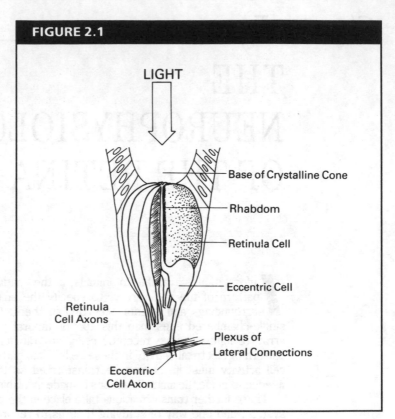

LIGHT

Base of Crystalline Cone

Rhabdom

Retinula Cell

Eccentric Cell

Retinula Cell Axons

Plexus of Lateral Connections

Eccentric Cell Axon

The first step in answering this question was taken by Hartline and Graham (1932), who recorded the activity of single axons in the optic nerve while shining a spot of light onto the corresponding ommatidia. They established that action potentials (impulses) pass down an axon at a rate roughly proportional to the logarithm of the intensity of light falling on its ommatidium. We saw in Chapter 1 that transduction of light by a rhabdomeric receptor generates a depolarisation of the membrane proportional to the logarithm of light intensity, and so this result is just what we would expect.

What is the significance of this *logarithmic* coding of light intensity by impulse frequency in an optic nerve axon? The intensity of light falling on *Limulus'* eye varies by a factor of about 10^{-6} or 10^{-7}, from dim light in deep water to bright light in shallow water under a clear sky. Linear coding would require the same range of impulse frequencies and therefore, since the maximum rate at which impulses can pass down an axon is about $1000 \ sec^{-1}$, the dimmest light would be coded by a frequency of one impulse every several thousand seconds.

Such slow rates of impulse transmission would make it impossible to follow changes in light intensity, and logarithmic coding solves the problem by compressing the range of intensities into a 6 or 7-fold range of impulse frequencies. Logarithmic coding of stimulus intensity is a common feature of many sensory systems, wherever a wide band of physical intensity must be coded by a narrow band of impulse rates.

So far, it seems that the pattern of light intensity over the eye of *Limulus* is reproduced faithfully in the pattern of activity of optic nerve axons, each one reporting light intensity in one part of the optic array. In fact, things are by no means so simple, and both the temporal and the spatial pattern of light undergo transformation in the retina.

Transformation of Temporal Pattern

Impulse frequency in a receptor cell axon does not follow changes in light intensity in a simple way, but shows the phenomenon called adaptation which we mentioned in Chapter 1. At the onset of light, impulse rate rises rapidly to a peak and then falls, after a second or so, to a steady level maintained while the light is on (Fig. 2.2a). Both the peak rate and the steady level are related logarithmically to the intensity of light (Fig. 2.2b). This process is called *light-adaptation*, and it means that a high impulse rate signals a sudden *increase* in light intensity and not a steady bright light.

Second, if a receptor is adapted to light and then left in darkness, its sensitivity to light gradually rises; the impulse rate generated in response to a test flash of light increases rapidly over the first few minutes in darkness, and then more gradually to reach a maximum after about an hour. This process of *dark-adaptation* is the much slower converse of light-adaptation. It means that the activity of an axon does not signal absolute light intensity but intensity *relative* to the degree of dark-adaptation of the receptor.

The effect of these two processes is that the output of a photoreceptor is quite stable over a wide range of light intensities, but that this stability can be disturbed by a sudden change in intensity. The temporal pattern of the output is therefore a

(a) The response of a single ommatidium to light. The frequency of discharge of impulses rises rapidly to a peak and then falls to a steady level within 0.5 sec (b) The peak response (A) and the steady response (B) of a single ommatidium to a flash of light at different light intensities. Note the logarithmic relationship between intensity and response. Adapted from Hartline and Graham (1932).

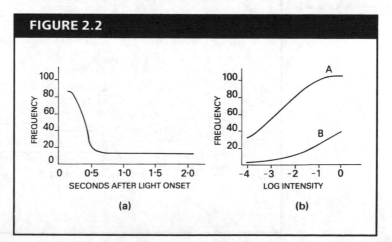

FIGURE 2.2

(a)

(b)

transformation of the temporal pattern of the input; slow changes in light intensity are filtered out while rapid ones are not. This means that the pattern of optic nerve activity will not carry information about gradual changes in the environment such as diurnal fluctuation in light level or gradual changes in turbidity of water, but it will carry information about events such as the shadow of an animal swimming overhead.

Transformation of Spatial Pattern

In their first experiments, Hartline and Graham used spots of light small enough to illuminate only one ommatidium at a time. What happens when, as in real life, light falls on all the ommatidia of the eye? Is the pattern of activity in the optic nerve simply the sum of the responses of individual photoreceptors to light, or do the signals from ommatidia interact with one another?

FIGURE 2.3

Experiments demonstrating lateral inhibition in the eye of Limulus. (a) Light falling on ommatidium B inhibits the response of ommatidium A to light. (b) Ommatidium C is too far from A for it to inhibit A's response. (c) Even so, light falling on C causes an inhibition of B's response and therefore lifts the inhibition imposed by B on A.

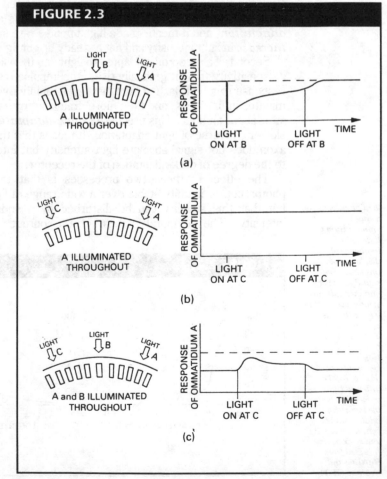

In a classical experiment, summarised in Fig. 2.3a, Hartline, Wagner and Ratliff (1956) demonstrated that the outputs of ommatidia do indeed interact with one another, through a process of *lateral inhibition* between neighbouring photoreceptors. Each cell inhibits the firing rate of those in a roughly circular area around it. The strength of the inhibition rises with increasing intensity of light falling on the inhibiting ommatidium, and falls with increasing distance between the ommatidia. Lateral inhibition is mutual, each photoreceptor being inhibited by its neighbours, which it in turn inhibits. Also, each photoreceptor inhibits its own activity, a process in part responsible for light-adaptation.

This model successfully predicts the effects of more complex patterns of light falling on the eye. For example, the inhibition imposed on ommatidium A by illumination of another B can be reduced by illumination of a third ommatidium C on the far side of B from A (Figs. 2.3b and 2.3c). The neuroanatomical basis of lateral inhibition is in collateral branches spreading sideways from each receptor cell axon in a layer just below the ommatidia, making inhibitory synaptic contacts with other nearby cells (Purple & Dodge, 1965).

Just as adaptation in receptors causes a transformation of the temporal pattern of light at the eye, so lateral inhibition causes a transformation of its spatial pattern. If the whole eye is evenly and diffusely illuminated, excitation of receptor cells by light will be largely cancelled by inhibition from neighbouring cells. The activity of optic nerve axons will therefore be low and will vary little with changes in light level.

Consider next what happens if there is a sharp boundary between a brightly and a dimly lit area of the eye. The output of those ommatidia lying just inside the bright area will be less inhibited, as their neighbours to the dim side are less active, while the output of those just across the boundary will be more inhibited, as their neighbours are more active. The result is shown in Figure 2.4; a steeper gradient in impulse rate at the boundary than would occur without lateral inhibition.

Just as adaptation transforms temporal pattern to give prominence to rapid changes in light intensity, so lateral inhibition gives prominence to rapid *spatial* changes in light intensity. Shallow gradients of intensity over the eye are smoothed out in the pattern of optic nerve activity, while steep gradients are maintained. The optic nerve will therefore carry information about some features of the crab's environment but not all. Are these features the important ones in organising the animal's actions?

The optic nerve will carry information about any aspect of the environment specified by sharp boundaries in the optic array. For example, one such boundary will be that between the bright disc of light reaching the animal direct from the sky and the dimmer ring around it scattered through the water. As a result of lateral inhibition, this boundary will be prominent in the pattern of optic nerve activity, and detection of its position could be useful to the

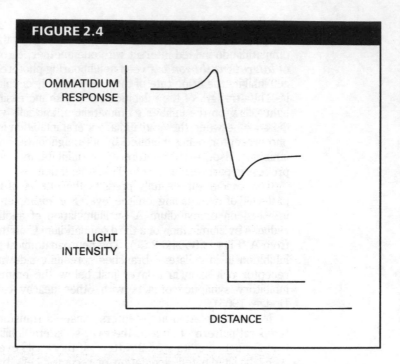

FIGURE 2.4

The responses of a row of ommatidia to a dark–light boundary falling on the eye. Note the sharpening of the response at the boundary caused by lateral inhibition.

OMMATIDIUM RESPONSE

LIGHT INTENSITY

DISTANCE

animal in keeping upright as it moves around an uneven seafloor.

Sharp boundaries in the optic array will also be caused by the shadows of animals swimming overhead. As a shadow moves over the crab's eye, lateral inhibition will generate steep gradients in the responses of ommatidia. Responses will be further increased at the trailing edge of the shadow by a burst of impulses in response to light onset. Again, information specifying an event of significance to the animal—a potential predator passing overhead—is made prominent in the pattern of optic nerve activity and can be used to organise defensive responses.

To conclude, there is a complex relationship between the spatiotemporal pattern of light falling on the eye of *Limulus* and the pattern of activity in the optic nerve. Transformations of pattern occur in the retina which filter out information about slow changes over space and time, and pass on information about rapid changes. These rapid changes specify events in the environment which are significant to the animal, and the challenge for physiological research is now to explore the further transformations which occur between the optic nerve and the pattern of commands to limb muscles.

THE VERTEBRATE RETINA

In Chapter 1, we described the vertebrate retina simply as a carpet of rods and cones covering the back of the eye. In addition, however, there is a layer of nerve cells between the photoreceptors and the vitreous humour filling the eye. It contains four classes of cell in addition to the rods and cones; *horizontal, bipolar, amacrine* and *ganglion* cells.

By detailed electron microscopy, Dowling (1968) established how these classes of neuron connect synaptically, and Figure 2.5 summarises his findings. Receptors synapse in the *outer plexiform layer* with both horizontal cells and bipolar cells, and bipolars synapse in the *inner plexiform layer* with both amacrine and ganglion cells. Some ganglion cells receive input directly from bipolars, while others are driven only by amacrines. The axons of ganglion cells run over the surface of the retina to the blindspot, where they form a bundle, the optic nerve, which runs to the brain. This pattern of synaptic connectivity is common to frogs, monkeys and other vertebrates, but there are important differences between species in the proportions of different types of synapse; a point we will return to later.

Although the vertebrate retina is more complex than that of *Limulus*, there is a basic similarity in structure. In both cases, there are nerve cell pathways running in two directions at right angles to one another; a receptor-brain pathway and a lateral pathway. The first pathway is represented in the *Limulus* retina by the axons of receptor cells, but in the vertebrate retina it

FIGURE 2.5

The structure of the vertebrate retina. RT— receptor terminals; H—horizontal cells; B—bipolar cells; A—amacrine cells; G—ganglion cells. Reproduced from Dowling (1968) with permission of the publishers.

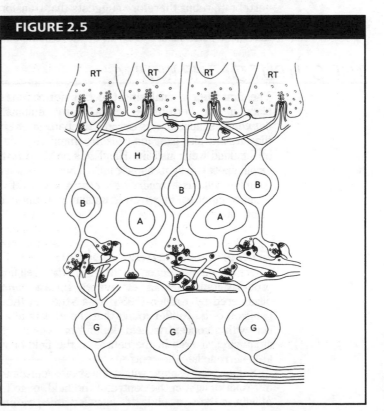

consists of a series of cells linking the receptors through the bipolars and amacrines to the ganglion cells.

Whereas in *Limulus*, each eccentric cell axon runs from one photoreceptor unit, the outputs of vertebrate photoreceptors are pooled together, so that a group of receptors acts as a functional unit. This occurs in two ways; through direct excitatory synaptic contact between neighbouring rods and cones, and through convergence of a number of receptor outputs to a single bipolar cell. The number of receptors pooled reflects the trade-off between acuity and sensitivity discussed in Chapter 1. In a primate eye, for example, each bipolar cell in the fovea connects to one or two cones, whereas in the periphery, a bipolar may connect to many rods. The ganglion cell axons leading from the fovea therefore have the potential to carry information about fine detail in the pattern of receptor excitation, whereas those leading from the periphery sacrifice this potential in order to achieve greater sensitivity to dim light.

The lateral pathway is also simpler in the retina of *Limulus*, and consists of the collaterals of receptor cell axons. In vertebrates, it is made up of two systems, the processes of horizontal cells ramifying in the outer plexiform layer and the processes of amacrine cells in the inner plexiform layer. The anatomy of the vertebrate retina therefore suggests that transformations of spatial pattern similar to those in *Limulus* are carried out, but also hints that these patterns are likely to be more complex.

THE OUTPUT OF THE RETINA

The first step in analysing the transformations of pattern taking place in the vertebrate retina is to establish the relationship between its input and its output; the pattern of light falling on it and the rate at which ganglion cells fire impulses. The first experiments of this kind were just like Hartline's on the *Limulus* retina, using small spots of light as stimuli. These demonstrated that each ganglion cell has a *receptive field*; a region of the retina, usually roughly circular, in which stimulation affects the ganglion cell's firing rate.

Concentric Receptive Fields

There are many different kinds of ganglion cell field, but one type is probably common to all vertebrates. It is the *concentric field*, first discovered by Kuffler (1953) in a study of the responses of cat ganglion cells. Kuffler found that the effects of a spot of light on a cell with a concentric field depend on whether the light falls in a small circular area in the centre of the field or in the ring-shaped area surrounding the centre.

Some cells respond with a burst of impulses to either the onset of a spot of light in the centre of the field, or to the offset of a spot of light in the surround; this is called a *centre-on* response. Other cells show the converse, *centre-off* response; offset of a spot of light in the centre of the field or onset in the surround causes a burst of impulses (Fig. 2.6).

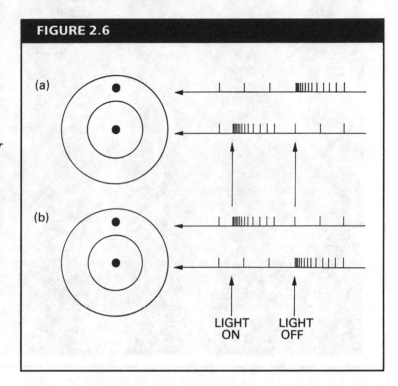

FIGURE 2.6

The responses of cat retinal ganglion cells to spots of light. A centre−on cell (a) responds with a burst of impulses to the onset of a spot of light in the centre of its field or to the offset of a spot of light in the surround area. A centre−off cell (b) responds in the opposite fashion.

(a)

(b)

LIGHT ON   LIGHT OFF

Enroth-Cugell and Robson (1966) found that both these categories of ganglion cell can in turn be divided into two sub-groups differing in their responses to sinusoidal gratings. Like the gratings described in Chapter 1 used to measure visual acuity, a sinusoidal grating is made up of parallel bright and dark bars. Their edges have a blurred appearance, however, as the brightness of the pattern varies sinusoidally with distance rather than changing sharply at the boundaries of the bars. Figure 2.7 shows a sinusoidal grating; the intensity of light reflected from it along a horizontal line follows a sine wave, in just the same way as the sound pressure near a vibrating tuning fork varies sinusoidally with time. A grating is described by the parameters of: *frequency*, expressed as cycles per degree of visual angle; *contrast*, expressed as the ratio of maximum to minimum intensity in the pattern; and *phase*, expressed in degrees, of the pattern relative to a fixed point.

Enroth-Cugell and Robson exposed an area of retina to a diffuse field of light alternating at regular intervals with a sinusoidal grating of the same average light intensity. What responses would be expected at onset and offset of the grating by cells with concentric receptive fields?

FIGURE 2.7

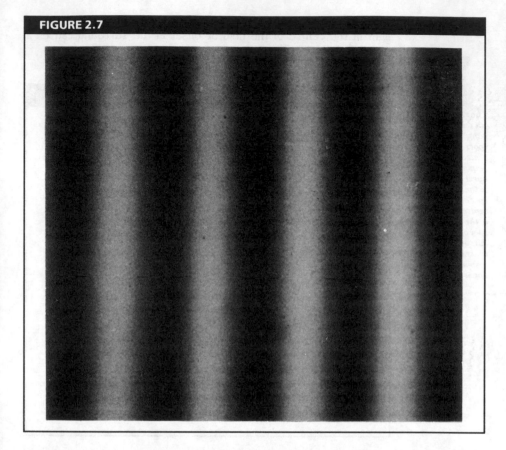

A sinusoidal grating. The brightness of the pattern varies sinusoidally along its horizontal axis. Photograph courtesy of Fergus Campbell, University of Cambridge.

Figure 2.8 shows the distribution of light intensity over the receptive field of an on-centre cell when it is illuminated by a grating of wavelength equal to twice the field diameter. In the first case, where the peak of the distribution falls on the centre of the field, a burst of impulses will occur at the onset of the grating, because the centre becomes brighter than the surround. If the phase of the grating relative to the centre of the field is shifted by 180°, there will be a response to grating offset, when the centre becomes dimmer than the surround. If the phase is shifted by 90° in either direction, however, there is no net change of light intensity over either the centre or the surround at grating onset or offset.

If the response of a ganglion cell is determined by the difference between light intensity in centre and surround, we would therefore expect to find two *null positions* as the phase of the grating relative to the field centre is changed through a full 360°. At these positions, in both on-and off-centre cells, there will be no response to onset or offset of a grating.

Enroth-Cugell and Robson found that some ganglion cells, which they called *X cells*, behave in exactly this way. They are said to have a *linear* response, as it is a linear function of the difference

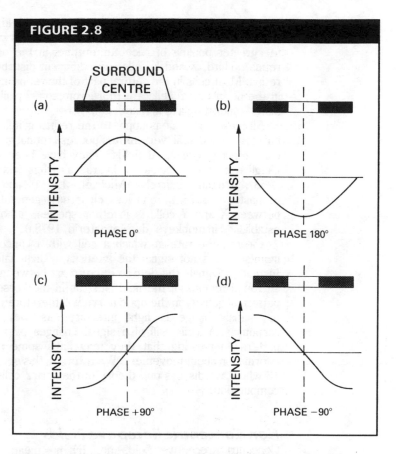

FIGURE 2.8

The distribution of light intensity over the concentric field of a retinal ganglion cell when a grating is projected onto it and the phase of the grating is varied. In (c) and (d), there is no change in total intensity in either centre or surround when the grating replaces diffuse light of the same average intensity; these are the null positions of the grating for an X cell.

between the intensities of light falling in the two areas. Others, called *Y cells*, behave differently, however. With these, no null position of a grating can be found, and the cell responds with a burst of impulses to on-and offset of the grating whatever its phase.

A further distinction between X and Y cells is in their response to moving gratings. As a sinusoidal pattern of light moves over an X cell's field, the cell's impulse rate rises and falls with the peaks and troughs of the pattern. The response of Y cells, on the other hand, shows a constant elevation to a drifting grating, with a modulation in phase with the grating superimposed on it. This test also shows that the response of a Y cell to the pattern of light in its receptive field is *non-linear*; it cannot be predicted by algebraic summation of excitatory and inhibitory influences from centre and surround.

X and Y cells differ in other ways besides linearity of response. First, an X cell gives a *sustained* response to a stationary grating, continuing to fire impulses while the grating is present. A Y cell, in contrast, gives a *transient* burst of impulses to the onset of such a stimulus. In order to evoke a sustained response from a Y cell, it must be stimulated with a moving grating.

Second, in any part of the retina the centres of Y cell fields are larger than those of nearby X cell fields (the fields of both types increase in size from the centre of the fovea outwards, reflecting the greater pooling of receptor outputs in the periphery of the retina). Third, X and Y cells have different distributions over the retina. Most cells in the central part of the retina are X type, while in the periphery Y cells are more common. Finally, Y cells have faster-conducting axons than X cells.

All these conclusions apply to the retinal ganglion cells of cats, but it is likely that all vertebrates possess retinal ganglion cells with concentrically organized fields. They have been found in retinal ganglion cells of species as diverse as frogs (Gaze & Jacobson, 1963), ground squirrels (Michael, 1968a) and monkeys (de Monasterio, 1978a). It is less clear how general the distinction between X and Y cells is in other species, although it is firmly established in monkeys (de Monasterio, 1978a).

Clearly, the rate at which a cell with a concentric field fires impulses does not signal the intensity of light falling in its field. Instead, it signals the degree of *contrast* between the centre and surround regions of the field. Just as in the horseshoe crab, the pattern of activity in the optic nerve will therefore give prominence to spatial change in light intensity. As they have transient responses, Y cells will also signal changes over time in spatial pattern, suggesting that they may have some role in carrying information about movement. We return to this question in Chapter 13 where we discuss one theory of the part Y cells play in motion computation.

Non-Concentric Receptive Fields

Concentric receptive fields are by no means the only kind possessed by the retinal ganglion cells of vertebrates. In addition to X and Y cells, the optic nerve of the cat contains a poorly defined class of *W cells*, which all have slowly-conducting axons but a variety of types of field.

Cleland and Levick (1974) and Stone and Fukuda (1974) found two relatively common types of W cell, together with other rarer types. The first, called "on-off" cells or "local edge detectors", respond with a burst of impulses both when a spot of light moves into the field centre and when it moves out again. Cells of the second group give no response to a stationary spot of light but respond strongly to one moving through the field. Many such cells show *direction selectivity* (or preference), giving their maximum response to a spot moving in a particular direction across the field and no response to movement in the opposite direction. The possible role of these direction selective cells in motion computation is also discussed in Chapter 13.

W cells are less common in the monkey than in the cat (de Monasterio, 1978b), but cells with similar responses are common in other vertebrates. Direction selective, on-off and "uniformity detector" cells make up a substantial proportion of the retinal output of frogs (Lettvin, Maturana, McCulloch & Pitts, 1959), pigeons (Maturana & Frenk, 1963), grey and ground squirrels (Cooper & Robson, 1966; Michael, 1968b), and rabbits (Barlow & Hill, 1963; Levick, 1967).

At one time it seemed that there was a clear distinction between the simple concentric fields found in cats by Kuffler (1953) and the more elaborate fields found in frogs by Lettvin et al. (1959), suggesting that more complex transformations are carried out in the retinas of simpler vertebrates. This distinction has become greatly blurred, however, with the discovery of non-concentric fields in cats, squirrels and other mammals, and the explanation of some apparently elaborate fields in simpler terms of concentric organisation (e.g. Gaze & Jacobson, 1963).

Even so, it appears that the *proportions* of different field types vary between species. In cats and monkeys the large majority of ganglion cells have concentrically organised fields and there are few on-off, directionally selective and other W cells. In squirrels, rabbits, pigeons and cold-blooded vertebrates, on the other hand, a greater proportion of cells have non-concentric fields. Although caution is needed in interpreting such data, because electrodes are selective in the types of axon from which they record impulses, it does seem that the information provided by the retina of a cat or monkey to the brain is a less complex transformation of the optic array than that provided in other vertebrates. Perhaps this is because greater flexibility and scope for learning is possible when the input to the brain is less highly transformed.

Opponent-Colour Retinal Ganglion Cells

As we saw in Chapter 1, many animals possess photoreceptors with more than one type of pigment, and so are potentially capable of colour vision. In this chapter, we have so far only described how retinal ganglion cells carry information about the spatial and temporal pattern of light intensity on the retina. For colour vision to be possible, these cells must also carry information about the spectral composition of light in their fields. One way of achieving this would be to connect each ganglion cell to receptors of one type; the result, in a primate, would be three classes of ganglion cells, each with a different peak wavelength sensitivity.

In fact, retinal ganglion cells transmit information about colour in quite a different way, by means of *opponent-colour* responses. A cell with this kind of response is excited by light of one wavelength but inhibited by light of a different wavelength. Opponent-colour responses are illustrated in Figure 2.9, which shows the responses of four such cells as the wavelength and intensity of light falling in their fields is varied. In one band of wavelengths, the cell's firing rate is increased, while in another it is decreased. Note that the boundary between these two bands remains roughly constant as light intensity varies, showing that these cells carry information about wavelength independently of light intensity.

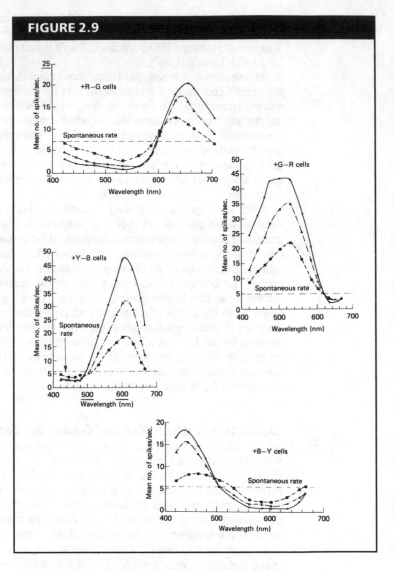

FIGURE 2.9

The relationship between wavelength of light and response for four different classes of opponent–colour cell in the monkey, each at three different levels of light intensity. The dashed lines show the cell's spontaneous firing rate in the absence of light stimulation. (+R– G–excited by red light and inhibited by green; +G–R– excited by green and inhibited by red; +Y–B– excited by yellow and inhibited by blue; +B–Y– excited by blue and inhibited by yellow). Reproduced from De Valois, Abramov and Jacobs (1966), with the permission of the publishers.

Some W cells in the monkey show opponent-colour responses throughout their fields (de Monasterio, 1978b). The responses of X cells are more complex, however, as they show opponent-colour responses superimposed on concentric fields; the centre and surround parts of the field have their peak sensitivities to different wavelengths. Centre-on and centre-off X cells in the monkey are each divided into four classes, according to their different opponent colour properties (de Monasterio, 1978a); the most common are the two types of red–green opponent cell, in which the centre is most sensitive to red light and the surround to green, or vice versa. Less common are the two types of blue–yellow opponent cell, in which the centre is most sensitive to blue light and the surround to yellow, or vice versa. Opponent-colour cells of these kinds have also been found in the ground squirrel (Michael, 1968c), and they carry a combination of spatial and colour information.

Finally, a more complex type of field still is the "dual-opponent" field, which has opposite antagonistic organisations in each part of the field. For example, red light might be excitatory and green light inhibitory in the centre, while green is excitatory and red inhibitory in the surround. No mammalian retinal ganglion cells have been found with such fields, but they have been found in the goldfish (Daw, 1968). Note that a dual-opponent cell would respond strongly to a simultaneous difference in wavelength between centre and surround, whereas an opponent-colour cell would not.

RETINAL MECHANISMS

How is it that retinal ganglion cells have such complex responses to the pattern of light falling on the retina? We can think of photoreceptors as measuring light intensity in each small part of the retina, and of these measurements being combined and transformed in the network of retinal cells and their synaptic connections. Here we discuss briefly the ways in which the wiring pattern of the retina organises concentric receptive fields.

Before tackling this problem, it is important to emphasise that it is an over-simplification to see receptors as simply measuring light intensity. Even before receptor signals pass to horizontal and bipolar cells, transformation of the input pattern occurs, as the hyperpolarisation of rods and cones in response to light is not a simple function of intensity. Instead, these receptors show adaptation in the same way as the photoreceptors of *Limulus*.

Normann and Werblin (1974) demonstrated adaptation in intracellular recordings from photoreceptors of the amphibian *Necturus*. They found that cones respond to light with a hyperpolarisation proportional to the logarithm of light intensity over an intensity range of 3.5 log units. The centre of this range continually shifts, however, to match the current background illumination. Figure 2.10 shows the intensity-response curves for

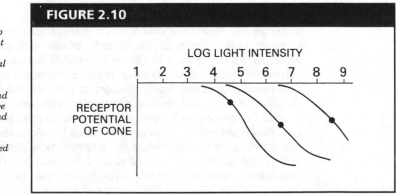

The relationship between log light intensity and receptor potential of a cone. The circles mark the light level around which each curve was obtained and to which the receptors were adapted. Adapted from Normann and Werblin (1974).

FIGURE 2.10

LOG LIGHT INTENSITY

1 2 3 4 5 6 7 8 9

RECEPTOR
POTENTIAL
OF CONE

cones adapted to three different background intensities. Note that the cell's response does not signal absolute light intensity but intensity relative to the current level of adaptation.

Even at this early stage, we see that receptors respond to changes in light intensity and not to absolute intensity. Diurnal animals are active in a wide range of light levels, and adaptation ensures that cones have maximum sensitivity to changes around whatever the current background light level may be. The situation is different with rods, where Normann and Werblin (1974) found that the operating range does not shift far above the dark-adapted level. Rods do not show as large a degree of adaptation because they are specialised for detecting a narrow range of low light intensities.

It should be noted that adaptation of the vertebrate visual system to variation in light level involves other processes in addition to adaptation of rods and cones. Light falling on one receptor causes the response of nearby receptors to adapt, showing that some further process must operate in the neural circuitry of the retina to adjust its sensitivity to light. The mechanisms involved are not yet fully understood, and a review of current theories can be found in Green (1986).

FIGURE 2.11

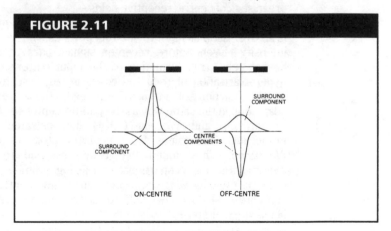

Enroth–Cugell and Robson's (1966) model of the organisation of X cell fields. The strength of the centre component depends on the light falling in the centre of the field and the strength of the surround component on light falling throughout the field. In both cases, the contribution of light intensity is weighted by a Gaussian function. The response of the cell is determined by the difference between the two components.

What processes in the retina bridge the gap between the responses of rods and cones and those of ganglion cells with receptive fields? The response of an X cell can be described by the model shown in Figure 2.11 (Enroth-Cugell & Robson, 1966). The output of the cell is determined by the algebraic sum of a centre and a surround component. Each component sums the total light falling in a circular area, and the contribution of each part of the area is weighted according to its distance from the centre, according to a Gaussian relationship. The curve obtained by taking the difference of the two Gaussians describes the antagonistic organisation of the field. Light falling in the outer part of the field has the opposite effect on the output to light falling on the inner part of the field.

What neural mechanisms perform this computation on the pattern of receptor signals over the retina? Werblin and Dowling (1969) made intracellular recordings from the retinal neurons of *Necturus*, and found that bipolar cells have centre-on or centre-off concentric fields. The linear spatial summation necessary to establish centre-surround organisation therefore occurs in the outer plexiform layer; the centre component is generated by the summed input of a group of neighbouring receptors to a bipolar cell, and the surround component by the input from a wider circle of receptors, mediated by horizontal cells. The two inputs act in an opposing way to generate a sustained slow potential in the bipolar cell. In *Necturus*, some ganglion cells are driven directly by bipolars, and therefore have concentric fields comparable to those of mammalian X cells.

Y cells share the basic concentric organisation of X cells, but have additional non-linear responses. Hochstein and Shapley (1976) showed that a further component added to the model in Figure 2.11 accounts for these non-linearities. Small subunits of the receptive field, distributed throughout it, respond in the same way as the centre of the field to either onset or offset of light. The responses of these units are not, however, summed together linearly with the responses of the centre and surround. Instead, a non-linear *rectification* takes place; in an on-centre cell, the response of the subunits adds to that of the centre at light onset but does not subtract from that of the surround at light offset (and vice versa in an off-centre cell). The result is that there is a response to light onset and offset whatever its spatial pattern.

This non-linear rectification probably occurs at synapses in the inner plexiform layer between bipolar, amacrine and ganglion cells. In *Necturus*, some ganglion cells do not synapse directly with bipolars but only with amacrine cells, and Werblin and Dowling (1969) suggest that these ganglion cells respond to changes in contrast. Victor and Shapley (1979) argue that the subunits of Y cell fields are bipolar cell responses, which are rectified at synapses with amacrine cells and then pooled by amacrines which in turn drive Y ganglion cells.

The evidence we have described so far provides a clear and consistent model of the neural interactions in the retina which determine the responses of cells with centre-surround receptive fields. The model is incomplete, however, and it is worth noting that it cannot account for evidence that retinal ganglion cells are often influenced by light falling on the retina *outside* the receptive field as we have defined it so far. This was first shown by McIlwain (1964), who found that a cell's threshold for responding to a dim spot of light falling in its field centre was lowered if a dark spot moved over the retina up to 90° or more away from the field centre. Further experiments demonstrated that some long-range interaction within the retina is responsible for this *periphery effect*, but its nature has not yet been discovered.

CONCLUSIONS

We have examined the processes taking place in the retina which transform a pattern of light intensity into a pattern of activity in optic nerve axons. We saw first the transformations of spatial and temporal pattern which occur through adaptation and lateral inhibition in the retina of the horseshoe crab and then the more complex variations on these themes in the vertebrate retina. Considerable progress has been made in deducing the patterns of synaptic interaction between cells responsible for these transformations, and a more detailed review of this research can be found in Tomita (1986).

As well as asking how the retina is organised to produce the responses of X, Y, and W cells, it is equally important to consider the functions of these responses. We have pointed out that the retina of *Limulus* filters out slow spatial and temporal changes in light intensity, and transmits information to the brain about rapid changes. In general, the same thing happens in vertebrates, but in a variety of ways in parallel. In Chapters 5 and 13 we consider the functions of some of these filtering operations of the retina in more detail, and particularly their roles in the detection of edges and of movement. Next, however, we complete our survey of physiological findings by following the optic nerves into the brain.

Chapter Three

VISUAL PATHWAYS IN THE BRAIN

The neural circuitry of the retina transforms the fluctuating pattern of light falling on it into a pattern of neural activity in the cells making up the optic nerve. This pattern carries information about the spatiotemporal structure of the optic array, and therefore about surfaces, objects and events in the surroundings. Many further transformations of this pattern are necessary, however, before the information is carried by neurons in a form which can control the animal's actions. The operations performed in the retina are only the first of a large number to take place in the central nervous system, and in this chapter we give an introduction to what we know of these further operations in the mammalian brain.

Neurophysiological research on the processing of visual inform- ation in the brain begins by tracing the pathways along which information travels from the eyes. In cold-blooded vertebrates, the axons of retinal ganglion cells making up the optic nerves project to the *optic tectum*, a structure in the midbrain. Their projection is orderly, with axons maintaining the same topographic relationship to each other as that of their receptive fields on the retina. This order is maintained in the tectum, where cells are arranged in layers called *retinotopic maps*, in which the positions of cells relative to one another corresponds to the relative positions of their fields on the retinal surface.

In mammals, there are several pathways from retina to brain. One is made up of a projection of some Y and most W retinal ganglion cells to the paired *superior colliculi* (Fig. 3.1), structures in the midbrain which are homologous to the optic tectum. They contain a number of layered retinotopic maps of the contralateral visual field. In the monkey superior colliculus, cells in the three superficial layers respond to moving stimuli but are not selective for direction of movement or for the form of a stimulus (Wurtz & Albano, 1980).

Another visual pathway is formed by the projection of X cells, most Y cells and a few W cells from the retina to the dorsal part of the two *lateral geniculate nuclei* (LGN) of the thalamus (Fig. 3.1). Optic nerve fibres terminate at synapses with LGN cells,

FIGURE 3.1

Schematic diagram of the primary visual pathway of a primate. Adapted from Gluhbegovic and Williams (1980).

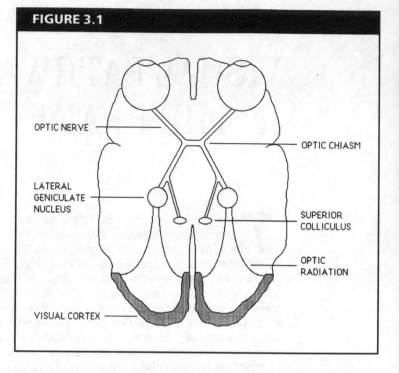

OPTIC NERVE

OPTIC CHIASM

LATERAL GENICULATE NUCLEUS

SUPERIOR COLLICULUS

OPTIC RADIATION

VISUAL CORTEX

which are arranged in layers, or laminae. Each lamina contains a retinotopic map of half of the visual field, those in the right LGN having maps of the left side of the visual field and those in the left LGN maps of the right side. In animals with laterally placed eyes, this is because there is complete crossing over of the optic nerves at the optic chiasm to run to opposite sides of the brain. In animals with binocular overlap, there is a partial crossing over, or decussation, of the optic nerves at the chiasm. The fibres of ganglion cells in the left halves of each retina (carrying information about the right half of the visual field) run to the left LGN, and conversely for fibres from the right halves of each retina, as illustrated in Figure 3.2. In the monkey, the LGN contains six laminae, three of which receive input from one eye and three from the other eye.

LGN cells have concentric receptive fields similar to those of retinal ganglion cells, and each is thought to be driven by one or more ganglion cells of the same receptive field type. The axons of LGN cells form the optic radiations (see Fig. 3.1) and project to the occipital lobe of the cerebral cortex—the highly folded sheet of nerve cells that forms the outer layer of the cerebral hemispheres. In the monkey, all LGN cells project to a region of the cortex in area 17 called the striate or visual cortex. The projection is more complex in the cat; X cell axons terminate in area 17 only, while Y and probably W cells have branching axons and project to adjacent areas of the cortex also. Although the similarity of LGN receptive

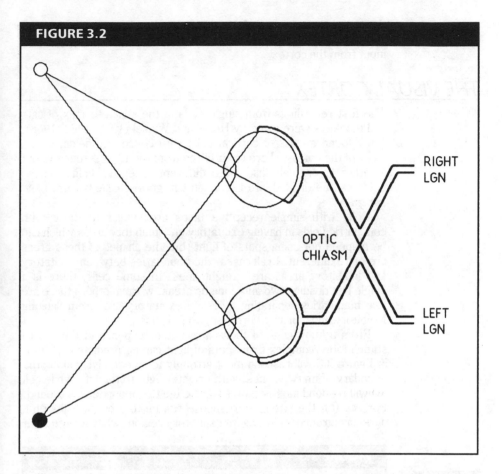

FIGURE 3.2

An illustration of the decussation of optic nerve fibres at the optic chiasm, showing how information about objects in one side of the visual field is transmitted to the opposite side of the brain.

fields to those of retinal ganglion cells suggests that the LGN acts as a simple relay of visual information to the cortex, the existence of a feedback path from cortex to LGN makes it likely that it has some more complex function, at present not understood.

Finally, other pathways are formed by some W cell axons which run to various structures such as the hypothalamus, tegmentum and ventral LGN, but little is known of these. The two main visual pathways in the mammalian brain are therefore those formed by projections from retina via LGN to striate cortex (the geniculostriate path), and from retina to superior colliculi (the retinotectal path). In humans, the first must be intact for conscious experience of vision to be possible, and someone with damage to the visual cortex will report complete blindness in part or all of their visual field. Even so, they will show some ability to locate or even identify objects which they cannot consciously see (Weiskrantz, Warrington, Sanders & Marshall, 1974), suggesting that, while most visual functions rely on the "primary" geniculostriate path, the "secondary" retinotectal path can carry enough information to guide some actions in an unconscious way. It should be noted, however, that the two pathways do not function independently in the intact brain, as there is a corticotectal path providing the superior colliculi with input from the cortex.

THE VISUAL CORTEX

The first recordings from single cells in the striate cortex of cats and monkeys were made by Hubel and Wiesel (1959, 1962, 1968). They found a class of cortical cells with concentric fields, in the layer of the cortex where input fibres from the LGN terminate, but in other layers cells had quite different receptive fields. These fields can be divided into two main categories, called *simple* and *complex*.

Cells with simple receptive fields are similar to those with concentric fields in having excitatory and inhibitory areas which can be mapped out using spots of light, but the shapes of these areas are quite different. In all cases, the boundaries between excitatory and inhibitory areas are straight lines. In some cells, there is a single line dividing two antagonistic areas, while in others there are two boundaries separating a central excitatory area from flanking inhibitory ones, or vice versa (see Fig. 3.3).

From a knowledge of these areas, the response of the cell to stimuli more complex than spots of light can be predicted. Cell (a) in Figure 3.3 will respond most strongly to an edge lying along the boundary of its two zones, with brighter light to the left, while cell (b) will respond most strongly to an edge the opposite way around. For cell (c), the strongest response will be to a bright "slit" on a dark background, covering its excitatory region, while for cell (d) it

FIGURE 3.3

Examples of four kinds of simple cortical cell fields (+ + excitatory region; − − inhibitory region).

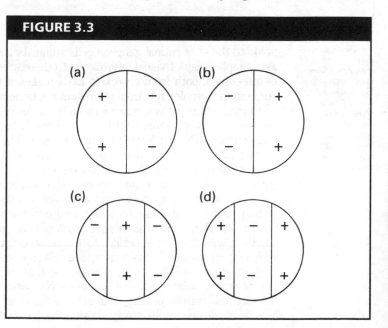

The orientation preference of a cortical simple cell. A light–dark edge falling on the vertical boundary between excitatory and inhibitory areas evokes the maximum response. As the edge is rotated, less of the excitatory and more of the inhibitory area is illuminated, and the response is reduced.

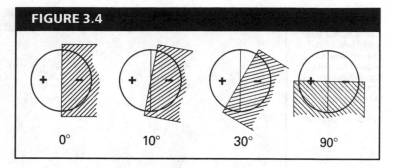

FIGURE 3.4

0°   10°   30°   90°

will be to dark bar on a bright background. In addition, most simple cells also show direction selectivity when tested with moving edges, responding most strongly to an edge moving in a particular direction.

Simple cells, like X cells, perform a linear spatial summation of light intensity in their fields, and their responses to stationary patterns of light can be predicted from the contrast, orientation and position of a stimulus falling in the receptive field. *Orientation preference* is a particularly important feature of simple cells; as would be predicted from their receptive fields, their maximum response is to a bar or edge oriented at a particular angle to the visual axis. This preference is quite a narrow one, and turning the stimulus through more than about 20° from the preferred angle greatly reduces the cell's firing rate (Fig. 3.4).

In the monkey visual cortex, the majority of simple cells are selective for wavelength (Thorell, De Valois & Albrecht, 1984). Some cells show a uniform opponent-colour organisation throughout the field, but the majority have dual-opponent responses (see p. 44) not present in the LGN, indicating that further processing of colour information takes place in the cortex.

For complex cells, the optimal stimulus is also a bar or an edge with a particular orientation, but falling anywhere within the cell's receptive field. The field of a complex cell cannot be marked out into excitatory and inhibitory regions using spots of light, and so there is no region in which the stimulus has to fall to cause a response. Like Y retinal ganglion cells, complex cells therefore have marked non-linearities in their responses. Some complex cells show direction selectivity in their responses to moving edges, while others do not. A full description and classification of simple and complex cells in monkey striate cortex is given by Schiller, Finlay and Volman (1976).

Hubel and Wiesel also described a third class of "hypercomplex" cell, with a receptive field much like that of a complex cell but with greatest response to a bar or edge not extending beyond the receptive field (Fig. 3.5). However, later studies (e.g. Schiller et al., 1976) found that both simple and complex cells possess this property of "end-stopping" or "end-inhibition" to varying extents, and so there is no evidence for a third distinct class of cell.

A cortical cell with "end–inhibition." The cell does not respond to a long edge extending beyond its field (a) but does respond to an edge ending within its field (b).

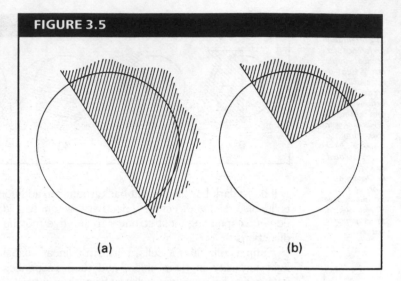

FIGURE 3.5

(a)   (b)

Functional Architecture in the Visual Cortex

Our description of Hubel and Wiesel's findings has so far ignored the structure of the visual cortex and the relationship between the arrangement of cells and their receptive fields. The visual cortex is by no means a homogeneous mass of tissue in which cells with different kinds of response are scattered randomly. Instead, it shows an astonishingly precise and regular arrangement of different cell types which Hubel and Wiesel (1962) call "functional architecture".

Like any region of cerebral cortex, the striate cortex is a folded sheet of cell bodies and fibres about 3 to 4 mm thick. Cell bodies tend to segregate into layers of greater and lesser density, and six main layers, some with subdivisions, can be recognised under the microscope (Fig. 3.6). Below these layers is the white matter, made up of the axons running between this region and other cortical regions or lower brain structures. Within the cortex, fibres run mainly perpendicularly to the surface, and the sideways spread of fibres across the cortex is limited to quite short distances.

So, the only visible structure in the striate cortex is the layering of cell bodies. What happens, however, when we probe with an electrode and ask what responses cells in each part of the cortex show? The first feature we find is an orderly retinotopic mapping of the visual world onto the surface of the cortex, just like that in the laminae of the LGN, with the left and right halves of the visual field mapped onto the right and left cortices respectively. Cortical cells therefore have the same topographic relation to each other as their receptive fields have in the visual field. However, the map is not metrically accurate, as the receptive fields of cells responding to stimuli in the centre of the visual field are smaller than those of cells with peripheral fields. Consequently, the cortical area devoted to the central part of the visual field is proportionally larger than that devoted to the periphery.

FIGURE 3.6

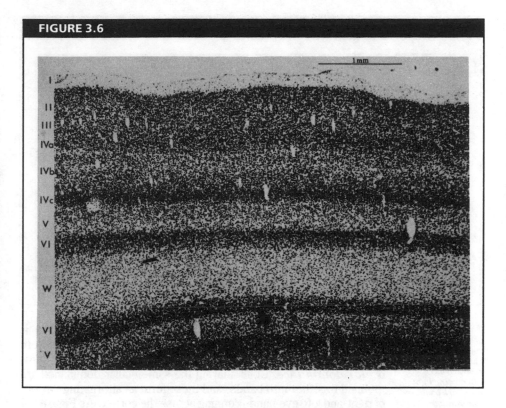

1 mm

I
II
III
IVa
IVb
IVc
V
VI
W
VI
V

Section of monkey visual cortex stained to show cell bodies. Note the layers into which the cortex is divided. Reproduced from Hubel and Wiesel (1977) with permission of the author and publishers.

Now, let us zoom in and concentrate on one small part of the cortex, in which all cells have fields from one part of the retina. As an electrode is moved gradually across the cortex, the fields of cells do not move across the visual field in a smooth way. Instead, roughly every millimetre, there is a jump from fields in one part of the visual field to fields in an adjacent part. Hubel and Wiesel (1977) explained this finding by suggesting that the cortex is divided into roughly square blocks of tissue, about 1 mm by 1 mm, extending from the surface to the white matter, which they call *hypercolumns*. Within a hypercolumn, cells have different receptive fields, which overlap a good deal, but all these fields fall within some single retinal area called the *aggregate field*. In the part of the cortex corresponding to the fovea, the aggregate field is about 0.1° across, while in the periphery it is 3° or more across. Note that the size of a field is measured as the angle subtended at the eye by an object just filling it.

In addition to this mosaic of hypercolumns, there are two further patterns of organisation in the visual cortex. First, cells fall into two groups according to which eye is most effective in eliciting a response. Recall that in the LGN, input from the two eyes is segregated into separate laminae. In layer IVc of the cortex, where fibres from the LGN terminate, this segregation is maintained; cells have concentric fields and respond to their optimal stimulus presented in one eye only. In other layers, however, cells have

FIGURE 3.7

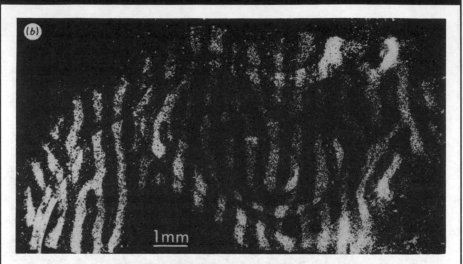

(b)

1mm

The pattern of ocular dominance columns in the visual cortex revealed as alternating light and dark bands by autoradiographic methods. Reproduced from Hubel and Wiesel (1977) with permission of the publishers.

binocular fields; they respond to their optimal stimulus if it is presented to either eye. Even so, cells always respond more strongly to stimuli in one eye than in the other, and are said to show *ocular dominance*. Cells sharing the same ocular dominance are grouped together into bands, and these form an alternating pattern of right-and left-eye bands running across the cortex. As Figure 3.7 illustrates, these can be made visible with appropriate staining techniques (LeVay, Hubel & Wiesel, 1975).

Second, cells are arranged in columns according to their orientation preference. If an electrode penetrates the cortex perpendicular to its surface, all the cells, both simple and complex, which it encounters have the same orientation preference. With an oblique penetration, a series of cells are found which have the same preference, then there is a jump to a new preference, and so on. Hubel and Wiesel (1962) explained these findings in terms of columns of cells sharing the same orientation preference. These are about 0.05 mm across and each hypercolumn contains about 20, so that the full 180° range of orientations is represented in each hypercolumn, in steps of about 10°. Orientation columns can also be made visible; Hubel, Wiesel and Stryker (1978) exposed monkeys to moving vertical stripes while injecting them with radioactively labelled 2-deoxyglucose, a substance taken up by active nerve cells. The resulting pattern of radioactivity in slices of striate cortex showed the positions of columns of cells with a vertical orientation preference (Fig. 3.8).

There are therefore three superimposed patterns of organisation in the striate cortex, but what is the relationship between them? Evidence on this question has been provided by Blasdel and Salama (1986), using voltage-sensitive dyes which bind to nerve cell

FIGURE 3.8

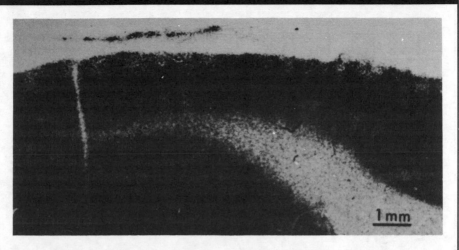

1 mm

Autoradiograph of section through visual cortex revealing columns of cells responding to vertical edges as dark stripes. The uniformly dark band across the centre of the cortex is layer IV, in which cells have no orientation preference. From Hubel, Wiesel and Stryker (1977). Reprinted with permission from NATURE Vol. 269 pp. 328–30. Copyright © 1977 Macmillan Journals Limited.

membranes and change their optical properties when the cell membrane potential changes. With this technique, it is possible to make visible the pattern of cell activity in a living animal over a wide area of the cortex. Blasdel and Salama found that orientation columns cluster into "modules" within which there is a smooth change in orientation preference, separated by "fractures", where orientation preference changes abruptly. Ocular dominance bands and fractures between modules are aligned in such a way that each module contains cells with both right-and left-eye dominance (Fig. 3.9). Hypercolumns are several times larger than modules, and probably therefore contain a number of them.

Spatial Frequency Tuning in the Visual Cortex

The properties of cells in the visual cortex which we have described so far have been discovered by using geometrical stimuli such as stationary or moving bars, slits or edges. Experiments testing the responses of cortical cells to sinusoidal gratings have also been an important source of information. In Chapter 2 (p. 39), we described how Enroth-Cugell and Robson (1966) used sinusoidal gratings to identify X and Y retinal ganglion cells, and explained that an important parameter of such a grating is its *spatial frequency*, measured in cycles per degree of visual angle. By projecting a grating on to the receptive field of a cell, we can discover whether it is "tuned" to a particular spatial frequency, to which it responds most strongly, and also how broad or narrow its tuning is.

A retinal ganglion or LGN cell shows broad spatial frequency tuning; its response to a grating varies little with spatial frequency between a minimum and a maximum value. Above the maximum

FIGURE 3.9

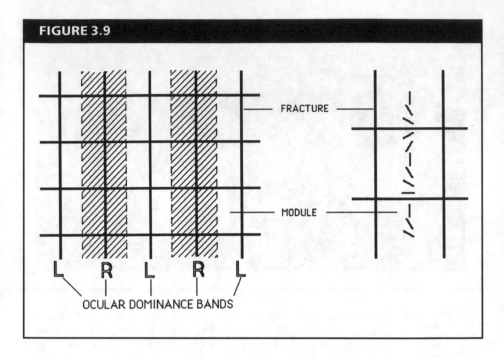

FRACTURE

MODULE

L   R   L   R   L

OCULAR DOMINANCE BANDS

The modular structure of the visual cortex. Left: Each module contains cells with both right and left eye preference. Right: Orientation preferences of cells change smoothly within a module, but abruptly at a fracture between modules. Note that modules and bands are not regular in shape, as they are in this illustration.

spatial frequency, there is no net change of illumination of either centre or surround at onset and offset of the grating and therefore no response from the cell. The smaller the receptive field of the cell, the higher this maximum spatial frequency will be. At any given distance from the centre of the cat retina, there is little variation in the field sizes of either X or Y cells (Peichl & Wässle, 1979) and consequently there is little variation in spatial frequency tuning.

The situation in the visual cortex is different; cells are more narrowly tuned to spatial frequency, and each hypercolumn contains cells with a wide range of optimum spatial frequencies (Fig. 3.10). In this example, the response of a cell to a grating is measured by its *contrast sensitivity*; the reciprocal of the threshold contrast required to obtain a criterion response from the cell. In the cat striate cortex, the optimum spatial frequencies of cells range from 0.3 to 3 cycles/deg, with all values represented at points out to about 10° eccentricity (Movshon, Thompson & Tolhurst, 1978). In the monkey, the range is rather higher, from 2 to 8 cycles/deg (De Valois, Albrecht & Thorell, 1982), presumably reflecting the monkey's greater visual acuity.

The breadth of tuning of cells can be measured by their *bandwidth*; the ratio of the spatial frequencies at which half the maximum contrast sensitivity is obtained. Bandwidths are measured in octaves by taking the logarithm to base two of the ratio (Fig. 3.11). In both cat and monkey striate cortex, bandwidths range from less than one to about three octaves, with a median value just

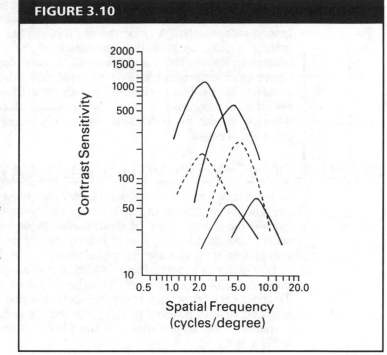

FIGURE 3.10

Responses of cells within one hypercolumn of visual cortex to sinusoidal gratings of different frequencies. Responses are expressed as contrast sensitivity, which is the reciprocal of the grating contrast required to elicit a criterion response from the cell. Note that peak sensitivities range from 2 to 8 cycles/ deg. From De Valois et al. (1982) with permission of the publishers.

over one. These bandwidths are considerably less than in the LGN.

Cortical cells are not only specific for the spatial frequency of sinusoidal gratings, but also for their orientation; unlike retinal and LGN cells, they respond to gratings only when they are oriented at a particular angle. These characteristics of cortical cells would be expected from what we have already described of their responses

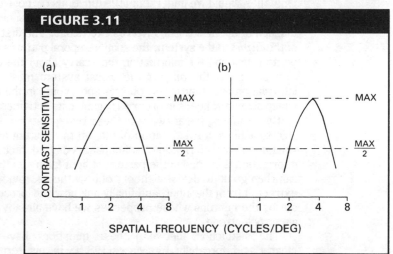

FIGURE 3.11

Measurement of the spatial frequency selectivity of a cortical cell. Cell (a) has peak sensitivity at 2.3 cycles/deg and a bandwidth of 2 octaves. Cell (b) has peak sensitivity at 3.2 cycles/deg and a bandwidth of 1.3 octaves.

to edge, bar and slit stimuli. A cell with a vertical bar as its optimum stimulus, for example, will give its peak response to a vertical grating with wavelength twice the width of the bar, provided the grating is lined up with the boundaries of the excitatory and inhibitory regions. There is no problem of reconciling the findings from experiments using the two types of stimuli. When we come to consider the possible functions of cortical cells in Chapter 5, we will see that the presence in each hypercolumn of cells tuned to different spatial frequencies is particularly important for the detection of edges.

THE FUNCTIONS OF THE VISUAL PATHWAY

So far, our description of the visual system has been a catalogue of the different responses of different types of neuron to light. One question which can be asked about these responses is *how* they occur, and in Chapter 2 we looked briefly at the synaptic connections in the retina which underly the fields of retinal ganglion cells. Equally as important as this kind of physiological analysis is the question of *why* single cells have the responses which they do. To answer this question, it is not enough to describe the responses of single cells to patterns of light. We must also interpret these responses in terms of a theory of the whole system of which the cell is a part.

As an analogy, imagine trying to understand how a clock works without knowing what it does. By dismantling the clock, it would be possible to describe each of its parts in turn and to explain how the movement of each one influences the next. But it would not be possible to understand the *function* of each part without knowing what the whole mechanism is doing. We would need to know that its purpose is to mark out fixed intervals of time and that an arrangement of pendulum and escapement is a way of doing this. Only then would we understand the functions of these components.

In the case of an animal's visual system, understanding the overall function of the mechanism involves two things. The first is the nature of the *input* to the system; the spatiotemporal patterns of light falling on its retina and the information they carry about the environment. The second is the *output* the visual system must provide; the information about surfaces, objects and events in the environment which an animal needs in order to organise its activities.

By combining the answers to these two questions, we should be able to achieve a specification of the job the system has to do. We will know what information the animal needs to detect and how that information is carried in the pattern of light falling on the retina. We can then go on to devise a theory of how the information is actually extracted from the input, and finally ask how this process is carried out by the neurons whose properties we have already studied with a microelectrode.

The distinctions between these questions have been made clearly and forcefully by Marr (1982). In his terms, the first problem is to devise a *computational* theory which specifies the job the visual system must do, the second problem is to find *algorithms* which can process information in the way required by the computational theory, and the third problem is to understand how these algorithms are *implemented* by neurons. All these stages are necessary for understanding the neurophysiology of vision. As Marr puts it:

> trying to understand perception by studying only neurons is like trying to understand bird flight by studying only feathers: it just cannot be done. In order to study bird flight we have to understand aerodynamics; only then do the structure of feathers and the different shapes of bird wings make sense (Marr, 1982, p.27.).

We have already introduced these principles in the case of the horseshoe crab's visual system. In Chapter 2, we suggested how a computational theory of crab vision would specify the information that the animal needs from the optic array to organise its activities, such as the direction of the water surface and the position of a moving predator. The second step would be to devise algorithms able to process the pattern of light at the eye so as to make the required information explicit. Finally, we would ask what role the processes of adaptation and lateral inhibition play in implementing these algorithms, and what further physiological processes are involved.

Clearly, we are some way from a full understanding of the functions of the horseshoe crab's visual system, and that of mammals is a greater challenge still. Here, we consider one particular theory of the function of the mammalian visual pathway, which holds that it acts as a hierarchical array of feature detectors. As we shall see, the theory has important flaws, but it provides a useful introduction to other interpretations which we consider in later chapters.

Single Cells as Feature Detectors

Vision provides us with the ability, so commonplace that we rarely reflect on it, to recognise an enormous variety of objects. In particular, our perception of something as a particular object or type of object remains stable despite variation in the pattern of light reflected from it and focused on to the retina. For example, we recognise a friend's face despite changes in their distance, the angle to which they are turned, the lighting, or their facial expression. All these variations cause large changes in the image of the face on the retina, and yet our perception of the particular person remains constant.

In Chapter 8 we discuss various theories of how perceptual constancy of this kind could be achieved, but for now we are concerned only with the theory that objects are recognised by a set of simple geometrical features, such as lines, angles, circles and so on, which remain invariant while the image of the object fluctuates. This "feature detection" theory proposes that the pattern of light on the retina can be transformed into an abstract, symbolic representation of the identities of the objects present in the visual field by a hierarchical series of feature detectors. These signal the presence of particular geometrical features; the higher the level in the hierarchy, the more complex the feature.

Barlow (1972) proposed that single cells in the visual pathway act as feature detectors. He argued that a neuron is tuned, through its synaptic connections to other cells, to respond when a particular feature falls in its receptive field. Firing of action potentials by the cell therefore signals the presence of this particular feature. Neurons are arranged in a hierarchy, those at each level taking their input from cells at the level just below. The higher its level in the hierarchy, the more abstract the feature to which the cell is tuned, and the less dependent is the cell's response on the retinal position of its feature.

This theory of the visual pathway as a hierarchical array of feature detecting cells was foreshadowed by Hubel and Wiesel's (1962) interpretation of retinal ganglion, LGN and cortical cells as a hierarchical system for detecting edges in the retinal image. They proposed that retinal ganglion and LGN cells make up the lowest level in the hierarchy, detecting light–dark edges falling within their fields at any orientation. An edge passing through the surround of a concentric field will alter the amount of light falling in the surround relative to that in the centre, and so cause a response in an X or Y cell. Simple cells in the cortex, according to Hubel and Wiesel, form the second level of the hierarchy. They are tuned to more specific features than are LGN cells, detecting edges with particular orientations. Simple cells in turn provide input to the third level, made up of complex cells. These also detect edges with particular orientations, but do not require them to be at fixed locations on the retina.

Barlow's (1972) theory is therefore an extension of Hubel and Wiesel's interpretation, proposing that cortical cells form the bottom layers of a hierarchy of cells which respond to progressively more and more abstract geometric features. The cells in the next level up might respond to simple geometrical patterns such as angles, defined by the activities of particular combinations of complex and hypercomplex cells. At the top of the hierarchy are cells responding only to stimuli such as particular items of food or particular social companions. Barlow's prediction that cells exist in the human nervous system which respond only to highly abstract stimulus classes has been dubbed the "grandmother cell" or "yellow Volkswagen detector" theory.

The Problem of Ambiguity in Feature Detection

Let us leave aside the possible higher levels of feature detectors for now, and consider whether the interpretation of the pathway from retina through LGN to striate cortex as a feature detection hierarchy is valid. First, is there evidence that cells in the pathway actually do connect according to a hierarchical scheme? In particular, do LGN cells provide input only to simple cells, which in turn connect only to complex cells? Intracellular recordings from cortical cells (e.g. Ferster & Lindström, 1983) show that the pattern is not this simple, and that LGN cells connect directly to both simple and complex cells. Even so, all simple cells receive input only from the LGN, while many complex cells have input from other cortical cells. Also, output from the striate cortex is provided only by complex cells. There is therefore some hierarchical organisation in the striate cortex, as the responses of complex cells are more shaped by cortical circuitry than are those of simple cells, but the actual pattern of connections is not as straightforward as Hubel and Wiesel predicted. A further problem for a hierarchical interpretation is the presence of feedback connections from the striate cortex to LGN, which indicates that information must pass in *both* directions along this part of the visual pathway.

A second question poses more serious difficulties for the feature detection theory; are single neurons really detectors of geometric features? Consider a centre-on X cell in the optic nerve or LGN. If an edge grazes its receptive field centre, the cell will respond as the illumination of the surround relative to the centre decreases. But for the cell to be an "edge detector" it must respond *only* to straight edges and *not* to any other pattern. A retinal ganglion or

FIGURE 3.12

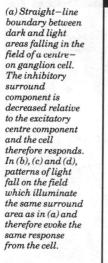

(a) Straight—line boundary between dark and light areas falling in the field of a centre—on ganglion cell. The inhibitory surround component is decreased relative to the excitatory centre component and the cell therefore responds. In (b), (c) and (d), patterns of light fall on the field which illuminate the same surround area as in (a) and therefore evoke the same response from the cell.

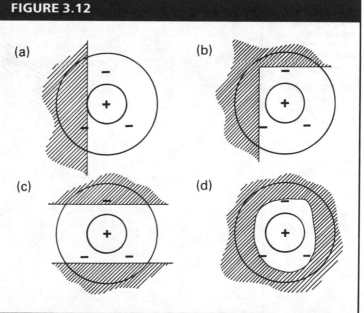

LGN cell does not meet this requirement, as there is an indefinite number of other patterns which would elicit an equally strong response. Figure 3.12 shows how a corner, bar or spot would elicit the same response from such a cell as an edge. The easiest way to see this point is to imagine you are trying to work out what is going on in the cell's field by monitoring its response. In this case, you would have little success, as the strength of the response would tell you how much centre–surround contrast was present, but not how it was distributed.

The feature detection theory would meet this argument by saying that the presence of an edge is not signalled by the activity of a single retinal ganglion or LGN cell but by the activity of a row of these cells. If simple cortical cells were connected to a row of LGN cells they would therefore act as edge detectors. Exactly the same argument can be made against the claim that cortical cells are detectors of geometrical features, however. The strength of a simple cell's response to an edge does vary with the orientation of the edge in its field, but it *also* varies with its contrast and position. The response of the cell therefore does not provide unambiguous information about the pattern of light in its field. A particular rate of response may mean that there is a low contrast edge of optimal orientation or a high contrast edge of a different orientation (Fig. 3.13a).

Similarly, the response of a cell to a bar or a slit is determined not only by the orientation of the stimulus but also by its contrast, position and width. Fig. 3.13b illustrates how a wide slit of optimal

Ambiguity in the response of a cortical simple cell. In (a), a low–contrast edge of optimal orientation and a high–contrast edge of a different orientation evoke the same response. In (b), a slit of optimal orientation but wider than the excitatory area evokes the same response as a slit of optimal width but different orientation.

FIGURE 3.13

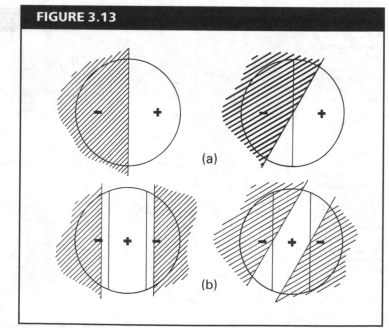

(a)

(b)

orientation can elicit the same response as a narrow slit of a different orientation. Finally, further ambiguity arises because the responses of many cortical cells are influenced not only by light but also by such things as sound (Fishman & Michael, 1973) and the angle of tilt of the animal's body (Horn & Hill, 1969).

This ambiguity of the responses of neurons is a serious problem for the feature detection theory, as it means that cells do not reliably signal the presence of particular geometrical features in the retinal image. Even if the brain is organised to carry out a hierarchical feature analysis, we cannot identify single cells with feature detectors. In Chapter 5 we consider in more detail the problem of locating edges of objects in an image, and discuss theories which give other explanations of the functions of retinal ganglion, LGN and cortical cells.

BEYOND THE STRIATE CORTEX

We have looked in some detail at the primary visual pathway as far as the striate cortex, and now we consider what transformations of visual information occur beyond it. Into what sort of pathways does the output of the striate cortex lead, and do they perform a hierarchical analysis of the retinal image? Single-cell recordings have revealed many regions of *extrastriate* (or *prestriate*) cortex, anterior to the striate cortex, in which the activity of neurons is influenced by light falling on the retina. Some of these "visual areas" can be marked out straightforwardly, as they contain retinotopic maps of the visual field similar to that in striate cortex. In other areas the map is partial, disorderly or both, and their identification therefore requires a variety of other methods (Van Essen, 1985). This leads to problems in defining visual areas, and so it is not yet possible to determine just how many areas there are in a particular species, or where all their boundaries lie.

Side view of the right cerebral hemisphere of a macaque monkey. Heavy lines show sulci (folds in the cortex), thin lines show established boundaries of visual areas and dotted lines show less well defined boundaries. All the areas shown extend into sulci, while a number of other areas are completely hidden within sulci. Note that area V1 is the striate cortex. Reproduced from Maunsell and Newsome (1987) with permission of author and publishers.

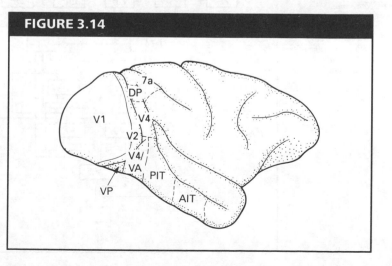

FIGURE 3.14

In the macaque monkey, a recent review (Maunsell & Newsome, 1987) describes 19 visual areas in the cortex, covering a large part of the occipital, temporal and parietal lobes (Fig. 3.14). The deep folding of the cortex means that some areas, lying within folds (or *sulci*), are not visible from the exterior. Two important areas not shown for this reason in Figure 3.14 are V3, lying in the lunate sulcus between V2 and V4, and the middle temporal area (MT) in the superior temporal sulcus anterior to V4.

How are all these areas connected to one another? The pattern of connections has proved not to be a simple chain from one area to the next; instead, each area sends output to several others, and most if not all connections are matched by reciprocal connections running in the opposite direction. In all, Van Essen (1985) lists some 92 pathways linking visual areas, which have been identified with varying degrees of certainty. An important feature of these pathways is that almost all can be classified according to the cortical layers in which they arise and terminate as either ascending (leading away from V1) or descending (leading towards V1), and when pathways are classified in this way a consistent hierarchical pattern emerges with areas placed at different levels (Fig. 3.15). The anatomy of the extrastriate cortex therefore suggests a hierarchical organisation, but one with a number of areas at each level and with extensive feedback from higher to lower levels.

The extrastriate visual areas appear to be arranged hierarchically,

FIGURE 3.15

The hierarchical organisation of extrastriate visual areas in the macaque monkey, as proposed by Maunsell and Newsome. Reproduced from Maunsell and Newsome (1987) with permission of author and publishers.

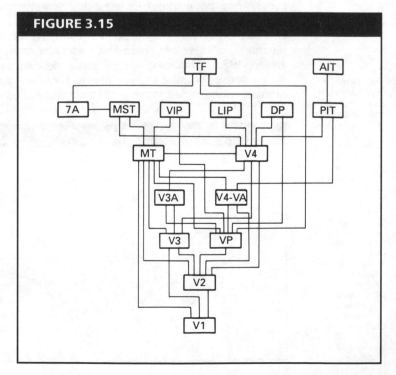

but is there any evidence that they function in the way envisaged by the feature detection theory? In particular, do neurons in successively higher level areas respond selectively to more and more abstract features of the retinal image? Zeki (1978) argued against this interpretation on the basis of single cell recordings. He found that cells in V2 have larger receptive fields than simple and complex cells in V1 (striate cortex), but show the same selectivity for orientation. In other areas, however, cells proved to be selective for different stimulus properties. For example, most cells in area MT are strongly selective for the direction and speed of motion, but not for colour or orientation, whereas in V4 the opposite is true. Zeki (1978) interpreted these results in terms of a "parcelling" model, in which the simple representation of the visual field in V1 and V2 is parcelled out to be analysed by a number of areas working in parallel, one analysing patterns of motion, another colour, and so on.

Further work has cast doubt on Zeki's view that each area has a clearly distinct function, as the differences between different areas in cell properties have turned out to be less clear-cut (Maunsell & Newsome, 1987; Van Essen, 1985). Instead, it seems possible that the extrastriate areas are grouped into two main pathways operating in parallel, one concerned with the analysis of motion and spatial layout, and the other with colour, form and object recognition. The motion pathway runs from V1 to MT, then to the medial superior temporal area (MST) and finally to area 7a in the parietal lobe, while the colour and form pathway runs to V4, then to the posterior inferotemporal area (PIT) and finally to the anterior inferotemporal area (AIT) in the temporal lobe. An examination of Figure 3.15 will show that the segregation between these pathways is by no means clear-cut; there is a degree of overlap and interconnection between them, and some areas do not fit into the scheme. Even so, a range of evidence reviewed by Maunsell and Newsome (1987) suggests that there is some segregation of these two sorts of analysis of visual information.

If the extrastriate areas do not function in a purely parallel fashion, but are instead grouped into two parallel pathways, does each of these pathways function hierarchically? If they do, then we would predict that cells in higher level areas would respond selectively to more abstract stimulus properties than cells at lower levels. There is some support for this prediction in the motion pathway, as cells in MT and MST are selective for more complex properties of motion than just its direction. We discuss the details of this evidence in Chapter 13 when we deal with the computation of motion in general.

In the colour and form pathway, the responses of cells do become progressively less dependent upon the retinal position of stimuli; receptive field sizes in V4 are typically 30 times the area of those in V1, while in AIT they are up to 100 times larger. Fields of IT cells often extend across the right and left visual fields, and always include the foveal region. Do cells in the colour and form pathway respond to progressively more abstract properties, however?

One claim for hierarchical processing in the colour and form pathway was made by Zeki (1980), who argued that cells in V4 show greater selectivity for wavelength than those in V1, and that their preferred wavelengths cover a wider range of the spectrum. Zeki's conclusion that further analysis of colour is carried out in V4 has been criticised, however, on the grounds that retinal ganglion cells have the same wavelength selectivity and distribution of preferred wavelengths as those in V4 (de Monasterio & Schein, 1982).

In further experiments, however, Zeki (1980) made the important discovery that some V4 cells show *colour constancy*. This term refers to the fact that we perceive a surface as having a constant colour despite changes in the spectral composition of light reflected from it. An everyday example of colour constancy occurs when we move from daylight into an artificially lit room. The composition of light from an electric bulb is markedly different from that of sunlight, and is relatively richer in long wavelengths. The same surface will therefore reflect more long wavelength light under a light bulb than in sunlight, and, if our perception of colour depended upon wavelength alone, it would appear redder. In fact, the colour we perceive remains largely constant; a white sheet of paper, for example, does not appear orange indoors or bluish outdoors (note that colour constancy is not perfect, as those with a good eye for colour know when choosing clothes under artificial light).

A powerful demonstration of colour constancy is provided by experiments in which two surfaces reflect light of identical spectral composition but are seen as having different colours (Land, 1977). In a typical experiment, a patchwork display of differently coloured surfaces is illuminated by mixed light from projectors with red, blue and green filters. The intensities of light from the three projectors are first adjusted to some arbitrary values—for example, so that the spectral composition of their mixed light falling on the display is equal to that of daylight—and the composition of light reflected from one surface A is measured. Now, by adjusting the intensities of the three projectors, it is possible to make the spectral composition of light reflected from another surface B equal to that reflected from A in the first stage. When this is done, B is *not* seen as having the same colour as A did in the first stage, as would be expected if perceived colour is determined by the spectral composition of reflected light alone. Further discussion of how the visual system might achieve this compensation for variation in ambient light, and more detailed descriptions of experiments, can be found in Land (1977) and Mollon (1982).

Returning to area V4, Zeki (1980) reported a number of cells which responded selectively to a surface of a particular colour, and which maintained this response as the spectral composition of light illuminating the surface changed. Under these circumstances, the composition of light falling in the cell's field changed, but its response, just like an observer's perception of colour, remained constant. Zeki (1983) compared the responses of cells in V1, and found no evidence of colour constancy; instead, all the cells studied were selective for wavelength alone. A possible explanation for this result is that the smaller receptive fields of V1 cells did not sample a sufficiently wide range of different colours in the patchwork display and therefore could not show colour constancy (Jacobs, 1986). Even so, Zeki's findings do demonstrate that some process takes place either in V1 or between V1 and V4 which converts wavelength-selective responses into ones selective for the more abstract property of perceived surface colour.

More firm evidence for hierarchical organisation of the form and colour pathway comes from the properties of some cells in the inferotemporal (IT) area. Many IT cells are like V1 cells in being selective for simple properties such as orientation, but some appear to be selective for quite elaborate stimuli. For example, Perrett, Rolls and Caan (1982) found that 10% of a sample of IT cells showed a preference for *faces*, of either people or monkeys. These were defined as cells which responded more than twice as vigorously to faces than to any of a wide variety of other simple or complex stimuli. Perrett et al. found that the responses of these cells were unaffected by transformations of faces which do not affect their recognition by people, such as changes in distance or colour, although their responses were reduced if faces were turned from a front to a profile view. The cells were also selective for the spatial configuration of features making up a face, giving weaker responses to scrambled photographs of facial features. Further work, reviewed by Perrett et al. (1986), has shown that different cells are selective for different views of a face. For example, a cell might respond strongly to profiles of faces but weakly to full face stimuli. Also, other cells respond most strongly to the faces of specific individuals; for example, some respond strongly to Dave Perrett's face but less strongly to faces of other familiar humans.

It is tempting to see Perrett et al's (1986) findings as evidence for Barlow's (1972) prediction of single cells acting as detectors of natural objects. We are certainly safe in concluding that these IT cells are selective for more abstract properties than are V1 cells, but are they indeed "grandmother" cells? For two reasons, we cannot draw this conclusion. First, the same face excites many cells, meaning that its presence is not signalled by a unique cell. Second, the problem of ambiguity which we discussed earlier in the context of the retina and striate cortex arises again here. Although the cells studied by Perrett et al. (1982) respond more strongly to faces than to any other objects, most show some response to other objects, and their activity does not signal unambiguously that a face is present in the visual field.

This problem of ambiguity is illustrated clearly in further experiments by Baylis, Rolls and Leonard (1985), who found that the majority of a sample of face-selective neurons in IT showed

FIGURE 3.16

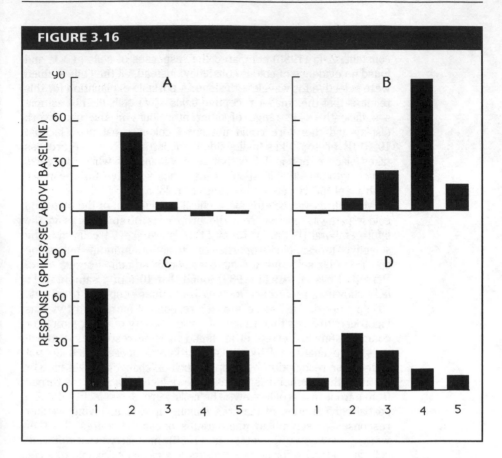

The responses of four different face–selective cells (A–D) in inferotemporal cortex to five different face stimuli (1–5). Cell A is strongly selective for face 2. Cells B and C are selective for faces 4 and 1 respectively, but less strongly. Cell D shows weak selectivity between faces. Adapted from Baylis, Rolls and Leonard (1985).

different responses to different individual faces. In particular, they found that some cells discriminate more sharply between faces than do others; Figure 3.16 shows examples of cells with varying degrees of selectivity. It is difficult to draw final conclusions from data of this kind about the validity of the theory that single cells act as feature detectors, as we cannot specify exactly what degree of selectivity is required by the theory. In Chapter 9, we come back to this problem and discuss a different framework for interpreting single cell responses, in which the presence of an object is held to be coded by the pattern of activity across a population of cells, and not in any one cell.

There is one further characteristic of cells in the form and colour pathway which has recently been discovered, and which poses an intriguing challenge to any interpretation of the pathway as a hierarchy. Most of the neurophysiological evidence we have described has been obtained in experiments using anaesthetised animals, and only recently have methods been developed for making single-cell records in alert, normally behaving animals. Now, if visual pathways are acting in a purely hierarchical way, transforming the pattern of light on the retina in a series of steps until some abstract representation of the visual field is achieved, we would not expect an animal's behavioural state to affect the responses of cells within these pathways (provided, of course, that head and eye movements are taken into account).

Evidence is now available, however, that an animal's behavioural state does influence the responses of cells in extrastriate cortex, in quite specific ways, and we describe two examples from the colour and form pathway to illustrate. First, Moran and Desimone (1985) studied cells in area V4 of macaque monkeys, asking whether their responses changed with changes in the animals' attentional state. For each cell, they first determined the boundaries of the receptive field and then the stimuli to which the cell responded. Both an effective and an ineffective stimulus were then presented together at different locations within the receptive field. If the monkey had previously been trained to attend to the location of the effective stimulus in order to detect a signal of some reward, the cell responded strongly. If, however, it had been trained to attend to the location of the ineffective stimulus, the response was much weaker, even though the pattern of light falling in the receptive field was identical in the two conditions. As Moran and Desimone put it, it was "almost as if the receptive field had contracted around the attended stimulus."

Moran and Desimone (1985) found that the receptive fields of about half of V4 cells were under this kind of attentional control, but could find no such effects in V1. A similar effect was found in AIT neurons by Fuster and Jervey (1982), who used a delayed match-to-sample task, in which a monkey is shown a coloured stimulus (the sample), and then, after a delay of more than 15 sec, is required to choose the same colour from among a number of stimuli in order to obtain reward. Fuster and Jervey found that over half of AIT cells responded differently from their resting level during the delay between sample and choice. Some of these cells showed colour-selective responses when the sample was presented, which persisted during the delay. More strikingly, other cells did not respond to the sample but did respond during the delay at a level dependent upon the sample colour. This last type of cell does not signal the presence in its field of a particular colour, but instead the colour which the animal will later choose. Some IT cells are therefore involved in the formation of visual memories lasting for many seconds.

The implication of findings such as these is clearly that extrastriate pathways do not function independently of other brain processes to deliver a representation of the visual world, but that their operation, beyond the earliest stages, is strongly influenced by processes responsible for attention, memory and the organisation of behaviour. Presumably one function of the extensive feedback connections between extrastriate areas, which we mentioned earlier, is to mediate such effects. As we discuss in later chapters, there is much psychological evidence to show that a perceiver's expectations and knowledge influence perception, and so there must be some interaction of such information with that from the retina at some stage in the brain.

CONCLUSIONS

In this chapter and the last, we have given an introduction to the wealth of knowledge obtained about the visual pathways of the mammalian brain, and have considered one theory of how they function. This feature detection theory provided a bold interpretation of early results, and its proposal that retinal input is transformed in a hierarchical series of stages has proved at least partly correct. In other respects, though, the theory has been inadequate. It dealt only with object recognition, ignoring the role of vision in obtaining information about spatial layout and motion; a role now being explored in the extrastriate motion pathway. The ambiguity of single cell responses presents serious problems for the theory, and a further challenge is posed by evidence that higher levels of the visual pathway can control the operation of lower levels.

The implication of these first attempts to understand the functioning of visual pathways is that a single principle such as feature extraction is unlikely to provide a general explanation, and that a more promising course is to explore how particular kinds of information are obtained from the retinal image, using more sophisticated algorithms to interpret single cell responses. This in turn means that progress requires more than just physiological methods, but also the development of models of visual processing based on psychological evidence, which are the subject of the remainder of this book. In Chapters 5 and 13, we describe recent advances in modelling how edges could be detected and how motion is computed in retinal images, and in both chapters we discuss how these models have been used to interpret physiological findings.

Part II

PROCESSING RETINAL IMAGES

INTRODUCTION: APPROACHES TO THE PSYCHOLOGY OF VISUAL PERCEPTION

*I*n Part I of this book we introduced you to some of the developments and theories which have emerged from the study of the neurophysiology of vision. The neurophysiological level has uncovered some important properties of cells in the visual pathway, but a proper understanding of the jobs that these cells are doing requires that we consider the process of visual perception at a different, more "computational" level. This was an argument put most forcefully by Marr (1976, 1982) whose work will be discussed extensively within this section.

As we discussed in the last chapter, Marr argued that three different levels of theory must be distinguished if we are to understand a complex information-processing task such as visual perception. For any process (and vision consists of very many processes), we should first formulate a *computational theory*, which describes what is being computed and why. Next we may consider the *algorithms* for achieving the computation, and the *representations* which form the input to and output from these algorithms. Finally, we may describe the *implementation* of the algorithm, whether in neural tissue or in a computer. In this part of our book, we turn to the level of computational theory, representation and algorithm in order to understand more adequately the problems and processes of visual perception. These higher levels of theory are essential to make sense of some of the physiological findings we encountered earlier, and to allow us to explore aspects of perception where neural mechanisms are as yet unknown. It is to the psychology, rather than the physiology, of vision that we must now turn.

In this part of the book we consider how the perception and recognition of three-dimensional objects might be achieved as a result of the processing of one or more retinal images. The retinal image has been seen as the input on which later processes operate in almost all accounts of visual perception. We are thus primarily concerned with those findings and theories that have emerged within this "traditional" approach to visual perception. The focus of much of this research has been on human perception, and this is undoubtedly due at least in part to the historical underpinnings of psychology in philosophy of mind. Before embarking on the details of the topics in this section, we feel we should outline very briefly how such theories of visual perception have evolved.

It is only relatively recently that a separate science of "psychology" has emerged. During the 17th and 18th centuries, scholars interested in natural philosophy made discoveries about light and eyes, and discussed epistemological issues in ways which were to colour subsequent thinking about visual perception well into this century. On the physical side, an understanding of image-formation by lenses, and the observation by Descartes of a retinal image formed on the back of a bull's eye, led to a long-standing belief that the eye functions much like a camera (or camera obscura in the days of da Vinci and Kepler), and that the starting point for vision is an image. However, it was obvious that the images produced by cameras and by eyes are clearly lacking in many of the qualities that we perceive in the world. Images are flat, static and meaningless. Visual perception reveals a solid, mobile and meaningful world. It seemed that perception must therefore involve processes that go beyond the information present in the image. On the philosophical side, the empiricists such as Locke (1690) and Berkeley (1709) argued that perception was somehow constructed from more primitive sensations through a process of learning through association. Though nativist philosophies were also voiced, in which knowledge of the entities of "space", or "time" were considered inborn, or divinely given, it is probably not too much of an overgeneralisation to say that it is the empiricist tradition which has dominated modern thinking in psychology. We will not delve here into the controversy between the "nativists" and the "empiricists", but simply agree with Boring (1942) that:

> No simple exposition of this great and largely fruitless controversy can, however, be adequate to its complexities. For one thing, almost every protagonist turns out, whatever he was called, to have been both nativist and empiricist. Everyone believed that the organism brought something congenitally to the solution of the problem of space; everyone believed that the organisation of space may be altered or developed in experience (p. 233).

The dominant empiricist position in the 19th century led to the attempted analysis (often using introspective methods) of perceptions into their component sensations by the *structuralists*, and considerable debate about which elements or attributes should be considered as fundamental (see Boring, 1942). By analysing elementary sensations it was hoped that eventually the complexities of human thought could be unravelled, since all complex ideas must ultimately have been derived through sensory experience. The mechanisms whereby perceptions were constructed from sensations, through reference to knowledge previously acquired through learning, were also discussed, most notably by Helmholtz (1866), whose idea of perception involving unconscious inference or conclusions is still echoed by contemporary theorists (e.g. Gregory, 1973). Compare their statements:

> such objects are always imagined as being present in the field of vision as would have to be there in order to produce the same impression on the nervous mechanism . . . The psychic activities that lead us to infer that there in front of us at a certain place there is a certain object of a certain character, are generally not conscious activities, but unconscious ones. In their result they are equivalent to a *conclusion* . . . (Helmholtz, 1866, trans. 1925, pp. 2–4).

> we may think of sensory stimulation as providing *data* for *hypotheses* concerning the state of the external world. The selected hypotheses, following this view, are perceptions (Gregory, 1973, pp. 61–63).

Thus a view of perception as indirect and inferential persists today, though the methods used to study vision have become more sophisticated, and some rather different ideas about perception have been voiced in the years between Helmholtz and Gregory. We will mention some of these landmarks in method and theory here very briefly.

Towards the end of the 19th century, the content of perception was commonly studied using the methods of analytic introspection—though Fechner's psychophysical methods (1860) saw the beginning of a more "objective" way to study the senses. However, introspectionist methods were largely abandoned in the United States, following J. B. Watson's lead in 1912. Watson put forward his case for behaviourism (Watson 1913, 1924), in which mentalistic notions such as "sensations" and "perceptions" were replaced by objectively observable "discriminative responses". The behaviourists argued that we can never know how animals, or other people, experience the world, and hence should only observe their behaviour, to examine how their responses are related to variations in the stimuli presented. Ironically, while classical behaviourism provided the methodological tools for the comparative study of perception, it considered it illegitimate to explain any observed differences in the perceptual capabilities of different species in terms of internal processes. The methods of contemporary psychology are still influenced by the behaviourist tradition, though students of perception, on the whole, now regard subjects' verbal reports of their perceptual experience as legitimate "responses" to be recorded and analysed.

At much the same time as Watson was developing behaviourism, the European Gestalt psychologists reacted against the structuralist assumptions that perception could be reduced to sensations. They retained an introspective, though phenomenological approach. They were nativist in philosophy, maintaining that perceptual experience was the result of certain dynamic field forces within the brain. We discuss Gestalt ideas further in Chapter 6.

Gestaltists apart, most other movements in the psychology of perception have been empiricist in flavour, and most have implicitly or explicitly assumed that perception should be regarded as some process of interpretation or construction from the incomplete information provided by the retinal image. Two movements, closely related to each other, which emphasised such complexities of human perception, flourished transiently during the 1940s and 1950s. The first of these, "transactional functionalism" (Kilpatrick, 1952), rested on the demonstrations of Ames (Ittelson, 1952). Ames' displays included a trapezoidal window which looked rectangular, a collection of sticks which could be seen as a chair, and perhaps best known, a curiously constructed room, which

The Ames room. The room is perceived as being of conventional shape, with right–angled corners and rectangular windows. The people standing inside the room appear to be of very odd sizes. In fact it is the room which is oddly shaped— the people are both of normal height. Photograph copyright © Eastern County Newspapers Ltd, Norwich. Used by permission.

FIGURE 4.1

(when viewed statically and monocularly) appeared room-shaped but did strange things to the apparent sizes of people standing or walking within it (see Fig. 4.1).

Such demonstrations were used to illustrate the apparently infinite number of objects which could give rise to any single retinal image, and to emphasise the probabilistic and inferential nature of seeing. What one sees will be what one expects to see, given one's lifetime of perceptual experience. While transactional functionalism stressed the individual's history as important in determining his or her perception, the "new look" (e.g. Bruner & Goodman, 1947) stressed the importance of individual differences in motivation, emotion and personality in influencing what they might see. Cantril (in Wittreich, 1959), for example, claimed that one observer, whose husband walked across the Ames room, persisted in seeing him remain constant in size, while the stranger accompanying him shrank or grew. Wittreich confirmed this observation with some of the married couples he tested.

During the 1960s, associationist explanations of perceptual learning and discriminative responding gave way to a new "cognitive psychology" of perception, attention and memory. Attempts were made to describe the stages which intervened between stimulus and response. The revolution in information technology provided a new metaphor for psychology, in which information from the senses was seen to be processed in ways not unlike the processing of information in a computer. Processes of sensory coding, storage and retrieval of information were all discussed, and the development of computer models of some of these processes was seen to be a legitimate goal of psychological theorising. If a machine could be designed which could "see", its computer program could constitute the implementation of a theory of how seeing is achieved by humans. (See Boden, 1987, or Garnham, 1987, for introductions to the field of artificial intelligence [A.I.]). Marr's (1982) theory represents perhaps the most sophisticated attempt yet to explain the information processing operations involved in vision within a framework which cuts across the boundaries between physiology, psychology and artifical intelligence.

In this very cursory discussion of the history of visual perception there has been one notable omission. We have here mentioned theories which have taken an "impoverished" retinal image as the starting point for perceptual processing. In Part III of this book we describe a quite different—controversial—theory, which was first proposed by J. J. Gibson (1950a, 1966, 1979). This theory suggests that the "input" to a perceptual system is structure in the entire optic array, and transformations in the array over time, Gibson denies that perception involves construction, interpretation or representation, and his theory thus stands apart from those that we have mentioned here. (Though, paradoxically, one can draw some parallels between some of Gibson's ideas and those of both the Gestaltists and the behaviourists—two diametrically opposed schools. We shall have more to say about this in Chapter 10.) In this part of the book, however, we are concerned to explore how far we can explain the perceptual accomplishments of people and animals when these perceptual activities *are* seen as the end-products of the processing of retinal images. This is the mainstream of theories of visual perception, and we defer any challenge to it for the moment.

A unifying principle in the psychology of visual perception has been that unless the perceiver makes assumptions about the physical world which gave rise to a particular retinal image, perception just isn't possible. The only dispute has been over how specific such assumptions need to be. For some contemporary theorists, these assumptions are thought to be quite specific and may be learned through an individual's lifetime experience, for example, the assumption that windows or rooms are rectangular. For others, the assumptions may be more general and hard-wired (that is, built into the central nervous system and not dependent on learning), such as the assumption that similarly oriented texture elements should be grouped together (see Chapter 6). Many theorists have argued that perceptual parsimony is achieved (at the cost of occasional error or illusion), by making use of specific world knowledge to infer, from sensory data, what it is that gave rise to those data. Thus tentative "object hypotheses," obtained by accessing stored information in memory, may constrain and guide the interpretation of incoming sensory data. Such perceptual theories may be described as involving a strong "top-down" or "conceptually-driven" component. Many A.I. models of perception fall into this category and some of these will be discussed in Chapters 6, 7 and 8. Other models (e.g. Marr 1976) have been developed largely along "bottom-up" or "data-driven" lines. In such theories very general constraints are incorporated within each stage of information processing, but specific world knowledge is only recruited into the act of seeing when relatively low-level stages of information-processing produce ambiguous results. One of Marr's many achievements is his demonstration that a great deal of the processing of images can be achieved without recourse to specific world knowledge (e.g. Marr, 1976).

OVERVIEW OF MARR'S THEORY OF VISION

In each of the chapters which follows in this section, we describe some of the ideas which have been important historically, including a description of Marr's theory of the topic under discussion. Of those theories which have emerged within the "information-processing" tradition, Marr's is the most compatible with our aim to account for animal, as well as human, perception. Although his aim has been to provide a theory which may be applicable to human perception, and hence he relies at least in part on human psychophysical evidence to support his statements, he stresses that the same kind of analysis could be applied to visual perception in other species. Most importantly, his level of "computational theory" demands that we always consider what is being computed from light, and why. Ecological, as well as physiological considerations would allow us to tailor a theory in the spirit of Marr to the beast in question:

> Vision, in short, is used in such a bewildering variety of ways that the visual systems of different animals must differ significantly from one another. Can the type of formulation that I have been advocating, in terms of representations and processes, possibly prove adequate for them all ? I think so. The general point here is that because vision is used by different animals for such a wide variety of purposes, it is inconceivable that all seeing animals use the same representations; each can confidently be expected to use one or more representations that are nicely tailored to the owner's purpose (Marr, 1982, p. 32).

Because Marr's theory is of some importance to this section of the book, but appears dotted around the different chapters contained here (which also discuss the work of people other than Marr), we take this opportunity to provide a brief summary of the important points that he makes.

An image, the input for visual processing, represents intensity over a huge array of different locations. This array of intensity values is created by the way in which light is reflected by the physical structures which the observer is viewing, and focused by the observer's eye. The goal of early visual processing is to create from the image a description of those structures—the shapes of surfaces and objects, their orientations and distances from the viewer. This is achieved by constructing a number of distinct representations from the intensity values in the image. The first representation is the *primal sketch*. The primal sketch describes the intensity changes present in the image and makes more global structures explicit. The first stage in this process is to locate discontinuities in light intensity because such "edges" will often coincide with important boundaries in the visual scene. In Chapter 5 we describe how a description of all these intensity changes, *the raw primal sketch* is formed. The raw primal sketch consists of a set of statements about the edges and blobs present, their locations, orientations and so on. From this complex and rather messy representation, larger structures—boundaries and regions —can be found through the application of grouping procedures. This more refined description is known as the *full primal sketch*, and in Chapter 6 we describe how it can be derived.

The full primal sketch captures many of the contours and textures within an image, but a description of an image is only one aspect of early visual processing, where the goal is to describe surfaces and shapes relative to the viewer. Marr sees the culmination of early visual processing as a *viewer-centred* representation, which he calls the *2½ D sketch*. This is obtained by an analysis of depth and motion and shading, as well as the structures assembled in the primal sketch. We describe some of the processes which contribute to the formation of the 2½ D sketch in Chapter 7.

The 2½ D sketch describes the layout of structures in the world from a particular vantage point. We need such a representation to guide any action we may need to take, whether simple eye movement or complicated locomotion. However, a further, and equally essential aspect of vision is the *recognition* of objects. In order to recognise what object a particular shape corresponds to, a third representational level is needed—one centred on the object, rather than on the viewer. This third level Marr terms the *3D model representations*, and these we describe in Chapter 8. It is at the stage of formation of the 3D model representations that a stored set of object descriptions is contacted. As far as possible, previous stages of visual processing proceed in a bottom-up fashion, making use of general constraints rather than any specific object "hypotheses."

Thus Marr's theory involves a number of distinct levels of representation, each of which is a symbolic description of some aspect of the information carried within the retinal image. A variety of different processes have been proposed by Marr and recent advocates of his philosophy, to transform one representation to another, and we describe some of these processes in the chapters which follow.

Marr's theory sees vision as proceeding by the explicit computation of a set of symbolic descriptions of the image. Object recognition, for example, is achieved when one of the descriptions derived from an image matches one that has been stored as a representation of a particular, known object class. Recently, there has been increasing interest in a rather different kind of computational model, in which "concepts" are represented as activities distributed over many elementary processing units. Such connectionist models provide convenient ways of implementing certain kinds of algorithm. We conclude this part of the book by introducing connectionist models and describing how they have been applied to problems of depth perception and object recognition.

Chapter Five

THE RAW PRIMAL SKETCH

The subject of this chapter is the very first stage of visual processing; the nature of the first representation built from a retinal image, and the algorithms which produce it. In Chapter 1, we explained how light provides information to a perceiver about their surroundings, through the relationship between the spatial structure of the optic array and surrounding surfaces and objects. A promising starting point for processing the retinal image, which is a projection of the optic array, is therefore to create a representation of it which makes its spatial structure explicit, specifying where changes occur in the intensity and spectral composition of light. Notice that we are making a simplifying assumption here, treating the retinal image as static and ignoring change in its structure over time caused by movement of the perceiver or of objects. In later chapters, we will return to the question of how motion in a retinal image can be processed and represented.

Clearly, there is a relationship between the places in an image where light intensity and spectral composition change, and the places in the surroundings where one surface or object ends and another begins, but this relationship is by no means a simple one. There are a number of reasons why we cannot assume that every intensity or spectral change in an image specifies the edge of an object or surface in the world. Consider first an imaginary environment in which all objects have *matte* surfaces, meaning that the light reflected in a particular direction from every point on a surface has the same intensity and spectral composition. Clearly, the edges of objects will give rise to intensity and spectral changes in an image of such a scene, but these changes will also arise for other reasons; an obvious example is the edge of a shadow falling on a surface.

Intensity changes also occur in the absence of edges as a consequence of the fact that the intensity of reflected light is a function of the angle of the surface to the direction of incident light. The intensity of reflected light is at a maximum if the surface is at right angles to incident light, and falls as it turns away. Consider a flat surface illuminated by a nearby light source (either an artificial lamp or another surface reflecting sunlight). The intensity of the light reflected from the surface will vary smoothly across it as its orientation to the direction of the light source changes. Intensity changes also arise when a surface is curved; unless it is lit by completely diffuse light, such a surface will also reflect a pattern of light with a smooth change in intensity. Similarly, a surface with a crease or a fold will reflect a pattern with an abrupt change in intensity.

Further complexities arise when we consider surfaces which, like almost all natural surfaces, are *textured* (see Chapter 1, p. 4). The intensity and spectral composition of light reflected in a particular direction from a textured surface varies across it, and, as a result, there is spatial change in the intensity of light within the patch of a retinal image which corresponds to a particular surface.

The complex relationship between natural surfaces and the intensity of light reflected from them is illustrated in Figure 5.1, which shows the intensity of light measured along a line across an image of a natural scene. Notice that, while intensity does change at the edge of the woman's head, it also fluctuates just as much

The intensity of light reflected from this scene has been measured along the horizontal line passing through the woman's head, and intensity values plotted in the graph above the line. Illustration courtesy of Mark Georgeson, University of Bristol.

FIGURE 5.1

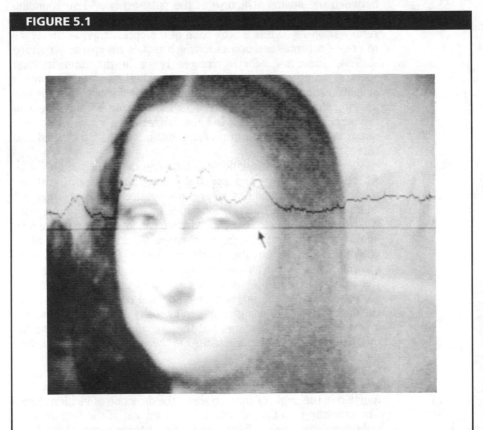

across its surface and across the background. These fluctuations arise from the texture of skin, hair and background, and from the varying orientation of the surface of the woman's face to the direction of incident light.

In Figure 5.1, or almost any natural image, the changes in light intensity and spectral composition associated with the edges of objects are embedded in a mass of changes caused by surface texture, surface shape, shadows and the layout of light sources. A fuller discussion of all these factors can be found in Watt (1988, Chapter 1), but their implication for present purposes is that there is no simple correspondence between the edges of objects in a natural scene and the intensity changes in an image.

It is worth noting that the feature detection theory of visual perception discussed in Chapter 3 did not take these problems into account, and considered only artificial patterns in which edges of objects are unambiguously specified by intensity changes. Figure 5.2 shows an example of a pattern meeting these requirements. In an image of it, patches of light reflected from the squares will be uniform, and changes in intensity will occur only at their edges. An algorithm which located changes in intensity in the image, such as the centre-surround comparison performed by retinal ganglion cells, would therefore be sufficient to produce a representation in which edges in such a pattern were made explicit.

More recent theories have recognised the complexity of the relationship between the structures of natural scenes and the structures of images, and have treated the problem of identifying the edges of objects as a more difficult one than did the feature detection theory. In particular, they have broken it down into two

FIGURE 5.2

Artificial pattern of dark and light areas.

*(a) A grey-level
representation of
an image,
specifying the light
intensity falling on
each pixel
(represented here
by the diameter of
a circle). (b) A
representation of
the differences
between light
intensity in
adjacent pixels in
(a). (c) A symbolic
description of the
significant
intensity change
as a diagonal edge
with a particular
location and
direction.*

main stages. The first of these is the creation of a representation in which changes in light intensity are made explicit, a representation which Marr terms the *raw primal sketch*. In the second stage, edges are identified by other algorithms taking the raw primal sketch as their input, and we consider this stage in Chapter 6. This approach has the advantage that the information about intensity changes in the raw primal sketch can also be used as input for other processes working in parallel which compute depth and motion in the retinal image. These are described in Chapters 7 and 13.

Before we consider algorithms which have been proposed for the construction of the raw primal sketch, it is important to make clear what task these are required to perform. They must take as their input a *grey-level* representation of the retinal image and transform it into an output, the raw primal sketch. A grey-level representation of the image is obtained by measuring light intensity in each of a large number of small regions of the image, called *pixels* (from picture elements). This representation is therefore simply a two-dimensional array of light intensity values, of the kind illustrated in Figure 5.3a. Such an input representation corresponds

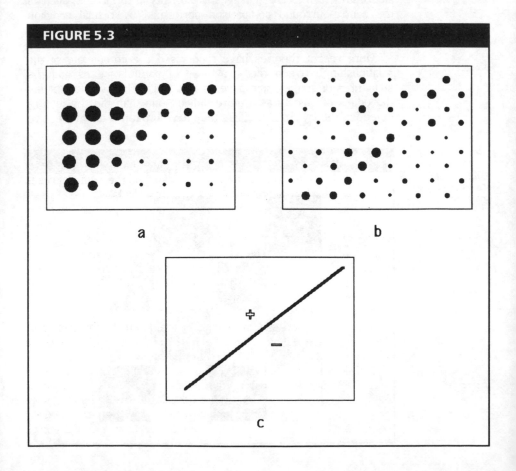

FIGURE 5.3

a

b

c

to that available to the visual pathway, with each pixel and its associated intensity value corresponding to a photoreceptor and its receptor potential.

The use of a grey-level representation as input involves a simplification, as it discards information about the spectral composition of light, and strictly is comparable to a retina with only one type of receptor pigment. This is a reasonable simplification to begin with, as we are able to perform most visual accomplishments in situations where the spectral composition of light does not vary independently of intensity (e.g. under monochromatic light or in a black-and-white picture). If we can understand how a grey-level representation is processed, then the processing of colour information can be tackled subsequently as a separate problem.

The raw primal sketch must specify where in the image significant changes in intensity occur. We mentioned in Chapter 1 (p. 21) an important property of light known as *photon noise*; a stream of photons is not steady but fluctuates in intensity around an average value. A patch of pixels illuminated by light from even the most uniformly reflecting surface will therefore at any instant have slightly different grey-level intensity values. It would not be useful to produce a raw primal sketch simply by calculating the differences between intensities in neighbouring pixels (as in Fig. 5.3b), as the significant changes in intensity will be swamped by noise which is still represented in the sketch. Instead, we need some means of producing a sketch such as that in Figure 5.3c, in which photon noise is filtered out and only those intensity changes associated with properties of objects and surfaces, such as texture or edges, are represented.

One means of filtering out noise in a grey-level representation such as Figure 5.3a is to smooth intensity values by replacing each one by the average of it and neighbouring values. If a grey-level representation is first smoothed in this way, and then differences in intensity between neighbouring pixels are calculated, differences due to noise will be attenuated and those due to significant features of the image will be more prominent. Now, this solution immediately begs another question; how widely around each pixel should intensity values be averaged? The wider the area in which averaging is carried out, the more the representation is smoothed, but what degree of smoothing is appropriate?

If the aim is to locate significant intensity changes in natural images, then there is no *single* degree of smoothing which is correct. This is because, in natural images, intensity changes occur over a range of different scales. There are large-scale changes in the intensity of light reflected from different surfaces, and smaller-scale changes in light reflected from texture elements within surfaces. Consider Figure 5.1 again, and notice that changes over different scales are present. There are large-scale changes from background to woman's face and back to background; intermediate scales of change between parts of the face lying at different angles to the direction of incident light; and small-scale changes within a surface between texture elements such as hairs. Smoothing a grey-level representation of an image is equivalent to blurring the image, and it is easy to see that as an image is blurred more and more, so successively larger-scale changes in intensity are eliminated from it.

It is convenient to express the effects of blurring in terms of filtering the spatial frequencies present in an image. Any pattern, such as a two-dimensional image, can be broken down into component sinusoidal patterns of different frequencies and amplitudes by a mathematical procedure known as Fourier analysis. It is therefore possible selectively to filter out spatial frequencies from an image. When an image is blurred, high spatial frequencies are attenuated. Alternatively, all spatial frequencies above a particular value could be filtered out completely, and the result would be similar in appearance to a blurred version of the original (see Fig. 5.4); the lower the cut-off frequency, the more blurred the result would appear. Notice that removing high spatial frequency components means exactly the same as removing small-scale intensity changes. Figure 5.4 also shows a second example of spatial frequency filtering, in which all components *below* a particular frequency are filtered out. The resulting image contains only small-scale intensity changes associated with edges of objects and texture elements, while large-scale changes across the boundaries of surfaces disappear.

We can conclude that the appropriate amount of blurring of an image in order to locate significant intensity changes in it depends on the scales of intensity change present in the particular image. Since, in natural images, this cannot be known in advance, an algorithm employing a single blurring process will not be successful. Theories seeking to explain how a raw primal sketch can be constructed have therefore proposed that multiple representations of the image are processed in parallel, each representation being obtained from the image by a different degree of blurring. By this means, it should be possible to identify intensity

Left: the result of filtering out high spatial frequencies from the photograph in the centre. Right: the result of filtering out low spatial frequencies. The first filtering blurs the picture while the second leaves its outlines. Original photograph copyright (1984) Bill Gillham and Sam Grainger. Filtered versions courtesy of John Frisby, University of Sheffield.

FIGURE 5.4

changes at a number of different scales simultaneously and then combine the results into the raw primal sketch.

Having considered these general requirements for algorithms capable of constructing a raw primal sketch, we now describe several proposed algorithms in more detail. We will see that they have much in common but that they also differ in some important respects.

THE MARR-HILDRETH ALGORITHM

The algorithm devised by Marr and Hildreth (1980) for constructing the raw primal sketch begins, for the reasons discussed above, by transforming a grey-level representation of an image into a number of independent representations, smoothed to different extents. A simple way to do this would be to average together all values lying in a circle around each pixel, but in Marr and Hildreth's algorithm the contribution of values to the average decreases the further they lie from the centre of the circle, according to a Gaussian (normal) distribution. The degree of blurring is determined by the width of the Gaussian distribution, measured by its standard deviation.

Why is a Gaussian function used to blur the image? The aim of the blurring operation is to limit the range of spatial frequencies present, but this aim is in conflict with the requirement that spatial information present in the image—the locations of gradients—is preserved in the raw primal sketch. The more extensive the filtering of spatial frequencies, the more spatial information will be lost as neighbouring gradients merge. For reasons which the mathematically skilled reader will find discussed in Marr and Hildreth (1980), the optimal trade-off between these requirements is achieved by using a Gaussian function in the blurring operation.

To sum up so far, Marr and Hildreth propose that the image is passed through a set of two or more *Gaussian filters*, which replace the array of grey-level intensity values (denoted by I) in the image with a set of arrays of values of G*I; the Gaussian-weighted averages of neighbouring values of I. These filters have Gaussian functions of different standard deviations, or widths. The wider a filter is, the lower is the highest spatial frequency it will pass and the larger is the smallest scale intensity change which is represented in its output. Figure 5.5 illustrates the effects of filtering an image with Gaussian filters of two different widths.

Now, we come to the second operation performed by Marr and Hildreth's algorithm; the location of intensity changes in the multiple, differently blurred representations of the image. The mathematical operation used to measure change is *differentiation*. If we take a function describing how one quantity *y* varies with another quantity *x* and differentiate it, we obtain a function describing how the *rate of change* of *y* varies with *x*. For example, consider a car travelling at constant speed. If we take the function relating its distance travelled to time, and differentiate it, we obtain a constant. This is the car's velocity, which does not vary with time.

FIGURE 5.5

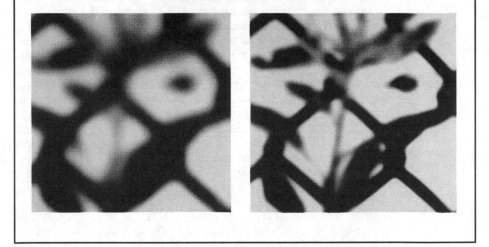

An image (above) blurred by Gaussian filters of two different widths (below). The more blurred picture is produced by the wider filter. Reproduced from Marr and Hildreth (1980) with permission of the author and publishers.

The result of differentiating a function is called its *first derivative*, and this can itself be differentiated to obtain the *second derivative*, which describes how the rate of change of y varies with x. If the function relating the distance travelled by a falling stone to time is differentiated, the first derivative (the stone's velocity) does vary with time; the stone's velocity increases as it falls. If this function is in turn differentiated, the second derivative is a constant, the stone's acceleration under gravity.

Gradients of light intensity in an image could be measured by taking the first derivative of intensity, but, for reasons of economy of computation, Marr and Hildreth's algorithm takes the second derivative. Figure 5.6 illustrates, for a one-dimensional intensity

FIGURE 5.6

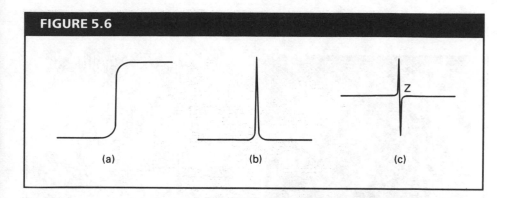

(a)   (b)   (c)

(a) A gradient of intensity. (b) Its first derivative. (c) Its second derivative, which crosses zero at point Z. Reproduced from Marr (1982) with permission of the publishers.

gradient, how the first and second derivatives change in the region of the gradient. Where the second derivative has a positive value, the gradient of intensity is increasing, and where it has a negative value the gradient is decreasing. Note particularly that values of the second derivative pass through zero (a *zero-crossing*) at the steepest point of the gradient.

In Marr and Hildreth's algorithm, this operation is carried out on a two-dimensional pattern of light intensity, using an operator called the Laplacian (∇^2). This gives the sum of the second derivatives taken in two orthogonal directions; its value measures the extent to which the intensity gradient is changing in the region of a point in the image, but does not convey any information about the direction in which this change occurs. Again, the interested reader will find detailed arguments for the use of the Laplacian in Marr and Hildreth (1980).

In the second stage of Marr and Hildreth's algorithm, the Laplacian operator is applied independently to each of the arrays yielded by the Gaussian filters. The result is a set of arrays of values of the Laplacian, denoted by $\nabla^2 G*I$. A wide $\nabla^2 G$ filter yields an array capturing only the large-scale changes in intensity in the image, while the output of a narrow $\nabla^2 G$ filter also contains information about small-scale changes. In order to locate gradients in the image, we now need to find, in each array, where the values of $\nabla^2 G*I$ pass through zero; that is, where positive and negative values of $\nabla^2 G*I$ are adjacent to one another. Once these zero-crossings are located, rows of zero-crossings sharing the same orientation (*zero-crossing segments*) are located.

We have now reached a stage where Marr and Hildreth's algorithm has yielded a set of representations of the image made up of zero-crossing segments. These make explicit the location and scale of intensity changes present in the original image, and Figure 5.7 illustrates the zero-crossings obtained from an image with $\nabla^2 G$ filters of three different widths. Note that no single one of these representations can give an adequate raw primal sketch. The output of a narrow filter represents noise together with significant intensity changes, while the output of a wide filter represents only

FIGURE 5.7

*The results of
passing an image
(upper left)
through ∇²G
filters of three
different widths.
Upper right, lower
left and lower
right: zero—
crossings obtained
with a narrow, an
intermediate and a
wide filter.
Reproduced from
Marr and Hildreth
(1980) with
permission of the
author and
publishers.*

significant changes but cannot localise them accurately. Marr and
Hildreth (1980) therefore propose a final step in which information
about zero-crossings from the separate ∇²G filters is *combined*.

In proposing rules for combining ∇²G filter outputs, Marr and
Hildreth (1980) argue that significant intensity gradients in a natural
image will give rise to zero-crossings in the output of more than
one filter. Although no evidence from systematic testing of images
is available, they give two reasons in support of this assertion.
First, a zero-crossing from a narrow filter which is not matched by
one from a wider filter is likely to represent noise. Second, the only
kind of intensity change which would give rise to a zero-crossing in
a wide channel not matched by one in a narrower channel would be
a diffuse, spread out change such as that caused by a diffraction
pattern, and such a change would not be produced by any important
feature of a natural scene.

The first rule for combining the outputs of ∇²G filters to
construct the raw primal sketch is therefore that, wherever zero-
crossing segments from filters of adjacent widths match, an *edge-
segment* is put in the sketch. In some situations, a zero-crossing

segment in a wide channel may be matched by two parallel ones of opposite contrast in a narrow channel; this situation is represented in the raw primal sketch by a *bar*. The ends of bars are represented by *terminations*, and closed loops of edge-segments are represented by *blobs*.

The raw primal sketch is therefore a symbolic representation of the image in terms of four different tokens—edge-segments, bars, terminations and blobs—denoting four different kinds of intensity change, and an example of a raw primal sketch is shown in Figure 5.8. As the example shows, the sketch does not pick out the outlines of objects, as the tokens present represent not only edges but also texture elements within surfaces. In the next chapter, we describe Marr's proposals for algorithms which take the raw primal sketch as input and extract object edges. What has been achieved at this stage is to extract from a noisy image a symbolic representation of the significant gradients of light intensity present.

Implementation

Marr and Hildreth (1980) implemented their algorithm for computing the raw primal sketch by taking photographs of natural scenes such as those in Figures 5.5 and 5.7, converting them to arrays of grey-level intensity values and applying the algorithm to these values. In principle, this could be done simply by calculation with pen and paper, but the huge number of calculations involved makes implementation by computer necessary. This approach makes it possible to judge the value of the algorithm by seeing the

FIGURE 5.8

The zero—crossings obtained from the picture in Figure 5.5 using a narrow and a wide ∇²G filter are shown in (a) and (b). These are combined to give the raw primal sketch; the locations of blobs, edge segments and bars are shown in (c), (d) and (e). Reproduced from Marr and Hildreth (1980) with permission of the author and publishers.

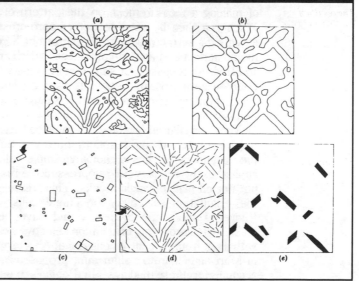

results it produces, but it does not tell us whether it is actually implemented in the nervous system. Does the mammalian visual pathway construct a raw primal sketch using this algorithm? Marr and Hildreth argue that at least the first stage of the algorithm—the detection of zero-crossings by independent ∇^2G filters—is implemented in the visual pathway, and we next discuss the physiological and psychophysical evidence for their argument.

Marr and Hildreth argue first that the function of X retinal ganglion cells is to compute ∇^2G*I. Recall from Chapter 2 that the response of an X cell is a linear function of the difference between the average intensities of light in the centre of the field and in the surround. The contribution of intensity to both components is weighted according to a Gaussian distribution (Enroth-Cugell & Robson, 1966).

Marr and Hildreth demonstrate that, given certain realistic assumptions, this computation of the difference of two Gaussians is equivalent to computing ∇^2G*I, and they argue that values of this function are signalled by the response rates of X cells. This hypothesis raises a problem; if zero-crossings are to be detected in an array of ∇^2G*I values, both positive and negative values must be available, but a nerve cell cannot give a negative response. Marr and Hildreth propose that this is why both on-and off-centre cells exist. The first type carries positive values of ∇^2G*I and the second negative values. A weakness in this hypothesis is that the relative sizes of centre and surround in the fields of X cells are not appropriate for the accurate computation of ∇^2G*I (Robson, 1983), but it is still possible that LGN cells, or cortical cells with concentric fields, perform the computation instead.

In Marr and Hildreth's interpretation, cells with concentric fields do not signal the presence of an edge, as the feature detection theory discussed in Chapter 3 holds. Their role is the humbler one of making a measurement on the pattern of light in their fields which can then be used to detect zero-crossings. One rule for detecting a zero-crossing in the pattern of X cell activity would be to find adjacent on-and off-centre cells which are both active. Marr and Hildreth propose that simple cells in the visual cortex measure oriented zero-crossing segments by signalling activity in parallel rows of on-and off-centre cells, according to the scheme shown in Figure 5.9.

Marr and Hildreth's model of simple cell organisation has proved to be incorrect in some respects, however. Schiller (1982) studied the responses of rhesus monkey simple cells when a drug was applied to the retina which suppressed the responses of on-centre but not off-centre ganglion cells. This treatment had no effect on the orientation selectivity of simple cells, whereas Marr and Hildreth's model predicts it would have been abolished. The mechanisms producing orientation selectivity can therefore operate with input from off-centre cells alone. An alternative implementation of Marr and Hildreth's algorithm, proposed by Poggio (1983), can account for these findings. In Poggio's model, a simple cell is

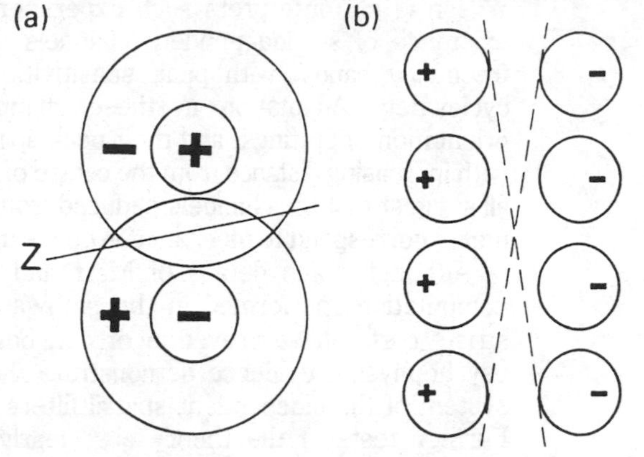

Marr and
Hildreth's scheme
for the detection of
zero—crossing
segments by
cortical simple
cells. In (a), the
fields of an on—
centre and an off—
centre LGN cell
overlap. If both are
active, then a
zero—crossing Z
must lie between
them and an AND
gate connected to
them would detect
it. In (b), an AND
gate connected to
parallel rows of
on— and off—
centre cells (field
surrounds not
shown) will detect
a zero—crossing
segment falling
between the
dashed lines.
Adapted from
Marr and Hildreth
(1980).

FIGURE 5.9

activated by a row of active on-centre (or off-centre) cells flanked by *silent* rows of the same type of cell. The basic unit is not an on- and an off-centre cell connected by an AND gate, as in Figure 5.9, but two cells of the same type connected by an AND-NOT gate.

One implication of Marr and Hildreth's (1980) theory is that the role of simple cells is to measure the positions, strengths and orientations of zero-crossing segments. They do not detect edges, as the feature detection theory held, but instead measure parameters from which the locations of edges can later be obtained. In this view, the known properties of the visual cortex therefore take us to only an early stage in visual perception; the computation of zero-crossing segments. How these are combined into the raw primal sketch by the nervous system is not known, though some simple cells may detect bars, and cells with "end-inhibition" (Chapter 3, p. 53) may be involved in the detection of terminations and blobs.

Another important feature of Marr and Hildreth's theory is that it provides an explanation for the existence of cells in the visual cortex tuned to a range of different spatial frequencies (see Chapter 3, p. 58), proposing that these act as $\nabla^2 G$ filters of different widths. The existence of multiple spatial frequency filters in the human visual system is also demonstrated by evidence from studies of the ability of observers to detect gratings and other spatial patterns of light. Campbell and Robson (1968) and Graham and Nachmias (1971) discovered that thresholds for detection of different components in compound gratings were the same as those for the detection of the components presented individually. These findings indicate that visual input is processed in multiple independent channels, each analysing a different band of spatial frequencies.

Spatial frequency channels have been analysed in more detail by measuring the increase in thresholds for detecting spatial patterns of light which occurs following exposure to sinusoidal gratings. Wilson (1983) interprets such experiments as demonstrating the existence of six independent channels tuned to different spatial frequency bands, with peak sensitivities ranging from 1 to 16 cycles/deg. Adaptation in these channels is specific for the orientation of gratings, and their peak spatial frequency tuning falls with increasing distance from the centre of the fovea. These findings all suggest that the channels deduced from psychophysical measurements correspond to mechanisms operating in the visual cortex.

Although some details of Marr and Hildreth's theory of the computations performed in the pathway from retina to LGN to striate cortex have proved incorrect, both neurophysiological and psychophysical evidence demonstrate the existence in the visual system of the independent spatial filters proposed by the theory. Further tests of the theory are clearly needed, and Marr and Ullman (1981) list a number of neurophysiological predictions which it makes. One prediction is that there must be pooling of X cell inputs from the LGN to form at least one wider $\nabla^2 G$ filter, and simple cells detecting zero-crossing segments should take their input from LGN cells with just one filter width. Another is that cells will exist which are driven by a set of cells with the same field and same orientation preference but with different spatial frequency sensitivities, and which therefore detect edge-segments from zero-crossing segments in adjacent $\nabla^2 G$ channels.

OTHER ROUTES TO THE RAW PRIMAL SKETCH

Marr and Hildreth's algorithm produces a "sketch" of all the edge-segments and blobs present from an original image. However, other routes to such a sketch are possible, and may provide a better account of the means by which the human visual system encodes intensity changes. Here we describe an interesting convergence by two different British groups towards a somewhat different account of this process.

Pearson and Robinson (1985) were disappointed with the results obtained with standard edge-finding algorithms when applied to the problem of automatic sketching of images of faces. Pearson's group was faced with the applied problem of compressing moving images of faces into a form economical for transmission down telephone lines to provide video-phones, particularly useful so that deaf people may communicate at a distance using sign language. An implementation of Marr and Hildreth's algorithm led to a cluttered, unusable sketch. This setback led them to consider in detail the nature of the edges that it was important for their artificial visual system to sketch.

Pearson and Robinson (1985) noted that the face is not a flat pattern (see also Bruce, 1988, and Chapters 8 and 16) but is a bumpy surface. The places where an artist draws lines in order to

Top: The luminance profile to which a valley-detector based upon a filter of this shape will respond most strongly. Bottom: A vertically orientated valley pattern has a column of darker elements (−) surrounded by lighter ones (+). Adapted from Pearson, Hanna and Martinez (1986).

FIGURE 5.10

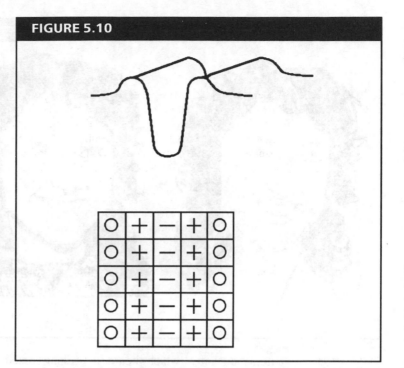

sketch the face correspond to places where the surface of the face turns sharply away from the line of sight, in addition to places where there is a sharp contrast such as at the hairline. Subject to certain lighting constraints, the former surface feature gives rise to a luminance (intensity) *valley* in an image (see Fig. 5.10), while the latter gives rise to a luminance discontinuity (a step edge). Pearson and Robinson devised a "valley-detecting" algorithm which found just these kinds of intensity changes in an image. It first applies a filter of the shape shown in Figure 5.10 to the image, and is able to use a single width of filter because input images are always of faces and of a standard size. The problem of intensity changes occurring over different scales therefore does not arise. Rather than detect zero-crossings in the output of this filter, as Marr and Hildreth's (1980) model does, Pearson and Robinson's algorithm then looks for the *peak* responses of the filter. The particular filter they use responds most strongly when it finds a luminance valley in the image. It will also respond, though less strongly, to a step edge. Valleys and edges at different orientations are found by separately applying filters oriented to detect horizontal, vertical and diagonal valleys.

Figure 5.11 shows examples of a line drawing of a face produced by Pearson and Robinson's system, next to an artist's sketch of the same face. The "automatic" sketch blacked in blocks of hair, eyebrows etc. using a simple procedure to darken any area whose mean intensity falls below some criterion. The result is an

FIGURE 5.11

(left) A cartoon produced by a human artist and (right) a cartoon produced automatically by the algorithm described in the text. Reproduced from Pearson et. al. (1986) with permission.

automatic sketch which bears a striking resemblance to that produced by the human artist.

An interesting additional feature of the "valley-detecting" algorithm is that it provides an account of why it appears more natural to the visual system to present a cartoon drawn in black on a white background, than one drawn in white on a black background, and why photographic negatives of human faces appear so difficult to recognise. An account of edge detection based upon zero-crossing location does not predict the asymmetry between positive and negative images, but this is easily accounted for in terms of the valley-detecting routine. A black-on-white cartoon reproduces the locations of luminance valleys from the original picture, whereas in a white-on-black cartoon these valleys have been turned into ridges. A black-on-white cartoon will pass through the valley detecting algorithm unaltered, whereas white-on-black cartoons and photographic negatives suffer distortions to the locations of facial features when passed through the same filter (Pearson, Hanna & Martinez, 1986).

Pearson and Robinson's cartoon-drawing algorithm is thus based on a similar initial step to Marr and Hildreth's (1980) algorithm, though it works at only a single level of spatial scale. The difference lies principally in what is detected from the output of the $\nabla^2 G$ filter. Watt and Morgan (e.g. Watt, 1988; Watt & Morgan, 1985) have also pointed out difficulties for the "zero-crossing" theory of edge detection, and have produced an alternative theory of the derivation of the primal sketch which bears some similarity to the scheme of Pearson and Robinson. Watt (1988) points out that the

FIGURE 5.12

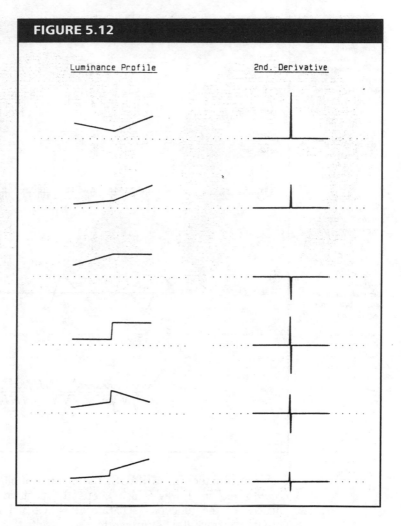

To the left are shown different profiles with discontinuities in gradient (top half of figure) or intensity (bottom half). To the right are shown the second derivatives of these waveforms. Note that zero-crossings arise in the second derivatives of the intensity discontinuities, but not the gradient discontinuities. Reproduced from Watt (1988) with permission.

detection of zero-crossings is only useful for locating the kind of intensity change (often intensity discontinuities) found at edges. However, there are other kinds of intensity change that the visual system might need to describe (see examples in Fig. 5.12). Watt and Morgan's MIRAGE algorithm allows any changes in intensity in the image to be fully described and also gives a rather better account of human psychophysical data than is given by theories based on the detection of zero-crossings in the second derivative. How does MIRAGE work?

The first stage of the MIRAGE system is the same as that of Marr and Hildreth's model—the image is convolved with a range of $\nabla^2 G$ filters. However, MIRAGE then differs from Marr and Hildreth's algorithm since there is no stage at which edges are detected from the output of each filter independently (as Marr and Hildreth achieve through finding zero-crossings from the output of

A luminance profile (resulting from two sets of stripes of different widths) is passed through ∇²G filters of two different widths. The output from the smaller filter has numerous zero−crossings, while the output from the larger filter has few. At the bottom is shown the result of separately summing the positive and negative portions of these filter outputs. Reproduced from Watt (1988) with permission.

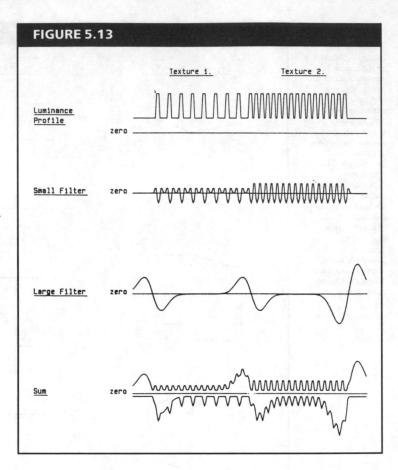

FIGURE 5.13

each spatial filter). In MIRAGE, the outputs of all the filters are *recombined* in a way which keeps the positive and negative portions of the functions separate. Positive and negative filter outputs are separately *summed* to yield results that Watt calls the S+ and S− signals (see Fig. 5.13). The locations of edges, bars and luminance plateaus are then determined from measurements made on these S+ and S− signals.

This occurs as follows. In Figures 5.13 and 5.14 each of the S+ and S− signals contain sections which depart from zero. Indeed each of the summed waveforms can be described as a set of "masses" each bounded by zero. We have marked these "zero-bounded masses" in Figure 5.14. The spatial sequence of the locations of the zero-values in the two summed signals can be used to interpret the intensity changes present. Edges give rise to one kind of sequence while lines give rise to another. Additionally, various measurements are made on these zero-bounded masses. The chevrons in Figure 5.14 mark the "centroids" (means) of these zero-bounded masses and these play a particularly important role in locating and describing an intensity change, in contrast to the zero-

FIGURE 5.14

The MIRAGE algorithm. A luminance profile (top) is passed through ∇²G filters of three different widths (second row). The positive and negative portions of these filter outputs are separately summed (third row). The zero‑bounded masses in these combined filter outputs are analysed and the apexes of the chevrons in the bottom row mark the locations of the centroids of these masses. Reproduced from Watt (1988) with permission.

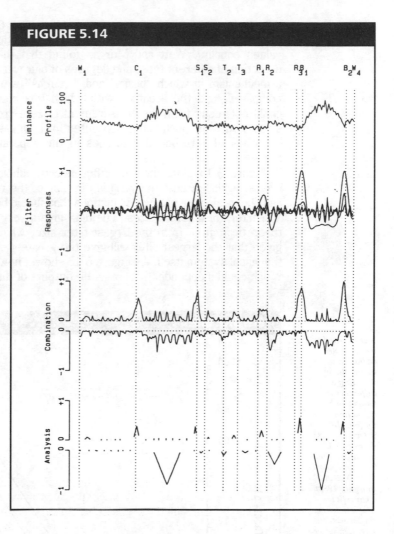

crossings of Marr and Hildreth's scheme. Centroids mark the point on an edge where the rate of intensity change is changing most rapidly, and mark the centre of a line. In Figure 5.14, the height of each chevron represents the mass of each zero-bounded portion of the filter responses, and the width of each chevron represents the spread of the zero-bounded mass. The masses and their spreads are also used to build a description of the intensity changes present (see Watt, 1988, for details).

Watt (1988) summarises a considerable amount of psycho-physical evidence that suggests the MIRAGE algorithm may provide a good account of edge detection in human vision. One example comes from an experiment by Watt and Morgan (1983), who asked subjects to say which of two edges looked most blurred. Watt and Morgan measured the smallest difference in blur that could be detected between the test and reference edge for different amounts, and different types of blur (e.g. Gaussian blur as described earlier, compared with a blurring function weighting all values equally). Watt and Morgan found that the thresholds of detection of different types and degrees of blur was consistent with a mechanism in which "peaks" and "troughs" were localised and compared, and the accuracy with which this could be achieved could not result from the measurement of zero-crossings or their slopes, but was much better accounted for by measurement of the centroids of zero-bounded masses in the separate S+ and S− signals.

Figure 5.15 plots the blur difference thresholds obtained for Gaussian blur against the variation in blur of the reference edge, and shows also the predicted functions that should be obtained from $\nabla^2 G$ filters of different sizes. The data give a very good fit to the theoretical curve from the largest filter size, which makes sense given that the largest filter will give the greatest spatial spread in the visual system itself. As Figure 5.15 shows, however, a system which could independently access the outputs of the smaller filters

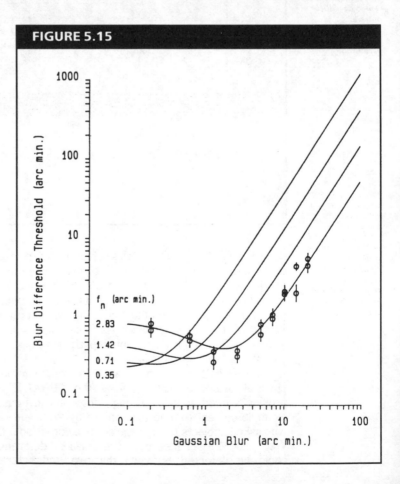

FIGURE 5.15

Solid lines show the predicted variation in the threshold for detecting a difference in Gaussian blur, as a function of blur, for four different filter sizes (2.83 down to 0.35 minutes of arc). The data points from Watt and Morgan (1983) clearly fit the prediction from the largest filter size. Reproduced from Watt (1988) with permission.

should be capable of greater sensitivity to differences in low degrees of blur (at less than 1 minute of arc in Figure 5.15). The observation that human observers cannot do any better than would be predicted from the largest scale filter is good evidence that the visual system cannot access the different filter outputs independently.

Further evidence for the MIRAGE algorithm comes from the data of Watt and Morgan (1984) who examined how accurately subjects could localise edges as a function of the contrast of the edge. Subjects were asked to decide whether or not two edges were aligned, and their accuracy as a function of contrast was compared with theoretical curves based upon the detection of peaks and zero-crossings from the second derivative, and the detection of centroids of zero-bounded masses in S+ and S− signals. As Figure 5.16 shows, the data give a much better fit to the curve predicted by centroid measurement than to the one predicted by measurement of peaks or zero-crossings.

While the MIRAGE algorithm as described seems to provide quite a good recent elaboration of an edge-finding mechanism based on initial $\nabla^2 G$ filtering, Watt (1988) goes on to show how filters of different sizes may be sequentially switched out of the system in order to conduct fine analysis of spatial structure. The initial product of MIRAGE is a *grouping* of the large scale structures in the image and the *detection* (without localisation) of the finer,

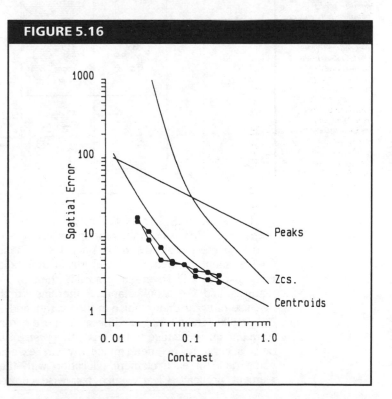

FIGURE 5.16

The data points (from Watt & Morgan, 1984) show the random error associated with judgements of edge location as the contrast of the edge is varied. The solid lines show theoretical predictions based on the detection of peaks, zero-crossings and centroids. Reproduced from Watt (1988) with permission.

FIGURE 5.17

At the top is an image of 16 dots. In the second row are shown the outputs of four different size ∇^2 filters. Immediately beneath this is shown the result of separately combining the positive (S+) and negative (S−) portions of all four filter outputs (row S4). The remaining rows reveal the results of progressively switching out the contributions of the larger filters. Thus S3 shows the results when the smaller three filters only are used, and so forth through to S1 which shows the positive and negative portions of the smallest filter alone. Reproduced from Watt (1988) with permission.

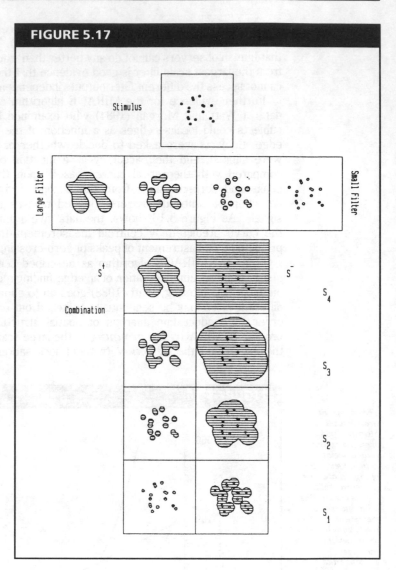

textural structures. For example, in Figure 5.17 we see how the output of MIRAGE describes groups or clusters of image features at the coarsest scale (from S+) and the statistical nature of the finer elements of texture as well (from the "holes" in S−; if the input pattern had reversed contrast, then S− would group the features and S+ would capture the finer texture). However, because of *error* due to noise in the system and errors introduced by sampling and filtering, and because these errors may propagate from one analytic stage to the next, the *positions* of elements can only accurately be determined by an extensive process of comparison of each element's location with that of each other element present. Clearly such pair-wise comparison processes could take a good deal of time, even in a parallel system, and the time will increase the more elements there are. For this reason, Watt suggests that grouping elements into clusters and solving for position at successively finer spatial scales can be highly economical, since there are generally fewer elements at a greater scale than at a finer one. If 12 dots are grouped into two larger clusters, it will be much faster to locate each cluster accurately than each dot within a cluster. In fact, Watt suggests that an optimally efficient system will work with progressively more finely resolved clusters, as illustrated in Figure 5.17.

Watt therefore argues that in order to go beyond just the detection of finer scale structure, and to *measure* the location of each texture element, the contribution of the coarser ∇^2G channels to the summed S+ and S− products must be progressively switched out. Each time a coarser channel is switched out, a slightly finer description is obtained whose own intrinsic spatial details may be economically measured. Progressing from the coarsest to the finest level of localisation will take time, however, and may not always be necessary. For many purposes a statistical description of texture may suffice and there may not be the need to complete the full spatial analysis. Watt (1988) suggests that the process of filter switching may be controlled either *automatically* or more flexibly by conscious *attention*. Automatic control may explain how the visual system copes with changes to the image (see Watt, 1988, for details), while the attentional route may explain how we can eventually spot an animal initially concealed from view by its camouflage. Watt (1988) therefore sees grouping, one aspect of perceptual organisation, as intimately connected with the formation of the raw primal sketch. This represents an additional point of departure from Marr and Hildreth (1980), for whom perceptual organisation builds upon the earlier establishment of the raw primal sketch, in ways we describe in Chapter 6.

CONCLUSIONS

Watt and Morgan's MIRAGE algorithm represents a promising advance upon that of Marr and Hildreth, since it gives a better account of certain psychophysical experiments. While no specific physiological implementation of MIRAGE has been suggested, the model hints at a possible role for the feedback connections between areas in the visual pathway. As we saw in Chapter 3 (p. 66), these are found in all connections between cortical visual areas, and even at the early stage of the pathway between LGN and striate cortex. Marr and Hildreth's theory does not propose any function for this feedback, whereas Watt's requires some mechanism responsible for controlling actively the width of the ∇^2G filters applied to the input. Although there is no physiological evidence on this issue at present, it is tempting to speculate that this is why feedback pathways are present at so early a stage in visual processing.

Even so, the MIRAGE algorithm, like Marr and Hildreth's, fails to accommodate an additional body of data which emphasises the orientation tuning of early stages of human vision. Recall from Chapter 3 the evidence that simple cells in the cortex are orientation selective. Spatial frequency tuning is also found to be orientation selective in human psychophysical experiments. For example, the classic study by Blakemore and Campbell (1969) showed that subjects who had adapted to a vertical grating of a particular spatial frequency by staring at it were less sensitive to contrast at the same or similar spatial frequencies, but only if the orientation of the grating remained the same.

While Marr and Hildreth attempt to explain orientation specificity in terms of the detection of oriented zero-crossing segments, the mechanism cannot accommodate recent findings of Georgeson and Shackleton (1989) on the perception of "plaid" patterns, formed by superimposing gratings of different spatial frequencies and different orientations. Georgeson and Shackleton showed that a sine- and a square-wave grating superimposed at ± 45° were perceived as separate patterns, and this is difficult to understand unless the spatial frequency filters are orientation-specific, which is not the case in either of the models described in this chapter.

Whatever the ultimate success of the different algorithms as accounts of human vision, all the research we have described in this chapter shares the assumption that the important job achieved by early visual processing is the representation of edges in a raw primal sketch. In the next chapter we turn to consider how more elaborate descriptions of an image can be constructed from the elements of the raw primal sketch.

Chapter Six

PERCEPTUAL ORGANISATION

*I*n Chapter 5 we considered how the raw primal sketch—a description of edge segments, terminations and blobs—may be derived from an array of intensities in the retinal image. In this chapter we turn to consider how such low-level descriptions may be organised into larger perceptual "chunks." When we view the world we do not see a collection of edges and blobs—unless we adopt a very analytical perceptual attitude—but see instead an organised world of surfaces and objects. How is such perceptual segregation achieved? How do we know which parts of the visual information reaching our sensory apparatus belong together? These are the questions addressed in this chapter. The first part of the chapter concentrates on human perception, since it was through the study of this that many of the principles of perceptual organisation became established. We return to the broader perspective of animal vision when we consider how such perceptual principles may be exploited in natural camouflage and advertisement. In the final part of the chapter we turn to artificial intelligence approaches to perceptual organisation.

As we discussed in Chapter 4, the psychology of human visual perception during the late 19th and early 20th century was dominated by associationism. It was assumed that perception could be analysed in terms of its component sensations, and that complex ideas were the result of associating together simpler ones. However, as the Gestalt psychologists pointed out, an analysis of perception into discrete sensations overlooks some important aspects of form and structure. Each of the arrangements shown in Figure 6.1 possesses the quality of "squareness" despite being composed of quite different elements. A tune is recognisable despite being played in a different key or at a different speed. The spatial and temporal relationships between elements are as important as the absolute size, location or nature of the elements themselves, and a sensation-based account of perception fails to capture this.

FIGURE 6.1

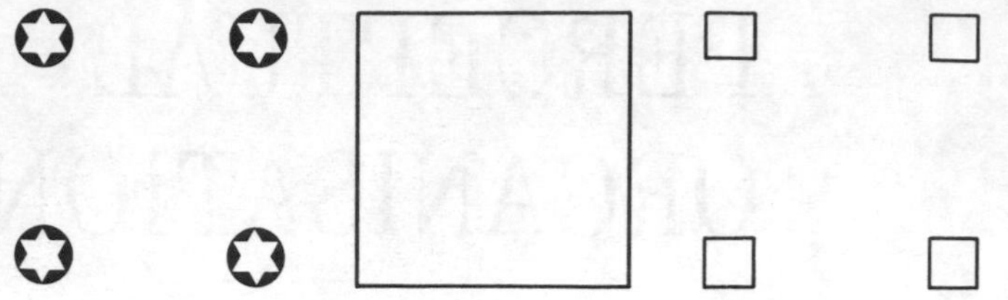

Each of these three forms is seen as being square, despite being composed of quite different elements.

Even Wundt (1896) recognised that a simple structuralist analysis failed to capture certain perceptual phenomena:

> A compound clang is more in its ideational and affective attributes than merely a sum of single tones (Wundt, 1896, trans. 1907, p. 368.)

But it was the Gestalt psychologists, notably Wertheimer (1923), Köhler (1947) and Koffka (1935), with whom the catch-phrase "the whole is greater than the sum of its parts" became identified. We will first describe the Gestalt ideas about perceptual organisation, and then go on to consider more recent accounts.

AMBIGUOUS PICTURES

The world that we view appears to be composed of discrete objects of various sizes which are seen against a background comprised of textured surfaces. We usually have no difficulty in seeing the boundaries of objects, unless these are successfully camouflaged (see later), and there is generally no doubt about which areas are "figures" and which comprise the "ground." However, it is possible to construct pictures in which there is ambiguity about which region is "figure" and which "ground." Edgar Rubin, one of the Gestalt psychologists, used the face/vase picture (Fig. 6.2) to illustrate this. The picture can be seen either as a pair of black faces in profile, or as a white vase, but it is impossible to maintain simultaneously the perception of both the faces and the vase. The contour dividing the black and white regions of the picture appears to have a one-sided function. It "belongs" to whichever region is perceived as figure. People viewing this picture usually find that their perception of it shifts from one interpretation to the other, sometimes quite spontaneously. The artist, M. C. Escher, exploited this principle of perceptual reversibility when he produced etchings in which there is figure/ground ambiguity (see Fig. 6.3).

It is also possible to construct pictures so that the internal organisation of a particular figure is ambiguous. Jastrow's

FIGURE 6.2

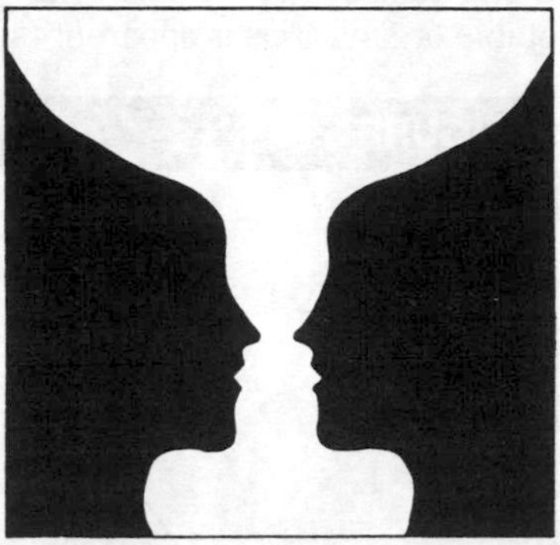

This picture, devised by E. Rubin in 1915, can be seen either as a pair of black faces in silhouette, or as a white vase.

M. C. Escher's "Circle Limit IV" © 1989 M. C. Escher Heirs/ Cordon Art – Baarn – Holland. Used by permission.

FIGURE 6.3

duck–rabbit picture (Fig. 6.4) may be seen as a duck (beak at the right), or a rabbit (ears at the right), but not both simultaneously. Some abstract and "op"-art may be perplexing to view because no stable organisation is apparent (see Fig. 6.5).

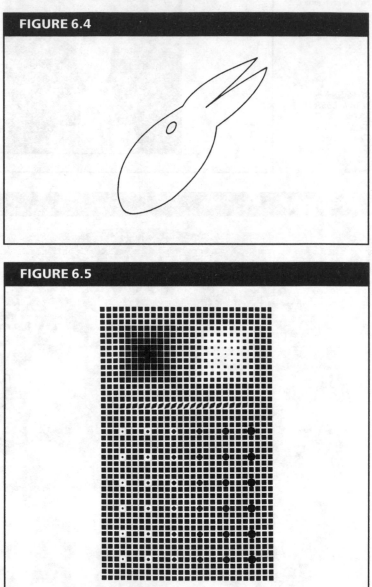

FIGURE 6.4

Duck or rabbit? This ambiguous picture was introduced to psychologists by J. Jastrow in 1900.

FIGURE 6.5

"Supernovae" 1959–61 by Victor Vasarely. Copyright DACS 1990. Used by permission.

The perception of such ambiguous displays is interesting in its own right, and psychologists have investigated the factors influencing which organisation of an ambiguous display will be preferred, and the factors determining perceptual reversals (e.g.

see Attneave, 1971; Hochberg, 1950; Pheiffer, Eure & Hamilton, 1956). In all these examples, the perceptual "data" remain the same, while the interpretation of it varies. It seems as though there must be a strong "top-down" component in such perceptions. Higher levels of perceptual interpretation appear to be continually constraining and guiding the lower levels of image analysis.

However, these ambiguous pictures have been cleverly constructed, and our perception of them is not necessarily typical of normal processing. Ambiguity generally does not arise in the real world, or in most pictures. Rather than having constantly shifting interpretations, we usually see a stable and organised world. For example, viewing Figure 6.6a in isolation, most people would report seeing a hexagon, while those viewing Figure 6.6b report seeing a picture of a three-dimensional cube, even though Figure 6.6a is an equally legitimate view of a cube, viewed corner on. Figure 6.7 is seen as a set of overlapping circles, rather than as one circle touching two adjoining shapes which have "bites" taken out of them. Why, given these possible alternative perceptions, do we see these pictures in these ways?

The form at (a) looks like a hexagon, while that at (b) looks like a cube. Of course (a) is also a legitimate view of a cube.

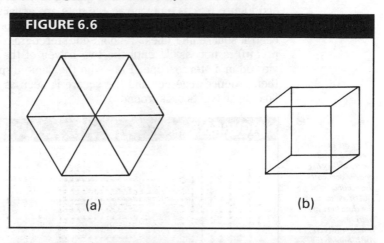

FIGURE 6.6

(a)

(b)

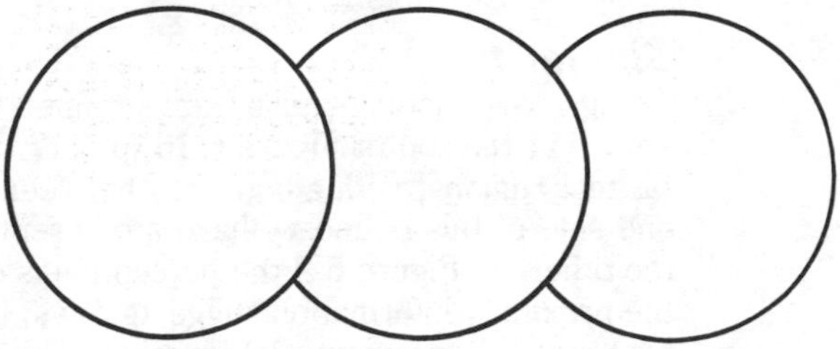

Most people would see this as a set of overlapping circles, although two of the shapes might have "bites" taken out of them.

FIGURE 6.7

GESTALT LAWS OF ORGANISATION

The Gestalt psychologists formulated a number of principles of perceptual organisation to describe how certain perceptions are more likely to occur than others. Some of their principles were primarily to do with the grouping of sub-regions of figures, and others were more concerned with the segregation of figure from ground. However, since sub-regions of a figure need to be grouped in order for a larger region to be seen as "belonging together" as figure, we will discuss all these principles together.

Proximity

One of the most important factors determining the perceptual organisation of a scene is proximity of the elements within it. Things which are close together are grouped together. In Figure 6.8a the perception is of columns, because the horizontal spacing of the dots is greater than their vertical spacing. In Figure 6.8b we see rows, because the horizontal spacing of the dots is the smaller, and Figure 6.8c is ambiguous; the dots are equally spaced in both directions. Proximity in depth is a powerful organising factor. The central square in a Julesz random-dot stereogram (see Chapter 7, p. 146) is not visible until the two halves of the stereo pair are viewed in a stereoscope. Dots with the same disparity values are then grouped together and the square is seen as a distinct figure floating above its background.

FIGURE 6.8

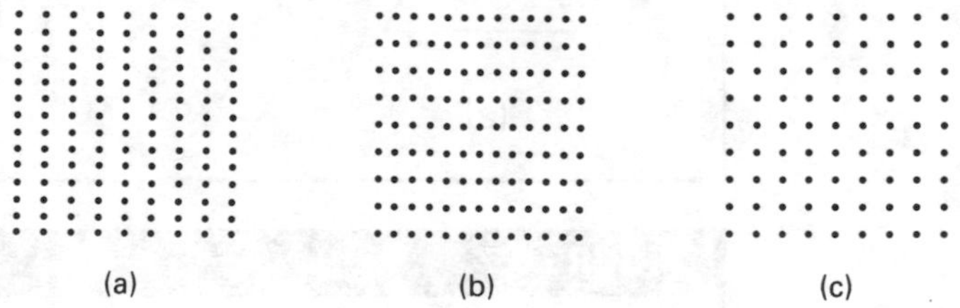

The dots in (a) form columns because they are nearer vertically than horizontally. At (b) we see rows, the dots here are nearer horizontally; (c) is ambiguous, the dots are equally spaced in both directions.

(a)   (b)   (c)

Similarity

Things which look "similar" are grouped together. The examples shown at the top of Figure 6.16 (p. 117) appear to consist of two distinct regions, with a boundary between them. The elements on one side of this boundary have a different orientation to those on the other. In Figure 6.9 the perception is of columns, even though the proximity information suggests rows, illustrating that similarity may override proximity information. The question of *how* similar items must be in order to be grouped together is an empirical one to which we will return.

This picture is seen as columns. Similarity in brightness of the dots over—rides proximity.

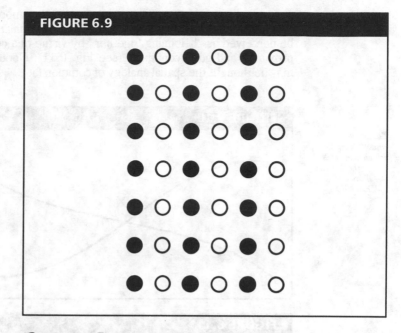

FIGURE 6.9

Common Fate

Things which appear to move together are grouped together. A camouflaged animal will only remain well-hidden if it remains stationary. As soon as it moves it is easier to see. Gibson, Gibson, Smith and Flock (1959) illustrated grouping by common fate with a simple demonstration. They sprinkled powder on two sheets of glass, and projected an image of the powder onto a screen. While the sheets were held still a single collection of powder was seen. As soon as one sheet was moved across the other, viewers saw the powder segregated into two independent collections, by virtue of the movement in the display. A further example is provided by random-dot kinematograms (see Chapter 7, p. 163), in which a central region of texture is revealed through the apparent motions of the elements it contains. Johansson (1973) has produced an even more dramatic demonstration of the power of movement to confer organisation. He attached lights to the joints of a darkly clothed actor and filmed him as he moved in a dark room, so that only the lights were visible. When the actor was at rest, observers reported perceiving a disorganised collection of points. As soon as the actor walked, their perception was that of a moving human figure. We shall return to discuss the perceptual organisation of such complex displays in Chapter 15.

Good Continuation

In a figure such as Figure 6.10, one tends to perceive two smooth curves which cross at point X, rather than perceiving two irregular V-shaped forms touching at X. The Gestaltists argued that perceptual organisation will tend to preserve smooth continuity rather than yielding abrupt changes. Quite dissimilar objects may be perceived as "belonging together" by virtue of a combination of proximity and good continuity (see Fig. 6.11). Good continuation may be thought the spatial analogy of common fate.

FIGURE 6.10

This is seen as two smooth lines which cross at X, rather than as two V−shapes touching at X.

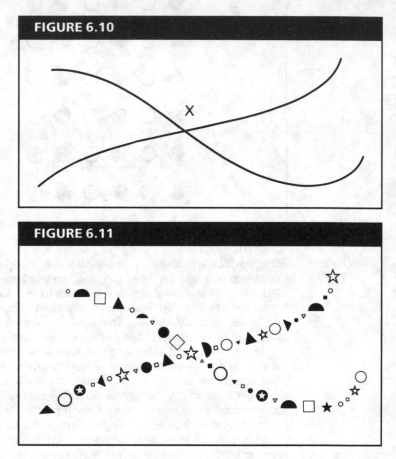

FIGURE 6.11

Quite dissimilar shapes may be grouped together through a combination of proximity and good continuation.

Closure

Of several geometrically possible perceptual organisations that one will be seen which produces a "closed" rather than an "open" figure. Thus the patterns on the left and right of Figure 6.1 are seen as squares rather than as crosses, because the former are closed. The Gestaltists suggested that the stellar constellation "the plough" might be seen as a plough because of closure and good continuation.

Relative Size, Surroundedness, Orientation and Symmetry

All other things being equal, the smaller of two areas will be seen as

FIGURE 6.12

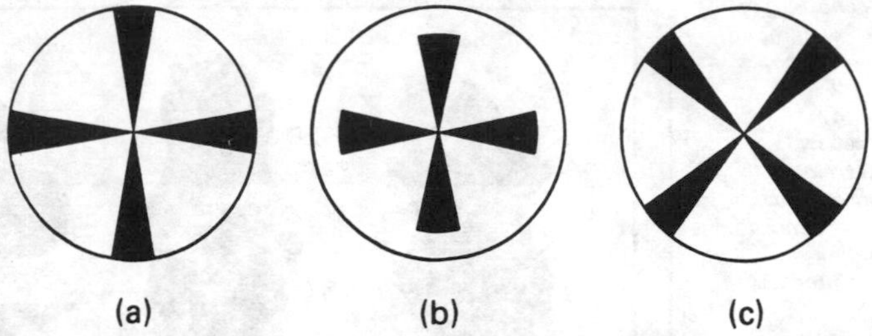

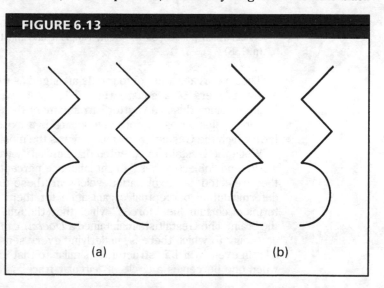

(a)   (b)   (c)

The preferred perception of (a) is a black propeller on a white background. This preference is enhanced if the white area surrounds the black as at (b). If the orientation of the forms is altered, so that the white area is oriented around the horizontal and vertical axes, as at (c), then it is easier to see the larger, white area as figure.

figure against a larger background. Thus Figure 6.12a will tend to be perceived as a black propellor shape against a white background since the black area is the smaller. This effect is enhanced if the white area actually surrounds the black as in Figure 6.12b, since surrounded areas tend to be seen as figures. However, if we orient the figure so that the white area is arranged around the horizontal and vertical axes then it is easier to see this larger area as a figure (Fig. 6.12c). There seems to be a preference for horizontal or vertically oriented regions to be seen as figures. Also note that both these sets of patterns are symmetrical. Symmetry is a powerful perceptual property, and may be more salient perceptually than non-reflected repetition (Bruce & Morgan, 1975). Examples of symmetry and repetition are shown in Figure 6.13. Symmetrical areas will tend to be perceived as figures, against asymmetrical backgrounds. Figure 6.14 shows how relative size, orientation, symmetry and surroundedness may all operate together so that it is difficult, if not impossible, to see anything other than the black

FIGURE 6.13

At (a) one form is repeated without reflection around a vertical axis. This arrangement is not as perceptually salient as the arrangement shown at (b), where repetition with reflection around the vertical axis produces bilateral symmetry.

(a)   (b)

This picture clearly shows black shapes on a white background. The black shapes are vertically oriented, symmetrical, small (relative to the background) and surrounded by the background.

FIGURE 6.14

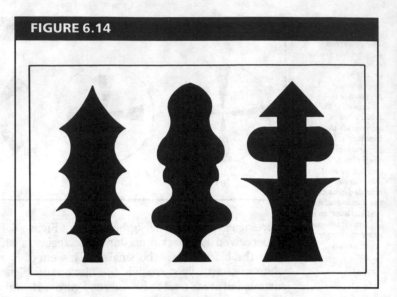

areas as the figures in this picture. The reader will note the perceptual stability of this picture compared with the ambiguity of Figure 6.2, where the relative sizes, surroundedness and symmetries in the display favour neither the "faces" nor the "vase" particularly strongly.

The Law of Prägnanz

For the Gestalt psychologists, many of these laws were held to be manifestations of the Law of Prägnanz, introduced by Wertheimer. Koffka (1935) describes the law:

> Of several geometrically possible organisations that one will actually occur which possesses the best, simplest and most stable shape. (p. 138)

Thus an organisation of four dots arranged as though they were at the corners of a square (Fig. 6.1, right) will be seen as a "square" since this is a "better" arrangement than, say, a cross or a triangle plus an extra dot. The square is a closed, symmetrical form which the Gestaltists maintained was the most stable.

While the Gestaltists accepted that familiarity with objects in the world, and "objective set," might influence perceptual organisation, they rejected an explanation solely in these terms. A major determinant of perceptual organisation for them was couched in terms of certain "field forces" which they thought operated within the brain. The Gestaltists maintained a *Doctrine of Isomorphism*, according to which there is, underlying every sensory experience, a brain event which is structurally similar to that experience. Thus when one perceives a circle, a "circular trace" is established, and so on. Field forces were held to operate to make the outcome as stable as possible, just as the forces operating on a soap bubble are such that its most stable state is a sphere. Unfortunately, there has been no evidence provided for such field forces, and the physiological theory of the Gestalts has fallen by the wayside, leaving us with a set of descriptive principles, but without a model of perceptual processing. Indeed some of their "Laws" of perceptual organisation today sound vague and inadequate. What is meant by a "good" or a "simple" shape, for example? Recent workers have attempted to formalise at least some of the Gestalt perceptual principles.

RECENT APPROACHES TO PERCEPTUAL ORGANISATION

Hochberg and Brooks (1960) tried to provide a more objective criterion for the notion of "goodness" of shape by presenting subjects with line drawings (Fig. 6.15) and asking them to rate the apparent tridimensionality in these figures. They argued that as the complexity of the figures as two-dimensional line drawings increased, so there should be a tendency for the figures to be perceived as two-dimensional representations of three-dimensional objects. They made a number of measurements on the figures

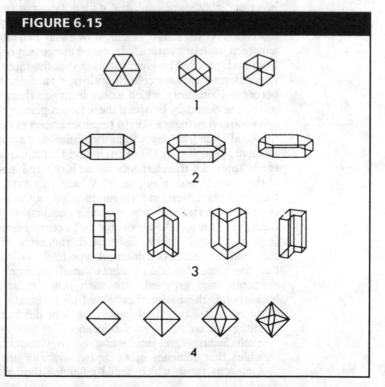

FIGURE 6.15

Examples of the forms used by Hochberg and Brooks (1960). In each of rows 1–4, the figure at the left is most likely to be seen as three-dimensional. From Julian E. Hochberg, PERCEPTION, 2e, copyright 1978, p.142. Reprinted by permission of Prentice Hall, Inc., Englewood Cliffs, New Jersey.

and looked for those which correlated well with perceived tridimensionality. The best measure was the number of angles in the figure. This measure seems to represent "complexity." The more angles the figure contains, the more complex it is in two dimensions, and the more likely it is to be perceived as a representation of a "simpler," three-dimensional object. A second measure which correlated well was the number of differently sized angles. This reflects the asymmetry in the 2D figure, since a figure in which many of the angles are of the same size is more likely to be symmetrical than one in which many differently sized angles are present. A final measure was the number of continuous lines. This reflects the discontinuity present, since the more continuous lines there are, the more discontinuities must be present between each. Thus the more complex, asymmetrical and discontinuous the 2D pattern, the more likely it was to be perceived as representing a projection of a 3D figure. Hochberg and Brooks then applied their measures to a set of new figures and found they correlated well with the perceived tridimensionality in these.

Thus it is possible to express Gestalt ideas such as "good shape" more precisely. In similar vein we now consider recent attempts to tackle the problem of grouping by similarity. How similar must items be before they are grouped together? It is unlikely that they must be *identical*, since no camouflage can ever perfectly match its surroundings, yet we know that camouflage can be remarkably successful. But if identity is not required, what are the important variables that determine grouping by similarity? This has been investigated by seeing how easily two different regions of a pattern, or more naturally textured image, segregate perceptually from each other. The logic of this is that the more the elements in two different regions cohere with one another, by virtue of the perceptual similarity which exists between them, the less visible will be the boundary between these two regions.

Olson and Attneave (1970) required observers to indicate where the "odd" quadrant lay within a circular display of simple pattern elements (see Fig. 6.16). They found that the quadrant was most easily spotted if the elements within it differed in slope from those of the rest of the display (e.g. $<$ $\vee$) and was most difficult to find if the elements differed in configuration, but not in the slopes of their component parts (e.g. $>$ $<$). Similar conclusions were reached by Beck (1972) who asked his subjects to count elements of one type (e.g. $<$) which were distributed randomly within a display containing elements of a different type (e.g. $>$). Again he reasoned that the more the odd elements stood out from the background elements, and grouped with each other rather than with the background, the easier they would be to isolate and count. Like Olson and Attneave, Beck found that slope differences led to faster counting than configurational differences.

Such findings are interesting as they demonstrate that the variables that influence grouping by similarity are not necessarily the same as those which would influence the judged *conceptual*

FIGURE 6.16

Some of the displays used by Olson and Attneave (1970) to investigate grouping by similarity. In the displays marked 1, 2 and 3, the lines in one region are of a different orientation to the rest, and the odd region is easy to spot. In display 4, odd elements are curved, and the odd region is reasonably evident. In displays 5 and 6, the configurations, but not the slopes, of the elements differ from one region to the next. Here it is much harder to spot the odd quadrant. Reprinted by permission from Olson & Attneave (1970). Copyright 1970 by the Board of Trustees of the University of Illinois.

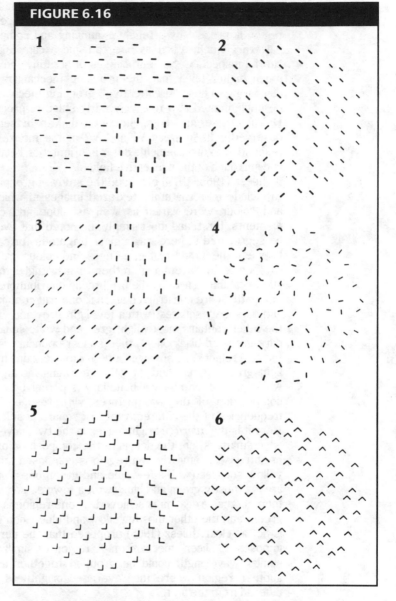

similarity of the same elements viewed individually by humans. Thus L and < might be considered more similar (both letter L, with one example tilted) when viewed as a single pair, than would L and ⌐. However, when large numbers of these elements are combined, it is the difference in the common orientations of two populations which is perceptually more salient than the difference between the conceptual identity of the individual members. Julesz (1965) stresses that in similarity grouping we are looking at spontaneous, preattentive visual processing, which precedes the identification of patterns and objects, and which is quite different from deliberate scrutiny. In some textures it is possible to discern that an odd region is present by carefully examining and comparing individual pattern elements, just as one can find a camouflaged animal by careful inspection. Such processes of scrutiny, however, are at a much higher level than the grouping mechanisms we are here discussing. These "preattentive" grouping mechanisms appear to be implemented at a relatively early stage of processing; indeed, DeYoe, Knierem, Sagi, Julesz and Van Essen (1986) have observed cells in areas V1 and V2 of the monkey cortex which respond if texture elements differ in orientation between the centre and surround of their receptive fields.

Julesz (1965; 1975) extended the study of grouping by similarity to include more naturally textured images in which brightnesses and colour were varied as well as slope and configuration of elements. First, and most simply, he noted that two regions would be segregated if there was a clear brightness or colour difference between them, and that brightness and colour grouping appeared to operate by "averaging" rather than taking detailed account of statistical differences in the brightness distributions. If two halves of a pattern are constructed so that one half contains mostly black and dark grey squares (with a few light grey and white ones), and the other contains mostly light grey and white squares (with a few dark grey and black ones), then a clear boundary is seen between the two regions. If, however, one region contains mostly black and light grey squares, and the other contains mostly dark grey and white ones, then no clear boundary is perceived even though the composition of the two pictures with respect to the relative frequencies of the different types of square is still quite different. Here it is the *average* brightnesses in the two halves of the pattern which matters, not the details of the composition of these average brightnesses. Similarly, if a region is composed mostly of red and yellow squares (with a few blue and green ones) and the adjacent area is mostly green and blue (with a few red and yellow squares) then good segregation is achieved. If one region is mostly red and green, and the other mostly yellow and blue, then the segregation is not as clear. Julesz (1965) proposed that the perceptual system imposes a "slicer" mechanism. A region of similar brightness or similar wavelength could be grouped together as distinct from another region where the "average" brightness or wavelength differed from the first.

The spatial distribution or "granularity" of different regions is also important however. If two regions have the same overall average brightness, but with the pattern elements distributed differently, so that they are spaced apart in one region and clumped together in the other (see Fig. 6.17), a perceptual boundary will be evident. Finally, in other work on region discrimination, Julesz confirmed the findings of Olson and Attneave, and Beck, in demonstrating the importance of differences in slope in perceptual segregation.

FIGURE 6.17

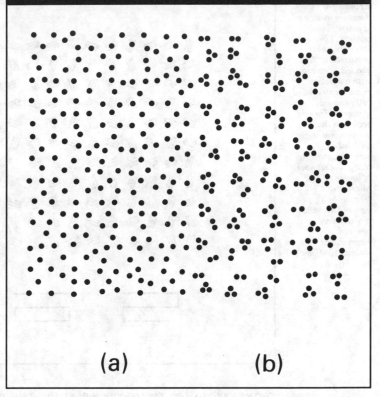

The average brightness in region (a) is the same as that in (b), but the dots in (b) are clumped together more than those in (a). A clear boundary is seen between the two regions.

(a)   (b)

Julesz tried to tie together a number of observations on perceptual grouping in terms of the formal statistical properties of the patterns being viewed. He initially made the strong claim that two regions cannot be discriminated if their first and second order statistics are identical—where these statistical properties are derived mathematically using either Markov processes (for generation in one dimension), or techniques from random geometry for two-dimensional generation (Frisch & Julesz, 1966; Julesz, Frisch, Gilbert & Shepp, 1973). Differences in the first order statistics of patterns capture differences in their overall brightness. Differences in second order statistics capture differences in granularity and slope.

Julesz's initial attempts to capture the variables determining similarity grouping in formal mathematical terms were thwarted by counterexamples, and this led him to devise his revised theory of "textons" (e.g. see Julesz, 1981). Julesz suggested that texture discrimination depended on whether or not differences could be detected in local features, where these features or "textons" were the basic elements of pre-attentive (i.e. early) vision. Textons are elongated blobs or line segments (with associated parameters such as aspect-ratio and orientation) and their terminators, and thus

FIGURE 6.18

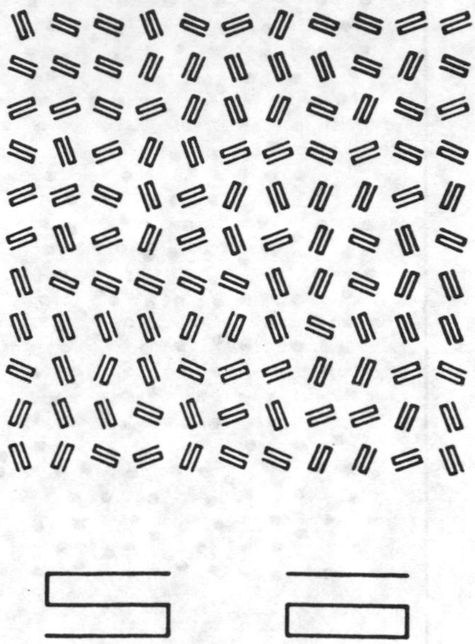

At the top is shown a texture made up of two different regions. The larger region is composed of "S-shaped" elements, with a smaller region composed of "10-shaped" elements. The odd region cannot be discriminated without close scrutiny, showing that if the number of lines and number of terminators agrees, their exact positions are ignored. Reproduced from Julesz (1981) with permission.

correspond to the representation in the raw primal sketch as conceived by Marr and others (as indeed they should, since such work on texture perception was an important influence on Marr). Julesz (1981) suggested that textures would only be discriminable where there were differences in the first order statistics of the textons. For example, two regions of texture containing different elements with the same numbers of terminators (see Fig. 6.18) do not segregate; only the number of textons (elongated features and terminations) seems to be important, while their spatial arrangement, and plausible candidate features such as closure and connectivity, appear to be unimportant:

> The preattentive visual system, evidently, cannot determine the location of terminators, but can count their numbers (or density) or their first order statistics. (Julesz, 1981, p. 95).

This statement is reminiscent of Watt's (1988) claim (see Chapter 5) that the first output of the MIRAGE system is a rough grouping of texture elements and a statistical description, without precise measurement, of the texture elements themselves. More precise measurements require attentional scanning, achieved by progressively dropping the contributions of coarser scale filters to the combined S+ and S− signals. However, it remains to be seen whether the MIRAGE system can provide a good account of which textures are easy and which are difficult to segregate.

The work of Julesz and his associates emphasises that pattern elements need not be identical in order to be treated together by grouping processes. Such grouping processes seem to operate between elements of similar brightness, wavelength, slope and granularity. These properties correspond to those which we know are extracted early on in visual processing (see Chapters 2 and 3), and correspond to the properties captured by the descriptions in Marr's "raw primal sketch." We return to consider Marr's work towards the end of this chapter.

Thus we have seen how recent work in the area of perceptual grouping has quantified the Gestalt principles of "good shape" and "similarity." All the above work has made use of artificial patterns and textures however. Can these laws of perceptual organisation be demonstrated in more natural settings?

CONCEALMENT AND ADVERTISEMENT

In this section of the chapter we return to the broader perspective of animal vision, to demonstrate how the Gestalt principles can give some insights into the ways in which the colouration and shapes of animals can help to conceal or to reveal them. The study of camouflage in nature in addition provides us with a way of exploring the ways in which perceptual grouping processes in other species may be similar to, or differ from, our own.

Animals which remain concealed from predators have a greater chance of surviving and reproducing, and a predator also stands a better chance of getting food if it is not easily visible to its own prey. In order to remain concealed an animal should not stand out as a figure against its background, but needs instead to blend with it. On the other hand, for the purposes of breeding or defending territory, animals may need to be conspicuous to potential mates or competitors. Under such circumstances the animal may need to stand out as a distinctive figure against its surroundings. Whether an animal will be camouflaged or conspicuous depends on its behavioural needs and the habitat in which it lives. Some animals may need to remain hidden for much of the time but have the potential of occasionally giving a highly distinctive display or warning sign. This can be achieved by temporarily revealing distinctive surface features which are normally hidden beneath wings or tails, or by changing skin colour, coat or plumage to meet changing circumstances. Thus to understand why a creature is coloured in a particular way we need to consider ecological factors as well as perceptual ones.

Merging and Contrasting

An animal that needs to be hidden should avoid standing out as figure against its background. An animal that needs to be seen should stand out as a figure distinctly from its background. The way in which this is achieved will depend upon the nature of the background habitat.

An animal can blend with a uniform background by being of similar average colour and brightness. Many species are coloured fairly simply to match the habitat in which they live, for example, tropical tree-snakes are green and polar bears are white. Some animals show seasonal variation in their colouration to match their changing habitats. The Arctic fox is white in the winter and brown during summer. In other species, different animals may be coloured differently in differing environments. The peppered moth is darker in urban than in rural areas for example.

A more radical way to prevent standing out as a figure, and one which is more effective against non-uniform habitats, is to break up the perceptual cohesiveness of the surface of the body by *disruptive colouration*. Dissimilar surface areas are less likely to be grouped together as a single figure. If some of the patches of surface colour are in turn similar to elements in the background this leads the animal's surface to be grouped together with its habitat. Disruptive colouration along with *background picturing* is an efficient method of camouflage where the habitat contains different coloured and shaped elements and variations in light and shade. The tree frog shown in Figure 6.19 is a good example of a creature whose surface markings incorporate these features. An artificial example is given by the green, brown and black mottled pattern

This African frog is well camouflaged when seen against the bark of the tree on which it habitually rests. Its asymmetrical markings show disruptive colouration along with background picturing. However, the shadow cast by the frog's head on the bark could reveal it. Photograph by P. Ward. Copyright © P.Ward/Bruce Coleman Ltd. Used by permission.

FIGURE 6.19

painted on tanks and combat jackets to achieve camouflage for human military purposes.

In these examples of camouflage we see exploitation of the principle that grouping by similarity (with the background habitat) may override grouping by proximity (of adjacent parts of the animal's surface). Effective disruptive colouration must match the background in terms of average brightness, colour and density of markings. Where the background texture elements have some intrinsic orientation, as in Figure 6.19, surface markings must be similarly oriented.

Conversely, in order to be conspicuous, an animal needs to have high brightness or colour contrast with its background. The all-black crow is a distinctive form against grassland or stubble field. In addition, the outline of an animal's body or of significant signs or structures can be enhanced by *outlining*. Many butterflies have contrasting borders around the edges of their wings, and some fish may have black edges to emphasise their distinctive fin shapes. Since flat structures are less conspicuous as figures than solid ones (see below), and solid bodies have no single contour line (the particular contour which will correspond to the animal's outline in an image of it will depend on vantage point), it makes sense that only "flat" structures such as butterfly wings or fish fins should be outlined in this way (Hailman 1977). More frequently, we find local outlining to emphasise the shape of a patch which serves as a courtship or warning signal. Such patches are often outlined in white or black in fish and birds.

Symmetry and Regularity

Symmetrical forms stand out more readily as figures against their backgrounds than do asymmetrical ones. Since animals are bilaterally symmetric, those that need to be hidden must reduce their apparent symmetry. Camouflaged snakes may rest in irregular coils so that the symmetry of surface markings is not evident. The frog in Figure 6.19 has asymmetrical markings which make it less visible as separate figure. Conversely, symmetry and repetition may be employed to enhance an animal's outline or internal features. Butterflies which have dramatic markings on their wings become highly salient symmetrical figures when their wings are spread. Signal patches can also be made conspicuous by virtue of their shape. Regular geometric forms such as circles, squares and triangles are perceptually salient figures, and they are also rare in the habitats of animals, so that surface markings which are geometrically regular will be additionally distinctive due to their dissimilarity to background elements. Hailman (1977) suggests that the common use of circular signal patches may be because they are regular, and hence unusual, rather than functioning as eye mimics. Triangular patterns can be seen on the breeding plumage of some male birds such as peacocks, and rectangular patches are found on the wings of some ducks. In many birds and fish we find another kind of regularity in the form of repeated markings—the series of tail spots on cuckoos and head stripes on sparrows for example.

Countershading and Reverse Countershading

A creature might be well camouflaged in terms of matching the colours and contrasts in its background, but could still be apparent as a distinct figure by virtue of its solidity. There will be a distinct depth difference between the upper part of a cylindrical body and the surface upon which it rests, which may be revealed to an observer by stereopsis or motion parallax (see Chapter 7). This will lead to grouping by proximity in depth and by common fate, just as central regions of texture can be revealed in random-dot stereograms and random-dot kinematograms (see Chapter 7). Many birds use sideways movements of their heads to reveal prey by motion parallax. A solution to this problem is to be as flat as possible, either behaviourally, by crouching, or structurally, by becoming flat during the course of evolution. Moths and flatfish, by virtue of their flat shapes, are at minimal depth differences from the surfaces on which they rest. Crouching also reduces the likelihood that an animal will be revealed by the shadow it casts. The head of the frog in Figure 6.19 casts such a shadow on the bark.

Creatures that inhabit environments where there is a strong light source have the additional problem of unequal illumination of their surfaces, leading to self-shading, which again will tend to reveal. This can be compensated for by *countershading*. A counter-shaded animal has its darkest surface areas where the most light strikes its body, and is lighter where less light is incident (Thayer, 1918). The zebra's stripes may in part serve a counter-shading function. The black stripes are at their broadest (and hence the coat on average is at its darkest) where the body receives most light.

The clearest examples of counter-shading are found among the fish, who often have dark dorsal and light ventral regions. This means that they are relatively concealed from airborne predators where their darker backs will be seen against the murk of the water, and also concealed when viewed by a predator swimming beneath them, as their light undersides are now seen against the brighter sky above. The countershading evident in an animal can usually be explained in terms of the direction of the habitual light source and the shape of its body. Caterpillars that live on the undersides of leaves have "reverse" coutershading, with their undersides which receive the most light, darker than their backs.

If appropriate countershading can serve to conceal an animal then reverse countershading could act to reveal it. There are some animals, who lead their lives in upright posture, who are lighter dorsally and darker ventrally. In the male bobolink (a kind of blackbird) reverse counter-shaded plumage, in which the head and back are white, is adopted for the breeding season, where the bird needs to be distinctive, but discarded during winter, when the bird's plumage is darker dorsally (Hailman, 1977).

Immobility and Camouflage

However well concealed a stationary animal may be, grouping by "common fate" would tend to reveal it if it moved. It therefore benefits a camouflaged animal if it can remain still for a large proportion of the time. In many species, while the adults may be brightly coloured for courtship or aggressive purposes, the young may have quite different plumage or coats which merge with their backgrounds. Whether the young of a species are camouflaged or not will depend on the habitat in which the nest or den is sited, and on the behaviour of both young and parents. For example, if the nest is on open ground, and both parents leave it to forage, then camouflage of the young is more important.

However, as Cott (1940) pointed out, while immobility is advantageous to concealment, it is not essential. A green tennis ball is harder to follow than a white one on a grass court. Thus even if an animal is active, it will be harder to spot or track if it merges with its background. Some creatures have markings which appear to make it harder to track their movement. Many snakes which flee in defence (Jackson, Ingram & Campbell, 1976), and some fish, have longitudinal stripes which may deceive observers since they appear to remain still as the animal moves forward. Of course movement is one of the easiest ways for an animal to reveal itself when it needs to be conspicuous. Some make use of temporal redundancy by making repetitive or stereotyped movements of their bodies in their displays, and others repeatedly flash signal patches beneath their tails or wings.

PERCEPTUAL ORGANISATION IN OTHER SPECIES

These examples of animal colouration thus illustrate how the Gestalt laws may be useful to help understand camouflage and concealment principles, at least when assessed by human vision. However, a successful camouflage for a particular species is not necessarily that which prevents its detection by a human visual system. It is the properties of the predator's, the prey's and the conspecific's visual systems which are important. Some species may not appear well-hidden to us, because their colours are different from those of their habitats. However, provided they need to be hidden from colour-blind species, only the brightness levels are important. Conversely, crab spiders which match the flowers on which they live may be well concealed to our eyes and to the eyes of many of their predators, but they may be detectable to any insect prey which have good sensitivity to ultra-violet radiation (Eisner, Silberglied, Aneshansley, Carrel & Howland, 1969). How can we find out whether an animal's colouration is having its apparent (to our eyes) effect of hiding an animal or making it conspicuous?

It is possible to examine how accurate are our own perceptual intuitions about the relative degrees of concealment attained by camouflaged animals by observing the "success" that different surface markings confer to an animal in terms of its survival. This can be done through natural observation or through experiment. For example, a radical change in the predominant colouration of the peppered moth has been observed in areas where industrial pollution is present. At one time, darker members of the peppered moth species were rare. Over the last 200 years or so, in areas where buildings and trees are polluted with soot and grime, the predominant colouration in the moths has changed. Darker members are much more frequent than lighter ones, while in rural areas the lighter moths are still common. This suggests that the avian predators which feed on such moths find light moths distinctive on dark backgrounds in the same way that we do. In industrial areas the gene for darker colouration has conferred an advantage on those possessing it, whose chances of surviving and reproducing have therefore been enhanced (Kettlewell, 1973).

As well as such "natural" experiments, it is possible to conduct controlled experiments in which members of a prey species are placed against different backgrounds and then exposed to predators. The success of a particular camouflage can be assessed in terms of the number of prey that survive! Sumner (1934), for example, reared mosquito fish in differently coloured tanks. These are fish that, in common with many others, adjust their colours to tone in with their surroundings. After seven to eight weeks those fish reared in a black tank were very dark, while those raised in a white tank were a much paler buff or grey. Equal numbers of the "black" and "white" fish were transferred into experimental tanks which were painted black or pale grey, and exposed to the Galapagos penguin as predator. Of the fish which were appropriately colour-adapted, 32% were eaten, as compared with 68% of those which were inappropriately colour-adapted. Thus the Galapagos penguin seems to find fish of high contrast to their background more easily than those of low contrast, again in agreement with our own perceptions. More dramatic experiments can involve artificially colouring the prey species before exposing them to predation (e.g. Croze, 1970).

Experiments such as these are not always ethically acceptable (most people would be unhappy if the prey used in such studies were mammals or birds rather than fish or insects). A further experimental way of assessing degree of concealment without the sacrifice of too many animals is illustrated by Pietrewicz and Kamil (1977). They conducted operant conditioning experiments in which blue jays were trained to detect moths in colour slides. Interestingly they showed that the birds were sensitive to the orientation of the moths (whether their heads were pointing up, down, or horizontally), as well as to the degree of visual similarity existing between the moth's markings and those of the bark against which it was photographed. Only the latter aspect is noticeable to us.

Observing the "success" of various surface markings is, of course, not the only way to study perceptual organisation in other species. Hertz (1928, 1929), for example, describes some delightful experiments with jays and bees in which she investigated aspects of their figural perception directly as they searched for food from arrangements of objects. She concluded that for the jay birds (though not for the bees), perceptual organisation was very similar to our own. To appreciate fully the adaptive significance of animal colouration requires continued research along these lines.

WHY DO THE GESTALT LAWS WORK?

We have shown that many of the Gestalt laws are useful descriptive tools for a discussion of perceptual organisation in the real world, but we are still some way from having an adequate theory of *why* the principles work and *how* perceptual organisation is achieved. We mentioned earlier how the Gestalt psychologists themselves attempted to answer both these points with their model of brain field forces. What alternative answers would contemporary theorists provide?

Marr's (1976, 1982) approach to vision would emphasise that we should always consider what general assumptions about the world can be brought to bear on visual processing to constrain the range of possible interpretations for any particular image. The Gestalt principles of organisation may work because they reflect a set of sensible assumptions that can be made about the world of physical and biological objects. Because the same kind of surface reflects and absorbs light in the same kind of way, the different subregions of a single object are likely to look similar. Because matter is cohesive, adjacent regions are likely to belong together, and will retain their adjacency relations despite movement of the object. The shapes of natural objects tend to vary smoothly rather than having abrupt discontinuities, and many natural objects (at least those which grow) are symmetrical. A solid object stands upon (and hence is at a different depth from) the surface on which it rests, and objects tend to be small compared with the ground. A perceptual system which made use of such assumptions to interpret natural images would generally achieve correct solutions to perceptual organisation, unless deceived by a camouflage exploiting these very same assumptions. It is perhaps not surprising that in our perception of unnatural displays (such as the patterns used by experimental psychologists or the authors of textbooks), we employ the same set of assumptions that serve us well in interpreting natural images.

However, having a set of descriptive principles, even if we know why they work, is still only a starting point for a full information processing theory of grouping processes. We need to know *how* such principles can be applied to primitive elements recovered from images—edges, blobs and so on, in order to recover the potentially significant structures present. It is research in artificial intelligence (A.I.), which has attempted to provide such a *process* theory of perceptual organisation, which is much more powerful than a purely *descriptive* theory, such as that of the Gestaltists or more recent workers like Julesz. Marr's (1976) early visual processing program implemented such a process theory and made extensive use of Gestalt principles to achieve perceptual organisation. Before describing Marr's work, we digress briefly to introduce other research in A.I. which has attempted to formalise organisational processes, by making use of a rather different set of constraints.

ARTIFICIAL INTELLIGENCE APPROACHES TO GROUPING

Scene Analysis Programs

Many researchers in A.I. during the 1960s and 1970s attempted to solve what became known as the *"segmentation problem."* This is the problem of dividing up a visual scene into a number of distinct objects. Most researchers avoided the complexities of natural images, and restricted their programs to a world of matt, white prismatic solids which were evenly illuminated. Figure 6.20 shows a line drawing of the outlines of such a collection of objects. Viewed analytically, Figure 6.20 is just a collection of straight lines in a variety of orientations. However, our spontaneous perception of such a scene is more likely to be of a collection of distinct *objects*. Thus this scene is readily described by our visual apparatus as being made up of two blocks and a wedge, with one block partially occluding the other two structures. Here again we have an example of perceptual organisation. Somehow we know that the regions labelled a, b and c belong together as one structure, distinct from d, e and f which belong to another. The Gestalt psychologists might argue that the perception of regions a, b and c as belonging to a "cube" provides a closed, simple and symmetrical interpretation, but this does not really address the question of *how* such a solution is achieved by visual processing.

This was the kind of problem tackled by Guzman (1968), Clowes (1971) and Waltz (1975) amongst others, who set out to try to write computer programs which could "see" objects from collections of lines such as these. The common principle in all their work was a consideration of the *junctions* present in these figures. A junction is a point where two or more lines meet. Different junction types have different implications for the possible arrangement of surfaces within the picture. Thus Guzman suggested that the presence of an *arrow* junction would generally imply that the edges which formed the fins of the arrow belonged to a single body, while a T junction generally implied that the shaft and the cross-bar of the T belonged to different bodies. Figure 6.20 shows how these principles apply in our example.

Guzman's program SEE considered only junctions, and incorporated his own informal intuitions about the interpretations of different junction types. Clowes tackled the problem of junction specification more systematically, and employed a more sophisticated

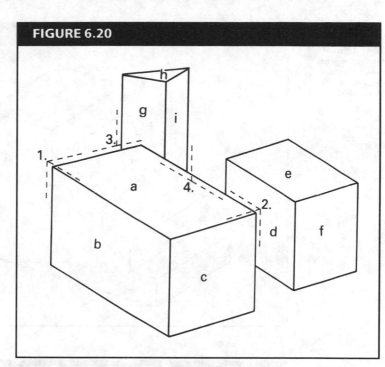

FIGURE 6.20

We have no difficulty in seeing that regions a, b and c belong together (likewise d, e and f; g, h and i). Guzman's program SEE interpreted pictures like this by examining the junctions present. Examples of arrow junctions are shown at 1 and 2, and T junctions are shown at 3 and 4. What other kinds of junction are there in this picture?

notion of how different junction types in the image relate to the organisation of *objects* in the "scene" depicted. This was achieved by considering the nature of the *edges* depicted by the junction lines (Clowes 1971, Huffman, 1971), as well as the nature of the intersection of these lines. Edges may be *convex, concave* or *occluding* (see Fig. 6.21). Only certain combinations of edge types are compatible with a particular configuration of lines at a junction. By ensuring that edges were consistently labelled along their entire length, Clowes' program OBSCENE was able to interpret pictures successfully provided that no more than three lines met at a single junction. The program was also able to "reject" certain pictures as "impossible" (see Fig. 6.22 for example), whereas SEE would simply accept such examples as objects.

The most elegant example of work of this type was that of Waltz (1975), who introduced a fourth edge type, the crack, and whose program accepted pictures of scenes containing shadows. Once shadows are introduced, the possible labellings for a particular type of junction increase dramatically, since a number of different types of edge could now be present. Nevertheless, Waltz's program was able successfully to parse scenes containing shadows. His work illustrates how adding more information in the form of light and shading may actually aid the interpretation of a scene by providing additional local constraints.

While such A.I. programs are intrinsically interesting, and point out the complicated processing which may underly our everyday ability to perceive patterns such as these, they are of limited

FIGURE 6.21

Three different kinds of edge are shown; concave (+), convex (−), and occluding (>).

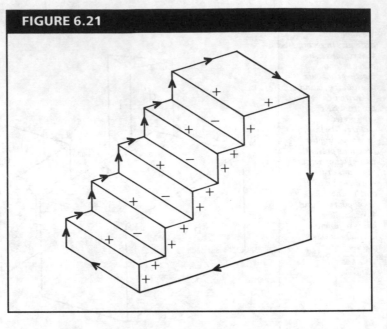

FIGURE 6.22

An impossible object. From Clowes (1971). Reproduced by permission of the North–Holland Publishing Company, Amsterdam.

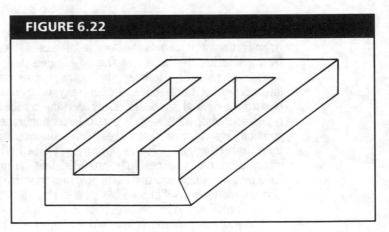

importance. The programs work by incorporating the constraints of their visual worlds, but the particular constraints employed are specific to the world of white prismatic solids—an artificially manufactured world which our visual systems did not evolve to perceive. The principles embodied within these segmentation programs would fail to recover the significant structures in natural images. Natural objects may have internal markings, texture and shading. Straight lines and angular junctions are rare. Indeed A.I. segmentation programs of the above type either start with a line drawing as input, or make use of initial programs to find the edges in images of prismatic solids by using the assumption that edges are straight, along with higher level knowledge about "likely" places to find lines (e.g. Shirai, 1973).

Marr's Program

Of more interest to our discussion is a processing model which can recover structures from natural images of everyday objects and surfaces, despite their noise, texture and shadow. Such a program was produced by Marr (1976, 1982), whose early visual processing program finds occluding and internal contours from images such as those shown in Figure 6.23. We have already considered some of Marr's ideas in Chapters 4 and 5. He proposes that cells in the retina and visual cortex of mammals function to locate *zero-crossings* (see p. 89) in the retinal image, which serve as the first step towards recovering information about edges in the world. A comparison of the zero-crossings found by sets of cells with different receptive field sizes leads to a set of assertions about the "features" present at each location in the image. This set of assertions is the *raw primal sketch*.

The primitives in the raw primal sketch are edges, bars, blobs and terminations which have the associated attributes of orientation, contrast, length, width and position. The representation of a straight line would consist of a termination, then several segments having the same orientation, then a final termination. The raw primal sketch is a very complex, messy affair (see the examples in Figs. 5.8, 6.30 and 6.31), from which we need to recover global structures as well as internal structures and surface texture.

This is achieved in the next stage of early visual processing by the recursive assignment of *place tokens* to small structures, or aggregations of structures, in the raw primal sketch. These place tokens are in turn aggregated together to form larger units, in a cyclical manner. Place tokens can be defined by the *position* of a blob, or of a short line or edge; by the *termination* of a longer edge, line or elongated blob, or by a small *aggregation* of tokens. Aggregation of these place tokens can proceed by *clustering* nearby place tokens on the basis of changes in spatial density (see Fig. 6.24), by *curvilinear* aggregation, which produces contours by joining aligned items which are near to one another (see Fig. 6.25) and finally by *theta aggregation*. Theta aggregation involves the grouping of similarly oriented items in a direction that relies upon, but differs from, their intrinsic orientation. Theta organisation can for example be used to recover the vertical stripes in a herring bone pattern where all the individual texture elements are oriented obliquely (see Fig. 6.26).

The grouping together of place tokens thus relies upon local proximity (adjacent elements are combined) and similarity (similarly oriented elements are combined), but more global considerations can also influence the structures detected. For example, in curvilinear aggregation, a "closure" principle could allow two edge segments to be joined even though the contrast across the edge

FIGURE 6.23

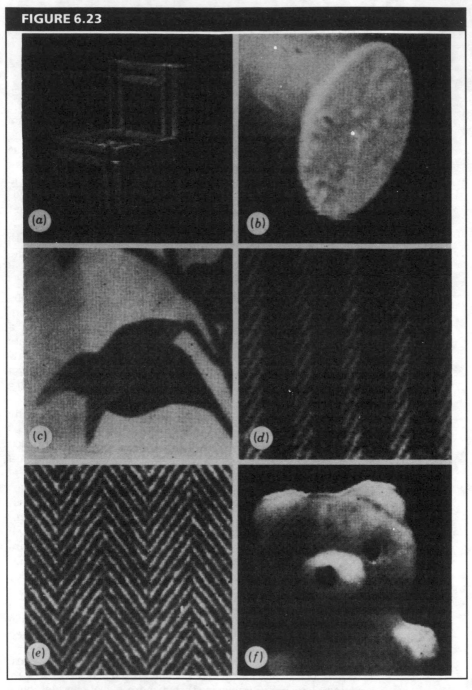

Examples of the images analysed by Marr's (1976) early vision program: (a) a chair; (b) a rod; (c) a plant; (d) and (e) textures and (f) a teddy bear. Reproduced with permission from Marr (1976).

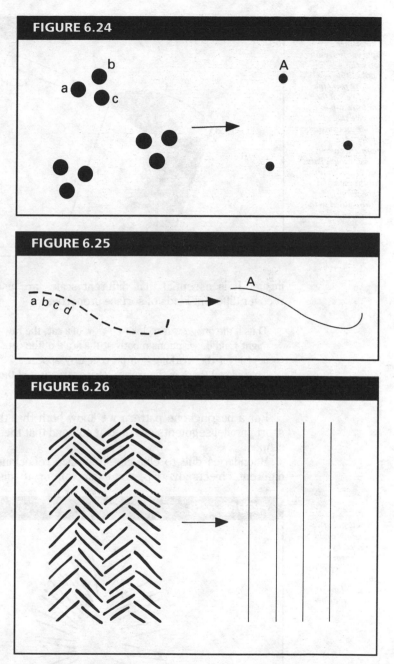

FIGURE 6.24

Place tokens corresponding to small dots can be grouped together by proximity to yield higher-order place tokens. Here, place tokens at a, b and c are grouped to yield a place token at A, and likewise for the other dots in this figure.

FIGURE 6.25

Curvilinear aggregation will group place tokens at a, b, c, d and so on to yield a single structure A.

FIGURE 6.26

Theta aggregation can recover the vertical orientation of the stripes of a herringbone pattern.

segments differed due to illumination effects (see the image in Fig. 6.27). Marr's program therefore embodies many of the Gestalt principles that we earlier discussed at length.

The grouping procedures use the construction of tokens at different scales to locate physically meaningful boundaries in the

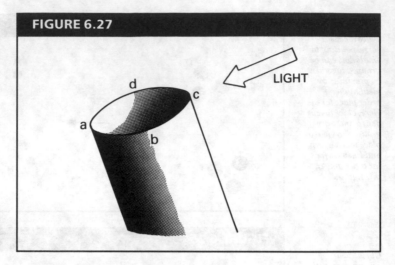

FIGURE 6.27

Curvilinear aggregation along with the application of a closure principle could reveal the contour a–b–c–d, despite the different contrasts of the edge segments along this contour. This pattern of shading might arise if a tube was illuminated in the direction shown.

image. It is essential that different scales are used in order to recover different kinds of surface properties.

> Thus if the image was a close-up view of a cat, the raw primal sketch might yield descriptions mostly at the scale of the cat's hairs. At the next level the markings on its coat may appear . . . and at a yet higher level there is the parallel stripe structure of these markings. (Marr 1982, p. 91).

For a herringbone pattern we know both that the "bones" are short parallel segments oriented at 45°, and that these form vertical stripes.

Boundaries due to changes in surface reflectance (where two different objects overlap, for example), or to discontinuities in

FIGURE 6.28

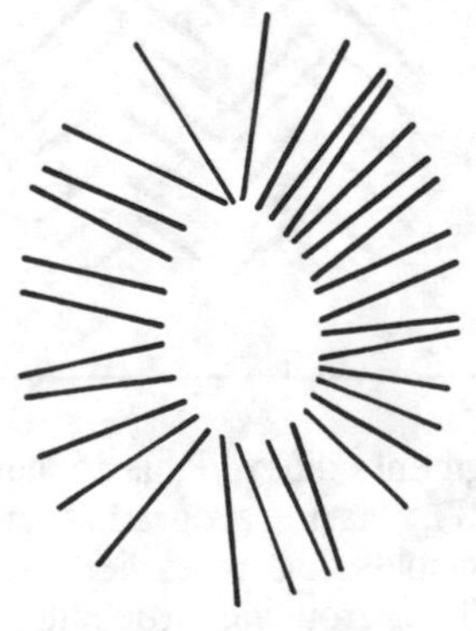

The elliptical boundary could be revealed by curvilinear aggregation of the place tokens assigned to the ends of the lines.

surface orientation or depth, can be revealed in two ways. First, boundaries may simply be marked by place tokens. The elliptical boundary perceived in Figure 6.28 may be produced by the curvilinear aggregation of the place tokens assigned to the termination of each radial line. Second, boundaries may be revealed by discontinuities in parameters that describe the spatial organisation of an image. Changes in the local density of place tokens, their spacing or their overall orientation structure could all be used to reveal such boundaries. Thus the boundary in Figure 6.29 cannot be defined by place tokens, but is revealed by the discontinuity in the common orientations of all the small elements in the image.

The boundary seen here could be revealed by discontinuities in the orientations of all the small elements in the two regions.

FIGURE 6.29

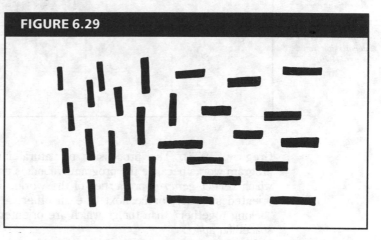

This last example also illustrates how Marr's theory can be applied to the problem of texture and region discrimination tackled by Julesz (see p. 118). While Julesz tried to arrive at a universal mathematical formula to explain why some texture boundaries were perceptually evident, although others were invisible without scrutiny, Marr provided a process theory which provides a more powerful explanation. Julesz's explanation was purely descriptive; Marr has shown *how* a set of descriptive principles can be used to recover texture and larger structures from images.

The successfulness of Marr's early visual processing program can be judged by its ability to recover the occluding contours from the image of a teddy bear (see Fig. 6.23), and to reveal the internal contours of the bear which correspond to eyes, nose and muzzle outlines (see Fig. 6.30). Such structures are recovered without recourse to high level knowledge. The program knows nothing of the usual shape of a teddy bear's head, and does not find the contours which correspond to its eyes because it "expects" to find them. Marr's theory of early visual processing thus contrasts strongly with some computer models, or more general theories of visual perception where expectations and "object-hypotheses" guide every stage of perceptual analysis (e.g. Roberts, 1965;

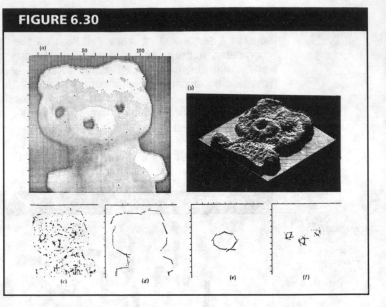

FIGURE 6.30

The image of a teddy bear (Fig. 6.23 (f)) is printed at (a), and shown as an intensity map at (b). At (c) is shown the location of all the small edge segments in the raw primal sketch. The structures which emerge after grouping operations are shown at (d), (e) and (f). Reproduced with permission from Marr (1976).

Gregory, 1973). The processing of natural images by Marr's program works because the program embodies grouping principles which reflect *general* properties of the world. Things which are oriented similarly, or lie next to each other, are more likely to "belong together" than things which are oriented dissimilarly and spaced far apart.

Marr's program resorts to higher-level knowledge only in cases of ambiguity. Thus in the image of a plant (see Fig. 6.31), the segmentation procedures fail to separate the contours of the two overlapping leaves. In this case the program needs to be "told" that the different contour segments do not belong together as a single structure. While this ambiguity is indeed present when starting from a static "monocular" image, the additional information gained from stereopsis or motion parallax from the leaves of a real plant would allow the correct grouping to be achieved without such downward-flowing information.

Segmenting Parts for Recognition

Marr's (1976) program showed how an object's occluding contour and internal markings could be assembled from the collection of more primitive descriptions comprising the raw primal sketch, on the basis of assumptions which generally hold true in the world of natural objects. Recently, other researchers have shown how similar general assumptions can be used to segment a complex occluding contour into different "part" components—a problem reminiscent of that originally tackled by Guzman and others with artificial objects.

FIGURE 6.31

The image of a plant (Fig. 6.23 (c)) is printed at (a). At (b) is shown the location of all the small edge segments in the raw primal sketch; (c) and (d) show some structures which are formed by curvilinear aggregation. The grouping procedures cannot separate the two leaves, and the single structure at (e) appears. If the program is told that segments 1 and 2 in the original image do not match, then the separate structures (f) and (g) are found. Reproduced with permission from Marr (1976).

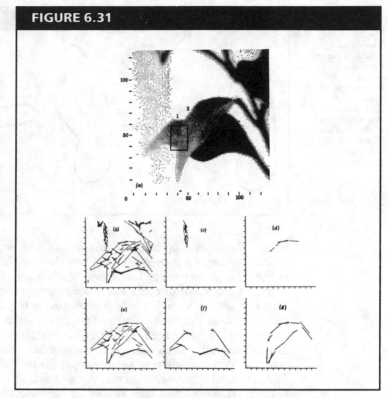

For example, Hoffman and Richards (1984) have provided a formal computational analysis of the role played by concavities in contour segmentation. They discuss *the transversality regularity*: distinct parts of objects intersect in a contour of concave discontinuity of their tangent planes. At any point around this intersection, a tangent to the surface of one part forms a concave cusp with the tangent to the surface of the other part (concave means it points into the object rather than into the background; see Fig. 6.32). This transversality regularity means that in an image of a complex shape, *concavities* mark the divisions between the contours of distinct parts. Concavities can be detected in contours of smooth shapes by seeking places where there is greatest negative curvature (see Fig. 6.34).

Hoffman and Richards provide some compelling demonstrations as evidence for the importance of these concavities in our segmentation of shapes. They have examined a number of classic ambiguous *reversing* figures, such as the Schröder staircase (Fig. 6.33) and the faces–vase figure that we introduced in Figure 6.2. Hoffman and Richards have shown how reversals of these figures are related to the possible alternative part segmentations. In the Schröder staircase (Fig. 6.33), for example, according to the partitioning scheme, "parts" of the figure must be "steps", since

FIGURE 6.32

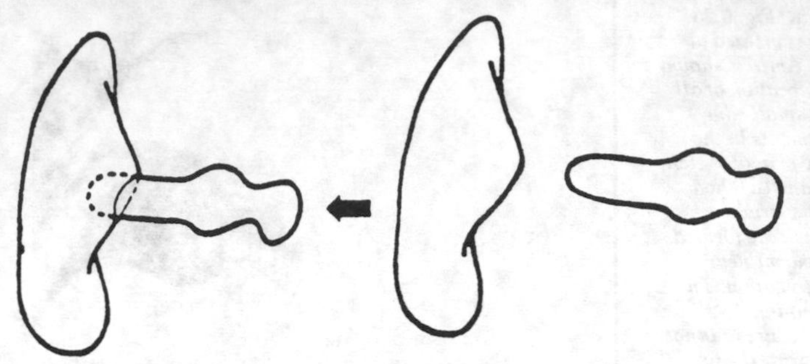

The "transversality regularity": when two surfaces interpenetrate they always meet in concave discontinuities. Reproduced from Hoffman and Richards (1984) with permission of the publisher.

each of the steps is bounded by two lines of concave discontinuity. When the staircase is seen in such a way that the plane marked "x" in Figure 6.33 appears to face upwards, then the steps which are defined by concave discontinuities pointing into the staircase are such that planes "x" and "y" are seen to belong together as faces of the same step. But when the figure reverses, so that the staircase now lies in the upper right of the picture, and plane "x" appears to face downwards, the concavities pointing into the body of the staircase define a different set of steps; planes "x" and "y" now form faces of different, adjacent steps. In the faces–vase figure (Fig. 6.34), when the figure is seen as the vase, then concavities pointing into it define its parts as the base, stem and bowl. When the figure is seen as a pair of faces, then the concavities pointing into them define parts as forehead, nose, and so forth. This demonstration shows how the same contour can be "recognised" as two distinct objects: what matters is the way in which the contour is partitioned prior to recognition, and this in turn seems to involve a simple search for concavities referred to the centre of whichever region is seen as figure.

Hoffman and Richards (1984) have shown how the kind of occluding contour that might result from the application of the

FIGURE 6.33

The Schröder staircase shows how part boundaries change as the figure and ground reverses. Reproduced from Hoffman and Richards (1984) with permission of the publisher.

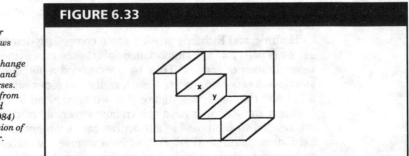

The faces—vase figure. When the vase region is taken as figure, then the concavities (minima of curvature) divide the vase into a base, stem, etc. When the faces regions are taken as figure, the concavities reveal parts corresponding to forehead, nose, etc. Reproduced from Hoffman and Richards (1984) with permission of the publisher.

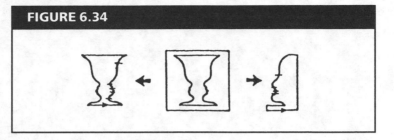

FIGURE 6.34

Gestalt grouping principles may be re-segmented into its parts. As we will see in Chapter 8, such segmentation forms an essential stage in Marr's theory of the analysis and recognition of occluding contours, and at that point we will return to take up the story of the part structure of objects.

CONCLUSIONS

The Gestalt psychologists, through the study of our perception of simple patterns, gave us insights into the organisational principles which may apply to the perception of the world. The study of natural camouflage and concealment shows that these principles fare well in describing the utility of various surface markings of animals. Marr has shown how such principles can be incorporated within a processing model which reveals the structures hidden in the messy data obtained from natural images. To the extent that other animals have similar figural perception to ourselves, we might similarly explain their early visual processing in terms of the elaboration of structures present in the primal sketch.

It should be noted here, however, that Marr (1982) does not regard his early visual processing program as solving the "figure-ground" or "segmentation" problem as traditionally conceived. The goal of early visual processing is not to recover the "objects" present within a scene—for the division of a scene into component objects is an arbitrary and ambiguous affair. Which should we regard as the "objects" to be recovered—a crowd of people, each individual person, or the eyes, ears and nose of each? Such consideration depends on the use to which the information is to be put. Marr instead sees the goal of early visual processing as to describe the surfaces present in the image. The recovery of the full primal sketch, in which some potentially significant structures such as occluding edges may be found, is only one aspect of early visual processing. Other valuable information about the kinds of surface discontinuities present can be gained from considering information about depth and motions present in the image. In this chapter we have largely ignored the problem of how depth and motion are analysed. We have merely mentioned their importance. It is to the analysis of depth and motion that we turn in Chapter 7.

Chapter Seven

PERCEIVING DEPTH AND MOVEMENT

Towards the end of the last chapter we described how Marr's early visual processing program recovers aspects of the structure of images from an initial array of intensities. As we pointed out, Marr sees the goal of early visual processing as furnishing a description of the surfaces being viewed by an observer. The recovery of occluding and internal contours is one aspect of this, but the full primal sketch is still essentially a description of the *image*, rather than of the *world*. The visual world which we view consists of surfaces extending away into the distance, and solid objects resting on them at different distances and with their surfaces inclined differently towards us. In addition, the pattern of light reaching the retina is never static. The eyes, heads and bodies of observers move, and objects and animals in the scene being viewed move likewise.

In this chapter we consider some of the optical information available to animals which allows them to perceive the layout of surfaces in the world, the relative distances of objects from themselves and the motions of these objects and of themselves. This is a theme to which we return at greater length in the third part of the book, where we consider how animals and people make use of varying optical information to control their actions in the world. In this chapter, we consider just that research that has arisen within the "retinal image" framework. Such research stresses that depth and motion perception require that *correspondences* be computed between retinal images displaced in space (from each eye) or in time (from one instant to the next).

PERCEIVING THE THIRD DIMENSION

The psychology of perception has been dominated by the apparent paradox of three dimensional vision. As we discussed in Chapter 1, the eye can for some purposes be thought of as a camera, with the lens and internal fluids acting to focus light onto a mosaic of retinal receptors. At any instant of time therefore one can conceive of the pattern of excitation of retinal receptors as a "picture," curved around the back of an eyeball. Though curved, the image is essentially two dimensional, and yet our perception is of a three dimensional world. How might depth be recovered?

The problem of how we recover the third dimension was tackled resolutely by the British Empiricist philosophers, notably by Berkeley (1709). Berkeley's views have come to dominate our thinking on many aspects of perception. The British empiricists rejected any notion that ideas were implanted in the mind at birth, saying instead that all complex ideas had to be built up by the association of simpler ones. Since all information is received via the organs of sense, ultimately all knowledge must be achieved by the associating together of simple sensations. It was assumed that the third dimension must be perceived by associating together visual "cues" with the position of objects felt by touch.

Convergence and Accommodation

The primary cues which Berkeley suggested could become associated with the felt positions of objects were the different angles of inclination of the eyes (see Fig. 7.1), different degrees of blurring of the image and different degrees of strain in the muscles around the lens.

Today we would refer to the different angles of inclination of the eyes as the degree of *convergence* and we would include both

The eyes swing inwards to focus on a near object.

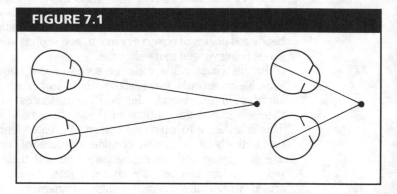

FIGURE 7.1

blurring and strain under the heading of the *accommodation* of the lens (see Fig. 7.2). Convergence and accommodation are often listed in introductory texts as "physiological" cues to depth. They are "cues" because these signals must be learned through association with non-visual aspects of experience. There is, however, a potentially much more important physiological source of information about relative distance for creatures with binocularly overlapping fields of vision.

Stereopsis

At close range, animals with overlapping visual fields have stereoscopic information available to them from the disparate

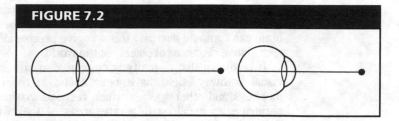

FIGURE 7.2

The lens accommodates, by becoming thicker, when the eye focuses on a near object.

images obtained at the two eyes. Each eye sees a slightly different view of the world due to the horizontal separation of the two eyes. You can confirm this by alternately opening and closing each eye. The world will appear to shift laterally.

Figure 7.3 shows the geometrical properties of the two retinal images which give rise to disparity. If the two eyes are focused on object A, the images in each eye cast by A are said to lie on *corresponding* points on the two retinas. The images cast by a nearer or more distant object, such as B, will fall on *disparate*

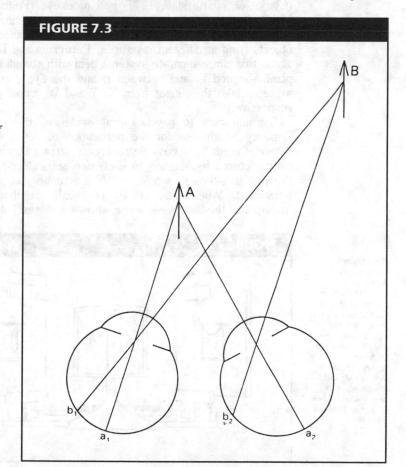

FIGURE 7.3

The eyes are focused on an object at A, and the image of A falls on corresponding points on the two retinas (a₁ and a₂). The images of a more distant object B, fall on disparate points on the two retinas (b₁ and b₂).

points on the two retinas, and the amount of disparity will depend upon the distance between B and A. Thus it can be seen that if the brain can compute disparity this will give precise information about the relative distances of objects in the world.

It is known that disparity is computed at an early stage in the visual pathway. Cells have been found in the cortex of cats, monkeys and other species which respond maximally when their optimal stimuli fall on disparate areas of the two retinas (e.g. Blakemore, 1970; Hubel & Wiesel, 1970). A cell selective for disparity would respond most strongly to a stimulus lying at a particular distance, or within a range of distances, from the eyes, and so would code depth information. As we described in Chapter 3 (p. 56), simple and complex cells in the primary visual cortex (area 17 of cats or V1 of monkeys) are driven by input from both eyes, but early evidence suggested that the additional property of selectivity for disparity was found only in cells in areas 18 or V2. However, more recent evidence has established that disparity-selective cells do exist in the primary visual cortex of both cats (Clarke & Whitteridge, 1977) and monkeys (Poggio & Poggio, 1984). In cats, there is further evidence suggesting that cortical cells are organised into separate systems coding information about objects lying at different distances. Pettigrew and Dreher (1987) argue that three separate systems deal with stimuli in the fixation plane, beyond it, and between it and the eyes, and that these systems take their input from X, Y and W retinal ganglion cells respectively.

Turning now to psychological evidence, the importance of disparity information for the perception of depth can easily be demonstrated. It is possible to create strong depth impressions from pictures by sending to each eye separately the projective drawing that the eye would see if an actual object in depth were presented. Wheatstone (1838) is usually attributed with the invention of the first *stereoscope*, shown in Figure 7.4.

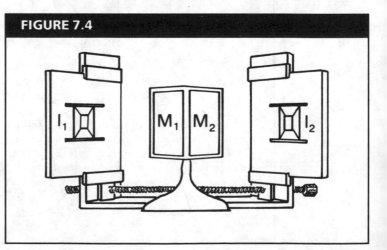

FIGURE 7.4

Wheatstone's stereoscope (1838). A picture of an object is drawn as it would appear to the left eye (I_1) and to the right eye (I_2). If these two images are sent to each eye separately, via mirrors M_1 and M_2, an observer sees a single object in depth. Adapted from Boring (1942).

He drew the view of a block as it appeared to each eye, and then with an arrangement of mirrors sent the left eye view to the left eye of an observer and the right eye view to the right eye. The result was that the observer saw a "solid" shape, in depth. It is possible to arrange such stereo demonstrations in a number of ways, all of which depend on separating out the left and right eye views, and then sending these separately to each eye. A common technique is to use *anaglyphs*. Here one view is drawn in red and one in green, and the two superimposed. The viewer looks through glasses containing a red filter to one eye and a green filter to the other, so that only one of the images is passed to each. The resulting perceptions of solid objects in depth are of course illusory. No actual solid object exists, but the disparities which would exist if an object were present have been captured in the anaglyphs. The brain thus receives the information that it would receive if an actual 3D object were presented, and the phenomenal impression reflects this. Frisby (1979) provides numerous examples of anaglyphs and his book is well worth consulting.

While it seems relatively easy to appreciate how disparity might be computed, and the neurophysiological evidence indicates that cells in the cortex may indeed measure the disparities present in the images to the two eyes, it is less easy to appreciate why our phenomenal impressions of objects in the real world, or of illusory forms in a stereoscope, are of single objects. If you focus on a pen held near your eyes, you will experience double images of more distant objects, but it is nonetheless true that within a certain range of distance a single percept is obtained. If the eyes fixate a given point, the region of space within which single vision is possible is known as Panum's fusional area. How is this fusion achieved?

To fuse images requires that disparities between the two eyes' images are interpreted in terms of single objects with unique locations in space. To achieve this interpretation in turn requires that we decide which parts of one eye's image *correspond* to particular parts in the other eye's image. This problem of establishing correspondences between one view and another slightly different one recurs in various forms throughout this chapter.

It used to be thought that the forms presented to each eye were recognised independently and then the images were matched and fused. For example, Sherrington (1906) suggested:

> During binocular regard of an objective image each uniocular mechanism develops independently a sensual image of considerable completeness. The singleness of binocular perception results from the union of these elaborated uniocular sensations. The singleness is therefore the product of a synthesis that works with already elaborated sensations contemporaneously proceeding (p. 380).

However, not all agreed with this—particularly given the strange results which could be obtained using stereoscopes: For example, Darwin received a communication from A. L. Austin in New Zealand:

> Although a perfect stranger to you, and living on the reverse side of the globe, I have taken the liberty of writing to you on a small discovery I have made in binocular vision in the stereoscope. I find by taking two ordinary carte-de-visite photos of two different persons' faces, the portraits being about the same sizes, and looking about the same direction, and placing them in a stereoscope, the faces blend into one in a most remarkable manner, producing in the case of some ladies' portraits, in every instance, a *decided improvement* in beauty (Galton, 1907, p.227).

Darwin passed this information on to Galton, who confirmed these observations. Ross (1976) suggests that Galton disagreed with the monocular combination explanation because the binocular perception of two different faces was so unlike an "optical" combination of the faces.

A more serious challenge to contemporary versions of the recognition and fusion theory (e.g. Ogle, 1964) came with the important work of Bela Julesz in the 1960s, summarised in his 1971 book. Julesz developed *random-dot stereograms* as a tool to explore the processes of stereopsis.

FIGURE 7.5

A random-dot stereogram of the kind devised by Julesz. If this pair was viewed in a stereogram, a square would be seen floating above the background. Photograph courtesy John Frisby, University of Sheffield.

A random-dot stereogram is shown in Figure 7.5. Both members of the stereo pair consist of a uniform, randomly generated texture of black and white dots. There is no recognisable form present in either member of the pair. However, if the stereogram shown in Figure 7.5 were to be viewed in a stereoscope, the viewer would see a central square of texture floating above the background. This is because the stereogram in fact contains disparate "forms" camouflaged by the background texture. Each half of the stereogram contains identical background elements. The central regions, corresponding to the perceived square, also match, but are displaced inwards from the background as shown in Figure 7.6. The gaps which remain after this lateral shifting are then filled in with more texture. Thus when viewed in a

FIGURE 7.6

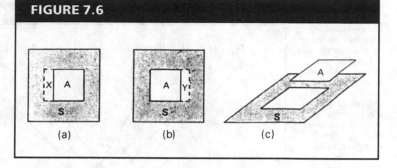

(a) (b) (c)

(a) and (b) are the two halves of a random−dot stereogram shown in simplified form. Both have the same surrounding texture (S). A central region (A) has been shifted to the right in (a) and to the left in (b). The gaps left have been filled in with more texture (X and Y). If such a stereogram was constructed, and viewed in a stereoscope, the central square would be seen floating above the background, as shown at (c). Adapted from Julesz (1965).

stereoscope the eyes are presented with the disparities which would be present if an inner square of texture were actually held above the background texture of random dots.

This simple demonstration makes it difficult to maintain any theory of stereopsis which depends on the recognition and fusion of monocular contours. It could be argued that *local* patterns of black and white dots are detected and matched, but Julesz (1971) provides evidence against this. For example, fusion can be achieved from stereograms in which one member of the pair is blurred, reduced in size, or has "noise" added to it such that any local patterns are disrupted.

Julesz proposes that stereopsis proceeds by a point-by-point comparison of dots of the same brightness value. He argues that brightnesses must be the same since fusion cannot be achieved if one member of a random-dot stereogram has reversed contrast to the other, i.e. if black dots in one image correspond to white dots in the other. If individual dots are matched, why is the percept obtained from a random-dot stereogram so stable? The number of possible matches between individual dots in such stereograms is huge; Figure 7.7 illustrates the problem of false targets in stereoscopic fusion. This figure shows how a viewer might in principle end up seeing any number of lace-like depth planes, yet in practice observers all reach the same, simple solutions to such stereoscopic puzzles.

Julesz suggests that the *global* stereopsis mechanism selects a match based on a uniform set of disparity measurements:

Thus, to obtain local stereopsis of a few edges or dots, one can visualize how the binocular disparity units will maximally fire for similar receptive fields in the two retinae of the same shapes, orientations and retinal ordinates. On the other hand, for complex textured surfaces, another level of neural processing has to be evoked that evaluates the possible local solutions and selects the densest firing units of the same disparity. This processing I will call global stereopsis, and it is on another level of complexity from the commonly quoted local stereopsis of the textbooks (Julesz, 1971, p. 150).

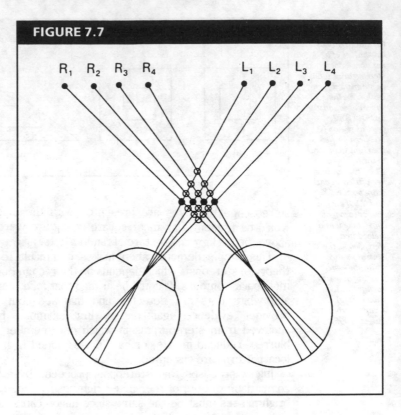

FIGURE 7.7

Both eyes look at four dots, but the correspondence between the two retinal projections is ambiguous. Each of the dots L_1 to L_4 could match any of the four projections of dots R_1 to R_4. "False" matches are shown as open circles in the projection field. Correct matches are shown as filled circles. Adapted from Marr and Poggio (1976).

In the monkey cortex, the further level of neural processing involved in global stereopsis seems to take place at an early stage. As we have already described, many cells in V1 are selective for the disparity in the retinal positions of isolated line or edge stimuli presented to both eyes. Some of these cells are also selective for disparity in random-dot stereograms, and this property is shown only by complex cells (Poggio & Poggio, 1984). Some process which finds matches in random dot patterns must therefore operate in V1, but physiological evidence has yielded no further details of the process involved. What progress has been made in understanding global stereopsis at an algorithmic level?

Julesz's own model of the process of global stereopsis is not couched in neurophysiological terms, but in the form of an elaborate mechanical metaphor—*the spring-coupled magnetic dipole model*. The model is designed to encompass amongst other things the phenomenon of *hysteresis* (Fender & Julesz, 1967). Normally stereograms can only be fused if the disparities presented to the two eyes are not too great, specifically not greater than Panum's fusional limit. Once a random-dot stereogram has been fused by an observer, however, the disparity can be increased to 20 times Panum's fusional limit, without loss of stereoscopic sensation. The phenomenon is rather like the attractiveness that is held between opposite poles of magnets once they have contacted — it becomes remarkably difficult to pull them apart.

The phenomenon of hysteresis has influenced several models of stereopsis which include *cooperativity* between local measures to achieve global stereopsis. However, as Marr (1982) points out, hysteresis may reflect the operation of a memory buffer rather than reflecting the mechanism of stereo fusion itself. Marr and Poggio (1976, 1979) have produced two different stereo algorithms, the first of which shows cooperativity and the second relying on a short-term memory system. These algorithms were both developed after a consideration of the constraints to be embodied in any theory of stereopsis. As we have already seen, in Marr's view, a computational theory, expressing what is being computed and why, must be formulated prior to any algorithms for achieving this computation (see also Chapters 4, 5 and 6). In addition, Marr points out that stereo matching should take place between elements which are reliably related to surface markings and discontinuities. Intensity arrays—which would be used to match "points of the same brightness level" (Julesz)—are thus poor candidates for the matching process. Raw primal sketch descriptions like edges and blobs might be candidates for stereo-matching, though in fact Marr and Poggio (1979) make use of zero-crossings for the matching process.

The computational theory of stereopsis formulated by Marr and Poggio takes into account the following constraints of the physical world:

1) A given point on a physical surface has a unique position in space at any one time and 2) matter is cohesive, it is separated into objects, and the surfaces of objects are generally smooth in the sense that the surface variation due to roughness, cracks, or other sharp differences that can be attributed to changes in distance from the viewer, are small compared with the overall distance from the viewer (Marr, 1982, p. 112).

These physical considerations give rise to three constraints in the matching of stereo images. First, the logic of the physical world dictates that a pair of candidate image elements to be matched must be physically similar if they are to have originated from the same point on an object's surface (the compatibility constraint). Secondly, any item in one image should only match one item in the other image (the uniqueness constraint). Finally, the disparity should vary smoothly almost everywhere in an image (the continuity constraint).

These matching constraints can be successfully embodied within an algorithm which can "solve" random-dot stereograms (Marr & Poggio 1976). The solution gradually drops out of a network of excitatory and inhibitory connections which take account of these three constraints simultaneously. We describe the operation of this network in more detail in Chapter 9, where we use it to introduce a particular class of connectionist models (see p. 204).

Marr and Poggio's (1976) algorithm provided a particularly clear example of how a proper understanding of the nature of a visual processing problem can lead to a workable solution to that problem. However, the particular algorithm proposed does not provide a good account of human stereo-matching, since it fails to account for a number of psychophysical observations. For example, Julesz and Miller (1975) showed that high spatial frequency "noise" added to stereograms did not disrupt the binocular fusion obtained between lower spatial frequency components in the image, provided that there was no overlap in the spatial frequencies of the noise and the image. This was one of a number of demonstrations that stereo matching may proceed within independent spatial-frequency tuned channels. Marr and Poggio (1979) produced a second stereo algorithm in which they attempted to account for such findings by suggesting that the image is analysed by a set of channels of successively finer resolution. This algorithm solves the problem of eliminating false stereo matches essentially by evasion.

The inputs to this stereo matching algorithm are the zero-crossings obtained using $\nabla^2 G$ filters of different widths (see Chapter 5). To satisfy the compatibility constraint, candidate matches must be zero-crossings of the same sign and orientation. The broadest width filters will produce relatively few zero-crossings (this is because the consequence of blurring an image is that only the larger scale intensity changes are preserved). Provided that matches are only tolerated within a particular disparity range related to the width of the filter, the probability of false matches occurring can be minimised. If the stereo images have a solution at all within the disparity range set then nearly 100% of the zero-crossings will find unique matches—if there is no solution possible within this disparity limit then a much smaller percentage of matches will be possible. The continuity assumption says that abrupt changes in disparity should be rare, and so it should be possible to find regions of the image where matches all fall within a given disparity limit. It is therefore possible to distinguish a successful from an unsuccessful match at a certain range of disparities.

Once a match has been achieved within a lower spatial frequency channel, this then constrains the range of disparities to be examined in the higher frequency channels. Lower spatial frequency channels control vergence movements of the eyes which cause finer channels to come into correspondence. Interim results are held in a temporary memory, the 2½ D sketch, and it is the operation of this memory to which Marr and Poggio attribute the phenomenon of hysterisis. Poggio and Poggio (1984) speculate about the possible physiological implementation of this model. They suggest that simple cells in the visual cortex—which are selective for the disparity of isolated lines or edges but not of random-dot patterns—represent the lower spatial-frequency channels which use large scale image features to establish matches and control eye movements, while complex cells are part of the system establishing matches between finer texture elements.

However, even Marr and Poggio's second (1979) algorithm does not easily accommodate all the psychophysical evidence on stereopsis. For example, if an outline is provided for the camouflaged square in a random-dot stereogram then stereo fusion is improved (Saye & Frisby, 1975). This facilitation occurs even if the stereogram is flashed very briefly (Mayhew & Frisby, 1981), and is thus unlikely to be given simply by the improved control of vergence movements. Mayhew and Frisby (1981, also Frisby & Mayhew, 1980) have developed a rather different computational model, in which the process of stereo matching was seen as intimately linked with the elaboration of descriptions in the raw primal sketch. This contrasts with Marr, who viewed stereopsis as a more-or-less separate module of visual information processing. The constraints that Mayhew and Frisby make use of are rather different from Marr's. Perhaps the clearest difference lies in their inclusion of a *figural continuity* constraint. For each zero-crossing in one eye's image, candidate matches are established from the other eye's image. Such candidates must be within a certain disparity, and they must be zero-crossings of the same sign and similar orientation to the target. If there are several candidate matches, most can be eliminated by checking whether other zero crossings in the near vicinity of the candidate bear the same *figural* relationship to it as those in the near vicinity of the target. Such a procedure successfully eliminates false matches from natural and random-dot stereo pairs. Mayhew and Frisby's (1981) algorithm also incorporated a rule that looked for correspondences between the different sized filter channels, just as Marr and Hildreth's (1980) edge-detecting algorithm looked for coincident zero-crossings between different channels (see Chapter 5). Like others (e.g. Pearson & Robinson, 1985; Watt & Morgan, 1984; see Chapter 5), however, Mayhew and Frisby argued that use of zero-crossings alone did not give a good account of human computation of intensity changes, and they suggested that peaks as well as zero-crossings were used.

More recently, Pollard, Mayhew and Frisby (1985) have proposed an alternative stereo algorithm ("PMF") that ensures figural continuity via a somewhat different route. The algorithm was developed to accommodate experimental findings of Burt and Julesz (1980) who found that human binocular fusion will only tolerate a disparity gradient of about 1. The disparity gradient (see Fig. 7.8) of two features (e.g. dots) presented to each eye, is the ratio of the difference between their disparities and their "cyclopean" separation (their distance apart in the cyclopean image that results from fusion). Pollard, Mayhew and Frisby (1985) argue that a binocular combination rule that only tolerates matches within a disparity gradient of 1 would preclude false matches and implicitly satisfy the constraints of surface continuity that we have discussed above.

There are numerous other contemporary models which attempt to account for stereoscopic fusion (Marr, 1982, criticises most of

FIGURE 7.8

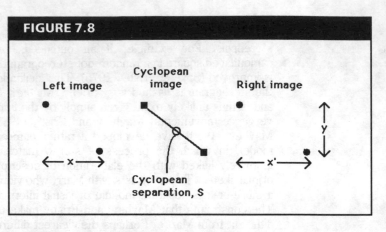

Left image   Cyclopean image   Right image

Cyclopean separation, S

The difference in disparities of the two dots is the difference in their horizontal separation (x' −x). The disparity gradient is the difference in disparity divided by the cyclopean separation (S), the distance separating the two dots when stereoscopically fused. S can be calculated from x, x' and y (see Pollard, Mayhew & Frisby, 1985, from which this figure is adapted).

them). Here we have examined some which have been developed in the spirit of Marr's computational theory, and ignored others which have been formulated in physical or mathematical terms (e.g. Julesz, 1971; Sperling, 1970). Many of the computational accounts we have discussed assume that stereopsis is achieved prior to, or in parallel with, the elaboration of the forms present in the image, and is therefore a relatively low-level process, operating as a separable module in Marr's theory, and uninfluenced by higher-level processes.

However, it may be that factors involved in the process of stereopsis are more cognitive than many such models imply. First, we should note that while fusion is impossible between reversed contrast random-dot stereograms, it *is* possible between reversed contrast *line* stereograms, where black lines in one member of the stereogram correspond to white lines in the other. This suggests that there may be some interaction between local stereopsis mechanisms operating on low-level measurements of the image, and other mechanisms which operate on disparities between more global *contours*. Mayhew and Frisby's (1981) approach, in which stereopsis and grouping processes are interlinked, may provide a way to explain such phenomena.

Secondly, Harris and Gregory (1973) produced stereograms in which each eye was stimulated with disparate *illusory contours* (illustrated in Fig. 7.9). They found that for forward-going contours, three-dimensional illusory contours were observed across the gaps between the sectors. Ramachandran and Cavanagh (1985) confirmed and extended this finding. They produced stereograms in which disparities were created between subjective contours in each eye's image. These larger form elements were superimposed upon a basic "wallpaper" pattern of texture (see Fig. 7.10a). Like Harris and Gregory (1973) they found that stereoscopic fusion could be obtained strongly from images where the disparities were consistent with the occlusion implied by the subjective contours. That is, subjects could see the illusory square floating above its background but would not see it as readily if the

FIGURE 7.9

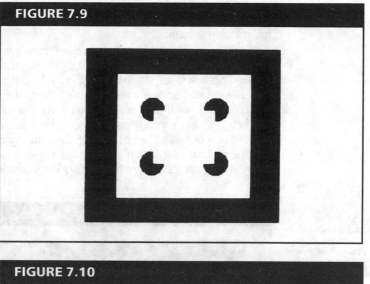

FIGURE 7.10

(a)

(b)

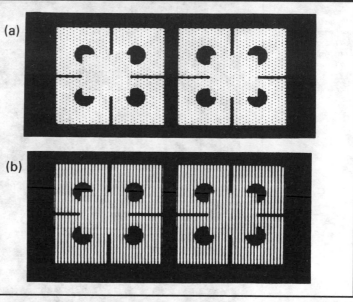

disparity suggested it should be behind its background. Additionally, the illusory contours in depth "captured" the background texture so that a square plane of texture was seen as floating above a background of similar texture, even though there was no explicit disparity present in the wallpaper texture itself. This capture effect was strong enough to carry a square of texture up from a background comprised of vertical lines, even though the stereo effect disrupts the continuity of the lines themselves (see Fig. 7.10b). This observation suggests that in some situations stereopsis may be based on the *apparent* configurations presented to each eye rather than relying solely on the actual figural information present.

That higher level cognitive factors may override local depth information is perhaps most strikingly demonstrated by Gregory's (1973) "hollow face" illusion (see Fig. 7.11). If a hollow mask of a face is viewed from a distance of a few feet, the impression is of a normal face, with the nose nearer to the observer than the forehead. Only at very close range indeed does the stereoscopic information dominate over the cognitive interpretative processes. It appears that "top-down" processes may need to be invoked to account fully for the processes of global stereopsis.

FIGURE 7.11

This is a picture of a hollow mask, illuminated from behind. In real life, as in this photograph, we see a normal face, with the tip of the nose nearer to us than the eyelids. Photograph by Sam Grainger.

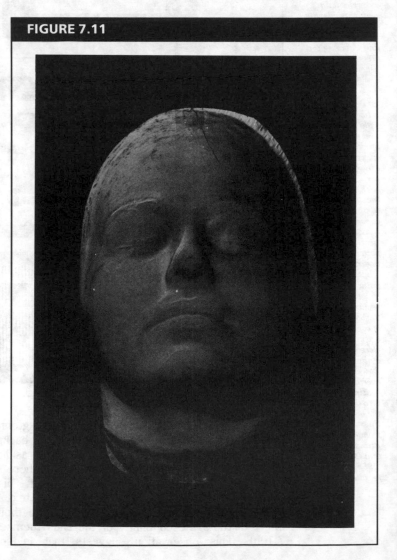

This account of stereopsis has necessarily been selective. Whole books have been devoted to the subject and the interested reader is advised to consult Julesz (1971), Gulick and Lawson (1976), Poggio and Poggio (1984) and the relevant sections of Kaufman (1974) and Marr (1982) for further details.

One-eyed humans can be accurate at gauging distance (as you will see if you close one eye and try reaching for objects), and creatures with panoramic vision and little binocular overlap include birds which can take flight, navigate and land. Convergence, accommodation and stereopsis can work only over relatively short distances. There must therefore be sources of information other than disparity to tell animals about the distances of objects in their world. Given the "flat" retinal image, what can these sources be?

Pictorial Cues to Depth

As well as the physiological cues, there are the "pictorial" cues to depth, so-called because artists since the Renaissance have employed them to convey an impression of depth in their work. If certain features can give depth information on a canvas then perhaps those same features may be used by the brain in its interpretation of the "flat" retinal picture.

Many of these pictorial cues are simple consequences of the geometry of the retinal image. Consider for convenience the properties of images cast by objects on a plane perpendicular to the line of sight, the "frontal plane" (see Fig. 7.12). We can think of such an image as capturing the geometrical properties of retinal images, ignoring the curvature of the latter.

The size of an image cast by an object is small if the object is far away, as at C in Figure 7.12, and becomes larger as the object approaches the frontal plane, as at A in Figure 7.12. Thus the

The size of the image cast by an object decreases with increase in distance.

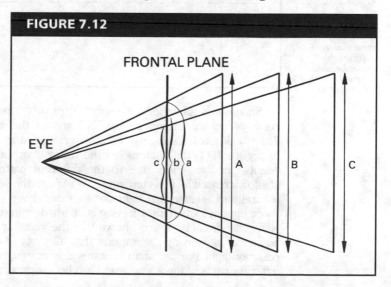

FIGURE 7.12

FRONTAL PLANE

EYE

relative size of an image depends upon its distance. If we consider naturally occurring surfaces, receding away from the frontal plane and consisting of large numbers of stochastically regular texture elements, the image cast by such a receding plane will contain a *gradient* of image size. As we will see in the third part of this book, the notion of a gradient is central to some approaches to space perception, but for the moment we are treating it as a "cue" for the perception of distance.

Perspective is perhaps the best known pictorial cue to depth. The horizontal separation of images cast by the two sides of a pair of railway tracks is larger for the nearer portions of the tracks and smaller for the more distant portions. The image cast by parallel lines at the frontal plane converges as the lines recede horizontally from the observer.

Because our eyes are elevated above the ground which supports us and other objects, there are also differences in the *height* in the visual field of images cast by objects at different distances. The further away an object is from the observer the higher in the visual field its image will be cast. The "cues" of relative size, perspective and relative height are all simple consequences of the geometry of the retinal image, and all three operate together whenever objects are viewed by the human eye (see Fig. 7.13).

In this diagram, an observer at P looks at a set of square units on the ground (paving slabs perhaps). The image formed at the frontal plane illustrates how the "cues" of relative size, perspective, and relative height are all simple consequences of the geometry of image formation. Adapted from J. J. Gibson (1950a). Used by permission of Houghton Mifflin Company.

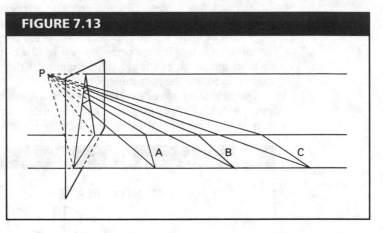

FIGURE 7.13

Shadow is an important aspect of pictures (or images) which conveys an impression of solidity, and in the last chapter we described how animals may be counter-shaded to counteract this. In Figure 7.14, the "humps" in the top row of the image become "dents" in the other, due to the different pattern of light and shadow created by inverting one row to form the second. We seem naturally to assume that light comes from above (from the sun or room lighting) when interpreting such shadow information. Indeed Ramachandran (1988) has shown that the visual system makes the additional simplifying assumption that all parts of a scene share a common light source, and maintains this assumption even though different parts of the scene may then be assigned different depths.

FIGURE 7.14

The shapes on the left are usually seen as bumps while those on the right are usually seen as dents, consistent with an overhead light source. Reproduced from Ramachandran (1988) with permission.

In Figure 7.14, for example, we see the top row as humps and the bottom row as dents, with the whole scene as illuminated from above, rather than seeing all the figures as humps. Such a bias towards common light sources and multiple depths makes sense given the evolution of our visual systems in a world with only one natural source of light. (However, even this bias can be overcome given sufficient additional expectations. When looking at the hollow face next to a normal one, both are seen as faces despite the fact that this involves assuming different light sources for the two adjacent objects.)

Just as the images cast by objects are smaller when they are at a distance so they are also less clear, less bright and have slightly different spectral properties. This is because light is scattered and absorbed by particles in the atmosphere and different wavelengths are scattered to different degrees (see Chapter 1). Figure 7.15 gives a powerful impression of depth because of the way in which the light reflected by the distant hills has been scattered though there are also other cues, such as relative size, operating here.

Another cue which operates when viewing most natural scenes is that of *interposition* or overlay. Figure 7.16 is seen as circles, with one on top of another. This is not the only possible interpretation; we might see the drawing as representing two adjacent shapes, one circular and the others with "bites" taken out of them. Usually, however, we interpret the irregular image as representing a "good" shape (cf. Gestalt principles discussed in Chapter 6) which is partially covered by another good shape.

Dynamic Cues

So far we have considered a static observer viewing an unchanging scene—an untypical situation. In addition to physiological cues to depth, and pictorial cues, modern cue theory also considers how movement of an observer, or of objects, can signal relative distance by *motion parallax*.

FIGURE 7.15

The image of the near hills is brighter and clearer than the image of the distant ones, from which the light has been scattered by the atmosphere. Photograph by Mike Burton.

FIGURE 7.16

Interposition.

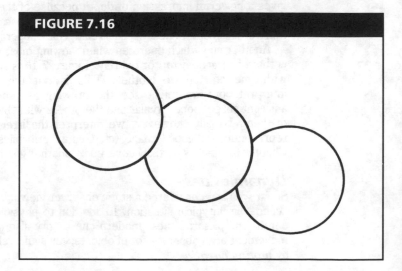

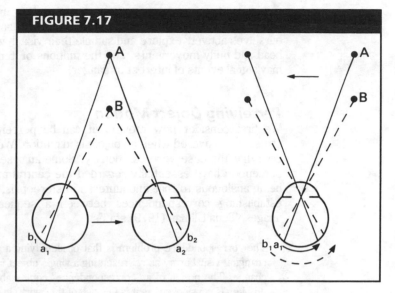

FIGURE 7.17

Motion parallax. The observer looks at two objects (A and B) at different distances. If the observer moves (as in the left diagram), or the objects move at equal speed (as in the right diagram), the image of the nearer object B, moves further across the retina $(b_1 - b_2)$ than does the image of A $(a_1 - a_2)$.

Consider Figure 7.17. Here we see an eye viewing two similar objects at different distances. As the eye moves, the image cast by object B travels further across the retina than that cast by object A. Conversely, if the eye were still, and objects A and B moved across the line of sight at constant and equal speed, the image cast by the nearer object would travel further across the retina than the image cast by the more distant one. Relative speed of motion of different portions of the retinal image could therefore signal relative depth. In Part III of this book we consider in great detail how information of this kind may inform an animal or person about the layout of the world and their own movements within it.

Thus while the retinal image contains many inherent ambiguities, various signs, cues or clues available in the total retinal picture are correlated with distances in the world and allow the "lost" third dimension to be recovered by the observer. At this point it should be noted that at least some aspects of depth perception appear to be innate rather than learned, even in humans, who are not independently mobile at birth. We will be considering some of this evidence in Chapter 12. For the moment we should simply point out that it does not seem as though all the "cues" to depth need to be learned through associating visual information with the felt positions of objects.

OBSERVER MOVEMENT AND OBJECT MOTION

In the context of our discussion of depth perception we have already mentioned one aspect of motion. We now move on to discuss further aspects of the perception of motion, again from the starting point of the retinal image. The problem of understanding the visual processing of retinal images becomes vastly more complicated once one begins to contemplate how movement in the world or by the observer is encoded. Most animals including ourselves actively explore and sample their visual worlds with eye, head and body movements, and the motions of items in the world may signal events of interest or danger.

Perceiving Object Motion

We first consider how movement can be perceived and object structure recovered when an object is in motion. We assume in this case that the observer is stationary. Some analyses of movement perception have essentially regarded the central problem here as being analogous to that encountered in stereopsis, namely that of establishing correspondences between a sequence of distinct images. Thus Ullman (1979) states:

> The correspondence problem is that of identifying a portion of the changing visual array as representing a single object in motion or in change. The notion of a "correspondence" comes about when the problem is considered (as it is in much of this work) in the context of a sequence of images, such as the frames of a motion picture. The problem then becomes one of establishing a match between parts of one frame and their counterparts in a subsequent frame that represents the same object at a later time (p. 4).

Thus for at least some workers in the field of artificial intelligence an understanding of motion perception starts with working out how correspondences are established between "snapshots" of the changing retinal pattern captured at different moments.

The justification for analysing the perception of motion in this way is given partly because it is possible to perceive movement in the absence of continuous translation of the retinal image. This phenomenon of *apparent motion* was extensively investigated by the Gestalt psychologists, notably by Wertheimer (1912). If an observer is presented with a display in which two lines in different locations are alternately exposed, at certain interstimulus intervals (which depend on the spatial separation, luminance and duration of the lines) the observer reports seeing the first line move across to the position of the second, i.e. the observer sees not two lines alternately appearing in different locations, but one line which moves smoothly from place to place. Thus it appears that change in retinal position can be a sufficient condition for the perception of movement (though note that it is not a necessary condition, as we see object motion when the eye tracks a moving target). Since apparent movement and real movement are phenomenally so similar, a strong case can be made for regarding the perception of real movement as the integration of a succession of discrete views.

Ullman's analysis of motion perception therefore starts with the correspondence problem in apparently moving displays. He argues that correspondences are established on the basis of matches between primitive *elements* of figures such as edges, lines and blobs, rather than between whole figures. That is, matches are built up between the kinds of descriptive units found in the raw primal sketch. (Note the similarity between this and the theories of Julesz (1971) and Marr and Poggio (1976, 1979), who establish matches between elements, rather than entire patterns, to achieve stereoscopic fusion.) Ullman presents a number of demonstrations to support his case. In one of these, observers were presented with a "broken wheel" display (see Fig. 7.18) in which every other spoke is incomplete. If the "wheel" is rotated by *x* degrees between successive frames, where *x* is greater than half the angle between the spokes of the wheel, the observer sees the wheel breaking into three distinct rings. The innermost and outermost rings rotate clockwise while the middle ring appears to rotate anticlockwise. This would be expected if matches were established between line segments, but would not be expected if the entire figure were being matched from frame to frame. If figural matching were occurring one would expect to perceive clockwise rotation of the whole wheel.

The solid lines show the first frame of Ullman's "broken wheel" configuration, and the dotted lines show the second frame when it is viewed in apparent motion. Under certain conditions the wheel is seen to split into three rings, with the outer and inner ones moving anticlockwise and the central one moving clockwise, as shown by the arrows. Adapted from Ullman (1979).

FIGURE 7.18

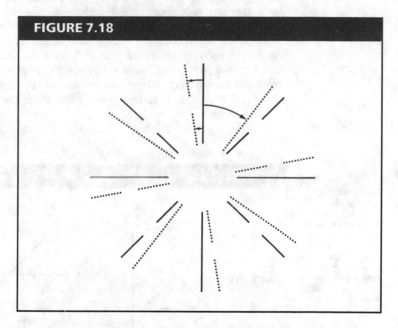

Ullman provides an elegant computational account of how correspondence can be achieved by making use of a principle of "minimal mapping." Suppose that one frame of a film consists of elements A and B, and a second frame consists of elements A' and B', displaced relative to A and B. The correspondence problem is to establish whether A or B is to be matched with A'. Ullman achieves this by establishing an *affinity measure* for each possible pairing. The closer together in space, and the more similar in description are the two elements in a pair, the greater will be their affinity (based on the simple assumption that near, similar matches are more likely to belong together than more distant, dissimilar matches). To solve the correspondence process for an entire display of several elements a solution is found which minimises matches with poor affinities and maximises those with strong affinities. A global solution is thus obtained through a set of local measures.

Once the correspondence problem has been solved (though Ullman's solution is not necessarily that used by the human visual system; see Marr, 1982), it is possible to recover the three dimensional structure which gives rise to a particular set of motions. The kinetic depth effect (Wallach & O'Connell, 1953) provides perhaps the best known example of the recovery of structure from motion. If a shadow is cast by a rotating wire shape onto a screen (see Fig. 7.19), a viewer can readily perceive the shape of the structure behind the screen from the dynamic shadow pattern. Ullman's own demonstration of the recovery of structure from motion involves the images of a pair of coaxial counter-rotating cylinders (see Fig. 7.20). When static, the display looks like a random collection of dots. Once it moves, however, the observer has a clear impression of one cylinder inside another, with the two rotating in opposite directions. Ullman has shown that it is possible to recover structure from motion if one assumes that the motion arises from *rigid* bodies. Given this rigidity assumption, his structure-from-motion theorem proves that structure can be recovered from three frames which each show four non-coplanar points in motion.

The interested reader is referred to Ullman's book (Ullman,

The kinetic depth effect (Wallach & O'Connell, 1953). When a wire shape is rotated behind a screen on which its shadow falls, observers see the dynamic shadow pattern as a solid shape in motion.

FIGURE 7.19

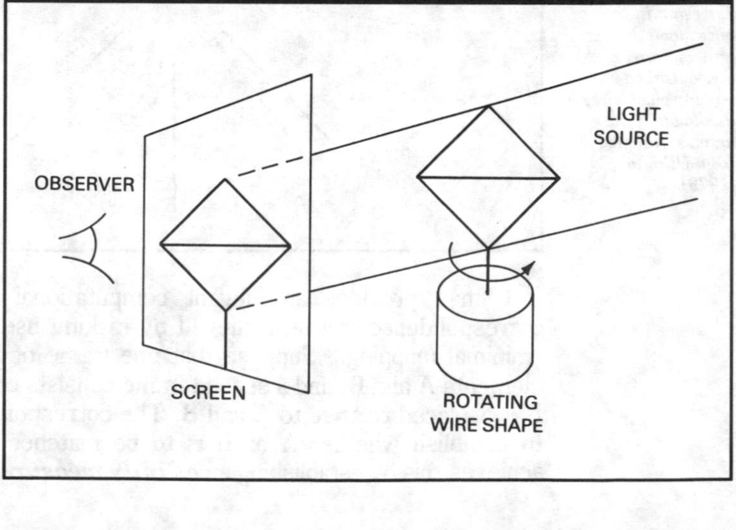

LIGHT SOURCE

OBSERVER

SCREEN

ROTATING WIRE SHAPE

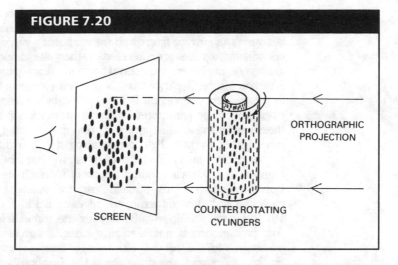

FIGURE 7.20

ORTHOGRAPHIC PROJECTION

COUNTER ROTATING CYLINDERS

SCREEN

Ullman's (1979) counter–rotating cylinders display. The screen shows the pattern of dots which would arise if the images of two, co–axial, glass cylinders covered with blobs were projected orthographically onto a screen. Observers who view a film of the screen can recover the structure of the counter–rotating cylinders from the pattern of apparent motions present.

1979) for a fuller discussion of the processes of establishing correspondences and recovering structure from motion. Throughout his book Ullman, like Marr, attempts to provide a computational account which makes use of general constraints (e.g. assume motion is of a rigid object) rather than knowledge of specific objects. We will return to consider the analysis of structure from motion in more detail later in the book when we describe the considerable body of work on the perception of biological motion and relative motion that has been conducted by the "ecological" perceptual theorists (see Chapter 15).

Motion Detectors Revisited

In Chapter 2 we described the directionally selective cells in the visual systems of rabbits, cats and monkeys which respond to motion within their receptive fields, indicating that motion might be considered a primitive property of the visual system to which detectors are directly attuned. In the preceding paragraphs, however, we have been considering a much less direct account of some aspects of motion perception.

These approaches may not be in opposition, however, since it is likely that several systems may be involved in the perception of motion. Braddick (1980), for example, has distinguished between two types of apparent motion, one which may depend on the stimulation of low-level "motion detectors," and the other which seems to depend on higher level, more cognitive factors.

Braddick has examined the factors which affect the perception of apparent motion in "random-dot kinematograms" (Julesz, 1971). A random-dot kinematogram (r.d.k.) is comprised of successive frames of random texture, in each of which there is no perceptible form. However, the dots in a central portion of each pattern are displaced by a constant amount from one frame to the next, while the background texture remains the same. The dots comprising the central region are seen to move as a whole revealing a boundary between the moving figure and the stationary surround. (Random-dot kinematograms are therefore rather like random-dot stereograms—in the latter, the central region is segregated by virtue of a common spatial disparity that the central elements possess, while in the former, the region is segregated by a common translation over time.) The parameters of apparent motion in r.d.k.s are not the same as those of apparent motion in line and figure stimuli as investigated by the Gestalt psychologists. In r.d.k.s the spatial displacement and inter-stimulus intervals must be much smaller than those which will produce apparent motion between two lines. For example, the inter-stimulus interval must be less than 100 msec for a 100 msec exposure of each r.d.k. frame (Braddick, 1973), but may be up to 300 msec for line stimuli (Neuhaus, 1930). Apparent motion is not seen in a r.d.k. if successive stimuli are presented to different eyes, though this is possible with line displays. Apparent motion in r.d.k.s is abolished if the inter-stimulus interval is bright, whereas in line displays it can be seen with dark or bright inter-stimulus intervals.

In classic line or configurational displays a number of interesting phenomena can be obtained which seem to demand a higher-level, more cognitive interpretation. For example, apparent motion can be seen between two different shapes, say a circle and a square, with the shape apparently changing as the form "moves" from one location to the other. Kolers (1963) showed that if the path of an apparently moving line was impeded by a third figure, the line would appear to move in depth to avoid the "obstacle." Finally, in the Ternus display (Ternus, 1926) illustrated in Figure 7.21, the entire configuration of elements is seen to move from place to place, even though the central element actually remains in the same location from frame to frame. This group movement occurs only if the inter-stimulus interval is greater than 40 msec (Pantle & Picciano, 1976). (While this last example might seem to counter Ullman's claim that correspondences are established between primitive elements rather than entire forms, his analysis is in fact able to account for "coherent" perception of the Ternus display [Ullman, 1979].)

A Ternus display. A and A₁ are the positions of two dots in the first frame of an apparent motion display. B and B₁ are the positions of dots in the second frame. Under certain conditions, observers see the entire configuration A–A₁ shift sideways to B–B₁. (N.B. The form of the dots from one frame to the next is identical. Open and filled circles have been used here to distinguish one frame from the next.)

FIGURE 7.21

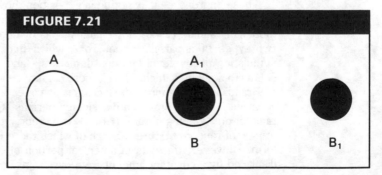

A
A₁
B
B₁

Therefore Braddick (1980) concludes that apparent motion in r.d.k.s. is:

a low-level "short-range" process (that) may tentatively be identified with the response of directionally sensitive neurons in the visual pathway to discontinuous stimulation. The more interpretative phenomena of apparent motion may then be associated with the higher-level process that determines the criterion of smooth perceived motion (Braddick, 1980, p. 140).

Braddick here suggests that it is only the short-range processes of apparent motion that may be a consequence of the firing of directionally selective neurons (see Chapter 2). Such neurons may underlie our ability to detect discontinuities in the direction of motions present in a dynamic display. Discontinuities in motion directions may themselves reflect discontinuities in the surfaces being viewed, and hence could give important information to aid the segmentation of a scene. Short-range processes of this kind may be quite distinct from the more sophisticated, "higher-level" analysis of correspondences and structure from motion, which we have been considering in this chapter. While long range motion seems to require the solution of the correspondence problem, short-range motion analysis poses a slightly different problem of computation, which will be considered in some detail in Chapter 13. In the third part of the book we will also consider other aspects of motion perception that have arisen naturally from the work of the ecological perceptual theorists.

It is in fact quite sensible that many different systems should seem to be involved in the perception of real and apparent motion. Different kinds of analysis are required for different types of moving stimulus. In the periphery of the visual field motion serves an orienting function. A flashing or moving light will cause human observers to turn their eyes and/or heads automatically to fixate the object. Such orienting functions may be mediated in part by the superior colliculus (see Chapter 3, p. 49). Once fixated, a moving object may need to be recognised and tracked, which will involve a number of different, presumably cortical, systems. To a large extent different contemporary theorists are attempting to explain different aspects of the perception of moving stimuli. The perception of object motion from changing retinal images is then, clearly, a complex topic. These transformations in the retinal image become yet more complex when we consider how changes may arise as a result of movements of the observer's eyes and body.

Eye Movements

The eyes themselves are never at rest. We can distinguish a number of different types of human eye movement, characterised by different sizes, latencies and speeds, and these were described in Chapter 1. While all these various eye movements are problematical for accounts of how it is that we perceive a stable visual world (since there is movement of the retinal image every time the eyes are moved), there is evidence that they are in fact essential for the perception of form. It is possible to examine perception without eye movements using the technique of *stabilised retinal images*. This can be achieved by attaching to the cornea of the eye a contact lens on which is mounted a miniature projector. Since the contact lens, and hence the projector, moves with the eye, the images of objects presented to the eye remain focused on identical retinal coordinates. Loss of perception of colour and contour occurs within seconds of stabilisation (Heckenmuller, 1965). Pritchard (1961) claimed that form perception is disrupted in a rather interesting manner. He presented observers with patterns, pictures and words and his subjects reported that they disappeared, and sometimes reappeared, in fragments, such that "meaningful" chunks were preserved. Thus the stimulus word BEER might be reported as PEER, BEE and BE at different times. While this again suggests a role for "top-down" processes, the effects may have been produced by occasional slippage of the lens system (Cornsweet, 1970), or may have resulted from reporting bias on the part of the observers. Nevertheless, the general conclusion from the stabilised image experiments is that movement of the image across the retina is *vital* for the maintenance of perception over time.

However, a consideration of eye movements alone immediately raises the problem of how it is that we know whether it is ourselves (eyes, head, body) or objects in the world moving, since movement of the image on the retina could be produced either by object movement or by movement of the observer.

Distinguishing Movement of the Eyes from Movement in the World

Consider a stationary eye viewing an isolated object as in Figure 7.22. As the object moves across the line of sight, the image it casts will move across the retina—it will be cast on different receptors as it travels. In this situation we correctly perceive ourselves as still and the object as moving. Now suppose we move the eye, but the object remains stationary. Again the image will move across the retina, but this time we will perceive the object at rest and ourselves as moving. Finally, consider what happens when the eye tracks a moving object. The image is cast on the same part of the retina, just as when neither the eye nor the object moves, but now movement *is* perceived.

It appears again that the information contained within the retinal image is ambiguous. In order to perceive correctly what is moving and what is at rest, the visual system as a whole must also take into account information about the way the eyes and body are moving. Gregory (1972) has suggested that two systems must be involved in movement perception—the image–retina system and the eye–

At (a), a stationary
eye views a moving
object O. As O
moves to O_1, its
image I moves
across the retina to
I_1. At (b) the same
image movement
($I–I_1$) is produced
when the eye
moves but the
object remains
stationary. At (c)
the eye moves to
track the
movement of the
object. O moves to
O_1, but its image
remains at the
same place, I.

FIGURE 7.22

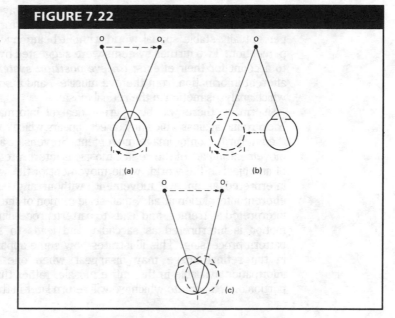

head system. Information from the eye–head system is used to disambiguate that from the image–retina system.

Account could be taken of the movement of eyes and body in one of two ways. Sherrington (1906) originally proposed an *inflow* theory in which afferent signals from the eye muscles are taken into account when movement in the retinal image is interpreted. Helmholtz (1866) proposed instead an *outflow* theory where it is efferent commands sent to the muscles (described by Helmholtz as an "effort of will") which are used in interpreting image movement. Early evidence seemed to favour Helmholtz's theory. If the eye is moved passively, by pressing on the side of the eyeball, the visual world appears to move. If signals from the muscles were being processed, such passive movement should be compensated for as easily as movement actively initiated by the observer. If the eye is immobilised by paralysing drugs or some mechanical wedge (Brindley & Merton, 1960; Mach, 1914), subjects report that the visual world appears to move when they attempt, unsuccessfully, to initiate eye movements. Here it appears that the commands to the muscles are being taken into account despite the fact that no actual change in the muscles results.

However, both these lines of evidence may be criticised. First, passive movement of the eye does not necessarily mimic normal changes in the muscles. Second, Stevens, Emerson, Gerstein, Kallos, Neufield, Nichols and Rosenquist (1976) report a more careful investigation of the effects of muscle paralysis. Following an attempted saccade, their subject reported a kind of displacement, or relocation of the visual *world* without movement. Stevens et al. suggest that a spatial system compares information from the retina with commands sent to the muscles, in the way suggested by Helmholtz, but that this system is responsible for maintaining a perceptually stable spatial world without being involved in motion perception. Two further systems were suggested by Stevens et al. to account for their effects; *an eye position system*, which uses afferent information from the eye muscles, and a *pattern system*, which analyses motion in the retinal mosaic.

Normally there will be a great deal of information from the background against which any object appears which can disambiguate the interpretation of image movement. Stevens et al. suggest that movement in part of the retinal mosaic is interpreted as movement of an object in the world, while movement of the whole mosaic is interpreted as an eye movement, without any need to involve efferent information at all. Small-scale motion of the entire array is interpreted as tremor, and leads to pattern processing. Large-scale motion is interpreted as saccadic, and leads to suppression of pattern processing. This illustrates how some apparent ambiguity in the retinal image may disappear when one considers the information available in the entire mosaic, rather than a restricted portion of it, a point to which we will return later in the book.

MARR'S THEORY OF THE 2½D SKETCH

Many of the issues that we have introduced in our discussion of the perception of depth and movement were incorporated within a single theoretical treatment by Marr (1982). Marr sees the goal of early visual processing as the production of a description of the visible surfaces of the environment, so that their dispositions and layouts are described with respect to the viewer. This description he terms the 2½D sketch, and it is built up from several different sources. The contour, texture and shading information available from the full primal sketch, stereopsis, and the analysis of motions present, all contribute to the 2½D sketch, which acts as a buffer store in which partial solutions can be stored as processing proceeds. The label "2½D" derives from the assumption that the sketch captures a great deal about the relative depths and surface orientations, and local changes and discontinuities in these, but that some aspects are represented more accurately than others:

> Very locally we can easily say from motion or stereopsis information whether one point is in front of another. But if we try to compare the distances to two surfaces that lie in different parts of the visual field, we do very poorly and can do this much less accurately than we can compare their surface orientations (Marr, 1982, p. 282).

For these and other reasons Marr concludes that the 2½D sketch represents surface orientation much more accurately than depth (see Fig. 7.23). Only local changes in depth may be represented to any degree of accuracy.

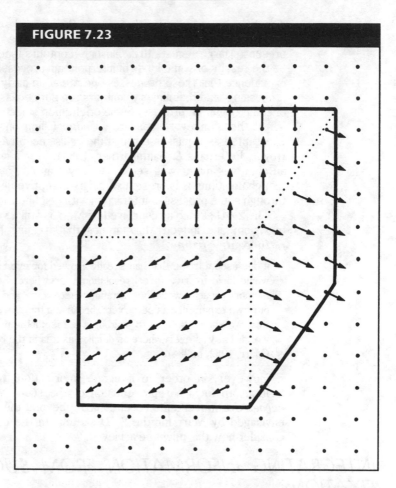

FIGURE 7.23

The 2½D sketch of a cube. The surfaces of the cube are represented by a set of vector primitives, like needles. The length of each needle represents the degree of tilt of the surface, and the orientation of the needle represents the direction in which the surface slants. From Marr (1982).

Discontinuities in depth are signalled primarily by stereopsis mechanisms and by the presence of occlusion. Occlusion may be specified by the presence of occluding contours in the primal sketch and by discontinuities in the pattern of motions present. Information about surface orientation is given by stereopsis, by surface and textural contours, and by an analysis of structure from motion.

Once these properties are obtained, Marr sees the representation in the 2½D sketch as comprised of a set of vector-like primitives, which may be depicted as a set of "needles" (see Fig. 7.23). The length of each needle describes the degree of tilt of that part of the surface, and the orientation of each needle describes the direction in which the surface slants. In addition, the distance from the viewer to each point on the surface could be represented very roughly by a third, scalar quantity (which is not shown in Fig. 7.23).

Where there is insufficient information present from the early visual processing modules to produce a full description in the 2½D sketch, various *interpolation procedures* may be invoked. For example, a uniform area when viewed by the two eyes contains no disparities. The depth of that part of the viewed surface must be obtained by interpolation from regions where contrasts are present. Marr suggests that "illusory" contours (see Fig. 7.9) may be the results of some kinds of interpolation processes. If so, there is evidence that these processes operate at an early stage in visual processing, and that illusory contours are not necessarily the result of some cognitive process. Some orientation selective cells in area V2 of the monkey respond to an edge falling on the retina but interrupted as it passes through the cell's receptive field (von der Heydt, Peterhans & Baumgartner, 1984). In this situation, where an observer might well see an illusory contour, a cell fires even though no stimulus is present within its receptive field, presumably through some process of interaction with neighbouring cells.

The 2½D sketch as conceived by Marr is still a very early stage of vision, and indeed Marr argues that it must be based on a *retinocentric frame*:

> if one used a frame that had already allowed for eye movements, it would have to have foveal resolution everywhere. Such luxurious memory capacity would be wasteful, unnecessary, and in violation of our own experience as perceivers, because if things were really like this, we should be able to build up a perceptual impression of the world that was everywhere as detailed as it is in the centre of gaze (Marr, 1982, p. 284).

However, in order to integrate information from successive fixations to form a representation of the scene which is stable *across* eye movements requires going beyond the representation envisaged by Marr for the 2½D sketch. In the next section we consider how this might be achieved.

INTEGRATING INFORMATION FROM SUCCESSIVE FIXATIONS

Human observers and other animals typically sample their visual worlds with a series of discrete fixations, separated by saccades. No visible blur is apparent when our eyes dart from location to location. Indeed there is evidence that processing during a saccade is suppressed (Volkmann, 1976), and Stevens et al. (1976) suggest that suppression is triggered by large-scale movement of the entire retinal mosaic. Somehow we must be able to integrate these successive "snapshots" to produce our perception of a stable visual world.

The problem of integrating successive slightly different retinal images may again be thought analogous to the problem of fusing two disparate images when stereopsis or apparent motion are achieved. In both cases the brain must discover which aspects of the retinal image "correspond" to the same objects and match them accordingly. We hope that the discussion of stereopsis and apparent motion above will have indicated that the correspondence problem is not trivial. It is no easier to solve when one considers integrating successive fixations.

If a view from one discrete sample of the visual world is to be matched with a second slightly different view obtained at a later point in time it is necessary to postulate some sort of memory to preserve the first view for comparison with the second. Information-processing psychologists have identified one such short-lived visual memory system which at first might seem a likely candidate to mediate the integration of successive glimpses. This short-lived visual memory system is known as *iconic memory* (named by Neisser, 1967). Its properties were first fully investigated by Sperling (1960).

Sperling conducted a series of experiments to investigate limits in the span of apprehension. If a human observer is presented very briefly with an array of, say, three rows each containing four letters, typically they can report only three or four of the total array of 12 letters. Observers state that they can "see" more letters than they can report. Sperling asked observers to report only a single row of such a display, by giving them a cue (high, medium or low-pitched tones for the top, middle and bottom rows respectively) *after* the offset of the display. If the cue followed the display immediately, then observers could report about three items from each four item row, suggesting that 75% of the letters were available for report immediately after presentation. As the delay between display offset and the presentation of the tone was increased so the number of items reported from any row declined, until at about 500 msec delay, with light pre-and post-exposure fields, there was no advantage to be gained by asking for partial report over full report.

Iconic memory therefore seems to preserve visual information from a briefly glimpsed scene for a period of 500 msec or more (depending on the pre-and post-field illumination levels). During this time iconic memory appears to decay passively. Information in iconic memory appears to be in an uninterpreted form, since only physical cues can be used to give a partial report advantage (Sperling, 1963; Von Wright, 1968, 1970; though see Merikle, 1980).

Could this be the memory system which serves to integrate successive views as observers fixate different portions of a scene? Hochberg (1968) and Turvey (1977b) argue strongly that it could not, since iconic memory is tied to anatomical, specifically retinal, coordinates. Thus, like Marr's 2½D sketch, it can serve no useful integrative function, since we have just replaced the problem of comparing different retinal snapshots with that of comparing different iconic snapshots. It seems that a memory system at a more abstract level than the iconic would be needed to serve this integrative function.

There is considerable, converging evidence for a post-iconic visual store which seems to play a role in visual imagery as well as in visual perception. For example, Phillips (1974) describes some elegant experiments in which he directly compared the properties of iconic memory with those of the short term visual store (STVS).

Iconic memory may be masked by the presentation of a bright light or pattern immediately after the test stimulus, is tied to anatomical coordinates and is not affected by pattern complexity. STVS is not disrupted by masking, not tied to anatomical coordinates but is affected by pattern complexity. In STVS, less is retained from complex than from simple patterns. These observations suggest that STVS is a limited capacity short term store at a more "schematic" level than iconic memory. Indeed there is now considerable evidence that the system underlying partial report superiority in the original "iconic memory" experiments might actually be based at this more "schematic" level (see Humphreys & Bruce, 1989, for a review).

Hochberg (1968) implicated such a schematic memory system in the integration of successive views of objects, labelling it a *schematic map*. Hochberg conducted a number of studies in which he mimicked successive local sampling of the entire visual field by revealing partial glimpses of objects to observers, in a technique called *successive aperture viewing*. A line drawing of an object might be displayed section by section through a slit as shown in Figure 7.24. Observers were able to recover object structure from these glimpses, see spontaneous reversals in depth and correctly notice the "impossibility" of certain configurations. Hochberg argued that the partial views were integrated at the level of the schematic map just as they would be if the observer were exploring a complete object with a succession of fixations.

However, Hochberg's schematic map does not serve to combine successive glimpses in a passive, "data-driven" way. Instead, he

FIGURE 7.24

(a) shows a figure which is ambiguous in depth and (b) shows an impossible figure. Observers notice ambiguity and impossibility if a figure is viewed piece by piece through an aperture, as illustrated in frames 1–7. Adapted from Hochberg (1968).

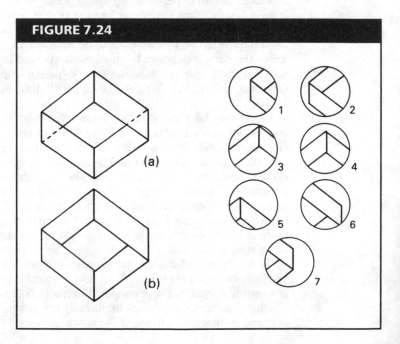

suggests that one may need previously acquired knowledge about the properties of objects to integrate successive views of them:

> It seems most plausible to me that they (schematic maps) are built up not only from the successive views of a given object or scene but from *previous experiences* as well (Hochberg, 1968, p. 325).

And elsewhere:

> A schematic map is a matrix of space-time expectancies (or assumptions) (Hochberg, 1968, p. 324).

Thus described, Hochberg's idea bears some similarity to Minsky's (1977) notion of "frame systems" (Turvey, 1977b). Minsky (1977) does not explicitly discuss the problem of integrating successive fixations made by the eyes alone, but addresses instead the broader problem of integrating successive views of an object or scene as the whole observer moves around or within it. He suggests that prior knowledge of an object such as a cube, leads to the establishment of a coherent interlinked system of frames. Each frame corresponds to a symbolic description of one view of the cube. As the observer moves around a cube, different faces of it become visible and others become concealed from view. Minsky suggests that rather than recomputing the description of each viewpoint anew, the correct frames in the system would become available when information about an impending movement became available.

An alternative way to conceptualise the operation of a schematic memory of this kind is to suggest that it reflects a representational level where information is encoded in a coordinate system which is not tied to the retina, but to some frame of reference which remains constant despite eye movements. Possible candidates for such a frame include a head-based "stable-feature" frame (Feldman, 1985) or an environment-based "scene" frame (Feldman, 1985; Pinker, 1984). Contemporary connectionist models provide a way of describing how information in a retinotopic frame might be mapped into a frame which would be stable across eye movements, and we will consider such models in more detail in Chapter 9.

An area of the cortex has been identified where recoding from a retinal-based to a head-based frame of reference may occur. This is area 7a of monkey parietal cortex, a part of the pathway processing motion and spatial information (Chapter 3, p. 67). Andersen, Essick and Siegel (1985) found that cells in this area, like those in other areas, have a receptive field defined by retinal co-ordinates, but that their responses are also modulated by the position of the eyes. Thus, for a particular eye position, a cell codes the location of a stimulus relative to the head, and Zipser and Andersen (1988; see Chapter 9, p. 220) have proposed that such cells may provide input to a further stage in which stimulus location is coded independently of eye position.

A Note on Modularity

Marr viewed the organisation of the visual system as inherently *modular*, so that stereopsis, structure from motion, shape from shading and so on, may all be studied in relative isolation, since they are processes which proceed largely independently of each other. Such a view of visual processing is consistent with the evidence that cortical pathways processing visual information are organised into separate "streams", dealing with form, colour, depth, motion and so on (see Chapter 3, p. 67). Yet somehow, these different aspects of a particular visual object—its distance, motion, colour and so forth, must be brought back together again in the act of perception. A number of different theorists suggest that it is the act of recognising a particular object at a particular location that knits together the separate descriptions, and we consider one such theory in Chapter 9 when we discuss the work of Feldman (1985). For converging perspectives from experimental psychology, the reader should consult the recent work of Treisman leading to her feature integration theory (for a review, see Treisman, 1988).

Marr sees the 2½D sketch as the end-product of *early* visual processing. While the 2½D sketch remains to be implemented in a working computer program, the suggestion is that it can be established largely without recourse to downward-flowing inform-ation. Recall the image of a plant (Chapter 6, p. 136) which could not be fully "solved" at the level of the primal sketch without knowledge that two separate structures were present. This knowledge would be available at the level of the 2½D sketch because of the discontinuities in depth at these "hidden" boundaries revealed by stereopsis and motion parallax. Thus when we start from the real input to human vision—which is binocular and dynamic—there are few ambiguities that cannot be resolved through a full consideration of the products of a number of early visual processing "modules." In Marr's theory, unlike many other contemporary ones, we do not need to know or hypothesise what we are looking at in order to describe at least some aspects of its shape fully. However, to describe the scene being viewed appropriately within a viewer-centred frame is still only an early stage in perception. There must be other processes which allow us to categorise the image of a plant as being that of a "plant," and a "rubber-plant" at that. It is to such processes of recognition that we turn next.

Chapter Eight

OBJECT RECOGNITION

An essential part of the behaviour of animals and people is their ability to *recognise* objects, animals and people which are important to their survival. People are able to recognise large numbers of other people, the letters of the alphabet, familiar buildings, and so on. Animals may need to recognise landmarks, suitable prey, potential mates or predators and to behave in the appropriate way to each category.

If we assume that the information available to a person or animal is a static two-dimensional image on the retina, a problem immediately arises in explaining visual recognition. Take the example of a person recognising letters of the alphabet; the problem is that an infinite number of possible retinal images can correspond to a particular letter, depending upon how the letter is written, how large it is, the angle at which it is seen and so on (Fig. 8.1). Yet somehow we recognise all these patterns of light as corresponding to the same letter. Or consider the problem of recognising a friend's face; the image of their face on the retina will depend upon the lighting conditions and their distance, angle and facial expression. Again, all these images are classified together, even though some (such as a full-face and a profile view) are quite dissimilar and more like the same views of different faces than they are like each other (Fig. 8.2).

FIGURE 8.1

All these different shapes are classified as the letter A.

FIGURE 8.2

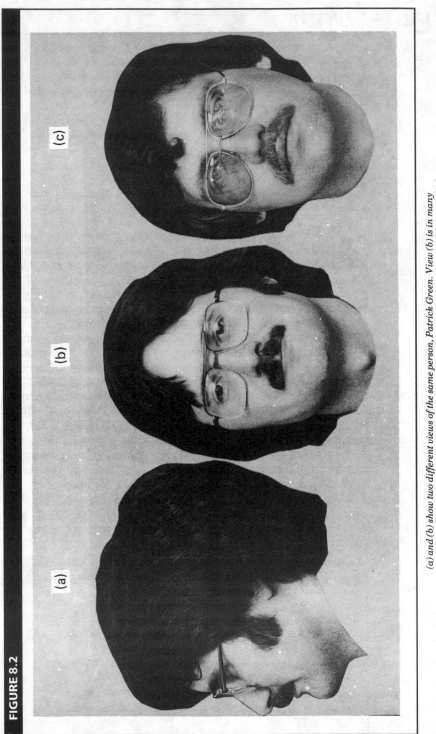

(a) and (b) show two different views of the same person, Patrick Green. View (b) is in many ways more like picture (c), which is of a different person, than it is like view (a). Photographs by Sam Grainger.

These are both illustrations of the problem of *stimulus equivalence*; if the stimulus controlling behaviour is a pattern of light, or image, on the retina, then an infinite number of images are equivalent in their effects, and different from other sets of images. Obviously, all the images corresponding to a particular thing, whether letter of the alphabet or face, must have something in common, but the problem is to find just what this is and how this thing in common is detected. It is this problem which we will be considering in this chapter.

SIMPLE MECHANISMS OF RECOGNITION

Many animals, particularly simpler ones such as insects and fish, solve the stimulus equivalence problem by detecting something relatively simple which all images corresponding to a particular object have in common. A good example is the three-spined stickleback. Males of this species build nests and defend them against other males by performing threat displays. A stickleback must therefore be able to recognise rival males and discriminate them from other fish and from objects drifting by. The retinal images of rival males will obviously vary greatly, depending upon the other fish's distance, angle and posture, and it seems that classifying these images separately from those of other fish will need elaborate criteria.

In fact, as Tinbergen (1951) discovered, the stickleback manages successfully with quite simple mechanisms of recognition. Tinbergen observed the strength of sticklebacks' aggressive responses to a range of models and found that they would readily attack a crude model of another fish, *provided* it had the red belly colour characteristic of male sticklebacks. Indeed, a crude model with a red belly elicited more attack than an accurate one without (Fig. 8.3).

A feature of an object or animal—such as the red belly of a stickleback—which elicits a response from an animal, is called a *key* or *sign stimulus*, and it greatly simplifies the problem of recognition. As long as red objects and fish with red markings are rare in the stickleback's environment, it can use the key stimulus to recognise rivals and does not need to use information about another fish's detailed structure and colouration.

The stickleback's recognition of a rival male does depend on more than just the presence of a patch of red of a certain size in the retinal image, as Tinbergen also found that a model with a red patch on its back was attacked less than one with an identical red patch on its belly, and that a model in the "head-down" posture of an aggressive fish was attacked more than one in a horizontal posture. Even so, the presence of this distinctive feature allows a much simpler means of recognition to be effective than would otherwise be the case.

Many other examples are known of key stimuli being important in the recognition by animals of other members of their species,

(a) and (b) show two different views of the same person, Patrick Green. View (b) is in many ways more like picture (c), which is of a different person, than it is like view (a). Photographs by Sam Grainger.

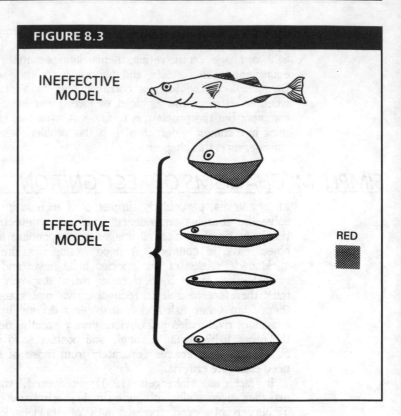

FIGURE 8.3

An accurate model of a stickleback without a red belly (top), is less effective as a stimulus to elicit aggression from a male stickleback than any of the cruder models below. Adapted from Tinbergen (1951).

INEFFECTIVE MODEL

EFFECTIVE MODEL

RED

and we will mention two other examples from Tinbergen's work. One is the recognition of female grayling butterflies by males. Tinbergen found that males would fly towards crude paper models moving overhead and that their response was not affected by the colour or shape of the model. The key stimulus turned out to be the pattern of movement of the model; males would fly towards it if it imitated the flickering and up-and-down movements of a butterfly, but not if it moved in a smooth way. Although butterflies do waste time chasing other males, or butterflies of the wrong species, this simple mechanism of recognition does prevent responses to other kinds of insect.

Another example is the recognition by nestling thrushes and blackbirds of their parents. When the parents bring food to the nest, the young birds turn towards them and gape, opening their mouths wide to be fed. Tinbergen found that gaping is elicited by a moving dark silhouette above the birds' eye level, of any shape and size. Presumably this simple mechanism of recognition is adequate because the chances of anything other than a parent resembling the key stimulus are low.

Key stimuli may also be important in the recognition of prey. Toads feed by snapping at insects flying past them, capturing them with their long sticky tongues, and Ewert (1974) found that they recognise insects by fairly simple criteria, as they will snap at small cardboard squares. Although Ewert's experiments used moving targets, toads will also snap at stationary models (Roth & Wiggers, 1983). While toads are selective for the size and speed of movement of model prey, these results show clearly that they are not able to recognise insects on the basis of finer details of their appearance.

Thus for some animals the problem of recognising significant objects may be reduced to the problem of detecting localised key stimuli or features which in the natural world are unambiguous cues to appropriate action. Such local features may be quite simple—it is easy to see how a "redness" detector might function in the stickleback, and not too difficult to conjecture how this might be coupled with a rather crude configurational analysis to explain observed preferences for the location of the red patch and the posture of the model. However, such mechanisms are also relatively inflexible, and depend for their success upon the predictability of the natural environment. When a scientist introduces a red dummy fish, a paper butterfly, or pieces of cardboard into an animal's surroundings, the assumptions about the properties of mates or prey on which the perceptual mechanism relies are violated.

Other animals, especially primates, have more flexibility in their perception and action and are able to recognise and discriminate on the basis of more complex and subtle criteria. In these cases, as in human perception, the problem of how stimulus equivalence is achieved is a difficult one, as we will see in the remainder of this chapter.

MORE COMPLEX RECOGNITION PROCESSES

We may speculate that at least some behaviour in humans may be under the control of key stimuli. For example, it has been shown (e.g. Goren, Sarty & Wu, 1975) that human neonates show innate following of face-like patterns, and we discuss this evidence in more detail in Chapter 16. On the whole, however, it is through a process of learning that we come to classify certain configurations as equivalent and distinct from others. The human infant learns to recognise the faces of its parents irrespective of angle, expression or lighting. A mother will still be "mummy" to her child after she has curled her hair, and a father will still be "daddy" if he hasn't shaved for a few days. Later, the child will learn to distinguish teachers and friends from strangers, family pets from strays, and the long process of formal education enables most to decipher the intricacies of human written language. What kinds of internal representations allow for the recognition of complex configurations, and what kinds of processes operate on the retinal image to allow access to these internal representations? These have been the questions posed in the study of human pattern and object recognition.

Much early work on pattern recognition focused on the problem of recognising alphanumeric patterns. There is good reason for such work, since researchers in computer science have had the applied aim of making computers able to recognise such patterns so that they might, for example, achieve automatic sorting of letters with hand-written postal codes. The emphasis on alphanumerics was unfortunate in other ways, since the problem of stimulus equivalence is rather different for alphanumerics than for objects. Letters must be recognised despite changes in their form, but they are only two-dimensional patterns, so that other problems in object recognition are minimised. Nevertheless the area of alphanumeric recognition is worth discussing briefly since it serves to introduce, and to dismiss, certain theoretical approaches to the broader area of object recognition.

Template Matching

The simplest account that we could offer of how we recognise alphanumeric characters would be that of *template matching*. For each letter or numeral known by the perceiver there would be a template stored in long-term memory. Incoming patterns would be matched against the set of templates, and if there were sufficient overlap between a novel pattern and a template then the pattern would be categorised as belonging to the class captured by that template. Within such a framework, slight changes in the size or angle of patterns could be taken care of by an initial process of standardisation and normalisation. For example, all patterns could be rotated so that their major axes (as discovered by other processing operations) were aligned vertically, with the height of the major axis scaled to unity (see Fig. 8.4). In addition, some pre-processing or "cleaning up" of the image would be necessary. Both humans and other animals (Sutherland, 1973) cope very well with broken or wobbly lines in the patterns they recognise.

Such a template-matching scheme could work provided that such normalising procedures were sufficient to render the resulting patterns unambiguous. Unfortunately this is almost impossible to achieve, even in the simple world of alphanumerics. An "R" could

Before matching to a template, a pattern could be standardised in terms of its orientation and size. This could be done by finding the major axis of the figure, rotating this to vertical, and scaling its size to some standard.

FIGURE 8.4

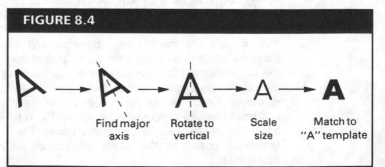

Find major axis   Rotate to vertical   Scale size   Match to "A" template

match an "A" template better than its own, and vice versa (see Fig. 8.5). The bar which distinguishes a "Q" from an "O" may be located in a variety of places (see Fig. 8.6). At the very least we would need more than one template for each letter and numeral, and it becomes difficult to see how children could learn letters and numbers in such a scheme.

FIGURE 8.5

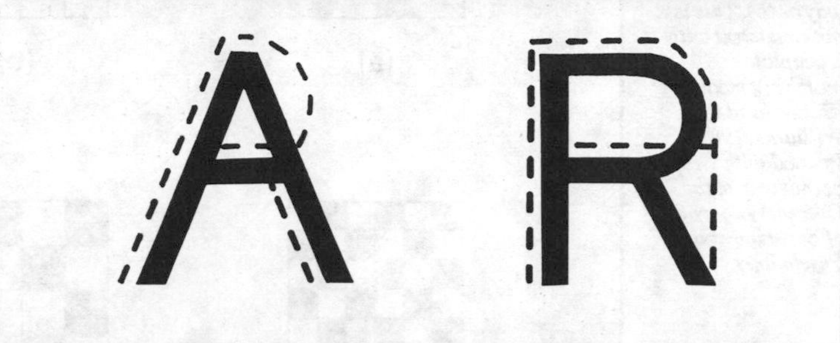

The bold figures show possible templates for an A (left) and an R (right). The dashed figures show how an R (left) and an A (right) could match another letter's template better than their own.

FIGURE 8.6

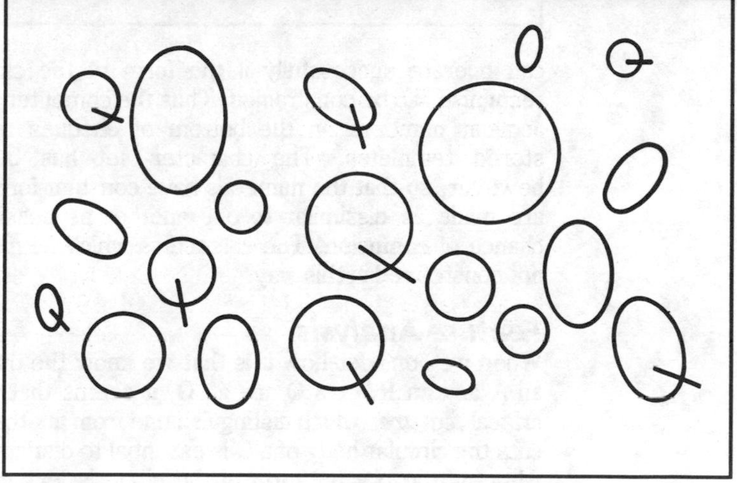

What distinguishes the Q's from the O's? Not the precise form of the circle, nor the precise location or orientation of the bar.

Template-matching schemes also fail to account for the facts of animal discrimination. Sutherland and Williams (1969) showed that rats trained to discriminate an irregular from a regular chequerboard pattern readily transferred this learning to new examples of random and regular patterns (see Fig. 8.7). As Sutherland (1973) points out, the configuration in Figure 8.7d should match better with a "template" for pattern 8.7a than for b, but it is treated by the rats as though it were more like b than a. It is also difficult to see how a template-matching model could possibly be applied to the more general area of object recognition, where the problem of stimulus equivalence is magnified. However, a template-matching process

Rats trained to respond in one way to pattern (a), and another way to pattern (b), later treat pattern (c) in the same way as (a), and pattern (d) in the same way as (b). This is not consistent with a template–matching model (Sutherland & Williams, 1969). Printed with permission of the Quarterly Journal of Experimental Psychology.

FIGURE 8.7

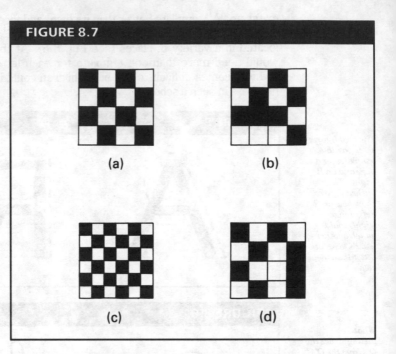

(a)   (b)

(c)   (d)

can operate successfully if the form of the characters it must recognise can be constrained. Thus the computer which recognises account numbers on the bottom of cheques matches these to stored templates. The character set has been constrained, however, so that the numerals have constant form, and in addition are made as dissimilar to one another as possible to avoid any chance of confusion. The characters which humans recognise are not constrained in this way.

Feature Analysis

When we consider how it is that we know the difference between an A and an R, or a Q and an O, it seems that there are certain critical *features* which distinguish one from another. The bar which cuts the circular body of a Q is essential to distinguish it from an O, whereas the precise form of the circle is less crucial. Perhaps a model in which combinations of features were detected would be more successful than one based on templates.

Feature analysis models of recognition were popular with psychologists and computer scientists during the 1960s while physiologists such as Hubel and Wiesel were postulating "feature detectors" in the visual cortex of cats and monkeys (see Chapter 3). Perhaps the most influential model for psychology was Selfridge's (1959) Pandemonium system, originally devised as a computer program to recognise Morse Code signals, but popularised as a model of alphanumeric recognition by Neisser (1967), and Lindsay and Norman (1972). An illustration of a Pandemonium system is shown in Figure 8.8.

FIGURE 8.8

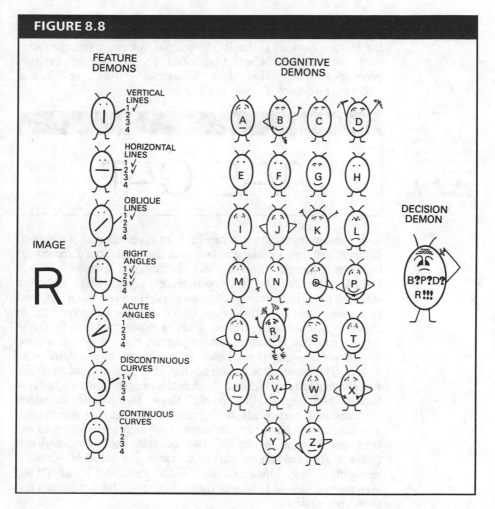

FEATURE DEMONS

VERTICAL LINES

HORIZONTAL LINES

OBLIQUE LINES

RIGHT ANGLES

ACUTE ANGLES

DISCONTINUOUS CURVES

CONTINUOUS CURVES

IMAGE

R

COGNITIVE DEMONS

DECISION DEMON

A Pandemonium system for classifying letters. Each cognitive demon represents a different letter, and "shouts" louder the more of its features are present. (Extra features inhibit the responses of cognitive demons.) The decision demon selects the letter which is being shouted the loudest. Liberally adapted from Selfridge (1959) and Lindsay and Norman (1972).

The system consists of a number of different classes of "demon." The most important of these for our purposes are the *feature demons* and the *cognitive demons*. Feature demons respond selectively when particular local configurations (right angles, vertical lines, etc.) are presented. The cognitive demons, which represent particular letters, look for particular combinations of features from the feature demons. Thus the cognitive demon representing the letter H might look for two vertical and one horizontal lines, plus four right angles. The more of their features are present, the louder will the cognitive demons "shout" to the highest level, the decision demon, who selects the letter corresponding to that represented by the cognitive demon who is shouting the loudest. Thus in this system individual characters are represented as sets of critical features, and the processing of any image proceeds in a hierarchical fashion through levels of increasing abstraction. It is this kind of model which Barlow (1972) and others used to interpret the properties of simple cells in the visual cortex (see Chapter 3, p. 62). Simple cells were thought to be acting as the feature demons in the Pandemonium system, passing information on to cells which responded to increasingly abstract properties. The notion of a "Grandmother cell" or "Yellow Volkswagen detector" arose in this context.

The same shape may be seen as an H in one context and an A in another (from a demonstration by Selfridge).

TAE CAT

A Pandemonium system can learn to give different weights to different features according to how well these features discriminate between different patterns, and in the next chapter we will consider a number of pattern recognition systems which learn in a similar way, by altering the weights between stimulus and response connections. A system of the Pandemonium type can in principle accommodate certain kinds of contextual effect. These are a ubiquitous feature of human pattern recognition and Figure 8.9 shows one example of how context affects the recognition of letters. The same shape can be seen as H or as A depending on the surrounding letters. Within a Pandemonium system we might allow higher level demons to "arouse" those at lower levels which correspond to particularly likely patterns, so that they would need less sensory evidence to make them shout sufficiently loudly to win over the decision demon (cf. the integration of contextual and physical feature information in a variety of models of word recognition, e.g. Morton, 1969). Humphreys and Bruce (1989) give more details of a range of context effects in human pattern and object recognition.

However, as a general model for human pattern and object recognition the Pandemonium system is unsatisfactory. Ultimately it rests on a description of patterns in terms of a set of features, which are themselves like mini-templates. One of the reasons that Pandemonium was so popular was that it seemed consistent with the neurophysiology of the visual cortex; but we have already seen that single cells cannot be thought of as "feature detectors" (see Chapter 3). While this may not matter for a purely psychological or computational theory of recognition, there are other problems. Feature-list descriptions fail to capture overall structural relations which are captured, but too rigidly, by more global templates. Thus the Pandemonium system depicted in Figure 8.8 would confuse an F with ⊣ and a T with ⊥, confusions that humans typically do not make. In addition, the Pandemonium system, in classifying patterns, discards all information which distinguishes different instances of the same pattern. The output of the decision demon would be the same irrespective of the particular version of the letter A shown. We need a way of talking about recognition which allows us to describe the differences between patterns as well as being able to classify together those which are instances of the same type. We need to preserve such differences so that other kinds of classifications can be made. We recognise someone's handwriting, for example, by the particular shapes of the letters they produce. Thus we need a representational format which captures aspects of structure which are essential for the classification of an item but preserves at some other level structural differences between different instances of the same class.

Structural Descriptions

A general and flexible representational format for human pattern and object recognition is provided by the language of structural descriptions. Structural descriptions do not constitute a theory of how recognition is achieved, they simply provide the right type of representation with which to construct such a theory. A structural description consists of a set of propositions (which are symbolic, but not linguistic, though we describe them in words), about a particular configuration. Such propositions describe the nature of the components of a configuration and make explicit the structural

(a) A structural description for a letter T. The description indicates that there are two parts to the letter. One part is a vertical line, the other a horizontal line. The vertical line supports and bisects the horizontal line. (b) A model for a letter T. This is like the description at (a), but the essential aspects of the description are specified. For something to be a T, a vertical line must support, and must bisect, a horizontal line, but the relative lengths are not important. (c) Shapes which would be classified as T's by the model. (d) Shapes which would fail to be classified as T's.

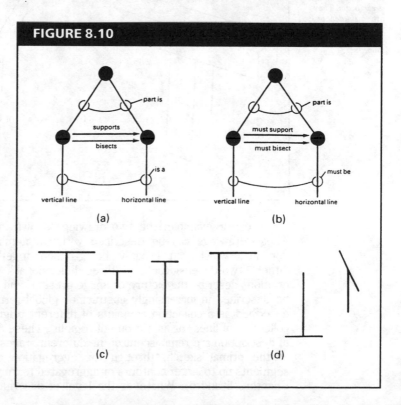

FIGURE 8.10

arrangements of these parts. Thus a structural description of a letter T might look like Figure 8.10a.

Using the language of structural descriptions it is possible to construct "models" for particular concepts and categories against which any incoming instance can be matched. Such models capture obligatory features of the structure but may be less particular about other details. Thus the "model" for a letter T might look like Figure 8.10b. It is essential that a horizontal line is supported by a vertical line, and that this support occurs about half way along the horizontal line. But the lengths of the two lines are less important. Figure 8.10c shows examples that would be classified as letter Ts by this model, and those that would fail.

Structural descriptions are also easier to apply to object recognition than templates or feature representations. A picture of an object can be described by a series of structural descriptions at increasing levels of abstraction from the original intensity distribution. There are thus a number of possible "domains" of description (Sutherland, 1973).

FIGURE 8.11

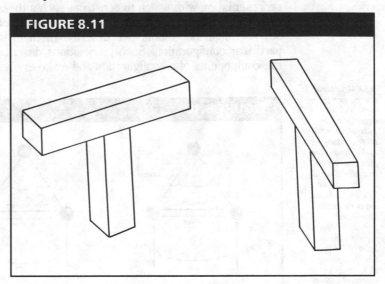

These two forms are quite different in terms of their two-dimensional description. They are equivalent only in the three-dimensional domain.

Take, for example, the two drawings shown in Figure 8.11. These drawings can be described within a number of distinct domains, which can broadly be grouped together as being either "two-dimensional" or "three-dimensional". The 2D descriptions describe the picture or image present, and this image can be described in increasingly abstract or global terms. It may be described as a collection of points of different brightnesses, as a collection of lines, or as a group of regions. These different levels of description are reminiscent of the different stages of elaboration of the primal sketch, through the aggregation of small edge segments up to larger contours or aggregated texture regions (see Chapters 5 and 6). Whatever the level of description in the 2D domain, whether points, lines or regions, the representations established for these two pictures would look very different. It is within the domain of 3D description that the equivalence of these two pictures can be established. 3D descriptions are couched in terms of surfaces, bodies and objects. The two pictures shown in Figure 8.11 are equivalent only at the level of an object description which is independent of the vantage point.

The description above again illustrates the thrust of Marr's term "2½D" sketch for the representation of *surfaces*, from the point of view of the observer. Marr's 2½D sketch falls somewhere in between the 2D and 3D groups of descriptions in Sutherland's scheme.

Thus two different projections of the same object will have different structural descriptions in the picture domain, but will be equivalent in the object domain (see Fig. 8.11). Provided that structural descriptions are established at all levels simultaneously, we can capture both the equivalences between different views of the same object and their differences. Our problem now is to consider how structural descriptions at the 3D level can be constructed, stored and matched, and to examine the extent to which the construction of 3D representations can proceed in a "bottom-up" fashion.

Winston (1975) provides an early illustration of the use of structural descriptions in object recognition to show how object concepts might be learned by giving examples. His program learns to recognise simple toy block structures such as those illustrated in Figure 8.12, which contains examples of an "arch", a "pedestal" and a "house".

The computer program is presented with examples of each, as well as "near misses", in order to build up models for each concept. The procedure for a pedestal might go as follows. First, the program would be presented with an example of a pedestal (Fig. 8.13a) to which it would assign the structural description shown in Figure 8.14a. Thus a pedestal is described as having two parts, with one part being a "brick" and the other part being a "board", with the former supporting the latter. Then the program would be presented with the sequence of "near misses" shown in Figure 8.13b–d. For Figure 8.13b, the description would again show two

Three of the toy block structures learned by Winston's program. Adapted from Winston (1973) with his permission.

FIGURE 8.12

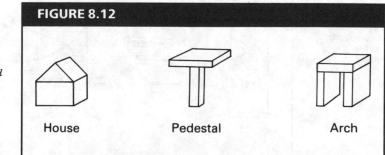

House   Pedestal   Arch

parts, with one a brick and the other a board, but the relationship between these is now different. The board is beside the brick, and the program was told that this is *not* a pedestal. By comparing this description of the near miss with that of the structure labelled pedestal, the program can construct a model for a pedestal in which the support relation is made obligatory. For something to be a pedestal one part *must be* supported by the other. The other examples in the training sequence (Fig. 8.13) further constrain the eventual model for a pedestal (Fig. 8.14b). The eventual model shows that for something to be a pedestal, an upright brick must support a lying board.

A pedestal training sequence. Adapted from Winston (1973) with his permission.

FIGURE 8.13

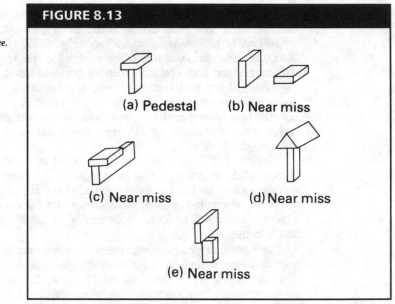

(a) Pedestal   (b) Near miss

(c) Near miss   (d) Near miss

(e) Near miss

(a) A description of the pedestal in 8.13a. (b) A model for a pedestal built up after training on a sequence of pedestals and near−misses. Adapted from Winston (1973) with his permission.

FIGURE 8.14

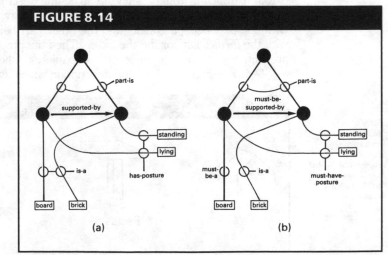

(a)   (b)

Our choice of a pedestal to illustrate this process of learning a structural model from examples was deliberate. The pedestal is like a three-dimensional letter T (see Fig. 8.10), and the structural description for a pedestal is very similar to that described for a T, except that the parts of the pedestal are themselves three-dimensional objects like a brick and a board, instead of the horizontal and vertical lines in the letter T. Thus, this kind of representation can be used for two-dimensional written characters, or three-dimensional objects.

To return to Winston's program, a process similar to that used for the pedestal can be used to derive a model for a house (Fig. 8.12). Here the eventual model would specify that a brick *must* support a wedge (the roof). As for the pedestal, both the support relations and the nature of the objects are quite tightly specified. However, in the case of an arch (Fig. 8.12) there is more flexibility. While the upright structures in the arch model *must* be bricks and *must not* touch each other, the structure which they support can be a brick, or a wedge, or maybe even any object at all. An arch is still an arch whatever the shape at the top.

Winston's program is here operating in the object domain. It can accept any projection of a brick or wedge and label these accordingly. However, the structural descriptions for brick and wedge must themselves be specified at a different level of the program. At an even lower level, the line drawing which serves as input must be parsed into separate objects using the procedures described in Chapter 6. The initial stages of the program make use of programs like Guzman's (see Chapter 6, p. 129) to group regions of the picture together.

The problems with Winston's system are buried within these low-level programs which furnish the descriptions on which the learning program operates. As we noted in Chapter 6, scene analysis programs of the kind developed by Guzman, Clowes and Waltz work by making use of the constraints inherent in the kinds of scene they describe. But the constraints of the mini-world of matt prismatic solids are not the constraints of the natural world. While something similar to Winston's learning program might provide a theory of visual object classification, we need a better way of furnishing structural descriptions for such procedures to operate on—one which is not restricted to an artificial world.

To do this, we must return to consider the fundamental problem of object recognition. To recap, the projection of an object's shape on the retina depends on the vantage point of the viewer. Thus, if we relied on a *viewer-centred* coordinate system for describing the object (one in the picture domain, to use Sutherland's terminology), descriptions would have to be stored for a great number of different vantage points. Minsky (1977) has in fact suggested that the linking together of a number of different views in the form of a *frame system* (see Chapter 7, p. 173) could provide the basis for recognition, and in the next chapter we will describe in some detail theories of recognition that involve the storage of discrete instances. However, if we can describe the object with reference to an *object-centred* coordinate system, (i.e. build a structural description in the "object" domain) then it would be possible to reduce the number of object models stored, ideally to only a single one per distinguishable object. This was what Winston attempted to do with an artificial world.

The problem is then to find a way of describing the object within its own coordinate system without confining the discussion to an artificial world, and/or using knowledge of an object-specific kind. If one has to rely on object-specific knowledge then we would have to know what an object was before we could recognise it—an obvious paradox. However, it seems likely that knowledge of *some* constraints is essential to parse objects—the question is, how specific are these?

MARR AND NISHIHARA'S THEORY OF OBJECT RECOGNITION

Marr and Nishihara (1978) outlined the foundations for one possible solution to this problem. An object must be described within a frame of reference which is based on the shape itself. To do this, we must be able to set up a canonical coordinate frame (a coordinate frame which is determined by the shape itself) for the shape before the shape has been described.

The appropriate set of descriptive elements (primitives) for describing a shape will depend in part on the level of detail that the shape description is to capture. The fingers of a human hand are not expressed in a system which uses primitives the size of arms and legs. To get around this problem, Marr and Nishihara suggest that we need a *modular* organisation of shape descriptions with different sized primitives used at different levels. This allows a description at a "high" level to be stable over changes in fine detail, but sensitivity to these changes to be available at other levels.

First we need to define an *axis* for the representation of a shape. Shapes which are elongated or have a natural axis of symmetry are easier to describe, and Marr and Nishihara restrict their discussion to the class of such objects which can be described as a set of one or more *generalised cones*. A generalised cone is the surface created by moving a cross-section of constant shape but variable size along an axis (see Fig. 8.15). The cross-section can get fatter or thinner provided that its shape is preserved. The class of generalised cones includes "geometric" forms like a pyramid or sphere, as well as natural forms like arms and legs (roughly). Objects whose shape is achieved by growth are often describable by one or more generalised cones, and so we can talk about object recognition in the natural world, rather than an artificial one. In the discussion which follows we will generally be talking about the recognition of shapes comprised of more than one generalised cone, so that there will be more than one axis in the

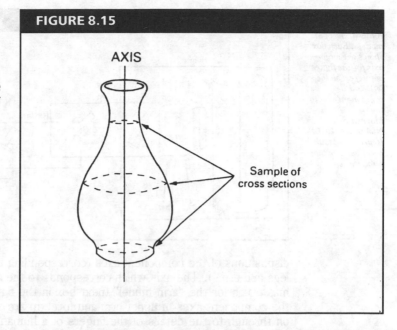

FIGURE 8.15

AXIS

Sample of
cross sections

One example of a generalised cone. The shape is created by moving a cross-section of constant shape but variable size along an axis.

representation. For example, a human figure can be described as a set of generalised cones corresponding to the trunk, head, arms and legs. Each of these component generalised cones has its own axis, and together these form the component axes for a representation of a human.

A description which uses axis-based primitives is like a stick figure. Stick figures capture the relative lengths and dispositions of the axes which form the components of the entire structure. The relative thicknesses of these components (e.g. the human trunk is thicker than a leg) could also be included in the representation, though for simplicity we will omit this detail here. Information captured by such a description might be very useful for recognition since stick figures are inherently modular. We can use a single stick to represent a whole leg, or three smaller sticks to represent the upper and lower limb segments and the foot. At a still finer level, we can capture the details of toes with a set of much smaller sticks. At each level of description we can construct a 3D model where each 3D model specifies:

1. A single model axis. This provides coarse information about the size and orientation of the overall shape described.
2. The arrangements and lengths of the major component axes.
3. Pointers to the 3D models for the shape components associated with these component axes.

This leads to a hierarchy of 3D models (illustrated in Fig. 8.16) each with its own coordinate system. The first "box" in Figure 8.16 shows the single model axis for a human body with the relative

FIGURE 8.16

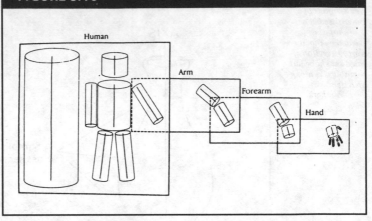

dispositions of the component axes (corresponding to head, body, legs and arms). The axis which corresponds to the arm forms the major axis for the "arm model" (next box in the figure), in which the component axes of upper arm and forearm are shown, and so on through to the details of the fingers of a human hand. Such a hierarchy of 3D models is called a 3D model description. Recognition is thought to be achieved when a match is established between a 3D model description derived from an image, and one of the stored catalogue of 3D model descriptions corresponding to known objects. These may in turn be organised hierarchically, in terms of the specificity of their descriptions (see Fig. 8.17). Thus a human figure can be matched to the general model for a biped, or the more specific model for a human. Ape and human are distinguished by the relative lengths of the component axes in the model description for a biped.

Now we need to address the question of how such 3D model descriptions can be derived *prior* to accessing the catalogue. We need to derive the axes from an image without knowing what object it is that the image represents. In fact it can be shown (Marr, 1977) that we can make use of the occluding contours of an image to find the axis of a generalised cone, provided the axis is not too foreshortened. The only assumption needed is that these contours come from a shape which is comprised of generalised cones.

We have already seen, in Chapter 6, how Marr's early visual processing program derives contour information from an image without knowing what shape it is looking for. Occluding contours in an image are those which show the silhouette of the object (see the outline of the head of the bear in Fig. 6.30, or the donkey in Fig. 8.20). As Marr points out, silhouettes are infinitely ambiguous, and yet we interpret them in a particular way:

Somewhere, buried in the perceptual machinery that can interpret silhouettes as three-dimensional shapes, there must lie some source

A catalogue of 3D
model descriptions
at different levels
of specificity.
Reproduced from
Marr and
Nishihara (1978)
with permission of
the publishers.

FIGURE 8.17

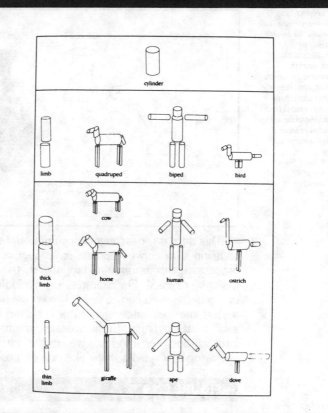

of additional information that constrains us to see silhouettes as we do. Probably . . . these constraints are general rather than particular and do not require a priori knowledge of the viewed shapes (Marr, 1982, p. 219).

Let us examine the assumptions which Marr suggests allow us to interpret silhouettes so consistently:

1. Each line of sight from the viewer to the object should graze the object's surface at exactly one point. Thus each point on a silhouette arises from one point on the surface being viewed. We can define the *contour generator* as the set of points on a surface that projects to the boundary of a silhouette (see Fig. 8.18).

2. Nearby points on the contour in an image arise from nearby points on the contour generator on the viewed object (see Fig. 8.19).

3. All the points on the contour generator lie in a single plane.

An object, its
silhouette and its
contour. The set of
points which
projects to the
contour (the
contour generator)
is shown. For this
figure, all three
assumptions (see
text) hold for all
distant viewing
positions in any
one plane.
Adapted from
Marr (1977) and
Marr (1982).

FIGURE 8.18

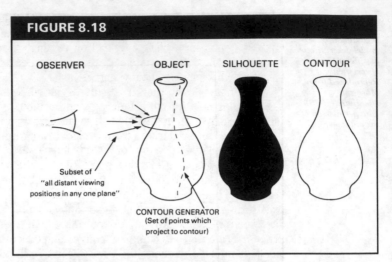

This third is the strongest assumption, but is necessary in order
to distinguish convex and concave segments in the interpetation
process. If this assumption is violated, then the wrong conclusion
might be reached. For example, the occluding contour in the image
of a cube, viewed corner on, is hexagonal (see Fig. 8.19). Because
we assume the contour generator is planar, we could interpret such
a silhouette wrongly. In the absence of any other information from
internal lines or motion, we might interpret the contour as
belonging to a spindle shape like one of those drawn, or simply as a

FIGURE 8.19

*A cube viewed
corner on gives
rise to the
silhouette and
contour shown.
The contour
generator
(a−b−c−d−e−f)
is not planar. This
silhouette might be
seen simply as a
hexagon, or
interpreted as one
of the spindle
shapes shown.*

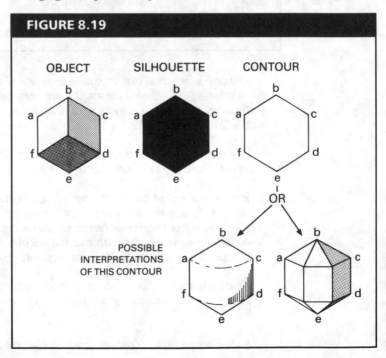

flat hexagon. In fact the points on the cube which gave rise to this contour do not lie in a single plane. It is this assumption of a planar contour generator which may lead us (wrongly!) to interpret the moving silhouette of someone's hands as the head of a duck, or an alligator, while playing shadow games.

Marr has shown that if a surface is smooth, and if these assumptions hold for all distant viewing positions in any one plane (see Fig. 8.18), then the viewed surface is a generalised cone. Thus shape can be derived from occluding contours *provided* the shape is a generalised cone, or a set of such cones. Vatan (cited by Marr, 1982) has written a program to derive the axes from such a contour. Figure 8.20 shows how his program derives the component axes from an image of a toy donkey. The initial outline was formed by aggregating descriptions from the raw primal sketch, in the same way as for the teddy bear's head (Chapter 6, p. 136). From this initial outline, convex and concave segments are labelled and used to divide the "donkey" into smaller sections. The axis is derived for each of these sections separately, and then these component axes are related together to form a "stick" represent-ation for the entire figure.

FIGURE 8.20

(a) An outline of a toy donkey. (b) Convex (+) and concave (−) sections are labelled. (c) Strong segmentation points are found. (d) The outline is divided into a set of smaller segments making use of the points found at (c) and rules for connecting these to other points on the contour. (e) The component axis is found for each segment. (f) The axes are related to one another (thin lines). Reproduced from Marr and Nishihara (1978) with permission of the publishers.

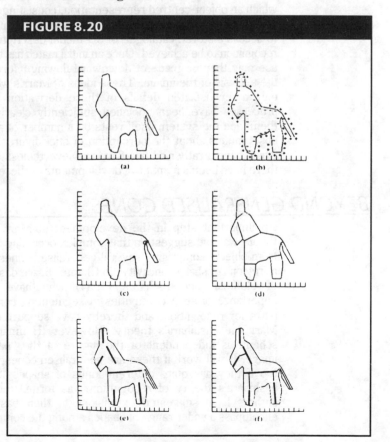

Now these axes derived from occluding contours are viewer-centred. They depend on the image which in turn depends on the vantage point. We must transform them to object-centred axes, and to do this we must make use of the *image-space processor*. The image-space processor operates on the viewer-centred axes and translates them to object-centred coordinates, so that the relationships between the different axes in the figure are specified in three, instead of two dimensions. Use may be made of information from stereopsis, texture and shading to achieve this, but it may also be necessary to use preliminary matches with stored 3D model descriptions to improve the analysis of the image. Thus, for recognition, Marr does envisage that there is a continuous interplay between the derivation of an object's description and the process of recognition itself:

> We view recognition as a gradual process that proceeds from the general to the specific and that overlaps with, guides, and constrains the derivation of a description from the image (p. 321).

In summary then, Marr and Nishihara outlined a scheme in which an object-centred representation, consisting of an axis-based structural description, could be established from an image and used to access a stored catalogue of 3D model descriptions in order for recognition to be achieved. Once an initial match has been established, use may then be made of downward-flowing information to refine the analysis of the image. These ideas of Marr's were speculative; only a few isolated details of these derivation and recognition processes have been specified sufficiently clearly to implement them; and the system itself rests on a number of assumptions and observations about the perception of stick figures and silhouettes which have a rather ad hoc flavour. Nevertheless, in recent years there have been a number of developments of these basic ideas.

BEYOND GENERALISED CONES

An important step in the development of Marr and Nishihara's theory was the suggestion that complex occluding contours formed from objects comprising several generalised cones are segmented at regions of sharp concavity. In Chapter 6, we described the work of Hoffman and Richards (1984) who have illustrated the importance of such concavities in segmenting contours to reveal parts for recognition, and thereby have supported one aspect of Marr and Nishihara's theory. However, Hoffman and Richards' scheme is independent of the nature of the "parts" within the image. It will work if these are generalised cones, but it will work too if they are quite different kinds of shapes. Since Marr and Nishihara's theory of recognition was formulated, a number of authors have suggested extensions to their basic approach, to encompass a wider range of shapes among the component parts.

FIGURE 8.21

A scene comprised
of superquadrics.
Reproduced from
Pentland (1987)
with permission.

For example, Pentland (1986a) has proposed a more flexible system of volumetric representation than can be achieved with generalised cones. Pentland suggests that most complex natural shapes are comprised of *superquadric* components and that these might be the basic components which we recover when analysing images of natural objects. Superquadrics include basic shapes such as spheres and wedges, and all kinds of deformations on these basic shapes which preserve their smoothly varying form and which do not introduce concavities. Figure 8.21 shows a scene constructed with superquadric components. While Pentland's theory is an interesting development for computer vision and graphics, as yet there has been no better evidence of the psychological validity of Pentland's scheme than there was for Marr and Nishihara's.

Biederman (1987) has also described complex objects as spatial arrangements of basic component parts. In Biederman's scheme, these parts come from a restricted set of basic shapes such as wedges and cylinders. Biederman calls these basic shape primitives "geons" (geometric ions), suggesting an analogy with words which are likewise constructed from combinations of basic primitives— phonemes. An occluding contour derived from an image of an object is segmented at regions of sharp concavity, and the resulting parts of the image are matched against representations of these primitive object shapes. The nature and arrangements of the geons found can then be matched with structural models of objects. The representation of each known object is a structural model of the components from which it is constructed, their relative sizes, orientations, place of attachment and so forth (see Fig. 8.22)

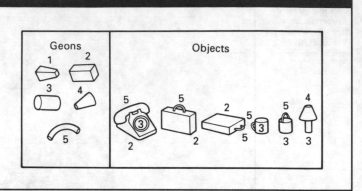

FIGURE 8.22

A selection of the volumetric primitives called "geons" (left hand panel) are used to specify objects in the right hand panel. The relations between the geons are important, as shown by the difference between a pail and a cup. Reproduced from Biederman (1987b) with permission.

A point of departure of Biederman's theory from Marr and Nishihara's is the suggestion that geons are defined by properties which are *invariant* over different views. According to this theory, it is not necessary to make use of occluding contours to recover an axis-based *three-dimensional* shape description. Instead, each different kind of geon has its own "key" features in the 2D primal sketch level representation. Biederman argues that there are a number of "non-accidental" properties of edges in images which can be used as reliable cues to related properties of edges in the world (cf. Kanade, 1981). The "non-accidental" principle is an assumption that when a certain regularity is present in an image, this is assumed to reflect a true regularity in the world, rather than an "accidental" consequence of a particular viewpoint. Take the example of a straight line in an image. This will usually result from an extended straight edge in the world, although it *could* result from other "accidental" consequences of viewpoint; for example, a bicycle wheel viewed end-on will give rise to a straight line image, even though it is a curved surface. The non-accidental assumption would lead to the wrong answer in this case, but will usually be correct. It leads us to assumptions such as that curved lines in images result from curved edges in the world, parallel edges in an image derive from parallel edges in the world; symmetry in the image signals symmetry in the world, and so forth. Non-accidental properties include collinearity, curvilinearity, symmetry, parallelism and co-termination (see Fig. 8.23).

A geon is identified by a particular set of defining features (such as parallel edges) which can be accessed via these non-accidental properties. Biederman suggests that the assumption of non-accidental properties could explain a number of illusions such as the Ames chair, and "impossible" objects, where, for example, the co-termination assumption is violated. Again, Biederman provides no specific evidence for the psychological validity of his particular representational scheme, though he does provide further evidence for the importance of concavities in defining the part structures of objects (cf. Hoffman & Richards, 1984).

Non—accidental
differences
between a brick
and a cylinder.
Reproduced from
Biederman
(1987a) with
permission.

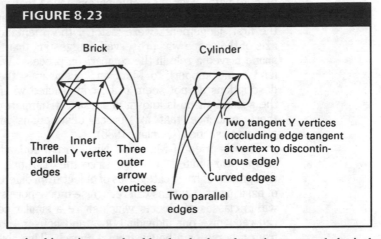

FIGURE 8.23

At this point we should ask whether there is any psychological evidence which can be brought to bear on the question of how objects are represented for recognition. The theories of object recognition we have discussed here emphasise the recognition of objects irrespective of viewpoint. In fact, there is evidence that not all views of objects are equally easy to recognise. Palmer, Rosch and Chase (1981) described how each of the different objects they examined appears to have a "canonical" viewpoint, which is often, though not always, something like a three-quarters view. People asked to imagine such objects report imaging them in their canonical views, and people asked which view they would choose to photograph, or which view of an object is "best," select canonical views. Importantly, Palmer et al. also found that these canonical views could be named more quickly than other views suggesting that such views play a privileged role in object recognition.

The advantage of canonical viewpoint could quite easily be accommodated by the theories above, even though these stress the recognition of objects independent of viewpoint. Marr and Nishihara (1978) emphasise that certain viewpoints will conceal important major axes which are needed to derive a shape description. For example, a top view of a bucket conceals the axis of elongation which is probably crucial to its description. For Biederman, certain views may conceal the non-accidental properties which define the "geons", and other views may better reveal them. It is thus not critical for "view-independent" models of object recognition that certain aspects of the process may be view-dependent. Indeed, a careful analysis of the content of canonical views, in terms of axes revealed or non-accidental properties, might be used as one route to assessing the psychological plausibility of these schemes.

The psychological validity of axis-based representations has already been investigated by other methods. For example, Humphreys (1984) asked subjects to decide whether or not two presented objects were the same shape (both elongated triangles or both parallelograms). Humphreys found that when subjects did not know exactly where the second shape would appear relative to the first, judgements were faster if the orientations of the major axis of the shape was preserved, suggesting that this aspect of the shape played a role in the comparison process. While such results lend some support to Marr and Nishihara's theory, axis-based descriptions do not seem to be constructed when the position of the second shape is known in advance (Humphreys, 1984), nor is there evidence that axis-based descriptions are used for all elongated shapes (Quinlan, 1988).

The theories of Marr and Nishihara, Pentland and Biederman also appear limited in scope, since they can only account for the recognition of basic categories of object from different configurations of basic parts. Humans can recognise much more subtle distinctions within classes of objects which share a similar configuration. We can recognise our individual dogs and houses, not just tell a dog from a horse or a house from a church. This ability to recognise objects from within a basic object category is not readily accommodated by any of the theories we have discussed thus far. It is at its most developed when we come to consider recognition of the human face.

Human faces must all be similar in overall configuration because of the other functions they subserve. Individual identity must be stamped upon this basic configuration, and, as we discuss at length in Chapter 16, there is now good evidence that faces are processed as "configurations" rather than as sets of independent features (e.g. Young, Hellawell & Hay, 1987). As yet we have no very good idea of the basic form of the representation used to tell one individual face from another. Psychologists and computer scientists alike have tended to view the problem of face recognition as one of *pattern* recognition, with structural descriptions for faces constructed from measurements made direct from the picture plane (see Bruce & Burton, 1989, for a review). However, faces are not flat patterns but are bumpy surfaces which we view from a range of different angles. Indeed, unfamiliar faces may be recognised and matched more readily in 3/4 views than in full face (e.g. Bruce, Valentine & Baddeley, 1987), a result which would not be expected if full face pictorial metrics formed the basis of face perception and recognition. Although Pentland (1986a) has considered faces to be comprised of a set of superquadric components, another possibility, discussed by Bruce (1988) is that *surface-based* rather than volumetric representations may play a role in face recognition. A rather different way of thinking about the problems of face recognition, which we elaborate in the following chapter, may arise from recent attempts to automate face recognition without involving the explicit construction of abstract symbolic descriptions at all.

A further class of objects which are not readily characterised in the simple, part-based way envisaged by Marr and Nishihara, Biederman and others include naturally rough, crumpled or

FIGURE 8.24

Examples of fractal patterns derived from different "generators" (left column) whose fractal dimension varies from 1.12 to 1.75. The patterns generated along the rows vary in terms of their depth of recursion—the extent to which the generation process is repeated at different scale. Reproduced from Cutting and Garvin (1987) with permission.

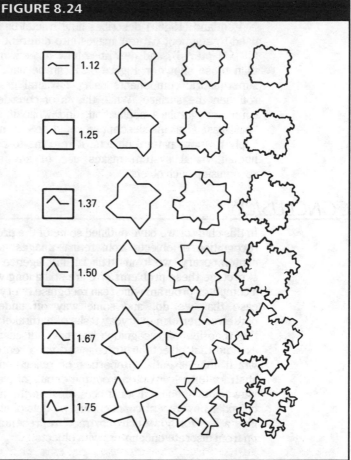

branching objects such as trees and clouds, and many textures such as rocky or sandy terrain. Some such "rough" patterns can be described as having a *fractal* structure (Mandelbrot, 1982). Fractals are patterns which have a fractional dimensionality. For example, a plane is two-dimensional while a cube is three-dimensional. A fractal pattern of dimension 2.1 would be almost smooth, like a plane, but with a slightly bumpy surface. As the fractal dimension increased towards 3, the surface would become increasingly craggy. Fractal patterns also have a recursive structure —they look the same at different scales. Figure 8.24 shows some examples of fractal patterns. Pentland (1986b) showed that human perception of the "roughness" of a surface was highly correlated with its fractal dimension as this ranged between 2 and 3 in the way described above, but did not compare the predictive power of fractal statistics with that of any other variable. Cutting and Garvin (1987) showed that ratings of the complexity of patterns like those shown in Figure 8.24 are well predicted by their fractal pattern statistics, but also found that other variables such as the number of sides, were equally good predictors of perceived complexity.

Pentland (1986b) describes how fractal-based methods can be used to segment natural images into different regions and objects (cf. Chapter 6), and describes how objects more natural-looking than those shown in Figure 8.21 can be built by adding together superquadric components using a fractal generation process to roughen the surface. While this is of considerable interest as a computer graphics application, and while it shows how a basic "part-based" shape description could be extended so that it could apply to more natural objects, it remains to be seen whether the human visual system makes use of any such system when recognising such objects.

CONCLUSION

In this chapter we have outlined some of the problems posed by the recognition of objects from retinal images, and have seen how contemporary work in artificial intelligence has attempted to overcome these problems. We are still a long way from developing a computer program which can recognise everyday objects with the ease that we do, and some way off understanding how we ourselves perform everyday tasks of natural object recognition. All the theories of recognition we have discussed in this chapter assume that objects are recognised via a representational level in which the essential properties of objects are stored in quite abstract form—divorced from the details of particular instances or viewpoints seen on distinct occasions. In the next chapter, we will consider how recent connectionist models of object recognition can give a feel for how such "abstract" representations might be built up from discrete encounters with objects.

Chapter Nine

CONNECTIONIST MODELS OF VISUAL PERCEPTION

Marr's theory of vision, which has provided a unifying framework for this section of the book, sees visual perception as involving the construction and manipulation of abstract symbolic descriptions of the viewed scene. In these terms, for example, an edge-detecting algorithm applied to a retinal image results in a *description* which is rather like a set of sentences describing which edge features are where in the image. In the brain, of course, there can be no such "sentences", but rather there are neurons, or collections of neurons, that are more or less active depending on the inputs they receive from other neurons. In recent years there has been increased interest in building neuron-like models of visual perception (and other sensory and cognitive processes) in which representations of the world are expressed in terms of activities in neuron-like units, rather than in terms of the construction and storage of abstract strings of symbols.

Such "connectionist" models have several apparent advantages over the conventional "symbol processing" model. First, they appear to be more biologically plausible (though, as we will see, some of this apparent plausibility is spurious). They also provide a relatively easy way to think about *parallel* computations which can be particularly convenient when a number of different constraints need to be satisfied simultaneously. Connectionist models additionally provide an interesting way of simulating how a system could *learn* to recognise certain categories from a collection of exemplars. This is not unknown in conventional models (e.g. Winston's work, discussed in Chapter 8) but becomes an important central feature of many connectionist models where learning occurs through weight adjustment—the reinforcement of certain excitatory or inhibitory "connections" between the neuron-like units and the weakening of others. Finally, a certain class of connectionist models have the additional property of "distributed" processing. In such models, there is no one-to-one correspondence between a "unit" and a "concept" as there is in more "localist" connection schemes (e.g. Feldman, 1985). Rather, a particular concept is represented in terms of a pattern of activity over a large set of simple units, and different patterns of activity in those same units represent different concepts. Such PDP (parallel distributed processing) versions of connectionist models have some attractive characteristics when applied to pattern and object classification, as we will see later in this chapter.

In this chapter, we introduce connectionist models of three main kinds in order to explore their potential for models of visual processing. First, we show how such models can provide a convenient means of satisfying constraints simultaneously. Secondly, we show how they can provide a way of *mapping* between different coordinate systems (e.g. retinal, scene-based, object-based). Thirdly, we examine pattern learning in connectionist models, and in particular we explore the potential of parallel distributed processing accounts of object and pattern recognition. We cannot attempt an exhaustive review of this rapidly expanding area. Rather, we aim to introduce the different topics with one or two examples, and the interested reader should consult Ballard, Hinton and Sejnowski (1983), McClelland and Rumelhart (1986), Rumelhart and McClelland (1986), and Morris (1989) for further details and examples.

SATISFYING CONSTRAINTS—MARR AND POGGIO'S (1976) ALGORITHM

Connectionist models provide a particularly effective way to implement an algorithm which has to satisfy many different constraints at once, and we start by introducing connectionist models with a description of their application to stereopsis. Recall from Chapter 7 that Marr and Poggio (1976) suggested that the correspondence problem in random-dot stereograms could be solved through the application of three matching rules which embody constraints of the physical world. Matches must be compatible (black dots with black dots and white with white), unique (a single match for each dot) and continuous (constant disparity values should be maintained).

The algorithm can be embodied in a competitive neural network where there is a unit for each possible disparity between a feature in one eye's view and another feature in the other eye's view (see Fig. 9.1). Thus each unit in the network *represents* a surface feature or patch at a particular depth. Each excited unit can in turn excite or inhibit the activity of other units, and have its own activity increased or decreased in turn by the excitation and inhibition it receives from other units. Marr and Poggio (1976) showed how the matching constraints could be satisfied in the patterns of excitation and inhibition in such a network. First, the compatibility constraint means that a unit will only be active initially if it is excited by similar features from both eyes' inputs (e.g. both must be black dots or both white dots in Fig. 9.1). Secondly, the uniqueness constraint is embodied by inhibition passing between units that fall along the same line of sight i.e. units which would represent *different* disparities for the *same* features inhibit one another. Finally, the continuity constraint is embodied by having excitation pass between units that represent *different* features at the *same* disparities. Thus unique matches that preserve areas of the same disparities are encouraged. Marr and Poggio showed that a simulation of such a network "solved" random dot stereograms. For example, if the network was presented with two patterns of random dots, corresponding to the two halves of a random dot stereogram in which human vision would see a central square at a different depth from its background, the pattern of excitation of the network gradually settled down to a state where adjacent units in a square-shaped region were active at a disparity distinct from that associated with units activated by dots from the background.

Although Marr and Poggio's is a parallel algorithm it was implemented in a serial computer by serial examination of the activity levels of each unit within a number of "rounds" or "iterations" of activity. In each iteration, the amount of excitation or activities present at the end of the previous iteration, and its

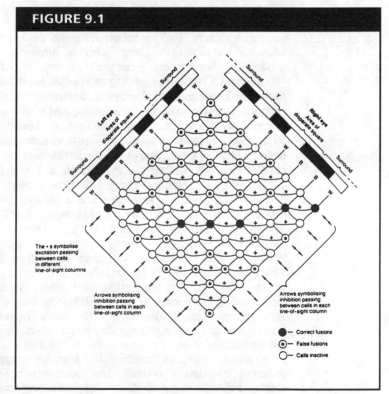

FIGURE 9.1

A small slice of a network for solving the correspondence problem in random–dot stereograms in the manner proposed by Marr and Poggio (1976). Black spots have been placed at nodes which are activated by the same features from both eye's inputs. Bigger black spots mark the nodes whose activation levels are greatest after excitation has passed between nodes representing the same disparity and inhibition has passed down lines of sight. Reproduced with permission from Seeing: Mind, Brain and Illusion by J.P. Frisby. Published by Oxford University Press 1979.

new activity computed. At the end of that iteration, new activity levels for all the units can be used to compute the amount of excitation and inhibition received by each unit in the next round. These iterations continue until the system reaches a steady state, i.e. one where there is no change in the pattern or amount of activity from one round to the next.

This type of parallel algorithm is finding increasing application in a range of applied visual processing tasks where a number of constraints must be satisfied. Other examples can be found in recent work on such topics as optic flow analysis and shape from shading, and in work on the satisfaction of constraints from multiple sources (e.g. Terzopoulos, 1986).

MAPPING BETWEEN COORDINATE SYSTEMS

In earlier chapters we have discussed how successive stages of visual perception might require that descriptions be built within different coordinate systems. Thus Marr (1982) argued that the primal sketch and 2½D sketch were based on retinocentric coordinates while the 3D models were based on object-centred coordinates. Connectionist models can provide a means of mapping between different coordinate systems.

For example, Hinton (1981) presented an early example of how a connectionist architecture could be used to recognise a letter irrespective of its tilt, by implementing a mapping from a particular view of a pattern, to a viewpoint-independent description, without knowing the identity of the letter in advance. This could be achieved by setting up a network of simple units, with some, "retina-based" units responding to specific local features falling at particular locations and orientations, and other "object-based" units responding to features oriented and located with respect to a frame centred on the letter rather than on the viewer (see Fig. 9.2). Activation within the retina-based units in turn excites the object-based units, but the degree of excitation will be modified by a separate set of "mapping units" which add in a bias towards a particular frame. Hinton suggests that there might normally be a bias towards a vertical reference frame, since, in the absence of other information, we would tend to recognise an "I" rather than an "H" from the same features (see Fig. 9.2). Hinton's system can be extended to recognise patterns when the mapping rules are not known in advance, because of inbuilt biases from the letter level which give more weight to combinations of features which define letters irrespective of orientation. Such biases can result in a letter being recognised even if oriented horizontally. Within such a scheme, an object's identity and the frame of reference for its description are recovered simultaneously through the converging pattern of activation.

A more ambitious attempt to describe mappings between different coordinate systems has been produced by Feldman (1985). Feldman suggests that visual processing involves establish-

FIGURE 9.2

A network for mapping from retina—based to letter—based units. Reproduced from Hinton (1981) with permission.

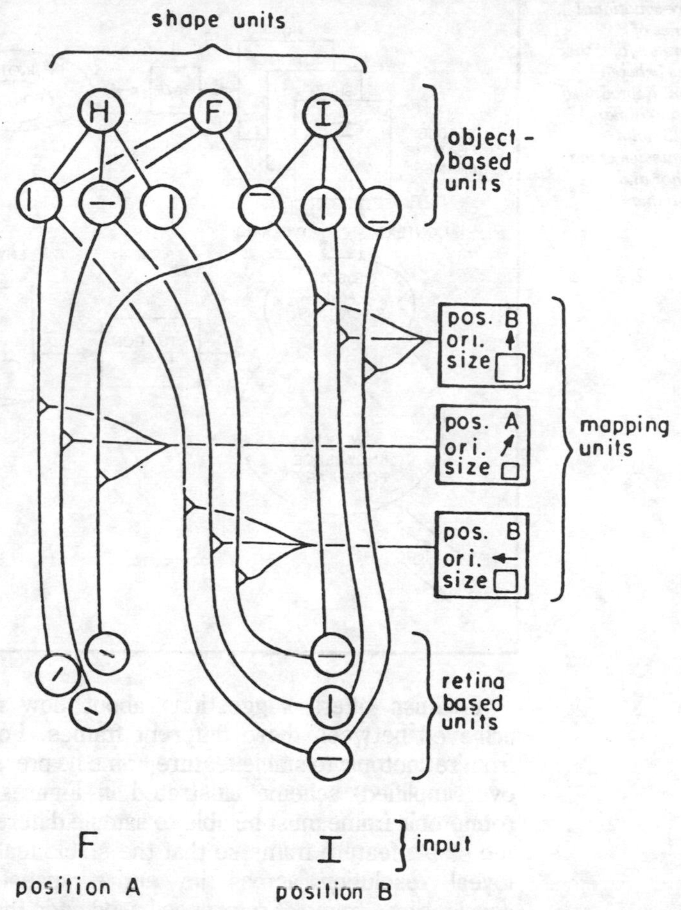

ing representations in four different "frames" of reference—the retinotopic frame, the "stable feature" or head-based frame, the environmental frame and the "world knowledge formulary" (see Fig. 9.3). The retinotopic frame finds edges, and computes disparity and motion within a retinally based coordinate system. As such, this frame resembles Marr's "2½D sketch" level. The stable feature frame encodes visual features in a way which is stable across fixations (unlike the retinotopic frame) and thus provides one means of integrating across different fixations (see Chapter 7). Features described in the stable feature frame are then used to address "world knowledge" where objects are represented in terms of their "appearance possibilities" (i.e. in viewpoint dependent rather than view-independent form). The environmental frame maintains a representation of where the recognised objects are located in the space around the viewer.

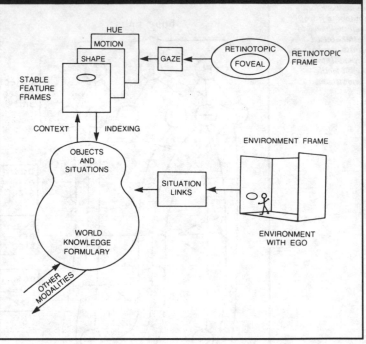

*Four
representational
frames of
reference, and the
links between
them. Reproduced
from Feldman
(1985) with
permission of the
author and
publishers.*

Feldman offers suggestions about how mappings could be achieved between these different frames. For example, to map from retinotopic to stable feature frame he presents the (deliberately oversimplified) scheme illustrated in Figures 9.4 and 9.5. The retinotopic frame must be able to sample different spatial regions of the stable feature frame so that the stable feature frame can have foveal resolution across its entire spatial extent. That is, considering a frame of reference based upon the head, the eyes can move so that different regions of this space are brought within the high resolution area of the retina. Knowledge of the current direction of gaze is needed to make the mapping between the retinotopic frame and appropriate coordinates within the stable feature frame. So, in Figure 9.4, retinal coordinate 64 maps to ("excites") stable feature frame coordinates 6,5 if gaze direction is 8,8; while retinal coordinate 65 maps to the same stable feature frame position if gaze is 7,8. (Fig. 9.4 shows only a portion of the retinotopic frame. The entire retinotopic frame is seen in Fig. 9.5 which shows how the frame is assumed to have a logarithmic coordinate structure in which fine spatial discriminations are possible in the fovea and increasingly coarse ones towards the periphery.)

Feldman suggests that the stable feature frame actually comprises a set of head-based spatial representations which separately describe the depths, motions, hues and so forth in the

FIGURE 9.4

Retinotopic coordinates map to different stable feature frame coordinates depending on the direction of gaze. Reproduced from Feldman (1985) with permission of the author and publishers.

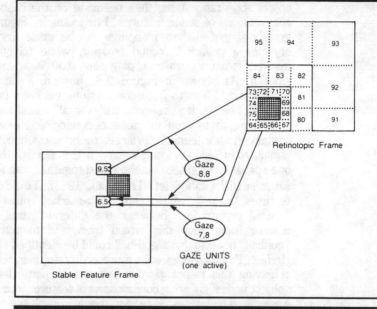

FIGURE 9.5

The logarithmic resolution of the retinotopic frame shown superimposed on the different representational components of the stable feature frame. Reproduced from Feldman (1985) with permission of the author and publishers.

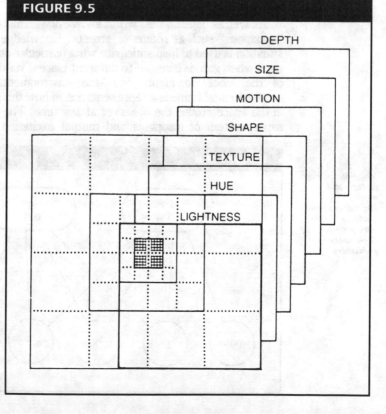

current visual scene (see Fig. 9.5). Mappings from the stable feature frame to the world knowledge formulary (catalogue of object appearances) can thus be made on the basis of particular combinations of stable features. For example, Figure 9.6 shows, greatly simplified, how mappings can be made from features to objects—a golfball is round (shape), white (colour) and pock-marked (texture) while a ping-pong ball is round, white and smooth. As shown in Figure 9.6, however, such an indexing scheme could lead to false conjunctions between the features of different objects. If a ping-pong ball is small, round and white, there is nothing to to stop its node becoming active when a scene contains both a tennis ball (large, round and white) and a marble (small, round and smooth). Clearly it is important that features at one spatial location are somehow tied together with features at the same spatial location (cf. Treisman, 1988). To achieve this, the features "round" "white" and "pock-marked" must be located in "spatial registration" between the different maps in the stable feature frame, and this would then lead to activation of the "golfball" node so that a golf-ball could be identified at this position. (In fact, Feldman suggests a more elaborate, hierarchical means of achieving this mapping from features at particular locations to "object nodes" by using conjunctions of features as an intermediate mapping. The interested reader should consult his paper for more details.)

As well as objects, the "world knowledge formulary" represents "situations" such as rooms or streets. Knowledge of the current situation is used to help anticipate what particular objects should be seen when gaze is directed to different places, via the fourth frame of the model in Figure 9.3—the environmental frame. The environmental frame is a representation of how things are arranged in the space around the observer at any time. The idea is that the same system of mappings and mutual excitation can lead to a

FIGURE 9.6

Mappings between features and objects. Reproduced from Feldman (1985) with permission of the author and publishers.

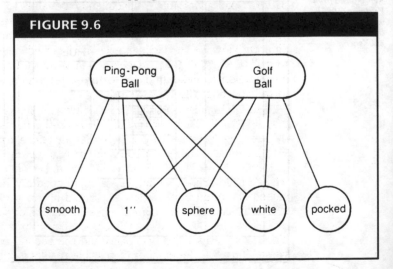

particular object or building to be expected (or "primed") when an observer's gaze is directed to a known location within a known situation.

Feldman's (1985) framework provides a general idea of how a connectionist model could be developed to build descriptions of objects within different coordinate systems. However, it should be noted that this model still begs all the questions about the basic "primitives" needed to compute disparity or represent objects, questions which are tackled more adequately at the "computational theory" level addressed by Marr. Nor does Feldman address in any detail the question of how these mappings were learned initially. In the next section we consider connectionist models which are directly concerned with the process of learning to recognise patterns.

LEARNING TO RECOGNISE PATTERNS

The networks described in the last section produce mappings between view-specific representations of objects and explicit representations of the defining characteristics of objects that might be view-independent. Neural networks have also attracted considerable attention for their apparent abilities to learn these "defining" or prototypical characteristics of objects from collections of instances, without apparently constructing any explicit representation of the defining characteristics themselves.

WISARD (Wilkie, Aleksander and Stonham's Recognition Device; e.g. Aleksander, 1983; Stonham, 1986) is a general-purpose pattern classifier constructed to model a neural network (though it is in fact implemented rather differently.) In WISARD there is no notion of "reference frame" or "features" at all. The WISARD system demonstrates how a network which stores the responses to a large number of different instances of different pattern exemplars may subsequently be able to classify novel patterns correctly. For example, Stonham (1986) describes how a WISARD system which had been trained on a large number of different views of the faces of each of 15 individuals, was then able to decide which of the 15 faces was shown, without any apparent computation or description of features, reference frames, and so forth. How does the system work?

WISARD takes as its input a large array of pixels, each of which may be either "black" or "white". This pixel array is then sampled by selecting "n-tuples" of pixels so that the entire array is sampled. For example, if there is a 100 x 50 array of pixels (5000 in total), and n=2, then 2500 pixel pairs will need to be taken to sample the whole image. Pixels within each n-tuple need not be adjacent and indeed are often quite widely separated in the pattern. When an n-tuple is sampled, there are 2^n possible results of sampling. When n=2, there are $2^2 = 4$ possibilities: the pair of pixels may be both black, both white, the first black and the second white, and vice versa. If $n = 3$, the number of possible results is $2^3 = 8$. Because of the statistical similarity between different exemplars of the same class, if a number of exemplars of the same pattern were sampled with the same n-tuples, some outcomes would never occur and others would often occur.

For example, consider the pattern "T" shown in Figure 9.7. If pixel triplets "a" and "b" shown in the figure were among those used to sample this pattern, then imagine what would happen to the results obtained from sampling as different example "T"s were shown. For triplet "a", the three pixels would never all be black if a T was shown; for triplet "b" the pixels will never show more than one black. Now if the same pixels were used instead to sample exemplars of a different pattern, the letter "O" (Fig. 9.7), a rather different pattern of outcomes would be obtained. Now triplet "b"

FIGURE 9.7

Pixel triplet (a) would never all be black if a T were shown, but could all be black if an O were shown. Pixel triplet (b) would never find more than one black pixel if a T is shown but could if an O was shown. Reproduced from Humphreys and Bruce (1989) with permission.

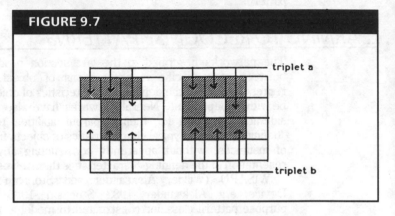

for example, could find three black pixels. WISARD learns different pattern categories by being exposed to many exemplars of each, and storing the results of the pixel sampling process on each occasion. It thereby builds up a representation of the responses obtained when sampling T's and another of the responses obtained when sampling O's. After training, an unknown pattern may be presented and categorised (as either a T or an O), by seeing whether the response obtained from the same sampling process more closely resembles those stored for T's or O's. Exactly the same principles are used to recognise faces as those described here for letters, but a very large array size is used, and a very large number of instances of each face are sampled in training. At no stage are facial "features" (eyes, lips, etc.) found and measured, or configural relationships between different features determined.

The WISARD system lends itself to a number of applications where, say, industrial parts must be recognised for sorting purposes. In such applications it is possible to ensure that lighting conditions and background surfaces remain the same. A WISARD trained to recognise objects placed against a white background would have problems if the background at test was dark, because the "features" sampled are raw pixel values. There are a number of further limitations to WISARD's powers to generalise to novel views not encountered during training, and these limitations are not characteristic of human vision. WISARD is an interesting and powerful pattern classifier, but it is not a good model of human object recognition processes.

Nevertheless, WISARD illustrates that much can be achieved by virtue of brute force, in the form of massive memory, but ignorance of any abstract defining characteristics of objects. In its current implementation, however, the WISARD system does not depart radically from current conceptions of memory as highly *localised*, since each category that WISARD learns has its own portion of memory assigned to it.

Recognising Patterns in a PDP Network

Of considerable recent interest is related work on *distributed* memory networks (Hinton & Anderson, 1981; McClelland & Rumelhart, 1985, 1986; Rumelhart & McClelland, 1986). In such networks, an object category is represented by a pattern of activity across a number of elementary processing units, each of which might, for example, represent a different "feature" in the image. The difference between this scheme and one like Feldman's (see earlier) is that these different "feature" units never activate a discrete "object" node—rather, the object is represented as nothing but a pattern of activity across the more elementary nodes. Successive instances of the same or different categories can be encoded over the *same* set of elementary processing units. This can be achieved if the weights on the connections between units are suitably adjusted, and the particular models differ in the way in which this is achieved.

One class of model makes use of what has been termed a "Hebbian" learning rule (after a suggestion made by Donald Hebb in 1949) to reinforce certain connections at the expense of others. An example is provided by Kohonen's matrix memory model (e.g. Kohonen, Oja & Lehtiö, 1981) of pattern association. In this model (see Fig. 9.8) there is a set of input units which are excited by a stimulus, and a set of output units that respond to these input patterns. All input units have connections to each output unit. The task of such a network is to learn to make distinct responses to each of a number of different patterns. This can be achieved if the weights between each input unit and each output unit are adjusted appropriately (to become either more excitatory or more inhibitory) to reinforce connections that produce the desired responses to certain inputs. A simple Hebbian learning rule adjusts the weights on the connection between each input and output unit in proportion to the product of the *input* activity to that unit multiplied by its desired *output* activity. The desired output activity is given by presenting a "forcing stimulus" to the output units along with the input patterns. The network's task is to learn to recreate the different forcing stimulus patterns when later presented with input patterns alone. This completely *local* learning rule (which adjusts

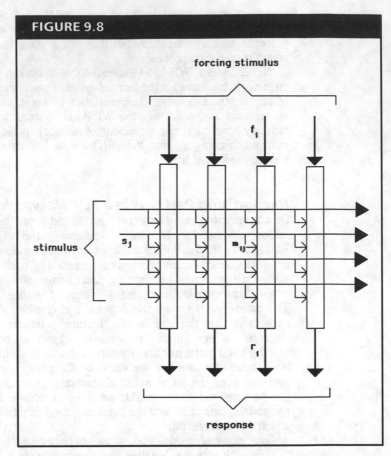

FIGURE 9.8

A set of four input units which encode the stimulus pattern s_j connect to a set of four response units which produce the response pattern r_i according to the matrix of weights (m_{ij}) set on the connections between each input unit and each output unit. These weights are set by associating the stimulus patterns with "forcing stimuli" f_i using a Hebbian learning rule. Adapted from Kohonen et al. (1981).

connection weights without taking account of activation anywhere else in the network) can fix the weights so that such a network can perfectly discriminate different input patterns provided these are "orthogonal" (orthogonality is a mathematical property related to linear independence). Even where patterns are not orthogonal, Kohonen has shown that there is a mathematical approximative technique for fixing the weights on the connections which can allow such a network to learn different responses to different patterns. This technique is known as *optimal linear associative mapping* and details can be found in Kohonen et al. (1981).

To demonstrate the performance and properties of such a network, Kohonen et al. presented such a network with different views of each of ten different faces. Each face was represented as a matrix of pixel intensity values, but this 2-dimensional matrix was strung out into a single row to provide a one-dimensional input pattern of intensity values which could be any one of 8 levels of grey. Views of the first face were associated with one response pattern (i.e. a "name" for that face), views of the second face were associated with a second response pattern and so forth. The network was then tested with novel views of these same ten individuals which were within the range of training views but slightly different from any that had been seen. The responses given to these novel views were much more like the correct names for each face than they were like any of the other names. The important point here is that the faces themselves were not represented anywhere within the network. Learning consisted of adjusting the weights on connections so that the correct responses were given to test patterns in the future, and a single set of weights thereby encoded all faces.

In that example, each face was associated with a response pattern roughly analagous to a name. However, such networks can also function as "autoassociators" so that each face (or any other input pattern) can be associated with itself (i.e. the forcing stimulus pattern equals the input stimulus pattern). The result of such autoassociative learning is that, given a future input of only part of the stimulus pattern or a noisy version of the stimulus, the "intact" stimulus output pattern will be re-created, and Kohonen et al. (1981) also illustrate this performance using pictures of faces.

A rather different rule is used to adjust the weights in single-layer nets of the type described by McClelland and Rumelhart (1985), whose network functions in an *autoassociative* fashion. Consider a simple processing module comprising an (artificially) small number of processing units (see Fig. 9.9). Each unit in the network is connected to each other unit. Additionally, there is an input to each unit from the stimulus pattern, and an output or

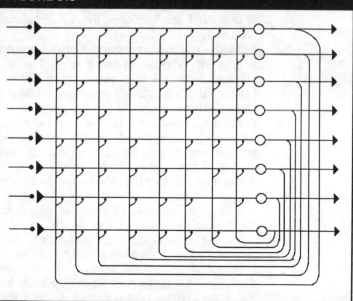

FIGURE 9.9

A set of eight processing units which receive external inputs (from stimulus patterns) and internal inputs, from all other processing units. Connections between the units have weights which are set using the delta rule, so that after learning a partial input pattern will tend to recreate the pattern of activation created by the whole input pattern. Adapted from McClelland and Rumelhart (1985).

"response" from each unit. Each unit has a "resting" activation level of 0, and non-resting activations can range from -1 to $+1$. When a pattern is presented to the network (i.e. one of a set of values ranging between -1 and $+1$ is input), each unit calculates its net input which is the sum of its external input and the inputs it receives from all other units. The input from each other unit equals that unit's activity multiplied by the weight on the connection between that unit and the one whose net input is being calculated. As in all the models we have considered, connections can be positive (excitatory) or negative (inhibitory). When the net input to a unit has been calculated, its activity is updated—positively if its net input is positive and negatively if its net input is negative, though a decay factor also operates to counteract this trend by sending activities back towards zero. The altered activity of the unit will in turn affect the activities of other units in the net and so the network is initially in a fluctuating state. Eventually, however, a network will settle into a state where the activities on the units remain stable from one iteration (cycle of activity summation) to the next.

After this steady state has been reached, the weights on the connections between the units are changed in a direction so that subsequent inputs of part of this stimulus pattern will tend to recreate the entire stimulus pattern. This is done by fixing the *internal* weights to each unit so that the total internal input equals the *external* input from the stimulus pattern. The result is that when the external input to that particular unit is missing (as it might be if a partial pattern was presented) the unit behaves as though it were present. To do this each unit calculates the difference Δ ("delta") between its internal and external input, and the weight change from another unit to this one is proportional to the activity of that other unit multiplied by Δ. This learning rule is called the "delta rule".

McClelland and Rumelhart (1985) have shown how, in principle, a network exposed to patterns of features corresponding to different instances of a category could both retain distinctions between the two different instances, while also learning the more general characteristics of the category from such examples. The patterns they use are simply sequences of $+1$s and -1s. If one of these patterns is called "Rover" and the other "Lassie", the problem is whether a network can learn the general characteristics of "dogs" from the examples, while at the same time retaining distinctions between the identities of the two "dogs" it has learned.

They illustrate their system by describing a simple module of just 24 processing units. One set of units is dedicated to encoding the "object" patterns, another set to the names. For example, to mimic the learning of "dog" prototypes, the first 16 units were given variations on a basic prototype pattern of $+$ and -1s. This prototype pattern was supposed to represent what is common to all dogs, while each presented instance actually learned by the network was some distortion of this basic pattern which was itself never seen. The remaining 8 units were given different (uncorrelated) patterns supposedly corresponding to the name of each of the different dogs that were learned. When later tested with a part of the prototype dog pattern (e.g. the first eight units) it will complete the prototype, i.e. its responses across the remaining eight units will tend to match the pattern for the rest of the prototype.

McClelland and Rumelhart go on to show how, in principle, the same network could learn *different* prototypes. In the example they choose, the network learns some patterns which are distortions around a hypothetical "dog" prototype, other patterns which are distortions around a "cat" prototype and a third set of patterns which are distortions around a "bagel" prototype. The dog and the cat pattern prototypes are not completely independent of each other (dogs and cats have some visual characteristics in common) while the bagel pattern prototype is completely independent (orthogonal) to that of the dog and the cat. As in the earlier example, the first 16 units were devoted to encoding these object patterns, while the last 8 units encoded patterns corresponding to the object labels—"dog", "cat" and "bagel". The pattern for each category name was orthogonal to each of the other two, to reflect the fact that while dog and cat visual shapes may be related, their names are not. After training on a series of hypothetical dog, cat and bagel instances produced from distortions on the dog, cat and bagel prototypes, the network can be tested by presenting each of the category prototypical visual patterns (the first 16 units) or names (last 8 units). The results obtained from such a simulation are shown in Table 9.1, where we see that presenting the pattern or name of each category leads to completion of the appropriate *pattern* of activation in the remaining units, though at decreased strength.

A network of this kind cannot only extract the general characteristics of the different categories to which it is exposed ("Lassie", "Rover", "dog") but it retains sensitivity to the patterns corresponding to particular recent or repeated instances. It will respond strongly to complete the "prototypical" Lassie, but will also respond more strongly to complete a recently or repeatedly encountered view of Lassie than to a novel or less recent view.

This ability both to extract the defining characteristics of concepts, and to retain details of particular instances of them, is a characteristic of human recognition. Most of the object recognition research we discussed in Chapter 8 concentrated on the problem of how we recognise that an object is, say, a dog, irrespective of its viewpoint. However, people do not just classify the instances of objects they recognise, they can also retain their individuating aspects in memory. For example, in repetition priming experiments, subjects are able to recognise a particular known object at a lower tachistoscopic exposure if that object has been recently seen (Warren & Morton, 1982). Although one view of an object will prime a quite different view, greatest priming is observed when an identical view of an object is repeated in the test phase (for related

TABLE 9.1

Pattern Recognition by a PDP network.

	Visual pattern	Name pattern
Prototype Dog:	+ − + + − − − − + + + + + − − −	+ − + − + − + −
Response to dog name:	+3−4+4+4−4−4−4−4+4+4+4+4+3+4−4−4−3	
Response to dog visual pattern:		+5−4+4−5+5−4+4−4
Prototype cat:	+ − + + − − − − + − + − + + − +	+ + − − + + − −
Response to cat name:	+4−3+4+4−4−3−3−4+4−4+4−4+4+4−4+4	
Response to cat visual pattern:		+5+4−4−5+4+4−4−4
Prototype bagel:	+ + − + − + + − + − − + + + + −	+ − − + + − − +
Response to bagel name:	+3+4−4+4−4+4+4−4+4−4−4+4+3+4+4−4	
Response to bagel visual pattern:		+4−4−4+4+4−4−4+4

The results of tests after learning hypothetical exemplars of the categories "dog", "cat" and "bagel". The prototype patterns are a series of + or − 1's (shown as + or − without the 1). The decimal points in the responses have been omitted for clarity – an entry of +4 represents an activation of +.4. Adapted from McClelland and Rumelhart (1985).

experiments using faces, see also Bruce & Valentine, 1985; Ellis, Young, Flude & Hay, 1987). An account of object recognition in which prototypical object descriptions emerge from the super-position of all encountered instances is readily able to account for such effects. Such "instance-based" models need not be couched in parallel distributed processing terms (e.g. Hintzman, 1986), but it is the PDP versions of instance-based models which have recently been attracting most attention.

However, these simple examples of "single layer" networks (where there is a single layer of units between input and response) have serious limitations as accounts of human pattern recognition as it can be proved that they cannot learn certain kinds of pattern categories. For example, such nets cannot learn to respond one way if A or B are present but not if *both* A and B or *neither* A nor B are present (the "exclusive or" condition: Minsky & Papert, 1969). However, networks with more than one layer can overcome these difficulties, provided that suitable learning rules can be devised. The "generalised delta rule" which employs a technique called "back-propagation of errors" provides one promising solution to this learning problem to allow a multi-layer network (now with a layer of "hidden units" between input and output) to learn pattern classifications (Rumelhart, Hinton & Williams, 1986). In such learning schemes activation from the input layer is generally squeezed through a narrow bottleneck of hidden units, where there are significantly fewer of these than input or output units. Such hidden units acquire interesting properties, appearing to make explicit abstract "features" of their inputs (e.g. Hinton, 1986, 1989). Other solutions for learning in multi-layer nets include *competitive learning* (Rumelhart & Zipser, 1986) and *simulated annealing* (Hinton & Sejnowski, 1986). The interested reader is referred to these papers for details of such systems which are beyond the scope of this introduction (see also the review by Hinton, 1989).

The "parallel distributed processing" models of object recognition clearly have some interesting properties which make them attractive as theories of human recognition processes. One weakness of such demonstrations at present is that they have generally not been applied to real objects. It is assumed that "Fido" is represented as a set of activities across a set of unknown encoding dimensions or features, and such assumptions beg many of the interesting questions about perception, questions which have been tackled more satisfactorily within the kind of computational framework proposed by Marr. Where distributed memory models have been tested on pictures rather than arbitrary sets of features, they have generally taken as their input raw pixel values (e.g. Kohonen, Oja & Lehtiö, 1981) rather than the oriented edge segments or blobs which seem to be delivered by the early stages of human vision. Another weakness is that a distributed memory system which represents two concepts with the same set of units, cannot recognise both categories at once (in our example, the network could not recognise Lassie and Rover at the same time).

CONCLUDING REMARKS

Despite the problems we have discussed, research on the properties of connectionist models is yielding exciting results at present, and we anticipate rapid progress over the next few years. One wider issue which connectionist theories raise is their relationship to theories which involve the explicit construction of a *symbolic* representation of the visual world. While some claim that connectionist models pose a fundamental challenge to conventional cognitive science, our own feeling is that developments in connectionist theory will complement (rather than challenge fundamentally) symbol-processing theories such as Marr's. For example, Hummel, Biederman, Gerhardsten and Hilton (1988) describe the development of a connectionist version of Biederman's theory of "recognition by components" which we outline in Chapter 8, and we have already mentioned Marr and Poggio's (1976) stereo algorithm as a good example of how a connectionist network might satisfy different constraints simultaneously. In neither of these examples does the connectionist model present a challenge to the symbol-processing perspective which spawned it, within which issues of computational theory and representational primitives were initially addressed. Similarly, it seems to us that parallel distributed models in particular provide a potentially powerful way to investigate the acquisition of "abstract" structural descriptions for object recognition. Connectionist models complement conventional models by addressing issues at a different level, one which is closer to Marr's notion of the "implementation" level of theory. This view is itself controversial, however, and the debate here focuses on the nature of representations constructed in traditional symbol-processing compared with connectionist modelling, a debate upon which we elaborate in Part IV of this book.

Another issue arising from the connectionist models we have described is whether they can help in the analysis of the *physiological* organisation of visual pathways in the brain. Although connectionist models are constructed from units and connections which look like neurons and synapses, it is important to treat this similarity cautiously. The models are based on assumptions about patterns of neural connections and the ways synapses are modified, and different models are based on different assumptions (for example, Hebbian and delta learning rules) which cannot yet be properly tested against physiological evidence. One interesting recent approach, however, has been to set up connectionist models and then compare the properties which model units develop through training with the properties of single cells in a part of the visual system. The reasoning involved is that similarities in the behaviour of units and of cells suggest that the cells are wired up in the way specified by the model.

Linsker (1986a; 1986b; 1986c) has investigated a multi-layer network in which there is a basic spatial structure so that inputs to a unit in layer n+1 tend (according to a Gaussian distribution) to come from nearby units in layer n. An unsupervised Hebbian learning procedure (in which there is no forcing stimulus, so that there is no model response for the system to learn), operates on initially random inputs. After learning, the network produces an impressive range of properties of receptive fields early in the visual system, including centre-surround fields in an early layer and orientation-tuned fields and orientation columns in later ones.

Rolls (e.g. 1987, 1990) has investigated the properties of a pattern recognition net similar to that of Kohonen et al. (1981), and has shown that the selectivity of individual units for input patterns represents a trade-off between two requirements. If selectivity is too low, interference between different inputs arises, whereas if it is too high, generalization and pattern completion are prevented. This theoretical expectation of units with an optimal intermediate selectivity for patterns is matched, Rolls argues, by the breadth of tuning observed in face-selective neurons (see Chapter 3, p. 69). Furthermore, Rolls suggests that these units may acquire their properties through a simple, unsupervised competitive learning procedure (cf. Rumelhart & Zipser, 1986).

Two other examples of this approach, using models which incorporate back-propagation algorithms, are provided by Lekhy and Sejnowski (1988) and Zipser and Andersen (1988). In the first study, a network trained to recognise the curvatures of simple geometrical surfaces from patterns of shading in their images generated hidden units which responded to bar and edge patterns and were selective for their orientation, in the same way as cells in the striate cortex. Zipser and Andersen's model was trained to convert an input specifying eye position and the retinal location of a stimulus to an output giving its location in head-centred co-ordinates. Here the properties of the hidden units came to resemble those of cells in area 7a (Andersen et al., 1985; see Chapter 7, p. 173).

Demonstrations of this kind provide powerful hypotheses about the organisation and function of regions of the visual pathway, but further physiological evidence is required to test them. In the case of models using back-propagation algorithms, there is the particular problem of finding a way in which these could be implemented physiologically. While this cannot be done by transmitting error signals back down a nerve cell axon, it is possible that it may be achieved through some mechanism involving the feedback pathways between cortical areas. Although this work is only at an early stage, there are equally good prospects for the relationship of connectionist theory with neurophysiology as for that with psychology which we have discussed more fully in this chapter.

So far in this book we have analysed how a human or other animal interprets a particular retinal image by constructing from it a representation of the scene being viewed. Most perception, however, particularly in simple animals, has an immediate consequence in terms of the animal's subsequent actions. One attractive feature of the connectionist models we have introduced briefly is that it becomes quite natural to consider how perception is translated into action since the models themselves are couched in terms of translations between stimuli and responses. This question of how perceptual processes contribute to the organisation of action is a major theme of the next part of this book.

Part III

DETECTING INFORMATION IN THE TRANSFORMING OPTIC ARRAY

Chapter Ten

INTRODUCTION TO THE ECOLOGICAL APPROACH TO VISUAL PERCEPTION

In the second part of this book we sketched an explanation of how an account of form, space and movement perception could be given in terms of the conventional starting point of the retinal image. The impression gained is that visual perception must involve large amounts of computation from instant to instant — building elaborate symbolic descriptions from primitive assertions, inferring distances from a variety of cues, taking account of signals to move eyes, and so on. The slightly different images reaching the two eyes must be combined to form a single three-dimensional percept, and views of the world glimpsed at different moments must also be integrated to result in the perception of a stable world containing objects in motion.

In this part of the book we consider a rather different framework for visual perception. The alternative, "ecological," approach emphasises the information which may be available in extended spatial and temporal pattern in the optic array, to guide the actions of animals and people, and to specify events of importance or interest. For the moment, we may regard the two approaches as complementary, with the "ecological" framework operating at a more global level of analysis than the computational accounts we have been considering until now. However, many of those working within the ecological framework regard their theoretical orientation as antithetical to that of information-processing theorists such as Marr. Inevitably we must confront some of these differences, though we leave the details of the arguments until Chapter 17.

The ecological approach to visual space perception was developed over a 35-year period by J. J. Gibson (Gibson, 1950a; 1966; 1979; see also Reed & Jones, 1982). Gibson's theory of perception takes as its starting point, not a "retinal image," which is passively sensed, but the ambient optic array, which an observer actively samples. In Chapter 1 we introduced the notion of an optic array and described how eyes have evolved to detect the spatial and temporal pattern contained within it. Gibson maintains that it is flow and disturbances in the structure of the total optic array, rather than bars, blobs or forms in an "image," which provide the information for perception, which unambiguously informs the observer both about the world and about him or herself simultaneously. In this ecological approach, perception and action are seen as tightly interlocked and mutually constraining. More controversially, Gibson's is a "direct" theory of perception, in which he maintains that information is "picked up" rather than "processed." Before we embark upon an introduction to Gibson's ideas, we should state that we disagree with his notion of "direct perception" in its strong form. Nevertheless, we feel that his theory has been important in inspiring some fascinating research, in which optical variables of higher order than local intensity values have been taken as the input to vision, and shown to provide important sources of information for the control of action (Chapters 11, 12 and 14), and the apprehension of events (Chapters 15 and 16). We think it appropriate to devote this chapter to a description of why and how Gibson developed his theory, before going on to make use of some of his ideas in the remaining chapters of this section.

J. J. GIBSON'S THEORY OF PERCEPTION

During World War II Gibson addressed himself to the problem of how to train pilots quickly, or how to discriminate potentially successful from unsuccessful pilots prior to training. The most difficult, and hence dangerous, aspects of flying are landing and take-off. To land a plane successfully you must know where you are located relative to the air strip, your angle of approach, and know how to modify your approach so that you are aiming for the right position at the right speed. Gibson felt therefore that good depth perception was likely to be a prerequisite of good flying. He discovered, however, that tests based on the pictorial cues to depth, and training measures devised to make people capitalise on depth information, had little success when applied to the problem of training pilots. Here was a clear practical example of the perception of relative distance, and yet attempts to improve "depth perception" were fruitless.

Such observations led Gibson to reformulate his views of visual perception radically. In his 1950 book he began by suggesting that the classical approach to "depth" or "space" perception be replaced by an approach which emphasised the perception of *surfaces* in the *environment*. This emphasis remained throughout his subsequent books. Gibson's theory emphasises the *ground* on which an animal lives and moves around, or above which an insect, bird or pilot flies. The ground consists of surfaces at different distances and slants. The surfaces are composed of texture elements. Pebbles, grains of sand, or blades of grass are all elements of texture which, while not identical, possess statistical regularity—the average size and spacing of elements of the same kind of texture will remain roughly constant for different samples. Some surfaces surround objects, and these objects may be attached to the ground (rocks, trees), or detached and independently mobile (animals). Object surfaces, like ground surfaces, have texture. The environment thus consists of textured surfaces which are themselves immersed in a medium (air). Gibson argues that we need an appropriate geometry to describe the environment, which will not necessarily be one based on abstractions such as "points" and "planes," as conventional geometries are. An ecological geometry must take surfaces and texture elements as its starting point:

> A surface is substantial; a plane is not. A surface is textured; a plane is not. A surface is never perfectly transparent; a plane is. A surface can be seen; a plane can only be visualized (Gibson, 1979, p. 35).

The structure which exists in the surfaces of the environment in turn structures the light which reaches an observer; we saw simple examples of this in Chapter 1. Gibson argues that it is the structure in the light, rather than stimulation by light, which furnishes information for visual perception. Stimulation per se does not lead to perception, as evidenced by perceptual experience in a Ganzfeld (Gibson & Dibble, 1952; Gibson & Waddell, 1952; Metzger, 1930). Diffuse unstructured light, as might be obtained by placing halves of table-tennis balls over the eyes and sitting in a bright room, produces perception of nothingness. To perceive things, rather than nothing, the light must be structured. In order to describe the structure in light we need an "ecological" optics (Gibson, 1961), rather than a description at the level of the physics of photons, waves and so on. The physics of photons coupled with the biochemistry of photoreceptor action can be used to explain how light is emitted and propagated and how receptors are stimulated by it, but not how the world is perceived. An ecological optics must cut across the boundaries between physical and physiological optics and the psychology of perception.

Gibson rejected the claim that the retinal image is the starting point for visual processing. Gibson argued that it is the total array of light beams reaching an observer, after structuring by surfaces and objects in the world, which provides direct information about the layout of those surfaces and objects, and about movement within the world and by the observer. Gibson pointed out that the total optic array contains information over space and time which unambiguously specifies layout and events. In Chapter 1 we described how light is structured in the optic array, and here we remind you briefly of the important points.

The ambient optic array at any point above the ground consists of an innumerable collection of light rays of different wavelengths and intensities. Some have been reflected by air particles, others by the surfaces in the world. These rays form a hierarchical and overlapping set of solid angles. The solid angles corresponding to the tiniest texture elements are nested within those which correspond to the boundaries of larger regions or objects. Changes in the pattern or properties of the light from one solid angle to another signal boundaries in the world, where for example one object partially conceals or occludes another object, or the ground.

Gibson maintained that the optic array contained *invariant* information about the world, in the form of higher-order variables, where traditional psychologists saw ambiguity and insufficiency in the retinal image. An example of an invariant is given by Sedgwick's (1973) "horizon ratio relation." The horizon "intersects" an object at a particular height, and Sedgwick showed that all objects of the same height, whatever their distance, are cut by the horizon in the same ratio. Further examples of invariants, and a fuller discussion of the concept, can be found in Cutting (1986).

An observer's task is to detect such invariant information by actively sampling the dynamic optic array. For example, the gradient of image size provided by the light reflected from textured surfaces receding away from an observer provides a continuous metric of the visual world. The rate of change of texture density, Gibson claims, can be detected directly, and unambiguously specifies the layout of surfaces in the world. In Chapter 7 we considered gradients of texture as one "cue" for depth perception. For Gibson, they are of more fundamental importance. Figure 10.1 shows examples of how texture gradients (of artificially regular proportions) can give impressions of surfaces receding into the distance. Figure 10.2 shows how the local shape of a surface may be given by the change in texture gradient.

FIGURE 10.1

Examples of texture density gradients.

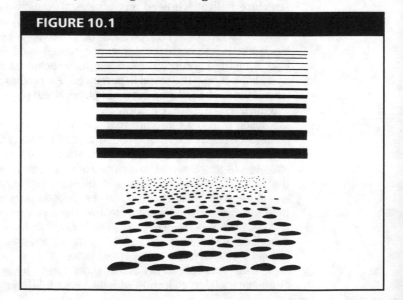

Surface shape and
slant can be
revealed by
texture.

FIGURE 10.2

Gibson and co-workers (Beck & Gibson, 1955; Gibson 1950b; Gibson & Cornsweet, 1952) have shown that changes in phenomenal slant are produced by changes in texture density gradients in viewed images, though the relationship between the two is not straightforward. Phenomenal slant is proportional to, but less than, actual slant. Gibson (e.g. 1975) later criticised these experiments on the grounds that they studied optical slant, i.e. the perceived slant about a plane perpendicular to the line of sight, rather than geographical slant — that relative to the ground surface. Hence the observer's task was not ecologically valid.

Surfaces which are flat and receding, or which are curved, are characterised by a number of texture gradients. One is in the *density* of texture elements; in a receding surface, the number of elements per unit of solid visual angle increases with distance. Others are the *perspective* and *compression* gradients, defined by changes in the width and height respectively of the projections of texture elements in an image plane. In a receding surface, these both decrease with distance. Perspective and compression gradients have proved to be more important than density gradients in producing the impression of a receding surface in displays, and in distinguishing flat and curved surfaces (Cutting & Millard, 1984).

Gibson originally termed his theory a "ground" theory of perception (Gibson, 1950a) in contrast with traditional "air" theories. In Gibson's view, the perception of objects should never be considered in isolation from the background texture on which they lie. Take the example of an observer viewing an object at a certain distance. Traditional "simplification" of this situation would lead to the schematisation in Figure 10.3 — where we can see that the same image could potentially be cast by an infinite number of objects of different sizes, inclinations and distances from the observer. Gibson (1950a) called this kind of theory an "air" theory

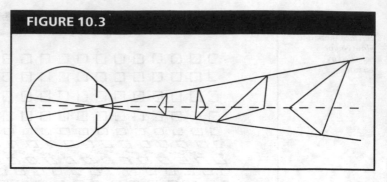

FIGURE 10.3

The kind of drawing typically used by students of visual perception to illustrate the ambiguity of the retinal image.

of visual perception because images are discussed as though cast by artificially smooth objects devoid of any background.

Gibsonian optics would depict the situation rather differently. Rather than considering an image cast by, for example, a tree suspended in a perceptual vacuum, Gibson would consider the total array of light reaching the observer. Assuming for the moment a stationary eye and world, the optic array would contain information about a continuous ground receding from the observer in the form of a texture density gradient. The size of this particular tree would be given by the amount of texture it conceals. Since a tree itself has texture, the fact that the tree is vertical, rather than inclined away from or towards the observer would also be specified by the lack of change in the texture density in the relevant portion of the optic array, that corresponding to the tree's trunk. Thus this particular pattern of light unambiguously specifies a tree of a particular size at a particular distance:

> Distance therefore is *not* a line endwise to the eye as Bishop Berkeley thought. To think so is to confuse abstract geometrical space with the living space of the environment. It is to confuse the Z-axis of a Cartesian coordinate system with the number of paces along the ground to a fixed object (Gibson, 1979, p. 117).

Gibson sees the important information about the layout of surfaces (he rejects the term "space" perception) as coming from a variety of gradients of information in the optic array, and gradients of texture, colour, brightness and disparity are all mentioned. However, it is misleading to consider the information available to such a "static" observer, since Gibson believes that movement is *essential* for seeing:

> What is clear to me now that was not clear before is that structure as such, frozen structure, is a myth, or at least a limiting case. Invariants of structure do not exist except in relation to variants (Gibson, 1979, p. 87).

Variants in information are produced by movement of the observer and the motion of objects in the world. The fact that observers *actively* explore their world allows powerful information from *motion perspective* to tell them both about their position relative to structures in the world and about their own movements. When an observer moves (as in Figure 10.4) the entire optic array is transformed. Such transformations nonetheless contain information about both the layout and shapes of objects and surfaces in the world, and about the observer's movement relative to the world:

Perception of the world and of the self go together and only occur over time (Gibson, 1975, p. 49).

FIGURE 10.4

When an observer moves the entire optic array is transformed. From Gibson (1966). Used by permission of Houghton Mifflin Company.

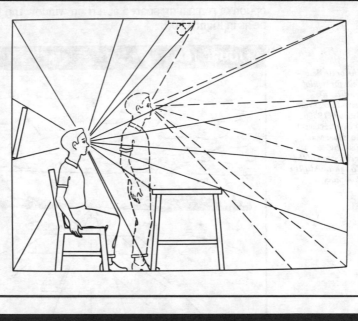

FIGURE 10.5

Successive views of a row of fence posts as an observer moves past them. The observer travels from right to left between each of the frames from left to right. From Gibson (1950a). The perception of the visual world. Used by permission of Houghton Mifflin Company.

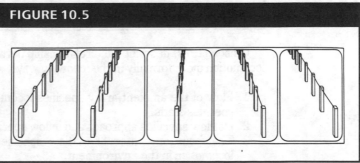

Figure 10.5 shows an example of motion perspective. As an observer walks past a collection of objects at different distances the relative motions present in the changing optic array will be specifically correlated with the layout of such objects. Indeed as an

observer moves in any way in the world this locomotion will always be accompanied by *flow* in the optic array. The nature of optic flow patterns is specific to certain types of movement (see Figs. 10.6–10.8). If a pilot is trying to land an aeroplane (Fig. 10.6) there will be streaming in the optic array radiating out from the point at which he is aiming. This point is known as the *pole* of the optic flow field. The array of optical texture elements (produced by light reflected from the texture elements in the world) expands centrifugally, with elements successively passing out of the bounded visual field of the observer and new elements emerging at the pole. If one was sitting on the roof of a train facing backwards there would be a continuous inward streaming of optical texture elements towards the point from which one was travelling (Fig. 10.7). If you chose the softer option of remaining seated at a train window the flow pattern would be as in Figure 10.8.

FIGURE 10.6

The optic flow field for a pilot landing an aeroplane. From Gibson (1950a). The perception of the visual world. *Used by permission of the Houghton Mifflin Company.*

Gibson (1979) described the relationship between optic flow and locomotion more formally in the following way:

1. Flow of the ambient array specifies locomotion and non-flow specifies statis.
2. Outflow specifies approach and inflow specifies retreat from.
3. The focus or center of outflow specifies the direction of locomotion in the environment.
4. A shift of the center of outflow from one visual solid angle to another specifies a change in the direction of locomotion, a turn, and a remaining of the center within the same solid angle specifies no change in direction (abridged from Gibson, 1979, pp. 227–9).

FIGURE 10.7

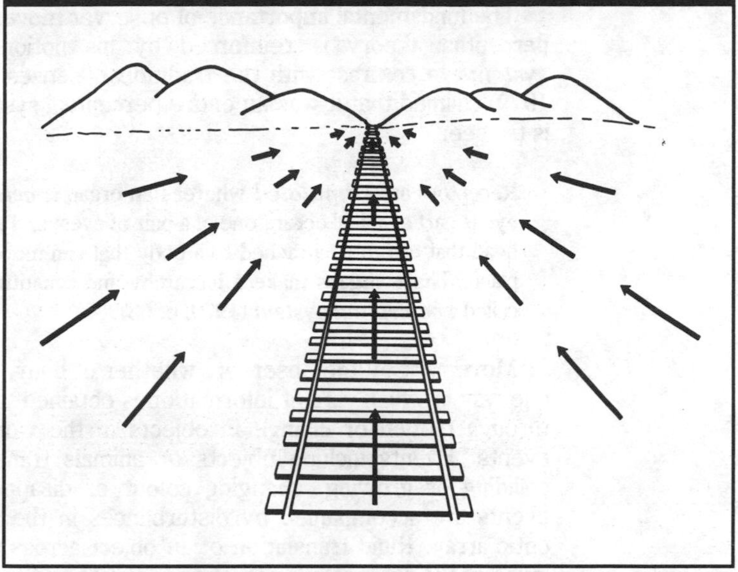

The optic flow field for a person sitting on the roof of a train, facing backwards.

FIGURE 10.8

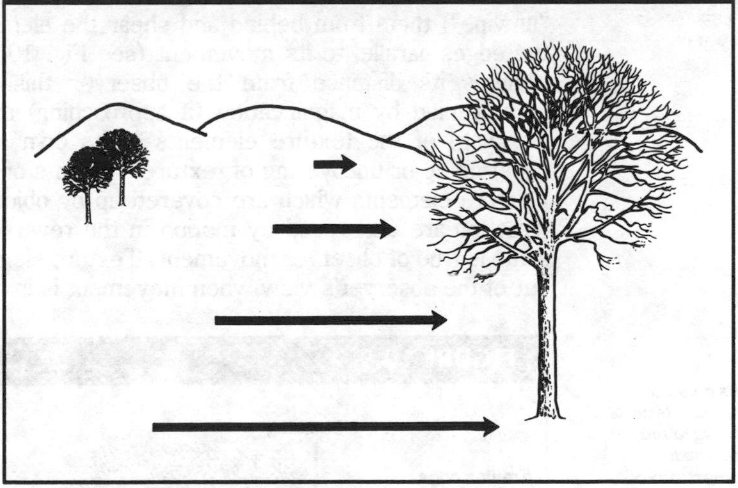

The optic flow field for a person sitting on a train and looking out of the window as they travel from right to left through this terrain.

That flow in the optic array may be sufficient to specify observer movement is dramatically demonstrated by the fairground amusement called the haunted swing. Here a person is seated in a stationary swing while the room rotates around them. The optical information is identical to that which would be produced if the observer, rather than the room, were being spun, and the subjective impression for the observer is the same—only by closing their eyes can they escape the nauseating sensation of being turned head over heels. In the next two chapters we will discuss in more detail how optical flow patterns may be used to inform animals and people of their actions in the world.

The fundamental importance of observer movement in Gibson's perceptual theory is reinforced by his notion of *perceptual systems* to contrast with the traditional "senses." Gibson (1966, 1979) claimed that it was an entire perceptual system whose job it is to "see:"

> Receptors are *stimulated* whereas an organ is *activated* . . . the eye is part of a dual organ, one of a pair of eyes, and they are set in a head that can turn, attached to a body that can move from place to place. These organs make a hierarchy and constitute what I have called a *perceptual system* (1979, p. 53).

Movement by the observer, whether of body, head or eyes, is one way in which variant information is obtained. The other way is through motion or change in objects in the world, i.e. through events. Events include objects or animals translating, rotating, colliding or growing, changing colour or disappearing. All such events are accompanied by disturbances in the structure of the optic array. Rigid translation of an object across the field of view involves the progressive accretion, deletion and shearing of texture elements. An object will progressively cover up (or "wipe out") texture elements in the direction of its movement, uncover (or "unwipe") them from behind and shear the elements crossed by the edges parallel to its movement (see Fig. 10.9). If the object changes its distance from the observer this change will be accompanied by magnification (if approaching) or minification (if receding) of the texture elements of its own surface, and the covering up or uncovering of texture elements of the background. Texture elements which are covered up by object motion in one direction are uncovered by motion in the reverse direction. The same is true of observer movement. Texture elements which pass out of the observer's view when movement is in one direction will

As an object moves, elements of background texture are progressively wiped out (covered up) by its leading edge, unwiped (revealed) by its trailing edge, and sheared by edges parallel to its direction of movement.

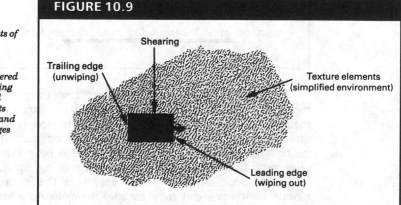

FIGURE 10.9

Shearing

Trailing edge
(unwiping)

Texture elements
(simplified environment)

Leading edge
(wiping out)

reappear if the movement is reversed. Gibson claims that this principle of *reversible occlusion* underlies the observer's impression of a constant and stable visual world where even those surfaces momentarily hidden are still "perceived."

Once one considers the total array of light there is no ambiguity about whether it is oneself or objects in the world which are moving. Eye movements do not change the structure of the ambient optic array, they simply allow a different portion of the array to be sampled. Movement of the head and body is always accompanied by a systematic flow pattern in the *total* array. Movement of an object within the world produces *local* disturbances in the structure of the array. Thus the major distinction between movement within the world or on behalf of the observer can be specified unambiguously by different flow patterns in the optic array. Note that Stevens et al. (1976; see Chapter 7, p. 167) also discussed how different patterns of motion in the entire retinal mosaic could be used to disambiguate motion perception, though the details of their argument are quite different from Gibson's.

Gibson's approach to the psychology of perception became progressively more radical. While in his 1950 book his major aim seemed to be to consider the nature of the visual information in the optic array within a psychophysical framework, in his later work (Gibson 1966, 1979) he became more interested in defining a totally new approach to perception. In the ecological approach to perception the animal and environment are viewed as intimately interlinked. The end product of perception is not seen as an internal representation of the visual world—a "percept." Rather the animal is seen as detecting *affordances*. The affordance of some surface or object in the environment is what it offers the animal—whether it can be grasped or eaten, trodden on or sat upon. The notion of an affordance can be traced back to the Gestalt psychologists, and particularly Koffka's idea of the "demand character" of an object:

> To primitive man each thing says what it is and what he ought to do with it . . . a fruit says "Eat me"; water says "Drink me"; thunder says "Fear me" (Koffka, 1935, p. 7).

A sawn-off tree trunk of the right flatness and size affords "sitting-on" by a human, or "hopping-on" for a frog; if a surface is flat, extended and substantial its property of affording support to terrestrial animals is implicitly given. Gibson makes the strong claim that there is information in the light to specify the affordances of the environment:

> This is a radical hypothesis, for it implies that the "values" and "meanings" of things in the environment can be directly perceived (Gibson, 1979, p. 127).

A detailed illustration of the concept of affordance is provided by Warren (1984), who studied people's judgements of whether staircases with differently proportioned steps, depicted in pictures, could be climbed in the normal way or not. Subjects taller and shorter than average differed in their judgements, which proved to be determined by the ratio of step height to the individual subject's leg length. Warren's subjects were therefore sensitive to the affordance of "climbability", but the results cannot tell us whether this is perceived directly or not. Gibson would have argued that an invariant property of the pattern of light reflected from a staircase which specifies "climbability" is picked up directly, but it could equally well be that inferential processes are involved in computing the three-dimensional structure of the steps and in relating their dimensions to information about stride length held in memory.

While it is relatively easy to appreciate that affordances like "supporting" or "graspable" might be specified in the optic array, it is much less easy to appreciate how qualities such as "eatable" or "writable-with" could be contained within the light. At the point where Gibson claims that a letter-box affords the posting of letters by humans of western culture, his theory is the most controversial. Nevertheless, the concept of affordances provides a powerful way to bridge the gap that exists in more cognitive theories between "perception" and "action." Within the theory of affordances, perception is an invitation to act, and action is an essential component of perception. However, Gibson's claim that all of perception can be understood without appeal to linguistic or cultural mediation is problematic, and we will return to this issue later.

Gibson thus asserts that optical information specifies surfaces of support, falling-off places, impending collision and so on. And, he claims, affordances are perceived directly, without the need for mediation by cognitive processes. The major task for the ecological psychologist is to discover the invariant information that animals have evolved to detect, and to discover the mechanisms by which they become attuned to this information. Gibson denies the need for "memory" in explaining perception. Incoming percepts are not matched against previously laid down traces, rather the perceptual system has evolved to "resonate" to certain invariant information. The concept of "resonance" is left rather vague by Gibson. For our purposes it is sufficient to stress that the theory suggests that there should be receptors or receptor networks which should be sensitive to variables of higher-order than "features" such as lines and edges.

Gibson decries the traditional laboratory experiment in perception in which observers are presented with "stimuli," devoid of context. In such situations the optical information is indeed impoverished but this will only tell us how a human observer copes with artificially impoverished inputs, and may tell us nothing of perception in the optically-rich real environment. He denies that ambiguous figures and illusions should be the starting point for a psychology of perception. While these may be interesting, and may be analysed in terms of the invariant information that they contain, they are not characteristic of normal perception. In the real world such perceptual distortions are rare. Additionally, Gibson regards the perception of *pictures* (the focus of much research in perception) as involving two components—the direct perception of the picture as a picture, i.e. as a flat surface, and the indirect perception of what it is that the picture represents. The picture of an apple, for example, as a flat surface, affords little apart from inspection. The affordances of the object depicted, the fact that it is an apple, can be grasped, thrown and eaten, are perceived indirectly and without ever fooling an adult observer into actually trying to reach for and eat the picture. Everyday perception is of the "direct," not the "indirect" kind.

Perhaps the best way to illustrate the difference between the approach of Gibson and his students and that of other perceptual theorists is to contrast their explanations of a number of specific topics. We have already seen how the problem of whether oneself or objects in the world are moving is dealt with by Gibson, but what about other "problems" in perception?

Size Constancy

Perceptual constancies have often been used to demonstrate the indirect and inferential nature of seeing. An object at distance $2x$ metres from an observer casts an image on the retina which is half the height of the image cast by that same object at distance x metres from the observer, and we have already seen (in Chapter 7) how relative size of retinal images may be thought of as a "cue" for the perception of depth. However if you watch a friend walk down the street he or she does not appear to shrink to half size each time their distance from you doubles. Our perception of the sizes of objects is remarkably constant, provided the distances are not too great.

The traditional view of this phenomenon is that the brain must take account of the perceived distance of objects (as given by various cues) and scale perceptual size up accordingly. The consequence of this is paradoxical. While relative image size may act as a cue to distance, the distance thus assessed is then used to judge the apparent size of the viewed object. Gibson views the problem differently. Because, he argues, texture gradients provide a continuous and constant scale for the perception of the world, there is no problem of size constancy scaling. The size of any object is given by the scale of the background at the point where the object is attached (Gibson, 1950a).

Size constancy breaks down over large distances. In the laboratory, perceived size tends towards image size, but Gibson (1947) showed that in an open, ploughed (and hence textured) field, estimates of the height of a distant stake merely became more variable at great distance rather than the error being in one direction. Size constancy also fails if we view objects from a height, rather than at a horizontal distance. Thus, from the top of a high building people on the pavement below us appear insect-like in their proportions. Traditional theory would explain this in terms of the absence of cues to distance. Gibson would say that when viewing from a height, the absence of the ground removes the continuous scale of texture necessary for accurate size perception.

Stereopsis

In Chapter 7 the reader was introduced to the problems associated with matching two disparate images into single three-dimensional percepts. It was suggested that global stereopsis was achieved on the basis of large numbers of computations and comparisons at a local level. Students of Gibson (e.g. Michaels, 1978) deny that visual perception involves the matching of two distinct images. No-one has ever suggested that tactile perception involves such a synthetic step—yet when one feels an object under a cloth, each hand must obtain a quite different tactile impression. It has always been implicitly assumed that we know objects directly by touch, and yet logically the problem of the resulting "singleness" of tactile perception is the same. Therefore if tactile images need not be compared and integrated, why consider binocular vision to involve the comparison and fusion of two retinal "pictures"? Michaels and Carello (1981) feel that perceptual theory has been misled by the camera metaphor:

> Just as Gibson took issue with the idea of discrete retinal snapshots, we will take issue with the supposition that the information has two parts, one to each eye, and that these two parts require fusion. And, just as he found it more convenient to consider the information for monocular motion perception to be transformations over a third dimension (time), we might reconsider binocular information in terms of transformations over a third dimension of space . . . Transformations over time describe the successive order of an optic array and so constitute monocular kinetic information. Similarly, transformations over space describe the adjacent order of two arrays and constitute binocular static information—what will be called the binocular array (Michaels & Carello, 1981, p. 119).

In these terms the task of the ecological perceptual theorist is to understand the invariant information obtained by binocularity, i.e. in the transformations which obtain from one eye's view to the other. It is claimed that invariants can be shown to specify the distances of objects, to remove the ambiguity of monocular shape information and can specify the shapes and sizes of particular objects (Michaels, 1978).

Perceiving Forms in Motion

In Chapter 6 we described the conditions in which "apparent" motion may be perceived when an item is displaced between successive frames of a film. The phenomenal similarity between real and apparent motion has justified the analysis of motion by perceptual theorists in terms of the comparison of successive retinal snapshots. In contrast, Gibson (1968) regarded the stimuli of apparent motion displays as preserving the transformational information which is present in a real moving display. In both cases, he would claim, the stimulus information contains transformations over time which specify the path of the motion. Gibson would argue that the perception of motion depends on the *direct* registration of this information. Clocksin (1980) has demonstrated that the types of edges present, and the orientations of surfaces in the world can be recovered "directly" from the optical flow information available to a locomoting observer. Thus a Gibsonian analysis of movement of objects or of observers would commence with an analysis of the information available in a continuously changing optic array. Clocksin starts with optical flow, and recovers edges.

We could contrast this with the approach of Ullman, considered in Chapter 7, who starts his analysis of motion perception with a sequence of static images, from which he recovers edges and then establishes correspondences between successive images over time. Both Clocksin and Ullman are researchers in artificial intelligence, concerned to provide explicit computational theories of perception. Both regard a consideration of the information available in the light reaching an observer to be fundamental to the development of adequate theories of perception, and both are attempting to avoid the use of object-specific, "downward-flowing" information in their accounts. Their difference lies in the nature of the information which forms the starting point for their analyses. For Ullman it is an image, for Clocksin it is flow.

Gibson's Theory in Perspective

Gibson's theory is radical indeed. It stands apart from the mainstream of perceptual theory. Some have likened Gibson's ideas to those of the Gestaltists, who took a similar phenomeno-logical approach to seeing. However, the Gestaltists were nativist in philosophy, while Gibson sees learning as important; and the Gestaltists sought to explain perceptual phenomena in terms of the physiology of the brain, unlike Gibson. It would be as legitimate to compare Gibson to the behaviourists, who looked at stimuli and responses but did not care to speculate on intervening stages of processing—but the behaviourists saw animals as prodded into action by discrete stimuli or sensations—while for Gibson, perception and action are intimately interlinked. Thus Gibson's approach is unique and has until recently been ignored by the vast majority of perceptual psychologists. This is largely because the difference between Gibsonian and traditional accounts of perception is more profound than might be appreciated from the preceding pages. The differences between the two approaches are not just psychological but verge on the philosophical. Traditional perceptual theory holds that perception is indirect and mediated by higher cognitive processes. We do not "just see" the world but actively construct it from fragmentary perceptual data. Gibson is a "direct realist". He holds that perception is direct and unmediated by inference and problem solving. However, at least some of the distinction between a "direct" and an "indirect" theory may be muddied by conceptual and logical confusion (Shaw & Bransford, 1977).

Much of the remainder of this book has a distinctly Gibsonian flavour, particularly in Chapters 11, 12 and 14, as we talk about the detection of information from optic flow patterns, and how this might be used to guide the actions of animals and humans in their worlds. However, unlike much of the work in ecological optics, we are concerned to describe physiological and computational models of how this information might be detected. We do not consider it adequate to claim that the observer just "resonates" to "invariants" picked up "directly", although we would concede that for some purposes one can demonstrate how patterns of light may be used to guide action, without detailed enquiry about how the information contained within light is processed. Different levels of analysis suit different purposes, and we return to these issues in Chapter 17. In addition, we see a distinction between the kinds of visual processing which might be used to guide locomotion through and manipulation of objects in the world, and the kinds of visual processing which might be involved in *understanding* the visual world in conceptual terms. For Gibson (1979), the two kinds of perception apparently do not differ. Thus just as a tree stump affords "sitting on", so a mail-box affords "posting letters", to a human being in a Western culture. In both cases perception is not mediated, in the inferential sense of the word, though humans may have to learn how to use the invariant information in the optic array. However, a fundamental aspect of human cognition is the ability to manipulate symbols and images in order to plan, reflect and reminisce. It seems likely that such "cognitive" activities are intimately involved in at least some aspects of human perception, and hence in this way too our approach is much less radical than Gibson's. In other animals we may wish to consider how "mental maps" of their environments are established and used. Such considerations appeal to notions of internal representations, "memories" of a kind, that Gibson would not consider appropriate to the subject matter of perception.

Our own aim is to present a pragmatic, rather than a theoretically "pure", account of a variety of perceptual accomplishments, and for many such accomplishments a "weak" version of the Gibsonian approach provides a more comfortable level of analysis than does the "retinal image" approach. In the remaining chapters of this section we will consider aspects of "dynamic" visual perception by animals and humans, but we will not adhere too strictly to a Gibsonian style of analysing these activities. Indeed, in Chapter 13 we consider explicitly computational analyses of the detection of variables of optic flow. However, it should be said that the majority of the research we will describe in this section has been conducted by people influenced by, and sympathetic to, Gibson's position. The subject matter and the approach of this section will feel very different to that of Part II. In Chapter 17 we tackle these differences explicitly and explore the possibilities for reconciliation and synthesis.

Chapter Eleven

VISUAL GUIDANCE OF ANIMAL LOCOMOTION

A crucial part of Gibson's critique of traditional theories of visual perception is his argument that they neglect the relationship between perceiver and environment. It is because of his emphasis on this relationship that Gibson came to describe his own approach as *ecological*. An ecological outlook on vision leads us to ask two kinds of question. First, what information is available in the spatiotemporal pattern of light to specify the structure of the environment and events in it? Secondly, what information does an animal or person *need* from the pattern of light in order to organise their actions?

We saw in Chapter 10 some of the ways in which Gibson tackled the first question, and in Chapters 11–16 we discuss further ways in which the optic array provides information for vision. We attempt to put this problem in the context of the second question, and stress the need to understand the role of visual perception in animals' and people's actions. We begin, in this chapter, by considering how animals use information in light to guide their movement around the solid objects and surfaces which surround them.

HOW ANIMALS MOVE ABOUT

The information which an animal needs to guide its movement through the environment—to perch on a branch, to detour around an obstacle, to jump over a ditch, and so on—will depend on the way in which it moves about; whether it burrows, runs, swims or flies. Means of locomotion are in turn constrained by the environment an animal lives in. The fundamental division of biological environments is into water and land. A watery environment—sea, lake or river—can in turn be divided into two kinds of potential habitat—the substrate and the open water. Many animals living in the substrate do not move about at all but are attached to the bottom and filter their food from water currents. Coral, sponges and bivalve molluscs such as oysters are examples of such sessile animals.

Many other species either move about on the surface of the substrate—examples include starfish and snails—or burrow in it, as do many annelid worms and some bivalve molluscs. For such animals, information about the chemical composition of the water, the chemistry and texture of the substrate and the direction of the force of gravity is often sufficient to control their movement around the environment and to enable them to locate sources of food and potential mates. The role of vision in guiding movement in such animals is often restricted to the detection of sudden changes in light level which specify possible predators.

One reason why many aquatic animals living on the substrate make only limited use of vision to guide locomotion is that they move slowly. Because of the viscosity of water, an animal like a lizard or rabbit, even if magically equipped with gills, would not be able to run about at its usual speed on the sea floor; animals such as lobsters and crabs are the fastest walkers over the bottom of watery environments. An animal moving slowly over the sea floor has less need to plan a course to avoid obstacles, because it is less likely to have enough kinetic energy to do itself any damage if it collides with one. A starfish or limpet encountering an obstacle simply creeps around it. The particular value of light is that it gives information about the positions of objects and surfaces beyond immediate tactile contact, and such information is not useful to a starfish or limpet.

Speed of movement is only one of a number of factors influencing the evolution of animals' visual capacities, however. Some bottom-living aquatic animals may make good use of vision. Crabs and octopuses live on the sea-floor, and locate nooks and crannies among rocks where they are relatively safe from predators, discriminate between different kinds of prey and engage in complex social behaviour. Vision plays some part in guiding these forms of behaviour, which rely on the ability to detect complex information in light.

In open water, animals can move at greater speeds, although whether a species can exploit this possibility depends upon its body size. The viscosity of water prevents small animals from generating sufficient power to move at any speed, and small planktonic animals such as shrimp simply swim to maintain their vertical position, often using the direction of maximum light intensity to orient themselves.

All larger animals which swim continuously in open water show similarly streamlined body shapes and modes of swimming, determined by the mechanics of moving through water; fish, sharks and marine mammals (whales and dolphins) swim by undulating movement of the body, whilst squid use a unique jet propulsion mechanism. These animals need to detect obstacles and other animals at a distance, and most of them use information available in light to do so. Dolphins and other cetaceans also use an echolocation system based on ultrasonic cries, while some fish species living in murky water detect objects in their surroundings by distortions of their own electric fields (Heiligenberg, 1973).

When we turn to consider the terrestrial environment, we again find species which move slowly over the surface of the earth, or burrow under it, but we also find a greater variety of ways of moving around the environment rapidly. Insects, spiders, reptiles, birds and mammals move by walking, running and jumping, while birds, bats and many insects can also fly.

As in water, light provides information specifying the layout of an animal's surroundings and, as light penetrates further through air than through water, information about surfaces is available up to greater distances than in water. We have seen in Chapter 1 the two kinds of eye which enable land animals to exploit this source of information; the vertebrate eye and the compound eye of arthropods. Only one group of land animals can move about at speed without vision; these are the bats, which, like dolphins, detect reflections of their own ultrasonic cries (Griffin, 1958).

This general survey of the animal kingdom shows us some ways in which the physical properties of an animal's habitat and the way it moves around it may influence the extent to which it will make use of information in light. This will depend upon many factors, including the amount of ambient light in its habitat, the extent to which it is absorbed by the medium, and the animal's mode of locomotion.

Environment and locomotion can constrain perception in more subtle ways than just determining which sensory modality is most appropriate. For example, animals which move about at speed in open water or air will have as a potential source of information variables in the optic flow field which are not available to animals which move only intermittently. In the rest of this chapter, we discuss examples of animals which move about at speed through air, and ask whether they do in fact detect variables of the optic flow field and use them to guide walking, running or flying. We will consider three problems which are posed for perception in such animals; maintaining a stable path through air currents, detecting surfaces in the surrounding environment and detecting the distances of surfaces.

HOW INSECTS STEER A STRAIGHT COURSE

An insect flies by beating its wings rapidly, twisting them as it does so, so that on each downstroke air is driven backwards and downwards. This generates a force on the insect with two components—an upwards force, or lift, and a forward force, or thrust. The aerodynamic principles by which these forces are produced are well understood, at least for larger insects (Pringle, 1974).

Simply beating the wings will not ensure *stable* flight, however. The direction and magnitude of the force produced by the wingbeat must be controlled to prevent the insect rolling, yawing or pitching (see Fig. 11.1). A degree of stability is provided by insects' anatomy. The abdomen, particularly if it is long, as in the locust, acts as a rudder to counteract pitch and yaw, and in all insects the centre of lift is above the centre of gravity, giving pendulum stability against roll. In these ways, deviation from a stable flight attitude generates a correcting force.

This inherent stability is augmented in all actively flying insects by "active reflexes"—negative feedback loops operating through the insect's nervous system and muscles. Receptors detect information specifying rotation around one of the axes, and the wings, limbs or abdomen move so as to correct the rotation. One source of information specifying rotation is the pattern of air flow over the insect. In the locust, for example, the rate of air flow over either side of the head during flight is detected by sensory hairs, and a difference in the two rates, which specifies yaw, generates steering movements of the legs and abdomen (Camhi, 1970).

In completely still air, or in air moving as a homogeneous mass at a uniform speed, this kind of change of pattern of air flow unambiguously specifies a rotation caused by the insect's own movement. Corrective movements of the wings, legs and abdomen will keep the insect on a straight and stable course.

Often, however, the air an insect flies through moves in irregular currents, gusts and eddies too small for us to detect but large enough to deflect a flying insect. For an insect flying through fluctuating air currents, air flow over the body provides ambiguous information about the insect's path relative to the environment. An

FIGURE 11.1

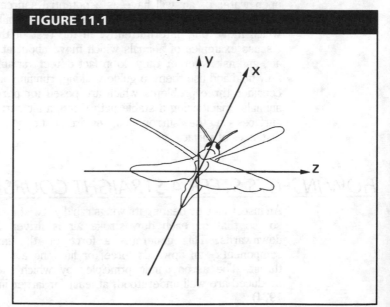

The three orthogonal axes through a flying insect. Rotation around axis x is rolling; around axis y is yawing and around axis z is pitching.

insect which simply regulated its path relative to the air around it would fly in an irregular, "drunkard's walk" path as it was blown about by fluctuating air currents. Such a flight path would be maladaptive for many insects, as they would be unable to fly any distance through the environment in order to reach new food sources.

We would therefore expect insects to be able to detect turns relative to the fixed environment around them as well as relative to the air in which they fly. What information in the optic flow field could specify such turns? Locusts maintain stability in the rolling plane by detecting both the direction from which diffuse light intensity is the greatest and the angle of the horizon relative to the body axis (Goodman, 1965). In a locust's natural environment, these two sources of information unambiguously specify the direction of the force of gravity, whatever the air around the insect is doing.

These two means of ensuring stable flight have their limitations. First, the orientation of the horizon is useful only to insects flying over open country, as locusts do when migrating, but not to insects flying through a cluttered environment of vegetation. Secondly, neither mechanism can correct yawing turns and prevent an insect flying round and round in circles. A further means by which insects can maintain stable flight, which overcomes both these problems, is through the *optomotor response*.

The first demonstration of the optomotor response (Kalmus, 1949) studied the control of walking rather than flying, and a typical experiment is shown in Figure 11.2. A fly walks on a platform surrounded by a cylinder with vertical stripes on its inside surface. As the cylinder is turned, the fly turns in the same direction, so that the velocity of flow of texture in the optic flow field is minimised.

Rotation of the cylinder causes a flow of optic texture in a uniform sideways direction throughout the optic flow field, but what would this pattern of flow specify about a fly's natural environment? It would not specify movement of the environment as, outside an optomotor experiment, the whole environment would never move in a uniform way (Gibson, 1966). Instead, it would unambiguously specify rotation of the fly due to movement of the surface it is resting on.

An illustration of this point is provided by situations where stationary human observers are presented with uniformly moving texture in a large part of the visual field. Such situations are rare, or must be contrived experimentally (note that forward locomotion does not produce *uniform* flow of texture), but they often cause a powerful impression of self-movement. The reader may have experienced such an effect by standing in shallow water at the seashore and looking straight down. As the water rushes out after each wave, an observer has a strong illusion of moving in the opposite direction. A similar effect can occur at a railway station, when uniform flow created by movement of a train on a nearby platform can be interpreted as movement of the observer's own,

Experiment to demonstrate the optomotor response of a walking fly.

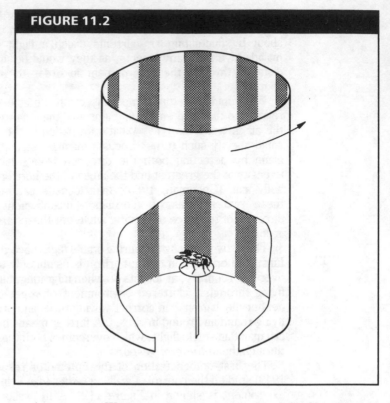

FIGURE 11.2

stationary train. We have more to say about control of posture and balance by vision in Chapter 12.

In an optomotor experiment, a fly detects a pattern of optic flow which specifies its rotation relative to the environment, and makes the appropriate turning movements of its legs to reduce sideways optic flow to a minimum. Can this ability to detect uniform flow throughout the optic flow field also be used to correct yawing turns during flight? Many insects, if suspended in the air by a rod glued to the back, will beat their wings as if flying, and their turning responses to artificial optic flow fields can be measured.

The fruitfly *Drosophila melanogaster* is one example of an insect which shows the same optomotor response during tethered flight as a walking fly does to a rotating striped drum. A fruitfly responds to a striped pattern moving sideways across its visual field with a yawing turn, made up of three components; an increase in the difference between the amplitudes of beat of the two wings, sideways deflection of the abdomen and hind legs, and inhibition of the "hitches", or transient reductions in wingbeat amplitude, which occur spontaneously and independently on the two sides of the body during normal flight (Götz, Hengstenberg & Biesinger, 1979).

There is no reason why uniform flow of optic texture should not also be used to detect pitching and rolling turns as well as yawing ones, and the fruitfly's optomotor response does indeed operate in these two planes also (Blondeau & Heisenberg, 1982; see Fig. 11.3). This means of detecting pitching and rolling will be effective in a cluttered environment where the horizon is not visible. It is important to stress that these rotating striped patterns simulate the optic flow caused by rotation of the insect, whether the rotation arises from its own movement or from an air current or from both. Since all these situations require the same corrective manoeuvres, there is no need for an insect to discriminate between them. We see here an example of the ecological principle that animals detect just the information in light which they need to control their actions.

It is obvious how these optomotor responses act to maintain stable flight by a fruitfly or other insect, but can they also keep an insect on a straight path through fluctuating air currents? In principle, they can play a part in doing this. Each time the insect is rotated by an air current, flow of texture will cause it to generate an opposing *torque*, or turning force. The insect will therefore keep the direction of its thrust constant relative to the environment. Its actual path will be determined by the resultant of its thrust and the air current, and the insect will therefore follow a zig-zag path. Nevertheless this path will have a component in a constant direction, and the insect will not fly around in circles.

This argument makes an unrealistic assumption, however,

The optomotor response of a tethered fly to rotation of a drum in all three planes. In each case, the fly turns to minimise velocity of flow of optic texture. Adapted from Blondeau and Heisenberg (1982).

FIGURE 11.3

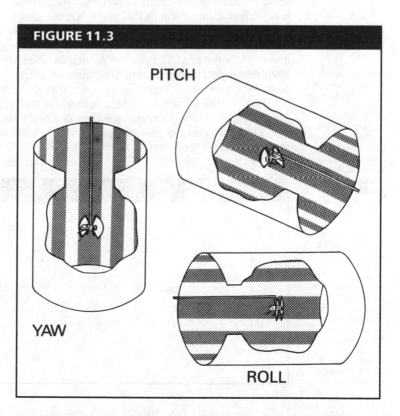

PITCH

YAW

ROLL

which is that there will be no optic flow unless the insect turns. This would be nearly true if the insect were at a considerable height above the ground and at a great distance from landmarks, so that motion parallax was only slight. If an insect flies near the ground, however, passing close to vegetation or other objects, there will be movement everywhere in the optic flow field, except at its *poles*, which specify the direction of movement (see Fig. 10.6). The rate of movement in any part of the optic flow field will depend on its angular separation from the poles, on the distance of corresponding landmarks from the insect and on the insect's velocity. These relationships are illustrated in Figure 11.4.

Unless an insect is flying at high altitude, the optic flow field will therefore be an elaborate pattern of regions of different rates of movement, generated by the insect's *translatory* movement, and the effects of *rotatory* movement will be superimposed on this pattern. If the optomotor responses we have been considering are to play a role in keeping an insect on a straight course by counteracting turns, then it appears that optic flow caused by rotation must in some way be filtered out from that caused by translation. How might this be achieved?

Reichardt (1969) has analysed the yawing optomotor response and has proposed a model of its control. In his model, receptor cells are connected to movement detectors, which respond to movement in a preferred direction in the same way as directionally selective retinal cells in vertebrates (Chapter 2, p. 41). We return to the mechanism of movement detection in Chapter 13, and our concern here is with the next stage of the model, in which the outputs of all movement detectors sharing the same preferred direction are summed together. Figure 11.5 illustrates how a "rotation detector" would compute the algebraic sum of signals from movement detectors, and our question is whether a mechanism of this kind can resolve the components of optic flow caused by rotation and by translation.

The relation between distance, angular position in the optic flow field and velocity of flow. (a) Objects A and B are equidistant to the observer but B is nearer to the pole of the optic flow field. As the observer moves in unit time from O to O', texture reflected from A moves through a greater angle. (b) Objects A and B are equidistant from the pole of the optic flow field, but B is nearer the observer than A. As the observer moves from O to O', texture reflected from B moves through a greater angle.

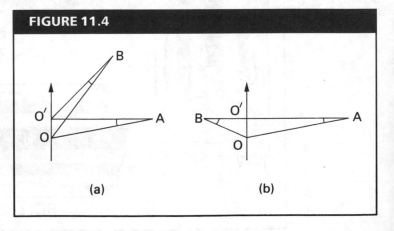

FIGURE 11.4

(a)

(b)

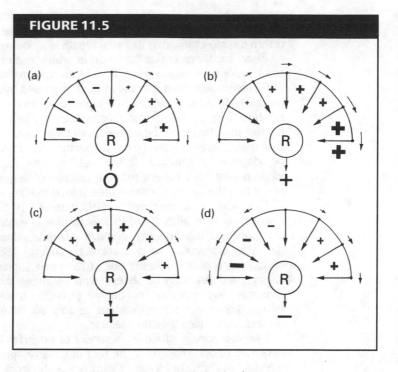

FIGURE 11.5

A model of the control of the optomotor response. Movement detectors signal the direction and rate of flow in each part of the optic flow field and a rotation detector R sums their outputs. (a) Optic flow during forward flight. (b) Effect of rotation superimposed on forward flight. (c) Optic flow caused by sideways movement. (d) Optic flow caused by a nearby surface on the left. Arrows indicate magnitude and direction of optic flow. Sizes of "+" and "–" symbols indicate magnitude of movement detector output.

In Figure 11.5, each movement detector gives a positive output to clockwise movement and a negative output to counter-clockwise movement, and the rotation detector sums their outputs. Consider undisturbed forward flight first; Figure 11.5a shows the directions and rates of flow over each part of the eye, and (as long as landmarks on the two sides are at approximately the same distance) it is apparent that the outputs of the detectors on the two sides will cancel out.

Consider next a counter-clockwise rotation of the insect, causing a uniform clockwise flow superimposed on the pattern in Figure 11.5a. The result of adding the two patterns is shown in Figure 11.5b, and the rotation detector now yields a positive output, which can be coupled to motor mechanisms to give a clockwise corrective turn. Similarly, a clockwise rotation will cause a negative output from the rotation detector and a counter-clockwise correction.

Disturbances to flight will not necessarily be purely rotatory, however, but will usually also involve a translatory component. Figure 11.5c shows the effects of a purely translatory disturbance, in which the insect is blown sideways, to the left. The optic flow will cause a positive response from the rotation detector and therefore a clockwise turn. The rotation detector therefore gives the same output to both translatory and rotatory disturbances to flight, but it can be argued that this failure to resolve the two components is not a problem for an insect. Whether it is blown to the left, or turned anti-clockwise, the appropriate manoeuvre to return the insect towards its original path is a clockwise turn.

Even so, there is one situation in which summation of signals from movement detectors will yield an inappropriate turn. Götz (1975) has pointed out that the optic flow caused by a nearby object on one side during undisturbed flight simulates that caused by a rotation (Fig. 11.5d). Some more complex model of insect flight control may therefore be needed, although Götz (1975) suggests that the apparent failure of the summation mechanism may in fact be adaptive for fruitflies. It will yield straight flight in an empty environment but frequent turns in patches of vegetation, with the result that the fly spends more time in food-rich areas.

One feature of Reichardt's (1969) model is that it assumes information from all parts of the visual field is summed equally. In one species, the hoverfly *Syritta pipiens*, there is evidence that this assumption is not correct (Collett, 1980). The flight performance of hoverflies is one of the most sophisticated among insects, and can easily be observed on a summer day. They can fly forwards, sideways or obliquely, through grass, flowers and foliage, hover in a stable position, and fly accurately towards the flowers from which they take nectar.

One component of Collett's model of hoverfly flight control is detection of optic flow over the part of the eye appropriate for the direction of flight. In forward flight, this is the front of the eye, but in sideways flight it is the side of the eye. The optic flow field is regulated so that its pole is kept over one of these areas, and this clearly involves a more complex and flexible model than that of Figure 11.5. Perhaps similar complexities occur in other insect species, although the ability of the hoverfly to fly with great accuracy in any direction may well mean that its perceptual capacities are unusually elaborate. We should be alert to the possibility of different mechanisms in different species of insect, related to different ecological demands.

The problem of maintaining a stable path or position in a moving medium is faced by other animals besides insects. Being larger and more powerful, birds will not be affected by small air currents, but stronger currents may be important in two sorts of situation. Hummingbirds, which hover in a stable position to feed from flowers, may need to detect and correct disturbances of their position by wind in the same way as hoverflies, and birds navigating over long distances must correct effects of crosswinds on their flight path.

Fish living in moving water face similar problems to those of airborne insects. Trout, for example, maintain their position in fast-flowing streams, and it seems likely that they do so by detecting information in the optic flow field specifying movement relative to their surroundings. The study of optomotor processes in fish and birds would present greater difficulty than in insects, but it would be interesting to know whether similar mechanisms are involved.

DETECTING SURFACES

Our next problem is one which is shared by a wider range of actively moving animals, including large terrestrial animals which are not troubled by air currents. It is the problem of detecting the surfaces of solid objects surrounding a moving animal, which is necessary in order to avoid collisions with obstacles and encounters with predators, or to orient towards landing surfaces, prey or mates. The three dimensional layout of the world can be retrieved from a stationary retinal image or a pair of images, in the ways discussed in Chapter 7, but we shall look at evidence that at least one insect species uses information in the optic flow field to do this.

The housefly, *Musca domestica*, as well as showing a standard optomotor response to a revolving striped drum, will also turn so as to follow the movement of a single vertical stripe on a drum (Reichardt & Poggio, 1976). As the stripe rotates, the fly follows its movement in such a way as to keep the stripe in the centre of its visual field.

What information in the pattern of light reaching its eyes might a fly be using to track a vertical stripe? Reichardt and Poggio (1976) found that the yawing torque of a fly presented with a single vertical stripe was determined by three factors. One is the angle between the stripe and the long axis of the fly's body. The second is the angular *velocity* of the stripe. For a given position of the stripe, the fly will turn more quickly if the stripe is moving away from the centre of the visual field more quickly. In this way, the fly has a simple ability to extrapolate from the stripe's rate of movement and predict its future position. Finally, the fly's torque shows small random changes causing it to turn irregularly, which can be observed either when the fly is placed in a homogeneously lit environment, or when it is fixating a stationary stripe.

Land and Collett (1974) were able to show that the same parameters of optic flow control turns when houseflies are in free flight. If two airborne flies come close to each other, they may buzz around in a brief flurry and then separate. Land and Collett filmed encounters of this kind between flies of the species *Fannia canicularis* and found that they take the form of a chase, lasting between 0.1 and 2 sec, in which the leading fly is closely followed by the pursuer. The record of one chase (Fig. 11.6) shows how each time the leading fly turns, the pursuer manoeuvres so as to follow it.

Land and Collett were able to reconstruct a pursuing fly's path accurately, given the leading fly's path, by applying two rules governing the pursuer's behaviour. First, as the leader's angular deviation from the pursuer's axis increases, the pursuer turns to reduce the angle. Secondly, when the leader is within 30° on either side of the pursuer's axis, the pursuer detects the leader's angular velocity and turns to reduce it also. As a result, the pursuer can begin its turn before the leader crosses its midline. These parameters of angular position and velocity are exactly those which

FIGURE 11.6

Record of a fly chase. Circles show positions of flies at 20 msec intervals (open circles—leader; closed circles—pursuer). Corresponding positions are numbered at 200 msec intervals. From Land and Collett (1974).

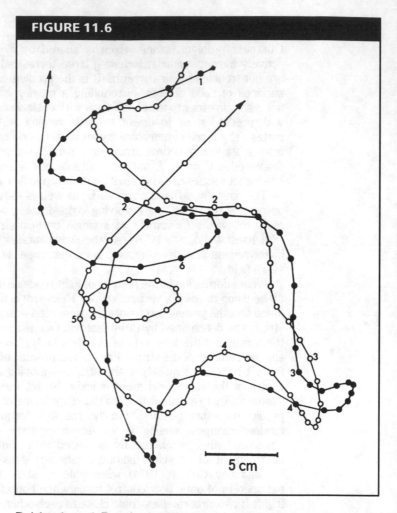

5 cm

Reichardt and Poggio (1976) demonstrated as controlling turns made by tethered flies.

Flies detect two simple parameters of optic flow in order to track small nearby targets such as black stripes, other flies or peas fired from a pea shooter. There are at least two possible reasons why this information is useful to a fly. First, Land and Collett (1974) argue that it enables male flies to locate and contact females. How, though, does such a simple form of visual guidance allow males to distinguish females from males, or to discriminate between females of different species? Part of the answer lies in the context of the fly's behaviour; Land and Collett suggest that a male fly can fly and turn more quickly than a female, so that a male pursuer can catch up with a female but not with a male. Likewise, a pursuer will be unlikely to catch up with a fly of another species because its aerodynamic properties will differ from those of a female of its own species. If the leader is smaller than a conspecific female and therefore able to turn more quickly, or if it is larger and therefore able to fly faster, the pursuer will fall behind.

Whether the pursuer catches up depends upon the size and aerodynamic properties of the two flies. If the leader is a female of the same species, these properties will be matched and the pursuer will catch up and mate. It seems unlikely, however, that this mechanism is foolproof, as flies of other species may well be present that are of the same size as females of the pursuer's species. Unless they have some further means of discriminating targets at a distance, houseflies will therefore waste some time in pursuit of the wrong target.

A second possible reason why flies track a moving or stationary vertical stripe is that they need to orient towards landing surfaces. Flies feed on a variety of kinds of organic matter, making short flights between potentially nutritious surfaces where chemo-receptors in their feet allow them to assess their luck in finding food (Dethier, 1955). Could fixation of a vertical stripe be the outcome of a system normally guiding the airborne fly towards a surface?

Imagine a fly in an artificial world of vertical dark cylinders against a diffuse white background. If the fly keeps aligned towards the edge of a cylinder in the same way as it does towards a stripe on a rotating drum, it will fly towards the surface of a cylinder, where it may land. If the cylinders move, or the fly is buffeted by air currents, control of torque by angular position and velocity will still guide it to the target. Now, let us make this artificial environment more realistic, in two stages. First, keeping all objects uniformly dark against a diffusely lit background, can the system deal with variation in shape and orientation of surfaces?

Wehrhahn and Reichardt (1973) have shown that similar principles control the lift/thrust responses of houseflies, so that a single horizontal stripe moving vertically can be fixated. The system therefore works around two axes and can guide the fly to a surface tilted at any angle. Further, Reichardt and Poggio (1976) show that patterns other than vertical stripes vary in their "attractiveness"; that is, the proportion of its time a fly spends fixating them. Perhaps the attractiveness of different geometrical patterns reflects in some way the likelihood that different sorts of natural surface will be nutritious.

Reichardt and Poggio (1976) argue that the random component in the fly's torque is important in preventing fixation of a sub-optimal pattern, or, in the natural environment, preventing flight towards an unpromising surface. We can imagine the airborne fly as surrounded by surfaces competing for fixation; as it switches its direction of flight about between them, through random fluctuations in torque, it will spend most time fixated on the optimal one and so fly towards it.

There is a second way, however, in which we must make this environment more realistic. The real world does not contain uniformly dark objects against a diffuse background, but objects with textured surfaces. Consider an insect flying about among the branches of a tree. At any instant, the optic array will contain a mass of solid angles of light reflected from texture elements such as veins or patches of colour on leaves. The *stationary* optic array does not now specify where the boundaries of objects lie, nor their relative distances. As soon as the insect moves, however, such information is available in the optic flow field. The boundaries of leaves are specified by boundaries between different rates of flow of optic texture. That reflected from a distant leaf will move at a different, lower rate from that reflected from a nearer leaf. In Gibson's (1966) terms, wiping and shearing of texture are available to specify three-dimensional layout.

In further experiments, Reichardt and Poggio (1979) demonstrated that flies have some ability to detect wiping of texture. They presented tethered flies with a vertical stripe of a random-dot texture against a background of the same texture (similar to that illustrated in Fig. 7.5). As we would expect, if both stripe and background either remained stationary or moved together, the flies did not fixate the stripe. Certain patterns of *relative* movement between stripe and background did, however, cause flies to fixate the stripe; the most effective patterns were oscillation of stripe and background at different frequencies or with the same frequency but with a phase difference of 90° or 270°. In a fly's natural environment, there would be relative movement in the optic flow field as it flew near a textured surface in front of a more distant, similarly textured background. Fixation of a small region of moving texture would therefore guide the fly towards a nearby landing surface.

The evidence we have described shows that houseflies turn to fixate small regions of the visual field which contrast with the background in either brightness or velocity of motion, and this behaviour guides the fly towards mates or towards landing surfaces. Recall from the previous section, however, that houseflies also respond to uniform sideways flow of optic texture by a turn in the opposite direction, and consider what will happen when a fly turns towards a small object against a textured background. The fly's turn will cause flow of texture in the opposite direction, and the resulting optomotor response will cancel out the original turn. How are flies able to make turns towards potential mates or landing surfaces when they are against a textured background?

A solution to this problem is proposed by Egelhaaf (1987), who argues that there are two distinct flight control mechanisms operating in parallel in the housefly. One, responsible for the optomotor response which stabilizes flight, is sensitive to image motion over a wide angle, while the other, responsible for orientation to objects, is sensitive to motion within a narrow angle. Egelhaaf demonstrates that these mechanisms also differ in their sensitivities to speed of motion; the response of the wide angle mechanism declines steeply over a range of image velocities in which the narrow angle mechanism continues to respond strongly.

Since flies fixate targets in a series of fast turns rather than a slow, smooth turn, the opposing signal generated by the wide angle mechanism is weak during a turn. In effect, according to Egelhaaf, the fly is able to turn to fixate objects by doing so at a speed too high for its flight stabilizing mechanism to respond.

To conclude, flies are able to detect the boundaries of surfaces by the relative motion between images of surface and of background and to turn to fixate them. The rules by which optic flow controls turns during flight which we have described are probably only a part of the fly's flight control system; it is possible, for example, that a fly switches between cruising flight, in which obstacles are avoided, and exploratory flight, in which they are approached. A combination of both experimental and observational analysis will be needed to explore further the ways flies and other insects steer between and towards obstacles.

It seems likely that other animals moving about through a cluttered environment—a fish swimming through coral, a deer running through a wood or a squirrel running between branches—use the same sources of information in the optic flow field to detect the layout of objects surrounding them. Many manoeuvres of this kind, however, will require information about the *distances* of surfaces from an animal, as well as their positions relative to one another; can the optic flow field provide distance information?

DETECTING DISTANCE

Distance Information in the Retinal Image

The ways discussed in Chapter 7 of extracting depth information from a static retinal image—accommodation, binocular disparity, image size and so on—are potentially available to animals, though to varying extents. The compound eye of insects does not accommodate, and this source of information is available only to animals with single-chambered eyes. The range of distances over which binocular disparity is useful depends upon the distance between the two eyes, and will be greater for vertebrates than for insects. Even so, at least one insect species does detect distance in this way; the extent of a preying mantis' strike at a small insect is determined by the disparity in positions of the image of the target in the two eyes (Rossel, 1983).

Vertebrate species which rely only on the "traditional" cues to depth in obtaining distance information are chameleons, toads and frogs. All these animals capture prey such as insects by orienting towards the target and striking at it with the tongue. The extent of the strike is accurately related to prey distance, and the chameleon obtains this information from the degree of accommodation of its lens when the prey is optimally focused (Harkness, 1977), while toads and frogs use both accommodation and binocular disparity (Collett, 1977). There are two ways in which an animal could detect the state of accommodation of the lens; by monitoring efferent commands to the muscles which move the lens, or by feedback

FIGURE 11.7

Path followed by a toad tracking a smoothly moving target. Each arrow represents a "walk" lasting about 2 sec.

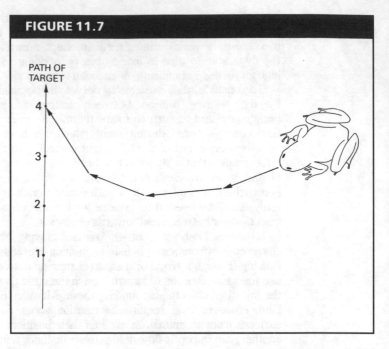

from sensory receptors. One way to distinguish between these alternatives is to use drugs which partially paralyse the lens muscles, so that for a given strength of efferent command the movement of the lens is reduced. If feedback from receptors is monitored, distance estimation will not be affected. In frogs, however, the result is underestimation of distance (Douglas, Collett & Wagner, 1986), implying that efferent commands to the muscles are monitored rather than the degree of movement which is actually achieved.

The use of information available in a static retinal image is particularly suitable to the technique of prey capture these animals employ, in which the direction and distance of a rapid strike is preset while the animal is stationary. This kind of control of movement is called *open-loop*, meaning that while the movement is executed no further information from the environment can modify it. In *closed-loop* control of movement, on the other hand, movement is continually modified by information from the surroundings; an insect's optomotor response is under closed-loop control, for example.

For the toad, obtaining depth information from a pair of static retinal images may reflect a more fundamental feature of its behavioural organisation, as Lock and Collett (1979) have obtained evidence suggesting that toads do not move through their surroundings under smooth, closed-loop control in the way that flies do, but in a series of "chunks" of movement controlled in an open-loop fashion by information detected at the start of the "chunk."

Lock and Collett found that toads approach a prey item which is beyond the 10 cm range of their strike in a series of walks and/or hops. Each of these "walks" lasts about 2 sec and takes the toad about 40 cm, but once it begins, moving the target does not alter the toad's bearing until the walk is completed. The bearing of the next walk is in the direction of the new position of the target. Likewise, a walk continues to completion even if the target disappears during it. Figure 11.7 illustrates how a toad tracks a moving target in a series of walks, each in the direction of the target's position at the outset.

A toad's approach to distant prey is therefore organised in a "chunked" way; information in the light reaching its eyes before a walk begins is used to set the bearing of that walk, which then is executed under open-loop control without further feedback control. This information could be obtained from the static optic array, or from the optic flow field during the previous walk, or both. The latter seems unlikely to be an important source of information, as a toad sets out on the correct bearing to an object as soon as it appears.

Lock and Collett found in further experiments that toads are able to detect the distance as well as the bearing of a target from the static optic array; there is a straightforward linear relation between target distance (if the target is outside snapping distance but inside the range of one walk) and walking distance. Again, moving the target or making it disappear during the walk did not affect the length of the walk.

These findings do not exhaust the toad's visual abilities, however; it can also detect the size and position of a barrier between itself and a target. Lock and Collett (1980) used two kinds of barrier, a chasm and a paling fence (Fig. 11.8). A toad confronted by a chasm will leap across it if it is not too wide, or step into it if it is not too deep. If it is both too wide and too deep, it turns away. In the case of the paling fence, a toad either sets out directly towards the prey or directly towards one end of the fence, depending upon the widths of the gaps in the fence. Again, the bearing of the first

Obstacles used by Lock and Collett (1979) to study a toad's approach to its prey.

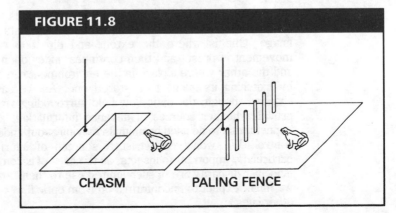

FIGURE 11.8

CHASM   PALING FENCE

walk is in one direction or the other, indicating that optic flow is not necessary to provide the information the toad needs.

Clearly, toads do not hop about at random snapping at prey items whenever they happen to fall within striking distance. Instead, they make their way through the obstacles surrounding them by means which are at the same time both remarkably efficient and apparently clumsy. It is a puzzle why organisation of the toad's movement should be "chunked" in this way; one possibility, suggested by Lock and Collett, is that it reflects some basic design principle of the amphibian nervous system. Whatever the reason, however, this kind of behavioural organisation is one which must rely on retrieving depth information from the static optic arrays at the two eyes.

Another source of distance information in the stationary optic array is the angular size of an object, provided of course that the absolute size of the object is known. The honeybee is an insect which uses angular size to obtain distance information, in the particular context of locating a familiar source of food. By training honeybees to feed from a dish at a certain distance from a landmark, and then varying the size and distance of the landmark, Cartwright and Collett (1983) showed that bees would search at the distance at which the angular size of the landmark at the eye was the same as during training.

Obtaining distance from angular size requires knowledge of the actual size of an object, and so this seems a surprising method for an insect to adopt. However, the bee does not need a general ability to detect distances of objects, but only the ability to return to a previously located food source. It achieves this by forming some representation of its retinal image, which Cartwright and Collett (1983) term a "snapshot", when it locates food. Its later flights to the food source are guided by matching the retinal image to that stored as a "snapshot" from the previous visit. Provided that the layout and position of large objects in the environment does not change over a period of hours or days, this simple method of navigation will return the bee to the food source over and over again.

In general, we have seen two sorts of situations where animals can rely exclusively on depth information in the stationary retinal image. One is where the extent and direction of a chunk of movement is preset and then continues under open-loop control, and the other where a place in the environment can be recognised by matching its image to a stored one. As we saw in the last chapter, though, the optic flow field surrounding a moving animal provides further sources of distance information, and we might expect these to be used by animals moving about under closed-loop control. We would expect such sources of information to be particularly important to insects, as the cues of accommodation and binocular disparity are of such limited use to them. In vertebrates, we might expect to find information from optic flow used alongside other cues.

Distance Information from the Optic Flow Field

The simplest kind of information in the optic flow field specifying distance is motion parallax; the further an object is from the eye the more slowly optic texture reflected from it moves (c.f. Fig. 11.4). Thus a flow field containing patches of texture moving at different rates provides information about the relative distances of surfaces around the animal. Honeybees also provide an example of an animal able to use motion parallax to detect relative distances. In experiments similar to those of Cartwright and Collett (1983), Lehrer, Srinivasan, Zhang and Horridge (1988) trained bees to feed from one of a number of discs mounted above the ground. The disc bearing food varied in size and position, but was always at the same height relative to the others. Lehrer et al. showed that bees detect the appropriate target from the motion of its image relative to those of the other targets as they fly above them.

Although motion parallax is useful to honeybees for the specific purpose of guiding return flights to food sources, it cannot specify *absolute* distances of surfaces, as the rate of optic flow is also a function of the animal's velocity. In many situations, an animal's speed relative to its surroundings will not be predictable; movement of the air or water, for a flying or a swimming animal, or the slope of the ground for a running animal, make the relationship between commands to muscles and actual velocity unpredictable. Since the animal's velocity cannot be obtained from image movement without knowing the distance of an object, motion parallax alone cannot yield distance information.

In some circumstances, an animal may be able to solve this problem through head or body movements of a fixed velocity. One such animal is the locust, which makes side-to-side swaying movements with its head before jumping from one surface to another. Wallace (1959) showed that the force of the jump is controlled by distance information obtained during the swaying movement; when he moved the target surface in time with the locust's head, but in the opposite direction, the insects consistently jumped short of the target. In the experiment, the opposing movement of the target caused its image to move more rapidly over the eye, at the velocity corresponding to a closer, stationary target. Similar head movements are seen in rodents; gerbils, for example, make vertical head movements before jumping over a gap, and Ellard, Goodale and Timney (1984) provide some indirect evidence that the behaviour enables motion parallax information to be used to control the distance jumped.

A well-known example of a stereotyped head movement is the head-bobbing of many bird species, including doves, pigeons and chickens. During walking, the head moves backwards and forwards relative to the body, and there is a brief "hold" phase in each cycle in which the head is almost stationary relative to the surroundings, followed by a "thrust" phase in which the head moves forward more quickly than the body. Notice that a walking bird's head never actually moves backwards relative to the surroundings; the powerful illusion that it does is an example of how we see motion of a figure in relation to nearby, larger figures (see Chapter 15, p. 322).

It is known that head-bobbing in doves and pigeons is controlled by optic flow produced by walking (Friedman, 1975; Frost, 1978), but its possible significance for vision is not fully understood. One possibility is that stabilization of the head relative to the surroundings during the hold phase aids detection of moving objects, but Davies and Green's (1988) finding that pigeons maintain rhythmic head movement in fast running or slow flight, when stabilization is not achieved, suggests that this cannot be the only function. The rapid forward movement of the head during the thrust phase will increase the velocities of texture patches over the retina, and so "amplify" relative motion between them; another function of head-bobbing may therefore be to aid the detection of small objects on the ground. Even so, the problem of obtaining absolute distances from optic flow remains, as the velocity of the head during the thrust phase is not predictable, but depends upon walking or flight speed.

So far, we have considered only velocity of flow as a parameter of the optic flow field. Lee (1980b) has demonstrated that distance information *can* be obtained independently of an animal's velocity if a more complex parameter of the optic flow field is detected. Strictly speaking, this parameter does not specify distance but *time to contact*; that is, the time that will elapse before the animal collides with a surface, assuming that it is moving with constant velocity. Time to contact is likely to be a useful piece of information to animals; for example, to a bird or insect approaching a surface and needing to time its landing manoeuvres correctly, or to a horse needing to time its jump over a fence.

FIGURE 11.9

Schematic representation of an animal's eye approaching a surface with velocity V(t). Adapted from Lee (1980b).

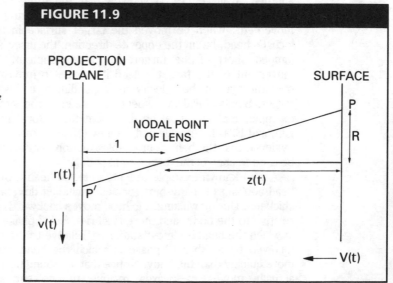

What is this parameter of the optic flow field, and how does it specify time to contact? Lee's argument goes as follows. Figure 11.9 shows a schematic representation of an animal approaching a surface with constant closing velocity. A surface on the right is approaching an eye on the left with velocity V. At time t it is a distance $Z(t)$ away, in units of the diameter of the eye, for convenience. A texture element P on the surface has an image P' projected on the retina. At time t, P' is a distance $r(t)$ from the centre of the expanding optic flow field and moving outwards with velocity $v(t)$.

From similar triangles,

$$\frac{1}{r(t)} = \frac{Z(t)}{R}$$

Differentiating with respect to time, and inverting,

$$\frac{r(t)^2}{v(t)} = \frac{R}{V}$$

Since

$$R = Z(t)r(t), \quad \frac{r(t)}{v(t)} = \frac{Z(t)}{V}$$

This ratio $r(t)/v(t)$, which Lee calls τ, is the ratio at time t of the distance of any point from the centre of an expanding optical pattern to its velocity away from the centre. Since it is equal to $Z(t)/V$, it specifies time to contact if V is constant. This result shows that the time elapsing until contact with a surface is specified by a simple ratio derivable from its dynamic projection on the retina. The ability to detect values of τ in the optic flow field could therefore provide an animal with a means of obtaining distance information, particularly in situations where it needs to time some action as it approaches a surface. An insect or bird approaching a surface might, for example, begin its landing manoeuvres when τ reaches some threshold value. Is there evidence that any animals do in fact use this information from the optic flow field?

Earlier in this chapter (p. 254) we saw how flies are guided towards potential landing surfaces by fixating a patch of texture moving relative to its background. As a fly approaches a surface, it does not simply crash into it (unless it is made of glass, for reasons which should be clear in a moment!) but performs a stereotyped series of landing manoeuvres, in which the fly decelerates and extends its forelegs forwards. A looming surface straight ahead is specified by centrifugal flow in a wide area of the optic flow field; a pattern which can be simulated by presenting a fly with a rotating disc on which a spiral is painted. Depending on the direction in which the disc is rotated, either inward or outward movement of edges is generated. If a housefly is suspended in front of a disc rotated so as to give an expanding pattern, it will immediately give the landing response, whereas a disc rotating in the opposite direction elicits no response (Braitenberg & Ferretti, 1966).

An expanding optic flow field is sufficient to cause a fly to carry out its landing manoeuvres, but does it use the parameter τ of this flow field to detect the correct point in its approach at which to start landing? The key prediction of the hypothesis that landing begins when τ reaches some threshold value is that the distance from the target at which landing begins will be greater for a fast approach than for a slow one (recall that τ is the ratio of the distance from a surface to the velocity of approach). Alternatively, if the fly detects the distance of the target and uses this to time its behaviour, then landing would be initiated at a *constant* distance from the target, whatever the velocity of approach.

Wagner (1982) has carried out a single-frame analysis of films of flies landing on small spheres in order to test the hypothesis that τ is used to time landing. He measured the variability over many landings of a number of parameters at the point when flies slowed their flight to begin landing, and found that the parameter with the least variation was the ratio of the rate of expansion of the image of the sphere to its size. This parameter is the inverse of Lee's τ, for the particular case where the point in the optic flow field considered is the edge of a looming object. Since it varied less at the point of deceleration than did the distance from the sphere, Wagner (1982) concluded that flies detect the value of τ of a looming target rather than its distance.

In further research on the fly's landing response, Borst and Bahde (1988) question whether Wagner's (1982) results do demonstrate that τ is detected. They propose an alternative "integration" model, in which the outputs of motion detectors across the whole visual field are summed together and the fly begins landing when this sum reaches a threshold value. They point out that this is a more economical model of the fly's visual system, as it involves the same processes as those underlying the optomotor response (see Fig. 11.5), and avoids the need for a separate system computing values of τ.

On the other hand, Borst and Bahde's (1988) model predicts less accurate timing of landing than does the τ hypothesis. Both predict that the distance at which landing begins will vary with approach velocity, and so both account for Wagner's (1982) results, but the integration model also predicts that landing distance will vary with the size of the target, its spatial structure and the structure of the surroundings. Borst and Bahde found that all these factors do influence landing distance, just as their model predicts. Their conclusion is that the fly uses a simple means of timing landing which does not achieve the ideal of triggering landing at a fixed distance or at a fixed time to contact, but which is nonetheless adequate for the fly's survival.

Experiments with a different animal, but giving results similar to those of Borst and Bahde (1988), were performed by Dill (1974). He studied the escape responses of a small tropical fish, the zebra danio (*Brachydanio rerio*) to looming discs, and found that the distance of the disc when the fish began to escape depended on both disc size and velocity. Further work is needed before concluding that these fish integrate velocity signals over the visual field in the same way as houseflies, however, as Dill's method did not fully control the position of the fish relative to the path of the disc. Even so, the results provide evidence against the hypothesis that escape is triggered by detecting τ.

In these two cases, it is likely that the requirements placed on the timing of behaviour are not strict. Provided a fly's feet are extended and its velocity is within a low range, its exact velocity when it contacts a surface is probably not critical (indeed, flies survive head-on collisions with sheets of glass). Similarly, a fish needs to escape from a predator as soon as it is detected, but not when it is at some particular distance. In cases such as these, the computation of τ is probably an unnecessary luxury, and we are more likely to find it used in situations where exact timing of behaviour is critical.

An example of animal which requires more reliable distance information is the gannet (*Sula bassana*), a seabird which hunts by flying over the sea at heights of up to 30 m. When it detects a fish below the surface, it dives almost vertically into the water to seize the fish in its beak. At the start of the dive, the gannet

FIGURE 11.10

Successive wing positions of a diving gannet. The wings are streamlined as the bird strikes the water. Drawing by John Busby, reproduced from Nelson (1978) with the permission of the publishers.

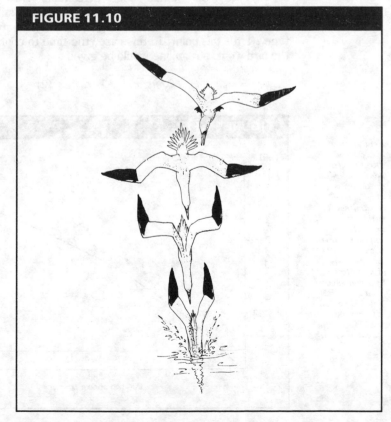

assumes a swept-back wing posture (Fig. 11.10) which allows it to steer, presumably keeping the fish at a fixed point in its visual field. Gannets enter the water at speeds of up to 24 m/sec (54 m.p.h.) and would be injured if they kept their wings extended at this speed. When less than a second away from the water surface their wings are therefore stretched back into a streamlined posture. If the wings are streamlined too soon, steering accuracy will be lost, whereas if they are streamlined too late, the bird will be injured. It is therefore crucial to the bird's hunting success and survival that its streamlining is accurately timed, and Lee and Reddish (1981) provide evidence that this is achieved by detecting τ.

If closing velocity is constant, τ directly specifies time to contact. The situation is more complex for the diving gannet, however, because the bird's velocity increases throughout its dive as it accelerates under gravity. Lee and Reddish show that, for an accelerating dive, the actual time-to-contact t_c is given by:

$$t_c = \tau(t) + t_d - \sqrt{t_d^2 + \tau(t)^2} \qquad (1)$$

Equation (1) shows that time to closing is given by both $\tau(t)$ and t_d, the duration of the dive, and so it appears that τ alone cannot specify when the gannet should streamline. However, Lee and Reddish argue that a strategy based on τ could still work, if the bird waited until τ reached a margin value τ_m and streamlined at a time t_i after this point. In this case, the time to contact t_c at which the bird would streamline would be given by:

$$t_c = \tau_m + t_d - \sqrt{\tau_m^2 + t_d^2} - t_i \qquad (2)$$

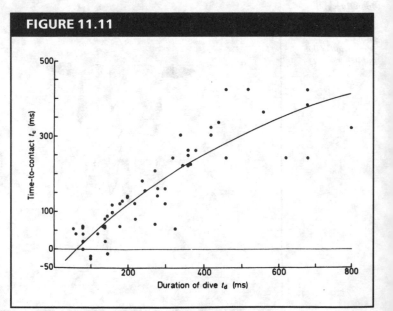

FIGURE 11.11

Relationship between the duration of a gannet's dive and the time to contact at which it streamlines. The curve is the best fit generated by equation (2) to the data. From Lee and Reddish (1981). Reprinted by permission from NATURE Vol. 293 pp. 293–4. Copyright © 1981 Macmillan Magazines Ltd.

Time-to-contact t_c (ms)

Duration of dive t_d (ms)

Lee and Reddish filmed gannets' dives and, by single frame analysis, obtained values of t_c and t_d for each of a large number of dives. Figure 11.11 shows the data they obtained and the curve generated by equation (2) which best fits the points. Lee and Reddish argue that strategies of timing streamlining which involve computation of the actual time to contact (from height, velocity and acceleration), or streamlining at a particular velocity or at a particular height, would all give relationships between t_c and t_d which match the data less well than does the τ strategy.

The gannet therefore appears to use the parameter τ to detect the optimum time to streamline its wings as it approaches the water, in contrast to the simpler method used by flies to time landing. An interesting problem for further research will be the factors which determine which actions of animals are timed by τ and which are not. In general, we might expect τ to be useful in situations where the timing of actions is critical, as when a large animal jumps or flies towards a small target. Animals such as squirrels and monkeys which jump between branches of trees may therefore be likely candidates. Accurate timing is also crucial in many skilled human activities, such as athletics, and we describe in Chapter 12 evidence that the detection of τ is involved in these.

CONCLUSIONS

The experiments we have described in this chapter provide evidence that Gibson's analysis of the information available in the optic flow field is useful for understanding how animals obtain information needed to guide movement through the environment. We have seen, for example, that flies detect uniform lateral flow and centrifugal flow in order to control flight and landing manoeuvres.

As well as showing that Gibsonian principles are useful in understanding animal vision, these examples make two further points. The first is that it is misleading to think of an animal perceiving the three-dimensional layout of its surroundings as constructing a metrically accurate representation of them. In many circumstances, animals will not need information about absolute distances of objects in order to control their actions successfully; a gannet does not need to know its height above the sea at each moment, but the optimum point at which to streamline its wings. We have seen that it is difficult to get absolute distance information from an optic flow field, because of the problem of independently gauging the animal's speed, but that heuristic strategies such as integration of velocity values, or computing τ, provide ecologically adequate means of timing approach to objects and surfaces.

The second point concerns a criticism often made of Gibson's theory, which is that it ignores the physiology of perception and is vague about how information available in light actually is detected. Although Gibson himself was not concerned with the physiology of vision, it would be mistaken to believe that his style of analysis of the information available in light is incompatible with neurophysiological analysis. Indeed, his emphasis on the information available for animals in the dynamic pattern of light in the optic flow field has played a part in stimulating research on physiological mechanisms involved in computing optical motion. We describe this research in Chapter 13, and show it has been particularly successful in determining how insects compute parameters of optic flow from a dynamic retinal image.

Chapter Twelve

VISUAL GUIDANCE
OF HUMAN ACTION

*I*n Chapter 11 we discussed how the flight paths of insects, the locomotion of toads and the diving of gannets may be guided by information obtained from patterns of optic flow. In this chapter we discuss aspects of locomotor behaviour in higher animals, particularly man. We describe how research conducted within an ecological framework has helped us to understand aspects of human action which were largely ignored by traditional approaches to human perception.

While the mental life of insects is presumably relatively uncomplicated, that of humans is complex and creative. We do not simply "respond" to the information which reaches our senses, but encode and reflect upon it, and can describe our world to others. Nevertheless, just like lower animals, we must maintain posture and safe footing, and negotiate obstacles while moving around the world. We duck to avoid missiles, or move our arms and hands appropriately to catch them. We stop at the edge of a cliff, jump over puddles, or brake the car when an animal darts across the road.

Following Lee (1977) we can classify the types of information necessary for controlling such locomotor activities into three kinds—*exteroceptive, proprioceptive* and *exproprioceptive.* Exteroceptive information about the layout of surfaces in the environment, and the position of objects or course of events within the environment is needed to guide action in the world. The most important source of exteroceptive information for humans and many other animals is vision. Proprioceptive information about the movement of body parts relative to one another is necessary for coordinated bodily actions, and is gained through mechanical receptors in joints and within the vestibular system, but also through vision (try bringing the tips of both your index fingers together with your eyes open and then with them closed). Exproprioceptive information about the position of the body or parts of it *relative to* the environment is also necessary for maintaining balance and guiding action through the world, and again vision provides powerful information of this kind.

Lee's classification departs from the traditional division of sensory systems into exteroceptors and proprioceptors, but his three-fold system is more suitable for discussions of locomotor behaviour. In the examples of locomotor behaviour we discuss below we will show how vision provides important information of all three kinds, this information being given by the dynamic properties of optic flow patterns.

In this chapter we first discuss how vision guides gross postural adjustments which allow us to duck to avoid missiles, or to maintain our balance while standing. We then consider finer aspects of locomotion and describe how it is that we negotiate a smooth path through a variable terrain. These are activities that humans share with other land-living animals, but we will go on to consider the visual guidance of behaviour peculiar to humans, such as driving cars or catching and hitting balls in sport. The way in which vision is used to guide this wide variety of activities appears to involve very general principles, some of which we have already met in Chapter 11.

POSTURAL ADJUSTMENTS

Avoiding Objects on Collision Course

An object approaching an observer on a collision path needs to be avoided. A strong empiricist tradition might suggest that infants would need considerable experience of the tactile consequences of an approaching object before reacting to the visual information specifying collision. However, it appears that infants may have an innate appreciation of particular patterns of optic flow. Bower, Broughton and Moore (1970) demonstrated that babies as young as eight days old would show defensive distress reactions when a foam rubber cube was pushed towards them. It appears that babies who are too young to have experienced the effects of colliding objects can respond appropriately to those apparently on collision course. Of course their reactions might be based on the change in air pressure created by the real approaching object rather than on the optical information specifying collision. However, Bower et al. (1970) and Ball and Tronick (1971) also tested young babies' reactions to dynamic optical displays in which no air pressure changes were present.

The displays were created by casting the shadow of a real object onto a screen in front of a supported infant. As the object was moved towards the light source, the shadow cast by it expanded in size, creating a "looming" image. Babies showed characteristic reactions to such displays. Their heads went back and their arms and hands were raised to cover their faces. Distress was also evident. While Bower et al. reported that the reactions exhibited were somewhat less strong to an apparent than to a real object, Ball and Tronick reported no difference in the strength of the reactions in the two cases. The reactions given to these looming patterns were in marked contrast to those shown when the pattern cast specified an object which was approaching on a non-collision path, or when it specified an object receding from the child (a shrinking as opposed to a looming pattern). Schiff, Caviness and Gibson (1962) reported similar responses in infant rhesus monkeys presented with looming patterns.

It may be that behaviour in this situation is based on detecting τ (see Chapter 11), the optic variable which specifies time to contact. Schiff and Detwiler (1979) have shown that adult humans are able to estimate when an object which had been approaching on a filmed collision course would have hit them, and that their judgements were influenced little by whether the object was filmed against a textured or a blank background. This suggests that adults can use the rate of looming of the image of an obstacle in the absence of information about the rate of background texture deletion to estimate τ. Adults do systematically underestimate τ in this situation, (see also McCleod & Ross, 1983), but this would seem an ecologically sound strategy. It is better to duck too soon than too late! It would be interesting to examine more microscopically the timing of reactions by infant humans and monkeys to patterns looming at different speeds to see whether there is evidence that their behaviour is controlled by the detection of τ.

Maintaining Balance

As adults (at least when sober) we take for granted our ability to remain upright on two feet. As every parent knows, however, the ability to stand and eventually to walk unsupported is an achievement which is gradually mastered by the infant with months of unsteadiness and falls on the way. The gymnast on the narrow beam, the ballet dancer on points or the circus artiste standing on a cantering horse must all learn to maintain balance in new and changing circumstances.

There are a number of different sources of information which may be used to control balance. These include information from receptors in the feet and ankle joints, information from the vestibular system—the organ of balance—and information received through the eyes. A simple demonstration suggests that visual information may be extremely important in maintaining posture. Try standing on one leg with eyes open and then with them closed. With eyes closed you will probably sway and perhaps even fall over, despite the information still being received from your feet, ankles and vestibular system.

The importance of vision in maintaining balance has been more formally demonstrated by Lee and his colleagues (Lee & Aronson, 1974; Lee & Lishman, 1975; Lishman & Lee, 1973) in an experimental arrangement known as the "swinging room." The room essentially consists of a bottomless box suspended from the ceiling. The subject stands on a floor and the walls of the room can be moved backwards or forwards around them, without their knowledge. The walls of the room are covered with wallpaper to provide a visual texture. When the room is moved towards the subject, this produces the same expanding optic flow pattern which would be produced if the observer were in fact swaying towards the wall. If the room is moved away from the observer this produces a contracting optical flow pattern as though the observer were swaying away from the wall. This is illustrated in Figure 12.1.

FIGURE 12.1

An adult or child stands in the swinging room. (a) The room is moved towards the subject and s/he sways or falls backwards. (b) The room is moved away, and s/he sways or falls forwards. (c) The expanding optic flow pattern which would result from movement of the room towards the subject. (d) The contracting optical flow pattern which would result from movement of the room away from the subject.

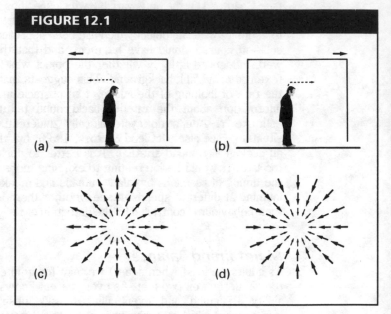

(a)   (b)

(c)   (d)

Using this apparatus Lee and his colleagues conducted a number of experiments in which they showed that vision could provide exproprioceptive information which could be used to control balance. In one experiment Lee and Aronson (1974) placed toddlers (aged 13–16 months) within the swinging room. After a period of acclimatisation in which the infant's normal stability while standing could be assessed, they tested the infant's reactions to slight movement of the wall of the room while the child was standing facing it. When the room was moved towards the subject he or she was observed to sway, stagger or fall in a direction away from the wall. This was not merely a defensive reaction to the "looming" pattern (cf. p. 268) because the child staggered or fell towards the wall when it was moved away from them (see Fig. 12.1). Indeed some of the children became distressed during the procedure and for them the experiment had to be prematurely terminated.

The responses shown by these children were entirely consistent with those that would be expected if the child interpreted the optic flow produced by movements of the room as resulting from its own postural sway. An outward flow, obtained when the room is moved towards the child, is consistent with sway towards the wall. The child then compensates for its apparent sway by moving backwards, and vice versa. It appears that in children acquiring the skill of balancing on two feet, visual information can over-ride the veridical information about actual posture obtained from the feet, ankles and vestibular system. Lee and Aronson suggest that it is vision which "tunes up" the sensitivity of these mechanical systems, and point out that visual information is a better source for the child to rely on while the feet and ankles are maturing and growing. Such observations may explain why congenitally blind children are slower than sighted ones in learning to stand and to walk, and blind adults show more body sway than sighted adults (Edwards, 1946).

Learning to stand upright is such an achievement for the child that we tend to forget earlier achievements, such as sitting upright. Vision seems to play a fundamental role in maintaining posture whether standing or sitting. Butterworth and Hicks (1977) showed that infants who have just learned to sit without being supported will sway with movements of the swinging room, and Butterworth (1983) showed that even two-month olds will move their heads with the room.

Even for adults it appears that visual information may over-ride that obtained from mechanical or vestibular receptor systems. A familiar example of this is when one experiences one's own stationary train as moving while another departs from the next platform, an example of induced movement (see Chapter 15). Lee and Lishman (1975) were able to affect body sway and stability in adults in normal and novel stances by movements of the swinging room. In one experiment they tested adults standing normally, on a sloping ramp, on a pile of foam pads (a "compliant" surface), or on their toes. Their degree of body sway was measured accurately with a sway meter when they stood with eyes open or eyes closed, or within the swinging room. Their body sway with eyes open could be "driven" by movements of the swinging room. Thus if the room was moved backwards and forwards in a regular, sinusoidal manner, the body was also seen to sway sinusoidally, linked to the movement of the walls. While this visual driving was observed in all four stances, it was greatest for adults standing on the compliant surface, where the information from the foot and ankle receptors was the most impoverished.

In a further experiment, Lee and Lishman had subjects adopt novel balancing postures such as the "Chaplin" stance (feet aligned at 180°) or the "pinstripe" stance (one foot angled behind the calf of the other leg while holding a weight in the hand opposite to the supporting leg). In such circumstances the adults, like the children in Lee and Aronson's study, could be made to stagger and fall by movements of the swinging room. They described the subject as like "a visual puppet; his balance can be manipulated by simply moving his surroundings without his being aware of it" (Lee & Lishman, 1975, p. 94).

The above examples monitored the forward and backward body sway of people facing the room as it moved towards or away from them. Lee and Young (1986) also describe studies by Anderson in

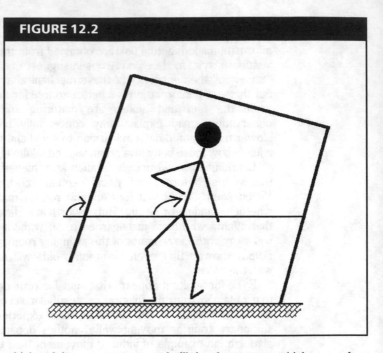

FIGURE 12.2

If the room is tilted as an adult or child walks or runs within it, their body tilts too. Adapted from Lee and Young (1986).

which adults ran on a treadmill in the room, which was then unexpectedly tilted around a horizontal axis (see Figure 12.2). The inclination of the room and of the subject's trunk was monitored using a Selspot movement measuring system, where infra-red light-emitting diodes are attached to key spots and a film of their positions over time is recorded. Using this method, it was possible to compare the sideways movements of the trunk in the normal room with the movements that occurred as the room was tilted. The trunk clearly tilted with the room, as though the runner were compensating for his or her perceived tilt in the opposite direction. Owen and Lee (1986) went on to test 3–5 year-old children walking on a solid floor as the walls of the room tilted around them. Like the adults, the children also tilted their trunks with the room.

We have seen that vision appears to play an important role in affecting gross postural adjustments. Babies respond to the exteroceptive information in looming patterns and try to avoid the "objects" which are about to collide with them. Toddlers and adults make use of exproprioceptive information from vision when maintaining balance. We now turn to consider how we use vision when we are actively negotiating terrain during locomotion.

WALKING, RUNNING AND JUMPING

It is obviously difficult to walk or run safely without adequate vision, but it is not necessarily obvious at how many different levels visual information is used to guide locomotion.

At the coarsest level, vision can inform moving animals of their direction of movement through the world. Any movement is accompanied by flow in the optic array, and the form of the flow pattern is precisely related to the direction of the movement. We have already considered, in Chapters 10 and 11, how patterns of flow specify the direction in which a human or animal is moving.

Visual information is also needed in order to avoid colliding with objects in the path of the movement or to steer a path through openings, and to specify the kind of terrain which lies ahead. At a coarse level, this includes discovering surfaces of support and avoiding "falling-off" places.

Detecting Falling-Off Places

From the moment they are independently mobile, young animals must avoid falling off dangerous edges. Adult humans generally avoid accidentally stepping over the edge of a cliff, but would an unattended infant avoid crawling off? This was the question posed by E. J. Gibson which led to her development of the "visual cliff" (Gibson & Walk, 1960). The apparatus is shown in Figure 12.3. It consists of a raised platform which divides two checkerboard surfaces (giving optical texture). One of these is at a similar level to the platform (the shallow side), the other is considerably lower (the deep side). Both sides provide surfaces of support, however, since the deep side is covered with a sheet of glass which is at the same level as that covering the shallow side. Thus both the shallow and deep sides have a surface which could safely support an animal or child, but the optical information given by the deep side specifies a sharp drop. Gibson and Walk showed that the young of all species which guide themselves mainly by vision, when placed on the central platform, would avoid venturing onto the glass covering the deep side. Human infants aged 6–14 months would not cross the glass even when encouraged by their mothers who were standing on the other side of it. Young animals placed on the glass showed defensive reactions.

By manipulating the size of the texture elements on the surfaces, and the distances of these from the central platform, Gibson and Walk were able to explore which variables were important in guiding the behaviour of the animals tested. If the squares on the deep side were made larger, so that the perceived density of the squares as seen from each side of the platform was equivalent, the animals still avoided the deep side, suggesting that motion parallax, rather than texture density, was the important variable. However, if the actual depth of each surface was made the same (i.e. both shallow), but one was patterned with smaller sized squares than the other, there was still a slight tendency to prefer the optically shallow side, suggesting some role for texture density. These observations suggest that by the time they are mobile (immediately for chicks and lambs, after 6 months or so for humans), young creatures can make use of motion parallax and also perhaps texture density changes in guiding themselves so that they

The visual cliff (Gibson & Walk, 1960). (a) Side view, (b) shows textured surfaces beneath the glass.

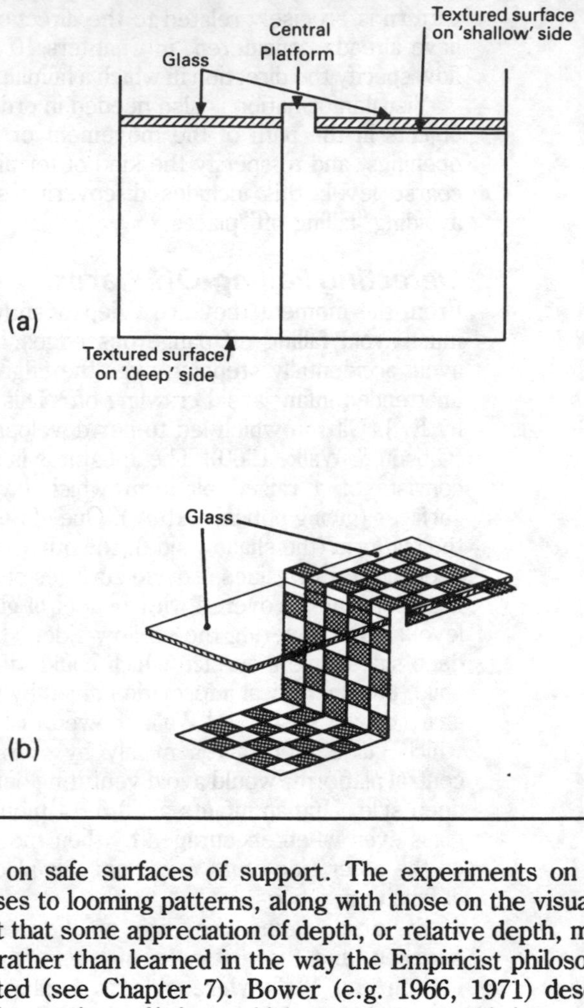

FIGURE 12.3

remain on safe surfaces of support. The experiments on infant responses to looming patterns, along with those on the visual cliff, suggest that some appreciation of depth, or relative depth, may be inborn rather than learned in the way the Empiricist philosophers suggested (see Chapter 7). Bower (e.g. 1966, 1971) describes other observations of infants which are relevant to this issue.

Regulating Gait

We have seen how vision may be used to detect gross aspects of layout, such as obstacles and cliffs, but vision is also necessary to guide finer aspects of locomotion. The movements of our limbs as we move through the world need to be tailored to the type of terrain we encounter, and the type of terrain needs to be anticipated and the limbs adjusted accordingly. To see why, we must briefly describe the nature of locomotor activity.

An animal or human walks or runs with a smooth and cyclically regular sequence of limb movements (Bernstein, 1967). It propels itself forwards by applying force backwards against the ground as each foot strikes it. When walking, one or more feet (depending on how many the walker possesses) remain in contact with the ground all the time; when running, the animal or human progresses by a series of leaps. The length of each leap ("flight") is determined by the speed at which the animal is travelling and the vertical thrust applied at each stride. Figure 12.4 illustrates this further for those familiar with vectors. For both walking and running it is important that the thrust being applied to the foot on contact is coordinated with the swing-through time of the foot which will next contact the ground, so that this meets the ground in the right way for maximum thrust. For example, if the foot is travelling forward relative to the ground when it contacts it, this will have a braking effect. Thus trained human runners try to lift their knees high so that they can thrust down hard and backwards relative to the ground as each foot strikes it just in front of the hips. The thrust applied at each stride must then give the runner sufficient vertical lift to ensure a long enough flight time so that the next foot can be swung through to its optimum strike position, and so on (Lee, Lishman & Thomson, 1982).

The striking of the ground needs not only to be timed, but the force exerted needs to be modified according to the type of surface encountered. If the ground surface is slippery then a large force will produce skidding rather than the desired propulsion forwards. If the surface is compliant rather than firm then much of the force will be absorbed by the surface rather than moving the animal (try running fast on soft sand), and so more force must be applied in

FIGURE 12.4

The distance travelled in each stride when running depends upon the vertical thrust (V) and a force reflected in horizontal velocity (H). At (a), both V and H are large, and the flight is long. At (b) the vertical thrust is reduced, and at (c) the horizontal velocity is reduced. In both cases, flight length is reduced. The flight path is not the resultant (R) of vectors V and H, because other forces are operating.

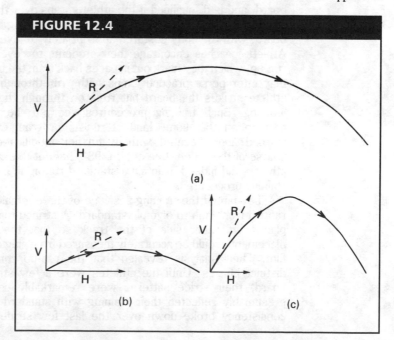

order to maintain speed. If the surface is uneven then the animal may fail to find adequate points of contact between its feet and the ground. Despite these difficulties humans and other animals can normally maintain fairly smooth progress through an environment of variable surfaces provided they can see properly. At night it can be an uncomfortably jarring experience to run across hilly or uneven ground, demonstrating how vision is needed to make fine adjustments to planned foot positions, postures and forces (Lee, 1980a).

It is thus essential that gait is regulated to meet the demands of a particular terrain. Theories of action which stress the "blind" running off of programs of locomotor activity have little to say about this:

> There will, in general, be unpredictable influences, both from within and without, which will deviate the activity from its intended course. The activity has, therefore, to be monitored in terms of the program and any deviation corrected by adjusting the ongoing program. It is in this continual process of formulating locomotor programs, monitoring their execution and adjusting them that sensory information plays its vital role (Lee & Lishman, 1977, p. 226).

Lee et al. (1982) have illustrated this adjusting of locomotor programs by sensory information in their studies of the sport of long-jumping. A long-jumper needs to maximise his or her horizontal velocity and vertical thrust at the point of take-off (refer back to Fig. 12.4). Since the jump is measured to the take-off board, and is disqualified if the athlete steps over this, the athlete must try to reach maximum speed as the launching foot strikes the board, with the body postured appropriately to give maximum lift. Athletic coaches encourage their students to develop a standard run-up, which they mark out in paces back from the board, and they may intersperse practice jumps with "run-throughs," where the athlete strikes the board but runs on through the sand without jumping. Such training procedures seem to be based on the assumption that some kind of run-up program can be set up, learned and executed without further modification during the course of the action. Lee et al. (1982) set out to examine whether athletes did indeed maintain a standard run-up in accordance with training procedures.

They filmed the training sessions of three female athletes who ranged from club to olympic standard. A striped marker strip was placed on either side of the track so that the athletes' foot placements could be accurately measured from single frames of the film. Their analysis revealed that the run-up consisted of two distinct phases. Until the athletes were a few strides from the board, their stride patterns were remarkably constant, which presumably reflected their training with standard run-ups. This consistency broke down over the last few strides however. It appeared that the cumulative effect of the small inconsistencies during the first phase meant that the athlete had to adjust her final few strides in order to strike the board accurately. There was a dramatic increase in the variability of stride lengths for the last three strides, while the standard error (a measure of variability) of the footfall positions decreased dramatically over these same few strides, to reach 8 cm at the board for the olympic athlete. It appeared that athletes were homing in on the board by adjusting the flight time of each of the last few strides. You will remember that flight length, and hence flight time, will be affected by changes in the vertical thrust applied if velocity remains constant (see Fig. 12.4). Lee et al. argue that these few strides are visually guided by the optic flow parameter τ which specifies time-to-contact with the board. In Chapter 11 (p. 261) we showed how τ was derived by considering the relative velocities of optical texture elements. For the examples we will discuss in this chapter:

$\tau(t)$ = 1/rate of dilation of retinal image of an obstacle

In the case of the long-jumper, τ would be given by the inverse of the rate of dilation of the image of the board. The average adjustment which is needed to the vertical thrusts of the last few strides (in order to modulate the flight times) is t'_f/t_f where t'_f is the required mean flight time of the remaining strides and t_f is the current flight time. t'_f is specified by time-to-contact.

Warren, Young and Lee (1986) were able to get more direct evidence that strides are adjusted by varying flight length (and hence flight time) through modulating the vertical thrust (see Fig. 12.4) on each stride. In an ingenious analogue of the task of running over variable terrain, they used a Selspot recording system to film trained athletes who had to place their feet on irregularly-spaced targets as they ran on a treadmill. Warren et al. confirmed that it was indeed flight length, rather than the trail and reach components of the stride length, that were adjusted by the athlete in such a situation. ("Trail" and "reach" refer to the extent to which the foot extends away from the body at take-off and landing respectively.) Furthermore, since flight velocity was kept roughly constant, it appeared that flight distance was indeed primarily adjusted by varying flight time. Consistent with this, they found that most of the variation in the step time was due to variations in vertical step thrust.

The long-jumpers and athletes studied by Lee and his colleagues represent extreme examples of precisely timed locomotion, but those of us of meagre athletic ability are still able to run to catch a bus, jumping over puddles and negotiating kerbs and other minor hurdles on the way. These activities are probably visually controlled in the same way as the more precise skill of long-jumping. For many of us, however, speedy transport is achieved by driving, rather than running. In the next section we consider how the control of some aspects of driving might also be given by the use of τ.

DRIVING CARS

Braking

Humans, unlike other animals, can propel themselves speedily and effortlessly through the world with the aid of machines. The motor-cyclist or car driver must learn to steer his or her vehicle around corners and obstacles, and must be able to slow down or stop as conditions dictate. A good driver will use the brake in good time, and with the correct force so that the car's speed can be reduced appropriately and smoothly. However, if brakes are applied too late (see unsafe driver 3 in Fig. 12.5), or too gently (unsafe driver 2 in Fig. 12.5), the driver will enter the "crash zone" shown in Figure 12.5, which may be fatal.

There are thus two components to braking—knowing when to start and knowing how hard to brake. When following fairly closely behind another vehicle a driver is usually given a clear visual signal to start applying brakes when the brake-lights of the car in front light up. He or she still has to decide how hard to apply the brakes, however, since normal brake lights give no indication about how much the car in front is slowing. The driver must therefore respond to the optic information which specifies how quickly he or she is closing on the car in front. It is better to brake strongly at first, since this minimises the stopping distance, but the driver must also avoid braking too severely for the car behind to respond in turn. Good drivers drive safe braking distances apart, and this also requires adjustment according to speed and road conditions.

When brakes must be applied to negotiate an "obstacle" (e.g. traffic lights) the driver must decide when to start braking as well

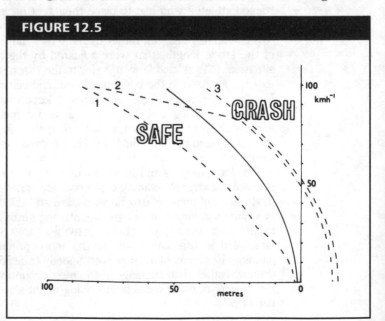

FIGURE 12.5

To stop safely, a driver must reduce speed (Km per hour) to zero before the distance to an obstacle (metres) reaches zero. The safe driver (1) in this figure achieves this by braking strongly at first, and then more gently. Driver 3 does not start to brake soon enough, and driver 2 brakes too gently. Reproduced from Lee and Lishman (1977), with permission of the publishers.

as how much pressure to apply. A potentially dangerous situation is encountered by the driver when leaving a fast highway where he or she may have adapted to travelling at a high constant velocity, and may fail to brake sufficiently to negotiate a steeply curved exit road or a roundabout (traffic circle). The driver's ability to reduce his speed accordingly can be enhanced by giving explicit advice on road signs about recommended exit or cornering speeds, or by augmenting the visual information which the driver responds to by constructing fences or painting lines across the road. One of the major through-routes in England, the A1, is particularly dangerous because it is almost of motorway (freeway) standard, hence people drive fast, but it is sometimes interrupted by roundabouts (traffic circles) which must be taken slowly. Yellow lines have been painted across the road on the approach to some of these roundabouts, and the lines get closer together nearer the roundabout. The lines themselves give one a vivid impression of speed after the relatively featureless miles preceding them, and the gradual change in the spacing of the lines gives drivers visual information that suggests they are decelerating less quickly than they actually are. This causes drivers to brake harder than they might otherwise.

It would appear that good drivers must be constantly monitoring their distance from other cars and obstacles, and must know about their own and other cars' speeds, acceleration and deceleration in order to brake effectively. However, Lee (1976) has argued that the control of braking can be more economically achieved if the driver responds directly to information about time-to-contact which is available in the optic flow field.

Lee suggests that a driver could register the value of $\tau(t)$ simply from the inverse of the proportionate rate of separation of the retinal images of any two points on the obstacle, e.g. the tail lights of a vehicle. That is:

$$\tau(t) = 1/(\text{rate of dilation of retinal image of obstacle})$$

$$\tau(t) = \frac{(\text{angular separation of the tail lights})}{(\text{rate of separation of the tail lights})}$$

In daylight the driver might make use of the image of the entire car in front, but only tail lights could be used at a distance at night. Lee suggests that drivers could make use of the optic variable τ and its derivative with respect to time, $\dot{\tau}$, to determine whether they are gaining on or receding from the car in front, and so to judge when to start braking for an obstacle or a moving vehicle, and to determine safe following distances and speeds. For example, Figure 12.6 shows a model which Lee (1976; also Lee & Lishman, 1977) suggests might describe how drivers make use of τ and $\dot{\tau}$ in deciding whether they need to brake (to avoid collision) or to accelerate (to keep up with traffic flow). This figure shows that a driver's deceleration is adequate if $\dot{\tau} > -\frac{1}{2}$ (a figure derived in detail in Lee 76). A driver could therefore function safely provided he or she maintained $\dot{\tau}$ at some marginal value greater than $-\frac{1}{2}$. Lee

FIGURE 12.6

Lee's (1976) model
illustrates how a
driver can
maintain a safe
distance by
maintaining τ
and τ̇ at safe
values. See Lee
(1976) for
derivation of these
values.
Reproduced from
Lee and Lishman
(1977), with
permission of the
publishers.

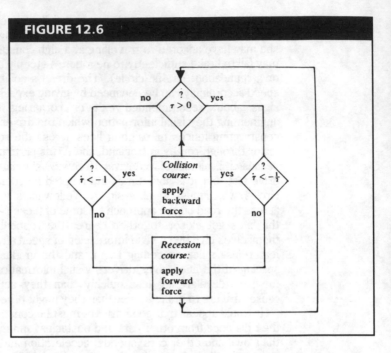

shows that such an assumption gives quite a good fit to data obtained in experiments where drivers were asked to stop at a specified point which they approached with varying speeds (Spurr, 1969).

Lee also suggests that road safety could be improved by amplifying or adding to the visual information gained from the rear ends of vehicles, particularly at night. By adding a reflectant strip so that the driver sees a progressively wider band of light the closer he or she approaches a vehicle at night, the information about rate of closure would be amplified, just as the yellow stripes painted across roads (see p.279) amplify information about speed. Information could be added by having an "imperative" brake signal, in addition to the normal brake lights, which would only operate when strong pressure was applied to the brake pedal by the driver in front.

Steering

We have already discussed in Chapter 10 how the optic flow pattern produced by movement along a straight path can inform an observer about the direction in which he or she is travelling. Lee and Lishman (1977) describe how optic flow can be used to guide steering. First, the optic flow line which disappears from view directly underneath the driver—the locomotor flow line—indicates the potential path that would be followed if no correction to the steering was applied. Second, the relationship between the images of the edges of the road and the optic flow lines can inform drivers whether they are on or off course. These two features of optical flow patterns could be used by drivers to adjust their steering. When steering on course, the locomotor flow line will lie down the centre of the road and the edges of the road will coincide with optic flow lines. When off-course, neither of these conditions will hold (see Fig. 12.7). A driver also has to anticipate bends, and begin to slow down before reaching sharp ones. Lee and Lishman suggest that information about time-to-contact (with the edge of the road,

FIGURE 12.7

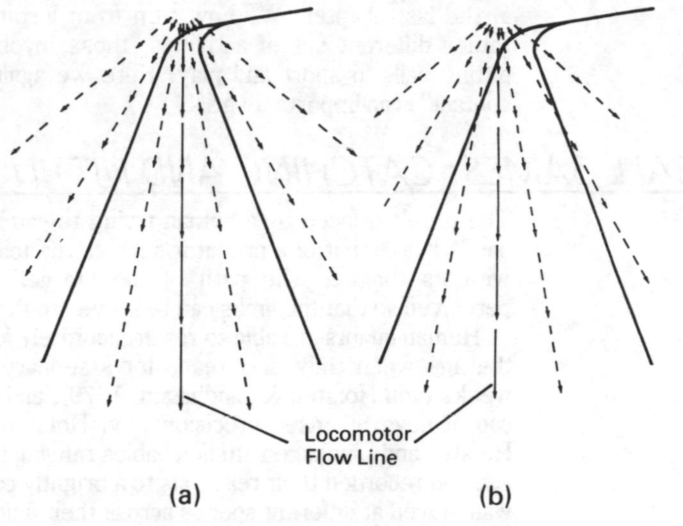

At (a) the driver is on course. The locomotor flow line lies down the centre of the lane on which the car travels, and optic flow lines coincide with the edges of the road. At (b) neither of these conditions holds, and the driver is off course. Adapted from Lee and Lishman (1977), with permission of the publishers.

Locomotor Flow Line

(a)   (b)

for example) could be used here in the same way as in braking on a straight path.

Drivers are not the only road-users who need to appreciate safe distances. Pedestrians crossing roads must also understand whether gaps between cars are large enough for safe crossing. This requires that pedestrians can perceive the difference between the times of arrival (time to contact) of the vehicles on either side of this gap, and can relate this difference to their own walking speed and distance across the road. Lee, Young and McLaughlin (1984) have devised a "pretend road" crossing task for children to practise this skill safely, by pretending that a stretch of pavement beside a road is the road itself. Children practise crossing the pavement successfully so that they get to the other side of the pavement well before cars on the real road reach the same target point. Young and Lee (1987) evaluated a training programme based upon the pretend road task extended to include two-way traffic. They found that after training, five year-olds developed road-crossing competence at a level normally shown by considerably older children. Practice with the task led five year-olds to set off to cross the pretend road more promptly when gaps were smaller, leading Lee and Young (1986) to suggest that five-year olds have developed an improved ability to detect τ and to use this information to guide their actions. The pretend road crossing task could thus prove an important component of road safety training, since it is at the ages of five and six that child pedestrian accidents are at a peak (Howarth, Routledge & Repetto-Wright, 1974).

A single variable, τ, therefore seems to be involved in a variety of locomotor activities, which include the defensive reactions of babies, the regulation of gait by long-jumpers, and timing of actions by road-users, as well as the control of diving in gannets described in the last chapter. We now turn from locomotion to consider a rather different set of activities, those involved in catching and hitting balls in sport and play. Here we again find that "time to contact" is an important variable.

BALL GAMES: CATCHING AND HITTING

The problem faced by a human trying to catch a ball in his or her hands is like that of a predator such as the toad catching an insect with its tongue. The path of the "target" must be correctly perceived so that the limbs can be moved to the right positions.

Human infants are able to reach accurately for a moving object at the age when they first reach for stationary ones, by about 18 weeks (von Hofsten & Lindhagen, 1979), and by 9 months infants can achieve 50 msec precision (von Hofsten, 1980, 1983). Von Hofsten and Lindhagen studied babies ranging from 12–36 weeks of age and recorded their reactions to a brightly coloured target which was moved at different speeds across their field of vision. Reaching occurred more frequently to slowly moving targets and more often in the older children. Across all age groups those reaches which were made were almost always accurate, suggesting that the babies only initiated a reach when they were likely to be successful. The youngest babies, at 12 weeks, hardly ever attempted to reach, and as they developed they reached first for the "easier," slowly moving targets.

A detailed film analysis of the reaches made by the babies (von Hofsten, 1980) revealed that they moved their arms in a series of ballistic (open-loop) movements to the point where contact would be made with the moving target. Babies at all ages were remarkably accurate at predicting the path of the target, but the older infants reached for it more "economically," using fewer ballistic steps. "While the infants seem to know where to go in order to catch the object most efficiently when they begin to reach, they do not seem to know quite how to get there" (von Hofsten, 1980, p. 381).

Even the youngest infants were able to "home in" on the target using discrete moves without looking back at their hands, suggesting that at this age they are able to define the position of their hands in perceived space using information from their joints and muscles.

Thus the prerequisites of catching or hitting appear to be at least partially pre-wired in the human. What seems to develop is the motor skill of getting to the target economically and grasping it, or hitting it, once there. In order to catch a moving ball, for example, the hand or hands must be oriented correctly and appropriate grasping movements initiated "before" the ball makes physical contact with the hand, while it is still in flight. Alderson, Sully and Sully (1974) studied one-handed catching of tennis balls and found that the fine orienting movements of the hand began 150–200 msec before the ball struck the palm and the grasping movement started 32–50 msec before contact.

While some vision is essential in order to assess the flight path and speed of a moving target in order to initiate these movements it does not seem to be necessary to view the entire trajectory. Whiting and Sharp (1974) studied one-handed catching of tennis balls which were only illuminated for 80 msec of their trajectory. The duration of the dark period which followed this brief illumination was varied from 125 to 445 msec (which included a period of 125 msec assumed to reflect CNS latency). They found that the function relating accuracy of catching and occlusion duration was U-shaped. Performance was poor if the occluded period was greater than 365 msec or shorter than 205 msec, peaking at 285 msec. It appears that there is an optimal point in the trajectory during which to view the ball in order to predict its path, this being when the time to contact is about 250–300 msec. If the ball is seen too early it gets "lost," possibly because of limitations on immediate memory. If it is seen too late there may be insufficient time to process the flight information and then begin the correct series of orienting movements.

Lee (1980a) has suggested that the 300 msec time-to-contact interval is critical because catchers standardise the duration of their movements and therefore need only to initiate these movements at a specific time to contact. Standard movement durations have been observed in a study by Schmidt (1969) where subjects had to move a slider to hit an approaching target, and also in ball-hitting by baseball batters. Hubbard and Seng (1954) filmed baseball batters and observed that they always began to step forward when the ball was released by the pitcher, but geared the duration of the step to the speed of the ball. The duration of the bat swing was kept constant but its initiation was dependent on ball speed, occurring about 40 msec after the forward foot was planted. Hubbard and Seng also tried to record the head and eye movements made by their sample of batters as they tracked the path of the ball. Though their methods were insensitive, their film analysis did suggest that batters did not track or fixate the ball during the final stage of its flight, nor when it actually made contact with the bat (contrary to the advice given in training manuals). Again it appears that it is information about time to contact picked up earlier in the flight path which is of more importance than the information gained in the final moments before contact occurs.

Lee, Young, Reddish, Lough and Clayton (1983) have explored the visual control of hitting in a situation where subjects had to leap up and punch balls which were dropped from varying heights above them, as in volleyball. A ball dropping towards the ground accelerates at a constant rate under the influence of gravity. Its velocity thus increases continuously. Lee et al. suggested that subjects might still make use of τ—the *instantaneous* time to contact at any point in the drop (cf. our discussion of gannets in Chapter 11). τ will always be greater than the *actual* time-to-contact (t_c) at that point, as illustrated in Figure 12.8. τ depends on the instantaneous velocity, and assumes that this remains constant for the remainder of the drop. But because the ball is accelerating, its average velocity for the remaining drop time will be greater than the velocity used to compute τ, and hence the actual time to contact, t_c, will be less than τ. The overestimation

FIGURE 12.8

The relationship between τ (instantaneous time to contact) and t_c (actual time to contact) for balls dropped from three different heights to yield three different drop times (0.78, 1.01 and 1.21 sec). From Lee et al. (1983). Published with permission of the Quarterly Journal of Experimental Psychology.

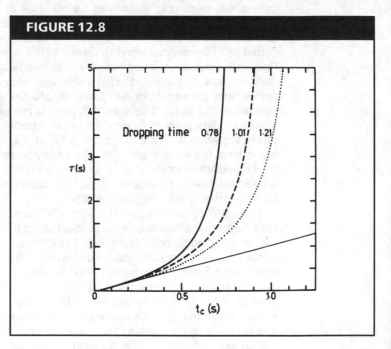

of t_c given by τ depends on the total drop time as illustrated in Figure 12.8.

If subjects were using τ to time their actions, one would predict that each stage of the punching action would occur earlier, the longer the drop time of the ball. For example, if the value τ of used to control a particular stage of the action were 1 sec, Figure 12.8 shows that this corresponds to a t_c of about 0.6 sec for a long drop and about 0.5 sec for a short drop. However, the action patterns for the different drop times should converge close to contact, since as Figure 12.8 shows, τ and t_c converge when actual time to contact is less than 250 msec. (It may be for this reason that 250–300 msec is an important time to contact during which to view a ball in flight, since it is at this point that τ can be used to give an accurate measure of the actual time to contact, while still allowing enough time for orienting movements to occur.) By measuring the changes occurring in the angles of the knee and elbow as these were flexed and extended in the punching act, Lee et al. were able to confirm these predictions, and produce evidence that the actions were indeed timed by making use of τ.

Here we have considered only a single component of the ball-game, that of striking the ball, and we have seen how timing of the actions seems to depend on the detection of time-to-contact earlier in the flight path. However, there is a further, crucial aspect of ball-game performance, which is directing the ball to some particular target. The volley-ball player need not just punch the ball, as in Lee et al's study, but punch it towards some target location or other. Rather than look at the ball in the last few moments of its flight, it seems success at directing it towards a target is achieved by looking at the target itself, and this in turn requires stabilisation of both head and eye (e.g. see Ripoll, Bard & Paillard (1986) for a study of shooting in basket-ball, and Bahill & LaRitz (1984) for a study of baseball strikers). Coordination of body, head and eye movements is an important ingredient of all action-oriented perception and the development and control of such coordination is a rapidly growing research topic (e.g. see Lee, Daniel & Kerr, 1988; Owen & Lee, 1986).

We have discussed at some length in this chapter and the previous one how a variety of animal and human activities may be regulated through the detection of fairly simple parameters derived from optic flow. To show that a particular variable, like τ, could be used to control action is much easier to do than to show how our physiology might function to compute τ, or to show *how* τ is involved at the level of regulating muscle actions. We have ignored both these problems in our discussion up till now. In the next two chapters we deal explicitly with some of the issues raised by the computation of motion and by the control of action.

Chapter Thirteen

THE COMPUTATION OF IMAGE MOTION

*I*n Chapters 11 and 12 we described evidence that variables of optic flow control posture and movement in animals and people, supporting Gibson's argument that a proper understanding of visual perception involves considering how the pattern of light reaching an observer transforms as the observer moves. Evidence of this kind establishes what parameters of optic flow are detected and what information they provide about an observer's surroundings. According to Gibson, this information is directly picked up by an observer, without any kind of processing of the fluctuating pattern of light reaching the eyes. Therefore, he argued, the task of explaining visual perception is complete once we have discovered the information in light to which the observer is attuned.

Alternatively, one could agree with Gibson that transformations in the structure of light reaching an observer are an essential source of information, but reject his arguments for a direct theory of perception. From this viewpoint, the evidence we have discussed in the preceding chapters establishes what information the visual system needs to extract from a retinal image as it changes over time; to use Marr's terms, introduced in Chapter 3 (p. 61), the evidence contributes to a computational theory of the information available in optic flow. In order to understand how this information is obtained, we need to devise algorithms capable of extracting it from a time-varying retinal image and then ask whether these algorithms are implemented in nervous systems.

It is important first to note a potential problem in obtaining properties of optic flow from a transforming retinal image. As defined by Gibson (1966), Lee (1980b) or Clocksin (1980), the optic flow field is a transformation in the optic array at a point or in its projection on a plane. It is therefore a pattern of velocities independent of any particular co-ordinate system tied to a projection surface. Now, if we are concerned with how optic flow properties are obtained from a time-varying retinal image, we must start by obtaining values for optical velocity tied to particular retinal co-ordinates. If this co-ordinate system *rotates* relative to the world, for example when the eye moves, then there will be optical motion relative to retinal co-ordinates, but no optic flow.

In consequence, the optical velocity at any point on the retina is made up of a rotatory and a translatory component, and so does not specify optic flow at that point unambiguously. To resolve the ambiguity, the two components of velocity must be determined separately. Longuet-Higgins and Prazdny (1980) have shown that this is possible, because the image velocity due to rotation is independent of object distance, whereas that due to translation is not. For an observer moving through rigid surroundings, motion parallax generated by objects at different distances lying along the same line of sight can therefore be used to resolve the two components. The solution is more complex for separately moving objects, but rotation and translation can still be resolved.

There has been considerable research on algorithms for processing time-varying images to obtain optical velocity, relative motion and more complex information. Before describing the results of this work, it is important to explain its relationship to the theories of motion perception based on retinal images which we described in Chapter 7. These theories take a series of discrete, static retinal images as input, and treat motion computation as a problem of establishing correspondences between features in these successive "snapshots" (e.g. Ullman, 1979). The justification for this approach lies in the phenomenon of apparent motion; an object is seen as moving smoothly when its position changes discretely from one frame of a display to another, as in a cine film.

As we discussed in Chapter 7 (p. 163), there is evidence that such high-level matching of abstract features over relatively large displacements is not the only process involved in motion perception. There is also a "short-range" process (Braddick, 1980) which operates over shorter time intervals and spatial displacements. Since the short-range process can operate on random-dot kinematograms, its input must be either light intensity values or low level features in the raw primal sketch, rather than the higher-level features which correspondence theories assume are matched between images. The existence of the short-range process therefore shows that a part of the explanation of motion perception lies in algorithms which can extract parameters of image motion from time-varying intensity values or edge information (Hildreth, 1984b).

We can therefore define an early stage of motion computation, which takes as its input a time-varying array of grey-level intensity values, and yields as its output the *velocity field*; an array of measurements of image velocity in each small region of the image, which can in turn be used as input to other processes computing higher-level properties of image motion. Since velocity is a vector quantity, each measurement must specify both direction and magnitude of motion (see Fig. 13.1).

FIGURE 13.1

(a) An image
consisting of a
moving square
against a
stationary
background. (b)
Its velocity field
representation,
specifying the
speed and
direction of motion
in each region of
the image.

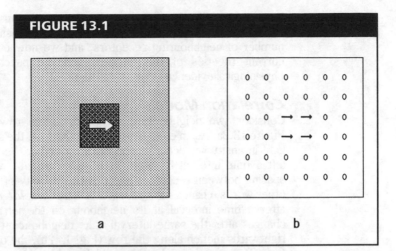

FIGURE 13.2

Gradients of light
intensity passing
over a row of
receptors.

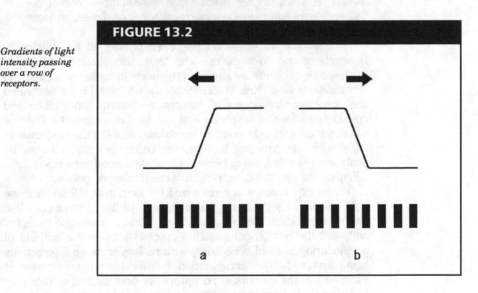

EARLY MOTION COMPUTATION

The goal of early motion computation is to obtain values for velocity from time-varying intensity values. How can this be done? Note first that velocity cannot be determined from changes in intensity at a single point. Figure 13.2a shows an intensity gradient moving over a row of light receptors. As it passes over each one, light intensity rises. This change provides no information about the direction of motion, however, as an increase in intensity could be caused by an edge of opposite contrast moving in the opposite direction (Fig. 13.2b). Nor does it provide information about the speed of motion of the edge; a particular rate of change in intensity could be caused by a slowly moving sharp edge or a fast moving fuzzy edge. Clearly, velocity measurements must be obtained through some computation performed on intensity values in a number of neighbouring receptors, and we now outline the main current theories of this process and the psychophysical and physiological evidence relevant to them.

Correlation Models

Consider two neighbouring receptors in the row illustrated in Figure 13.2a. As an edge passes along the row, the same change in light intensity will occur at one receptor and at the receptor to its left a time interval δt later (δt is given by x/v, where x is the spacing between receptors and v is the velocity of the image). In other words, changes at a receptor will be *correlated* with changes after a time interval at its neighbour on the left, but not with changes after the same interval at its neighbour on the right. For rightwards motion along the row (Fig. 13.2b), the opposite will be true. Therefore, any algorithm which could compute correlations in this way between neighbouring receptors could yield at least the direction of image motion as output.

An algorithm of this kind has been developed by Reichardt, Braitenberg and co-workers, who have also obtained extensive evidence that it is implemented in the nervous systems of flies and other insects (e.g. Reichardt, 1969). In Chapter 11 we described the optomotor response of insects to uniform optic flow and considered how this response acts to stabilise an insect's flight or to keep it on a straight course. Reichardt has used the response as a means of determining how insects compute image motion, by analysing the relationship between spatiotemporal patterns of light falling on the eye and the strength of the turning response.

These experiments are reviewed by Reichardt (1969), and we will consider only their main conclusions. All the retinula cells in a single ommatidium (see Chapter 1, p. 12) act as a single receptor unit, and the motion computation process acts on the outputs of neighbouring pairs of receptors, with no longer range interactions being involved. The computation follows the stages shown in Figure 13.3; the outputs of receptors are first filtered so that only fast changes in intensity are passed, with steady components being filtered out (the effect is the same as that of adaptation described in Chapter 2, p. 32). The outputs of these filters are then multiplied together with those from neighbouring receptors a short time before. Within a pair of receptors, two multiplications are performed and the difference between the results is the output of the whole motion detection unit.

To understand how this computation works, consider an edge moving to the left over the pair of receptors and follow through the signals produced at each stage (Fig. 13.3). The output has a positive value as the edge passes over the unit, whereas with rightward motion the output is negative. The output therefore gives the direction of image motion by comparing the correlation between intensity changes in one direction with that in the other

FIGURE 13.3

Left: Reichardt's motion computation model. R— receptors. F— filters. D—delay units. X— multiplication units. C—unit comparing results of multiplications (subtracts output of X₂ from that of X₁). Right: An illustration of the model's operation. A dark edge passes from right to left over the row of receptors. The graphs show the change in the output of each unit over time, starting from the same point in time. The final output of unit C is positive; the reader should confirm that left— and rightwards motion give positive and negative outputs respectively, whether the moving edge is light or dark.

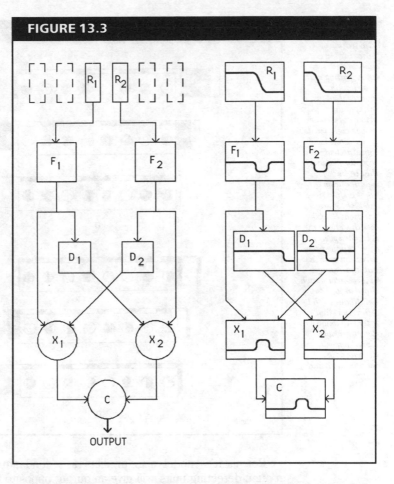

OUTPUT

direction. Note that the unit cannot give a reliable measure of the speed of motion. Although the output does vary with speed, it is also a function of the contrast of the moving pattern and of the spatial frequencies present in it, and so is ambiguous.

The description of Reichardt's model in Figure 13.3 is simplified, giving its key features without the mathematical specifications which enable it to predict precisely the optomotor responses of insects. These details are also given in Reichardt (1969), together with further tests of the model. We will briefly mention two of these. First, a critical feature of the model is that the signals from neighbouring receptors are multiplied; note that if they were summed instead the model would fail, giving opposite outputs to edges of opposite contrasts but moving in the same direction. This multiplication process is demonstrated in an experiment where an increase in light intensity at one ommatidium O_1 is followed by a decrease in its neighbour O_2. Although the direction of successive stimuli is from O_1 to O_2, the insect responds by turning in the opposite direction, as the model predicts.

FIGURE 13.4

Illustration of "aliasing" in a motion detector. (a) A grating with wavelength greater than twice the spacing between receptors moves rightwards. The change in light intensity at a receptor matches that in its neighbour on the right a short time later. (b) A grating with wavelength less than twice the receptor spacing moves in the same direction as in (a), but now changes at a receptor match those in its neighbour on the left a short time later. A motion detector would signal opposite directions of motion in (a) and (b).

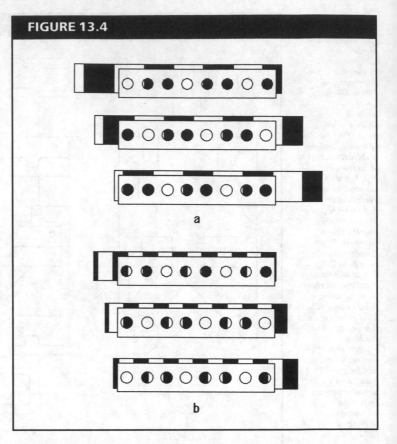

Reichardt's model also predicts a second situation in which motion detecting units will give an output opposite to the direction of image motion. This is when the spacing of light intensity changes in the image becomes so close that edges are closer together than the distance between receptors. For example, if the image of a grating moves over the eye, reversal of motion detector output will occur when the wavelength of the grating falls below twice the receptor spacing (see Fig. 13.4). This prediction of reversal of the optomotor response, or *aliasing*, with high spatial frequency gratings has been confirmed experimentally.

The physiological processes which perform the correlation algorithm in insects have not yet been identified. Direction selective cells have been found in the lobula plate of the fly, a stage of the visual pathway separated from receptors by several synaptic steps (Hausen, 1982). These cells presumably carry the output of motion detection units, but the way in which their synaptic input carries out the correlation algorithm is not known. Neurophysiological evidence for physiological implementation of the correlation algorithm has instead come from direction selective cells in vertebrate retinas (see Chapter 2, p. 41). These are relatively common in some species, such as rabbits, but less so in cats and monkeys, where they are classed as a type of W cell.

Barlow and Levick (1965) proposed a model of the organisation of the fields of direction selective retinal ganglion cells, which works on the same correlation principle as Reichardt's model. As Figure 13.5 shows, the cells have an excitatory input from one receptor R_1 and a delayed inhibitory input from a neighbouring receptor R_2. Movement in the direction R_1 to R_2 therefore excites the cell, while movement from R_2 to R_1 causes coincident inhibition which cancels the response. Barlow and Levick (1965) obtained evidence that this interaction occurs separately in many small regions in the cell's field, and so the cell sums the outputs of many units of the kind shown in Figure 13.5. Torre and Poggio (1978) have proposed that the inhibition involved is of the "silent" or "shunting" type, where an inhibitory synapse does not hyperpolarise the cell membrane but stabilises its membrane potential near the resting level, so abolishing any depolarisation produced at an excitatory synapse. Marchiafava (1979) has obtained evidence for this mechanism from intracellular recordings from direction selective cells in the turtle retina. Subsequent research has indicated that the excitatory and inhibitory inputs come from two types of amacrine cell releasing different neurotransmitters; a review is given by Hildreth and Koch (1987).

The correlation model gives a good account of motion detection in insects and in directionally selective retinal ganglion cells, but does it provide an adequate model of human motion detection? One problem is that aliasing, or motion reversal, does not occur when people see high-frequency moving gratings, but van Santen and Sperling (1984) show that a straightforward modification of Reichardt's model can account for this. They replace the point

Barlow and Levick's (1965) model of directionally selective ganglion cells. If receptor R_1 is stimulated and then receptor R_2, the signal from R_1 arrives ahead of inhibition from R_2 and the cell responds. With movement in the opposite direction, inhibition from R_2 coincides with the signal from R_1 and there is no response.

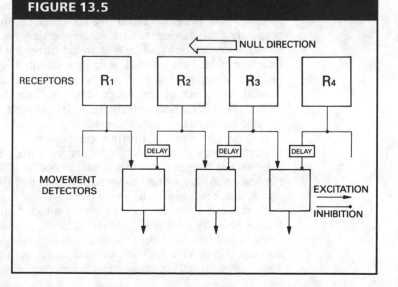

FIGURE 13.5

samples of light intensity which provide input in the original model by spatially extended receptive fields which filter out high spatial frequencies. Van Santen and Sperling show that the results of a variety of experiments on motion detection are consistent with predictions of their model.

A problem in interpreting psychophysical evidence such as that obtained by van Santen and Sperling (1984) is that other models of motion detection can yield the same results through the operation of different algorithms. An important example is the model proposed by Adelson and Bergen (1985), which yields a direction selective response without a multiplicative interaction of the kind used in Reichardt's model. Adelson and Bergen instead use filters which weight intensity values depending upon their location in the filter's receptive field and then sum the weighted values linearly. The principle is the same as that underlying linear summation in X retinal ganglion cells (Chapter 2, p. 39), but broadened to encompass fields extended in time as well as space; the contribution of intensity values to the output is weighted according to their times of occurrence as well as their spatial positions. A particular class of these spatiotemporal filters are direction selective, but, unlike the Reichardt model, their output fluctuates as a pattern moves with constant velocity. Adelson and Bergen (1985) show how further steps can be added to the model to correct this, and the final result turns out to be equivalent to van Santen and Sperling's (1984) version of Reichardt's model, yielding the same result for a particular input, but through a different series of steps (see also van Santen and Sperling, 1985).

The motion detectors of Adelson and Bergen (1985) and van Santen and Sperling (1984) yield the same predictions and cannot be distinguished through psychophysical methods alone. They do, however, make different predictions about the responses and interconnections of single cells involved in motion computation. Adelson and Bergen (1985) would predict two types of cell responding to moving stimuli, corresponding to two stages of spatiotemporal filtering. The first would correspond to "separable" filters, in which the overall weighting of intensity values is the product of separate spatial and temporal weightings, while the second would act as "non-separable" or "oriented" filters, and would show direction selectivity. McLean and Palmer (1989) provide evidence that motion-sensitive cells in cat striate cortex fall into these two classes. Further information is needed about the pattern of connections between cells in order to determine whether Adelson and Bergen's model is implemented in the cortex; if so, an implication is that motion detection is achieved through different algorithms in retinal W cells and in cortical cells.

Another model of motion computation based on linear filters is proposed by Watson and Ahumada (1985). If modified to give a constant output to a pattern moving with constant velocity, it is also equivalent to Reichardt's correlation model (van Santen & Sperling, 1985). Watson and Ahumada argue, however, that the fluctuating output of linear filters is a desirable property in a motion detector, as the frequency of fluctuation codes for image velocity independent of contrast, unlike the output amplitude of the Reichardt model.

Gradient Models

We have seen that the rate of change of light intensity at a receptor cannot provide information about the direction or the speed of image motion (see Fig. 13.2). The ambiguity in direction of motion could be resolved if the sign of the spatial gradient of light intensity were computed; an increase in intensity together with a positive spatial gradient unambiguously signals leftwards motion, for example. Further, if the steepness of the spatial gradient is known, the speed of image motion can also be determined. The relationship between velocity, rate of change of intensity at a point and the spatial gradient of intensity around that point is given by

$$v = - \frac{\partial I}{\partial t} \cdot \frac{\partial x}{\partial I}$$

where v is the image velocity and $\partial I/\partial t$ and $\partial I/\partial x$ are the partial derivatives of intensity with respect to time and to distance along an axis x. If these two derivatives can be computed, velocity along a single axis can be measured unambiguously. The time derivative can be obtained from the changing intensity at a single receptor, but computation of the spatial gradient must involve intensity values from two or more neighbouring receptors.

This "gradient" algorithm for measuring velocity offers the advantage over the correlation method of giving an accurate value for image speed, but is it implemented in any visual systems? Marr and Ullman (1981) have proposed that an algorithm of this kind provides a second process of motion computation in the mammalian visual pathway, in parallel with that represented by the W retinal ganglion cells described above. Marr and Ullman argue that this second process is seen in the direction selective responses of some simple cells in visual cortex (Chapter 3, p. 53) and that, unlike the correlation-based motion system in W cells, it is closely integrated with the detection of edges. In particular, they propose that as gradients in intensity are measured by Marr and Hildreth's (1980) $\nabla^2 G$ algorithm (Chapter 5, p. 87), the velocity of motion of these gradients is computed at the same time. The presence of a spatial gradient is already signalled in a zero-crossing in the output of a $\nabla^2 G$ filter, and Marr and Ullman propose that this is differentiated with respect to time to yield a velocity measurement.

Figure 13.6a shows the profile of $\nabla^2 G*I$ values around a zero-crossing at X; if the whole pattern of light is moving to the right, the values of $d(\nabla^2 G*I)/dt$ are as in Figure 13.6b, while if it is moving to the left they are as in Figure 13.6c. Movement to the right gives a positive value of the time derivative at point X while movement to the left gives a negative value. The algorithm can therefore compute the direction of motion along one axis.

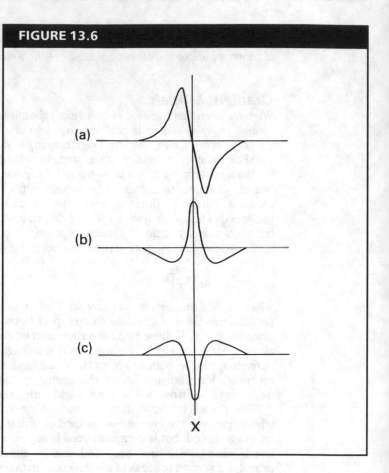

FIGURE 13.6

A gradient of light intensity at X gives the profile of $\nabla^2 G*I$ values in (a), with a zero–crossing at X. If the gradient is moving to the right, the time derivative of $\nabla^2 G*I$ is as in (b), while if it is moving to the left it is as in (c). The sign of the time derivative at a zero–crossing therefore specifies direction of movement. Adapted from Marr and Ullman (1981).

Marr and Ullman argue that the time derivative of $\nabla^2 G*I$ is computed in the retina and signalled by Y retinal ganglion cells, positive and negative values of the derivative being carried by on- and off-centre cells respectively. Richter and Ullman (1982) argue that this computation is carried out in the inner plexiform layer of the retina (Chapter 2, p. 36). Bipolar cells have fields similar to those of on-and off-centre X cells, and so, according to Marr and Hildreth (1980), signal values of $\nabla^2 G*I$. Richter and Ullman propose that recurrent synapses between bipolar and amacrine cells perform an operation equivalent to differentiation on the bipolar cell signals. The resulting output is then rectified at bipolar-ganglion cell synapses and pooled by Y ganglion cells, in the way proposed by Hochstein and Shapley (1976) (see Chapter 2, p. 46). The non-linearity of Y cell responses means that the magnitude of the time derivative cannot be signalled accurately by Y cells, and so they provide only the direction of motion.

In the visual cortex, Marr and Ullman (1981) propose that X and Y cell signals are combined to give simple cells which are both orientation and direction selective, according to the scheme shown

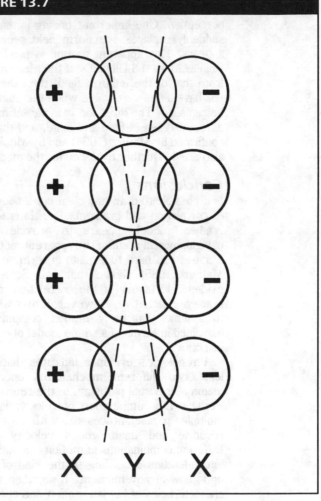

FIGURE 13.7

Marr and Ullman's scheme for simple cortical cells detecting a zero−crossing moving in a particular direction. Parallel rows of on− and off−centre X LGN cells are connected to an AND gate as in Figure 5.9. The larger overlapping fields between them are of Y cells, also connected to the AND gate. If these are on− centre, the system will respond when a zero−crossing segment moving to the right falls between the dashed lines, while if they are off−centre it will respond to one moving to the left (field surrounds not shown). Adapted from Marr and Ullman (1981).

in Figure 13.7. An AND gate is connected to parallel rows of on- and off-centre X cells and also to an overlapping row of Y cells. If these are on-centre, an output from the AND gate will indicate a zero-crossing segment of the correct orientation moving to the right, while if they are off-centre it will indicate one moving to the left. The model therefore predicts that each direction-selective simple cell will be driven by *both* on-and off-centre X cells and by *either* on-or off-centre Y-cells. These predictions differ from those made by McLean and Palmer's (1989) interpretation of direction-selective cells in terms of Adelson and Bergen's (1985) motion computation model, and more knowledge of the responses and connections of these cells is needed in order to decide between the two models.

Psychophysical experiments have provided support for Marr and Ullman's (1981) algorithm as a model of human motion perception. One important finding is that a stationary edge which suddenly replaces a uniform field seems to move slightly as it appears. This apparent motion is predicted by a gradient model such as Marr and Ullman's; if the mean intensity of the edge differs from that of the uniform field, then the time derivative of $\nabla^2 G * I$ will have a non-zero value when the edge appears, and motion will be signalled. The direction of apparent motion can be predicted for different types of field and edge, and these predictions have been confirmed by Mather (1984) and by Moulden and Begg (1986), who also provide further evidence for the model.

Conclusions

Is it possible to draw any clear conclusion about the relative merits of correlation and gradient algorithms for motion detection? The gradient model appears to provide a better explanation of psychophysical results; the apparent motion of a stationary edge as it appears is hard to explain in terms of a correlation model, and Mather (1985) shows that van Santen and Sperling's (1984) evidence in favour of the correlation model does not reject the gradient alternative. However, it may well be an oversimplification to assume that early motion computation in humans can be explained in terms of a single model of either kind, as is the case in insects.

Physiological evidence indicates that motion is detected by at least two different mechanisms operating in parallel in the mammalian visual pathway, in the retina and in the striate cortex. Perhaps the computation of velocity is therefore performed by multiple, parallel processes, with no one process able to yield accurate and unambiguous velocity information in isolation. Different combinations of motion computation processes may come into operation according to the kind of information needed from optic flow at any moment. If so, then we would expect that the characteristics of human motion detection would follow more than one type of model, depending upon subtle features of experimental conditions.

THE INTEGRATION OF MOTION MEASUREMENTS

So far, we have considered ways of measuring optical motion along a single axis. In order to compute a velocity field, however, it is necessary to obtain the components of the direction of motion in two dimensions. Imagine a gradient algorithm applied to each intensity measurement in a two-dimensional array rather than just along a row. Would the result be an array of velocity measurements? The answer is no, because any motion detecting device with a field of view which is small relative to an edge moving through it can only detect the component of velocity at right angles to the edge, while the component parallel to the edge is invisible. This constraint will

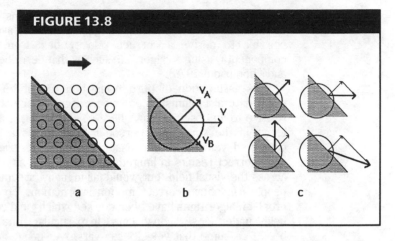

FIGURE 13.8

The aperture problem. (a) An edge moving over an array of motion detectors. (b) The field of a single motion detector. V_A and V_B are the components of the velocity V of the edge. The motion detector is sensitive only to the component V_A. (c) Four different velocities of an edge which all give the same perpendicular component and therefore the same response from a motion detector.

apply to motion computation in animal visual systems, where the images of edges of moving objects are large relative to the fields of motion sensitive cells.

Figure 13.8 illustrates this constraint, known as the *aperture problem*. In Figure 13.8a, an edge moves rightwards over an array of motion detectors, with a velocity with components V_A and V_B perpendicular and parallel to the edge respectively. A single motion detector can only measure the component V_A (Fig. 13.8b). This measurement does not give the true velocity accurately; as Figure 13.8c illustrates, many different true velocities could yield the same perpendicular component V_A. All that a single detector can reliably give is the direction of motion with a resolution of 180°. Further discussions and illustrations of this problem can be found in Marr and Ullman (1981), Hildreth (1984a, 1984b) and Hildreth and Koch (1987). The implication is that computation of the velocity field must require a second stage, taking the initial measurements of motion, or *perpendicular components* of velocity and integrating them into accurate velocity measurements.

If there are no constraints on the true pattern of motion in the image, and so no predictable relationships between velocity at one point and at any other, then the task of integrating perpendicular components is impossible and an infinite number of velocity field solutions are possible. However, consideration of the motion which occurs in natural images suggests possible useful constraints. The most obvious is that image motion arises from solid objects and surfaces which move coherently relative to the observer, so that there will in fact be predictable relationships between velocity in different points. How can these relationships be expressed?

First, let us make the simplifying assumption that image motion arises only from the translatory motion of rigid bodies in planes perpendicular to the line of sight (that is, bodies do not rotate, deform or move towards or away from the observer). If these constraints apply, then all the images of elements on the surface of one object will move with the same velocity, and it can be assumed that velocity will be constant over small regions of the image, changing abruptly at occluding edges. Given this assumption, it is possible to derive a correct velocity field from perpendicular components, using an algorithm such as that described by Fennema and Thompson (1979).

This assumption of pure translation cannot be maintained in many natural circumstances, where rigid objects rotate or loom relative to an observer, or where objects deform, as when a tree blows in the wind or a person moves. A visual system which computed velocity on the assumption of pure translation would yield correct results in limited situations, such as a target moving across the visual field, but would fail in many circumstances where people can obtain correct motion information. To deal with this problem, algorithms have been devised which yield correct velocity fields under looser constraints. In particular, one approach has been to assume that velocity can vary over images of objects, but that it does so *smoothly*. This is a reasonable assumption for most natural scenes, as the surfaces of objects are smooth relative to their distance from the observer. Sudden changes in distance, and therefore in velocity, will occur only at occluding edges. For example, if a cylinder rotates around its long axis, the velocity of images of elements on its surface varies smoothly from zero at the edges to a maximum along the centre. An algorithm which assumes pure translation would compute uniform velocities over the surface and so would not distinguish a rotating cylinder from a translating one, while the smoothness assumption allows the two to be discriminated.

The smoothness assumption does not in itself allow the correct velocity field to be computed, and it is necessary to make a further assumption that some particular measure of velocity variation is minimised. For example, an algorithm which assumes that velocity variation is minimised over areas of the image is described by Horn and Schunck (1981). They show that it computes correct velocity fields for both translating and rotating objects, but also, not surprisingly, that it yields errors at occluding edges where the smoothness constraint does not hold. Another model of this kind is proposed by Yuille and Grzywacz (1988).

An alternative approach is that of Hildreth (1984a; 1984b), who demonstrates that an algorithm minimising variation in velocity along a contour in the image yields correct velocities for objects with straight edges. Evidence that an algorithm of this kind operates in human vision is provided by Hildreth's discovery that the errors it produces for moving curves match a number of visual illusions. Two of Hildreth's (1984b) examples are shown in Figures 13.9. and 13.10. The computed velocity field for a rotating ellipse differs somewhat from the true field (Fig. 13.9); in particular it has a stronger radial component than it should. Hildreth points out that this corresponds to the illusion of pulsating radial movement seen in a rotating ellipse under some conditions. Similarly, the computed velocity field for a rotating cylinder with a helix on its surface (a

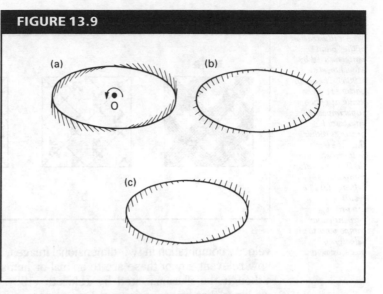

FIGURE 13.9

(a) An ellipse rotating rigidly around its centre O. The velocities of points on its edge are shown by straight lines. (b) The components of these velocities perpendicular to the edge. (c) The velocity field obtained from the perpendicular components which minimises variation in velocity along the edge. Reproduced from Hildreth (1984b) with permission of author and publishers.

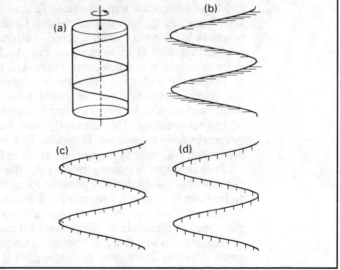

FIGURE 13.10

(a) A cylinder with a helix on its surface ("barberpole"), rotating around its vertical axis. (b) The two-dimensional projection of the helix with the velocities of points along it shown by straight lines. (c) Perpendicular components of velocity. (d) The velocity field which minimises variation in velocity along the edge. Reproduced from Hildreth (1984b) with permission of author and publishers.

barberpole) shows strong vertical components absent in the true velocity field (Fig. 13.10). Again, the same error occurs in human vision, as the rotating barberpole is seen to move upwards or downwards. Further examples of illusions which seem to reflect a process of minimising velocity variation can be found in Hildreth (1984a; 1984b).

While much progress has been made with algorithmic theories of

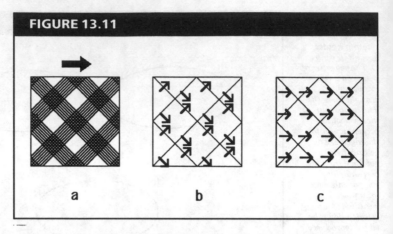

FIGURE 13.11

a   b   c

(a) An illustration of the "plaid" patterns used by Movshon et al. (1985). The actual patterns were made up of two superimposed sinusoidal gratings rather than the bar patterns shown. (b) Perpendicular components of velocity. (c) The result of integrating perpendicular components to give velocity measurements.

velocity computation in two-dimensional images, it remains unclear how relevant any of these are to animal or human visual systems, although the illusions cited by Hildreth (1984a; 1984b) provide evidence that human vision involves a process minimising velocity variation. However, there is evidence to show that one basic assumption of all these models is relevant to biological systems; the assumption that the measurement of perpendicular components and their integration into a velocity field are two distinct stages in visual processing. Movshon, Adelson, Gizzi and Newsome (1985) presented observers with "plaid" patterns, made up of two gratings crossed at an angle (see Fig. 13.11a). When the whole pattern moves in one direction, observers report seeing coherent motion of the pattern in that direction, provided that the contrast and spatial frequency of both gratings is similar. If the gratings differ sufficiently, observers report seeing two gratings sliding across one another. This is exactly what would be expected if the perpendicular components of motion had been computed but not integrated into velocity measurements (see Figs. 13.11b and c).

The fact that separate motion of the two gratings can be perceived suggests that it is possible for perpendicular components to be detected but not integrated. Movshon et al. (1985) obtained further evidence that these are separate processes by showing that the contrast threshold for detection of a moving plaid is raised by exposure to an adapting plaid but not a single grating moving in the same direction. Note that the single grating has the same velocity as the plaid but not the same perpendicular components. On the other hand, exposure to a single adapting grating does raise the threshold for detection of coherent motion of a plaid moving in the same direction. These findings show that the detection of perpendicular components and of velocity are separate processes which undergo adaptation independently.

Movshon et al. (1985) also found physiological evidence for these two stages by testing the responses of cells in the monkey visual system to moving plaids. They first identified direction selective cells by testing their responses to moving single gratings. If a cell responds to a rightwards moving grating, for example, then two alternative predictions can be made about its response to a plaid. If the cell is sensitive only to perpendicular components, then it will show two response peaks as the plaid is rotated through 360° around its direction of motion, corresponding to each of the two component gratings moving rightwards. On the other hand, if it is sensitive to velocity, it will show only one peak, when the whole pattern is moving rightwards. Movshon et al. (1985) found that all direction selective cells in V1 (visual cortex) have responses of the first kind, but in the middle temporal area (MT), an extrastriate area forming part of the "motion pathway" (Chapter 3, p. 67), some cells have responses of the second type. This striking discovery implies that cells in V1 analyse only perpendicular components of motion and that their integration into velocity measurements occurs in MT or between V1 and MT.

Relative Motion and Velocity Computation

We saw in Chapter 11 that boundaries between regions of the retinal image with different velocities are used by insects to detect objects against backgrounds of similar texture. People also can detect object edges when no other information besides relative motion is available. For example, Rogers and Graham (1979) presented observers with a random-dot pattern in which parallel bands of the pattern moved at different speeds as observers moved their heads. The result was a powerful illusion of a corrugated surface in depth. The importance of relative motion for vision leads us to ask at what stage in the processing of image motion it is detected. One possibility is that it is detected relatively late, from a full velocity field representation. Nakayama and Loomis (1974) propose a model of this kind, in which units with centre-surround organisation are excited by motion in one direction in the field centre and inhibited by motion in the opposite direction in the surround. A number of these units, with overlapping fields but different direction preferences, are linked to a single "convexity detector" which sums their ouptuts. Nakayama and Loomis show that the activity of a convexity detector signals the presence of an image velocity boundary passing through its field.

Nakayama and Loomis' (1974) model appears to receive some physiological support. Cells sensitive to relative motion between a target in the central part of the field and either a similar target or a background texture in the field surround have been discovered in the visual systems of several species, including area MT in the owl monkey (Allman, Miezin & McGuinness, 1985). The response to motion in a preferred direction in the field centre is facilitated by motion with a different velocity in the surround but suppressed by motion with the same velocity. Further, Frost and Nakayama (1983) discovered cells in the pigeon optic tectum which respond to opposite directions of motion in centre and surround, whatever these directions are, as Nakayama and Loomis' (1974) proposed convexity detectors do.

Even so, there are some important discrepancies between the physiological evidence and Nakayama and Loomis' theory. The theory assumes a linear summation of velocities in centre and surround, which does not appear to occur in the cells studied. Frost, Scilley and Wong (1981), for example, found that the response of cells in pigeon tectum to a moving dot in the field centre could be suppressed equally by motion in the same direction in the surround of a dot or of a texture filling the entire field. A linear summation of velocity measurements would cause greater suppression in the second case. Second, the inhibitory surrounds of these cells are often strikingly large, even covering the entire visual field in owl monkey MT (Allman et al. 1985). With a velocity field containing many relative motion boundaries, the inhibitory surround of virtually every cell would therefore contain motion discrepant to that in the centre. With non-linear summation, all cells would be activated and no information would be available to localise relative motion boundaries in the way that Nakayama and Loomis' model aims to do. These cells do not appear to represent the convexity detectors of this model, and further evidence is needed to clarify their role in the computation of relative motion.

An alternative possibility is that relative motion is computed *before* the velocity field, directly from perpendicular components. From a theoretical point of view, such a scheme offers a solution to the problem of using smoothness constraints to compute the velocity field. As we have seen, these yield incorrect results at occluding edges where velocity changes abruptly. Hildreth (1984b) suggests that relative motion information obtained from perpendicular components of motion could be used to constrain velocity computation so that variation is minimised only within relative motion boundaries and not across them. The algorithm which she proposes for detecting relative motion in perpendicular components first operates on a number of ranges of orientations of zero-crossings independently. It locates boundaries where the average sign of motion of zero-crossings changes, and then combines the results from all zero-crossing orientations. If such a boundary is present in zero-crossings of more than one orientation, then relative motion is present.

Despite these theoretical proposals, the relationship between computation of velocity and of relative motion in vertebrate visual systems remains unclear at present. Rather more progress has been made in the case of insects, however. Reichardt, Poggio and Hausen (1983) have developed a model for the computation of relative motion from the outputs of the motion detectors described earlier (see Fig. 13.3). In this model, the output of each motion detector is inhibited in a non-linear fashion by the summed outputs of all motion detectors in a region around it. The signals resulting from this interaction are then summed to give an output which controls the insect's turning response. The system has the property of responding to incoherence in the input pattern of motion signals, giving a stronger output the less uniform these are. The fully specified model predicts accurately several properties of flies' responses to textured figures moving against similar backgrounds, such as the fact that the size of the figure has little effect on the strength of the response. Some progress has also been made towards identifying particular classes of cell in the fly visual system which implement this means of detecting relative motion (Egelhaaf, 1985).

Reichardt et al's (1983) model detects relative motion in an image without computing accurate velocity values. Instead, relative motion is computed directly from the outputs of motion detectors which give only the direction of motion reliably. As we have seen, the magnitude of an insect motion detector's output is a function both of image speed and of the spatial structure of the image, which in turn means that the output of the relative motion detecting system is also influenced by spatial structure. For example, it will respond to a patch of texture moving with the *same* velocity as the background, if the spatial components of the textures differ. Reichardt et al. (1983) argue that this feature of the model is in fact valuable to an insect, which does not need to locate accurately all the occluding contours in its visual field but to detect small objects moving relative to the background. The ability to detect differences in both texture and velocity in the same process confers added efficiency in carrying out this figure-ground discrimination.

It seems certain that the mechanisms of motion computation which Reichardt and co-workers have identified in insects are much simpler than those operating in human vision or that of other mammals. The fly's visual system is dedicated to processing image motion for a few purposes only, such as figure-ground discrimination or detection of uniform whole-field flow, and so relies on fast, simple mechanisms built for these purposes only. In particular, these do not require the computation of the accurate velocity field required to explain human motion perception. One illustration of the difference is that flies are not able to detect a figure and ground oscillating together in antiphase, despite the strong relative motion generated, whereas this form of motion is readily detected by people (Baker & Braddick, 1982). In the remainder of this chapter, we deal with more complex parameters of relative motion than the simple velocity boundaries we have considered so far, and ask how they are computed in visual systems.

MORE COMPLEX PROPERTIES OF OPTIC FLOW

We described in Chapters 10 and 11 how a variety of different properties of optic flow specify such things as occluding edges, relative distance, direction of motion and time to contact. In comparison to work on the simple properties of velocity and relative motion, much less progress has been made in under-standing how visual systems compute these more complex properties. In this concluding section, we will survey a variety of findings and models which hint at possible answers.

Two main approaches to the problem of obtaining optic flow information can be distinguished. One assumes that a velocity field representation is first computed, and then, after resolving global rotatory components caused by eye movements, higher order properties of optic flow are computed. In particular, it is possible to show that any pattern of spatial variation in a small region of the optic flow field can be decomposed into three simple transformations; isotropic expansion, rigid rotation and shear (see Fig. 13.12). Since both the rate and the axis of shear need to be specified, any optic flow pattern can therefore be represented as the sum of these two quantities together with the rates of expansion and rotation. These four components are all invariant with global rotatory motion in the velocity field caused by eye movement, and can be obtained by differentiating the optic flow field in four different ways (Koenderink, 1986). In principle, therefore, the structure of the optic flow field could be separated from global rotatory motion and represented fully and economically in terms of these four differential components.

This mathematical result may have little relevance to the operation of biological systems, however, as the computation of a velocity field is sensitive to noise in the image, and differentiation of the velocity field even more so. Koenderink (1986) therefore suggests a second way of considering the problem, proposing that visual systems rely on less economical but more robust means of computing properties of optic flow. In particular, there may be a number of mechanisms operating in parallel, each built to compute

FIGURE 13.12

A simple pattern (a) subjected to three different transformations: (b) pure expansion, (c) pure rotation and (d) pure deformation or shear. Any transformation of a patch in the optic flow field can be expressed as a sum of four components; the rates of expansion, rotation and shear, and the axis of shear. Note that only in (d) does the relative orientation of contours change. Adapted from Koenderink (1986).

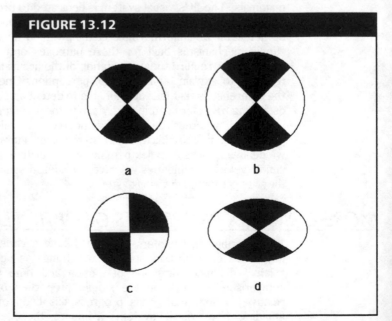

a

b

c

d

one particular property for a particular behavioural purpose. Koenderink further suggests that these need not require the prior computation of a velocity field. For example, one means of detecting shearing deformation in optic flow is through changes in the relative orientation of texture elements (see Fig. 13.12d), which are available in the output of the visual cortex without any further motion computation.

Single cell recordings provide some evidence that motion computation may involve multiple processes operating in parallel. One example is seen in the *accessory optic system* (AOS), a region of the vertebrate midbrain to which some optic nerve fibres project (Ch. 3, p. 51). Cells in the AOS respond to large slowly moving textured patterns and are selective for both direction and speed of motion (Simpson, 1984). These properties suggest that AOS cells are involved in the computation of *global* motion, in contrast to the analysis of *local* motion performed in visual cortex or area MT (see p. 303). On the basis of the distribution of preferred directions in AOS cells, Simpson (1984) argues that the function of this structure is to analyse global rotatory movement in the retinal image into three perpendicular components, and thereby contribute to the stabilization of eyes and head.

In contrast, other regions appear to be involved in the analysis of global translatory motion. Cells in the lateral suprasylvian area of cat cortex are direction selective, and Rauschecker, von Grünau and Poulin (1987) found that their preferred directions were mainly away from the area centralis. These cells would therefore be maximally stimulated by the looming retinal motion produced by forward movement of the cat. More complex properties of individual cells are seen in the superior temporal polysensory area (STP) of monkey prestriate cortex, where many cells have very large fields which cover nearly the entire visual field (Bruce, Desimone & Gross, 1981). Of these, some have different direction selectivities in different parts of the field, responding to motion either towards the area centralis or away from it. Others show selective responses for objects moving in depth, producing either looming or contracting patterns of motion in the field.

There is also psychophysical evidence for a system in human vision which is specifically sensitive to looming and contracting patterns of optic flow. Regan and Beverley (1978) tested observers' thresholds for detecting two types of motion of square stimuli, either oscillating in position or in size. They found that exposure to a square oscillating in size caused adaptation which was specific to this pattern of motion; the exposure did not affect thresholds for detecting oscillation in position. The frequency, direction and amplitude of motion in the two displays were equal, and so the results cannot be explained in terms of adaptation of motion detectors. Instead, Regan and Beverley concluded, adaptation must have occurred in some higher level "looming detector" which is sensitive to the specific pattern of relative motion of the four edges.

It is fascinating to speculate about the role of prestriate areas such as STP in computing properties of looming optic flow fields, and about their possible relationship to Regan and Beverley's (1978) proposed "looming detectors." If these do represent a system specialized for obtaining information from global patterns of translatory motion, not only more physiological evidence but also specific algorithmic theories are required to understand how it operates. One variable of a looming optic flow field which we would expect visual systems to compute is time to contact, and results obtained by Buxton and Buxton (1983) may be important in determining how this is achieved.

Buxton and Buxton (1983) are concerned with the problem of how depth information could be computed from the projection on to the retina of a looming flow field. Like Marr and Ullman (1981; see p. 295), they extend Marr and Hildreth's (1980) algorithm for edge detection to consider the case of a time-varying image, but differ from Marr and Ullman in arguing that a model of visual processing should incorporate a limit to the fineness of resolution of intensity changes over time. They devise an algorithm which smooths intensity changes with a temporal Gaussian filter as well as the spatial Gaussian filters of Marr and Hildreth's model, and which then computes second derivatives of smoothed intensity values with respect to time as well as to spatial co-ordinates.

The output of Buxton and Buxton's algorithm proves to have some important properties; in particular, zero-crossings can arise in it for two different reasons. First, an intensity gradient in the image causes a zero-crossing at the same position in the output array, in just the same way as in Marr and Hildreth's model. Buxton and Buxton term this type of zero-crossing a "static edge," as it appears whether the gradient moves over the retina or not. If it does move, the gradient may give rise to a second zero-crossing, at a point in the periphery of the output array remote from the static edge. The position of this "depth zero" is determined by the distance of the object feature causing the gradient in the image, and by its velocity relative to the observer.

The depth zeroes in the output of Buxton and Buxton's algorithm provide a possible solution to the problem of computing time to contact. The position of a depth zero gives directly the time to contact with the object feature producing it, but a correspondence problem arises in matching a particular depth zero to the image of that feature. Buxton and Buxton propose a straightforward way of solving this; as an object approaches, the depth zero moves inwards and may cross the corresponding static edge. When this happens, the sign of the zero-crossing at the static edge reverses. Provided such a cross-over in the sign of a static edge can be detected, the position of the edge when it happens gives directly the time to contact with the object feature producing the static edge.

A limitation to Buxton and Buxton's (1983) model for the computation of time to contact is that it works only for features in the periphery of the retinal image, and therefore only for objects far from the line of travel or close to the observer. They argue that their algorithm could therefore provide two mechanisms for obtaining depth information working in parallel; one to obtain accurate depth information from image motion near the centre of the visual field, and another, based on depth zeroes, to compute rapidly the information needed to avoid looming objects. Their model is therefore an example of the approach proposed by Koenderink (1986), which envisages a variety of specialised systems operating in parallel to extract different kinds of information from transformations over time in the retinal image. It is tempting to interpret the psychophysical and physiological evidence discussed above as indicating a specialised system for computing time to contact using the algorithm proposed by Buxton and Buxton, but a great deal more evidence will be needed to test this hypothesis.

CONCLUSIONS

The research which we have described in this chapter illustrates one way in which some aspects of Gibson's theory of perception can be brought together with information-processing theories into a common framework. This involves accepting Gibson's arguments for optic flow as a source of information about an observer's surroundings but rejecting his claim that variables of optic flow are picked up "directly." Instead, in this view, they are computed from the fluctuating intensity values in the retinal image as it changes with an observer's motion. We have considered in some detail how the simplest variable of optic flow—optical velocity—could be computed from intensity values, and have seen that considerable progress has been made on this problem. For more complex variables, we have seen a variety of models and findings which have yet to fall into a consistent pattern.

One important issue arising from this discussion is the role of the velocity field. We have seen how two lines of argument assume that a representation of optical velocities over the retina has a key role in motion computation. First, work on early motion processing (e.g. Hildreth, 1984b) assumes that a velocity field is the output representation for these processes, and, second, investigations of the higher order information available in optic flow takes such a representation as given. Although we know that velocity information is computed in the human visual system, we have seen hints that other analyses computing relative motion, time to contact or components of rotation may proceed in parallel, using simpler measurements than the velocity field as their input. These ideas suggest an alternative view, in which the flexibility of human motion processing arises from the operation of many specialised systems together rather than a single general-purpose one. Whether this view eventually proves correct or not, one consequence is that it leads us to consider the particular purposes of motion computation for the control of action, and in the next chapter we follow up this aspect of Gibson's theory in more detail.

Chapter Fourteen

THEORIES OF THE CONTROL OF ACTION

*I*n Chapters 11 and 12, we saw that both animal and human perception do involve the detection of some of the parameters of the optic array and optic flow field which Gibson believed to be important. Chicks and babies avoid precipices by detecting motion parallax and texture gradients; flies find landing sites by detecting wiping of texture in the optic flow field and gannets and people time movement by monitoring the relative rate of expansion of parts of the flow field. The description of the information available in light developed by Gibson is therefore useful in explaining some perceptual processes.

These examples reflect another feature of the "ecological" approach to perception, which is its emphasis on the role of perception in an animal's or person's action. The traditional approach treats perception and action as quite distinct processes; perception is the processing of information in the retinal image to yield a symbolic representation of the world, and action is the generation of commands to the muscles. This generation of responses must obviously draw on information about the environment, but the traditional view would be that the two processes could be analysed independently of one another.

In the ecological view, however, perception and action are tightly interlocked processes. Animals and people do not passively perceive the world but move about in it actively, picking up the information needed to guide their movement. There is a continuous cycle between organism and world. The consequence of this viewpoint is that the role of perception is to furnish the information needed to organise action, which in turn implies that an understanding of perception requires an understanding of the systems controlling action. In this chapter, we therefore intend to explore the relationship between perception and action in two contexts; first, the optomotor response of insects and, secondly, the control of human action. We will not be able to provide a clear answer to the question of how vision controls action, but we hope to introduce you to the kind of framework which might be useful for answering this question in the future.

THE OPTOMOTOR RESPONSE

In Chapter 11, we described the turning response of a tethered insect in a rotating drum (p. 245) and argued that the role of this response is to keep an insect on as straight a path as possible through the environment. We discussed in Chapter 13 the progress that has been made in uncovering the neurophysiological basis of this response, with the discovery of neurons that respond to uniform movement of a pattern of light over the eye. If the insect's nervous system transforms the spatiotemporal pattern of light intensity at the eye into a pattern of neural activity representing the distribution of movement over the eye, then what is the next stage? How are commands to muscles modulated in order to generate the appropriate turn?

Von Holst (1954) explained the optomotor response in terms of the model shown in Figure 14.1; a command to carry out a movement originates in a "higher centre" of the nervous system and an "efference copy" of the commands to the muscles is retained in a "lower centre". As the movement is executed, there

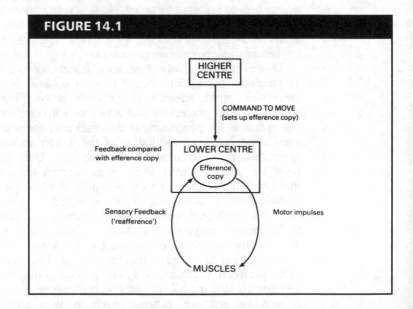

FIGURE 14.1

Von Holst's efference copy model.

HIGHER CENTRE

COMMAND TO MOVE
(sets up efference copy)

Feedback compared with efference copy

LOWER CENTRE

Efference copy

Sensory Feedback ('reafference')

Motor impulses

MUSCLES

will be a flow of optic texture over the eye and this movement-induced input is called "reafference". The reafferent input can be compared with the input expected from the commands stored as an efference copy in the lower centre. Note the similarity between this model and the one we discussed in Chapter 7 (p. 167), which attempted to explain how the human nervous system compensates for effects of the movement of the eye on the retinal image

How does Von Holst's "efference copy" model explain the optomotor response? If the insect is stationary, no optic flow over the eye is expected and so a discrepancy is registered if the drum rotates. The discrepancy indicates that the source of the movement is outside the insect and so it turns in order to reduce the discrepancy caused by relative movement. If, on the other hand, the insect initiates a movement in a stationary environment, the resulting reafference corresponds to that predicted from the efference copy and so there is no discrepancy. The theory can therefore account for the insect's ability to initiate movement without being locked into position by the optomotor response.

We have already discussed one problem with this theory in Chapter 11, arguing that the sensory information provided by a rotating drum would, in the insect's normal environment, unambiguously specify rotation of the insect. The more important problem for now, however, is that Von Holst's efferent copy theory assumes that reafference *can* be predicted from motor commands. In the case of the human eye, this may well be so; given the mechanics of the muscles, inertia of the eyeball and so on, a particular pattern of muscle contraction will yield a predictable rate, direction and extent of movement over the retina. But this will not necessarily be so for a flying or walking animal. The same set of commands to the flight or leg muscles can generate quite different results depending upon patterns of air flow around the animal or the terrain it is walking on. This is a problem of "context conditioned variability," to which we will return later in this chapter.

If an "efferent copy" cannot reliably predict the effect of motor commands, what are the consequences of eliminating it from the model of the optomotor response? We are now left with a simpler model, in which uniform image motion caused by rotation of the insect is measured and appropriate motor commands are generated to return this motion to zero. One difference between this model and that of Von Holst is that it does not include any means of resolving whether the source of image motion is the animal's own movement or an external disturbance. As we have argued, however, there is no reason, in many circumstances, for an insect to resolve this ambiguity; all it needs is information specifying what corrective change in its flight is needed.

A second difference concerns the initiation of movements. In Von Holst's model, self-initiated movements are generated by a "higher centre" lying outside the feedback loop controlling movement, which effectively suppresses the optomotor response while a turn is made. The simpler model appears, on the other hand, to leave the insect locked into a fixed position or path of movement and unable to initiate turns. Although this problem seems to require the introduction of some higher level process of the kind proposed by Von Holst, it could be solved in other ways. We have already seen in Chapter 11 two properties of the fly's optomotor response which offer other solutions.

First, Reichardt and Poggio (1976) observed a semi-random fluctuation in a fly's torque as it fixated a visual pattern (p. 251). In natural circumstances, where an airborne fly is surrounded by many objects competing for fixation, this instability in the optomotor response would result in occasional turns as the fly "jumped" from fixation of one object to another. Second, Egelhaaf (1987) showed how a small moving target elicits a turn despite the opposing flow of background texture, because the mechanisms sensitive to local and global motion have different velocity sensitivities (p. 254). In both these cases, the stabilizing effect of the optomotor response to global image motion is briefly suppressed while a turn to fixate an object is made, but no "higher centre" is required to explain how this happens.

While feedback mechanisms of the kind proposed by Von Holst (1954) may be involved in some types of insect optomotor response, recent research has challenged the argument that such processes are necessary in order to prevent an insect being locked in position or on a straight course. Whatever the particular mechanisms prove to be in any one insect species, this discussion of Von Holst's model provides an illustration of some important assumptions underlying the traditional view of the relationship between perception and action. In this view, perceptual processes operate to produce an internal representation of the environment, which a "central executive" uses to make decisions about which pieces of behaviour to execute. Von Holst's proposed "higher centre" is one example of this implicit assumption that behaviour is controlled hierarchically, with decisions emanating from a central executive.

In the case of the fly's optomotor response, we have seen findings which point to an alternative model, in which behavioural "decisions" are the outcome of fluctuating interactions between mechanisms of visuomotor co-ordination. When we turn to consider the control of human action, alternatives to the "central executive" assumption have to be far less specific. Even so, an important strand in ecological theory has been the search for such alternatives, and in the remaining part of this chapter we review what has been achieved in this search.

THE CONTROL OF HUMAN ACTION

Most theorists are agreed that actions must ultimately be controlled at a high level in the nervous system where something like an "action plan" must be formulated and executed. When we consider the nature of action plans it is clear that at some level the representation must be sufficiently flexible and abstract to allow equivalent ends to be achieved in a variety of ways. Turvey (1977a) gives as an example the observation that we can draw a letter A with a pen on paper, with a finger on someone's back or with a toe in the sand. At least some of these activities may be novel, but are not difficult for us. In the same way we can recognise a letter A drawn in different ways by different people (see Chapter 8). Some abstract representation of the letter perhaps allows for the way in which we can generalise both when perceiving and when acting. Here we see one contrast with the organisation of insect behaviour, where such flexibility of motor control is largely absent.

Suppose then we wished to draw an A in the sand with a toe. Somehow the abstract representation which we wish to particularise must be translated into a specific pattern of motor (i.e. muscle) activity. It might be possible, in principle, to conceive of each muscle involved in this action being independently instructed by commands issued from a high level in the nervous system. Thus our abstract conception of the letter A might be translated into a series of independent commands to a variety of muscles in the leg, foot and toes. This kind of "push-button" metaphor for the control of action has been criticised by Bernstein (1967) whose arguments have been summarised and extended by Turvey and his colleagues (Fitch, Tuller & Turvey, 1982; Tuller, Turvey & Fitch, 1982; Turvey, 1977a; Turvey, Fitch & Tuller, 1982; Turvey, Shaw & Mace, 1978).

There are two different, but closely associated problems with the push-button metaphor. The first is known as the *degrees of freedom* problem. An "executive" issuing independent efferent commands to all those muscles involved in even the simplest of movements would have a very great deal of moment to moment computation to perform. This first problem is possibly compounded by the second—that of *context-conditioned variability* (Turvey et al. 1982). We have already met this problem in discussing the insect optomotor response, where we pointed out that the consequences of a particular pattern of commands to leg or wing muscles would not be predictable, but would depend upon the external forces acting on the limbs. In the human case, the problem is even greater, as the context in which any particular muscle contraction occurs affects the actual limb movement achieved. The movement produced by a given contraction depends on the current configuration of the parts of the limb, the current motions of the adjoining limb segments, and the external forces against which each muscle must work. An executive pressing the buttons, in such a model, would have to have moment to moment information available about the external forces and the dynamic and static aspects of the current configurations of the limb segments.

Turvey et al. (1978) liken the problem of the push-button executive to that which an air pilot would face if he or she had to control individually each of the mechanical segments used to guide the flight of an aeroplane. At a minimum, an aeroplane has two ailerons at the back of the wings which can be moved up or down to control roll; two elevators on the tail which if moved up or down control pitch, and a rudder at the back which can be moved left or right to control yaw (cf. insect flight in Chapter 11). There is thus one degree of freedom for each of these five hinged parts. If each of these parts had to be altered individually the pilot would be faced with an impossible informational load. Even if the mechanical parts could only be moved to one of eight positions the control system would still have to keep track of 8^5 (32,768) independent states.

Of course no air pilot actually has to cope with this task because the mechanical components of the guidance system are in fact linked. The ailerons are yoked so that when one moves up the other moves down. The rudder is linked to the ailerons so that it moves left when the right aileron goes down: and the elevators on the tail section move together—both up or both down. This linkage reduces the degrees of freedom to two, and the guidance of the aircraft can be achieved with a joystick which also has two degrees of freedom (it can be moved forward or backward for ascent or descent and from side to side to bank or turn.)

Turvey et al. (1978) and Turvey (1977a) suggest that combinations of muscles in animals are similarly linked and constrained to act together as "coordinative structures" which can function relatively autonomously. Spinal reflexes are seen as simple examples of coordinative structures, though even these can involve quite complicated actions. For example, an animal with the upper part of the spinal cord completely sectioned will still repeatedly scratch an itch on its body with whichever foot can most easily reach it.

The concept of coordinative structures goes beyond simple reflex acts, however, to include patterns of inter-limb coordination in voluntary acts. An everyday example is given by the difficulty we experience if we try to beat out two quite different rhythms simultaneously with different hands. The hands seem constrained to act together in this situation. Kelso, Putnam and Goodman (1983) have demonstrated this more formally. If two hands are required to make movements of different difficulties and directions, the movement of each hand is influenced by that of the other. Such patterns of mutual constraint and interaction would not be expected if an "executive" independently commanded each muscle. Turvey therefore suggests that the executive commands a group of muscles which function cooperatively together.

Coordinative structures thus reduce the degrees of freedom problem, and they may also solve some of the problems of context-conditioned variability. Coordinative structures can take care of the local context in which an action takes place if they behave like mass-spring systems. The equilibrium point of a spring to which a mass is attached is not affected however the mass is pushed or pulled. The spring always returns to rest at the same length, without any executive monitoring its movements over time. There is some evidence that human limb movements exhibit similar properties. More radically, coordinative structures may be viewed as *limit-cycle oscillators* (a different kind of oscillator from the familiar mass-spring system). Limit-cycle oscillators are mutually synchronising—they influence one another's behaviour. We have just described how movement in one hand may influence the movement in the other, and such observations suggest that this model of coordinative structures may be a fruitful one to pursue (see Tuller et al., 1982 for a good introduction to these ideas).

Thus coordinative structures may drastically reduce the number of instructions and monitoring that the executive must perform. However, coordinative structures must still be set into action, and their parameters altered to cope with changing environmental circumstances, so our executive still has a role to play. From the above discussion it follows that the instructions issued from the executive must be at a more abstract level than instructions to individual muscles. The executive is seen as controlling the modes of interaction of lower centres. Turvey argues that this form of control should not be viewed as hierarchically organised, with the executive issuing commands which pass unidirectionally and without modification to lower levels. Rather he suggests that the system must be organised as a *heterarchy*, or, more radically, as a *coalition* (see Turvey et al., 1978). In a heterarchical organisation no one part of the system should be seen as dominating the others. All levels in a heterarchy contribute equally to hypothesis-testing and decision-making.

An important structure which contributes to the organisation and control of action is the segmental apparatus of the mammalian spinal cord. The spinal cord can be seen as a set of "segments" (marked out by the vertebrae), within each of which there are neuronal loops which control simple reflexes (like the knee jerk), without involving any "communication" with the brain. Complex voluntary activities may involve the recruitment, modification and elaboration of these simple reflexes, which form the bases for coordinative structures. This may be achieved in part by *tuning* of the segmental apparatus prior to a movement occurring. Turvey (1977a) cites evidence from Gurfinkel, Kots, Krinsky, Pal'tsev, Feldman, Tsetlin and Shik (1971) in support of the notion of tuning. If a subject is asked to flex one leg, it typically takes about 170 msec between the command and the flexion occurring. If, during this latency period, the knee-jerk reflex is elicited, its amplitude is enhanced relative to a control condition where no command is present. It therefore appears that an instruction issued from the brain to the leg involves the preparation or tuning of the segmental apparatus prior to the actual movement of the leg occurring.

If we continue to consider leg movements, in the more complex activity of walking or running, there is evidence that the organisation of the segmental apparatus of the spinal cord allows the initiation and maintenance of stepping movements of the limbs without sensory input. However, the form of the stepping pattern must be tailored to the external forces. This can be achieved by using afferent information obtained from reflex structures and also by tuning the segmental apparatus on the detection of relevant information obtained primarily through vision. In this way a basic pattern of activity can be attuned to the current contextual demands.

Thus the control of action involves both the activation of the relevant coordinative structures and their tuning to meet environmental conditions. Both of these functions can be seen as dependent on the pickup of information from the optic array. The detection of *invariants* may underlie the perception of significant structures towards which the animal or person must manoeuvre, or upon which it must act. The detection of *variation*, i.e. the pattern of change in the optic flow, will determine the precise form that the action must take:

> evolution has thoroughly exploited the principle of separating action-plan specification from tuning. The instinctive rituals are released by stimulation of a simple kind—the red belly of the stickleback, the spot under the herring-gull's beak—but the unfolding stereotypic behaviour is flexible; it relates to the lie of the land, to the contingencies of the local environment. We should suppose that these species-specific action plans are adjusted by the pickup of information about the environment, that is to say, that tuning is environment-related (Turvey, 1977a, p. 246).

Once again, however, the details of tuning need not be specified absolutely at a cortical level. Much of it can be achieved by the segmental apparatus. Indeed given the nature of the interactions at lower levels, many aspects of locomotor adjustment may take care of themselves. This can be achieved in part by some types of *tuning reflex*. An example of this is the tonic neck reflex, which biases the motor apparatus for a movement in the direction of gaze. In humans, directing the eyes and head towards an item of interest may effect reorganisation of the segmental apparatus appropriate to changing the direction of locomotion. Detailed information about the layout of the environment, which modifies the form of the locomotion in the new direction may likewise be taken account of at a segmental level. The executive (something of a misnomer in a heterarchically organised system) cannot, given the degrees of freedom problem, be responsible for the detailed metrical prescription for an act. This must be realised at lower levels, but there is good evidence that the spinal and muscular systems are functionally organised to achieve this.

Thus visual information of different kinds (invariants and variants) must be injected into unfolding activities at appropriate points, after which the coordinative structures which have been activated and tuned can take care of themselves to a large extent. However, Turvey and his colleagues go even further, and devolve the responsibility for these "injections" of visual information to the coordinative structures:

> We do not want a model in which the brain interprets the perceptual information, decides what portion of the information to supply a given coordinative structure, and when to supply it. Instead, the organisation of the coordinative structure should be such as to accept only certain information at certain times (Fitch et al. 1982, p. 272).

Coordinative structures do seem to be organised so that a minimal change in one of their parameters has a maximum effect on behaviour. An animal's speed of running is altered only by the thrust it applies to the ground, other aspects of the step cycle remaining constant, and in Chapter 12 we saw how visual information is used to modify thrust in humans. To return to baseball batters, we described (see p. 283) how Hubbard & Seng (1954) showed that batters keep the timing of their swings constant, and deal with balls of varying speed by altering only the speed with which they step forward. Time to contact assessed during the ball's flight thus affects only a single aspect of a complex activity.

The baseball batter serves as an example to summarise the ideas of Turvey and his colleagues which we have presented here. The invariants of the ball-pitching situation (those that specify a ball, a pitcher etc.) inform the batter that a striking action would be appropriate. The action plan for "striking" will be abstract, and rather than consisting of detailed instructions to individual muscles, will serve to recruit the appropriate coordinative structures. The variants in the situation (e.g. the speed of the ball) will determine how the batter should strike it, but are used to modify only certain components of the action, leaving others constant.

Turvey's arguments remain controversial, and we have given no more than their flavour in this chapter. The details of the anatomical, physiological and experimental evidence for his position have been omitted. However, it is hoped that this brief account will serve to illustrate how perception and action might be related within an ecological theory. Indeed in such an approach they cannot be separated. Within this framework an "action plan" is seen as one and the same as a projection of the environment, the product of "perception".

Although we started this chapter by pointing to the weaknesses of a certain kind of information-processing model of action, this is not to deny computational perspectives any role. One interesting direction for the future may come from attempts to use connectionist modelling to examine how the different constraints from the environment and muscles may combine to determine action. For example, Hinton (1984) has successfully modelled the process of reaching for a target without losing one's balance, using a simple two-dimensional model person reaching out in front of them. The problem is to avoid swinging the arm out in a way which shifts the centre of gravity of the person as a whole to an unstable position—to avoid this, other limb and trunk movements must occur to compensate. Hinton found that a connectionist model could satisfy these two constraints (touch the object, while maintaining centre of gravity above the foot) simultaneously, and that the solution was much more elegant when combinations of joint angles were adjusted synergistically (see also our discussions of coordinative structures elsewhere in this chapter).

CONCLUSIONS

A fundamental part of the ecological view of perception is that perception and action are interlocked processes. If we are to understand perception, we must know what it is for, and that means we must understand how action is organised. In simple animals such as insects, the principle that perception is for the control of movement may well be sufficient to give us a full understanding of perception. In more complex animals, and especially people, this viewpoint is relevant only to certain aspects of perception; those involved in the moment-by-moment control of movement – taking strides, hitting a ball, applying brakes and so on. It is not directly relevant to understanding how perception yields information which is not used in the immediate control of activity but instead stored in some way to influence activity later. The principle of perception being constrained by action is not obviously relevant to a person watching a television programme, for example. In the next chapter we follow up this point, and ask what the ecological approach has to offer the study of human perception outside the context of moment-by-moment control of movement.

Chapter Fifteen

EVENT PERCEPTION

In this part of the book we discuss ways in which a variety of animals, including humans, may detect specific patterns of flow or local change in the optic array in order to guide their actions in the world. The kind of perception that we have been discussing is that which demands immediate action—to locomote smoothly, to avoid collision or to steer a straight course. However, a great deal of human perception results in comprehension and reflection rather than in immediate action. The film-goer, tennis umpire, the spectator at a football match, the air-traffic controller—all must interpret the complex dynamic visual information in the events they are viewing, although their immediate actions are not necessarily affected. We spent some time in Part II of this book discussing how it is that we recognise significant forms, from the conventional starting point of the static retinal image. We now turn to consider how it is that we interpret *dynamic* optical information, and thus consider event perception in terms of analysing transformations in optical flow.

In this chapter we will deal with human perception, since it is not clear to what extent animals contemplate in the way that we do the events in their world, though Humphrey and Keeble (1974) have shown that monkeys will work in order to be shown films, even when the films show events that monkeys find frightening. However, as will become clear later on in the chapter, human perception of events may result in attributional processes which may at least in part be culturally and linguistically mediated. We begin this chapter by describing how human observers interpret patterns of motion in fairly simple and artificial dynamic displays. Here we outline some of the principles which are needed to account for the perception of such displays, principles that we will find useful as we go on to consider the complex patterns of motion given by more natural events.

THE PERCEPTION OF RELATIVE MOTION

People are more sensitive to relative motion than to absolute motion. Suppose a spot of light is moved very slowly in a dark room. There will be a particular threshold velocity at which the point is seen to be moving rather than stationary. Aubert (1866; cited in Kaufman, 1974) found that this threshold velocity was between 10 and 20 mins of arc per second if a luminous dot was moved in the dark. This is the threshold for *observer-relative* motion, which for a static observer corresponds to "absolute" motion. However, if a second spot of light is introduced, the velocity that the first must reach in order for movement to be seen in the display is lower. The threshold for "object-relative" motion is lower than that for observer-relative. Aubert showed that there was a 10-fold decrease in the threshold for motion perception when a dot was moved against a pattern of lines, rather than a uniform field (Kaufman, 1974). In a situation where the velocity of one dot is below the observer-relative threshold, and a second, stationary dot is present, the perception of movement in the display is ambiguous. Either one, or the other, or both dots may appear to be moving.

When motions are above the observer-relative motion threshold, perceptions are rarely ambiguous, but they do seem to be dominated by the relative motions in the display. For example, if a stationary dot is surrounded by a rectangle which moves to and fro around it, the dot may appear to be moving in a direction opposite to that of the rectangle (see Fig. 15.1). This movement of the dot is *induced* by that of the rectangle. Induced motion can be seen in natural situations, when the moon appears to race in a direction opposite to that of the clouds on a windy night. On a cloudless night

FIGURE 15.1

Induced movement. A stationary dot appears to move to the left as the rectangle surrounding it is moved to the right.

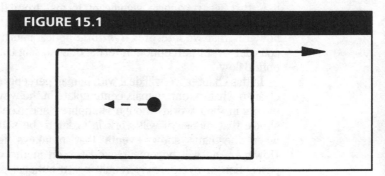

the moon appears perfectly still (its actual movement is too slow to be detected as it is below the threshold for observer-relative movement). It is interesting that the moon's movement is seen relative to the clouds even if the stationary buildings nearby could provide an alternative frame of reference. The Gestalt psychologist Duncker (1929) suggested that there was a "separation of systems" in such perception. The movement of any one part of a display is seen relative to its immediate surrounding frame, but is not affected by more remote influences. A demonstration by Wallach (1959) supports this (see Fig. 15.2). Here a dot is surrounded by a rectangle which is in turn enclosed by a circle. The perceived motion of the dot is influenced only by the actual movement of the rectangle, and little by that of the circle. That of the rectangle in turn is influenced only by the circle.

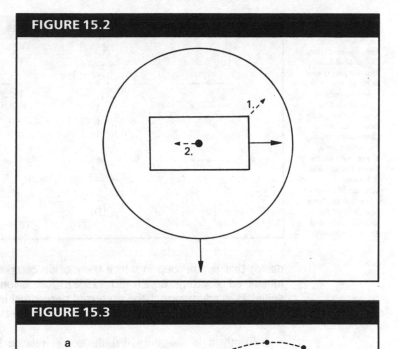

FIGURE 15.2

The circle is moved downwards and the rectangle is moved to the right (solid arrows). The perceived motion of the rectangle (1) is influenced by the actual movement of the circle. The perceived motion of the stationary dot (2) is influenced only by the actual movement of the rectangle. Adapted from Wallach (1959).

FIGURE 15.3

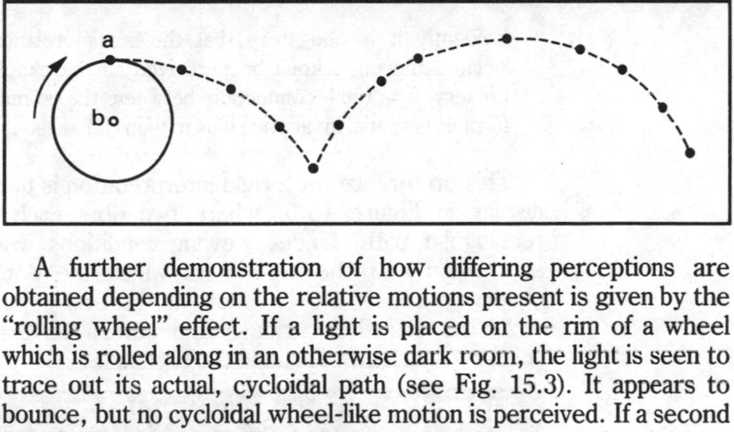

The cycloidal path traced out by a light (a) placed on the rim of a wheel which rolls in the dark. If only (a) is illuminated, this path is perceived. If the hub (b) is also illuminated, than (a) appears to cycle around (b).

A further demonstration of how differing perceptions are obtained depending on the relative motions present is given by the "rolling wheel" effect. If a light is placed on the rim of a wheel which is rolled along in an otherwise dark room, the light is seen to trace out its actual, cycloidal path (see Fig. 15.3). It appears to bounce, but no cycloidal wheel-like motion is perceived. If a second light is illuminated on the hub, however, the one on the rim now seems to trace out a path which revolves around the hub, and the two lights now form a wheel-like configuration which translates across the field of view. The rolling wheel is one of a number of examples where the perceived configuration of the motion of one element is affected by the presence of another. A final example is shown in Figure 15.4. The central dot, which moves on a diagonal path, is flanked by two dots, which move horizontally. The presence of these alters the way in which the central dot is seen to move. It appears to move vertically, between the flanking dots, while all three dots together move horizontally as a unit.

The perception of many such displays seems to conform to a "simplicity" or "minimum" principle. Of many possible interpretations of a display of separately moving elements, the simplest is

FIGURE 15.4

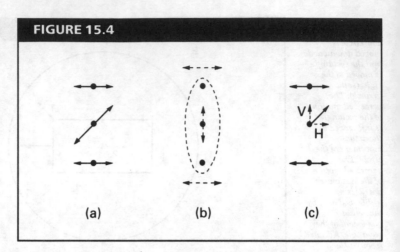

(a) Three dots move to and fro on the paths shown, but the perception is as shown at (b). The central dot appears to travel on a vertical path between the two flanking dots, as the entire set of three dots moves from side to side. This can be explained in terms of vector analysis (c). See text for details. Adapted from Johansson (1975).

(a)   (b)   (c)

made; that is, the one in which the motion components seen are minimised (Cutting & Proffitt, 1982). Johansson (1973, 1975) suggests in addition that the preferred perceptual interpretation of dynamic displays is in terms of the motion of rigid structures:

> Evidently it is obligatory that the spatial relation between two isolated moving stimuli be perceived as the simplest motion that preserves a rigid connection between the stimuli. The general formula is spatial invariance plus motion (Johansson, 1975, p. 73).

This preference for a rigid interpretation is demonstrated in the display in Figure 15.5, where two dots each follow the same rectangular path. Under viewing conditions which minimise the impression that the screen on which the dots appear is flat, observers report the two dots as the end points of a rigid stick which moves rather curiously in depth, rather than seeing them as "chasing" each other around the rectangle.

FIGURE 15.5

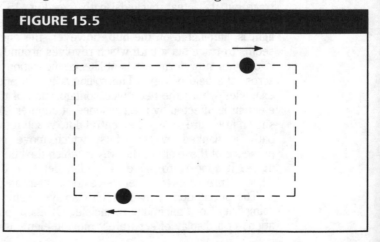

Two dots move on a rectangular path in the dark, as shown. The dots appear to form the ends of a stick which moves curiously in depth. Reproduced by permission from Johansson, 1975.

Such phenomena of relative motion perception have been extensively investigated by Johansson (1973, 1975) who suggests that the perception of many such displays can be accounted for if it is assumed that the visual system performs some kind of *perceptual vector analysis*. Let us examine this notion by starting with one of Johansson's own displays. As we have already described, when the display in Figure 15.4 is shown to human observers, they report seeing the central dot moving up and down a vertical path between the two horizontal "flanking" dots. Thus the resulting perception is of the vector which results after the components of *common motion* of the three display elements have been subtracted. To elaborate, the two horizontally moving flanking dots are moving together and therefore share a common horizontal translatory motion, against which other relative motions can be perceived. The diagonal motion of the central dot can be resolved into two vector components (see Fig. 15.4c), one (H) in the horizontal direction of the common motion of the flanking dots, and the other (V) perpendicular to this (i.e. vertical). If the common motion component of the whole display is partialled out, the motion which is "left over" (the residual) is a vertical motion of the central dot, which is what people report when shown such a display.

The same kind of analysis can be applied to the perception of the lights attached to a rolling wheel, described above. When a light is placed on the hub in addition to that on the rim, there is a common motion component shared by the two lights which corresponds to the direction in which the wheel is moving. This common motion component completely accounts for the motion of the light on the hub, and when partialled out of the motion of the light on the rim, the residual left to this light is cyclical motion around the hub. This kind of description suggests that common motions are abstracted from a display first, leaving relative motions as the residual, though Cutting and Proffitt (1982) point out that Johansson has not always made such a strong claim.

Cutting and Proffitt (1982) argue that not all perceptions of such displays are consistent with the "common-motion-first" principle. For example, observers occasionally report the rolling wheel display with a single rim and hub light as appearing like a "tumbling stick" (Duncker, 1929). Here the two lights appear to be the end-points of a stick which rotates about a point halfway along its length. The stick is tumbling because the imaginary midpoint itself traces out a "hobbling" path (see Fig. 15.6). In such a situation relative motion analysis appears to take priority, with common motion left as residual.

There are thus two possible ways in which any given set of absolute motions can be resolved into a perception of relative and common motions. Either common motion can be detected first, in such a way as to minimise (give the simplest account of) the common motion present, and then, after abstraction of the common motion, the relative motions may be perceived as residual. Or relative motion can be detected and its components minimised, and

FIGURE 15.6

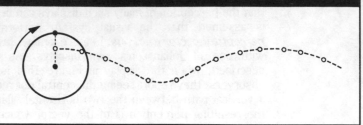

The path traced out by the midpoint of an imaginary line joining lights on the rim and hub of a wheel. Observers occasionally report this display as like a stick tumbling along this path.

after abstraction of this the common motion will be left as residual. These two possibilities make different predictions about the resulting perceptions of most displays of the "wheel-rolling" kind. As already mentioned, the "common-motion-first" theory predicts that a display with a hub light and a single rim light should appear wheel-like, while the "relative-motion-first" theory predicts that it should appear as a tumbling stick. While the rolling wheel perception is preferred (Duncker 1929; Johansson 1975; Cutting & Proffitt 1982), the tumbling stick may be seen, particularly if subjects are not fixating on one of the lights (Duncker, 1929). For other displays the "relative-motion-first" theory gives a much better account of what is perceived. Consider the configuration of lights in Figure 15.7. Here two lights are placed 90° apart on the rim of a wheel. The common motion in the display is again linear translation, and if this were abstracted first then we would expect observers to report both lights cycling around the imaginary centre of the wheel. However, if the relative motion were minimised, the two lights could be seen revolving around the midpoint of the imaginary line which joins them. After abstraction of this relative motion, the common motion left would be the prolate cycloidal motion of this midpoint—a kind of tumbling stick again. In fact, observers report the latter perception of such a display.

We seem to be left in a dilemma. For some displays it looks as though common motion is minimised and abstracted first, and for others it seems that relative motions are first detected and common motion seen as residual. Cutting and Proffitt suggest that both processes may proceed simultaneously, with the one

FIGURE 15.7

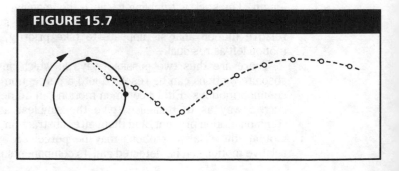

The path traced out by the midpoint of an imaginary line joining two lights placed 90° apart on the rim of a wheel.

achieving solution first dominating the perception. That is, the perceptual system may seek to minimise both common and relative motions at the same time. The one which is solved first determines that the other be perceived as residual. This theory seems to give the best account of the perception of this type of display, and certainly reinforces the idea that *absolute* motions are rarely seen as such.

Thus we have seen that the visual system resolves simple dynamic displays into components of common and relative motions. In the next section we will apply these ideas to a more natural kind of display—that which depicts biological motion.

BIOLOGICAL MOTION

The most dramatic demonstrations of the visual system's application of a "minimum" principle were produced by Johansson (1973) in his biological motion displays. Johansson produced films of people walking, running and dancing in which the only visible features were lights attached to the actors' joints. Lights might be attached to the shoulders, elbows, wrists, hips, knees and ankles, to form a total of 12 moving lights in the dynamic displays (see Fig. 15.8). Such a display is easy to produce by wrapping reflectant tape around the joints and filming with a video camera set up to pick up only high contrast. In the film which results, all information about the contour of the human figure has been removed, and if a still frame of such a film is shown it looks like a meaningless jumble of dots, or, at best, a Christmas tree. However, as soon as the actor is shown moving, the impression is immediately of a human figure. The perception of a moving human can be achieved with as little as 100 msec of film, or with as few as six lights shown. Not only can the figure be clearly seen (with the invisible contours of arms and legs present in a ghostly way), but the posture, gait and activities of the actor can be clearly described. It is clear from the displays whether the person is walking, running, jumping, limping, doing push-ups, or dancing with a partner likewise portrayed by a set of moving lights.

Sensitivity to the figural coherence of such displays of biological motion appears either to be innate, or to develop very quickly. Bertenthal, Proffitt and Cutting (1984) found that three-and five-month old infants were able to discriminate between upright and inverted walking point-light figures, though not between static frames from the upright and inverted conditions. Infants at this age were also able to discriminate a "coherent" point-light display of a person walking a treadmill from the same display with the dot motions scrambled to form what adults judged to look like "a swarm of bees".

Runeson and Frykholm (1981; 1983) have demonstrated the extraordinary subtlety of perception possible by adults viewing moving point-light displays. In their experiments, they filmed the movements of actors throwing sand-bags to targets at different distances. Runeson and Frykolm (1981) showed that observers can accurately judge differences in the weight carried by an actor, where both the actors and load together are depicted by a total of 21 points of light. In later experiments (Runeson & Frykholm, 1983), point lights were placed on the actors' joints, but no lights were placed on the bags, so that observers viewing the film had no information from the bags themselves about their motions. Nevertheless, observers were extremely accurate at judging how far the actors had been trying to throw the bag on each attempt.

FIGURE 15.8

Lights are attached to the joints of an actor who walks or runs in the dark. The changing pattern of lights is immediately interpreted as a human figure in motion.

Johansson considered the perception of biological motion in displays like these to be consistent with perceptual vector analysis, applied hierarchically. Let us take the case of an actor walking across a screen in front of the observer. The entire configuration of moving dots has a common motion component in the horizontal direction in which the actor is moving. Against this, the shoulders and hips make slight undulatory motions. Against this undulatory motion of the hips, the knee describes a pendular motion. Once the pendular motion of the knee has been partialled out, the ankle can be seen to describe a further pendular motion about this. Thus the dynamic configuration can be resolved into a set of hierarchical, relative motions of rigid limb segments. These walking figure displays again show how the visual system apparently "prefers" to interpret moving elements as representing the end-points of *rigid* structures in motion, even if the resulting rigid structures may then appear to have quite complex motions in depth. It should be stressed that Johansson considers the perceptual decoding principles of the vector analytic type, and the preference for rigid motions, to be "hard-wired" rather than derived from experience with real moving objects. We might note at this point a similarity with Ullman's theory (described in Chapter 7), who likewise made use of a rigidity assumption to interpret structure from moving point configurations.

Johansson's moving figures have been subjected to a more rigorous analysis by Cutting and his co-workers. In particular they have investigated how observers may detect subtle differences in gait from these displays. In preliminary work, Cutting and Kozlowski (1977) showed that observers performed well above chance at identifying themselves and their room-mates from such dynamic displays. In a number of subsequent experiments (Barclay, Cutting & Kozlowski, 1978; Kozlowski & Cutting, 1977; Kozlowski & Cutting, 1978) they have gone on to show that observers are 60–70% accurate on average at detecting the *sex* of a walker from a display. In order to judge sex to this accuracy observers need to see about 2 secs of the display which corresponds to about two step cycles, suggesting that such judgements rely on some dynamic invariant rather than on static configurational cues. The detection of the sex of a walker does not seem to depend crucially on any particular elements in the display. Above chance level judgements can be made if only points on the upper body or lower body are illuminated (but see Kozlowski & Cutting (1978) for a reinterpretation of the lower-body findings), though performance is best when joints on both upper and lower halves of the body are shown. Thus the information on which such judgements are made appears to be given by some *global* invariant, rather than by particular elements in the display.

Barclay, Cutting and Kozlowski (1978) began the search for such an invariant with the observation that male and female bodies differ in the ratio of shoulder width to hip width. Men have broad shoulders and narrow hips compared with women. However, in the kinds of displays typically used, where the actor walks across the line of sight, only a single shoulder light and hip light are visible, so this ratio cannot be detected. Therefore the shoulder to hip width ratio cannot provide the basis for judgements of sex. This ratio does have consequences for other aspects of the relative motion in the display, however (Cutting, Proffitt & Kozlowski, 1978). During locomotion, the hips and shoulders work in opposition to one another. When the right leg is forward in the step cycle, the right hip is also forward relative to the right shoulder which is back. Likewise, when the left leg is forward, so too is the left hip, with the left shoulder back. The relative widths of the shoulders and hips should thus affect the relative side to side motion of the hip and shoulder joints when viewed from the side. A measure based on this relative swing was found to correlate reasonably well with the consistency with which different walkers were rated as male or female.

However, Cutting et al. (1978) went on to derive a more general invariant from their displays which correlated better with the ratings given to different walkers. This measure was the relative height of the *centre of moment* of the moving walkers. The centre of moment is the reference point around which all movement in all parts of the body have regular geometric relations: it corresponds to the point where the three planes of symmetry for a walker's motion coincide. Its relative location can be determined by knowing only the relative widths (or relative swings) of the hips and shoulders (see Fig. 15.9). The centre of moment for male walkers is lower than that for females, and therefore provides a possible basis for judgements of sex.

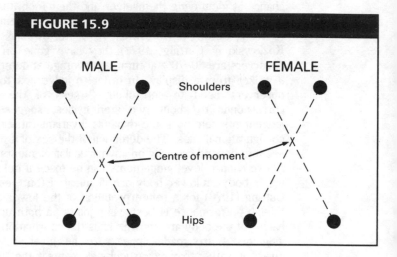

FIGURE 15.9

The relative location of the centre of moment for male and female walkers. Adapted from Cutting and Proffitt (1981).

Cutting (1978a) was able to show the validity of the centre of moment as a determinant of gait perception by synthesising artificial dynamic dot displays which mimicked the movements of walkers. In this way it was possible to vary *only* the centre of moment in such displays, holding all other variables constant. The synthetic "male" and "female" walkers produced were correctly identified on 82% of trials, though if the lights corresponding to the hips and shoulders were omitted performance dropped to about 59%, still above chance. These results are compatible with those obtained with real walkers, where above chance, but reduced, performance was obtained when some of the lights were removed. Thus it appears that a simple biomechanical invariant, the centre of moment, can be recovered from a display such as this and could be used to specify reasonably accurately the sex of the walking figure.

We should note here that the centre of moment of a dynamic configuration can serve as the origin for an object-centred coordinate system about which the relative motions of the other elements can be described. We saw in Chapter 8 how Marr and Nishihara (1978) tackled the problem of deriving an object-centred coordinate system from the occluding contours obtained from the image of a static object. The problem was to derive an axis for the figure without prior knowledge of what the shape represented. With the work of Cutting and colleagues we see that the relative motions in a dynamic display, in the absence of contour information, may also be used to derive an object-centred coordinate system about which to describe movement, and the resulting description might then provide the basis for recognising the form depicted.

The centre of moment is a general invariant which can be found for other kinds of dynamic display. To return to the rolling wheel configurations (see p. 323), the centroid—the centre of the configuration of lights—is directly analogous to the centre of moment. Proffitt and colleagues (Proffitt & Cutting, 1979; Proffitt, Cutting & Stier, 1979) have shown that the relationship between the centroid, and the centre of the wheel, determines how wheel-like is the motion observed. When the two coincide (as when two lights are placed 180° apart on the rim), "perfect" wheel-like motions are seen. When the centroid and the centre of the wheel are far apart, as when the two lights are placed 90° apart on the rim (see Fig. 15.7), "hobbling" motions are seen.

The centre of a radially expanding optical flow field, which as we have seen (Chapters 10, 11 and 12) is very important in guiding locomotor activity, also comprises the centre of moment for that dynamic display, and Cutting and Proffitt (1981) have also argued that the centre of moment is a useful concept when applied to slow events, such as the ageing of a face (see Chapter 16) or the movement of stars in the night sky which migratory birds use to steer their course. Furthermore, Cutting (1982) has demonstrated that viewers may be sensitive to alterations in *second-order* centres of moment (the centres of moment of component structures), when perceiving the bending motions present in "tree" and "bush"-like configurations.

A Grammar for Event Perception

Cutting and Proffitt (1981) argue that it is possible to construct a "grammar" for event perception, like a grammar in language. From the dynamic visual information presented, observers "parse" out different components (see Fig. 15.10). From a total visual scene (used here to refer to information which changes over time, rather than in its more traditional, "static" sense), the first division made is between an event and the ground against which it occurs. For example, an event might consist of a person walking along a crowded shopping precinct. The precinct would be the "ground" for this event, and might itself contain other potential events. Once an event has been parsed, it can then be described as having figural and action components. The action of a figure is its action *relative to the observer*, to be distinguished from the movement of parts of a figure *relative to itself*. In our example, the action of the person consists of their translation across the precinct. The swinging arms and legs constitute the movement of the figure relative to itself.

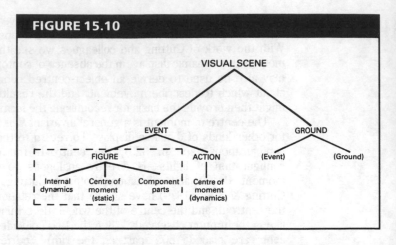

A grammar for event perception. A visual scene can be divided into event and background. The event consists of a figure and its action. Adapted from Cutting and Proffitt (1981).

FIGURE 15.10

The action of a figure is captured by the dynamics of its centre of moment, while the "static" centre of moment itself serves as a reference point for the description of the motions and locations of the different parts of a figure.

If the figure contains component structures, a hierarchical set of centres of moment can be abstracted, each serving as the reference point about which the motion and topography of the component structure can be described (see Fig. 15.11). For the description of a walking figure, Cutting and Proffitt's analysis is very similar to Johansson's. After the centre of moment for the torso is obtained, about which the hip and shoulder movements are

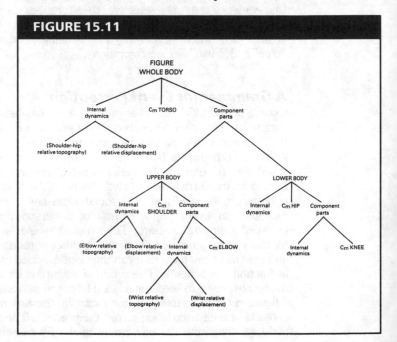

An expansion of the boxed section of Fig. 13.10, showing how a moving human figure can be broken down into a hierarchical set of components, each with its centre of moment, internal dynamics and component parts. Adapted from Cutting and Proffitt (1981).

FIGURE 15.11

described, the limb movements are described as a nested set of pendulum actions. The motion of the elbow is described relative to its "static" centre of moment at the shoulder (which is a second-order centre), and the motion of the wrist is described relative to its third-order centre of moment at the elbow, and so on. A different example in which there are component structures to describe would be given by the perception of a tree swaying in the wind (Cutting, 1982). The centre of moment for a tree is the point where its trunk meets the ground. Since the tree does not move as a whole, there is no action component here. Second-order centres are present where each limb meets the trunk, and third-order centres would be present at minor branch points along each limb.

This "grammatical" approach to event perception is still highly speculative, and in places problematical. For example, what should be seen as an "event" and what should be seen as "ground"? However, it may well provide a useful framework in which the perception of static scenes can be seen as a special case of dynamic events, rather than vice versa.

In all the above examples, observers have viewed displays and reported the *motions* present, or identified the structures (e.g. walking figures) which give rise to these motions. One aspect of natural event perception which we have yet to consider is how we go beyond the motions present to attribute causality to the motions. It is to this topic that we turn next.

THE PERCEPTION OF CAUSALITY

When we watch a football match we are in no doubt about why the football suddenly speeds up and changes direction— it was kicked. That is, the change in the movement of the ball was *caused* by the action of one of the players' feet. Likewise, in boxing or judo, we see the action of one of the combatants as causing the other to fall to the floor. We might suggest that it is our previous experience of seeing footballs kicked, or opponents thrown, which allows us to make causal *inferences* in new situations. However, Michotte (1946, translated 1963) made the strong claim that causality is perceived *directly*.

Michotte experimented with simple displays. In one situation (Fig. 15.12a), subjects viewed a display in which a black square (A) moved towards a red square (B) at constant speed. At the moment when A came into contact with B, A stopped and B moved off, either at the same speed or at an appreciably slower one. After a short time B also came to rest. Michotte reports that in this situation observers see the black square bump into the red square and set it into motion: "The impression is clear; it is the blow given by A which *makes B go*, which *produces* B's movement." (p.20). This has been termed the "launching effect." In another demonstration (Fig. 15.12b) A again moves towards B, but continues its course without changing speed. When the two objects contact, B in turn moves off at the same speed as A until both objects finally come to rest together. In this situation Michotte describes the impression as of A carrying B along or pushing it ahead. This effect is known as "entraining." Michotte backs up his claim that phenomenal causality is directly apprehended by demonstrating that the impression is critically dependent on the temporal, spatial and formal properties of the display. In the first experiment described, if an interval is introduced between A contacting B, and B moving off, the impression of causing, or launching, B's movement is eradicated. If B moves off faster than A then the impression is of B being "triggered" rather than launched, while if B moves off more slowly it appears to be launched rather than triggered. However, whether launching or triggering is seen also depends on the length of the path that B subsequently follows as well as on the ratio of the objects' speeds, an observation which was confirmed by Boyle (1960).

According to Michotte, the launching effect depended not only on these spatial and temporal aspects but also on the similarity between the paths of the motion of the two objects. As object B's path was shifted in angle away from the direction of A's path so the reported perceptions of launching declined. If B went off at a direction at right angles to A (Fig. 15.12c), Michotte claimed that launching was almost never observed. While the impression of launching is thus crucially dependent on the temporal and spatial parameters, Michotte claimed that it was unaffected by the *nature*

FIGURE 15.12

Frames of a film of the kinds of display used by Michotte. ■ *Black square A,* □ *Red square B. (a) Launching; (b) Entraining; (c) A display where B moves off at 90° and launching is not perceived.*

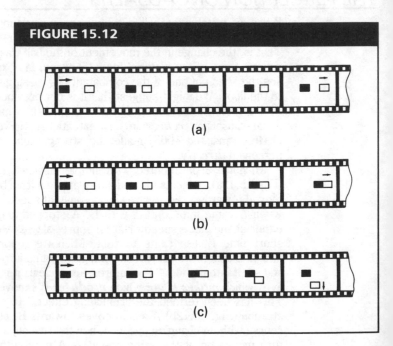

(a)

(b)

(c)

of the items used. If A was a wooden ball, and B a small, brightly coloured circle, Michotte reported that the launching effect was unchanged. Michotte regards this as important evidence for the "direct" perception of causality, since if previous experiences of cause and effect were responsible there should be no reason to see a causal relationship between two quite dissimilar items.

While few would doubt that such causal impressions can be gained from displays of the types used by Michotte, there has subsequently been some doubt about the universality of observers' impressions. Michotte himself was often vague about the precise numbers of subjects he tested, or the instructions he gave them, and in places based strong claims on the results obtained with a very small number of highly practised subjects. Boyle (1960) reported having to discard 50% of his subjects on the basis of a pre-test in which these subjects failed to report "launching" or "entraining" from standard displays. Beasley (1968) assessed formally the extent of individual differences in the perception of these displays and reported that only 65% and 45% of his subjects responded respectively to "launching" and "entraining" displays in causal terms. Contrary to Michotte's claim, 45% *did* report causal impressions when object B departed at 90° from A in the launching display. In addition, and again contrary to claims made by Michotte, Beasley found that the nature of the objects used—squares, discs or cars—did have an effect on the nature of the responses elicited.

It seems that we should doubt Michotte's claims of the universality of such causal impressions, and this casts doubt upon the idea that such effects are perceived "directly." It seems as likely that the perception of such displays *is* in line with acquired perceptual and cultural experience of the world. We have learned that certain event sequences imply causal relations between the participants, and the language we use to describe such events reflect, but may also influence, such perceptual learning. Having abandoned the idea that causality is perceived through the *direct* pick up of spatial and temporal invariants, it is still interesting, nevertheless, to enquire how such causal impressions are obtained through reference to acquired experience.

Weir (1978) has developed a computer model which interprets displays like those of Michotte, in ways similar to human observers. Her approach is a transactionalist one, in which there is a continuous interaction between the stimulus pattern and stored internal representations in the form of action "schemata." It is thus nearer in conception to the kind of framework we presented in Part II of this book. Her computer program accepts a symbolic description of each of a sequence of static images, corresponding to different frames of a film of a Michotte display, so that the movement of each display element has to be computed by comparing elements from one frame to the next. This means that she has to tackle the "correspondence problem" (see Chapter 7) in order to match the objects in each frame:

*Schemas for
Launching (a) and
Entraining (b).
Adapted from
Weir (1978).*

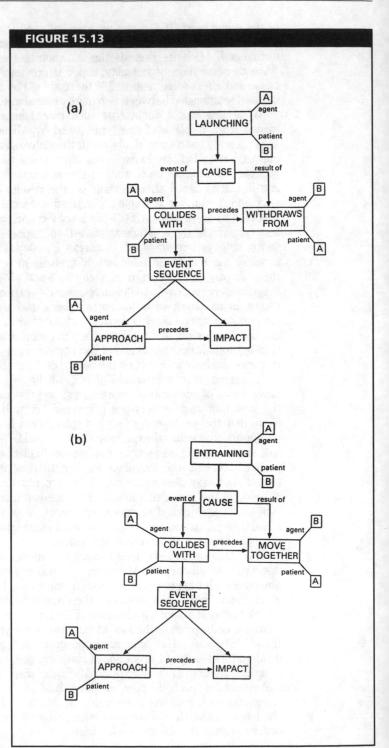

FIGURE 15.13

There will in general be more than one way of pairing the picture regions in two adjacent frames and a way of choosing which of the possible pairings correspond to an *enduring object in motion* must be provided (Weir, 1978, p. 249).

Weir makes use of partial matches between incoming event sequences and stored action schemata to help solve this correspondence process, and so "top-down" processes (see Chapter 4) play a central role in her theory. This is unfortunate for our purposes here, since although we have rejected the hypothesis that causal relations may be directly perceived, we would not want to deny that object motions may be detected in a bottom-up way. Nevertheless some features of Weir's program are worth describing here since a modification of her theory could quite easily be applied to motions which had been computed without involving higher-level concepts.

The object motions are compared with stored "schemata" for different actions, which are dynamic descriptions for actions rather like the structural descriptions for objects which we considered in Chapter 8. An action schema contains units like "approaches" and "withdraws." The action schema for "Launching" is shown in Fig. 15.13a, and that for "Entraining" in Fig. 15.13b. For each action there is an *agent*, and an object on which the agent acts (here called the *patient*).

The schema consists of several components. Launching consists of collision followed by withdrawal, and the schema specifies the event sequence that defines a collision. Entraining consists of collision followed by movement together. If the first few frames of the film match the "collision" sequence, then both the launching and entraining schemas are activated. The subsequent actions in the display will allow a decision to be reached about which interpretation is correct.

Weir's simulation allows the possibility of anticipation of expected actions, by the activation of "demons" which look out for expected sequences. It can also incorporate individual differences in perception. For example, some subjects may report launching only if B's speed after impact is substantially below A's before impact. This can be incorporated by restrictions in the definitions of actions like "withdraws from."

Leslie (1984; Leslie & Keeble, 1987) has also analysed the computational basis of causality perception, in order to interpret the results of his developmental studies showing that by 27 weeks infants can perceive causal relations such as launching. Leslie suggests that causal perception results from a visual mechanism that takes its input from lower-level motion processors, analyses the sub-movements to produce higher-level descriptions of the spatial and temporal properties of the event and finally describes its causal structure. Unlike Weir's analysis, however, Leslie's sees causality computation as entirely impervious to higher beliefs or expectations.

We have seen how causal impressions may be obtained from simple displays, and argued that such impressions are likely to be gained by a process of computation, rather than "directly" as Michotte claimed. We now turn to consider how *intentions* and *dispositions* may be perceived in the objects which move in simple dynamic displays.

PERCEPTION AND ATTRIBUTION

Observers who view displays of the type used by Michotte may describe the actions of the objects in animate terms. Thus A may be seen to "kick" or to "shove" B. B may be seen to "escape" from A who is "chasing" it. Therefore, in addition to perceiving causality, we may also perceive intentionality in the action of inanimate objects, just as in everyday life we interpret the actions of animate beings in terms of what they are trying to do. In addition, these momentary intentions which we observe may lead us to attribute enduring dispositional traits to the actors we observe. If person A kicks B, chases him, then kicks him again, A may be seen as a "bully."

The classic study of such attributional processes in perception was conducted by Heider and Simmel (1944) who showed observers a film in which two triangles of different sizes (the larger and smaller hereafter referred to as T and t respectively) and a circle (c) were seen to move in the vicinity of a rectangular frame (the house) with a moveable flap in one side (the door)(see Fig. 15.14). The first few frames of the film sequence depicted the following movements (illustrated roughly in Fig. 15.14, and described here, as in the original article, in "anthropomorphic" terms for simplicity): T moved toward the house, opened the door, moved inside and closed the door. t and c appeared and moved around near the door. T moved out of the house towards t; the two fight, with T the winner; during the fight, c moved into the house.

Heider and Simmel showed the entire film to 34 subjects who were simply asked to "write down what happened in the picture". All but one of their subjects described the film in terms of the movements of animate beings. A typical subject's description of the first few frames was:

> A man has planned to meet a girl and the girl comes along with another man. The first man tells the second to go; the second tells the first, and he shakes his head. Then the two men have a fight, and the girl starts to go into the room to get out of the way and hesitates and finally goes in. She apparently does not want to be with the first man (pp. 246–247).

In a second experiment Heider and Simmel asked their subjects to interpret the movements of the figures as actions of persons and then to answer a series of questions which included such items as "what kind of a person is the big triangle". Such questions were

FIGURE 15.14

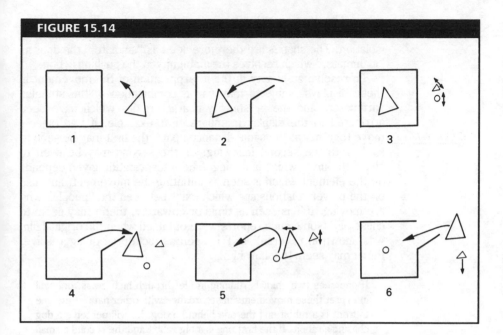

A sequence of events from the early part of Heider and Simmel's (1944) film. The film shows a big triangle, a small triangle, and a small circle moving around near a box with a moveable flap (the door). See text for a description of the event sequence.

answered with high consistency. Both triangles were usually perceived as male, with the larger one seen as "aggressive," a "bully," "bad-tempered," etc. The circle was seen as "frightened," "meek" or "helpless." Even in the first experiment, where no specific direction to see the objects as people was given, subjects tended to describe the objects as being of different sex and with differing dispositions.

Like Michotte, Heider and Simmel suggested that causal impressions were given by the spatial, temporal and figural aspects of the display. Thus when T is seen to "hit" t, the stimulus parameters are very similar to those in the "launching" experiment of Michotte. T approaches t until it comes into contact with it. Then T stands still while t starts to move in the same direction as T's earlier movement:

> This phenomenal relationship is obviously determined by temporal succession and spatial proximity. The good continuation of the line — the fact that the direction of t's movement continues the direction of T's probably plays a role in the convincing appearance of this apparent energetic movement. (p. 253).

The movement of T and the door which result in the impression of T "opening" or "closing" the door are similar to Michotte's "entraining" displays, since the movement of T is imparted to the door by prolonged contact rather than sudden impact. The question arises as to why it is always T who appears to push the door (rather than the door pushing T). Heider and Simmel suggest that here the interpretation is influenced by the context in which such movements occur. The door never moves *without* contact from T or one of the other shapes, whereas each of the shapes *is* seen to move in isolation. The shapes are therefore seen as "animate," the door as "inanimate," which resolves the ambiguity in the pushing action.

To resolve ambiguity in the interpretation of the movement in these displays, subjects may use a combination of the stimulus parameters and the personality characteristics which have been attributed to the display members. For example, if two objects move together at the same distance apart, the first may be seen to lead, with the second following, or the second may be seen to chase the first, which is fleeing. The interpretation given depends on the element which is seen as initiating the movement, and also on the power relationships which exist between the "people" who are moving. If T is seen as timid or cowardly, then t may seem to chase him (some such reports were obtained when the original film was shown in reverse). If T is seen as dictatorial or aggressive, then t may seem to follow him:

> If one sees two animals running in file through high grass, one will interpret these movements in accordance with other data. If the one in front is a rabbit and the one behind a dog, he will perceive a dog chasing a rabbit. If the first one is a big rabbit and the second a small one, he will not see "chasing" but "leading" and "following" (p. 254).

Thus while Heider and Simmel see some aspects of the interpretation as given by the stimulus parameters, other aspects, while "constrained" by these features, will additionally be influenced by the total context in which the individual action is embedded. Intention as well as action is involved in the interpretation of their film. If T is hitting t, then T wants to hurt t. If T chases t into the house, then t may be trying to hide from T. Such intentional attributions themselves influence the dispositions which are accorded to the individual elements, and these dispositions may in turn influence how a new action sequence is interpreted.

These examples illustrate that even in the perception of the movements of simple shapes in a relatively neutral context, we see the application of quite complex and subtle attributional processes by humans. What we see happening will depend not only on the momentary motions in the display, but on expectations built up over a sequence of actions, expectations which are derived from our broader social experiences. It would seem to be stretching the Gibsonian line too far to say that all the qualities imparted to these simple objects are specified in the light. The pattern of activity present doubtless constrains the range of possible interpretations, but cannot specify which interpretation will be given (would contemporary women see the circle as female?).

Nevertheless, it is still interesting to explore the ways in which different stimulus parameters influence the perception of such displays. Heider and Simmel's study was limited to a single film.

Unlike Michotte, they made no attempt to vary spatial or temporal parameters systematically. Indeed the film which they constructed probably reflected their own intuitions about the phenomenological processes they wished to study. However, Bassili (1976) has conducted a study in which aspects of a Heider and Simmel type of display were systematically varied.

In Bassili's computer-generated displays, a black and a white circle were filmed undergoing various movements. Five different films were produced which ranged from a "chase," in which the temporal and spatial characteristics of the following (black) circle were tightly linked to those of the leading (white) one, down to a film in which both elements moved randomly and independently about the screen. Thus the temporal and spatial linking of the movements were progressively relaxed. Subjects who viewed the films were initially required to "Describe what you saw in one concise sentence" and then asked more specific questions about their perceptions of the film. The effect of temporal contingency was assessed by comparing the responses to two films, in both of which the directions of the motions were random. In one, however, a change in direction of one element was quickly followed by a change in direction of the other. In the other no such temporal contingency held.

It was found that temporal contingency between the changes in direction of the two figures was critical for the perception of an interaction between them, while the motion configuration (the spatial contingencies) were an important factor in the *kind* of interaction and the intentionality attributed to the figures. For example, subjects were much more likely to report that the black circle was chasing or following the white circle, and to ascribe intention to either or both of the circles, when the direction of the changes in the black circle's path were tightly linked to those of the white circle. When the directions were random, but temporally linked, subjects saw the circles as interacting in some unspecified way, but were less likely to describe this interaction in intentional terms.

It is interesting to contrast the *interactive* nature of the perception of these displays with the *relative motion* perceptions described earlier in this chapter. For example, Johansson (p. 324) describes the perception of two white dots following one another around a rectangle (Fig. 15.5) as being of the dots forming the end-points of a rigid stick which itself moves in depth, while in the work of Michotte, Heider and Simmel, and Bassili, similar elements are seen as independent elements which influence the actions of each other. It seems likely that the nature of the elements, the viewing conditions and the instructions given to subjects will all influence how such moving displays are interpreted. If the display elements are identical, as in Johansson's displays, they may be more likely to be grouped together as parts of a single object than if they are dissimilar as in Bassili's. If the display is viewed under conditions where the flatness of the screen, and the screen edges, are not apparent, then it is more likely that movement in depth will be seen. Finally, if subjects are requested to describe the *motions* in the display they may be less likely to respond in terms of animate interactions than if they are asked to state "what happened."

In this chapter we have examined how we perceive motion in relatively simple displays. We have concluded by considering how relatively simple display elements may be perceived in causal interrelationships, and endowed with "human" qualities of intention and personality. These complex attributional processes undoubtedly derive from our everyday social experiences, but the social attributions that we make in everyday life will themselves depend at least in part on information obtained from non-verbal aspects of a perceived interaction or situation. In the next chapter we turn to explore aspects of interpersonal perception in their own right, as we move from a discussion of event perception to social perception.

Chapter Sixteen

PERCEPTION OF THE SOCIAL WORLD

*I*n Chapter 15, we considered how people can perceive events by detecting complex transformations in patterns of light. In the case of Johansson's experiments, we described evidence that people are particularly sensitive to biological patterns of motion, such as those characteristic of a walking person. Johansson's evidence illustrates one way in which information in light about the *animate* world—the other people or other animals surrounding an observer—can be detected. In contrast, most of our discussion of the role of vision in guiding animals' and people's actions has so far been concerned with problems of manoeuvring through the inanimate world, such as those faced by diving gannets or by long jumpers which we considered in Chapters 11 and 12. In this chapter, we discuss more fully how vision guides action in the animate world, taking examples from both animal and human vision.

An animal needs information about the activities of other animals around it which in some way affect its chances of survival and reproduction. These fall into three categories. The first is *prey*, which carnivorous animals must detect, pursue and capture. Secondly, most species are themselves prey for other species, and they must be able to detect and evade *predators*. Thirdly, most animals need information about the activities of other members of their own species, or *conspecifics*, with which they engage in various forms of social behaviour. This includes mating and the courtship behaviour which may precede it, parental care, play and various forms of competition such as aggression and territoriality. In some species, particularly the social insects and some mammals, it includes elaborate forms of co-operative behaviour in which many individuals engage together in hunting, nest building and other activities.

In all these situations, an animal must be able to perceive what other animals are doing and adjust its own behaviour accordingly. The ways in which people obtain food, protect themselves and interact with other people involve many further complexities arising from culture and language, but, even so, human social interaction requires the same basic abilities to recognise other people and detect what they are doing. Our discussion in this chapter deals primarily with the role of vision in guiding animal and human *social* behaviour, although we consider some examples of ways in which animals obtain information about prey or predators. We will discuss two main problems; first, how do animals detect what other animals are doing? Second, how do animals and people recognise other members of their species individually?

PERCEIVING OTHER ANIMALS' BEHAVIOUR

Consider one animal engaged in some social interaction, such as courtship or a territorial dispute, with another. How can we categorise the aspects of the other animal's behaviour which it needs to detect? First, information about the other animal's *posture*—the orientations of different parts of its body relative to each other—may be needed. For example, the angles of a dog's ears relative to its head, and of its tail relative to its body, provide information about its aggressiveness. Similarly, gulls involved in aggressive encounters threaten other gulls by adopting an upright posture with the bill pointing downwards and the wings held forwards, and signal submission with the opposite, crouching posture (Fig. 16.1).

Second, an animal may also need to be able to detect the *orientation* relative to itself of another animal's whole body or of a part of its body such as its head or a limb. An example is provided by the aggressive displays of Siamese fighting fish. In a threat display, a fish spreads its dorsal, tail and anal fins (Fig. 16.2). It may turn broadside to its opponent and lower and twitch its pelvic fin (Fig. 16.2c). At the same time it may beat its tail and flashes of bright colour may occur on the tail and body. Alternatively, it may face its opponent head-on and open its gill covers (Fig. 16.2d). Simpson (1968) analysed these encounters and discovered that a fish's behaviour is influenced by the orientation of its opponent relative to itself. A fish is more likely to turn to a broadside

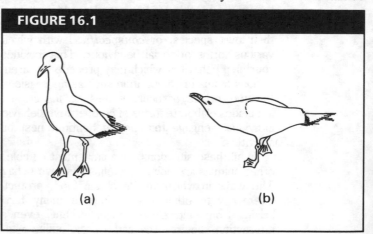

FIGURE 16.1

Threat (a) and appeasement (b) postures of the lesser black-backed gull. Drawn from photographs by N. Tinbergen in Manning (1978).

(a)   (b)

(a) and (b) Non-displaying Siamese fighting fish. (c) Display posture with fins spread out and pelvic fin lowered. (d) Display posture with gill covers opened. Adapted from Simpson 1968.

FIGURE 16.2

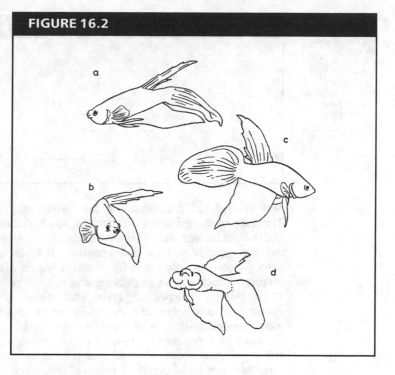

orientation if its opponent is facing it than if it is broadside, so that the two fish often take up a "T" shaped configuration. Also, a fish is more likely to flicker its pelvic fin if the opponent is facing it than if it is broadside.

In both the gull's and the fighting fish's aggressive interactions, it is almost certain that a bird or fish detects both the posture and the orientation of its rival, and this is likely to be true of all but the simplest social behaviour. A question we can ask about the perceptual processes involved in cases like these is whether information about posture and orientation is obtained from a static retinal image, or whether animals detect transformations over time in these parameters. Does a Siamese fighting fish process a static retinal image to determine whether a particular configuration, such as a fish with extended fins, is present, or does it process a time-varying image to detect transformations in posture and orientation such as a flickering fin or a 90° turn?

To determine whether an animal detects static or dynamic properties of another animal's behaviour, we would need to compare behaviour towards appropriate stationary and moving models. This is technically difficult, but an example of such an experiment is provided by Turner (1964). Young chicks learn to feed by pecking at small objects on the ground and they have a strong tendency to peck close to the spot where the mother is pecking. Turner made a model hen (Fig. 16.3) which could be made to "peck" at the ground and found that chicks would approach it and

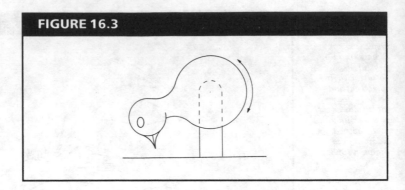

FIGURE 16.3

Flat cardboard model of a hen. "Pecking" movements of the model elicit pecking by chicks. Adapted from Turner (1964).

peck around its bill as readily as they would approach a real hen. This only happened when the model made "pecking" movements, and the chicks were much slower to approach a stationary model in either an upright or head-down posture. It looks as if chicks may detect a simple change in optic structure—a downwards wiping of texture—which specifies a pecking action.

Less direct evidence suggesting that animals detect changes in posture and orientation of conspecifics is provided by experiments which demonstrate a close temporal relationship between such a change and some specific response. For example, Bossema and Burgler (1980) observed rapid and reliable responses by jays to turns of other birds' heads. A group of jays adopts a peck order in which each pair of birds has a strict dominant-subordinate relationship. When the group is given food, the dominant eats first while the others mill about near the food. If a subordinate approaches closely, the dominant turns its head to fixate it either binocularly or monocularly. The subordinate often hops backwards when this happens, and is more likely to do so if the dominant bird fixates it binocularly than if it fixates it monocularly.

Bossema and Burgler's (1980) observations could be explained in two ways, either as detection of the static configuration of another jay's head in a particular orientation, or as detection of a transformation in posture, and experiments with artificial displays would be needed to decide between these (provided jays could be induced to respond to them!). Firmer evidence is provided by observations of animals responding differently to different transformations of posture leading to the same end result. Davis (1975) filmed the responses of small groups of pigeons when one of the group received a mild footshock. The alarmed bird immediately took flight, followed in most cases by the other birds in the group. The delay between the first bird and the next one starting to take off was very short, typically 100 msec. Davis then asked why it is common in normal circumstances to see one pigeon in a group take flight while the others remain completely unaffected. He compared films of take-offs which did and did not induce flight in other pigeons and could find no visual or auditory differences between them. The differences turned out to lie in the pigeon's behaviour immediately before take-off; if the bird crouched, stretched its neck or looked upwards just before taking off, other birds rarely responded. If these movements did not occur, they did.

Davis' (1975) experiments demonstrate clearly that pigeons do not just recognise a snapshot-like configuration of a bird with outspread wings, and suggest that they can instead distinguish two patterns of transformation of another pigeon's posture. A similar response to other birds' behaviour occurs when birds flying in a flock all execute a turn in the same direction at the same time. Observed directly, the degree of synchrony of such turns is striking and has even inspired speculation about thought transference in birds!

Potts (1984) has provided an alternative explanation by filming turns made by large flocks of dunlin in response to an approaching object. The flock's turn begins with a turn by one bird, followed by a wave of turns in the same direction spreading in all directions through the flock. The first birds to respond to the initiator of the turn did so with a delay of 67 msec, well above the reaction time of 38 msec recorded to a startling stimulus in laboratory conditions. However, the average interval over the whole flock between a bird's turn and that of its nearest neighbour was only 14 msec, which shows that the birds cannot simply be responding to their neighbour's turns. Potts (1984) proposed instead that each bird detects the *wave* of turns approaching it and times its turn to coincide with it, in the same way as dancers in a chorus line do. If this hypothesis is correct, it involves an ability to detect not just a transformation in one animal's posture, but a higher-order pattern of transformation in a number of animals.

We have seen examples from jays, pigeons and dunlin where transformations in birds' postures are tightly locked to responses by other birds. In all these cases, the interaction involved is brief, as one individual responds to another's movement by hopping back, taking flight or turning. Some social interactions between animals involve longer periods of tightly meshed movement of two individuals, in which each individual's change in posture and orientation is closely followed by the other. The rough and tumble play of two puppies, for example, appears to have this characteristic, and Golani (1976) has analysed social interactions of this kind in more detail from film records.

Figure 16.4 shows drawings made by Golani from single frames of a film of two Tasmanian devils (dog-like marsupial mammals) play-fighting. In this sequence, the animals roll and tumble about in elaborate ways, but through much of the sequence a constant relative orientation of the animals' heads is maintained. Golani terms such a constant relative configuration a "joint", around which the animals move, and says:

> The heads of a pair of Tasmanian devils "wag" their bodies into a multitude of postures and movements. In a context of cheek-to-cheek joint maintenance, the two animals move in unison as one kinetic chain (Golani, 1976, p. 117).

FIGURE 16.4

Drawings from single frames of a film of two Tasmanian devils in courtship play. Numbers refer to frames of film taken at 16 frames/sec. Until frame 249, the male (in the background until frame 147, in the foreground after frame 212) keeps the female's head adjacent to his right cheek. Reproduced from Golani (1976) with permission of the author and the publishers.

Another illustration comes from an analysis of wolf social interaction carried out by Moran, Fentress and Golani (1981). They filmed "supplanting" interactions, in which a dominant wolf approaches a subordinate one, they interact for a period, and then the subordinate moves away. Moran et al. found that the relative orientations of the two wolves' bodies fell into four main categories. In each of these, as the animals moved, some aspects of their relative orientations remained constant. In *circling*, the dominant's head is maintained at a distance of at least half a wolf-length from the hindquarters of the subordinate, and the two take up an antiparallel orientation (Fig. 16.5a). In *following*, the dominant keeps its head at the same distance from the subordinate's hindquarters, but both animals are oriented in the same direction (Fig. 16.5b).

A more complicated pattern is *twist and turn*. Here, the two animals maintain contact or near contact at the shoulder and a relative orientation of between 45° and 90°. The dominant appears to push the subordinate around in a circular path as this relative configuration is maintained (Fig. 16.5c). Finally, in *hip-thrust*, the wolves maintain a near-parallel orientation and contact at the hips. Periods of no movement are interspersed with sideways pushes of the dominant's hip against the subordinate's, accompanied by snarling and baring of the teeth (Fig. 16.5d).

Notice that these patterns are not static displays such as the threat displays of gulls or fighting fish described earlier. Instead, they are descriptions of those aspects of the joint orientation of two animals which remain constant as the animals move. For such stability to occur, each animal must continually monitor the positions of parts of the other's body relative to its own and adjust its own movement to keep the appropriate variables constant. It is likely that senses of smell, sound and touch, play a role in achieving this, but likely too that it involves the use of vision to detect elaborate transformations of posture and orientation.

As well as raising questions about perceptual processes, the close meshing of movement in social interaction illustrated by Tasmanian devils and wolves poses interesting problems for theories of the control of movement (see Chapter 14). An indefinite number of different patterns of commands are sent to the Tasmanian devil's muscles, all with the effect that its head keeps the same joint orientation with the other animal's head. The concept of "coalitional organisation" which we outlined in Chapter 14 may be relevant to this problem.

Perceiving Paths of Travel

So far, we have discussed cases where an animal obtains information about another's behaviour which does not necessarily involve any movement of the other animal relative to the observer. Changes in posture and orientation can occur without any change in the relative positions of the two animals. We therefore now turn to

FIGURE 16.5

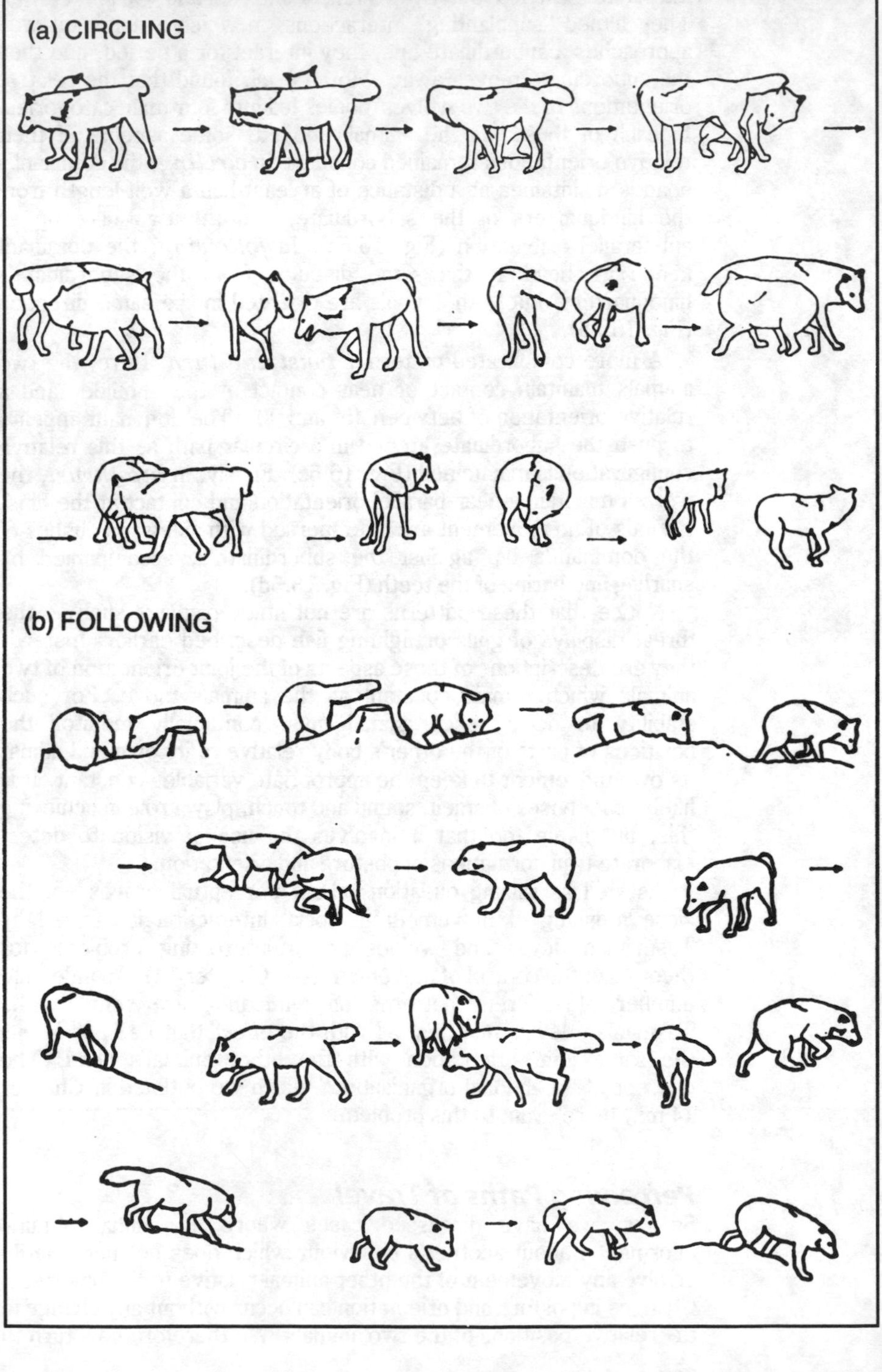

(a) CIRCLING

(b) FOLLOWING

FIGURE 16.5 (continued)

(c) TWIST-AND-TURN

(d) HIP-THRUST

Drawings made from single frames of a film of two wolves. Numbers refer to frames of film taken at 24 frames/sec. (a) Circling (b) Following (c) Twist and turn (d) Hip−thrust. From Moran et al. (1981) with permission.

consider what information animals are able to obtain through vision about another animal's direction of movement.

Many simple forms of interaction between animals do not require one to detect the other's direction of movement. In order to pursue either prey or a conspecific, a simple tactic is to keep moving while orienting towards the target, as a fly does in pursuing a potential mate (Chapter 11, p. 251). Similarly, an animal could escape from a predator by moving as fast as possible while orienting away from it. A more complex variant of this tactic has been described in blue crabs by Woodbury (1986). These animals swim in the shallow water of the intertidal zone, and, if a predator approaches, start to swim rapidly. Acting as a model predator, Woodbury walked towards crabs and recorded the bearing they took when they first responded to him. He discovered that they do not simply swim directly away from a predator, but that their bearing is an average of two component directions weighted differently. The stronger component is a directly offshore bearing carrying the crab into deeper, and presumably safer, water, while the weaker is a bearing away from the predator.

Woodbury showed that the resulting escape route maximises the distance offshore the crab attains before being intercepted by the predator. Woodbury (1986) always approached crabs directly, and so did not obtain any evidence whether they could discriminate different directions of a predator's movement relative to themselves. It is easy to see how this information could be useful; the same predator moving directly towards an animal is more dangerous than one the same distance away but moving in some other direction. In order to make this discrimination between directions of motion relative to the observer, information from a static snapshot is not sufficient and some information about the transformation in the other animal's position is needed.

An experiment testing for the ability to discriminate direction of movement is reported by Burger and Gochfeld (1981), who compared the responses of nesting gulls to people either walking directly towards the nest or walking on a tangential route passing a minimum of one metre from the nest. Herring gulls nesting in the open showed alarm responses when the directly approaching person was at a greater distance than a person travelling tangentially. Clearly, the gulls did not detect just the instantaneous distance of the person, but unfortunately it cannot be firmly concluded that they detected direction of travel. The directly approaching person looked straight at the gulls, but the tangentially walking person did not, making it possible that the gulls discriminated different orientations of the person relative to themselves.

A second way in which we might expect animals to use information about another animal's direction of travel is to intercept it. As we have already seen, a simple way for an animal A to catch up with an animal B is to move directly towards it, as a housefly does in pursuing a potential mate. This would result in the approach path shown in Figure 16.6a. As Menzel (1978) points out, interception is a more complex process, as it requires A to *extrapolate* from B's path of movement to predict a point at which it could intercept it (Fig. 16.6b). Is there evidence that animals are capable of doing this?

FIGURE 16.6

(a) Animal B approaches animal A by keeping its bearing at zero. (b) B extrapolates from A's path of movement and moves straight to an interception point. Adapted from Menzel (1978).

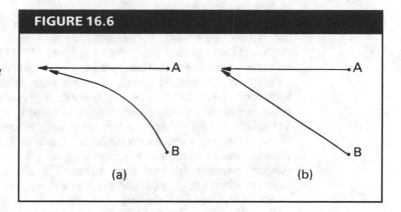

Observation of dogs hints strongly that they are able to extrapolate the paths of target objects, dogs and people in the way shown in Figure 16.6b. Dogs are strikingly accurate in jumping to intercept a ball and catch it in their jaws; they run to intercept or head off the path of movement of a dog or person; and they will run on ahead of their owner, looking back to check the owner's path of travel and adjust their own accordingly. Chimpanzees behave similarly (Menzel, 1978); if a number of chimps are travelling together and there is a clear leader of the group, which determines its direction of travel, other chimps will run on ahead and look back from time to time to adjust their direction to keep on the same route as the leader.

Why should the ability to extrapolate other animals' paths of movement be useful to a dog in catching prey or in social interaction? Dogs are closely related to wolves, which, like lions and other large carnivorous mammals, capture large prey by hunting in packs. An individual dog or wolf would have little success in catching large animals such as deer or caribou because it would be outdistanced or injured by a kick from the intended prey. A dog's abilities to detect and extrapolate from paths of movement are therefore likely to have evolved for more complex tasks than just running to intercept fleeing prey; in particular, for the task of co-operative pack hunting. What information about prey and conspecifics do dogs or wolves need to perform this task?

Observations of pack hunting predators have demonstrated a striking degree of co-ordination between individual animals. Lions fan out as they stalk their quarry (Schaller, 1972, Chapter 8), while Mech (1970, Chapter 7) describes wolves surrounding a caribou standing at bay or pursuing a running caribou in single file.

Behaviour of this kind suggests that each animal in a pack is able to detect the positions and paths of movement of both the prey and the other members of the pack relative to itself, and to use this information to plan its own path. It is clearly difficult to determine the specific information used by pack hunting animals, but some features of the behaviour of sheepdogs provide evidence for some of the processes involved.

The ways in which a shepherd and a sheepdog control a group of sheep draws on behavioural predispositions of dogs which evolved as part of pack-hunting behaviour, and Vines (1981) has described how the trainer builds on these predispositions when training a dog to respond to whistled commands. Our main interest is in the behaviour shown by a naive dog towards a group of sheep; the behaviour on which either pack-hunting skills or co-ordination with a shepherd is built. There are two particularly interesting features of this behaviour. First, an untrained dog tends to "herd" sheep, by circling around them, moving from side to side while keeping a roughly constant distance from them. The sheep draw closer together when a dog is near and move as a group, keeping beyond a minimum distance from the dog.

Second, a naive dog tends to position itself on the opposite side of a group of sheep from its trainer. If the trainer moves either to his right or to his left, the dog matches his move so as to keep the group of sheep directly between them. A shepherd exploits this tendency in training by giving the right or left turn whistle while the dog makes the appropriate turn relative to the sheep.

In these situations, the dog is moving so as to maintain its position relative to both the group of sheep and the trainer. On its own, it moves about a good deal but keeps a roughly constant distance from the sheep, while they keep a constant (and much smaller) distance from each other and a minimum distance from the dog. With the trainer present, the dog keeps the centre of the group of sheep on a line between itself and the trainer.

Are these rules regulating position relative to sheep and trainer part of a pack-hunting strategy? Predators such as dogs or wolves stand little chance of taking an animal such as a sheep from a group without risking injury from other prey. They therefore face the problem of splitting off one sheep from its group. Once this is done, they can move between it and the rest of the group and then attack it. To achieve this, however, they must overcome the sheep's strong tendency to keep close to other sheep.

The dog's tendency to keep a position opposite the trainer gives a clue as to how two dogs might be able to break up a group of sheep and split one off. The chances of this happening will be greater if they can make the sheep mill about and increase their distances from neighbouring sheep. Two dogs circling about a group of sheep in an unco-ordinated way would not achieve this to any extent, as most of the time the sheep would be able to move as a group away from both dogs at once, maintaining close contact as they do so (Fig. 16.7).

FIGURE 16.7

Two dogs (closed circles) circling a group of sheep (open circles) in an unco-ordinated way. There is always a consistent direction in which the sheep can move to escape from both dogs.

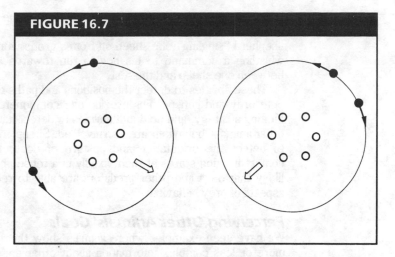

If the dogs maintain positions opposite each other as they circle about, however, there will always be two directions in which each sheep could move to escape from the dogs (Fig. 16.8). The chances of splitting the group of sheep in two, or of splitting one off from the rest, will therefore be greater. All that needs to be added

FIGURE 16.8

Two dogs circling a group of sheep and maintaining positions diametrically opposite each other (a). As the dogs move, there are two possible escape routes for the sheep. In (b), one sheep moves in the opposite direction to the rest of the flock and is then pursued by the dogs (c,d).

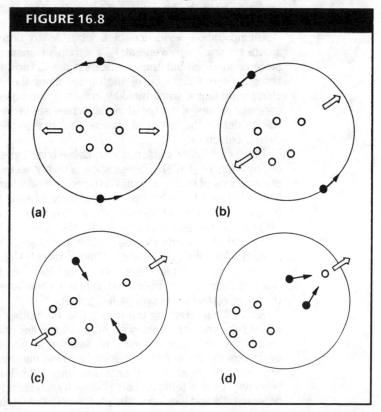

(a)   (b)

(c)   (d)

is for the dogs to detect a large gap between one sheep and the others and drive a wedge between them by running into the gap. A shepherd "singling" one sheep off from a group works in this way, whistling a command to his dog to run towards him into a gap between one sheep and the rest.

These abilities to detect the positions and paths of movement of both prey and conspecifics provide one component of dogs' pack hunting strategy, and no doubt abilities to detect further aspects of other animals' behaviour are also involved. Sheep are certainly able to detect the orientation and posture of dogs, keeping closer contact if a dog stares at them fixedly in a tense posture, and it is likely that dogs and other predators are able to recognise similar aspects of prey behaviour.

Perceiving Other Animals' Goals

We have seen examples where animals show the ability to obtain more or less complex information about other animals' postures, orientations and paths of travel. In none of these, however, have we seen any evidence that the orientation or movement of other animals *relative to the environment* is detected. This is an everyday human ability—we can readily detect what another person is looking at, pointing at or walking towards—and there is evidence from the behaviour of some primates that they have the same ability.

Chimps show evidence of being able to detect the goal of another animal's movement; if a group of chimps approaches a piece of food, all but the one nearest it will turn away, as if each recognises the distance of the others from the goal. A band of chimps hunting a small monkey in a tree spreads out to block its potential routes of escape along branches, suggesting that they are able to detect the layout of branches relative to the quarry as well as to themselves.

More conclusive evidence is available from experiments carried out by Menzel (1978). Chimps show a highly accurate memory for the locations of pieces of fruit scattered around a familiar enclosure. Menzel showed one chimp where a piece of fruit was hidden and then locked it in a hut adjoining the enclosure with its companions. On release, the group emerged from the hut and all the chimps set out together towards the food, some running on ahead to search along the knowledgeable chimp's line of travel. Control procedures showed that the other chimps were not simply finding the fruit by smell or sight, and so they must have been able to extrapolate from the knowledgeable chimp's path of travel.

As well as detecting the orientation of another animal's line of travel relative to the environment, monkeys and apes seem able to detect the direction of gaze of another animal relative to the environment. Packer (1977) describes how one male olive baboon will solicit the help of another in attacking a third male and driving him away from a female. This is done by alternately looking at the potential ally and looking at the rival, with a threatening expression.

This suggests that the animal whose help is being solicited perceives the orientation of the head relative to the rival as well as to itself. Similarly, a subordinate chimp which knows the location of a piece of food will not approach it directly if a dominant chimp is present but takes a roundabout route so that it approaches the food from a direction out of the dominant's line of sight.

Again, Menzel's (1978) experiments provide more conclusive evidence. In one, Menzel asked whether a chimp could tell where a piece of food was hidden by observing a person either taking a few steps towards it or pointing at it. In both cases, a chimp which had watched the person ran straight to the food. Further, chimps were able to distinguish different kinds of goal according to how far the person had walked towards them. Presumably they are able to pick up information in the same way from the postures and gestures of other chimps.

In another experiment, Menzel and Halperin (1975) showed that other chimps' posture and movement can specify not only where an object is but also how interesting it is to chimpanzees. They hid a piece of fruit and a novel toy in an enclosure; of these two objects, chimps prefer the fruit. One chimp was shown the location of the fruit and another the location of the toy, before both were returned to the group. On release, all the group followed the individual which knew the location of the fruit, demonstrating that some subtle features of the chimps' behaviour must have indicated how desirable a goal they were approaching.

These observations raise interesting questions about the ability of animals to detect other animals' *intentions*, in the sense of the purpose or goal of another animal's actions. A simple form of detection of intention would be one chimp detecting the goal to which another is travelling, but Premack and Woodruff (1978) have argued that chimpanzees are capable of more elaborate perception of intention. They showed chimps videotapes of people attempting to solve various problems. These included trying to open a door or trying to get at bananas just out of reach. The chimp subject was given a set of photographs of various objects such as a key or a pole, and almost always chose the one of the object which would solve the person's problem. Premack and Woodruff argue that a chimp's natural mode of perceiving its animate environment is in terms of intentions; not simply the moment-by-moment behaviour of other chimps (or people) but where their behaviour is going in the world. Note the similarity between this argument and that of Heider and Simmel (1944) discussed in Chapter 15 (p. 338) that people spontaneously attribute intentions to parts of artificial moving displays.

RECOGNITION OF INDIVIDUALS

All social behaviour relies on some means of recognising conspecifics, and of discriminating them from other objects or animals in the surroundings. We saw examples in Chapter 8

(p. 177) of how simple "key stimuli" are used by animals such as butterflies and sticklebacks to recognise their conspecifics. Some social animals have considerably greater powers of discrimination than these, and are able to recognise different members of their species as *individuals*. We see illustrations of this ability in cases where group-living birds and mammals discriminate between their own offspring and those of other animals in the group, or discriminate which individuals are dominant to them and which are subordinate.

Laboratory experiments can be devised to confirm that animals are able to discriminate between individual other animals on the basis of visual information. For example, Ryan (1982) has shown using an operant conditioning procedure that chickens can discriminate slides of one bird in a variety of poses from slides of other birds and could transfer this discrimination to novel sets of slides. Similarly, Rosenfeld and Van Hoesen (1979) have shown that monkeys can easily learn to discriminate slides of one monkey's face seen from many angles from slides of other monkeys' faces. Any skepticism that chickens or monkeys vary enough in their appearance to make individual recognition possible is weakened by the fact that human observers are able, with sufficient experience, to discriminate individual members of these and similar species. Bateson (1977) provided evidence that an observer, familiar with a large colony of Bewick's swans, was able to recognise from photographs at least 52, and probably several hundred individual swans, using subtle differences in the markings on their bills.

Humans are an especially social species, with striking abilities to recognise large numbers of other people. In the remainder of this chapter, we discuss what is known of the visual processes involved in individual recognition, beginning with research on the development of recognition in both young animals and infants, and then considering how human adults recognise faces.

The Development of Individual Recognition

In order to study the processes involved in learning to recognise individual conspecifics, we need to find situations in which a young animal learns rapidly and reliably. A case which has been studied in some detail is that of young birds learning to recognise their mothers. The young of some bird species, such as chickens and ducks, are able to move about independently a short time after hatching, and, within a few days, to find their own food. For some time, however, the young birds are dependent upon their mother as a source of warmth, protection from predators and help in finding food. It is therefore essential for their survival that they keep close to her, which in turns means that they must recognise her and discriminate her from other adults of their species. This is achieved in part through recognition of the mother's calls, but there is evidence that vision is involved as well.

If a chick or duckling is hatched in an incubator, kept in darkness until it is about a day old, and then exposed to a conspicuous moving object, it approaches and follows it. After exposure to this object for an hour or so, it will later approach it in preference to any other object. This phenomenon is known as *imprinting* (Bateson, 1966), and demonstrates that birds form some representation of the visual characteristics of a familiar object which enables them to recognise and keep close to it. Imprinting therefore provides a means by which a bird could learn to recognise its mother. In the first day or two after hatching, it will be exposed to her far more than to any other conspicuous, moving object, and so will learn to recognise and follow her.

The fact that young birds in the laboratory will imprint on a wide variety of artificial objects suggests that, at hatching, they have no representation of the visual properties of the mother bird and so will be equally likely to learn the characteristics of any object they are exposed to. Further research has demonstrated that this is not so. Dark-reared chicks with no previous visual experience follow a blue or red object more readily than a green or yellow one (Kovach, 1971), and this predisposition to avoid imprinting on green objects is presumably adaptive in a natural world full of moving foliage. Chicks' innate preferences between objects are even more specific than these, however. Johnson, Bolhuis and Horn (1985) tested chicks' preferences between two moving objects; a rotating bright red box or a stuffed jungle fowl hen moving with a rocking motion. They found that chicks not previously exposed to either of these objects showed a preference for the stuffed fowl which, provided the chicks had some visual experience during their first day, emerged gradually over the second day after hatching.

The preference for a stuffed fowl observed by Johnson et al. (1985) is not strictly speaking innate, as it requires a period of time and some non-specific visual experience before it appears. The crucial point, however, is that the preference develops *without* any exposure to the fowl. In experiments using artificial objects, in contrast, imprinting only occurs following exposure to an object. Clearly, chicks must have some representation of the visual properties of a fowl before they have any opportunity to learn them. In other experiments, Johnson et al. found that this developing preference for the stuffed fowl interacts with the process of acquiring a preference for a familiar object. They concluded that two processes are responsible for young birds' ability to recognise their mother. First, an initial representation of the visual characteristics of mother birds in general is built into the nervous system in some way which does not require experience of a mother bird. Second, exposure to one particular bird causes this representation to be refined, so that details specifying a young bird's own mother as distinct from others are incorporated.

Johnson and Horn (1988) went on to identify which features of a hen are specified in a chick's initial representation. They tested chicks' initial preference for a stuffed fowl over a variety of models in which some characteristics of a hen were removed and others maintained. Their results indicate that chicks do not recognise a hen on the basis of her overall outline or the colour and texture of her feathers, but recognise specifically the configuration of the head and neck region. Any model in which this part of the fowl was intact was equally as attractive to chicks as the complete fowl. Further experiments showed that chicks were equally attracted to a stuffed duck or polecat as to the fowl. These results indicate that the initial representation does not specify the head and neck shape of the young bird's own species precisely, but must instead be a cruder representation of a "generalised" head and neck.

HUMAN FACE PERCEPTION

So far in this chapter we have separated our discussion of the perception of what another animal is doing from our discussion of how its individual identity is recognised. In human perception such a separation can also be maintained to some extent. We may use some information such as overall posture and gait to inform us of another's actions or even intentions (e.g. Runeson & Frykholm, 1983; see Chapter 15), while recognising individual identity largely through other sources such as clothing, the voice and particularly the face. However, both voice and face inform us not just about identity but also about a person's intentions, desires and emotional state. Voice and face perception mediate social perception in a number of different ways, telling us about what a person is doing and feeling as well as who they are. In this final section we consider the different uses made of facial information within a broadly ecological framework.

Development of Face Perception

There is now good evidence that face learning in the infant is guided by some innate specifications of what faces look like, in the same way as young birds possess an innate representation of the visual properties of hens. Goren, Sarty and Wu (1975) showed that new-born infants (with an average age of 9 minutes) would track schematic face-like patterns more than control patterns with the same features re-arranged, a result that has been replicated more recently by Dziurawiec and Ellis (1986). This result suggests that human infants may come equipped with knowledge of roughly what heads and faces look like, and this innate knowledge may allow them to attend selectively to such objects so that they can subsequently learn more about the appearance of their own caregivers.

A more controversial claim is that human neonates are able to discriminate and imitate facial expressions. Field, Woodson, Greenberg and Cohen (1982) showed that infants aged 1–2 days looked less at faces whose expressions remained constant than at faces whose expressions changed, suggesting that the infants must have been able to discriminate between the different expressions. Meltzoff and Moore (1977) found that neonates would imitate facial expressions such as mouth opening and tongue-poking. The facility to imitate requires that the infant is not only able to tell the difference between two different expressions, but is able to map a particular seen expression onto a particular pattern of muscle activity. Such a mapping involves a rather sophisticated kind of expression recognition ability. These demonstrations are not always replicated (e.g. McKenzie & Over, 1983), but they do remind us that face perception is not a unitary task but involves many different processes. As we elaborate later, identifying a particular person from their face is not the same as identifying an expression, and it would be quite possible, in principle, to have an innately specified facial expression system which was quite independent of the face identification system. Facial expressions (though not the rules for displaying them) are culturally universal (Ekman, 1982) so there is no reason why some knowledge of them should not be hard-wired.

It would be much more controversial to suggest that an infant was born with a knowledge of the detailed appearance of their own particular family members, and it seems likely instead that learning of individual appearances occurs after birth. The ability to learn the appearances of strangers develops gradually over the first seven months of life (Fagan, 1979). Although there is evidence that 1-month olds (Sai & Bushnell, 1988) and even two-day olds (Bushnell, Sai & Mullin, 1989) can discriminate visually between their mother's and a stranger's face, their ability to do so seems likely to be based on hair-style and colour, rather than on internal facial features, since even infants aged 12 weeks cannot discriminate their mother's from a stranger's face when the hair region is concealed with a bathing cap (Bushnell, 1982). Nevertheless, the younger infants must be capable of rapid learning of quite subtle characteristics of hair and head outline, since Bushnell et al. (1989) were careful to pair mothers with strangers who had broadly similar hair length and colour.

The human infant thus appears to have an innate knowledge of "faceness" plus, possibly, some innate knowledge of certain facial gestures and how to map these onto its own action patterns. Other face-processing abilities are gradually learned during the first few months of life, and a review of this topic can be found in Flin and Dziurawiec (1989). We now turn to consider what is known about the processes of face perception when fully developed in the adult.

Adult Face Perception and Identification

The dynamic configuration of the human face is endowed with a number of different kinds of meaning, all of which need to be extracted in the course of social interaction. The extraction of these different kinds of meaning must rely on the abstraction of different invariant and variant information. A face first serves as the most reliable way to identify an individual, but in addition to identifying *known* faces, we can derive other information even from unknown faces. We can decide that a face looks young or old, male or female, intelligent or friendly. This information is also important in our social interaction—we may decide to go and talk to someone at a party because they look attractive or interesting to us, we take account of a child's apparent age when choosing topics of conversation, and so forth. Because the face and head are mobile, we must somehow identify structural information from a face which remains invariant despite these transformations in pose and expression.

As well as serving to identify or categorise an individual, a person's face also conveys expressive information, which may inform us about his or her emotional state, intentions towards or attentiveness to an observer, and which may help to disambiguate verbal information during conversation. Movements of the face may help a listener to know whether a remark is intended seriously or in jest, and whether it is a request or a command. People are reasonably accurate at identifying emotions from facial expressions, and this ability must rely on the detection of a different kind of information from that which subserves face recognition. That is, we must be able to encode from faces both information which specifies an individual's age, sex or identity (irrespective of pose or expression), and information which specifies a particular expression (irrespective of the identity of the person whose expression it is.)

In addition to such expressive motions of the face, lip movements can also be important to help derive phonology in speech perception (for a review see Dodd & Campbell, 1987). Phonemes which may be difficult to distinguish auditorally, such as /f/ from /s/ and /n/ from /m/ are often readily distinguished visually from movements of the lips. It has been known for some time that seeing the face can aid speech perception in noisy conditions (e.g. Sumby & Pollack, 1954), but more recent evidence suggests that lip movements are taken into account in speech perception even when the acoustic speech signal alone is quite unambiguous (e.g. McGurk & MacDonald, 1976).

Experimental evidence obtained with normal adults, combined with patterns of neuropsychological impairment, have led to the suggestion that different processing "modules" are responsible for the different uses made of facial information (e.g. see Bruce & Young, 1986; Bruce, 1988). Expression analysis, for example, proceeds independently of face identification, and lipreading proceeds independently of both these other modules. In the next sections we discuss very briefly what is known about the visual processing of faces within the expression and identification modules that allow us to derive these different kinds of meaning from such subtle differences in configuration.

Perceiving Facial Expressions

In the natural world the human face is in almost continuous motion. Some movements of the head involve rigid transformations, as when the head is turned from side to side, but expressive movements of the face, such as smiles and frowns, are not rigid. Such non-rigid motions include stretching and bulging of different parts of the face, produced by complex sets of muscles. Bassili (1978; 1979) has used a technique like Johansson's (see Chapter 15, p. 327), in which small illuminated spots are scattered over a face which is then filmed in the dark, to show that observers can identify a "face" from a moving configuration of lights without seeing any structural information about the facial features. Not only can a "face" be identified, but observers also have some success in identifying different emotions portrayed in such displays. Quite specific information about faces can be gleaned simply from the pattern of transformations present, without any need for information about the *form* of the face, just as human walkers can be identified in Johansson's displays, without any detail of the form of their limbs.

Despite the dynamic nature of facial expressions, most work in this area has used photographs of posed expressions to determine how accurately human observers can perceive the different emotions portrayed (for a review see Ekman, 1982). People are fairly accurate at assigning posed emotional expressions to one of a few fairly broad categories, such as happiness, surprise, anger and disgust. There is a good degree of universality in such judgements. People from a variety of literate and some pre-literate cultures judge such displays in similar ways (Ekman & Oster, 1982). While less is known about the accuracy with which observers can judge spontaneous expressive movements, there is evidence that at the very least, positive and negative emotions can be distinguished in natural situations (Ekman, Friesen & Ellsworth, 1982).

What processes might underly our ability to judge emotional expressions? One possibility is that information about different facial "postures" is encoded and compared to some kind of stored catalogue, just as we suggested earlier in this chapter that an animal might recognise another's posture by recognising different "snapshot" configurations. A particular emotion might be characterised by the relative dispositions and shapes of the component parts of the face, perhaps with respect to the major axis of symmetry, in a manner analogous to the part-based theories of object recognition (e.g. Biederman, 1987; Marr & Nishihara, 1978) which we discussed in Chapter 8.

It would be difficult to apply such a scheme in natural situations where there is continuous movement in the face, and where expressions must be *meshed* in social interaction. A better way to describe the information which underlies expressive judgements might be to make use of dynamic rather than static cues. Ekman and Friesen (1982) have developed a *Facial Action Coding System* (FACS) to describe in detail the movements made by different parts of a face. The FACS consists of an inventory of all the perceptually distinct actions which can be produced by the facial muscles. Using such an inventory, we are in a position to ask whether unique combinations of actions (independent of who the actor is) underly the perception of different emotions.

The kind of analysis is illustrated here for the eyebrows alone (Ekman, 1979). Figure 16.9 shows the distinguishable action units for the brows and forehead together, and the distinguishable combinations of these units. These patterns have been "frozen" for the purposes of illustration, and it is important to emphasise that Ekman and Friesen are concerned to code *actions* rather than configurations. Ekman has shown that different action units are indeed involved in different emotions. For example, action unit 1 alone, or with 4, indicates sadness, 4 alone yields anger or distress, 1 with 2 gives surprise, and 1 + 2 + 4 gives fear.

Ekman has thus shown that distinct patterns of activity are related to changes in emotional state, and it may be these patterns of activity that observers detect in the face. While momentarily frozen expressions might be compared with some stored catalogue of facial postures, it may be more profitable to think of observers matching transformations in expression over time to dynamic emotion "schemata," like the action schemas in Weir's work that we described in Chapter 15 (p. 335). Expressions are never all-or-none, but are graded and blended. A person's momentary expression of faint surprise may represent a point of increasing or decreasing amazement, so we need to know its relationship both to

The different action units for the brow and forehead identified by the Facial Action Coding System (Ekman & Friesen, 1978). Action units 1, 2 and 4 may occur alone (top) or in combination (bottom). The drawings were obtained by tracing photographs. From Ekman, P. (1979) About brows: Emotional and conversational signals. In M. von Cranach, K. Foppa, W. Lepenies, & D. Ploog (Eds.) Human ethology, Cambridge: Cambridge University Press. Reproduced with permission of the publishers.

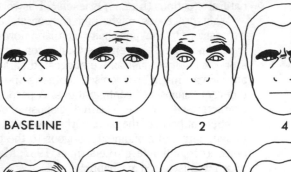
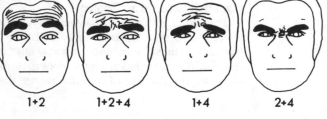

FIGURE 16.9

BASELINE   1   2   4

1+2   1+2+4   1+4   2+4

prior and subsequent expressive movements, and to concurrent events in the world, in order to interpret it properly.

To reinforce this point, consider the following scenario. Suppose someone pulls out a gun, aims it at you, squeezes the trigger, and thereby releases a flag on which is written the word "BANG." Your emotions are likely to swing rapidly through the range from horror and fear to surprise followed by mirth (if you appreciated the joke) or anger (if you didn't). These emotions are likely to be revealed in rapidly changing and blending expressions. A stored catalogue of facial postures would not help an observer decipher your feelings here. Some representational system sensitive to unfolding *events* would be more appropriate.

Identifying Faces

As we mentioned in Chapter 8, most researchers have treated the problem of how faces are recognised in ways similar to the research on pattern recognition described in that chapter. The stimuli used in face recognition research have usually been photographs of real faces or composite faces constructed from Photofit or Identikit. While early research in the area was primarily directed at understanding factors that influenced recognition *memory* for previously unfamiliar faces, recent work has additionally examined carefully the visual and cognitive processes which influence the recognition of already familiar faces. We will not delve into more cognitive issues here (for a review see Bruce, 1988), but will concentrate on discussing the nature of the visual information which sustains our recognition decisions.

We now know that it is the *configuration* of facial features, as much as the features themselves, which specifies individual identity (e.g. Sergent, 1984; Young, Hellawell & Hay, 1987). Sergent (1984) found that subjects could decide that two Identikit faces were different more quickly when they differed on two dimensions than when they differed on any single facial dimension (the dimensions of the face that were varied in this study were the type of eye, the shape of the chin, and the placement of the internal features in the face). This result suggests that the dimensions of variation may be processed interactively rather than independently, since if they were processed independently a decision could never be made more quickly than by the fastest of the independent analysers. This suggestion of configural processing was supported by the results of a multi-dimensional scaling analysis of perceived similarities between the different faces. Young et al. (1987) made new composite faces from the top halves and bottom halves of different famous faces. When the two halves of the composite were closely aligned, to form a new face, subjects found it very difficult to name the top halves. When the two halves were misaligned, subjects were much quicker to name the top halves. The top and bottom half configurations together produced a new configural identity, within which it was very difficult to recognise a familiar sub-set of features.

It seems to be the processing of configural information that makes face recognition memory particularly susceptible to inversion (Valentine, 1988; Yin, 1969). Sergent (1984) found evidence of configural processing only for upright faces, and Young et al. (1988) found that halves of facial composites were recognised more quickly when the faces were inverted than when the faces were upright, their explanation being that the configural processing which blended the two halves when upright was less effective when the two halves were inverted.

To recognise an individual from their face requires sensitivity to more than the "first-order" configuration of eyes, nose and mouth that specifies "a face". It is the "second-order" configuration relative to the basic face pattern which is important (Diamond & Carey, 1986). Diamond and Carey showed that the recognition of individual members of a breed of dogs by expert breeders was as disrupted by inversion as was face recognition, and argued that the dog-breeders had also developed second-order configural sensitivity for members of this other perceptual category.

The particular importance of the overall configuration of the face can help us understand why face recognition can be remarkably robust despite a variety of unnatural as well as natural transformations (such as expressive movements). For example, faces can be identified from relatively low spatial frequency information (e.g. see Harmon, 1973), or from simple line-drawn cartoons. In both cases, overall configuration is preserved while fine details are discarded. Even more interesting is our ability to recognise grossly distorted caricatures, which can be more recognisable than veridical line drawings of the same faces (Rhodes, Brennan & Carey, 1987). Caricatures seem to be effective because they exaggerate the relationship between an individual face and the "average" or "norm" of all faces, and an artificial caricature-generator that works on this principle produces highly effective caricatures (Brennan, 1985; Rhodes, Brennan & Carey, 1987).

Thus far, we have emphasised the importance of configural information in face recognition. However, the parts of the face are not themselves equally important for recognition (for a review see Shepherd, Davies & Ellis, 1981). The external features of the faces (hairstyle and face outline) seem most important in the recognition of unfamiliar faces, though recognition of familiar faces seems to rely more on internal features (Ellis, Shepherd & Davies, 1979). A multi-dimensional scaling study of similarity judgements to unfamiliar faces revealed three main dimensions of hairstyle, face shape and age (Shepherd et al. 1981), which again stresses the importance of external features and/or global configural variations in our perception of unfamiliar faces. Of the internal features, the eye region seems most salient for identification and the nose the least, and this result is found for both familiar and unfamiliar faces (e.g. Haig, 1986; Roberts & Bruce, 1988).

All the above research has made use of full-face views of static faces. The use of static faces does not necessarily invalidate research into face recognition, since a photograph of a real face must itself capture structural information about that face which remains invariant across a variety of different views (or photographs). However, the use of such materials has perhaps prevented researchers from thinking carefully about the kind of physical information which could be used to distinguish one face from another in the real world. For example, many memory experiments have confounded picture recognition with face recognition, by presenting identical photographs of faces at study and test. Face recognition can only be seen to have occurred if a face is recognised *despite* changes between presentation and test. Recognition memory for briefly presented unfamiliar faces is significantly impaired if these are tested in a different view (Bruce, 1982), suggesting only a limited ability to abstract invariant information from a single photograph. Therefore, even if experiments manipulating the "features" of composite faces reveal that the hair or eyes are preferentially attended to, and/or better remembered, we still have to establish how it is that eyes could be recognised from different angles or when altered as in frowning.

It is perhaps not too difficult to construct hypotheses about the kinds of structural information about a face which might remain invariant under rigid transformations. For example, the ratio of nose length to overall head height could be recovered fairly easily from any viewing angle, and would give a measure of "nose size" which did not depend on viewing angle or distance. The ratio of inter-ocular distance to width of the head could give an invariant measure of how close together the eyes were set in the head. As yet, however, we have little insight into what information could remain invariant when a face undergoes *non*-rigid transformations, such as smiling, frowning or grimacing, where there will be less preservation of metrical properties. The ratio of nose length to head height, for example, would be altered whenever the nose was wrinkled in disgust.

One way around this problem would be simply to propose that such expressive movements just add "noise" to the process of extracting invariants, and that when we view faces under natural conditions we concentrate on their more passive moments in building up enduring representations which can be used to identify people (e.g. Ekman, 1978). There may even be some kinds of information that we can extract from a face that are affected relatively little by expressive movements. Such information might include (for Caucasian faces) hair length, texture and style, overall face shape, age-level, skin tone etc. It is interesting to note again that dimensions roughly corresponding to "hair style," "face shape" and "age" were found to account for similarity judgements made between pairs of unfamiliar faces (Shepherd, Davies and Ellis, 1981). Therefore we could argue that there are a number of potential sources of information in the face to specify identity, so that expressive movements could simply be regarded as a complicating nuisance.

An alternative approach would be to propose that invariant information about an individual's identity may be given by, and be preserved in, patterns of expressive movement. Strong evidence to support such an idea would be provided if observers could identify their friends from the Bassili displays we described above. Bruce and Valentine (1988) examined this by filming expressive (smiling, frowning and gasping) and rigid (e.g. nodding, shaking and rocking) movements of the heads of three male and three female colleagues whose faces were displayed using Bassili's technique. Subjects in the experiment were told whose heads might appear (all the actors were known to subjects) and what motions they might make, and were asked to decide on each trial how the face was moving, whether it was male or female, and whose face it was. Like Bassili, we found that subjects were highly accurate at identifying expressive movements from these dynamic displays, and were at ceiling identifying the rigid movements. Subjects were above chance performance at identifying the sex and identities from these displays, but performance levels were very low compared with the identification of expressions. It appears that patterns of expressive movement per se convey rather little invariant information to specify identity.

While motion per se may not yield information important for face recognition, this does not mean that an "ecological" approach to face recognition could not yield important insights. As argued elsewhere (e.g. Bruce, 1988; Bruce, 1989; Bruce & Burton, 1989), the "pattern recognition" approach to the problem of face recognition has treated faces as though they were static *flat* patterns, whose individual variations are captured by distances on the picture plane of full-face images. However, faces are not flat patterns, but bumpy surfaces, whose structures are constrained by the growth of the bones underneath. The processes of growth may themselves produce global changes to which observers are sensitive, and we may develop a better understanding of the important dimensions of individual variation by considering the head as a growing, rubbery three-dimensional object rather than a flat, static pattern. It may be that the above-chance performance at recognising the sex and identities of faces in our Bassili-type displays (Bruce & Valentine, 1988) arose because motion reveals aspects of the three-dimensional shape of the face which contribute to its identification. In the next section we consider examples of such an approach in relation to perceived variations in the age and sex of the face.

Judging the Age and Sex of Faces

As an example of an ecological approach to face perception which takes the three-dimensional pattern of growth of the head into account, we will consider Shaw and Pittenger's work on *ageing*. Shaw and Pittenger (1977) examined the non-rigid transformation which the profile of a human head undergoes while it ages, and have identified information which remains invariant under this transformation.

Shaw and Pittenger have shown that people are very consistent at rank ordering profile outlines according to their apparent relative age, suggesting that head shape provides at least one of the sources of information which we use when establishing a person's age. Consider the set of profiles shown in Figure 16.10. You will probably agree that the one on the right looks "young" and the one on the left looks "old." How can we describe the nature of the transformation which relates the older to the younger profiles ? Shaw and Pittenger have demonstrated that the growth process transforms the human head in a similar way to that which occurs in dicotyledonous plants. The profile of a human head is very similar in shape to a dichotyledonous structure (see Fig. 16.11). Ignoring facial detail, the shape is like an inverted heart with a rounded top—a cardioid.

Shaw, McIntyre and Mace (1974) demonstrated that a single transformation, if applied to the outline of the skulls of infant, child

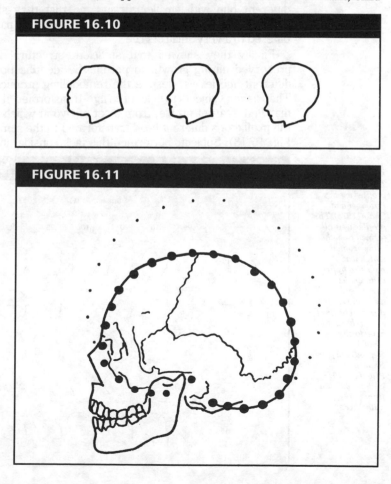

FIGURE 16.10

The profile on the right looks younger than the one on the left, and the central one appears intermediate in age.

FIGURE 16.11

The small dots show a regular cardioidal shape lying above a profile of a human skull. Appropriate transformation of this shape gives a good fit to the shape of the skull, as shown by the large black dots. From Shaw, McIntyre and Mace (1974). Copyright © 1974 by Cornell University. Used by permission of the publisher, Cornell University Press.

and adult, could map one skull continuously onto the other. They hypothesised that there might be a cardioidal shape invariant for growth space, with ageing representing cardioidal *strain*. Strain is imposed on the bones of the skull by stresses produced by growth of softer, highly elastic tissues. Pittenger and Shaw (1975) tested the extent to which perceived changes in relative age level are captured by a strain transformation as opposed to a shear transformation (which modifies the angle of the facial profile). Subjects were shown a series of profiles produced by modifying a single outline profile over seven levels of strain and five levels of shear (Fig. 16.12). They found that 91% of the relative age judgements made by their subjects were consistent with the hypothesis that a strain transformation was responsible for these perceived age changes, while only 65% of the judgements were consistent with a shear transformation, which confirmed their intuition that it was strain that was the important determinant. In further experimental work they demonstrated that observers were consistent in perceiving a profile with larger strain as "older" than a different one with smaller strain, and that they showed a high sensitivity in these judgements even when the pairs of profiles differed to a very small degree.

Finally they showed that sufficient structural invariants are preserved during growth to permit the identification of heads at different age levels, despite the remodelling produced by ageing. They asked subjects to select the age-transformed skull profile that matched a target profile, from a set of two in which the "foil" was the profile of a different head transformed to the same degree (see Fig. 16.13). Subjects performed this task considerably better than

FIGURE 16.12

The series of profiles used by Pittenger and Shaw (1975). The profiles were all formed from the same original, which was modified by five different levels of shear (vertical axis) and seven different levels of strain (horizontal axis) to give this set of 35. Reproduced from Shaw and Pittenger (1977) with permission from the publisher.

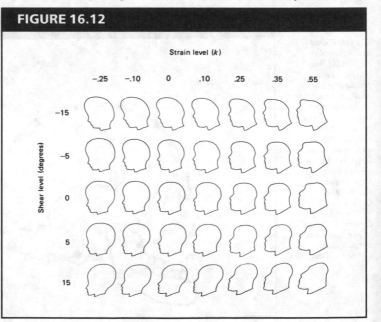

chance. It thus appears that the ageing transformation preserves invariant information which might specify individual identity. We are indeed able to match pictures of people taken at different ages, provided the age spans are not too great (Seamon, 1982), and Shaw and his colleagues have shown how one source of information — skull profile shape — might contribute to these judgements.

FIGURE 16.13

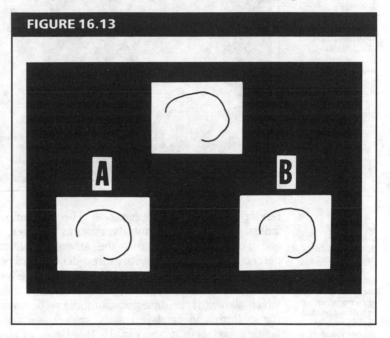

The skull outline at the top is the same as B, but age–transformed to a different extent. Skull A is a different individual, at the same transformational level as B. Reproduced from Shaw and Pittenger (1977) with permission from the publisher.

We have omitted all the mathematical detail from this account of Shaw and Pittenger's work, and you are referred to their articles for a full discussion of this, (see also Todd, Mark, Shaw & Pittenger, 1980). It is worth pointing out here that the invariant they claim accounts for age transformations is *topological* rather than *metrical*. The former requires a different kind of geometry from the familiar Euclidean geometry we learn at school. The concept of "shape" which emerges from a weaker (non-metrical) geometry is qualitative rather than quantitative, but may provide the right way to handle the changes in shape provided by non-rigid transformations.

The early work on cardioidal strain that we have just reviewed was rather restricted in its application of the growth transformation to simple, line-drawn cranio-facial profiles, and as such said rather little about the perception of age from normal faces. Mark and Todd (1983) published an interesting extension of this work in which the cardioidal strain transformation was applied in three dimensions to a three-dimensional representation of the head of a 15-year old girl (see Fig. 16.14). A computer-sculpted bust of the girl is shown to the right of Figure 16.14, and to the left is a bust that was cut from the same data-base, age-transformed in a direction that should

Right: a computer-sculpted bust of a girl aged about 15 years. Left: the bust which was cut after age-transforming the data-base in a direction which should make the girl appear younger in age. Reproduced from Mark and Todd (1983) with permission.

FIGURE 16.14

Left: a three-dimensional data-base of a head obtained from laser-scanning. Right: the same head, age-transformed in a direction that should make it appear younger.

render it younger in appearance. The vast majority of subjects indeed saw the transformed version as younger, which led Mark and Todd to conclude that the strain transformation could be perceived from more realistic, three-dimensional heads.

Bruce, Burton, Doyle and Dench (1989) have examined this claim more recently, using computer-aided design techniques which allow a three-dimensional model to be constructed in wire-frame form and displayed as a smooth surface using standard lighting models (e.g. see Fig. 16.15). Bruce et al. obtained a data-

FIGURE 16.15

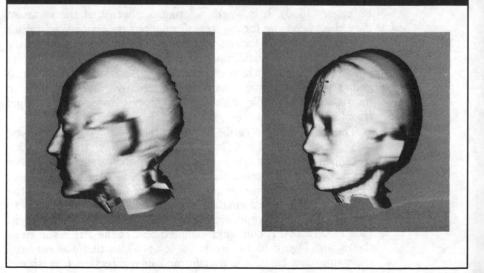

base of 3D head measurements from a laser-scan of an adult head and age-transformed this to different extents in a direction that should have rendered the resulting head younger in appearance. Subjects were asked to judge which member of each of a pair of heads looked the younger, and their ability to do this was assessed as a function of the amount of difference in age levels between the two heads shown, and the views in which these were shown (two profiles, two three-quarter views or one profile and one three-quarter view). Subjects made relative age judgements equally accurately when shown two different views (a profile and a three-quarter view) and when shown two identical views (e.g. two profiles) which allowed comparison between the shapes of the occluding contours; these results were consistent with Mark and Todd's (1983) conclusion that subjects can detect the strain transformation in three dimensions.

However, Bruce et al. (1989) also found that many subjects did not spontaneously see the supposedly "younger" versions of the head as younger, but needed to be given some information about the range of ages that were to be anticipated. Without this guidance, some subjects saw the "younger" heads, for example, as belonging to "little old ladies who had lost their teeth". It seems, then, that richer data structures such as 3D models of heads present wider opportunities for interpretation. Cardioidal strain level is only one possible route to judging age and does not necessarily lead to the "direct" perception of age level. Our argument here is similar to that used against the "direct" perception of causality in the displays used by Michotte (see Chapter 15, p. 333). Because naive subjects are not universal in the impressions formed of such displays of varying age level, we would argue that cardioidal strain is but one of a number of *cues* which *constrain* the judgement of age.

The orthodontist Enlow (1982) suggested that the difference between female and male faces was related to the difference between immature and mature heads, with female faces having somewhat more "babyish" proportions. In particular, Enlow claimed that because males have greater lung capacities than females, their nose region develops more, so that males have larger noses and more protruberant brow regions than females who have more concave profiles. Consistent with this, Roberts and Bruce (1988) obtained evidence for the importance of the configuration of the nose relative to the rest of the face in making sex judgements. Masking the nose had a large detrimental effect on sex judgements, and a much greater effect than masking eyes or mouths. A different pattern was found with the same masks on a familiarity judgement task, where, consistent with other results on feature saliency in identification, masking the noses had no observable effect on performance but masking the eyes had a significant detrimental effect.

In recent research in our laboratory (e.g. see Bruce, Burton & Doyle, in press) we have shown that altering the shape of the noses of 3D head models can have a reliable effect on the rated masculinity and femininity of the heads. Making the nose more concave in shape makes the head look more feminine and making it more protruberant in shape makes it look more masculine. Here we have a clear example of how an "ecological" approach to face perception promotes a rather different perspective on the kind of individuating dimensions that may be important in face perception. Altering the shapes of features of a 3D head can reveal aspects of face perception which are not evident when working with front-view face "patterns".

The ecological approach to face perception has also been extended in a different way by Berry and McArthur (1986; see also the collection edited by Alley, 1988) who have argued that invariant structural information leads to the "direct" perception of subtle social attributes. This work has again concentrated on the effect of cardioidal strain on the face, and has shown, for example, that "baby-faced" adults, whose facial features are relatively low down the face, are seen as more weak and submissive than adults whose features are placed relatively higher up the face.

CONCLUDING REMARKS

This chapter has briefly surveyed the perceptual bases of social perception, suggesting ways in which the ecological approach to perception might be applied to problems as diverse as hunting in packs to judging a person's age. We concluded with a more detailed survey of the processes of face perception in humans, and suggested ways in which an ecological approach might add to this research area. In this context it is interesting to note the overlap between the "ecological" perspective we have here urged as important for theories of face processing, and the "computational" level of theory which Marr (1982) advocated as an important initial step before the development of algorithmic levels of theory (see Part 2 of this book). More traditional, pattern-processing theories of face processing have lacked such a computational theory, and the important work of Pearson and Robinson (1985) which we described in Chapter 5 was probably the first account of face processing that spelled out what needed to be computed from facial images and why. Interestingly, Pearson and Robinson stressed that the goal of a cartoon-drawer was to describe the three-dimensional facial surface, and their automatic cartoon-drawer does just this (see Chapter 5 for further details). This example makes it clear that there can be much in common between the "computational" level of theory and the "ecological" approach that we have explored in this part of the book. Indeed we have implicitly treated the "ecological" level as a "higher" level of theory, but one that can guide the details of an algorithmic specification of some process. However, in making this assumption we have glossed over some important issues which have sustained deep divisions between researchers of perception to which we now turn.

Part IV

CONCLUSIONS

Chapter Seventeen

CONTRASTING THEORIES OF VISUAL PERCEPTION

We have now considered the current state of knowledge of visual perception as it has been built up from research within three traditions. The physiological tradition, which we introduced in the first part of this book, studies the nervous system directly, seeking to establish how the pattern of light falling on receptor cells is transformed by networks of nerve cells into patterns of electrical activity. The second approach, which we described in Part II, moves away from this physiological level and asks what processes operate on the retinal image to yield perceptual experience. The third, "ecological" approach, which we introduced in Part III, also seeks explanation at a more abstract level than physiology, but differs from the second in taking the starting point for vision as the spatiotemporal pattern of light in the optic array.

So far, we have treated these different traditions as frameworks for research and have asked what knowledge has been gained within each. In fact, there is a great deal more to the difference between the second and third approaches than simply whether it is more useful to treat the input for vision as an image or as an optic array. This issue is only one aspect of a much wider theoretical debate concerning the nature of perception and the proper ways to explain it, and it is time now to deal with this debate. For simplicity, we will contrast two positions, which we will call "traditional" and "ecological," although there is much diversity of opinion within each viewpoint. By "traditional" theorists we mean psychologists and computational theorists of the tradition which emphasises the inferential and constructive nature of perception. By "ecological" theorists we mean those theorists who claim that perception involves the direct pick-up of information from the time-varying optic array. In Chapters 4 and 10, we introduced these two theoretical positions before going on to describe the research they have each inspired. In this chapter we try to summarise the important differences between them and ask where reconciliation is and is not possible. Our discussion falls under two headings; the nature of the input for vision and the question of whether perception is direct or indirect.

THE NATURE OF THE INPUT

First, we sum up and clarify the issues at stake in choosing the retinal image or the optic array as the starting point for visual perception. Obviously, there is no argument over the facts that a single chambered eye forms an image on the retina and that the image has to be there for vision to occur. The image is a projection of a segment of the optic array and the spatiotemporal pattern of light is reproduced in it, within limits imposed by the eye's acuity. For many practical purposes, image and optic array are interchangeable. As we saw in Chapter 11, for example, the optical parameter τ can be equally well used to describe a pattern of flow in the optic array or in its projection on a retina.

So, what difference *does* it make to introduce the concept of the optic array? One advantage is in the comparative study of vision, where it helps us to understand that image-forming eyes are not the only light-sensitive structures which can achieve a degree of directional selectivity (Chapter 1, p. 9). A more significant consequence of Gibson's concept of the optic array is that it leads to a quite different conception of the information available in light to a perceiver. The traditional view took the input to be nothing more than a mosaic of point-light intensities on the retina, each characterised by its intensity and wavelength. Gibson attacked this belief on several grounds, but particularly because it makes the mistake of describing the input for a perceiver in the same terms as the input for a single photoreceptor.

The input for a receptor is a stream of photons, but the input for a perceiver is a *pattern* of light extended over space and time. Gibson therefore argued that ways of describing this pattern should be devised, and examples of the terms he introduced are gradients and rates of flow of optic texture. Although descriptions of spatial structure can be applied equally easily to an optic array or to a retinal image, it is important to avoid artificially "freezing" the retinal image and losing sight of the temporal pattern of light in the changing optic array.

Once the possibility of describing the input for vision in terms of structure is accepted, it becomes possible to ask what relationships hold between a perceiver's environment and the structure of the optic array. Gibson's "ecological optics" sets out to explore these relationships, and we have seen examples of them throughout the third part of this book. In the traditional view, there was no obvious place for such questions; input was made up of elements of point intensity, and the intensity of light falling on a single receptor provides no information about the environment.

On these issues, our sympathies are with Gibson's position. He was right, we believe, to argue that the input for vision can be described in terms of the structure of light and not just in terms of point intensities of light. He was right also to argue that there are relationships between the environment surrounding a perceiver and the structure of light in the optic array and that information to specify the structure of the environment is therefore available in the optic array. But this conclusion begs another question; are *all* objects and events in the environment fully specified by the pattern of light in the optic array, or only a limited class of simple properties such as distances, slants and textures of surfaces? We shall see later that Gibson's answer to this question is more difficult to accept.

DIRECT AND INDIRECT THEORIES OF PERCEPTION

As well as defining the nature of the input for vision, a theory of perception must also have something to say about how it is that the structured light reaching a perceiver gives rise to perceptual experience and to visually guided action. The answers given by traditional and ecological theories diverge sharply at this point, and are far less easily reconciled than the differences we have considered so far. The roots of the difference can be found in the history of Gibson's theory.

Gibson's early work was concerned with the perception of the layout and distances of the surfaces surrounding an observer. Since the time of Helmholtz, traditional theory had argued that such perception required processes of *inference* to supplement the supposedly impoverished nature of the flat, static retinal image. These processes of inference were held to *mediate* between retinal image and perception. From his analysis of the structure of the optic array and optic flow, Gibson argued that the problem was wrongly conceived and that processes of inference are required only if a restricted kind of description of the input for vision is adopted.

Gibson therefore argued that, since the structure of light directly specifies surface layout, mediating processes of the kind proposed by Helmholtz are not necessary for perception of "distance". From this conclusion, he went on to argue against *any* role for mediating or inferential processes in perception and to claim that invariant properties of the optic array specifying structures and events in the environment are detected *directly*.

The claim that perception is direct and unmediated has been taken up by "ecological" theorists, but strongly criticised by others, and in the remainder of this chapter we will set out the points at issue between them. First, however, it is worth mentioning the points where there is no disagreement between the two approaches. At a philosophical level, both direct and indirect theorists subscribe to *realism*, maintaining that we are in sensory contact with a real world and that perception reveals this world to us. Both positions also agree that visual perception is mediated by light reflected from surfaces and objects in the world, and both agree that some kind of physiological system is needed to perceive this light. Finally, there is also agreement that perceptual experience can be influenced by learning.

The issue which divides the direct from the indirect accounts of perception is the question of *how* physiological systems must be organised to perceive the world. The traditional approach to visual perception maintains that the world of objects and surfaces that we see must be reconstructed by piecing together more primitive elements such as edges or blobs. To carry out this reconstruction, knowledge of the world is needed, and various kinds of knowledge have been proposed in different "indirect" theories. Examples are knowledge of the sizes of objects in order to detect their distance, or knowledge that natural objects approximate to generalized cones. The process of reconstruction can, the traditional approach maintains, be broken down into stages and analysed both physiologically (as we saw in Part I) and psychologically (as we saw in Part II).

In contrast, the ecological approach maintains that qualities such as surface slant or object shape are perceived directly. An object's shape is not perceived by adding up a set of "features" like edges or blobs, using knowledge of the world to do so. There is information to specify shape in higher-order invariants in the light, and it is not necessary, or even possible, to decompose such processes into more primitive psychological operations or "computations". It may be a task for physiologists to unravel the complexities of how nervous systems are attuned to such higher order invariants, but the ecological psychologist need enquire no further once invariant information has been described.

Now any theory of indirect perception must allow *something* to be detected "directly", and traditionally it is assumed that photoreceptors detect changes in light intensity directly. A biochemist would wish to decompose the process of intensity detection further, but traditional theorists would treat it as an elementary process closed to further analysis, and certainly would not claim that the detection of changes in intensity involved "mediation" by knowledge of the world. They would, however, claim that higher order properties of the world must be reconstructed by making use of those properties which *are* directly detected, and "gluing" them together by making use of knowledge of the world. In contrast, a direct theory of perception maintains that the perception of *all* properties of the world is like the detection of light intensity. The system is attuned to higher order variables, and the only task for psychology is to discover what these higher-order variables are.

What are the important issues dividing these two positions and is there any possibility of reconciling them? We see two important senses in which perception is regarded as "mediated" in the traditional view, and we will consider the objections of ecological theorists to each in turn. The first is the sense that perception of higher-order variables is mediated by processes of computation from low-level properties, and the second is the sense that perception must involve the formation, matching and storage of representations of the world.

Mediation of Perception by Computational Processes

The first issue between direct and indirect theories of perception concerns the levels at which perception can properly be explained. For a direct theory of perception, there are two, the ecological and the physiological. The ecological level is concerned with the information an animal needs from the environment in order to organise its activities, and with the ways in which the changing optic array can provide the information needed. The physiological level is concerned with how networks of nerve cells are organised so as to detect invariants in the optic array. Gibson was concerned to work at the first of these levels, and had little to say about the second, speaking simply of an animal being "attuned" or "resonating" to invariants. Taking the case of the parameter τ as an example, an explanation at the ecological level would be concerned with how τ specifies time to contact with a surface, and with the evidence showing that the timing of animals' and people's actions relies on detection of τ. A direct theory of perception would say that there is nothing more for psychology to ask about this situation, but would accept as valid a physiological investigation of how nerve cells are organised so as to "resonate" to τ.

We would agree with "direct" theorists that the control of action by information in the structure of light can be studied without reference to physiological processes, but we differ with their assertion that there is no level of explanation lying between the ecological and the physiological. Consider what actually happens when we come to ask how an animal's nervous system is built to detect τ. A physiologist would not simply search for τ-detectors but would ask what sort of model of neural interactions could yield a value of τ as output given a fluctuating pattern of light intensities as input. This model would involve processes computing direction and velocity of movement in different parts of the flow field, and others summing these outputs to yield τ. In Chapter 13 we reviewed the recent progress that has been made in developing such computational accounts of motion perception.

This would be an algorithmic level of explanation, to use Marr's terminology discussed in Chapters 4 and 5. Ullman (1980) argues that the "direct" theory is mistaken in believing that there are two distinct levels of explanation, the ecological and the physiological, and concurs with Marr in believing that an algorithmic theory must come between the two in order to organise physiological knowledge. We agree with Ullman's position, and feel that "direct" theorists have not paid sufficient attention to the problem of the relationship between ecological and physiological levels of explanation.

Marr (1982) makes a similar argument, accepting the value of ecological optics but asserting the need for algorithmic explanations of how properties of the optic array are detected. Marr suggested that:

In perception, perhaps the nearest anyone came to the level of computational theory was Gibson (1966) (1982, p. 29).

This is not at all a paradoxical claim, since Marr's notion of a "level one" or "computational theory" is an abstract understanding of the structure and constraints of the visual information processing problem and must not be confused with the algorithmic level which spells out actual computations. It is Gibson's denial of the algorithmic level with which Marr quarrels:

Gibson's important contribution was to take the debate away from the philosophical consideration of sense-data and the affective qualities of sensation and to note instead that the important thing about the senses is that they are channels for perception of the real world outside, or, in the case of vision, of the visible surfaces. He therefore asked the critically important question. How does one obtain constant perceptions in everyday life on the basis of continually changing sensations? This is exactly the right question, showing that Gibson correctly regarded the problem of perception as that of recovering from sensory information "valid properties of the external world" (Marr, 1982, p. 29).

Although one can criticise certain shortcomings in the quality of Gibson's analysis, its major, and, in my view, fatal shortcoming lies at a deeper level and results from a failure to realize two things. First, the detection of physical invariants, like image surfaces, is exactly and precisely an information-processing problem, in modern terminology. And second, he vastly underrated the sheer difficulty of such detection (Marr, 1982, p. 30).

If Ullman's and Marr's arguments are accepted, we can then go on to ask how the variables of optic flow which Gibson and others have identified are computed from a fluctuating pattern of light intensities in a time-varying image. As we discussed in some detail in Chapter 13, progress has already been made in devising algorithms which might specify, for example, time to contact a surface from an expanding pattern of optic flow (e.g. Buxton & Buxton, 1983). We believe that the work reviewed in that chapter represents a promising start to the study of how variables of optic flow are computed. We cannot agree with the radical Gibsonian argument that analyses of this kind are irrelevant to the explanation of perception, and that matters must be left at the assertion that any information available in light is "directly" perceived. For the purposes of an ecological level of analysis, they can be left at that point, but, if links to a physiological level are to be made, they cannot.

Perhaps some common ground between the two positions can be found by agreeing with the "direct" position that properties of the world can be detected without "cognitive" processes of inference, interpretation and judgement *but* arguing, with "indirect" theorists such as Marr and Ullman, that such processes of detection nonetheless rely on computation. The term *cognitively impenetrable* (Fodor & Pylyshyn, 1981; Pylyshyn, 1981) has been used to refer to perceptual processes which cannot be influenced by beliefs, expectations and the like. Examples of such processes might be the analysis of optic flow, or the elaboration of forms in the primal sketch in Marr's theory (see Chapter 6).

Cognitive impenetrability does not necessarily imply direct detection in the sense that no computational explanation is possible. Indeed, Fodor (1983) suggests that it is the data-driven, cognitively impenetrable sensory modules which will be most profitably explored with current computational techniques, and is much more pessimistic about our prospects for understanding more central cognitive processes. Fodor and Pylyshyn's (1981) notion of *compiled detectors* is a useful one here, referring to computational processes which run in an autonomous, data-driven way. At a higher level of analysis, compiled detectors can be regarded as detecting properties of the world directly, but at a lower level of analysis their operations can be unpacked. At a behavioural level, it does not matter whether one argues that τ, for example, is perceived directly, or whether it is computed by compiled detectors. What does matter is that its detection need not rely on inferences of the hypothesis-testing variety.

For the purposes of ecological analysis we can proceed simply by saying that τ is detected, and leave others to work out the details of how this detection is accomplished. Much of the research we described in Part II of this book can be seen as attempts by researchers such as Marr to work out these details; while much of that in Part III asks simply what the ecologically relevant variables are, and how they are used, but does not address the issue of how they can be recovered.

Does Perception Require Representations?

We have concluded that the problem of whether perception is mediated by computational processes should be understood in terms of levels of explanation. At an ecological level, structures in light can be regarded as directly detected, and at a physiological level, light intensity can be regarded as directly detected. The two levels are not neatly separable, however, and to explore perception at a physiological level requires theories of algorithms which enable the detection of structures in light and which are implemented by the nervous system.

There is a second sense in which traditional theory regards perception as mediated, however, and this raises issues which extend beyond problems of perception to questions of the nature of our knowledge of the world. The argument is that in order to perceive the world an animal or person must form an internal representation of it. We have seen examples of representations of the world which theories of perception have postulated; Marr's 2½D sketch (see Chapter 7) represents the layout of the surfaces surrounding an observer, while theories of object recognition (see Chapter 8) have postulated catalogues of stored descriptions of objects held in memory. The term "representation" is used in a wide variety of senses. It is used to refer to any symbolic description of the world—whether this is the world as it has been in the past (as in stored "memories"), as it is now (the 2½D sketch, or structural descriptions), or as it might be in the future (as in certain kinds of imagery). It is also used by "connectionist" theorists (see Chapter 9) to refer to non-symbolic patterns of activation in simple networks, which, nevertheless *represent* some object, feature, distance or other property of the surroundings.

Direct theories of perception completely reject *all* such representations as further examples of mediating processes standing between the world and the perceiver. The counter-argument would run as follows. Just as sizes, slants and distances of surfaces surrounding an observer are specified by invariant properties of optic flow patterns, so any object we can recognise, from a pencil to a painting, is specified by as yet unidentified "high-level" invariants. Therefore, just as we can, at an ecological level, regard detection of distance specified by a texture gradient as direct, so we can equally well regard perception of a pencil or painting as direct. There is no need for any processes of constructing or matching representations.

A further argument against a role for representation in perception is that the direct fit between perception and action is broken. The invariants to which an animal is attuned are those specifying the actions it must perform to ensure its survival, and Gibson (1979) devised the term *affordance* to express this point. An affordance is an opportunity for action provided by an object, such as support by a firm surface, grasping by a limb of a tree, or mating by an animal of the opposite sex. Gibson claimed that affordances such as these are specified by the structure of the light reflected from objects, and are directly detectable. There is therefore no need to invoke representations of the environment intervening between detection of affordances and action; one automatically leads to the other.

We have already argued in similar terms (see Chapter 14, p. 314) that an insect's vision does not work to build up a representation of its surroundings, but instead to provide just the information required to modulate its flight. A female fly (or anything resembling one) could be said to afford pursuit, and the fly to detect the information in the optic array specifying this affordance. In these terms, where is the need for a representation of a female fly to which input is matched?

It is clear that if an algorithmic level of explanation is allowed (as we have argued it must be), then "representations" of some sort are inevitably involved, for the purpose of an algorithm is to transform one representation into another. Thus, Marr (1982) states that the algorithms involved in fly vision:

> deliver a representation in which at least three things are specified: 1) whether the visual field is looming sufficiently that the fly should contemplate landing; 2) whether there is a small patch—it could be a black speck or, it turns out, a textured figure in front of a textured ground—having some kind of motion relative to its background; and if there is such a patch, 3) ψ and $\dot{\psi}$ for this patch are delivered to the motor system (Marr, 1982, p34). [ψ is the angular bearing and $\dot{\psi}$ the angular velocity of the patch; see Chapter 11, p. 251].

What Marr is doing here is to analyse the link between the fly's perception and action into a series of algorithms and representations, and we would argue that such an explanation is not only legitimate but necessary if a physiological analysis is to be undertaken. It is not at all the same as saying that a conceptual representation of the world is built up which a "little fly in the head" consults before taking action, although by using the word "contemplate" Marr could mislead us into thinking that this is what he intends. The representations are patterns of activity in networks of neurons.

In this situation, it becomes difficult to distinguish the ecological and representational positions. The first states that the tuning of the fly to the invariances in the light reaching it fits it to its environment, while the second states that properties of the fly's environment are represented in the neural networks detecting the structure of light. If the term representation is used in this sense, it seems there is really nothing to argue about. It is only if we wanted to claim that the fly had a "concept" of something to pursue that there should be any dispute. If we allow algorithms we must allow representations, but for many examples of animal vision in particular we should consider these to be non-symbolic patterns of activity in the nervous system rather than "concepts" or "memories". We return to consider the issue of non-symbolic representations a little later.

By choosing the example of a fly's visual perception, however, we have avoided more difficult issues raised by the "representation" debate. In this example, we are dealing with the *direct* control of activity by a known invariant in the light *currently* reaching the fly's eyes. Let us consider an example from animal perception not meeting these criteria; Menzel's demonstration of chimpanzees' memory for the location of pieces of food (Chapter 16, p. 356). If a chimp is carried around a familiar field, shown the locations of 20 pieces of food and then released, it will move around the field gathering up all the pieces. Control experiments show that the locations of food cannot be detected by a chimp which has not previously been shown them. What are we to make of this phenomenon?

The first difference from the fly example is that control of activity is not direct; information obtained from light specifying where food is hidden is used later to guide travel around the field. The second is that there is no information in the light reaching the chimpanzee while it is gathering up the food to specify where food is. In an indirect theory of perception, these facts are accommodated by saying that the chimp forms a representation of the information specifying the locations of food, and this representation is later used to guide travel around the field.

A direct theorist would reply that the representational explanation makes the mistake of putting over-narrow bounds on the sample of light in which information can be detected. If we take the sample of light to be that stretching over both sessions of the experiment, then there are invariants specifying the locations of food and there is no need to invoke representations. There is no difference in principle, to a "direct" theorist, between this situation and one in which a chimpanzee's view of a piece of food while approaching it is briefly interrupted by an obstacle. In both cases, activities extended over time are guided by directly detected invariants in a sample of light extended over time. The difficulties many have in accepting this formulation are typified by Menzel's comment that:

> I am an ardent admirer of Gibson, and I don't doubt that his theory could explain much of the data cited in this chapter; but when he starts talking about how animals can "see" things that are hidden from sight or even located in a different room he loses me (Menzel, 1978, p. 417).

The disagreements become sharper when we move to human perception. The Gibsonian position is that anything we perceive must be specified by invariant properties of stimulation, directly detected without any need for representation of information. There are invariants specifying a friend's face, a performance of *Hamlet*, or the sinking of the *Titanic*, and no knowledge of the friend, of the play or of maritime history is required to perceive these things. Gibson also applied the concept of affordance to human perception; a pen, he argued, affords writing and a mailbox the posting of a letter. No knowledge of writing or of the postal system needs to be represented in memory, as invariants specifying these affordances are directly detected.

An important difference between these examples and those we used earlier is that we are now dealing with situations where no invariants specifying objects, events or affordances have been demonstrated or seem likely to be demonstrated. The calm with which Gibsonian theorists contemplate this difficulty is captured in Michaels and Carello's (1981) reply to the question:

How can the ecological approach account for experiential dimensions of hedonic tone (humor, pleasure, amusement) that appear to have no physical stimulus referent?

with the answer:

The invariants must be very higher-order indeed (Michaels & Carello, 1981, p. 178).

Critics of the Gibsonian position do not accept that this answer is adequate, and we will outline the objections made to it by Fodor and Pylyshyn (1981). Their principal criticism is that the terms "invariant" and "directly detected" are left so unconstrained in their meanings in Gibsonian theory as to be meaningless. They take the example of an art expert detecting the fact that a painting was executed by Da Vinci and not by an imitator. To explain this by stating that the expert has directly detected the invariant property "having been painted by Da Vinci" is, they argue, to use the term "invariant" in a trivial way. For any percept, if a sufficiently large sample of available light is considered, there can in principle be some invariant to specify a property of this sort; here, a sample including the light reflected from all Da Vincis, imitations of Da Vincis, books on Da Vinci, and so on.

Fodor and Pylyshyn argue that the notions of invariant and direct detection can be constrained by what they term a "sufficiency criterion". The pattern of light reflected from a looming surface is sufficient to cause the perception of impending collision, as shown by experiments with artificial simulations of such a pattern. Therefore, it makes sense to speak of an invariant property of this pattern being detected directly. In contrast, we have no reason to believe that a sample of light reflected from a Da Vinci is sufficient to cause recognition of it. Rather, Fodor and Pylyshyn argue, further information beyond that in the light is necessary, and this must be information about the properties of Da Vinci's paintings represented in memory.

This sufficiency criterion therefore restricts the notion of direct perception to situations where structured patterns of light with particular invariant properties can be shown to be sufficient to explain perception and behaviour (although, as we argued earlier, the processes involved in detecting them can be analysed at an algorithmic level). On this criterion, perception of other people, familiar objects and almost everything we perceive falls on the Da Vinci rather than the looming surface side of the boundary, and therefore requires additional kinds of representation of the perceived object.

Thus for most of human perception we must advocate that information in light is compared with stored knowledge of the world. There are some compelling demonstrations to testify to this, such as the "hollow face" illusion (Chapter 7, Fig. 7.11). There is sufficient information here to see the mask as hollow, but we stubbornly fail to do so. If we move our head from side to side the face appears to follow us, in blatant disregard for the actual motion perspective present. The hollow face is not an example of an illusion which involves static observers or monocular viewing, and is a difficult one for the ardent Gibsonian to dismiss as a laboratory trick. We must invoke a memory of some sort here to explain why we see what we are used to seeing despite useful information to the contrary.

However, we do feel that the ecological psychologists make some very pertinent criticisms of current conceptions of memory, and it is worth examining these here. First, the kinds of representational schemes used in research into object recognition, which we discussed in Chapter 8, are not easy to adapt to the recognition of dynamic configurations like moving human figures. Marr and Nishihara's axis-based representations are derived from the occluding contours in static images, and it may be that different representational schemes could be constructed which are based on information in a transforming optic array. Two rather different approaches to this problem were introduced briefly in Chapter 15, where we talked about Cutting's analysis of the centres of moment in moving displays, and Weir's action "schemas", in which temporal relations such as "approach" and "withdrawal" were specified. These kinds of ideas seem worth pursuing.

Secondly, and more generally, ecological psychologists (e.g. Bransford, McCarrell, Franks & Nitsch, 1977) object to the notion of memory as a set of associated locations which must be searched through. This particular metaphor for memory is ingrained in our everyday language (we talk of trying to "find" a name that we've forgotten) and entrenched in many contemporary models of memory (Roediger, 1980). Ecological psychologists object that such conceptions of memory often imply that we must search exhaustively through our memories to discover that something is novel, and make it difficult to articulate the nature of the novelty once this is discovered.

They point instead to the subtle interactions between the context in which something is perceived and the meaning attributed to it. To take one of Bransford et al's examples, consider an outstretched hand. This could mean "come with me", "I have five children", "read my palm" etc, and Bransford et al. consider it absurd that every possible meaning for this configuration should be stored as a different potential association, yet this is precisely how many models of memory are described. We feel that these are important points, and that it is well worth seeking alternative formulations for memory. However, while the criticisms made by direct theorists are valid, they have yet to present any adequate alternative.

Perhaps, though, the connectionist movement that we discussed in Chapter 9 may provide a computational metaphor more acceptable to the Gibsonian ecological theorist, by avoiding the necessity for *symbol processing* and *symbolic* representations, even for longer term "concepts" and "memories". At first glance, the connectionists (e.g. McClelland, Rumelhart & Hinton, 1986) seem to make a number of points that echo those of the Gibsonians. *Symbolic* representations of the world are replaced by *patterns of activity*, in networks whose operation is (roughly) like the activity of neurons. Memories are *content addressable*— a fragment of a known pattern as input will lead to the restoration of the whole pattern of activity, without any process of *search*. Contextual sensitivity is built into connectionist models since the co-activation of two or more units will tend to recur again in the future. Memory is not a set of explicit traces stored at identifiable addresses, but, particularly in distributed memory models, is more a set of potentialities of the entire network. Given one cue, one "memory" will be retrieved, given some other cue, a quite different memory will be retrieved from the same set of connections between the same set of units. To the extent that parallel distributed processing models provide alternative explanations of the same psychological phenomena, perhaps here is a computational metaphor for the Gibsonian notions of "resonance" and "attunement"?

Connectionist models are certainly geared to action, but Fodor and Pylyshyn (1988) have recently argued that they suffer from the same short-comings as other purely *associative* (S-R) accounts of cognitive phenomena. Because of this, Fodor and Pylyshyn (1988) suggest that connectionist models *cannot* provide an alternative to traditional symbol-processing models since they cannot embody syntactic constraints to which cognition is sensitive. Many of the arguments that they level against the connectionist revival are similar to the arguments levelled by Chomsky (1959) against the behaviourist account of language acquisition and we will not repeat these arguments here. Their conclusion, however, is that connectionism should only be an *implementation* level theory, not an algorithmic level theory. Connectionist models may show us how, for example, the brain maps from a viewer-centred to an object-centred coordinate system (cf. Chapter 9), but they do not do away with the *psychological* level of theory at which the brain must be seen as constructing and manipulating *symbolic* representations.

The distinction between algorithm and implementation is important, and there is much debate over which of these levels connectionist models are tackling (e.g. Broadbent, 1985; Rumelhart & McClelland, 1985). While connectionist theorists might disagree with Fodor and Pylyshyn (1988), they do generally agree that they are tackling cognitive processes at a different level from that of traditional theories. Rumelhart and McClelland (1985), for example, contrast traditional "macrostructural" level theories with the "microstructural" level addressed by parallel distributed processing models, while Smolensky (1987, 1988) suggests that connectionist models operate at the "subsymbolic" level, from which representations emerge that have properties approximately the same as those of symbolic representations at a higher level. Thus even for committed connectionists, in contrast to the Gibsonians, there is a level of theory at which it may be legitimate, and possibly more convenient, to consider the construction, manipulation and storage of explicit "symbolic" representations.

While connectionist models appear to provide a different metaphor for memory, it is important to note that many of the attractive properties of these models are neutral with respect to the connectionist/traditionalist contrast (cf. Fodor & Pylyshyn, 1988). For example, a compelling feature of PDP memory models is that they can abstract the prototype of a category *and* retain sensitivity to recent instances, yet traditional non-connectionist models can show similar properties (e.g. Hintzman, 1986). Traditional models can be instance-based or abstractive in their learning properties and so can connectionist models.

We have implicitly agreed with Fodor and Pylyshyn (1988) by assigning connectionist models to a subordinate role in Part II of this book, where we introduced them as a means of achieving particular levels of description discussed elsewhere in more traditional terms. This is not to imply that these models will play a subordinate role in the development of visual science—on the contrary some of the most exciting developments in theoretical and applied vision may be driven by this school. However, we agree with Fodor and Pylyshyn's argument that such models do not provide an *alternative* to traditional accounts at the *psychological* level of theory.

We have so far considered two senses of the term "representation"; a momentary pattern of activity in a neural network, and a relatively long term "memory" which allows us to know the meanings of things. There is also an intermediate kind of memory that we should discuss. In Chapter 6 we discussed representations such as Hochberg's "schematic maps" and Marr's 2½D sketch, which have been postulated to allow a representation of the immediate visual world to be established. We would agree with ecological theorists (e.g. Turvey, 1977b) that at least some such "short term" visual memories may be wrongly conceived, because they are built up from static "snapshots" of the world. If we place more emphasis on the recovery of structure from optic flow, some kinds of "store" may become unnecessary.

However, there is some interesting evidence to suggest that the visual guidance of human locomotion does not involve a direct meshing of optic flow and activity but a time-limited storage process of some kind. Thomson (1983) asked subjects to view a target, then close their eyes and walk or run to the target "blind". He found they could locate a target at a distance greater than 5 metres, provided it took them less than 8 seconds to get to it. If it took longer than that, either because it was too far, or because of a delay before they started, then they got lost. To explain results like this, it seems reasonable to propose that there is some "representation" or "memory" for the location of the target which can be used in the formulation and control of motor programs for journeys of short duration, but which cannot be maintained for longer ones. It may be this kind of representation which allows us to "see" that part of the visual world we are not currently looking at as we pursue our daily activities.

CONCLUDING COMMENTS

Our aim in this chapter has not been to review thoroughly the debate between Gibsonian and traditional theories, or to offer new insights, but rather to organise and sift the issues, and to offer our own resolution of them. The debate is a furious one, and the reader is referred to the papers by Ullman (1980), Fodor and Pylyshyn (1981), Turvey (1977b) and Turvey et al. (1981), and even to reviews of the first edition of this book (Pittenger & Mace, 1985; Sutherland, 1985) for further detail of it. In some respects current arguments about the status of connectionist models are concerned with the same, central debate about the necessity for a cognitive or psychological level of theory to stand between the "stimulus" and the "response" (see the collection edited by Pinker & Mehler, 1988). Some points of argument are, we feel, relatively easily settled, particularly by recognising the different levels at which perception can be explained and the relationships between them. We have argued that Gibson's early insights into the nature of the input for vision, and the ecological optics he formulated, have been of enormous value, and the insights into perception we have discussed in the third section of the book testify to their productivity.

On the other hand, we find that the Gibsonian approach is not helpful in dealing with the relationship between ecological optics and physiological levels of explanation. Gibson's concern to avoid mediation and inference led him to shy away from these problems, and we find their clearest treatment in discussions such as Ullman's (1980) and Marr's (1982). We must stress that Marr's work shares a good deal with Gibson's views. He places great emphasis on understanding the relationship between the structures in the world which a perceiver needs to detect and the ways in which they structure light, just as Gibson's ecological optics does. In Marr's approach, assumptions about the world are built into algorithms for perceiving it, and explicit forms of "inference" avoided wherever possible. In comparison, Marr's use of an image, rather than optic flow, as a starting point is no important barrier between them.

In addition, we find it difficult to accept that Gibson's formulation does away with any role for memory in understanding perception. We find it unconvincing to explain a person returning after ten years to their grandparents' home and seeing that a tree has been cut down as having detected directly an event specified by a transformation in the optic array. At this point, we concur with Fodor and Pylyshyn (1981) that the terms of Gibson's theory are being extended to the point of becoming empty. Even so, we believe that Gibsonian criticisms of traditional views will continue to be valuable in forcing a re-examination of the models of the role of memory in perception.

A further comment we have on the debate between direct and indirect theorists is that the examples in which their arguments carry most force are quite different. The Gibsonian concept of affordance, for example, is at its most powerful in the context of simple visually guided behaviour such as that of insects. Here it does indeed make sense to speak of the animal detecting the information available in light which is needed to organise its activities, and the notion of a conceptual representation of the environment seems redundant.

For more intelligent creatures, and for people, we can make the same kinds of argument about detection of distance, falling-off places and so on in the guidance of locomotion. It is in these contexts where Gibsonian arguments carry most conviction. Indeed, some "direct" theorists, such as Turvey et al. (1981), seem to claim that it is only these kinds of activities which fall within the scope of an "ecological" theory of perception, and with this we would have no argument. It is only if they wished to argue that these activities alone constitute perception that we would be unhappy.

Proponents of the representational view, however, challenge Gibsonian theory by invoking human abilities to perceive objects, events and meanings which are bound up in a rich cultural context. Fodor and Pylyshyn's (1981) discussion of the recognition of a genuine Da Vinci is an example. Here, two aspects of Gibsonian ideas become a good deal less convincing. First, the mere assertion that there are high-level invariants in the structure of light which allow the direct perception of such objects dilutes the concept of invariant away. Secondly, the argument of animal-environment mutuality, which was so useful when we considered the classes of information a fly might need to survive and reproduce, becomes vague and even trivial when we consider human beings perceiving and acting in a cultural rather than a physical environment.

We feel that a distinction made by Fodor and Pylyshyn (1981) between "seeing" and "seeing as" captures the difference between the two kinds of situation:

> What you see when you see a thing depends upon what the thing you see is. But what you see the thing as depends upon what you know about what you are seeing . . .

> Here is Smith at sea on a foggy evening, and as lost as ever he can be. Suddenly the skies clear, and Smith sees the Pole Star. What happens next? In particular, what are the consequences of what Smith perceives for what he comes to believe and do? Patently, that depends upon what he sees the Pole Star as. If, for example, he sees the Pole Star as the star that is at the Celestial North Pole (plus or minus a degree or two), then Smith will know, to that extent,

where he is; and we may confidently expect that he will utter "Saved!" and make for port. Whereas, if he sees the Pole Star but takes it to be a firefly, or takes it to be Alpha Centauri, or—knowing no astronomy at all—takes it to be just some star or other, then seeing the Pole Star may have no particular consequences for his behaviour or his further cognitive states. Smith will be just as lost after he sees it as he was before (Fodor & Pylyshyn, 1981, p. 189).

We believe that the ecological approach has little useful to say about *seeing as*, although it has given us useful insights into *seeing*. For animals, we can be fairly specific about the information needed from the environment to guide activity, because we can refer to their requirements for survival and reproduction. For people, we cannot do this, apart from simple requirements such as avoiding cliffs, walking upright and dodging or catching flying objects. Most human activity takes place within a culturally defined environment, and we see no alternative to the assumption that people see objects and events *as* what they are in terms of a culturally given conceptual representation of the world.

In these pages we have set down our own reasons for rejecting the strong claim that perception is *direct*, as ecological psychologists would have it. We have argued that perception involves computations and that it involves representations, and that it is a legitimate task of psychology to enquire into the nature of these computations and representations. Having said this, we would stress that the nature of the computations performed may seem different once one considers the transforming optic array as the input to visual processing, rather than the retinal image. Different kinds of computations require different sorts of representation, and many of the traditional ideas may need re-thinking in the light of the findings of ecological psychologists.

The importance of describing what animals and people *do* in their worlds and *how* they do it cannot be understated, and this is the greatest strength of the ecological level of analysis. This demands that we study real behaviour in real situations. We should never assume that by stripping down real world activities into tractable laboratory tasks that we will find out the right things. Consider an experiment by Ebbeson et al. (1977). They examined how drivers decided whether to cross an intersection depending on the speed and distance of an oncoming car. They did this in two ways; in the laboratory, using model cars, and in the field, with real cars, and real risks. In the laboratory it appeared that "drivers" were making a complex decision about when to cross, based on the estimation of the distance and velocity of the approaching car. These subjects made 9% errors. In the field, it seemed that drivers simply made use of temporal headway (time to contact) with the approaching car, which does not require the separate computation of distance and velocity. These drivers made no errors.

By studying drivers, long-jumpers or gannets carrying out visually guided activities in a natural setting, we can gain rich insights into the optic variables which are used to guide activity, and it is this kind of research that we have considered in Part III of this book. Once the important variables have been discovered, however, we still need to know *how* they are detected, and this is the role of the kind of research described in Part II, and in Chapter 13 of Part III. Although the theories inspiring the two kinds of research differ strongly on fundamental issues, we feel that there is considerable scope for using the insights of both to solve smaller, more defined problems in visual perception.

It is in understanding how simple animals such as flies perceive their surroundings that a combination of the two approaches has achieved most success, specifying the ecological problems vision must solve for the animal, devising appropriate algorithms and unravelling their implementation by nervous systems. In human beings, this enterprise is vastly more difficult, particularly because human perception operates in a cultural as well as a physical environment. The formulation and testing of algorithmic theories, and the investigation of their physiological bases, is therefore a difficult task, but nonetheless a fascinating one.

REFERENCES

Adelson, E.H., & Bergen, J.R. (1985). Spatiotemporal energy models for the perception of motion. *Journal of the Optical Society of America, A2*, 284-299.

Alderson, G.H.K., Sully, D.J., & Sully, H.G. (1974). An operational analysis of a one-handed catching task using high speed photography. *Journal of Motor Behaviour, 6*, 217-226.

Aleksander, I. (1983). Emergent intelligent properties of progressively structured pattern recognition nets. *Pattern Recognition Letters, 1*, 375-384.

Alley, T.R. (Ed.), (1988) *Social and applied aspects of perceiving faces*. Hillsdale, N.J.: Lawrence Erlbaum Associates Inc.

Allman, J., Miezin, F., & McGuinness, E. (1985). Stimulus specific responses from beyond the classical receptive field: Neurophysiological mechanisms for local-global comparisons in visual neurons. *Annual Review of Neuroscience, 8*, 407-430.

Andersen, R.A., Essick, G.K., & Siegel, R.M. (1985). Encoding of spatial location by posterior parietal neurons. *Science, 230*, 456-458.

Attneave, F. (1971). Multistability in perception. *Scientific American, 225*, 63-71.

Baker, C.L., & Braddick, O.J. (1982). Does segregation of differently moving areas depend on relative or absolute displacement? *Vision Research, 22*, 851-856.

Bahill, A.T., & LaRitz, T. (1984). Why can't batters keep their eyes on the ball? *American Scientist, 72*, 249-253.

Ball, W., & Tronick, E. (1971). Infant responses to impending collision: Optical and real. *Science, 171*, 818-820.

Ballard, D.H., Hinton, G.E., & Sejnowski, T.K. (1983). Parallel visual computation. *Nature, 306*, 21-26.

Barclay, C.D., Cutting, J.E., & Kozlowski, L.T. (1978). Temporal and spatial factors in gait perception that influence gender recognition. *Perception and Psychophysics, 23*, 145-152.

Barlow, H.B. (1972). Single units and sensation: A neuron doctrine for perceptual psychology? *Perception, 1*, 371-394.

Barlow, H.B., & Hill, R.M. (1963). Selective sensitivity to direction of motion in ganglion cells of the rabbit's retina. *Science, 139*, 412-414.

Barlow, H.B., & Levick, W.R. (1965). The mechanism of directionally selective units in rabbit's retina. *Journal of Physiology, 178*, 477-504.

Barlow, H.B., & Mollon, J.D. (1982). *The Senses*. Cambridge: Cambridge University Press.

Barnes, R.D. (1968). *Invertebrate zoology*. Second edition. Philadelphia: W.B. Saunders.

Bassili, J.N. (1976). Temporal and spatial contingencies in the perception of social events. *Journal of Personality and Social Psychology, 33*, 680–685.

Bassili, J.N. (1978). Facial motion in the perception of faces and of emotional expression. *Journal of Experimental Psychology: Human Perception and Performance, 4*, 373-379.

Bassili, J.N. (1979). Emotion recognition. The role of facial movement and the relative importance of upper and lower areas of the face. *Journal of Personality and Social Psychology, 37*, 2049-2058.

Bateson, P.P.G. (1966). The characteristics and context of imprinting. *Biological Review, 41*, 177-220.

Bateson, P.P.G. (1977). Testing an observer's ability to identify individual animals. *Animal Behaviour, 25*, 247-248.

Baylis, G.C., Rolls, E.T., & Leonard, C.M. (1985). Selectivity between faces in the responses of a population of neurons in the cortex in the superior temporal sulcus of the monkey. *Brain Research, 342*, 91-102.

Beasley, N.A. (1968). The extent of individual differences in the perception of causality. *Canadian Journal of Psychology, 22*, 399-407.

Beck, J. (1972). Similarity grouping and peripheral discriminability under uncertainty. *American Journal of Psychology, 85*, 1-20.

Beck, J., & Gibson, J.J. (1955). The relation of apparent shape to apparent slant in the perception of objects. *Journal of Experimental Psychology, 50*, 125-133.

Berkeley, G. (1709). An essay towards a new theory of vision. In *A New Theory of Vision and other writings*, Introduction by A.D. Lindsay. London: J.M. Dent and Sons Ltd. (1910).

Bernstein, N. (1967). *The coordination and regulation of movements*. Oxford: Pergamon Press.

Berry, D.S., & McArthur, L.Z. (1986). Perceiving character in faces: The impact of age-related craniofacial changes on social perception. *Psychological Bulletin, 100,* 3-18.

Bertenthal, B.I., Proffitt, D.R., & Cutting, J.F. (1984). Infant sensitivity to figural coherence in biomechanical motion. *Journal of Experimental Child Psychology, 37,* 213-230.

Biederman, I. (1987a). Recognition by components: A theory of human image understanding. *Psychological Review, 94,* 115-145.

Biederman, I. (1987b). Matching image edges to object memory. *Proceedings of the First International Conference on Computer Vision.* IEEE Computer Society, London.

Blakemore, C. (1970). The representation of three-dimensional visual space in the cat's striate cortex. *Journal of Physiology, 209,* 155-178.

Blakemore, C., & Campbell, F.W. (1969). On the existence of neurones in the human visual system selectively sensitive to the orientation and size of retinal images. *Journal of Physiology, 203,* 237-260.

Blasdel, G.G., & Salama, G. (1986). Voltage-sensitive dyes reveal a modular organization in monkey striate cortex. *Nature, 321,* 579-585.

Blondeau, J., & Heisenberg, M. (1982). The three-dimensional optomotor torque system of Drosophila melanogaster. *Journal of Comparative Physiology, 145,* 321-329.

Boden, M. (1987). *Artificial intelligence and natural man.* 2nd Edition. Hassocks: Harvester Press.

Boring, E.G. (1942). *Sensation and perception in the history of experimental psychology.* New York: Appleton-Century-Crofts.

Borst, A., & Bahde, S. (1988). Spatio-temporal integration of motion. *Naturwissenschaften, 75,* 265-267.

Bossema, I., & Burgler, R.R. (1980). Communication during monocular and binocular looking in European jays (Garrulus garrulus glandarius). *Behaviour, 74,* 274-283.

Bower, T.G.R. (1966). The visual world of infants. *Scientific American, 215,* December, 80-92.

Bower, T.G.R. (1971). The object in the world of the infant. *Scientific American, 225,* 30-38.

Bower, T.G.R., Broughton, J.M., & Moore, M.K. (1970). Infant responses to approaching objects. An indicator of response to distal variables. *Perception and Psychophysics, 9,* 193-196.

Boyle, D.G. (1960). A contribution to the study of phenomenal causation. *Quarterly Journal of Experimental Psychology, 12,* 171-179.

Braddick, O.J. (1973). The masking of apparent motion in random-dot patterns. *Vision Research, 13,* 355-369.

Braddick, O.J. (1980). Low-level and high-level processes in apparent motion. *Philosophical Transactions of the Royal Society of London, Series B, 209,* 137-151.

Braitenberg, V., & Ferretti, C.L. (1966). Landing reaction of Musca domestica induced by visual stimuli. *Naturwissenschaften, 53,* 155.

Bransford, J.D., McCarrell, N.S., Franks, J.J., & Nitsch, K.E. (1977). Toward unexplaining memory. In R. Shaw & J. Bransford (Eds.), *Perceiving, acting and knowing: Toward an ecological psychology.* Hillsdale, N.J.: Lawrence Erlbaum Associates Inc.

Brennan, S.E. (1985). The caricature generator. *Leonardo, 18,* 170-178.

Brindley, G.S., & Merton, P.A. (1960). The absence of position sense in the human eye. *Journal of Physiology, 153,* 127-130.

Broadbent, D.E. (1985). A question of levels: Comment on McClelland & Rumelhart. *Journal of Experimental Psychology: General, 114,* 189-192.

Bruce, C., Desimone, R., & Gross, C.G. (1981). Visual properties of neurons in a polysensory area in superior temporal sulcus of the macaque. *Journal of Neurophysiology, 46,* 369-384.

Bruce, V. (1982). Changing faces: Visual and non-visual coding processes in face recognition. *British Journal of Psychology, 73,* 105-116.

Bruce, V. (1983). Recognizing faces. *Philosophical Transactions of the Royal Society of London, Series B, 302,* 423-436.

Bruce, V. (1988). *Recognising Faces.* London: Lawrence Erlbaum Associates Ltd.

Bruce, V. (1989). The structure of faces. In A.W. Young & H.D. Ellis (Eds.), *Handbook of research on face processing*. Amsterdam: North Holland.

Bruce, V., & Burton, M. (1989). Computer recognition of faces. In A.W. Young & H.D. Ellis (Eds.), *Handbook of research on face processing*. Amsterdam: North Holland.

Bruce, V., Burton, M., Doyle, T., & Dench, N. (1989). Further experiments on the perception of growth in three dimensions. *Perception & psychophysics, 46,* 528–536.

Bruce, V., Burton, M., & Doyle, T. (in press). Faces as surfaces. To appear in V. Bruce & M. Burton (Eds.), *Processing images of faces*. Norwood, New Jersey: Ablex.

Bruce, V., & Morgan, M.J. (1975). Violations of symmetry and repetition in visual patterns. *Perception, 4,* 239-249.

Bruce, V., & Valentine, T. (1985). Identity priming in the recognition of familiar faces. *British Journal of Psychology, 76,* 373-383.

Bruce, V., & Valentine, T. (1988). When a nod's as good as a wink: The role of dynamic information in facial recognition. In M.M. Gruneberg, P.E. Morris, & R.N. Sykes (Eds)., *Practical aspects of memory: Current research and issues, Vol. I.* Chichester: Wiley.

Bruce, V., Valentine, T., & Baddeley, A. (1987). The basis of the 3/4 view advantage in face recognition. *Applied Cognitive Psychology, 1,* 109-120.

Bruce, V., & Young, A. (1986). Understanding face recognition. *British Journal of Psychology, 77,* 103-327.

Bruner, J.S., & Goodman, C.C. (1947). Value and need as organising factors in perception. *Journal of Abnormal and Social Psychology, 42,* 33-44.

Burger, J., & Gochfeld, M. (1981). Discrimination of the threat of direct versus tangential approach to the nest by incubating herring and great black-backed gulls. *Journal of Comparative and Physiological Psychology, 95,* 676-684.

Burt, P., & Julesz, B. (1980). Modifications of the classical notion of Panum's fusional area. *Perception, 9,* 671-682.

Bushnell, I.W.R. (1982). Discrimination of faces by young infants. *Journal of Experimental Child Psychology, 33,* 298-308.

Bushnell, I.W.R., Sai, F., & Mullin, J.T. (1989). Neonatal recognition of the mother's face. *British Journal of Developmental Psychology, 7,* 3-15.

Butterworth, G. (1983). Structure of the mind in human infancy. In L.P. Lipsett (Ed.), *Advances in infancy research. Vol. II.* Norwood, New Jersey: Ablex.

Butterworth, G., & Hicks, L. (1977). Visual proprioception and postural stability in infancy. A developmental study. *Perception, 6,* 255-262.

Buxton, B.F., & Buxton, H. (1983). Monocular depth perception from optical flow by space-time signal processing. *Proceedings of the Royal Society of London, Series B, 218,* 27-47.

Camhi, J.M. (1970). Yaw-correcting postural changes in locusts. *Journal of Experimental Biology, 52,* 519-531.

Campbell, F.W., & Robson, J.G. (1968). Application of Fourier analysis to the visibility of gratings. *Journal of Physiology, 197,* 551-566.

Carpenter, R.H.S. (1977). *Movements of the Eyes*. London: Pion Press.

Cartwright, B.A., & Collett, T.S. (1983). Landmark learning in bees: Experiments and models. *Journal of Comparative Physiology, 151,* 521-543.

Chomsky, N. (1959). Review of *Verbal Behaviour* by Skinner. *Language, 35,* 26-58.

Clarke, P.G.H., & Whitteridge, D. (1977). A comparison of stereoscopic mechanisms in cortical visual areas V1 and V2 of the cat. *Journal of Physiology, 272,* 92-93P.

Cleland, B.G., & Levick, W.R. (1974). Properties of rarely encountered types of ganglion cells in the cat's retina and an overall classification. *Journal of Physiology, 240,* 457-492.

Clocksin, W.F. (1980). Perception of surface slant and edge labels from optical flow: A computational approach. *Perception, 9,* 253-271.

Clowes, M.B. (1971). On seeing things. *Artificial Intelligence, 2,* 79-112.

Collett, T.S. (1977). Stereopsis in toads. *Nature, 267,* 349-351.

Collett, T.S. (1980). Some operating rules for the optomotor system of a hoverfly during voluntary flight. *Journal of Comparative Physiology, 138,* 271-282.

Cooper, G.F., & Robson, J.G. (1966). Directionally selective movement detectors in the retina of the grey squirrel. *Journal of Physiology, 186*, 116-117P.

Cornsweet, T.N. (1970). *Visual perception.* New York: Academic Press.

Cott, H.B. (1940). *Adaptive coloration in animals.* London: Methuen.

Croze, H. (1970). Searching image in carrion crows. *Zeitschrift für Tierpsychologie supplement 5,* cited in M. Edmunds, (1974). *Defence in Animals.* New York: Longman.

Cutting, J.E. (1978a). Generation of synthetic male and female walkers through manipulation of a biomechanical invariant. *Perception, 7,* 393-405.

Cutting, J.E. (1978b). Perceiving the geometry of age in a human face. *Perception and Psychophysics, 24,* 566-568.

Cutting, J.E. (1982). Blowing in the wind: Perceiving structure in trees and bushes. *Cognition, 12,* 25-44.

Cutting, J.E. (1986). *Perception with an eye for motion.* Cambridge, Mass.: M.I.T. Press.

Cutting, J.E., & Garvin, J.J. (1987). Fractal curves and complexity. *Perception and Psychophysics, 42,* 365-370.

Cutting, J.E., & Kozlowski, L.T. (1977). Recognizing friends by their walk: Gait perception without familiarity cues. *Bulletin of the Psychonomic Society, 9,* 353-356.

Cutting, J.E., & Millard, R.T. (1984). Three gradients and the perception of flat and curved surfaces. *Journal of Experimental Psychology: General, 113,* 198-216.

Cutting, J.E., & Proffitt, D.R. (1981). Gait perception as an example of how we may perceive events. In R.D. Walk, & H.L. Pick, Jr (Eds.), *Intersensory perception and sensory integration.* New York: Plenum.

Cutting, J.E., & Proffitt, D.R. (1982). The minimum principle and the perception of absolute and relative motions. *Cognitive Psychology, 14,* 211-246.

Cutting, J.E., Proffitt, D.R., & Kozlowski, L.T. (1978). A biomechanical invariant for gait perception. *Journal of Experimental Psychology: Human Perception and Performance, 4,* 357-372.

Dartnall, H.J.A., Bowmaker, J.K., & Mollon, J.D. (1983). Human visual pigments: Microspectrophotometric results from the eyes of seven persons. *Proceedings of the Royal Society of London B, 220,* 115-130.

Davies, G., Ellis, H., & Shepherd J. (1981). *Perceiving and remembering faces.* London: Academic Press.

Davies, M.N.O., & Green, P.R. (1988). Head-bobbing during walking, running and flying: Relative motion perception in the pigeon. *Journal of Experimental Biology, 138,* 71-91.

Davis, J.M. (1975). Socially induced flight reactions in pigeons. *Animal Behaviour, 23,* 597-601.

Daw, N.W. (1968). Colour-coded ganglion cells in the goldfish retina: Extension of their receptive fields by means of new stimuli. *Journal of Physiology, 197,* 567-592.

De Monasterio, F.M. (1978a). Properties of concentrically organized X and Y ganglion cells of macaque retina. *Journal of Neurophysiology, 41,* 1394-1417.

De Monasterio, F.M. (1978b). Properties of ganglion cells with atypical receptive-field organization in retina of macaques. *Journal of Neurophysiology, 41,* 1435-1449.

De Monasterio, F.M., & Schein, S.J. (1982). Spectral bandwidths of colour-opponent cells of geniculocortical pathway of macaque monkeys. *Journal of Neurophysiology, 47,* 214-224.

Dethier, V.G. (1955). The physiology and histology of the contact chemoreceptors of the blowfly. *Quarterly Review of Biology, 30,* 348-371.

De Valois, R.L., Abramov, I., & Jacobs, G.H. (1966). Analysis of response patterns of LGN cells. *Journal of the Optical Society of America, 56,* 966-977.

De Valois, R.L., Albrecht, D.G., & Thorell, L.G. (1982). Spatial frequency selectivity of cells in macaque visual cortex. *Vision Research, 22,* 545-559.

DeYoe, E., Knierem, J., Sagi, D., Julesz, B., & Van Essen, D. (1986). Single unit responses to static and dynamic texture patterns in macaque V2 and V1 cortex. *Investigative Ophthalmology and Visual Science, 27,* 18.

Diamond, R., & Carey, S. (1986). Why faces are and are not special: An effect of expertise. *Journal of Experimental Psychology: General, 115,* 107-117.

Dill, L.M. (1974). The escape response of the zebra danio *(Brachydanio rerio).* I. The stimulus for escape. *Animal Behaviour, 22,* 711-722.

Dodd, B., & Campbell, R. (1987, Eds.). *Hearing by eye: the psychology of lipreading*. Hillsdale, N.J.: Lawrence Erlbaum Associates Inc.

Douglas, R.H., Collett, T.S., & Wagner, H.-J. (1986). Accommodation in anuran Amphibia and its role in depth vision. *Journal of Comparative Physiology, 158*, 133-143.

Dowling, J.E. (1968). Synaptic organization of the frog retina: An electron microscopic analysis comparing the retinas of frogs and primates. *Proceedings of the Royal Society of London, Series B, 170*, 205-228.

Duncker, K. (1929). Über induzierte Bewegung (Ein Beitrag zur Theorie optische wahrgenommener Bewegung). *Psychologische Forschung, 12*, 180-259. Translated and abridged as "Induced Motion" in W.D. Ellis (Ed.). *A source book of Gestalt psychology*. London: Routledge and Kegan Paul (1955).

Dziurawiec, S., & Ellis, H.D. (1986). Neonates' attention to face-like stimuli: A replication of the study by Goren, Sarty and Wu (1975). Manuscript in preparation cited in Ellis, H.D., & Young, A.W. (1989). Are faces special? In A.W. Young & H.D. Ellis (Eds.), *Handbook of research on face processing*. Amsterdam: North Holland.

Ebbesen, E.B., Parker, S., & Konēcni, V.J. (1977). Laboratory and field analyses of decisions involving risk. *Journal of Experimental Psychology: Human Perception and Performance, 3*, 576-589.

Edwards, A.S. (1946). Body sway and vision. *Journal of Experimental Psychology, 36*, 526-535.

Egelhaaf, M. (1985). On the neuronal basis of figure-ground discrimination by relative motion in the visual system of the fly. III. Possible input circuitries and behavioural significance of the FD-cells. *Biological Cybernetics, 52*, 267-280.

Egelhaaf, M. (1987). Dynamic properties of two control systems underlying visually guided turning in houseflies. *Journal of Comparative Physiology, 161*, 777-783.

Eisner, T., Silberglied, R.E., Aneshansley, D., Carrel, J.E., & Howland, H.C. (1969). Ultraviolet videoviewing: The television camera as an insect eye. *Science, 146*, 1172-1174.

Ekman, P. (1978). Facial signs: Facts, fantasies and possibilities. In T. Sebeok (Ed.), *Sight, sound and sense*. Bloomington: Indiana University Press.

Ekman, P. (1979). About brows: Emotional and conversational signals. In M. von Cranach, K. Foppa, W. Lepenies and D. Ploog (Eds.), *Human ethology*. Cambridge: Cambridge University Press.

Ekman, P. (1982). *Emotion in the human face. Second edition*. Cambridge: Cambridge University Press.

Ekman, P., & Friesen, W.V. (1978). *Facial Action Coding System: A technique for the measurement of facial movement*. Palo Alto, California: Consulting Psychologists Press.

Ekman, P., & Friesen, W. (1982). Measuring facial movement with the Facial Action Coding System. In P. Ekman (Ed.), *Emotion in the human face*. Second edition. Cambridge: Cambridge University Press.

Ekman, P., Friesen, W.V., & Ellsworth, P. (1982). Does the face provide accurate information? In P. Ekman (Ed.), *Emotion in the human face*. Second edition. Cambridge: Cambridge University Press.

Ekman, P., & Oster, H. (1982). Review of research, 1970-1980. In P. Ekman (Ed.), Emotion in the human face. Second edition. Cambridge: Cambridge University Press.

Ellard, C.G., Goodale, M.A., & Timney, B. (1984). Distance estimation in the Mongolian gerbil: The role of dynamic depth cues. *Behavioural Brain Research, 14*, 29-39.

Ellis, A.W., Young, A.W., Flude, B.M., & Hay, D.C. (1987). Repetition priming of face recognition. *Quarterly Journal of Experimental Psychology, 39A*, 193-210.

Ellis, H.D. (1975). Recognising faces. *British Journal of Psychology, 66*, 409-426.

Ellis, H.D., Shepherd, J.W., & Davies, G.M. (1979). Identification of familiar and unfamiliar faces from internal and external features: Some implications for theories of face recognition. *Perception, 8*, 431-439.

Enlow, D.H. (1982). *Handbook of facial growth*. 2nd edition. Philadelphia: W.B. Saunders.

Enroth-Cugell, C., & Robson, J.G. (1966). The contrast sensitivity of retinal ganglion cells of the cat. *Journal of Physiology, 187*, 517-552.

Ewert, J.P. (1974). The neural basis of visually guided behaviour. *Scientific American, 230*, 34-49.

Fagan, J. (1979). The origins of facial pattern recognition. In M.H. Bornstein & W. Keesen (Eds.), *Psychological development from infancy: Image to intention*. Hillsdale, N.J.: Lawrence Erlbaum Associates Inc.

Fantz, R.L. (1961). The origin of form perception. *Scientific American, 204*, 66-72.

Fechner, G.T. (1860). *Elemente der Psychophysik*. Leipzig, Germany: Brechtkopf and Härtel.

Feldman, J.A. (1985). Four frames suffice: A provisional model of vision and space. *The Behavioural and Brain Sciences, 8*, 265-289.

Fender, D.H., & Julesz, B. (1967). Extension of Panum's fusional area in binocularly stabilized vision. *Journal of the Optical Society of America, 57*, 819-30.

Fennema, C.L., & Thompson, W.B. (1979). Velocity determination in scenes containing several moving objects. *Computer Graphics and Image Processing, 9*, 301-315.

Ferster, D., & Lindström, S. (1983). An intracellular analysis of geniculo-cortical connectivity in area 17 of the cat. *Journal of Physiology, 342*, 181-215.

Field, T.M., Woodson, R., Greenberg, R., & Cohen, D. (1982). Discrimination and imitation of facial expressions by neonates. *Science, 281*, 179-181.

Fishman, M.C., & Michael, C.R. (1973). Integration of auditory information in the cat's visual cortex. *Vision Research, 13*, 1415-1419.

Fitch, H.L., Tuller, B., & Turvey, M.T. (1982). The Bernstein perspective III. Timing of coordinative structures with special reference to perception. In J.A.S. Kelso (Ed.), *Human motor behaviour: An introduction*. Hillsdale, N.J.: Lawrence Erlbaum Associates Inc.

Flin, R., & Dziurawiec, S. (1989). Developmental factors in face processing. In A.W. Young & H.D. Ellis (Eds.), *Handbook of research on face processing*. Amsterdam: North Holland.

Fodor, J.A. (1983). *The modularity of mind*. Cambridge, Mass.: M.I.T. Press.

Fodor, J.A., & Pylyshyn, Z.W. (1981). How direct is visual perception? Some reflections on Gibson's "ecological approach". *Cognition, 9*, 139-196.

Fodor, J.A., & Pylyshyn, Z.W. (1988). Connectionism and cognitive architecture: A critical analysis. *Cognition, 28*, 3-71.

Fox, R., Lehmkuhle, S.W., & Westendorff, D.H. (1976). Falcon visual acuity. *Science, 192*, 263-265.

Friedman, M.B. (1975). Visual control of head movements during avian locomotion. *Nature, 255*, 67-69.

Frisby, J.P. (1979). *Seeing: Mind, brain and Illusion*. Oxford: Oxford University Press.

Frisby, J.P., & Mayhew, J.E.W. (1980). Spatial frequency tuned channels: Implications for structure and function from psychophysical and computational studies of stereopsis. *Philosophical Transactions of the Royal Society of London, Series B, 290*, 95-116.

Frisch, H.L., & Julesz, B. (1966). Figure-ground perception and random geometry. *Perception and Psychophysics, 1*, 389-398.

Frost, B.J. (1978). The optokinetic basis of head-bobbing in the pigeon. *Journal of Experimental Biology, 74*, 187-195.

Frost, B.J., & Nakayama, K. (1983). Single visual neurons code opposing motion independent of direction. *Science, 220*, 744-745.

Frost, B.J., Scilley, P.L., & Wong, S.C.P. (1981). Moving background patterns reveal double opponency of directionally specific pigeon tectal neurons. *Experimental Brain Research, 43*, 173-185.

Fuster, J.M., & Jervey, J.P. (1982). Neuronal firing in the inferotemporal cortex of the monkey in a visual memory task. *Journal of Neuroscience, 2*, 361-375.

Galton, F. (1907). *Inquiries into human faculty and its development*. London: J. M. Dent and Sons Ltd.

Garnham, A. (1987). *Artificial intelligence: An introduction*. Routledge and Kegan Paul.

Gaze, R.M., & Jacobson, M. (1963). "Convexity detectors" in the frog's visual system. *Journal of Physiology, 169*, 1-3P.

Georgeson, M., & Shackleton, T. (1989). *What's the use of Fourier filters? A new theory of edge computation in vision*. Paper presented to the Experimental Psychology Society, Swansea, April 1989.

Gibson, E.J., & Walk, R.D. (1960). The "visual cliff". *Scientific American, 202*, 64-71.

Gibson, E.J., Gibson, J.J., Smith, O.W., & Flock, H.R. (1959). Motion parallax as a determinant of perceived depth. *Journal of Experimental Psychology, 58*, 40-51.

Gibson, J.J. (1947). *Motion picture testing and research*. AAF Aviation Psychology Research Report No. 7. Washington, D. C. Government Printing Office.

Gibson, J. J. (1950a). *The perception of the visual world*. Boston: Houghton Mifflin.

Gibson, J.J. (1950b). The perception of visual surfaces. *American Journal of Psychology*, *63*, 367-384.

Gibson, J.J. (1961). Ecological optics. *Vision Research*, *1*, 253-262.

Gibson, J.J. (1966). *The senses considered as perceptual systems*. Boston: Houghton Mifflin.

Gibson, J.J. (1968). What gives rise to the perception of motion? *Psychological Review*, *75*, 335-346.

Gibson, J.J. (1975). *The implications of experiments on the perception of space and motion*. Final Report to Office of Naval research, Arlington, Va.

Gibson, J.J. (1979). *The ecological approach to visual perception*. Boston: Houghton Mifflin.

Gibson, J.J., & Cornsweet, J. (1952). The perceived slant of visual surfaces—optical and geographical. *Journal of Experimental Psychology*, *44*, 11-15.

Gibson, J.J., & Dibble, F.N. (1952). Exploratory experiments on the stimulus conditions for the perception of a visual surface. *Journal of Experimental Psychology*, *43*, 414-419.

Gibson, J.J., & Waddell, D. (1952). Homogeneous retinal stimulation and visual perception. *American Journal of Psychology*, *65*, 263-270.

Gluhbegovic, N., & Williams, T.H. (1980). *The human brain: A photographic atlas*. Hagerstown, Md.: Harper & Row.

Golani, I. (1976). Homeostatic motor processes in mammalian interactions: A choreography of display. In P.P.G. Bateson & P.H. Klopfer (Eds.), *Perspectives in ethology, Vol. II*. New York: Plenum, pp. 69-134.

Goodman, L.J. (1965). The role of certain optomotor reactions in regulating stability in the rolling plane during flight in the desert locust *Schistocerca gregaria*. *Journal of Experimental Biology*, *42*, 385-407.

Goren, C.C., Sarty, M., & Wu, R.W.K. (1975). Visual following and pattern discrimination of face-like stimuli by newborn infants. *Pediatrics*, *56*, 544-549.

Götz, K.G. (1975). The optomotor equilibrium of the *Drosophila* navigation system. *Journal of Comparative Physiology*, *99*, 187-210.

Götz, K.G., Hengstenberg, B., & Biesinger, R. (1979). Optomotor control of wingbeat and body posture in *Drosophila Biological Cybernetics*, *35*, 101-112.

Graham, N., & Nachmias, J. (1971). Detection of grating patterns containing two spatial frequencies: A comparison of single-channel and multiple-channel models. *Vision Research*, *11*, 251-259.

Green, D.G. (1986). The search for the site of visual adaptation. *Vision Research*, *26*, 1417-1429.

Gregory, R.L. (1972). *Eye and brain*. Second edition. World University Library.

Gregory, R.L. (1973). The confounded eye. In R.L. Gregory & E.H. Gombrich (Eds.), *Illusion in nature and art*. London: Duckworth.

Gregory, R.L. (1980). Perceptions as hypotheses. *Philosophical Transactions of the Royal Society of London, Series B*, *290*, 181-197.

Griffin, D.R. (1958). *Listening in the dark*. New Haven, Connecticut: Yale University Press.

Gulick, W.L., & Lawson, R.B. (1976). *Human stereopsis: A psychophysical analysis*. New York: Oxford University Press.

Gurfinkel, V.S., Kots, Ya.M., Krinsky, V.I., Pal'tsev, Ye. I., Feldman, A.G., Tsetlin, M.L., & Shik, M.L. (1971). Concerning tuning before movement. In I.M. Gelfand, V.S. Gurfinkel, S.E. Fomin & M.L. Tsetlin (Eds.), *Models of the structural-functional organisation of certain biological systems*. Cambridge, Mass. M.I.T. Press.

Guzman, A. (1968). Decomposition of a visual scene into three-dimensional bodies. *AFIPS Proceedings of the Fall Joint Computer Conference*, *33*, 291-304.

Haig, N.D. (1986). Investigating face recognition with an image-processing computer. In H.D. Ellis, M.A. Jeeves, F. Newcombe, & A. Young (Eds.), Aspects of face processing. Dordrecht: Martinus Nijhoff.

Hailman, J.P. (1977). *Optical signals: Animal communication and light*. Bloomington: Indiana University Press.

Harkness, L. (1977). Chameleons use accommodation cues to judge distance. *Nature*, *267*, 346-349.

Harmon, L.D. (1973). The recognition of faces. *Scientific American*, *229*, 71-82.

Harris, J.P., & Gregory, R.L. (1973). Fusion and rivalry of illusory contours. *Perception*, *2*, 235-247.

Hartline, H.K., & Graham, C.H. (1932). Nerve impulses from single receptors in the eye. *Journal of Cellular and Comparative Physiology*, *1*, 227-295.

Hartline, H.K., Wagner, H.G., & Ratliff, F. (1956). Inhibition in the eye of Limulus. *Journal of General Physiology, 39*, 651-673.

Hausen, K. (1982). Motion sensitive interneurons in the optomotor system of the fly. II. The horizontal cells: Receptive field organization and response characteristics. *Biological Cybernetics, 46*, 67-79.

Hebb, D.O. (1949). *The organisation of behaviour*. New York: Wiley.

Heckenmuller, E.G. (1965). Stabilization of the retinal image: A review of method, effects and theory. *Psychological Bulletin, 63*, 157-169.

Heider, F., & Simmel, M. (1944). An experimental study of apparent behaviour. *American Journal of Psychology, 57*, 243-259.

Heiligenberg, W. (1973). Electrolocation of objects in the electric fish *Eigenmannia*. *Journal of Comparative Physiology, 87*, 137-164.

Helmholtz, H. von (1866). *Treatise on physiological optics, Vol. III* (trans. 1925 from the third German edition, Ed., J.P.C. Southall). New York: Dover (1962).

Hertz, M. (1928). Figural perception in the jay bird. *Zeitschrift für vergleichende Physiologie, 7*, 144-194. Translated & abridged in W.D. Ellis (1955). *A source book of Gestalt Psychology*. London: Routledge and Kegan Paul.

Hertz, M. (1929). Figural perception in bees. *Zeitschrift für vergleichende Physiologie, 8*, 693-748. Translated & abridged in W.D. Ellis (1955). *A source book of Gestalt Psychology*. London: Routledge and Kegan Paul.

Hildreth, E.C. (1984a). Computations underlying the measurement of visual motion. *Artificial Intelligence, 23*, 309-354.

Hildreth, E.C. (1984b). *The measurement of visual motion*. Cambridge, Mass.: M.I.T. Press.

Hildreth, E.C., & Koch, C. (1987). The analysis of visual motion: From computational theory to neuronal mechanisms. *Annual Review of Neuroscience, 10*, 477-533.

Hinton, G.E. (1981). A parallel computation that assigns canonical object-based frames of reference. *Proceedings of the International Joint Conference on Artificial Intelligence*. Vancouver, Canada.

Hinton, G.E. (1984). Parallel computations for controlling an arm. *Journal of Motor Behaviour, 16*, 171-194.

Hinton, G.E. (1986). Learning distributed representations of concepts. In *Proceedings of the Eighth Annual Conference of the Cognitive Science Society*. Amherst, Mass.

Hinton, G.E. (1989). Connectionist learning procedures. *Artificial Intelligence, 40*, 185-234.

Hinton, G.E., & Anderson, J.A. (1981, Eds). *Parallel models of associative memory*. Hillsdale, N.J.: Lawrence Erlbaum Associates Inc.

Hinton, G.E., & Sejnowski, T.J. (1986). Learning and relearning in Boltzmann machines. In D.E. Rumelhart, J.L. McClelland and the PDP Research Group (Eds.), *Parallel distributed processing: Explorations in the microstructure of cognition, Vol. I: Foundations*. Cambridge, Mass.: MIT Press.

Hintzman, D.L. (1986). "Schema abstraction" in a multiple-trace memory model. *Psychological Review, 93*, 411-428.

Hochberg, J. (1950). Figure-ground reversal as a function of visual satiation. *Journal of Experimental Psychology, 40*, 682-686.

Hochberg, J. (1968). In the mind's eye. In R.N. Haber (Ed.), *Contemporary theory and research in visual perception*. London: Holt, Rinehart and Winston Inc.

Hochberg, J. (1978). *Perception*. Second edition. Englewood Cliffs, New Jersey: Prentice Hall.

Hochberg, J., & Brooks, V. (1960). The psychophysics of form: Reversible perspective drawings of spatial objects. *American Journal of Psychology, 73*, 337-354.

Hochstein, S., & Shapley, R.M. (1976). Linear and nonlinear spatial subunits in Y cat retinal ganglion cells. *Journal of Physiology, 262*, 265-284.

Hoffman, D.D., & Richards, W.A. (1984). Parts of recognition. *Cognition, 18*, 65-96.

Horn, B.K.P., & Schunck, B.G. (1981). Determining optical flow. *Artificial Intelligence, 17*, 185-203.

Horn, G., & Hill, R.M. (1969). Modification of receptive fields of cells in the visual cortex occurring spontaneously and associated with bodily tilt. *Nature, 221*, 186-188.

Howarth, C.I., Routledge, D.A., & Repetto-Wright, R. (1974). An analysis of road accidents involving child pedestrians. *Ergonomics, 17*, 319-330.

Hubbard, A.W., & Seng, C.N. (1954). Visual movements of batters. *Research Quarterly, 25,* 42-57.

Hubel, D.H., & Wiesel, T.N. (1959). Receptive fields of single neurons in the cat's striate cortex. *Journal of Physiology, 148,* 574-591.

Hubel, D.H., & Wiesel, T.N. (1962). Receptive fields, binocular interaction and functional architecture in the cat's visual cortex. *Journal of Physiology, 160,* 106-154.

Hubel, D.H., & Wiesel, T.N. (1968). Receptive fields and functional architecture of monkey striate cortex. *Journal of Physiology, 195,* 215-243.

Hubel, D.H., & Wiesel, T.N. (1970). Stereopsis vision in the macaque monkey. *Nature, 225,* 41-42.

Hubel, D.H., & Wiesel, T.N. (1977). Functional architecture of macaque monkey visual cortex. *Proceedings of the Royal Society of London, series B, 198,* 1-59.

Hubel, D.H., Wiesel, T.N., & Stryker, M.P. (1977). Orientation columns in macaque monkey visual cortex demonstrated by the 2-deoxyglucose autoradiographic technique. *Nature, 269,* 328-330.

Hubel, D.H., Wiesel, T.N., & Stryker, M.P. (1978). Anatomical demonstration of orientation columns in macaque monkey. *Journal of Comparative Neurology, 177,* 361-380.

Huffman, D.A. (1971). Impossible objects as nonsense sentences. In B. Meltzer & D. Michie (Eds.), *Machine intelligence 6.* Edinburgh: Edinburgh University Press.

Hummel, J.E., Biederman, I., Gerhardstein, P.C., & Hilton, H.J. (1988). From image edges to geons: A connectionist approach. In D. Touretsky, G. Hinton & T. Sejnowski (Eds.), *Proceedings of the 1988 Connectionist Models Summer School.* San Matreo: Morgan Kaufman.

Humphrey, N.K., & Keeble, G.R. (1974). The reactions of monkeys to "fearsome" pictures. *Nature, 251,* 500-502.

Humphreys, G.W. (1984). Shape constancy: The effects of changing shape orientation and the effects of changing focal features. *Perception and Psychophysics, 35,* 361-371.

Humphreys, G.W., & Bruce, V. (1989). *Visual cognition: Computational, experimental and neuropsychological perspectives.* London: Lawrence Erlbaum Associates Ltd.

Ittelson, W.H. (1952). *The Ames demonstrations in perception.* Princeton, New Jersey: Princeton University Press.

Jackson, J.F., Ingram, W., & Campbell, H.W. (1976). The dorsal pigmentation pattern of snakes as an antipredator strategy: A multivariate approach. *American Naturalist, 110,* 1029-1053.

Jacobs, G.H. (1986). Cones and opponency. *Vision Research, 26,* 1533-1541.

Johansson, G. (1973). Visual perception of biological motion and a model for its analysis. *Perception and Psychophysics, 14,* 201-211.

Johansson, G. (1975). Visual motion perception. *Scientific American, 232,* 76-89.

Johnson, M.H., Bolhuis, J.J., & Horn, G. (1985). Interaction between acquired preferences and developing predispositions during imprinting. *Animal Behaviour, 33,* 1000-1006.

Johnson, M.H., & Horn, G. (1988). Development of filial preferences in dark-reared chicks. *Animal Behaviour, 36,* 675-683.

Julesz, B. (1965). Texture and visual perception. *Scientific American, 212,* 38-48.

Julesz, B. (1971). *Foundations of cyclopean perception.* Chicago: University of Chicago Press.

Julesz, B. (1975). Experiments in the visual perception of texture. *Scientific American, 232,* 34-43.

Julesz, B. (1981). Textons, the elements of texture perception, and their interactions. *Nature, 290,* 91-97.

Julesz, B., Frisch, H.L., Gilbert, E.N., & Shepp, L.A. (1973). Inability of humans to discriminate between visual textures that agree in second-order statistics—revisited. *Perception, 2,* 391-405.

Julesz, B., & Miller, J. (1975). Independent spatial-frequency-tuned channels in binocular fusion and rivalry. *Perception, 4,* 125-143.

Kalmus, H. (1949). Optomotor responses in *Drosophila* and *Musca. Physiologia Comparata et Oecologia, 1,* 127-147.

Kanade, T. (1981). Recovery of the three-dimensional shape of an object from a single view. *Artificial Intelligence, 17,* 409-460.

Kaufman, L. (1974). *Sight and mind: An introduction to visual perception.* New York: Oxford University Press.

Kelso, J.A.S., Putnam, C.A., & Goodman, D. (1983). On the space-time structure of human inter-limb coordination. *Quarterly Journal of Experimental Psychology, 35A,* 347-375.

Kettlewell, B. (1973). *The evolution of melanism.* Oxford: Oxford University Press.

Kilpatrick, F.P. (1952, Ed.), *Human behaviour from the transactionalist point of view.* Princeton, New Jersey: Princeton University Press.

Kirschfeld, K. (1976). The resolution of lens and compound eyes. In F. Zettler & R. Weiler (Eds.), *Neural principles in vision.* Berlin: Springer.

Kirschfeld, K. (1982). Carotenoid pigments: Their possible role in protecting against photo-oxidation in eyes and photoreceptor cells. *Proceedings of the Royal Society of London, Series B, 216,* 71 -85.

Koenderink, J.J. (1986). Optic flow. *Vision Research, 26,* 161-180.

Koffka, K. (1935). *Principles of Gestalt psychology.* New York: Harcourt Brace.

Köhler, W. (1947). *Gestalt psychology: An introduction to new concepts in modern psychology.* New York: Liveright Publishing Corporation.

Kohonen, T., Oja, E., & Lehtiö, P. (1981). Storage and processing of information in distributed associative memory systems. In G.E. Hinton & J.A. Anderson (Eds.), *Parallel models of associative memory.* Hillsdale, N.J.: Lawrence Erlbaum Associates Inc.

Kolers, P.A. (1963). Some differences between real and apparent visual movement. *Vision Research, 3,* 191-206.

Kovach, J.K. (1971). Interaction of innate and acquired: Colour preferences and early exposure learning in chicks. *Journal of Comparative and Physiological Psychology, 75,* 386-398.

Kozlowski, L.T., & Cutting, J.E. (1977). Recognizing the sex of a walker from a dynamic point-light display. *Perception and Psychophysics, 21,* 575-580.

Kozlowski, L.T., & Cutting, J.E. (1978). Recognizing the gender of walkers from point-lights mounted on ankles: Some second thoughts. *Perception and Psychophysics, 23,* 459.

Kuffler, S.W. (1953). Discharge patterns and functional organization of mammalian retina. *Journal of Neurophysiology, 16,* 37-68.

Land, E.H. (1977). The retinex theory of colour vision. *Scientific American, 237,* 108-128.

Land, M.F. (1968). Functional aspects of the optical and retinal organization of the mollusc eye. *Symposia of the Zoological Society of London, 23,* 75-96.

Land, M.F. (1981). Optics and vision in invertebrates. In H. Autrum (Ed.), *Comparative physiology and evolution of vision in invertebrates. B: Invertebrate visual centres and behaviour I.* Berlin: Springer-Verlag.

Land, M.F., & Collett, T.S. (1974). Chasing behaviour of houseflies (*Fannia canicularis*). A description and analysis. *Journal of Comparative Physiology, 89,* 331-357.

Lee, D.N. (1976). A theory of visual control of braking based on information about time-to-collision. *Perception, 5,* 437-459.

Lee, D.N. (1977). The functions of vision. In H.L. Pick & E. Saltzman (Eds.), *Modes of perceiving and processing information.* Hillsdale, N.J.: Lawrence Erlbaum Associates Inc.

Lee, D.N. (1980a). Visuo-motor coordination in space-time. In G.E. Stelmach & J. Requin (Eds.), *Tutorials in motor behaviour.* North-Holland Publishing Company.

Lee, D.N. (1980b). The optic flow field: The foundation of vision. *Philosophical Transactions of the Royal Society of London, Series B, 290,* 169-179.

Lee, D.N., & Aronson, E. (1974). Visual proprioceptive control of standing in infants. *Perception and Psychophysics, 15,* 529-532.

Lee, D.N., Daniel, B.M., & Kerr, D.J. (1988). Looking: The development of a fundamental skill. In *The Wenner-Gren Center International Symposium Series, Report of International Wallenberg Symposium 1988 on the Neurobiology of Early Infant Behaviour.* Macmillan.

Lee, D.N., & Lishman, J.R. (1975). Visual proprioceptive control of stance. *Journal of Human Movement Studies, 1,* 87-95.

Lee, D.N., & Lishman, J.R. (1977). Visual control of locomotion. *Scandinavian Journal of Psychology, 18,* 224-230.

Lee, D.N., Lishman, J.R., & Thomson, J.A. (1982). Regulation of gait in long-jumping. *Journal of Experimental Psychology: Human Perception and Performance, 8,* 448-459.

Lee, D.N., & Reddish, P.E. (1981). Plummeting gannets: A paradigm of ecological optics. *Nature, 293,* 293-294.

Leé, D.N., & Young, D.S. (1986). Gearing action to the environment. *Experimental Brain Research, Series 15.* Berlin: Springer-Verlag.

Lee, D.N., Young, D.S., & McLaughlin, C.M. (1984). A roadside simulation of crossing behaviour. *Ergonomics, 27*, 1271-81.

Lee, D.N., Young, D.S., Reddish, P.E., Lough, S., & Clayton, T.M.H. (1983). Visual timing in hitting an accelerating ball. *Quarterly Journal of Experimental Psychology, 35A*, 333-346.

Lehrer, M., Srinivasan, M.V., Zhang, S.W., & Horridge, G.A. (1988). Motion cues provide the bee's visual world with a third dimension. *Nature, 332*, 356-357.

Lekhy, S.R., & Sejnowski, T.J. (1988). Network model of shape-from-shading: Neural function arises from both receptive and projective fields. *Nature, 333*, 452-454.

Leslie, A.M. (1984). Spatiotemporal continuity and the perception of causality in infants. *Perception, 13*, 287-305.

Leslie, A.M., & Keeble, S. (1987). Do six-month-old infants perceive causality? *Cognition, 25*, 265-288.

Lettvin, J.Y., Maturana, H.R., McCulloch, W.S., & Pitts, W.H. (1959). What the frog's eye tells the frog's brain. *Proceedings of the Institute of Radio Engineers, 47*, 1940-1951.

LeVay, S., Hubel, D.H., & Wiesel, T.N. (1975). The pattern of ocular dominance columns in macaque visual cortex revealed by a reduced silver stain. *Journal of Comparative Neurology, 159*, 559-576.

Levick, W.R. (1967). Receptive fields and trigger features of ganglion cells in the visual streak of the rabbit's retina. *Journal of Physiology, 188*, 285-307.

Lindsay, P.H., & Norman, D.A. (1972). *Human information processing*. New York: Academic Press.

Linsker, R. (1986a). From basic network principles to neural architecture: Emergence of spatial opponent cells. *Proceedings of the National Academy of Sciences U.S.A., 83*, 7508-7512.

Linsker, R. (1986b). From basic network principles to neural architecture: Emergence of orientation-selective cells. *Proceedings of the National Academy of Sciences U.S.A., 83*, 8390-8394.

Linsker, R. (1986c). From basic network principles to neural architecture: Emergence of orientation columns. *Proceedings of the National Academy of Sciences U.S.A., 83*, 8779-8783.

Lishman, J.R., & Lee, D.N. (1973). The autonomy of visual kinaesthesis. *Perception, 2*, 287-294.

Lock, A., & Collett, T. (1979). A toad's devious approach to its prey: A study of some complex uses of depth vision. *Journal of Comparative Physiology, 131*, 179-189.

Lock, A., & Collett, T. (1980). The three-dimensional world of a toad. *Proceedings of the Royal Society of London, Series B, 206*, 481-487.

Locke, J. (1690). *An essay concerning human understanding*. Edited from the fourth (1700) and fifth (1706) Editions by P.H. Nidditch. Oxford: Oxford University Press (1975).

Longuet-Higgins, H.C., & Prazdny, K. (1980). The interpretation of moving retinal images. *Proceedings of the Royal Society of London, Series B, 208*, 385-397.

McArthur, L.Z., & Baron, R.M. (1983). Toward an ecological theory of social perception. *Psychological Review, 90*, 215-238.

McClelland, J.L., & Rumelhart, D.E. (1985). Distributed memory and the representation of general and specific information. *Journal of Experimental Psychology: General: 114*, 159-188.

McClelland, J.L., & Rumelhart, D.E. (1986). *Parallel distributed processing: Explorations in the microstructure of cognition. Vol. II: Psychological and Biological Models*. Cambridge, Mass.: Bradford Books.

McClelland, J.L., Rumelhart, D.E., & Hinton, G.E. (1986). The appeal of parallel distributed processing. In D.E. Rumelhart & J.L. McClelland (Eds.), *Parallel Distributed Processing: Explorations in the Microstructure of Cognition. Volume 1: Foundations*. Cambridge, Mass.: MIT Press.

McCleod, R.W., & Ross, H.E. (1983). Optic-flow and cognitive factors in time-to-collision estimates. *Perception, 12*, 417-423.

McGurk, H., & MacDonald, J. (1976). Hearing lips and seeing voices. *Nature, 264*, 746-748.

McIlwain, J.T. (1964). Receptive fields of optic tract axons and lateral geniculate cells: Peripheral extent and barbiturate sensitivity. *Journal of Neurophysiology, 27*, 1154-1173.

McKenzie, B., & Over, R. (1983). Young infants fail to imitate facial and manual gestures. *Infant Behaviour and Development, 6*, 85-89.

McLean, J., & Palmer, L.A. (1989). Contribution of linear spatiotemporal receptive field structure to velocity selectivity of simple cells in area 17 of the cat. *Vision Research, 29*, 675-679.

Mach, E. (1914). *The analysis of sensations*. Republished, 1959, Dover Publications.

Mandelbrot, B.B. (1982). *The fractal geometry of nature*. San Francisco: W.H. Freeman.

Manning, A. (1978). *An introduction to animal behaviour*. Third edition. London: Edward Arnold.

Marchiafava, P.L. (1979). The responses of retinal ganglion cells to stationary and moving visual stimuli. *Vision Research, 19*, 1203-1211.

Mark, L., & Todd, J.T. (1983). The perception of growth in three dimensions. *Perception and Psychophysics, 33*, 193-196.

Marr, D. (1976). Early processing of visual information. *Philosophical Transactions of the Royal Society of London, Series B, 275*, 483-524.

Marr, D. (1977). Analysis of occluding contour. *Proceedings of the Royal Society of London, Series B, 197*, 441-475.

Marr, D. (1982). *Vision: A computational investigation into the human representation and processing of visual information*. San Francisco: W.H. Freeman and Co.

Marr, D., & Hildreth, E. (1980). Theory of edge detection. *Proceedings of the Royal Society of London, Series B, 207*, 187-216.

Marr, D., & Nishihara, H.K. (1978). Representation and recognition of the spatial organization of three-dimensional shapes. *Proceedings of the Royal Society of London, Series B, 200*, 269-294.

Marr, D., & Poggio, T. (1976). Cooperative computation of stereo disparity. *Science, 194*, 283-287.

Marr, D., & Poggio, T. (1979). A computational theory of human stereo vision. *Proceedings of the Royal Society of London, Series B, 204*, 301-328.

Marr, D., & Ullman, S. (1981). Directional selectivity and its use in early visual processing. *Proceedings of the Royal Society of London, Series B, 211*, 151-180.

Martin, G.R. (1985). Eye. In A.S. King & J. McClelland (Eds.), *Form and function in birds, Vol III*. London: Academic Press, pp. 311-374.

Mather, G. (1984). Luminance change generates apparent movement: Implications for models of directional specificity in the human visual system. *Vision Research, 24*, 1399-1405.

Mather, G. (1985). Apparent motion from luminance change: Further comments on candidate mechanisms. *Vision Research, 25*, 2005-2006.

Maturana, H.R., & Frenk, S. (1963). Directional movement and horizontal edge detectors in the pigeon retina. *Science, 142*, 977-979.

Maunsell, J.H.R., & Newsome, W.T. (1987). Visual processing in monkey extrastriate cortex. *Annual Review of Neuroscience, 10*, 363-401.

Mayhew, J.E.W., & Frisby, J.P. (1981). Psychophysical and computational studies towards a theory of human stereopsis. *Artificial Intelligence, 17*, 349-385.

Mech, L.D. (1970). *The wolf: The ecology and behaviour of an endangered species*. Garden City, New York: The Natural History Press.

Meltzoff, A.N., & Moore, M.K. (1977). Imitation of facial and manual gestures by human neonates. *Science, 198*, 75-78.

Menzel, E.W. (1978). Cognitive mapping in chimpanzees. In S.H. Hulse, F.Fowler & W.K. Honig (Eds.), *Cognitive processes in animal behaviour*. Hillsdale, N.J.: Lawrence Erlbaum Associates Inc.

Menzel, E.W., & Halperin, S. (1975). Purposive behaviour as a basis for objective communication between chimpanzees. *Science, 189*, 652-654.

Merikle, P. (1980). Selection from visual persistence by perceptual groups and category membership. *Journal of Experimental Psychology: General, 109*, 279-295.

Metzger, W. (1930). Optische Untersuchungen in Ganzfeld II. *Psychologische Forschung, 13*, 6-29.

Michael, C.R. (1968a). Receptive fields of single optic nerve fibres in a mammal with an all-cone retina. I. Contrast-sensitive units. *Journal of Neurophysiology, 31*, 249-256.

Michael, C.R. (1968b). Receptive fields of single optic nerve fibres in a mammal with an all-cone retina. II. Directionally sensitive units. *Journal of Neurophysiology, 31*, 257-267.

Michael, C.R. (1968c). Receptive fields of single optic nerve fibres with an all-cone retina. III. Opponent colour units. *Journal of Neurophysiology, 31*, 268-282.

Michaels, C.F. (1978). *The information for direct binocular stereopsis*. Unpublished manuscript (cited in Michaels & Carello, 1981).

Michaels, C.F., & Carello, C. (1981). *Direct perception*. Englewood Cliffs, New Jersey: Prentice Hall.

Michotte, A. (1963). *The perception of causality.* Translated by T. & E. Miles from (1946) Edition. London: Methuen.

Millott, N. (1968). The dermal light sense. *Symposia of the Zoological Society of London, 23,* 1-36.

Minsky, M. (1977). Frame-system theory. In P.N. Johnson-Laird & P.C. Wason (Eds.), *Thinking: Readings in cognitive science.* Cambridge: Cambridge University Press.

Minsky, M., & Papert, S. (1969). *Perceptrons.* Cambridge, Mass.: M.I.T. Press.

Mollon, J.D. (1982). Colour vision and colour blindness. In H.B. Barlow & J.D. Mollon (Eds.), *The senses.* Cambridge: Cambridge University Press, pp. 165-191.

Moran, G., Fentress, J.C., & Golani, I. (1981). A description of relational patterns of movement during "ritualized fighting" in wolves. *Animal Behaviour, 29,* 1146-1165.

Moran, J., & Desimone, R. (1985). Selective attention gates visual processing in the extrastriate cortex. *Science, 229,* 782-784.

Morris, R.G.M. (1989, Ed.). *Parallel distributed processing: Implications for psychology and neuroscience.* Oxford University Press (in press).

Morton, J (1969). The interaction of information in word recognition. *Psychological Review, 76,* 165-78.

Moulden, B., & Begg, H. (1986). Some tests of the Marr–Ullman model of movement detection. *Perception, 15,* 139-155.

Movshon, J.A., Adelson, E.H., Gizzi, M.S., & Newsome, W.T. (1985). The analysis of moving visual patterns. In C. Chagas, R. Gattass & C. Gross (Eds.), *Pattern recognition mechanisms.* Vatican City: Vatican Press, pp. 117-151.

Movshon, J.A., Thompson, I.D., & Tolhurst, D.J. (1978). Spatial and temporal contrast sensitivity of neurones in areas 17 and 18 of the cat's visual cortex. *Journal of Physiology, 283,* 101-120.

Nakayama, K., & Loomis, J.M. (1974). Optical velocity patterns, velocity-sensitive neurons and space perception: A hypothesis. *Perception, 3,* 63-80.

Neisser, U. (1967). *Cognitive psychology.* New York: Appleton-Century-Crofts.

Neisser, U. (1976). *Cognition and reality.* San Francisco: Freeman.

Nelson, B. (1978). *The Gannet.* Berkhamsted: T. & A.D. Poyser.

Neuhaus, W. (1930). Experimentelle Unterschung der Scheinbewegung. *Archiv für die Gesamte Psychologie, 75,* 315-458.

Nilsson, D.E. (1988). A new type of imaging optics in compound eyes. *Nature, 332,* 76-78.

Normann, R.A., & Werblin, F.S. (1974). Control of retinal sensitivity. I. Light and dark adaptation of vertebrate rods and cones. *Journal of General Physiology, 63,* 37-61.

Ogle, K.N. (1964). *Researches in binocular vision.* New York: Hafner.

Olson, R.K., & Attneave, F. (1970). What variables produce similarity grouping? *American Journal of Psychology, 83,* 1-21.

Owen, B.M., & Lee, D.N. (1986). Establishing a frame of reference for action. In M.G. Wade & H.T.A. Whiting (Eds.), *Motor Development in Children: Aspects of coordination and control.* Dordrecht: Martinus Nijhoff.

Packer, C. (1977). Reciprocal altruism in *Papio anubis. Nature, 265,* 441-443.

Palmer, S.E. (1975). Visual perception and world knowledge. In D.A. Norman, D.E. Rumelhart and the L.N.R. Research Group, *Explorations in Cognition.* San Francisco: Freeman.

Palmer, S.E., Rosch, E., & Chase, P. (1981). Canonical perspective and the perception of objects. In J. Long & A.D. Baddeley (Eds.), *Attention and performance IX.* Hillsdale, N.J.: Lawrence Erlbaum Associates Inc.

Pantle, A., & Picciano, L. (1976). A multistable movement display: Evidence for two separate motion systems in human vision. *Science, 193,* 500-502.

Pearson, D.E., Hanna, E., & Martinez, K. (1986). Computer-generated cartoons. Proceedings of the Rank Prize Funds Symposium on *Images and Understanding.* Royal Society, London, October 1986. To be published by Cambridge University Press.

Pearson, D.E., & Robinson, J.A. (1985). Visual communication at very low data rates. *Proceedings of the IEEE, 73,* 795-812.

Peichl, L., & Wässle, H. (1979). Size, scatter and coverage of ganglion cell receptive field centres in the cat retina. *Journal of Physiology, 291,* 117-141.

Pentland, A. (1986a). Local shading analysis. In A.P. Pentland (Ed.), *From pixels to predicates.* Norwood, New Jersey: Ablex.

Pentland, A. (1986b). Perceptual organisation and the representation of natural form. *Artificial Intelligence, 28,* 293-331.

Pentland, A. (1987). *The parts of perception* (Report No. CSLI-87-77). Menlo Park, California: Center for Study of Language and Information.

Perrett, D.I., Mistlin, A.J., Potter, D.D., Smith, P.A.J., Head, A.S., Chitty, A.J., Broennimann, R., Milner, A.D., & Jeeves, M.A. (1986). Functional organisation of visual neurones processing face identity. In H.D. Ellis, M.A. Jeeves, F. Newcombe & A. Young (Eds.), *Aspects of face processing.* Dordrecht: Martinus Nijhoff.

Perrett, D.I., Rolls, E.T., & Caan, W. (1982). Visual neurones responsive to faces in the monkey temporal cortex. *Experimental Brain Research, 47, 329-342.*

Pettigrew, J.D., & Dreher, B. (1987). Parallel processing of binocular disparity in the cat's retinogeniculocortical pathways. *Proceedings of the Royal Society of London Series B, 232,* 297-321.

Pheiffer, C.H., Eure, S.B., & Hamilton, C.B. (1956). Reversible figures and eye movements. *American Journal of Psychology, 69,* 452-455.

Phillips, W.A. (1974). On the distinction between sensory storage and short term visual memory. *Perception and Psychophysics, 16,* 283-290.

Pietrewicz, A.T., & Kamil, A.C. (1977). Visual detection of cryptic prey by blue jays. *Science, 195,* 580-582.

Pinker, S. (1984). Visual cognition: An introduction. *Cognition, 18,* 1-63.

Pinker, S., & Mehler, J. (Eds.). (1988). *Corrections and symbols.* Cambridge, Mass.: M.I.T. Press.

Pittenger, J.B., & Mace, W.M. (1985). Visual perception as a text. Scientific correspondence in *Nature, 317,* 22.

Pittenger, J.B., & Shaw, R.E. (1975). Ageing faces as viscal-elastic events: Implications for a theory of non-rigid shape perception. *Journal of Experimental Psychology: Human Perception and Performance, 1,* 374-382.

Poggio, T. (1983). Visual algorithms. In O.J. Braddick & A.C. Sleigh (Eds.), *Physical and biological processing of images.* Berlin: Springer, pp. 128-153.

Poggio, G., & Poggio, T. (1984). The analysis of stereopsis. *Annual Review of Neuroscience, 7,* 379-412.

Pollard, S.B., Mayhew, J.E.W., & Frisby, J.P. (1985). PMF: A stereo correspondence algorithm using a disparity gradient limit. *Perception, 14,* 449-470.

Potts, W.K. (1984). The chorus-line hypothesis of manoeuvre co-ordination in avian flocks. *Nature, 309,* 344-345.

Premack, D., & Woodruff, G. (1978). Does the chimpanzee have a theory of mind? *Behavioural and Brain Sciences, 4,* 515-526.

Pringle, J.W.S. (1974). Locomotion: Flight. In M. Rockstein (Ed.), *The Physiology of Insecta, Vol. III.* London: Academic Press, Second Edition, pp. 433-476.

Pritchard, R.M. (1961). Stabilized images on the retina. *Scientific American, 204,* 72-78.

Proffitt, D.R., & Cutting, J.E. (1979). Perceiving the centroid of configurations on a rolling wheel. *Perception and Psychophyics, 25,* 389-398.

Proffitt, D.R., Cutting, J.E., & Stier, D.M. (1979). Perception of wheel-generated motions. *Journal of Experimental Psychology, 5,* 289-302.

Pugh, E.N., & Cobbs, W.H. (1986). Visual transduction in vertebrate rods and cones: A tale of two transmitters, calcium and cyclic GMP. *Vision Research, 26,* 1613-1643.

Purple, R.L., & Dodge, F.A. (1965). Interaction of excitation and inhibition in the eccentric cell in the eye of *Limulus. Cold Spring Harbor Symposia on Quantitative Biology Volume 30.*

Pylyshyn, Z.W. (1981). The imagery debate: Analog media *versus* tacit knowledge. *Psychological Review, 88,* 16-45.

Quinlan, P. (1988). *Evidence for the use of perceptual reference frames in two-dimensional shape recognition.* Unpublished PhD thesis, University of London.

Ramachandran, V.S., (1988). Perception of shape from shading. *Nature, 331,* 163-166.

Ramachandran, V.S., & Cavanagh, P. (1985). Subjective contours capture stereopsis. *Nature, 317,* 527-531.

Ratliff, F., Hartline, H.K., & Lange, D. (1966). The dynamics of lateral inhibition in the compound eye of *Limulus.* In C.G. Bernhard (Ed.), *The functional organisation of the compound eye.* Oxford: Pergamon.

Rauschecker, J.P., von Grünau, M.W., & Poulin, C. (1987). Centrifugal organization of direction preferences in the cat's lateral suprasylvian visual cortex and its relation to flow field processing. *Journal of Neuroscience, 7,* 943-958.

Reed, E., & Jones, R. (1982)., (Eds.), *Reasons for realism. Selected essays of J.J. Gibson.* Hillsdale, N.J.: Lawrence Erlbaum Associates Inc.

Regan, D., & Beverley, K.I. (1978). Looming detectors in the human visual pathway. *Vision Research, 18,* 415-421.

Reichardt, W. (1969). Movement perception in insects. In W. Reichardt (Ed.), *Processing of optical data by organisms and by machines.* New York: Academic Press.

Reichardt, W., & Poggio, T. (1976). Visual control of orientation behaviour in the fly. Part I. A quantitative analysis. *Quarterly Review of Biophysics, 9,* 311-375.

Reichardt, W., & Poggio, T. (1979). Figure-ground discrimination by relative movement in the visual system of the fly. *Biological Cybernetics, 35,* 81-100.

Reichardt, W., Poggio, T., & Hausen, K. (1983). Figure-ground discrimination by relative movement in the visual system of the fly. Part II: Towards the neural circuitry. *Biological Cybernetics, 46,* 1-30.

Rhodes, G., Brennan, S., & Carey, S. (1987). Recognition and ratings of caricatures: Implications for mental representations of faces. *Cognitive Psychology, 19,* 473-497.

Richter, J., & Ullman, S. (1982). A model for the temporal organization of X-and Y-type receptive fields in the primate retina. *Biological Cybernetics, 43,* 127-145.

Ripoll, H., Bard, C., & Paillard, J. (1986). Stabilisation of head and eyes on target as a factor in successful basketball shooting. *Human Movement Science, 5,* 47-58.

Roberts, A.D., & Bruce, V. (1988). Feature salience in judgements of sex and familiarity of faces. *Perception, 17,* 475-481.

Roberts, L.G. (1965). Machine perception of three-dimensional solids. In J.T. Tippett, D.A. Berkowitz, L.C. Clapp, C.J. Koester & A. Vanderburgh (Eds.), *Optical and electro-optical information processing.* Cambridge, Mass.: M.I.T Press.

Robson, J.G. (1983). Frequency domain visual processing. In O.J. Braddick & A.C. Sleigh (Eds.), *Physical and biological processing of images.* Berlin: Springer, pp. 73-87.

Roediger, H.L. (1980). Memory metaphors in cognitive psychology. *Memory and Cognition, 8,* 231-246.

Rogers, B., & Graham, M. (1979). Motion parallax as an independent cue for depth perception. *Perception, 8,* 125-134.

Rolls, E.T. (1987). Information representation, processing and storage in the brain: Analysis at the single neuron level. In J.-P. Changeux & M. Konishi (Eds.), *The neural and molecular bases of learning.* Wiley, pp. 503-540.

Rolls, E.T. (1990). The processing of face information in the primate temporal lobe. In V. Bruce & M. Burton (Eds.), *Processing images of faces.* Norwood, New Jersey: Ablex (in press).

Rosenfeld, S.A., & Van Hoesen, G.W. (1979). Face recognition in the rhesus monkey. *Neuropsychologia, 17,* 503-509.

Ross, J. (1976). The resources of binocular perception. *Scientific American, 234,* 80-86.

Rossel, S. (1983). Binocular stereopsis in an insect. *Nature, 302,* 821-822.

Roth, G., & Wiggers, W. (1983). Responses of the toad *Bufo bufo* to stationary prey stimuli. *Zeitschrift für Tierpsychologie, 61,* 225-234.

Rumelhart, D.E., Hinton, G.E., & Williams, R.J. (1986). Learning internal representations by error propogation. In D.E. Rumelhart & J.L. McClelland, J.L. (Eds.). *Parallel distributed processing: Explorations in the microstructure of cognition, 1. Foundations.* Cambridge, Mass.: M.I.T. Press.

Rumelhart, D.E., & McClelland, J.L. (1985). Levels indeed! A response to Broadbent. *Journal of*

Experimental Psychology: General, 114, 193-197.

Rumelhart, D.E., & McClelland, J.L. (1986). *Parallel distrubuted processing: Explorations in the microstructure of cognition, 1. Foundations.* Cambridge, Mass.: M.I.T. Press.

Rumelhart, D.E., & Zipser, D. (1986). Feature discovery by competitive learning. In D.E. Rumelhart & J.L. McClelland (Eds.), *Parallel distrubuted processing: Explorations in the microstructure of cognition, 1. Foundations.* Cambridge, Mass.: M.I.T. Press.

Runeson, S., & Frykolm, G. (1981). Visual perception of lifted weights. *Journal of Experimental Psychology: Human Perception and Performance, 7,* 733-740.

Runeson, S., & Frykolm, G. (1983). Kinematic specifications of dynamics as an informational basis for person-and-action perception: Expectation, gender-recognition and deceptive intention. *Journal of Experimental Psychology: General, 112,* 585-615.

Ryan, C.M.E. (1982). Concept formation and individual recognition in the domestic chicken (*Gallus gallus*). *Behaviour Analysis Letters, 2,* 213-220.

Sai, F., & Bushnell, I.W.R. (1988). The perception of faces in different poses by 1-month-olds. *British Journal of Developmental Psychology, 6,* 35-41.

Saye, A., & Frisby, J.P. (1975). The role of monocularly conspicuous features in facilitating stereopsis from random-dot stereograms. *Perception, 4,* 159-171.

Schaeffel, F., & Howland, H.C. (1987). Corneal accommodation in chick and pigeon. *Journal of Comparative Physiology, 160,* 375-384.

Schaller, G.B. (1972). *The Serengeti lion: A study of predator-prey relations.* Chicago: Chicago University Press.

Schiff, W., Caviness, J.A., & Gibson, J.J. (1962). Persistent fear responses in rhesus monkeys to the optical stimulus of "looming". *Science, 136,* 982-983.

Schiff, W., & Detwiler, M.L. (1979). Information used in judging impending collision. *Perception, 8,* 647-658.

Schiller, P.H. (1982). Central connections of the retinal ON and OFF pathways. *Nature, 297,* 580-583.

Schiller, P., Finlay, B.L., & Volman, S.F. (1976). Quantitative studies of single-cell properties in monkey striate cortex. I. Spatiotemporal organization of receptive fields. *Journal of Neurophysiology, 39,* 1288-1319.

Schmidt, R.A. (1969). Movement time as a determiner of timing accuracy. *Journal of Experimental Psychology, 79,* 43-47.

Seamon, J.G. (1982). Dynamic facial recognition: Examination of a natural phenomenon. *American Journal of Psychology, 95,* 363-381.

Sedgwick, H.A. (1973). *The visible horizon.* PhD thesis, Cornell University.

Selfridge, O.G. (1959). Pandemonium: A paradigm for learning. In *The mechanisation of thought processes.* London: H.M.S.O.

Sergent, J. (1984). An investigation into component and configural processes underlying face perception. *British Journal of Psychology, 75,* 221-242.

Shaw, R.E., & Bransford, J.(1977). Introduction: Psychological approaches to the problem of knowledge. In R.E. Shaw & J. Bransford (Eds.),*Perceiving, acting and knowing: Toward an ecological psychology.* Hillsdale, N.J.: Lawrence Erlbaum Associates Inc.

Shaw, R.E., McIntyre, M., & Mace, W. (1974). The role of symmetry in event perception. In R.B. MacCleod & H.L. Pick (Eds.), *Perception: Essays in honor of James J Gibson.* Ithaca New York: Cornell University Press.

Shaw, R.E., & Pittenger, J.B. (1977). Perceiving the face of change in changing faces: Implications for a theory of object recognition. In R.E. Shaw & J. Bransford (Eds.), *Perceiving, acting and knowing: Toward an ecological psychology.* Hillsdale, N.J.: Lawrence Erlbaum Associates Inc.

Shepherd, J., Davies, G., & Ellis, H. (1981). Studies of cue saliency. In G. Davies, H. Ellis & J. Shepherd (Eds.), *Perceiving and remembering faces.* London: Academic Press.

Sherrington, C.S. (1906). *Integrative action of the nervous system.* New Haven: Yale University Press (reset edition, 1947).

Shirai, Y. (1973). A context sensitive line finder for recognition of polyhedra. *Artificial Intelligence, 4,* 95-120.

Simpson, J.I. (1984). The accessory optic system. *Annual Review of Neuroscience, 7,* 13-41.

Simpson, M.J.A. (1968). The display of the Siamese fighting fish *Betta splendens. Animal Behaviour Monographs, 1,* 1-73.

Sivak, J.G. (1978). A survey of vertebrate strategies for vision in air and water. In Ali, M.A. (Ed.), *Sensory ecology: Review and perspectives.* New York: Plenum.

Smolensky, P. (1987). Connectionist AI, symbolic AI and the brain. *Artificial Intelligence Review, 1,* 95-110.

Smolensky, P. (1988). On the proper treatment of connectionism. *The Behavioural and Brain Sciences, 11,* 1-74.

Sperling, G. (1960). The information available in brief visual presentations. *Psychological Monographs, 74,* whole no. 498.

Sperling, G. (1970). Binocular vision: A physical and neural theory. *American Journal of Psychology, 83,* 461-534.

Spurr, R.T. (1969). Subjective aspects of braking. *Automobile Engineer, 59,* 58-61.

Stevens, J.K., Emerson, R.C., Gerstein, G.L., Kallos, T., Neufield, G.R., Nichols, C.W., & Rosenquist, A.C. (1976). Paralysis of the awake human: Visual perceptions. *Vision Research, 16,* 93-98.

Stone, J., & Fukuda, Y. (1974). Properties of cat retinal ganglion cells: A comparison of W cells with X and Y cells. *Journal of Neurophysiology, 37,* 722-748.

Stonham, J. (1986). Practical face recognition and verification with WISARD. In H.D. Ellis, M.A. Jeeves, F. Newcombe & A. Young (Eds.), *Aspects of face processing.* Dordrecht: Martinus Nijhoff.

Sumby, W.H., & Pollack, I. (1954). Visual contribution to speech intelligibility in noise. *Journal of the Acoustical Society of America, 26,* 212-215.

Sumner, F.B. (1934). Does "protective coloration" protect? Results of some experiments with fishes and birds. *Proceedings of the National Academy of Science, 10,* 559-564.

Sutherland, N.S. (1973). Object recognition. In E.C. Carterette and M.P. Friedman (Eds.), *Handbook of perception. Volume III: Biology of perceptual systems.* London: Academic Press.

Sutherland, N.S., & Williams, C. (1969). Discrimination of checkerboard patterns by rats. *Quarterly Journal of Experimental Psychology, 21,* 77-84.

Sutherland, S. (1985). Vision as a guide to action. Book review in *Nature, 315,* 258.

Ternus, J. (1926). Experimentelle Untersuchung über phänomenale Identität. *Psychologische Forschung, 7,* 81-136. Trans. as "The problem of phenomenal identity" in W.D. Ellis (1955). *A source book of Gestalt psychology.* London: Routledge and Kegan Paul.

Terzopoulos, D. (1986). Integrating visual information from multiple sources. In A. Pentland (Ed.), *From pixels to predicates.* Norwood, New Jersey: Ablex.

Thayer, G.H. (1918). *Concealing coloration in the animal kingdom.* New York: Macmillan.

Thomson, J.A. (1983). Is continuous visual monitoring necessary in visually guided locomotion? *Journal of Experimental Psychology: Human Perception and Performance, 9,* 427-443.

Thorell, L.G., de Valois, R.L., & Albrecht, D.G. (1984). Spatial mapping of monkey V1 cells with pure colour and luminance stimuli. *Vision Research, 24,* 751-769.

Tinbergen, N. (1951). *The study of instinct.* Oxford: Clarendon Press.

Todd, J.T., Mark, L.S., Shaw, R.E., & Pittenger, J.B. (1980). The perception of human growth. *Scientific American, 242,* 106-114.

Tomita, T. (1986). Retrospective review of retinal circuitry. *Vision Research, 26,* 1339-1350.

Torre, V., & Poggio, T. (1978). A synaptic mechanism possibly underlying directional selectivity to motion. *Proceedings of the Royal Society of London Series B, 202,* 409-416.

Treisman, A. (1988). Features and objects. The fourteenth Bartlett memorial lecture. *Quarterly Journal of Experimental Psychology, 40A,* 201-237.

Tuller, B., Turvey, M.T., & Fitch, H.L. (1982). The Bernstein perspective II. The concept of muscle linkage or coordinative structure. In J.A.S. Kelso (Ed.), *Human motor behaviour: An introduction.* Hillsdale, N.J.: Lawrence Erlbaum Associates Inc.

Turner, E.R.A. (1964). Social feeding in birds. *Behaviour, 24,* 1-46.

Turvey, M.T. (1977a). Preliminaries to a theory of action with reference to seeing. In R. Shaw & J. Bransford (Eds.), *Perceiving, acting and knowing: toward an ecological psychology.* Hillsdale, N.J.: Lawrence Erlbaum Associates Inc.

Turvey, M.T. (1977b). Contrasting orientations to the processing of visual information. *Psychological Review, 84,* 67-89.

Turvey, M.T., Fitch, H.L., & Tuller, B. (1982). The Bernstein perspective I. The problems of degrees of freedom and context-conditioned variability. In J.A.S. Kelso (Ed.), *Human motor behaviour: An introduction.* Hillsdale, N.J.: Lawrence Erlbaum Associates Inc.

Turvey, M.T., Shaw, R.E., & Mace, W. (1978). Issues in the theory of action: Degrees of freedom, coordinative structures and coalitions. In J. Requin (Ed.), *Attention and performance VII*. Hillsdale, N.J.: Lawrence Erlbaum Associates Inc.

Turvey, M.T., Shaw, R.E., Reed, E.S., & Mace, W.M. (1981). Ecological laws of perceiving and acting: In reply to Fodor & Pylyshyn (1981). *Cognition, 9*, 237-304.

Ullman, S. (1979). *The interpretation of visual motion*. Cambridge, Mass.: M.I.T. Press.

Ullman, S. (1980). Against direct perception. *Behavioural and brain sciences, 3*, 373-415.

Uttal, W.R. (1981). *Taxonomy of visual processes*. Hillsdale, N.J.: Lawrence Erlbaum Associates Inc.

Valentine, T. (1988). Upside-down faces: A review of the effect of inversion upon face recognition. *British Journal of Psychology, 79*, 471-492.

Van Essen, D.C. (1985). Functional organization of primate visual cortex. In A. Peters & E.G. Jones (Eds.), *Cerebral cortex. Vol. 3: Visual cortex*. New York: Plenum, pp. 259-329.

van Santen, J.P.H., & Sperling, G. (1984). Temporal covariance model of human motion perception. *Journal of the Optical Society of America A, 1*, 451-473.

van Santen, J.P.H., & Sperling, G. (1985). Elaborated Reichardt detectors. *Journal of the Optical Society of America, A2*, 300-321.

Victor, J.D., & Shapley, R.M. (1979). The nonlinear pathway of Y ganglion cells in the cat retina. *Journal of General Physiology, 74*, 671-689.

Vines, G. (1981). Wolves in dogs' clothing. *New Scientist*, 10th Sept., 1981.

Volkmann, F.C. (1976). Saccadic suppression: A brief review. In R.A. Monty & J.W. Senders (Eds.), *Eye movements and psychological processes*. Hillsdale, N.J.: Lawrence Erlbaum Associates Inc.

von der Heydt, R., Peterhans, E., & Baumgartner, G. (1984). Illusory contours and cortical neuron responses. *Science, 224*, 1260-1262.

von Hofsten, C. (1980). Predictive reaching for moving objects by human infants. *Journal of Experimental Child Psychology, 30*, 369-382.

von Hofsten, C. (1983). Catching skills in infancy. *Journal of Experimental Psychology: Human Perception and Performance, 9*, 75-85.

von Hofsten, C., & Lindhagen, K. (1979). Observations of the development of reaching for moving objects. *Journal of Experimental Child Psychology, 28*, 158-173.

Von Holst, E. (1954). Relation between the central nervous system and the peripheral organs. *British Journal of Animal Behaviour, 2*, 89-94.

Von Wright, J.M. (1968). Selection in visual immediate memory. *Quarterly Journal of Experimental Psychology, 20*, 62-68.

Von Wright, J.M. (1970). On selection in immediate visual memory. *Acta Psychologica, 33*, 280-292.

Wagner, H. (1982). Flow-field variables trigger landing in flies. *Nature, 297*, 147-148.

Wallace, G.K. (1959). Visual scanning in the desert locust *Schistocerca gregaria*. *Journal of Experimental Biology, 36*, 512-525.

Wallach, H. (1959). The perception of motion. *Scientific American, 201*, 56-60.

Wallach, H., & O'Connell, D. N (1953). The kinetic depth effect. *Journal of Experimental Psychology, 45*, 205-217.

Walls, G.L. (1942). *The vertebrate eye and its adaptive radiation*. New York: Hafner.

Waltz, D.L. (1975). Generating semantic descriptions from scenes with shadows. In P.H. Winston (Ed.), *The psychology of computer vision*. New York: McGraw-Hill.

Warren, C., & Morton, J. (1982). The effects of priming on picture recognition. *British Journal of Psychology, 73*, 117-129.

Warren, W.H. (1984). Perceiving affordances: Visual guidance of stair climbing. *Journal of Experimental Psychology: Human Perception and Performance, 10*, 683-703.

Warren, W.H., Young, D.S., & Lee, D.N. (1986). Visual control of step length during running over irregular terrain. *Journal of Experimental Psychology: Human Perception and Performance, 12*, 259-266.

Watson, A.B., & Ahumada, A.J. (1985). Model of human visual-motion sensing. *Journal of the Optical Society of America, A2*, 322-341.

Watson, J.B. (1913). Psychology as the behaviourist views it. *Psychological Review, 20*, 158-177.

Watson, J.B. (1924). *Psychology from the standpoint of a behaviourist*. Philadelphia: Lippincott.

Watt, R.J. (1988). *Visual processing: Computational, psychophysical and cognitive research.* London: Lawrence Erlbaum Associates Ltd.

Watt, R.J., & Morgan, M.J. (1983). The recognition and representation of edge blur: Evidence for spatial primitives in human vision. *Vision Research, 23,* 1457-1477.

Watt, R.J., & Morgan, M.J. (1984). Spatial filters and the localisation of luminance changes in human vision. *Vision Research, 24,* 1387-1397.

Watt, R.J., & Morgan, M.J (1985). A theory of the primitive spatial code in human vision. *Vision Research, 25,* 1661-1674.

Wehrhahn, C., & Reichardt, W. (1973). Visual orientation of the fly *Musca domestica* towards a horizontal slope. *Naturwissenschaften, 60,* 203-204.

Weir, S. (1978). The perception of motion: Michotte revisited. *Perception, 7,* 247-60.

Weiskrantz, L., Warrington, E.K., Sanders, M.D., & Marshall, J. (1974). Visual capacity in the hemianopic field following a restricted occipital ablation. *Brain, 97,* 709-728.

Werblin, F.S., & Dowling, J.E. (1969). Organization of the retina of the mudpuppy *Necturus maculosus.* II. Intracellular recording. *Journal of Neurophysiology, 32,* 339-355.

Wertheimer, M. (1912). Experimentelle Studien über das Sehen von Bewegung. *Zeitschrift für Psychologie, 61,* 161-265. Translated in T. Shipley (Ed.), *Classics in Psychology.* New York, Philosophical Library, 1961.

Wertheimer, M. (1923). Untersuchungen zur Lehre von der Gestalt, II. *Psychologische Forschung, 4,* 301-350. Translated as "Laws of organisation in perceptual forms" in W.D. Ellis (1955). *A source book of Gestalt Psychology.* London: Routledge and Kegan Paul.

Wheatstone, C. (1838). Contributions to the physiology of vision. Part I: On some remarkable and hitherto unobserved phenomena of binocular vision. *Philosophical Transactions of the Royal Society of London, 128,* 371-394.

Whiting, H.T.A., & Sharp, R.H. (1974). Visual occlusion factors in a discrete ball-catching task. *Journal of Motor Behaviour, 6,* 11-16.

Wigglesworth, V.B. (1964). *The life of insects.* London: Weidenfeld & Nicolson.

Wilson, H.R. (1983). Psychophysical evidence for spatial channels. In O.J. Braddick & A.C. Sleigh (Eds.), *Physical and biological processing of images.* Berlin: Springer, pp. 88-99.

Winston, P.H. (1973). Learning to identify toy block structures. In R.L. Solso (Ed.), *Contemporary issues in cognitive psychology: The Loyola symposium.* Washington, D.C.: Hemisphere Publishing.

Winston, P.H. (1975). Learning structural descriptions from examples. In P.H. Winston (Ed.), *The psychology of computer vision.* New York: McGraw-Hill.

Wittreich, W.J. (1959). Visual perception and personality. *Scientific American, 200,* 56-75.

Wood, D.C. (1976). Action spectrum and electrophysiological responses correlated with the photophobic response of *Stentor coeruleus. Photochemistry and Photobiology, 24,* 261-266.

Woodbury, P.B. (1986). The geometry of predator avoidance by the blue crab *Callinectes sapidus* Rathbun. *Animal Behaviour, 34,* 28-37.

Wundt, W. (1896). *Grundriss der Psychologie.* Translated by C.H. Judd (1907) as *Outlines of Psychology.* New York: G.E. Stechart and Co.

Wurtz, R.H., & Albano, J.E. (1980). Visual-motor function of the primate superior colliculus. *Annual Review of Neuroscience, 3,* 189-226.

Yin, R.K. (1969). Looking at upside-down faces. *Journal of Experimental Psychology, 81,* 141-145.

Young, A.W., Hellawell, D.J., & Hay, D.C. (1987). Configurational information in face perception. *Perception, 16,* 747-759.

Young, D.S., & Lee, D.S. (1987). Training children in road crossing skills using a roadside simulation. *Accident Analysis and Prevention, 19,* 327-341.

Yuille, A.L., & Grzywacz, N.M. (1988). A computational theory for the perception of coherent visual motion. *Nature, 333,* 71-74.

Zeki, S.M. (1978). Uniformity and diversity of structure and function in rhesus monkey prestriate visual cortex. *Journal of Physiology, 277,* 273-290.

Zeki, S. (1980). The representation of colours in the cerebral cortex. *Nature, 284,* 412-418.

Zeki, S. (1983). Colour coding in the cerebral cortex: The reaction of cells in monkey visual cortex to wavelength and colours. *Neuroscience, 9,* 741-765.

Zipser, D., & Andersen, R.A. (1988). A back-propagation programmed network that simulates response properties of a subset of posterior parietal neurons. *Nature, 331,* 679-684.

GLOSSARY

This glossary gives definitions of technical terms, particularly physiological and mathematical ones, not defined in the text, and also of terms used in sections of the book distant from those in which they are explained. Terms in italics are defined elsewhere in the glossary.

Absorption spectrum The relationship between the wavelength of light striking a *pigment* and how strongly the light is absorbed.

Accommodation Adjustment of the optics of an eye to keep an object in focus on the retina as its distance from the eye varies. In the human eye this is achieved by varying the thickness of the lens.

Action potential The interior of a nerve cell has a negative electrical charge relative to the exterior. If the *axon* of a nerve cell is stimulated electrically, the membrane allows current to cross it and the charge is momentarily reversed. This change in membrane behaviour spreads rapidly down the axon and the wave of change in voltage across the membrane which it causes is called an action potential.

Acuity See *visual acuity*.

Adaptation A change in the sensitivity to light of either a *photoreceptor* or of the visual system as a whole, so as to match the current average light intensity. Adaptation to bright light (e.g. when you wake up and switch on a light) occurs rapidly, while dark adaptation (e.g. when you walk from daylight into a dark cinema) is a slower process.

Affordance A term introduced by Gibson, which refers to a possibility for action afforded to a perceiver by an object. The affordances of an object depend upon the perceiver as well as upon the characteristics of the object. For example, a stream affords such actions as jumping and paddling to a person, but to a frog it affords swimming.

Aggregate field The area within which the *receptive fields* of cells in a single *hypercolumn* of the *visual cortex* fall.

Algorithm A specified procedure for solving a problem.

Amacrine cell A type of cell in the vertebrate retina (see Fig. 2.5).

Ambient optic array See *optic array*.

Area centralis Area in a vertebrate retina rich in *cones*, with little pooling of receptor outputs. In the human eye, the area centralis corresponds to the *fovea*, but this is not so in all species.

Axon The long, slender process of a nerve cell leading away from the cell body and ending at *synapses* with other cells.

Bipolar cell A type of cell in the vertebrate retina (see Fig. 2.5).

Bottom–up process See data–driven process.

Centre–off response A cell with a *concentric receptive field* that responds to a reduction of light intensity in the centre of its field relative to that in the surround is said to have a centre–off response.

Centre–on response A cell with a *concentric receptive field* which responds to an increase in light intensity in the centre of its field relative to that in the surround is said to have a centre–on response.

Closed–loop control A control system in which the output is continuously modified by feedback from the environment. An example is a person maintaining balance on a surfboard; their posture (the output) is continually adjusted in response to movement of the board (feedback).

Complex cell Cell in the *visual cortex* responding either to an edge, a bar or a slit stimulus of a particular orientation falling anywhere within its *receptive field*.

Computational theory A term introduced by Marr. Computational theories of vision are concerned with how, in principle, particular kinds of information such as the shapes of objects or distances of surfaces can be extracted from images. Solutions to such problems involve consideration of the constraints which apply to the structures of natural objects and surfaces and the ways in which they reflect light. An example is the demonstration that the shape of an object can be recovered from its silhouette if the shape approximates to a *generalised cone*.

Concentric field A *receptive field* divided into an inner circular region and an outer ring–shaped region. Light falling in each of the two regions has opposite effects on the response of the cell.

Conceptually driven process A process of extraction of information from sensory input which relies for its operation on prior knowledge of the properties of objects or events to be detected. For example, a conceptually driven process for recovering the structures of solid objects represented in an image would require prior information about the geometrical properties of objects (such as the nature of cubes and cylinders) which could be present.

Cone Vertebrate *photoreceptor* with short outer segment, which does not respond to light of low intensity.

Connectionist model Model of the operation of the nervous system or some part of it made up of a large number of units, each taking input from many of the others as well as from external sources. Inputs and outputs of units are numerical values—not symbols—and the operations performed by units on their inputs are relatively simple.

Contrast Difference between maximum and minimum intensities in a pattern of light.

Data driven process A process of extraction of information from sensory input which relies only on information available in the input. For example, a data driven process for recovering the structures of solid objects represented in an image would require no knowledge of the geometrical properties of particular kinds of object.

Dendrites The processes of nerve cells which carry *slow potentials* from *synapses* to the cell body.

Depolarisation A change in the *membrane potential* of a nerve cell such that the interior becomes less negatively charged relative to the exterior. If the membrane of an *axon* is depolarised, *action potentials* are generated with increased frequency.

Derivative The result of differentiating a function. A time derivative is obtained if a function relating some quantity to time is differentiated with respect to time. For example, the time derivative of a function relating the volume of water in a bath to time expresses how the rate of emptying or filling of the bath varies with time.

Diffraction The scattering of rays of light by collision with particles of matter as they pass through a medium such as air or water.

Direction preference An alternative term to *direction selectivity*.

Direction selectivity A difference in the response of a cell to a pattern of light moving through its *receptive field* according to the direction of movement.

Directional sensitivity A single *photoreceptor* is stimulated by light arriving through a segment of the *optic array*. In this book, we have used the term directional sensitivity to refer to the size of this segment. The smaller it is, the greater the directional sensitivity of the photoreceptor. In order to achieve a high degree of directional sensitivity, some means of forming an image is required. The term is used by some authors as a synonym of *directional selectivity*.

Eccentric cell Type of *photoreceptor* in the eye of the horseshoe crab (see Fig. 2.1).

Eccentricity Angular distance of a point on the retina from the centre of the *fovea*.

Edge segment In Marr's theory of early visual processing, a token in the *raw primal sketch* formed where *zero−crossing segments* from ∇^2G *filters* of adjacent sizes coincide.

Electrotonic spread The spread of a *slow potential* over the membrane of a *dendrite* or nerve cell body.

End−inhibition A property of some cells in the *visual cortex* which respond strongly to either an edge, a bar or a slit which ends within the *receptive field*.

Exproprioceptive information Information about the position of a perceiver's body, or parts of the body, relative to the environment. Lee (1977) introduced this term to give a three−fold classification of types of sensory information, along with the traditional classes of *exteroceptive* and *proprioceptive* information.

Exteroceptive information Information about surfaces, objects and events in a perceiver's environment.

Fibre See axon.

Extrastriate cortex Region of primate cerebral cortex anterior to *striate cortex* (see Fig. 3.14).

Filter, ∇^2G An *algorithm* which smooths an array of light intensity values in an image with a *Gaussian filter* and then applies a *Laplacian* operator to each region of the smoothed image. The wider the filter, the greater the degree of smoothing of the image by the Gaussian part of the filter.

Firing rate The frequency at which *action potentials* pass down the *axon* of a nerve cell.

Fixation In the case of an animal with mobile eyes, alignment of the eyes so that the image of the fixated target falls on the *area centralis*. Otherwise, alignment of the head to point towards the fixated target.

Fourier analysis Fourier's theorem proves that any one−dimensional pattern can be fully described as the sum of a number of sine–waves of different frequencies and amplitudes. The same is true of a two–dimensional pattern provided that horizontal and vertical components of each sinusoid are analysed. Fourier analysis is a procedure for breaking down a pattern into its sinusoidal components.

Fourier transform The description of a pattern in terms of the frequencies and amplitudes of its sinusoidal components which is obtained by applying *Fourier analysis*.

Fovea Pit–shaped depression in a vertebrate retina, usually in an *area centralis*.

Ganglion cell A type of cell in the vertebrate retina (see Fig. 2.5). The *axons* of ganglion cells are packed together in the *optic nerve* and carry information from retina to brain.

Gaussian filter Algorithm smoothing spatial or temporal variation in an image by averaging neighbouring values of light intensity, the contribution of values to the average being weighted according to a Gaussian (normal) function.

Generalised cone The surface created by moving a cross–section of constant shape but variable size along an axis (see Fig. 8.15).

Grating A pattern of parallel dark and bright bars of equal widths. In a sinusoidal (or sine–wave) grating, brightness varies sinusoidally across the pattern, so that the stripes are blurred (see Fig. 2.7).

Horizontal cell A type of cell in the vertebrate retina (see Fig. 2.5).

Hypercolumn A block of the *visual cortex* in which all cells have *receptive fields* falling in a single area of the retina.

Hypercomplex cell A *complex cell* with the property of *end–inhibition*.

Hyperpolarisation A change in the *membrane potential* of a nerve cell such that the interior becomes more negatively charged relative to the exterior. If the membrane of an *axon* is hyperpolarised, *action potentials* are generated with lower frequency.

IT (Inferotemporal area) Visual area in *extrastriate cortex* (see Fig. 3.14).

Impulse See *action potential*.

Interneuron Nerve cell in the central nervous system which is neither a *receptor* nor a *motor neuron*.

Intracellular recording Recording the *membrane potential* of a nerve cell by means of an electrode penetrating the membrane.

Invariant In Gibson's use of the term, some measure of the pattern of light reflected from an object, event or scene which remains constant as other measures of the pattern vary. An invariant therefore provides information for a perceiver about some aspect of their surroundings. For example, the size of elements of optic texture in the light reflected from a surface varies with the nature of the surface and with its distance from the perceiver, and therefore does not provide information to specify the slant of the surface relative to the perceiver. For a particular slant, however, the rate of change of the size of texture elements is invariant for different surfaces and different distances.

LGN (lateral geniculate nucleus) The part of the mammalian brain where the *axons* of retinal *ganglion cells* terminate, and from which axons run to the *visual cortex* (see Fig. 3.1).

Laplacian (∇^2) If a quantity such as light intensity varies along one dimension, then the second derivative of that quantity describes the rate at which its gradient is changing at any point. For example, a positive value of the second derivative would indicate that the gradient of light intensity is becoming more positive. Where light intensity varies along two dimensions (as it does in an image), the Laplacian is the sum of the second derivatives of intensity taken in two orthogonal directions (i.e. at right angles).

Linearity A device with a single input and output is said to operate in a linear fashion if the relationship between the value x of the input and and the value y of the output has the form $y = mx + c$ (and therefore can be represented graphically as a straight line). For a linear device with multiple inputs, the relationship between output and the values x_1, x_2, . . . of the inputs has the form $y = m_1 x_1 + m_2 x_2$ . . . + c. Examples of non–linearities are where the output is a function of a higher power of x, log x, or the absolute value of x.

Luminance Light intensity.

MT (Middle temporal area) Visual area in *extrastriate cortex* (see Fig. 3.14).

Membrane potential The difference in electrical potential between the interior and the exterior of a nerve cell. In the resting state, the interior is always negative relative to the exterior.

Motion parallax Movement of the image of an object over the retina. The rate of movement depends upon the velocity of the object relative to the eye, and its distance from the eye.

Motor neuron A nerve cell which *synapses* with a muscle cell. *Action potentials* passing down the *axon* of the motor neuron cause the muscle to contract.

Neuron Nerve cell.

Non—linearity See *linearity*.

Ocular preference Cells in the *visual cortex* which respond more strongly to a stimulus presented to one eye than to the other are said to show ocular preference.

Off—centre cell Cell with a *centre—off response*.

On—centre cell Cell with a *centre—on response*.

Ommatidium Unit of the compound eye containing a light—sensitive rhabdom (see Fig. 1.8).

Open—loop control Control system in which the output is not continuously modified by feedback from the environment. An example is a person swatting a fly; once the swing of the arm begins, it is completed whatever the fly does.

Operant conditioning A term introduced by Skinner. In an operant conditioning procedure, an animal's behaviour is changed by pairing a piece of behaviour (the operant) with reinforcement. For example, if a rat receives food each time it presses a bar, it will come to press the bar more frequently. Such methods can be used to determine whether an animal can discriminate two stimuli. For example, if a rat can learn to press a bar when it hears a tone of one pitch and not to press when it hears one of another pitch, then it must be able to discriminate the tones.

Opponent—colour response If light of one wavelength falling in its *receptive field* causes a cell to fire more frequently than its resting rate, and light of a different wavelength causes it to fire less frequently, the cell is said to have an opponent—colour response.

Opsins A group of *pigments* found in *photoreceptor cells*.

Optic array Term introduced by Gibson, to refer to the instantaneous pattern of light reaching a point in space from all directions. In different regions of the optic array, the spatial pattern of light will differ, according to the nature of the surface from which it has been reflected.

Optic flow field The fluctuating patterns of light intensity reaching an observer caused by any relative movement between observer and environment.

Optic nerve Nerve running from retina to brain.

Optic texture The spatial pattern of light reflected from a textured surface.

Optomotor response The turning response of an animal presented with uniform flow of *optic texture*, in the direction which minimises rate of flow relative to the animal.

Orientation preference Variation in the response of a cell in the *visual cortex* with the orientation of an edge, bar or slit. The preferred orientation is that giving the greatest response.

Peak spectral sensitivity The wavelength of light to which a *photoreceptor* responds most strongly.

Perpendicular component The component of the velocity of motion of an edge which is perpendicular to the edge.

Photon Unit of energy in electromagnetic radiation.

Photopic vision Vision in light sufficiently bright to excite *cones*.

Photoreceptor cell A *receptor cell* sensitive to light.

Pigment A chemical substance which absorbs light. Pigment molecules change in shape as they absorb light and, in a *photoreceptor*, this change begins a series of biochemical processes which lead to the *receptor potential*.

Pitch Rotation of a flying insect or bird in a "head—up" or "head—down" manner (see Fig. 11.1).

Plexiform layer Layer of nerve cell processes and *synapses* in the vertebrate retina (see Fig. 2.5).

Poles (of optic flow field) These are the two points in the *optic flow field* surrounding an observer moving through the environment at which there is no flow of *optic texture*. One is the point towards which the observer is moving (see Fig. 10.7) and the other is the point away from which the observer is moving.

Prestriate cortex See *extrastriate cortex*.

Projection Light rays are said to be projected to the image plane when an image is formed. The word also has a quite different meaning in neurophysiology, to refer to the region where the *axons* of a group of nerve cells in the brain terminate and make *synaptic* contact.

Proprioceptive information In Lee's use of the term, information about the positions of parts of the body relative to one another.

Psychophysics The analysis of perceptual processes by studying the effect on a subject's experience or behaviour of systematically varying the properties of a stimulus along one or more physical dimensions.

Raw primal sketch In Marr's theory of vision, a rich representation of the intensity changes present in the original image.

Receptive field The area of the retina in which light causes a response in a particular nerve cell.

Receptor cell A nerve cell sensitive to external energy.

Receptor potential The change in *membrane potential* of a *receptor cell* caused by external energy impinging on it.

Refraction The bending of rays of light as they cross a boundary between two transparent media of different optical densities.

Retinal ganglion cell See ganglion cell.

Retinotopic map An array of nerve cells which have the same positions relative to one another as their *receptive fields* have on the surface of the retina.

Retinula cell A *photoreceptor* in the eye of an insect or other arthropod (see Figs. 1.8 and 2.1).

Rod Vertebrate *photoreceptor* with long outer segment, sensitive to light of low intensity.

Roll Rotation of a flying insect or bird around the long axis of the body (see Fig. 11.1).

Saccade Rapid movement of the eye to fixate a target.

Scalar A quantity which has magnitude only.

Scotopic vision Vision in dim light, sufficiently bright to excite *rods* but not *cones*.

Sensitivity spectrum The relationship between the wavelength of light striking a *photoreceptor* and the size of the *receptor potential*.

Simple cell Cell in the visual cortex showing *linear spatial summation* of light intensities in parts of its *receptive field* separated by straight line boundaries.

Sinusoidal grating See *grating*.

Slow potential A small change in the *membrane potential* of a nerve cell, such as a *receptor potential*, which decays as it spreads passively over the membrane. In contrast, an *action potential* is propagated by an active change in membrane properties and does not decay in amplitude as it is transmitted.

Spatial frequency The frequency, expressed as cycles per unit of visual angle, of a sinusoidal pattern of light such as a *grating*. At a particular viewing distance, the spatial frequency of a grating depends upon the width of its bars; the narrower these are, the higher the frequency.

Spatial frequency tuning A nerve cell in a visual pathway which responds more strongly to sinusoidal *gratings* which have *spatial frequencies* in a particular range than to gratings of other frequencies is said to show spatial frequency tuning.

Spatial summation If the response of a cell to a pattern of light is a function of the difference in the amounts of light falling in different regions of its *receptive field*, then it is said to show linear spatial summation.

Stereopsis Perception of depth dependent upon disparity in the images projected on the retinas of the two eyes.

Stereoscopic fusion The process whereby the two disparate retinal images are combined to yield a single percept in depth.

Striate cortex See *visual cortex*.

Superior colliculus Structure in mammalian midbrain where some *W cell axons* terminate.

Synapse A point where the membranes of two nerve cells nearly touch and where electrical activity in one cell influences the *membrane potential* of the other cell.

3–D model representation An object–centred representation of shape, organized hierarchically (see Fig. 8.16).

Top–down process See *conceptually driven process*.

Topology A branch of geometry describing the properties of forms which are unaffected by continuous distortion such as stretching. For example, a doughnut and a record have the same topology.

Torque Turning force, equal to force applied multiplied by the distance of its point of application from the centre of rotation.

Transduction The process by which external energy impinging on a *receptor* cell causes a change in its *membrane potential*.

2½D sketch A viewer–centred representation of the depths and orientations of visible surfaces (see Fig. 7.23).

V1 Primary *visual cortex* of a primate.

V2, V3, V4 Visual areas in *extrastriate cortex* (see Fig. 3.14).

Vector A quantity which has both magnitude and direction.

Vergence movements Movements of the eyes making them either more or less convergent.

Velocity field A representation of the velocity of image motion at any instant in each of many small regions of a time–varying image (see Fig. 13.1).

Vestibular system The organ in the inner ear involved in the *transduction* of angular acceleration of the body into nerve impulses.

Visual acuity An observer's visual acuity is measured by the angle between adjacent bars in the highest frequency *grating* which they can distinguish from a plain field of the same average brightness as the grating.

Visual angle The angle which an object subtends at the eye (see Fig. 1.13).

Visual cortex, primary Region of the mammalian cortex in the occipital lobe receiving input from the LGN. Cells in the primary visual cortex respond to light falling on the retina and are arranged in a *retinotopic map*. In primates, this region is also known as the striate cortex or V1.

W cells The *ganglion cells* of the mammalian retina which do not have *concentric fields*.

X cells The *ganglion cells* of the mammalian retina with *concentric fields* which show *linear spatial summation* of light intensities in centre and surround areas of the *receptive field*.

Y cells The *ganglion cells* of the mammalian retina with *concentric fields* which show non–*linear* responses to changes in light intensity.

Yaw Rotation of a flying insect or bird around the vertical axis (see Fig. 11.1).

Zero–crossing A point where values of a function change sign (see Fig. 5.6).

Zero–crossing segment A series of *zero–crossings* obtained from an image which share the same orientation (see Fig. 5.9).

AUTHOR INDEX

Adelson, E.H. 294, 297, 302, 303
Ahumada, A.J. 294
Albano, J.E. 49
Albrecht, D.G. 53, 58
Alderson, G.H.K. 283
Aleksander, I. 211
Alley, T.R. 374
Allman, J. 303, 304
Andersen, R.A. 173, 221
Anderson, J.A. 213,
Aneshansley, D. 125
Aronson, E. 269, 270
Attneave, F. 109, 116
Baddeley, A. 200
Bahde, S. 262
Bahill, A.T. 285
Baker, C.L. 305
Ball, W. 268
Ballard, D.H. 204
Barclay, C.D. 329
Bard, C. 285
Barlow, H.B. 28, 42, 62, 69, 183, 293
Bassili, J.N. 363, 341
Bateson, P.P.G. 358, 359
Baumgartner, G. 170
Baylis, G.C. 69
Beasley, N.A. 335
Beck, J. 116, 227
Bergen, J.R. 294, 297
Berkeley, G. 74, 142
Bernstein, N. 274, 315
Berry, D.S. 374
Bertenthal, B.I. 327

Beverley, K.I. 307, 308
Biederman, I. 197, 220, 363
Biesinger, R. 246
Blakemore, C. 104, 144
Blasdel, G.G. 56, 57
Blondeau, J. 247
Boden, M. 77
Bolhuis, J.J. 359
Boring, E.G. 74, 75
Borst, A. 262
Bossema, I. 346
Bower, T.G.R. 268, 274
Boyle, D.G. 334, 335
Braddick, O.J. 163, 164, 165, 288, 305
Braitenberg, V. 261
Bransford, J. 238
Bronsford, J. 286
Brennan, S. 366
Brindley, G.S. 167
Broadbent, D.E. 387
Broennimann, R. 69
Brooks, V. 115
Broughton, J.M. 268
Bruce, V. 94, 113, 172, 200, 218, 362, 364, 366, 367, 368, 372, 373
Bruce, C. 307
Bruner, J.S. 77
Burger, J. 352
Burgler, R.R. 346
Burton, M. 200, 368, 372, 373
Bushnell, I.W.R. 361
Butterworth, G. 271
Buxton, B.F. 308, 380

Buxton, H. 308, 380
Caan, W. 68
Camhi, J.M. 244
Campbell, F.W. 93, 104
Campbell, H.W. 125
Campbell, R. 362
Carello, C. 236, 384
Carey, S. 366
Carpenter, R.H.S. 26
Carrel, J.E. 125
Cartwright, B.A. 258, 259
Cavanagh, P. 152
Caviness, J.A. 269
Chase, P. 199
Chitty, A.J. 69
Chomsky, N. 387
Clarke, P.G.H. 144
Clayton, T.M.H. 286
Cleland, B.G. 41
Clocksin, W.F. 237, 287
Clowes, M.B. 128, 129
Cohen, D. 360
Collett, T.S. 250, 251, 252, 255, 256, 258/9
Collett, T. 256, 257
Cooper, G.F. 43
Cornsweet, T.N. 166
Cornsweet, J. 227
Cott, H.B. 125
Croze, H. 126
Cutting, J.E. 201, 226, 227, 324, 325, 326, 329, 332, 333
Cutting, J.F. 327
Daniel, B.M. 285
Davies, G. 366, 367
Davies, M.N.O. 260
Davis, J.M. 346, 347
Daw, N.W. 45
De Monasterio, F.M. 42, 44, 68
De Valois, R.L. 53, 58
Dench, N. 372
Desimone, R. 71, 307
Dethier, V.G. 253
Detwiler, M.L. 269
DeYoe, E. 118
Diamond, R. 366
Dibble, F.N. 225
Dill, L.M. 262
Dodd, B. 362
Dodge, F.A. 35
Douglas, R.H. 256
Dowling, J.E. 37, 47
Doyle, T. 372, 373
Dreher, B. 144
Duncker, K. 322, 325, 326
Dziurawiec, S. 360, 361

Ebbesen, E.B. 391
Edwards, A.S. 271
Egelhaaf, M. 254, 304, 305, 314
Eisner, T. 125
Ekman, P. 361, 363, 364, 367
Ellard, C.G. 259
Ellis, H.D. 360, 366, 367
Ellis, A.W. 218
Ellsworth, P. 363
Emerson, R.C. 167, 170, 233
Enlow, D.H. 373
Enroth-Cugell, C. 39, 46, 57, 92
Essick, G.K. 173, 221
Eure, S.B. 109
Ewert, J.P. 178
Fagan, J. 361
Fechner, G.T. 75
Feldman, A.G. 317
Feldman, J.A. 173, 174, 204, 206, 211
Fender, D.H. 148
Fennema, C.L. 300
Fentress, J.C. 349
Ferretti, C.L. 261
Ferster, D. 63
Field, T.M. 360
Finlay, B.L. 53
Fishman, M.C. 63,
Fitch, H.L. 315, 317, 318
Flin, R. 361
Flock, H.R. 111
Flude, B.M. 218
Fodor, J.A. 381, 385, 387, 388, 389, 390, 391
Fox, R. 20
Franks, J.J. 386
Frenk, S. 43
Friedman, M.B. 260
Friesen, W.V. 363
Frisby, J.P. 145, 151, 152
Frisch, H.L. 119
Frost, B.J. 260, 303, 304
Frykholm, G. 327, 328, 360
Fukuda, Y. 42
Fuster, J.M. 71
Galton, F. 146
Garnham, A. 77
Garvin, J.J. 201
Gaze, R.M. 42, 43
Georgeson, M. 104
Gerhardstein, P.C. 220
Gerstein, G.L. 167, 170, 233
Gibson, E.J. 111, 273
Gibson, J.J. 4, 77, 111, 223, 225–239, 245, 254, 269, 287, 380, 382
Gilbert, E.N. 119
Gizzi, M.S. 302, 303

Gochfeld, M. 352
Golani, I. 347, 348, 349
Goodale, M.A. 259
Goodman, L.J. 245
Goodman, D. 316
Goodman, C.C. 77
Goren, C.C. 179, 360
Gotz, K.G. 246, 250
Graham, N. 93
Graham, C.H. 32, 34
Graham, M. 303
Green, D.G. 46
Green, P.R. 260
Greenberg, R. 360
Gregory, R.L. 75, 136, 152, 154, 166
Griffin, D.R. 243
Gross, C.G. 307
Grzywacz, N.M. 300
Gulick, W.L. 155
Gurfinkel, V.S. 317
Guzman, A. 128
Haig, N.D. 366
Hailman, J.P. 123
Halperin, S. 357
Hamilton, C.B. 109
Hanna, E. 96
Harkness, L. 255
Harmon, L.D. 366
Harris, J.P. 152
Hartline, H.K. 32, 34, 35
Hausen, K. 292, 304, 305
Hay, D.C. 200, 218, 365, 366
Head, A.S. 69
Hebb, D.O. 213
Heckenmuller, E.G. 166
Heider, F. 338, 357
Heiligenberg, W. 243
Heisenberg, M. 247
Hellawell, D.J. 200, 365, 366
Helmholtz, H. von 74, 167
Hengstenberg, B. 246
Hertz, M. 127
Hicks, L. 271
Hildreth, E.C. 87, 89, 90, 91, 93, 96, 103, 151,
    288, 293, 295, 296, 299, 300, 301, 302, 304,
    308, 309
Hill, R.M. 42, 63
Hilton, H.J. 219
Hinton, G.E. 204, 206, 213, 219, 319, 387
Hintzman, D.L. 218, 388
Hochberg, J. 109, 115, 171, 172, 173
Hochstein, S. 47, 296
Hoffman, D.D. 136, 138, 196, 198
Horn, G. 63, 359
Horn, B.K.P. 300

Horridge, G.A. 259
Howarth, C.I. 282
Howland, H.C. 19, 125
Hubbard, A.W. 283, 319
Hubel, D.H. 52, 53, 54, 55, 56, 62, 144
Huffman, D.A. 129
Hummel, J.E. 220
Humphrey, N.K. 321
Humphreys, G.W. 172, 199, 200
Ingram, W. 125
Ittelson, W.H. 76
Jackson, J.F. 125
Jacobs, G.H. 69
Jacobson, M. 42, 43
Jeeves, M.A. 69
Jervey, J.P. 71
Johansson, G. 111, 324, 325, 326, 327
Johnson, M.H. 359
Jones, R. 223
Julesz, B. 117, 118, 119, 120, 147, 148, 150,
    152, 155, 161, 163
Kallos, T. 167, 170, 233
Kalmus, H. 245
Kamil, A.C. 126
Kanade, T. 198
Kaufman, L. 155, 321, 322
Keeble, G.R. 321
Keeble, S. 337
Kelso, J.A.S. 316
Kerr, D.J. 288
Kettlewell, B. 126
Kilpatrick, F.P. 76
Kirschfeld, K. 16, 27
Knierem, J. 118
Koch, C. 293, 299
Koenderink, J.J. 306, 309
Koffka, K. 106, 114, 233
Köhler, W. 106
Kohonen, T. 213–215, 219, 220
Kolers, P.A. 164
Konëcni, V.J. 391
Kots, Ya.M. 317
Kovach, J.K. 359
Kozlowski, L.T. 329, 330
Krinsky, V.I. 317
Kuffler, S.W. 38, 43
Land, M.F. 14, 15, 251, 252
Land, E.H. 68
LaRitz, T. 285
Lawson, R.B. 155
Lee, D.N. 260, 261, 267, 269, 270, 271, 272,
    275, 276, 277, 279, 285, 287
Lehmkuhle, S.W. 20
Lehrer, M. 259
Lehtiö, P. 213–215, 219, 220

Lekhy, S.R. 221
Leonard, C.M. 69
Leslie, A.M. 337
Lettvin, J.Y. 43
LeVay, S. 56
Levick, W.R. 42, 43, 293
Lindhagen, K. 282
Lindsay, P.H. 182
Lindström, S. 63
Linsker, R. 220
Lishman, J.R. 269, 271, 275, 276, 279
Lock, A. 256, 257
Locke, J. 74
Longuet-Higgins, H.C. 288
Loomis, J.M. 303, 304
Lough, S. 286
MacDonald, J. 362
Mace, W.M. 315, 316, 317, 369, 389, 390
Mach, E. 167
Mandelbrot, B.B. 201
Marchiafava, P.L. 293
Mark, L. 371, 373
Marr, D. 60, 73, 77, 78, 79, 87, 89, 90, 91, 93,
   94, 96, 103, 127, 128, 131, 136, 138, 149,
   150, 151, 155, 161, 162, 168, 170, 190, 192,
   195, 199, 204, 206, 220, 295, 296, 298–299,
   308, 330, 363, 374, 380, 383, 389,
Marshall, J. 51
Martinez, K. 96
Mather, G. 298
Maturana, H.R. 43
Maunsell, J.H.R. 66, 67
Mayhew, J.E.W. 151, 152
McArthur, L.Z. 374
McCarrell, N.S. 386
McClelland, J.L. 204, 213, 215, 387
McCleod, R.W. 269
McCulloch, W.S. 43
McGuinness, E. 303, 304
McGurk, H. 362
McIlwain, J.T. 47
McIntyre, M. 369
McKenzie, B. 361
McLaughlin, C.M. 281
McLean, J. 294, 297
Mech, L.D. 353,
Meltzoff, A.N. 361
Menzel, E.W. 353, 356, 357, 384
Merikle, P. 171
Merton, P.A. 167
Metzger, W. 225
Michael, C.R. 42, 43, 45, 63
Michaels, C.F. 236, 384
Michotte, A. 333
Miezin, F. 303, 304

Millard, R.T. 227
Miller, J. 150
Millott, N. 8
Milner, A.D. 69
Minsky, M. 173, 189, 219
Mistlin, A.J. 69
Mollon, J.D. 28, 68
Moore, M.K. 268, 361
Moran, J. 71
Moran, G. 349
Morgan, M.J. 96, 99, 101, 113, 151
Morris, R.G.M. 204
Morton, J. 217
Moulden, B. 294
Movshon, J.A. 58, 302, 303
Mullin, J.T. 361
Nachmias, J. 93
Nakayama, K. 303, 304
Neisser, U. 171, 182
Neufield, G.R. 167, 170, 233
Neuhaus, W. 164
Newsome, W.T. 66, 67, 302, 303
Nichols, C.W. 167, 170, 233
Nilsson, D.E. 12
Nishihara, H.K. 190, 199, 330, 363
Nitsch, K.E. 386
Norman, D.A. 182
Normann, R.A. 45, 46
O'Connell, D. N. 162
Ogle, K.N. 146
Oja, E. 213–215, 219, 220
Olson, R.K. 116
Oster, H. 363
Over, R. 361
Owen, B.M. 272, 285
Packer, C. 356
Paillard, J. 286
Pal'tsev, Ye. I. 317
Palmer, S.E. 199
Palmer, L.A. 294, 297
Pantle, A. 164
Papert, S. 219
Parker, S. 391
Pearson, D.E. 94, 96, 151, 374
Peichl, L. 57
Pentland, A. 197, 200–202
Perrett, D.I. 69
Peterhans, E. 170
Pettigrew, J.D. 144
Pheiffer, C.H. 109,
Phillips, W.A. 171
Picciano, L. 164
Pietrewicz, A.T. 126
Pinker, S. 173
Pittenger, J.B. 368, 369, 370, 371, 389

Pitts, W.H. 43
Poggio, T. 92, 144, 148, 149, 150, 151, 161, 204, 220, 251, 252, 253, 254, 293, 304, 305, 314,
Poggio, G. 144, 148, 150, 155
Pollack, I. 362
Pollard, S.B. 151
Potter, D.D. 69
Potts, W.K. 347
Poulin, C. 307
Prazdny, K. 288
Premack, D. 357
Pringle, J.W.S. 243
Pritchard, R.M. 166
Proffitt, D.R. 324, 325, 326, 327, 329, 330, 331
Purple, R.L. 35
Putnam, C.A. 316
Pylyshyn, Z.W. 381, 384, 387, 388, 389, 390, 391
Ramachandran, V.S. 152, 156
Ratliff, F. 35
Rauschecker, J.P. 307
Reddish, P.E. 264, 284
Reed, E.S. 223, 389, 390
Regan, D. 307, 308
Reichardt, W. 248, 250–252, 253, 254, 290–291, 304, 305, 314
Repetto-Wright, R. 282
Rhodes, G. 366
Richards, W.A. 136, 138, 196, 198
Richter, J. 296
Ripoll, H. 285
Roberts, A.D. 366, 373
Roberts, L.G. 135
Robinson, J.A. 94, 151, 374
Robson, J.G. 39, 43, 46, 57, 92, 93
Roediger, H.L. 386
Rogers, B. 303
Rolls, E.T. 69, 220
Rosch, E. 199
Rosenfeld, S.A. 358
Rosenquist, A.C. 167, 170, 233
Ross, J. 146
Ross, H.E. 269
Rossel, S. 255
Roth, G. 179
Routledge, D.A. 282
Rumelhart, D.E. 204, 213, 215–219, 221, 387
Runeson, S. 327, 328, 360
Ryan, C.M.E. 358
Sagi, D. 118
Sai, F. 361
Salama, G. 56, 57
Sanders, M.D. 51
Sarty, M. 179, 360

Saye, A. 151
Schaeffel, F. 19
Schaller, G.B. 353
Schein, S.J. 68
Schiff, W. 269
Schiller, P.H. 92
Schiller, P. 53
Schmidt, R.A. 283
Schunck, B.G. 300
Scilley, P.L. 304
Seamon, J.G. 371
Sedgwick, H.A. 226
Sejnowski, T.J. 204, 219, 221
Selfridge, O.G. 182
Seng, C.N. 283, 319
Sergent, J. 365
Shackleton, T. 104
Shapley, R.M. 47, 296
Sharp, R.H. 283
Shaw, R.E. 238, 315, 316, 317, 368, 369, 370, 371, 389, 390
Shepherd, J. 366, 367
Shepp, L.A. 119
Sherrington, C.S. 146, 167
Shik, M.L. 317
Shirai, Y. 131
Siegel, R.M. 173, 221
Silberglied, R.E. 125
Simmel, M. 338, 357
Simpson, M.J.A. 344
Simpson, J.I. 307
Sivak, J.G. 20
Smith, O.W. 111
Smith, P.A.J. 69
Smolensky, P. 387
Sperling, G. 152, 171, 293, 294, 298
Srinivasan, M.V. 259
Stevens, J.K. 167, 170, 233
Stier, D.M. 331
Stone, J. 42
Stonham, J. 211
Stryker, M.P. 56
Sully, D.J. 283
Sully, H.G. 283
Sumby, W.H. 362
Sumner, F.B. 126
Sutherland, N.S. 180, 181, 186, 289
Ternus, J. 164
Terzolpoulos, D. 206
Thayer, G.H. 124
Thompson, I.D. 58
Thompson, W.B. 300,
Thomson, J.A. 275, 276, 388
Thorell, L.G. 53, 58
Timney, B. 259

Tinbergen, N. 177
Todd, J.T. 371, 373
Tolhurst, D.J. 58
Tomita, T. 48
Torre, V. 293
Treisman, A. 174, 210
Tronick, E. 268
Tsetlin, M.L. 317
Tuller, B. 315, 317, 318,
Turner, E.R.A. 345
Turvey, M.T. 171, 173, 314, 315, 316, 317, 318,
    388, 389, 390
Ullman, S. 94, 160, 162, 164, 288, 296, 298–299,
    308, 379, 389
Valentine, T. 200, 218, 366, 368
van Santen, J.P.H. 293, 294, 298
Van Essen, D.C. 65, 66, 67, 118
Van Hoesen, G.W. 358
Victor, J.D. 47
Vines, G. 354
Volkmann, F.C. 170
Volman, S.F. 53
von der Heydt, R. 170
von Hofsten, C. 282
Von Holst, E. 312, 314
Von Wright, J.M. 171
von Grünau, M.W. 307
Wässle, H. 58
Waddell, D. 225
Wagner, H. 262
Wagner, H.-J. 256
Wagner, H.G. 35
Walk, R.D. 273
Wallace, G.K. 259
Wallach, H. 322
Walls, G.L. 27, 28
Waltz, D.L. 128, 129

Warren, W.H. 233, 277
Warren, C. 217
Warrington, E.K. 51
Watson, J.B. 75
Watson, A.B. 294
Watt, R.J. 83, 96, 99, 101, 103, 120, 151
Wehrhahn, C. 252
Weir, S. 335, 337
Weiskrantz, L. 51
Werblin, F.S. 45, 46, 47
Wertheimer, M. 106, 160
Westendorff, D.H. 20
Wheatstone, C. 144
Whiting, H.T.A. 283
Whitteridge, D. 144
Wiesel, T.N. 52, 53, 54, 55, 56, 56, 56, 62, 144
Wiggers, W. 179
Williams, R.J. 219
Williams, C. 181
Wilson, H.R. 94
Winston, P.H. 187
Wittreich, W.J. 77
Wong, S.C.P. 304
Wood, D.C. 8
Woodbury, P.B. 352
Woodruff, G. 357
Woodson, R. 360
Wu, R.W.K. 179, 360
Wundt, W. 106
Wurtz, R.H. 49
Yin, R.K. 366
Young, A.W. 200, 218, 362, 365, 366
Young, D.S. 271, 277, 281, 282, 285
Yuille, A.L. 300
Zeki, S. 67, 68, 69
Zhang, S.W. 259
Zipser, D. 173, 219, 221

SUBJECT INDEX

AIT (anterior inferotemporal area)   see *IT*
Absorption spectrum,   12, 26-28
Accessory optic system (AOS),   307
Accommodation:
  as cue to depth,   142, 255, 256
  of vertebrate eye,   19, 20
Action schema,   337, 364, 386
Acuity – see *Visual acuity*
Adaptation,   23, 33, 45, 46, 48
Affordance,   233-235, 238, 382, 384, 390
Ageing of head profiles, 368-373
Algorithmic level,   61, 73, 287, 374, 379-383, 389
Aliasing,   292-294
Amacrine cells,   37, 38, 47, 293, 296
Ambient optic array – see *Optic array*
Ambiguous pictures,   106-109, 137-139
Ames' demonstrations,   76, 77, 198
Anaglyph,   145
Aperture problem,   299
Apparent motion – see *Motion*
Artificial intelligence,   77, 78, 127, 128, 129, 130
Attention,   70, 71, 103
Attribution,   338-340, 342
Back-propagation,   219, 220, 221
Balance,   269-272
Bandwidth,   58, 59
Behaviourism,   75-77, 238
Binocular disparity – see *Stereopsis*
Bipolar cells,   37, 38, 45, 47, 296
Blur,   86, 87
  detection of,   99-101
Bottom-up processing,   78-80, 187

(see also *Data driven processing*)
Braking,   278-280
Camera analogy,   28, 29, 74, 141, 236
Camouflage,   103, 116, 121-126, 139
  background picturing,   122, 123
  countershading,   124
  disruptive colouration,   122, 123
Cardioidal strain,   370, 371, 373, 374
Catching,   283, 284
Causality, perception of,   333-338, 373
Centre of moment,   330-333, 386
Centre-off response,   39, 40, 44, 46, 47, 92, 93, 296, 297
Centre-on response,   38-40, 44, 46, 47, 63, 92, 93, 296, 297
Children's perception of:
  biological motion,   327
  causality,   337
  exproprioceptive information,   270-272
  faces,   360, 361
  looming,   268
  moving targets,   282, 283
  time to contact,   281, 282
  visual cliff,   273, 274
Ciliary muscles,   14, 19
Closure, grouping by,   112, 131
Coalition,   317, 349
Cognitive impenetrability,   381
Colour constancy,   68, 69
Colour vision,   12, 26-28, 43, 67-69, 85
  (see also *Opponent-colour responses*)
Common fate, grouping by,   111, 124, 125
Compiled detectors,   381
Complex cells,   52, 53, 62, 63, 148, 150

Compound eye, 11-13, 255
of *Limulus*, 31-38, 47
Computational theory, 61, 73, 78, 79, 149, 163, 287, 374, 380
Concentric receptive field:
centre-surround organization, 38, 39, 45, 221
of cortical cells, 52, 55
as $\nabla^2 G$ filter, 92
as edge detector. 62-64
of LGN cells, 50, 57, 58
as relative motion detector, 303, 304
of retinal ganglion cells, 38-44, 46, 47, 57, 58
Conceptually driven processing – see *Top-down processing*
Cone, 14, 15, 21-23, 45, 46
absorption spectra of pigments, 27, 28
oil droplets in, 27
Connectionist models, 80, 203, 204, 382, 386-389
of mapping between co-ordinates, 206-211
of movement control, 319
of pattern recognition, 211-220
physiological evidence, 220-221
of stereopsis, 204-206
and symbol-processing models, 219, 386-388
Context-conditioned variability, 313, 315, 316
Continuation, grouping by, 111, 112
Contrast sensitivity, 58
Convergence of eyes, 25, 26, 150, 151
as cue to depth, 142
Co-ordinate systems, mapping between, 173, 206-211, 221
Co-ordinative structures, 316-319
Correspondence problem:
in integrating fixations, 170
in motion perception, 160-165, 288, 335-337
in stereopsis, 145, 161, 204
Cues to depth – see Depth perception
Data driven processing, 78, 172, 381
(see also *Bottom-up processing*)
Degrees of freedom problem, 315, 316, 318
Delta rule, 216, 219, 220
Depth perception:
(See also *Stereopsis, Time to contact, 2½D sketch*)
by accommodation, 142, 255, 256
in animal locomotion, 256-259
by convergence, 142
development of, 273, 274
Gibson's analysis of, 224, 227, 228, 235, 377
by image size, 155, 156, 235, 257, 258
by motion parallax, 157, 159, 259, 265, 273, 303

by pictorial cues, 155-158
by shading, 156, 157, 174, 206, 221
by texture gradients, 156, 226-228, 235, 236, 273
Direct perception:
arguments against, 379-381, 383-386, 389-391
of causality, 333-335, 338, 373
theory of, 224, 233-235, 237, 238, 375, 377, 378, 382, 387, 389, 390
Direction-selective responses:
in accessory optic system, 307
of cortical cells, 53, 67, 294, 295, 303, 307, 308
in insect nervous system, 248, 292, 305
of retinal ganglion cells, 42, 163, 165, 248, 292-295
Displays of animals, 177, 344, 345, 349
Distance perception – see *Depth perception*
Distributed memory, 213, 387
Dual-opponent response, 45, 53
Eccentric cell, 31, 32
Edges:
detection by:
Marr-Hildreth algorithm, 87-91, 151, 295, 308
MIRAGE algorithm, 96-104
single cells, 62-65, 92, 93
and intensity gradients, 81-83, 85, 86, 95
localisation of, 101
and relative motion, 254, 255, 303, 305
Edge-segment, 90, 91, 94, 105
Emotion, perception of, 362-365
Empiricism, 74, 76, 142, 268, 274
End-inhibition, 53, 93
(see also *Hypercomplex cell*)
Event perception, 232, 331-333, 365
Exproprioceptive information, 267, 270, 272
Exteroceptive information, 267, 272
Extrastriate cortex:
(see also MT, V2, V3, V4)
colour processing in, 67-69
motion processing in, 67, 72, 173, 303, 307, 308
pathways, 66, 67, 70, 71, 103, 174, 221
visual areas, 65-71
Eye:
(see also *Vertebrate eye*)
apposition, 11
compound, 11-13, 31, 255
evolution of, 10-28
single-chambered:
of cephalopods, 14
image formation by, 13, 14, 17, 18
pinhole eye, 13

reflecting eye, 13, 14
superposition, 11-12
Eye-cups, 9, 10
Eye movements:
classification, 25, 26
distinguishing from object motion, 166-168,
233, 312, 313
integration of fixations, 170-173
necessity for vision, 166
Eyes, stabilisation of, 285, 307
Eyespots, 8, 9
Faces:
age judgements of, 368-373
automatic sketching of, 94-96, 374
caricatures, 366
cells selective for, 69, 70, 221
expressions of, 360-365, 367, 368
inversion effect, 366
recognition of, 175, 176, 179, 200, 217, 358,
362, 366-368, 371
computer models for, 211, 212, 214, 215
configural information in, 365, 366
development of, 360, 361
from expressive movements, 367, 368
sex judgements of, 373, 374
Facial Action Coding System, 363, 364
Feature detection:
(see also *Recognition*)
by single cells, 62, 83, 92, 93, 184
ambiguity problem, 63-65, 69, 70
theory of recognition, 61, 62, 182-185
Figure-ground discrimination, 106, 113, 114,
139
(see also *Edges, Relative motion*)
Filter, $\nabla^2 G$, 89, 90, 96, 97, 100, 101, 150, 295
active control of, 103, 120, 121
in visual pathway, 92-94
Fourier analysis, 96
Fovea, 23, 42, 55, 67, 208
Fractal, 201, 202
Frame system, 173, 189
Functional architecture, 54-57
Gait:
perception of, 327-330
regulation of, 274-277, 317, 319
Ganglion cells – see *Retinal ganglion cells*
Ganzfeld, 225
Gaussian filter, 87, 89, 100, 308
Gaze direction, detection of, 346, 356, 357
Generalised cone, 190-192, 195, 196, 378
Geon, 197-199
Gestalt psychology, 76, 77, 105, 106, 139,
237, 322
laws of organisation, 110-116, 121-125, 127-
128, 133, 157

Goodness of shape, 115, 116, 157
Grating:
plaid patterns, 104, 302, 303
resolution of, 17
sinusoidal, 39, 40
response of cells to, 39-41, 57-60
thresholds for detection, 93, 94, 104
Grouping processes, 101-103, 116-121, 128,
152, 341
(see also *Camouflage, Gestalt psychology*)
in Marr's theory, 131, 133, 136
in other species, 125-127
Head-bobbing – see *Head movements*
Head movements, 259, 260, 346
Head, stabilisation of, 260, 285, 307
Hebbian learning rule, 213, 220
Heterarchy, 317
Hidden units, 219, 221
History of theories of perception, 74-78
Horizontal cells, 37, 38, 45, 47
Hypercolumn, 55-58, 60
Hypercomplex cells, 53, 62
(see also *End-inhibition*)
Hypothesis-testing, 75, 78, 174, 381
(see also *Mediation of perception, Top-
down processing*)
Iconic memory, 171, 172
Illusions:
Ames' demonstrations, 76, 77, 198
Gibson's criticisms, 234, 235
hollow face, 154, 385, 386
illusory contours, 152, 153, 170
in moving figures, 300, 301
Imprinting, 359, 360
Indirect theory of perception – see *Inference,
Mediation of perception*
Induced motion – see *Motion*
Inference, 75, 77, 238, 375, 377, 381, 389
(see also *Mediation of perception, Top-
down processing*)
Infra-red, sensitivity to, 22
Insect flight, 243-245
(see also *Optomotor response*)
fixation of objects, 251-253, 314, 352, 382,
383
landing response, 261-263, 383
return to food sources, 258, 259
Intention, perception of, 338, 340-342, 356,
357
Invariant, 198, 226, 234, 236, 238, 318, 329-
331, 367, 368, 370, 371, 374, 378, 379, 382-
385, 390
Isomorphism, doctrine of, 114
IT (Inferotemporal area), 69-71
Key stimulus, 177, 178, 358

Kinetic depth effect, 162
Laplacian, 89
Lateral geniculate nucleus (LGN), 49-55, 57-59, 62-65, 92, 94, 103
Lateral inhibition, 35, 36, 48, 61
Lens:
　aberrations of, 20, 27, 29
　accommodation of, 19, 20
　of eye-cups, 9, 10
　image formation by, 10, 13, 14, 17, 18
　power of, 18
　of vertebrate eyes, 14, 18-20, 27
Light:
　and animal locomotion, 242, 243
　physics of, 2, 3
　plane of polarisation, 12
　reflection by natural surfaces, 3, 4, 81, 82
　refraction, 3, 18
　spectrum of wavelengths, 2
Logarithmic coding, 32, 33, 45
Long jumping, 276, 277
Looming, detection of, 261, 268, 269, 274, 307, 308, 385
MT (Middle temporal area), 66, 67, 303, 304, 307
Macula lutea, 23, 27
Mediation of perception, 234, 238, 377-379, 381, 382, 389
　(see also *Inference*)
Memory:
　distributed, 213, 387
　for faces, 365, 367
　in integration of fixations, 171-173, 388
　localised, 386
　matrix model, 213-215
　PDP models, 213-219, 388
　in single cell responses, 71
　spatial, 258, 356, 383, 384, 388, 389
MIRAGE algorithm, 97-103, 120, 121
Modularity, 174, 362
Modules (in visual cortex), 57
Motion:
　(see also *Eye movements, Optic flow, Relative motion*)
　apparent, 111, 160, 163-165, 236, 288, 298
　cells sensitive to – see *Direction-selective responses*
　computation (detection) of:
　　correlation models, 290-295, 298
　　in cortical areas, 67, 72, 173, 294, 303, 307, 308
　　gradient models, 295-298, 308
　　in insects, 248, 249, 290-292, 304, 305
　　integration of measurements, 298-303
　　multiple mechanisms, 298, 306, 307, 309
　　by spatiotemporal filters, 294, 295

from successive images, 160-163, 237, 288, 337
　induced, 271, 322
　parallax, 124, 136, 157, 159, 248, 259, 260, 273, 288
　perspective, 229, 386
　structure from, 162, 169, 174, 368
Nativism, 74, 76
Neural net – see *Connectionist models*
Ocellus – see *Eyecup*
Ocular dominance, 56, 57
Ommatidium, 11, 12, 31-36, 290
Opponent-colour responses, 43-45, 53
　(see also *Wavelength-selective responses*)
Optic array:
　as input for vision, 77, 224-226, 376, 377
　sampling of, 24-26
　structure of, 4-7, 225, 226
　transformations of, 229, 232, 233, 254, 287, 389
Optic chiasm, 50, 51
Optic flow field:
　(see also *Motion computation, Time to contact*)
　analysis of:
　　algorithms for, 206, 237, 287, 306-309, 380
　　physiological, 307, 308
　　resolution of rotation, 248-250, 287, 288, 306
　direction of motion from, 230-232, 245-248, 280, 281
　distance information in, 259, 260, 265
　exproprioceptive information in, 269-272
　structure of, 230, 248, 254, 331, 382, 388
　time to contact information in, 260, 261
Optic nerve:
　of *Limulus*, 31-36
　of vertebrates, 37, 38, 49, 50, 307
Optic tectum, 49, 303, 304
Optomotor response, 245-250, 254-256, 262, 290-292
　efference copy model, 312-315
Orientation preference (selectivity), 53, 56, 57, 59, 60, 67, 92, 94, 104, 170, 221, 296
Outlining, 123
PDP models – see *Parallel Distributed Processing*
PIT (Posterior inferotemporal area) – see *IT*
Pandemonium model, 182-184
Panum's fusional area, 145, 148
Parallel distributed processing, 204, 211-219, 388
Path of travel, perception of, 282, 283, 349, 352-356
Perpendicular component, 299-304

Photoreceptors:
(see also *Cone, Rod*)
ciliary,   14, 15
directional sensitivity of,   8-10, 15, 16
of *Limulus*,   31-35
rhabdomeric,   11-13, 31
wavelength sensitivity,   12, 26-28
Pigments,   8, 12, 26-28
(see also *Rhodopsin*)
Pixel,   84, 85, 211, 212, 214, 219
Place token,   131, 133, 135
Point-light displays,   327-329, 363, 368
Prägnanz, law of,   114, 115
Predators, escape from,   262, 263, 352
Prestriate cortex – see *Extrastriate cortex*
Prey capture,   178, 179, 255, 353, 354
Primal sketch,   79, 139, 174, 186, 206
see also *Raw primal sketch*
Proprioceptive information,   267
Proximity, grouping by,   110-112, 123, 124, 131
Pupil,   20, 23
Random-dot kinematogram,   111, 124, 163-165, 288
Random-dot stereogram,   110, 124, 146-149, 164, 204, 205
Raw primal sketch,   79, 84-87, 94, 96, 103, 104, 120, 121, 131, 136, 149, 195, 288
computation in visual pathway,   92-94
Marr-Hildreth algorithm,   87-91
Reaching,   282, 283
Reafference,   312
Recognition:
of block structures,   186-189
canonical viewpoint in,   199
connectionist models of,   211-221
of faces,   61, 175, 179, 200, 211, 212, 214, 215, 217, 360-362, 365-368
of individual animals,   177-179, 357-360, 366
of letters and numbers,   175, 180-186, 206, 212
physiological basis,   61, 62, 69, 70
representations for:
axis-based,   190-192, 196, 198-200, 386
feature sets,   182-186, 210
geons,   197-199
structural descriptions,   185-189
surface-based,   200
templates,   180-182, 186
3D model,   80, 191, 192, 196, 206
from silhouettes,   192-19
Relative motion:
biological patterns,   327-333, 345, 346, 367, 368
and causality,   333-335

cells sensitive to,   303-305
computation of,   303-305
and events,   331-333
and figure-ground discrimination,   254, 255, 260, 303, 305, 383
and intentions,   338, 340-342
rigidity assumption,   323, 324, 328, 329
thresholds for detection,   321, 322
vector analysis of,   324-328
Representation:
(see also *Recognition: representations for*)
distributed,   204
grey-level,   84, 85
of motor patterns,   315, 318, 319, 349
role in perception,   77, 79, 238, 382-385
snapshot,   258
symbolic,   219, 386-388
viewer-centred,   79, 80, 174, 189, 196, 207, 208, 387
Resonance,   234, 238, 379, 387
Retina:
of *Limulus*,   31-36
of vertebrates,   14, 15, 20-23
adaptations in structure,   21-24
cellular structure,   37, 38
synaptic interactions,   46-48, 293, 296
Retinal ganglion cells:
(see also *W cells, X cells, Y cells*)
concentric receptive fields,   38-44, 46, 47
direction selective,   42, 163, 165, 248, 292-295
as feature detectors,   62-64, 83, 92
opponent colour responses,   43-45, 68
periphery effect,   47
spatial frequency tuning,   57-59
species differences,   43, 293
synaptic connections,   37, 38, 47, 48, 50, 293, 296
Retinal image:
(see also *Depth perception, Stimulus equivalence*)
discovery of,   74
formation of,   13, 14, 17, 18
imperfections of,   29
relationship to optic array,   223, 224, 376, 377
stabilisation of,   166, 260
Retinomotor response,   23
Retinotopic map,   49, 50, 54, 65, 173, 207, 208
Retinula cell,   11, 12, 15, 30, 290
Rhabdom,   11, 12, 31
Rhodopsin,   12, 15
Rod,   14, 15, 21-23, 27, 28, 38, 46
Rolling wheel display,   323-326, 331
Saccade,   25

suppression of processing during, 170
Scene analysis programs, 128-131
Schematic map, 172, 173
Segmentation of shapes, 136-139, 195-197, 202
Sensation-based theories, 75, 105
Shading:
  as cue to depth, 156, 157
  shape from, 174, 196, 206, 221
Sheepdogs, 354-356
Short-term visual store, 171, 172
Shunting inhibition, 293
Sign stimulus – see *Key stimulus*
Signal patches, 123, 124
Similarity, grouping by, 110, 111, 116-121, 123, 131, 341
Simple cells, 52, 53, 104, 150
  connections, 63, 296
  as feature detectors, 62, 64, 65
  as movement detectors, 295-297
  as zero-crossing detectors, 92-94
Single celled animals, 7-8
Size constancy, 235, 236
  (see also *Ames' demonstrations*)
Smoothness assumption, 300, 304
Social interaction of animals, 343, 344
  aggression, 177, 344-346, 349-351, 356, 357
  group co-ordination, 346, 347, 353, 356, 357
  individual recognition, 357-360
  pack hunting, 353-356
  parent-offspring, 345, 346, 358-360
  play, 347, 348
Spatial frequency, 39, 57, 86
  channels, 93, 94, 104, 150
  Gaussian filtering of, 87
  tuning of cells, 57-59, 93, 94
Speech perception, 362
Spinal cord, 316, 317
Steering, 280, 281
Stereopsis, 124, 136, 142-147, 168, 169, 174, 196, 255
  algorithms for, 149-152, 161, 204-206, 219
  cognitive processes in, 152-154
  Gibsonian analysis of, 236
  local vs. global, 147, 148
  physiological basis, 144, 148, 150
Stereoscope, 144, 145
Stimulus equivalence, 61, 177, 179, 180
  (see also *Recognition*)
Striate cortex – see *Visual cortex*
Structural descriptions, 185-189
Structuralism, 75, 76, 106
Superior colliculus, 49, 51, 52, 165
Superquadric components, 197, 200, 202
Swinging room, 269-272

Symmetry, 113, 114, 123
Tapetum, 22
Template matching, 180-182
Textons, 119, 120
Texture:
  discrimination, 116-121, 135
  gradients of, 156, 226-228, 235, 236, 273, 382
  optical, 230
  of surfaces, 4, 82, 225
3D model representation, 80, 191, 192, 196, 206
Time to contact:
  computation of, 262, 308, 309, 379, 380
  detection of, 262-265, 269, 277, 279-285, 319, 379, 391
  specification by optic flow, 260, 261, 379
Top-down processing, 78, 109, 135, 136, 154, 166, 337
  (see also *Visual pathway: feedback connections*)
Transactional functionalism, 76, 77, 335
Transduction, 8, 12, 15
2½D sketch, 79, 80, 150, 168-171, 174, 206, 207, 382, 388
V1 – see *Visual cortex, primary*
V2, 66, 67, 118, 144, 170
V4, 66-68, 71
Valley, luminance, 95, 96
Vector analysis, 324-328
Velocity computation – see *Motion computation*
Velocity field, 288, 289, 299, 300, 304-307, 309
Vertebrate eye:
  accommodation, 19, 20
  adaptations for dim light, 20-24
  image formation, 13, 14, 17, 18
  placement in head, 24, 25, 50
  structure, 14, 15
Visual acuity, 17, 20, 21, 58
  relationship to sensitivity, 21-24, 38
Visual angle, 17
Visual cliff, 273, 274
Visual cortex, primary, 50-52
  connections between cells, 63, 94
  functional architecture, 54-57
  input from LGN, 63, 64
  outputs from, 51, 52, 63, 65-67, 103
  responses of cells:
    to binocular disparity, 144, 148, 150
    direction selective, 53, 294-297, 303, 307
    to line stimuli, 52, 53, 104, 221
    to non-visual stimuli, 65
    to spatial frequencies, 58-60, 93

to textures,   118
wavelength-selective,   53, 68, 69
Visual pathway, mammalian:
extrastriate,   66, 67
feedback connections,   51, 63, 66, 71, 103,
221
primary,   49-52
hierarchical model of,   61-63, 65
Marr-Hildreth model of,   92-94
secondary,   49, 51, 52
W cells,   42-44, 49-51, 144, 293, 295
Wavelength-selective responses,   67-69
(see also *Opponent colour responses*)
WISARD,   211-213
X cells,   40-42, 44, 144, 294

as ∇^2G filters,   92, 296, 297
projection,   49, 50, 296, 297
retinal mechanisms,   46, 47
spatial frequency tuning,   57, 58
Y cells,   41, 42, 144
motion computation by,   48, 296
projection,   49, 50, 296, 297
retinal mechanisms,   47, 296
spatial frequency tuning,   57, 58
Zero-bounded mass,   98, 99, 101
Zero-crossing,   89, 90, 92, 95-99, 101, 131,
295, 304, 308
in stereopsis,   149-151
Zero-crossing segment,   89, 90, 92-94, 104,
297